IDEOLOGY AND STATUS OF SANSKRIT

Contributions to the History of the Sanskrit Language

IDEOLOGY AND STATUS OF SANSKRIT

Contributions to the History of the Sanskrit Language

Edited By

JAN E.M. HOUBEN

MOTILAL BANARSIDASS PUBLISHERS
PRIVATE LIMITED • DELHI

First Indian Edition : Delhi, 2012
First published by E. J. Brill *in 1996*

ISBN : 978-81-208-3501-6

MOTILAL BANARSIDASS
41 U.A. Bungalow Road, Jawahar Nagar, Delhi 110 007
8 Mahalaxmi Chamber, 22 Bhulabhai Desai Road, Mumbai 400 026
203 Royapettah High Road, Mylapore, Chennai 600 004
236, 9th Main III Block, Jayanagar, Bangalore 560 011
Sanas Plaza, 1302 Baji Rao Road, Pune 411 002
8 Camac Street, Kolkata 700 017
Ashok Rajpath, Patna 800 004
Chowk, Varanasi 221 001

Printed in India
By Jainendra Prakash Jain at Shri Jainendra Press,
A-45, Naraina, Phase-I, New Delhi 110 028
and Published by Narendra Prakash Jain for
Motilal Banarsidass Publishers Private Limited,
Bungalow Road, Delhi 110 007

CONTENTS

ACKNOWLEDGEMENTS

The present volume is an outcome of the seminar "Ideology and Status of Sanskrit in South and Southeast Asia" organized under the auspices of the International Institute for Asian Studies (IIAS), Leiden, 17-19 November 1994. When working on the organization of the seminar and on the publication of this volume, the editor incurred a pleasant debt of gratitude to numerous individuals and institutions. The generous support and assistance provided by the then newly founded IIAS made the seminar possible, and the active and enthusiastic participation of a considerable number of scholars made it a success. Apart from the contributors to this volume, the following persons deserve special mention: Professors L. Leertouwer, D.H.A. Kolff and H.W. Bodewitz, Professor Hannes Kniffka, Mrs. Iwona Milewska, Dr. Max Nihom, Professor Peter Raster, Dr. Herman Tieken, Dr. J.-M. Verpoorten, Professor T.E. Vetter and Dr. J.H.A. Vivekanand. Thanks to the organizational skills of Mrs. Esther Guitjens, latent practical problems during the seminar were already solved before they manifested themselves.

Professor Johannes Bronkhorst (Lausanne) should be mentioned as the one who guided me through all critical phases in planning and organizing the seminar and in solving organizational problems in the publication of this collective work. All participants contributed to the formulation of the concept of the present volume, which attempts to provide an overview of the historical depth and geographical and cultural extension of the ideology and status of Sanskrit, as well as of the major themes and theoretical problems associated with it in modern research.

When working on this volume as an IIAS research fellow, I received all the necessary support and facilities from the IIAS, personalized for me in the enthusiastic members of its Staff, Prof. W.A.L. Stokhof, Mrs. Sabine Kuiper, Mrs. Karin van Belle, Mrs. Kitty Yang and Mrs. Maya Gal, and the editor-in-chief of all IIAS-publications, Paul van der Velde. It is hoped that this volume will serve as a fitting tribute to their commitment to academic quality, continuity and innovation in Asian Studies.

Here I would also like to record my gratitude to Prof. Paul Dundas (Edinburgh) for writing an excellent contribution to this volume even though he could not be present at the seminar. The staff of the library of the department of South and Central Asia (Kern Institute) was always helpful in providing material and bibliographical assistance. Of all others who helped in various ways in the realization of this book I would here like to mention especially my friends Dolf J.B.F. Hartsuiker (Utrecht), and Frans H.P.M. Janssen (Utrecht), as well as Prof. J.G. de Casparis (Leiden), Dr. Marijke Klokke (Leiden), Prof. K.R. van Kooij (Leiden), Prof. E. te Nijenhuis, and Prof. T.E. Vetter (Leiden).

Finally, I am grateful to the staff of E.J. Brill publishers for giving this volume a place in their series "Brill's Indological Library."

Leiden, May 1996 Jan E.M. Houben

LIST OF CONTRIBUTORS

ASHOK N. AKLUJKAR; Department of Asian Studies, University of British Columbia; 2075 Wesbrook Mall, Vancouver, B.C., Canada V6T 1W5.

SAROJA BHATE; Department of Sanskrit and Prakrit Languages, University of Poona; Pune 411007, India.

VICTOR A. VAN BIJLERT; Department of Languages and Cultures of South and Central Asia, University of Leiden; P.O. Box 9515, NL-2300 RA Leiden, The Netherlands.

JOHANNES BRONKHORST; Section des Langues et Civilisations Orientales, Université de Lausanne, BFSH 2; CH-1015 Lausanne, Switzerland.

CORSTIAAN VAN DER BURG; Department of Religious Studies, Vrije Universiteit; De Boelelaan 1105, NL-1081 HV Amsterdam, The Netherlands.

MADHAV M. DESHPANDE; Department of Asian Languages and Cultures, University of Michigan; Ann Arbor, Michigan, 48109-1285; U.S.A.

PAUL DUNDAS; Department of Sanskrit, University of Edinburgh; 7 Buccleuch Place, Edinburgh, EH8 9LW, United Kingdom.

TEUN GOUDRIAAN; Hondsrug 123, NL-3524 BW Utrecht, The Netherlands.

HANS HENRICH HOCK; Department of Linguistics, University of Illinois; 707 S. Mathews, Urbana IL 61801, U.S.A.

JAN E.M. HOUBEN; Department of Languages and Cultures of South and Central Asia, University of Leiden; P.O. Box 9515, NL-2300 RA Leiden, The Netherlands.

JOHN D. KELLY; Department of Anthropology, University of Chicago, 1126 East 59th Street, Chicago IL 60637, U.S.A.

A.G. MENON; Department of Languages and Cultures of South and Central Asia, University of Leiden; P.O. Box 9515, NL-2300 RA The Netherlands.

SHELDON POLLOCK; Department of South Asian Languages and Cultures, University of Chicago, Foster Hall, 1130 East 59th Street, Chicago IL 60637, U.S.A.

ANNA RADICCHI; Universita' di Cagliari, Istituto di Glottologia; Viale Avignone 19, 53100, Siena, Italy.

BAAS J. TERWIEL; Thai Studies Department, University of Hamburg; Von-Melle-Park 6, D-20146 Hamburg, Germany.

PIETER C. VERHAGEN; Department of Languages and Cultures of South and Central Asia, University of Leiden; P.O. Box 9515, NL-2300 RA Leiden, The Netherlands.

ALBRECHT WEZLER; Institut für Kultur und Geschichte Indiens und Tibets, Neue Rabenstrasse 3, D-20354 Hamburg, Germany.

PREFACE TO THE INDIAN EDITION

Jan E.M. Houben,
École Pratique des Hautes Études, Paris

Unlike the large majority of language names, the name 'Sanskrit' is not the name of a people or country or nation.[1] The name *saṁskṛta,* which literally means 'polished, well-formed', points to its socio-linguistic position throughout the ages: it was the cultured language of the well-educated, of the social and religious elite. The term Sanskrit properly applies to the regulated language which developed some centuries after Pāṇini's grammar, and access to which was not limited by ethnicity or belief system (Brahmanism, Buddhism, Jainism, Cārvāka, etc.). By extension, however, it refers to closely related earlier forms of the language which are used in the Vedic texts (cf. Whitney 1888: xi-xv; Thieme 1994). Certain attestations of the name *saṁskṛta* with reference to language and usually in opposition to *prākṛta* and *apabhraṁśa*[2] appear relatively late, from the first centuries before and after the first millennium Common Era. From its earliest

---

[1]Renou 1956: 6: 'Le mot <<sanskrit>> est ainsi l'une des rares désignations de langue qui ne soit pas de provenance ethnique.' At least, the ancient and modern, indigenous and external names of most well-known languages, English, French, German, Dutch, Greek, Latin, Hebrew, Hindi, Marathi, Hindustani, etc. are either derived from or identical with the names of a people, country or nation. (These proper names may next have well-established or uncertain etymologies as significant words.) I did not try to verify this for the more than 6900 languages listed in the last edition of the *Ethnologue* (Lewis 2009). Notable exceptions from South Asia, apart from Sanskrit, are the literary languages Prakrit, the religious language Pali, the commercial lingua franca Urdu. More recent times saw the construction of languages such as Esperanto and Interlingua which are from the beginning meant for communication between people of different mother tongues and which have significant names not derived from the name of a people, country or nation.

[2] See contributions of Aklujkar and Houben in the present volume.

attestations to the present day,[3] Sanskrit has been participating in complex, multilinguistic contexts.

Regarding the history of the Sanskrit language, Louis Renou observed that 'the questions posed by [its] development ... and the almost paradoxical conditions of its survival have not yet been tackled in detail' (1956: 1[4]). This is as much true now as it was more than fifty years ago, even if significant contributions have been made to various crucial aspects. We still have to confirm, that '... the time has not yet come (if it would ever come) for a definitive work in this area. Too many preparatory studies are missing, too many elements remain unknown' (Renou, ibid.[5]).

In his review of the volume *Ideology and Status of Sanskrit* (henceforth: ISS)[6], the Spanish linguist Luján remarked that 'since Renou's (1956) *Histoire de la langue sanskrite* there has not been any booklength study dealing with the history of Sanskrit. Besides, linguistic thought has changed to a great extent since the date of publication of Renou's book; accordingly, it was high time to undertake a profound revision of the ideas on the history of Sanskrit.' The contributors to the volume ISS take up for discussion several problematic points pertaining to the early beginnings, the development and stabilization and to the latter days of what we may call the 'Sanskrit tradition' – if, for the sake of simplicity, we are ready to use a term that leaves implicit

---

[3] The *Ethnologue* (Lewis 2009), under the lemma 'Sanskrit', informs the reader that Sanskrit is a language of India and that a surprisingly high number of 2950 persons registered as first language speakers in the 2001 Census. More credibility can be accorded to the number of second language speakers, which is said to be 194.433. The comment is added that it is a 'Classical language of learning, liturgical language.' It is unclear why the *Ethnologue* mentions only 'Sharada, Sinhala' as its scripts, skipping several other old scripts formerly used for writing Sanskrit and omitting the script that is dominantly used for this purpose at present, Devanāgarī.

[4] 'On n'avait pas encore abordé avec quelque détail l'ensemble des questions que pose l'évolution de cette langue, les conditions presque paradoxales de sa survie.'

[5] 'Sans doute le temps n'est pas venu (s'il doit jamais venir) pour une oeuvre définitive en ce domaine. Trop de travaux préparatoires manquent, trop d'éléments resteront inconnus. Jusqu'ici on a surtout éclairé les débuts, les origines indo-européennes, la structure des hymnes védiques, certains points de l'usage ultérieur.'

[6] Other reviews that came to my notice are: Colas 1998, Goldman 1997, Jamison 1997, Patyal 1997, Polomé 1999, Scharf 1997, Smith 2002, Squarcini 2002, Verpoorten 1998.

the internal heterogenity and dynamics of what could also be referred to in the plural as 'Sanskrit traditions.'

The aim of ISS was to contribute especially to the social and sociolinguistic history of Sanskrit. A few updates can be made for the current Indian edition. Three publications are central in these updates. One appeared actually a few years before the publication of ISS, in 1989, two appeared recently, in 2006 and in 2009.

A. The volume *Dialectes dans les Litératures Indo-Aryennes* ('Dialects in the Indo-Aryan Literatures,' ed. C. Caillat 1989) was the outcome of an international Colloquium organized in Paris in 1986. Its subject-matter partly overlapped with that of ISS. Several articles of this volume were referred to in contributions in ISS. A contribution that in the course of the years has turned out to be particularly influential is Michael Witzel's 'Tracing the Vedic Dialects,' which forms a series with other publications by the same author on this subject and in the same line of approach.[7]

Before the publication of 'Tracing the Vedic Dialects' the general consensus was that the Vedic texts in general and the Ṛgveda in particular show a strong presence of linguistic norms and little dialectal variety.[8] Michael Witzel, however, summarizing and adding to dispersed research results of preceding decades, simply posited the existence of localized dialects in Vedic, which can be traced through the available Vedic texts. In the domain of Vedic studies, his article contained the promise of a new, fruitful direction of research. Witzel sketched the consensus and his new departure as follows:

> It is believed ... that the Vedic language had no dialects. One usually admits that the archaic poetic language of the Ṛgveda is a mixture of many dialects which had influenced each other. On the other hand, the educated speech of post-Ṛgvedic times, found in the prose texts, the so-called Brāhmaṇas, is regarded as the contemporary, the living language of the priests and other

---

[7] 'On the Localization of Vedic Texts and Schools' (1987), 'Notes on Vedic Dialects (1)' (1991) and 'Notes on Vedic Dialects (2)' (2005).

[8] Cf. Renou 1956: 10 on the Ṛgveda: 'Bien que dû à des auteurs multiples, préparé dans des localités séparées, il ne présente guère de diversité dialectale. Autrement dit, nous avons affaire dès l'origine à une sorte de norme linguistique.'

> well-educated men, while the rest of the population spoke various degrees of early Middle-Indian, i.e., archaic Prākṛts. But this is as far as one will go. My contention will be that even this standard North Indian Koine, 'Vedic', which does not seem to have regional variations at all, shows traces of the local dialects – if only one looks carefully enough. (Witzel 1989: 99).

The divergent linguistic features, for instance several ways of dealing with euphonic combination (*sandhi*), can usually be understood from different theoretical perspectives. Those of Middle and Late Vedic texts seem most promising with regard to dialectal differences. However, 'especially Renou and Caland regarded many of the variations in grammar, to be treated below, as mere variations in the style of Vedic, viz. of the various Vedic schools' (Witzel 1989: 99 n. 3). Of special interest is the attribution of a quite distinct mode of recitation, with two instead of three basic pitches, to a specific text, the Śatapatha-brāhmaṇa, of which it is known that it has at least partly an eastern origin: Videha (Videgha), not the larger Punjab area as other ancient Vedic texts. This could have confirmed the existence of different dialects in Middle and Late Vedic. However, the relationship beween other Vedic ways of accentuation and the one of the Śatapatha-brāhmaṇa remains unclear and difficult to analyze B.B. Chaubey (1975, 1978) and George Cardona (1993) devoted important studies to the accentuation of the Śatapatha-brāhmaṇa. Especially the latter detailed proposal is not entirely convincing to Witzel.[9]

On the basis of an overview of the available evidence and arguments brought forward till now, including some that have been unduly neglected in recent discussions, it becomes clear, however, that the accent system represented in the Bhāṣika-sūtra, while perfectly valid for the later tradition of SB recitation (in Benares), does not correspond to any early dialectal development in Vedic Sanskrit –

[9] After having expressed his doubt on technical aspects of Cardona's account, Witzel adds: 'The exact mechanism of the Eastern dialect's substitution of a low tone for an originally rising tone of the more Western Vedic dialects cannot be described here in detail' (Witzel 1997: 327).

least of all to a dialectal development of major teachers of the ŚB such as Yājñavalkya (Houben, forthcoming). This removes a crucial argument for accepting 'Vedic dialects' (Witzel 1989 and 1997), which are rather to be considered regional variations of a 'sociolect' or of a language belonging to a particular sociological stratum of ancient Indian society. As for the Bhāṣika-sūtra, it is a *pariśiṣṭa* of a *pariśiṣṭa,*[10] not mentioned in the traditional list of supplementary Śukla-yajurveda texts. It was probably written in Benares and it need not be earlier than the 16th century Common Era.

Earlier grounds for scepticism brought forward by, among others, Caland, Renou and Minard have therfore not been removed: the results from 'dialectic,' 'stylistic,' school differences and the role of social strata can hardly be distinguished. In view of the strong suggestion of a settled speaking community that is associated with the term 'dialect' and in view of the 'habitual travelling' of Brahmins of which also Witzel is well aware (e.g., 1989: 231), it is more realistic to speak of a *bhāṣā* and of early and late Vedic as 'sociolects' with regional variations, with dynamic change over time. Area-wide convergence covering Witzel's three centres, Kurukṣetra, Pañcāla and Kosala-Videha, was here more important than regional divergence. The great sage of the Vājasaneyins, Yājñavalkya, may have used a Brahminical *koinē* without recognizable accent; and if he had any accent, this had nothing to do with the accentuation-system as described in the Bhāṣika-sūtra.

Also at the early Vedic stage, Sanskrit or rather its predecessor formed a language for which 'ideology and status' were more important than variations according to geographical localization. Witzel's conclusion in these articles regarding the localization of *schools* and *texts* is more convincing than his proposal that it was the Vedic *language* itself which had specific dialects. Regional variations are there and they may be attributed partly to artefacts of the school transmission of the various texts, partly to underlying early Middle Indo-Aryan dialects, 'Vedic Prakrits' or 'proto-Prakrits', and even to Dravidian

[10] Pt. Yugal Kishore Pāṭhaka in his edition of the Vājasaneyi-prātiśākhya, Benares 1888, p. 412.

and Austro-Asiatic languages; but on the level of the learned and sophisticated, priestly language of the Vedas and Brāhmaṇas the dominant characteristics are homogeneity and convergence.

The difficulties with respect to our judgement of systematic distinctions well-known since the times of Wackernagel, Caland and Renou – whether we have to attribute them to stylistic variation, to sociolinguistic differences, to differences in the transmission through various schools, or, as Witzel proposed, to geographically localizable dialects – cannot be separated from theoretical choices that are necessary in our understanding of languages in general and Indian languages in particular. In one way of thinking about Sanskrit it is a discrete unit that forms a 'node' in a tree of related languages, with, for instance, ancient Persian and esp. the language of the Avesta as 'sister' language, and Hindi, Urdu, Marathi, Oriya, etc. as 'daughter' languages of Sanskrit. Since M.B. Emeneau and F.B.J. Kuiper, a 'field' approach to languages of India including Sanskrit (see Hock, present volume) has received some attention, but as a secondary model, superimposed on a classical 'family' model. Basically, we have to decide whether we want to see languages as particles (discrete units), waves, or fields. As we know from physics, in some experiments light appears to be a wave phenomenon, in other experiments, equally convincing and equally repeatable, it consists of particles. The status of exclusive 'truth' can be claimed by neither of these two distinct and seemingly mutually contradictory ways of understanding light. Recently, the following methodological observations have been made regarding fundamentally different ways of seeing languages.

> Scholars are recognizing that languages are not always easily nor best treated as discrete, identifiable, and countable units with clearly defined boundaries between them ... . Rather, a language is more often comprised of continua of features that extend across time, geography, and social space. There is growing attention being given to the roles or functions that language varieties play within the linguistic ecology of a region or a speech community. ... Languages can be viewed, then, simultaneously as discrete units (particles) amenable to being listed and counted, as continua of features across time and

> space (waves) that are best studied in terms of variational tendencies as examples of 'change in progress', and as parts of a larger ecological matrix (field), where functional roles and usage of the linguistic codes for a wide range of purposes are more in focus. (Lewis 2009)

Deshpande (2006: 141) rightly explains that

> The notion of language family implies that languages B and C are branchings of a common ancestor A, and this fact of a genetic connection accounts for certain features. On the other hand, the notion of a linguistic area implies that languages A and B, though belonging to different language families and originally possessing different linguistic features come to share some of each others features over a long period of time through intense contact.

But here too, the 'linguistic area' model (in which languages appear in a 'field') is superimposed on a 'family' model (in which languages are discrete units generating new units over time), as if the latter's priority would have been well-established. Recent researches suggest that within the period that interests us, from the second millennium B.C.E. till the present, Vedic and classical Sanskrit evolved from 'linguistic area' to 'linguistic area' (with several shifts of the geographical point of gravity, from the northwest of the Indian subcontinent to the central Gangetic plains, and India's southern states). The appropriateness of attributing primary status to a model of 'family' relationships between languages as 'particles' or discrete units, can therefore be questioned, especially because the same problem applies to what can be reconstructed for earlier periods (cf. Pinault 2002).

B. An important recent publication demonstrates how the dichotomy between a carefully maintained priestly language[11] and the language

[11] Basically, the difficulty and obscurity of the language of the seers of hymns and priests who employ them in Vedic rituals is not so much a matter of our lack of background information (this may create some difficulties but no fundamentally unsurmountable ones), and even less of a conscious effort directly aiming at obscurity (although such efforts were no doubt undertaken when social demands for truly inspired poetry could no longer be fulfilled). Rather, the attempt to express the inner connection of things

of daily use emerges from a belief system that attributes highest value and even soteriological efficacy to 'the words of the gods'. Alexis Pinchard's *Les langues de sagesse dans la Grèce et l'Inde anciennes* (2009, based on a thesis defended in 2005; cf. also Bader 1989) studies this dichotomy not only from an Indian perspective but from a comparative Indo-European perspective, with special emphasis on ancient Greece. In India, the dichotomy is subject to a continuous 'inflation' that can be easily traced back to very early stages: at first, the 'secret words or footsteps of the cows' are preserved in 'human' hymns addressed to the gods; subsequently, the entire collection of 'human' hymns, skillfully composed by trained poets, acquire the status of divine texts which through their metre, etc., are demarcated from all other language use, including the comments and explanations of difficulties associated with these divine texts; the next stage is the acquisition of divine status by both the hymns and their explanations, the stage reflected in the dictum *mantra-brāhmaṇayor veda-nāmadheyam* 'Mantras and Brāhmaṇas have the designation "Veda" ' (Āpastamba Śrauta-sūtra 24.1.31). The auxiliary disciplines such as grammar, etc., which develop in order to bridge the increasing distance between the language of the Veda and even the polished language of daily life, are the next candidates to receive divine status; the last observed stage is the attribution of divine status not only to Vedic literature and its auxiliary disciplines but to the entire Sanskrit language, a view which we find already clearly formulated by the 5th century grammarian-philosopher Bhartṛhari. But we have to infer that this view remained in his time by no means uncontested, as Bhartṛhari juxtaposes it to the opposing view that Sanskrit is an artificially regulated derivation from a more widely and more 'naturally' spoken language, Prakrit.

Problems such as those analysed by Ashok Aklujkar in this volume and in subsequent studies (esp. Aklujkar 2003 and 2009), appear in a

---

forced the poets and thinkers to use a special language, which unavoidably created a distinction between those who understood it and those who did not, somewhat in the way technical terminology developed within a scholarly or scientific discipline facilitates communication among specialists but excludes the non-initiated. Cf. Porzig 1925: 656 and Houben 2000.

different perspective both in the light of the 'inflation' of divine status to which Pinchard has drawn attention, and in the light of Vedic thought and Indo-European comparison applied to philosophy (and vice versa), according to the methodology proposed by Pinchard. The results for Indian thought have our first interest here, but the starting point of Pinchard is the philosophy of Plato and the Sophists, and their common indebtedness to the Mysteries, especially those of Orpheus and Eleusis. For several of the steps taken on the way of tracing back philosophical challenges implicitly accepted by Plato, Socrates and the Sophists, Pinchard points to striking parallels with elements in Indian thought. In case of the Mysteries, these parallels are found in the rituals of the Ṛgveda. The importance of Pinchard's work – a work which searches system rather than new data[12] – lies not only in the substance of the collection of materials (in ancient Greek, Sanskrit and Vedic texts), but also in the method developed to address the problems[13]. The work helps to make visible broader parallels for seeming anomalies in Indian cultural history. For instance, the almost obsessive preoccupation with memorization in ancient India, is clarified by the glorification of memory as a path to knowledge by Plato which appears in the context of the intense preoccupation with memorization in ancient Greece. The other side of the coin is the avoidance of the use of writing for significant literature, not only religious but also legal.[14] Hence, Pinchard observed: 'It should by no means surprise us, therefore, that the evidence of a refusal of writing by members of the priestly or divinatory class in Indo-European civilizations is so abundant, even when writing was often known and used in other contexts. Such a refusal is merely a matter of recognizing

[12] The author sees himself in the 'tradition française d'un comparatisme indo-européen à fonction systématisante plutôt qu'archéologique' (Pinchard 2009: 129). For the background of his ideas see also Watkins 1994 and 1995.

[13] Even if someone would disagree with several decisions and conclusions of the thesis, it would be difficult to refute the author without using at least partially his method.

[14] For the legislator Lycurgus, education of the citizens was the only thing that can guard important matters for the common wealth, but he refused to put into writing the details of litigations (Pinchard 2009: 306).

the natural impossibility of wisdom to be passed on as a book. Wisdom is what it is only as long as it establishes by itself its distance from writing.' [15]

Another important problem area that appears in a new perspective is that of the relationship between language and reality (or: word and object), discussed in ISS by J. Bronkhorst and later on in *Langage et Réalité: sur un épisode de la pensée indienne* (1999). Whether Sanskrit is considered a divine language (by Brahmanical thinkers) or not (by Buddhist thinkers), one property of the ancient Indo-European 'language of the gods' is attributed to its words: the capacity to express the true, though perhaps not ultimate, nature of the object.

Pinchard's book raises anew the old question of Indo-European and other relations that link Indian cultural and intellectual history with the world beyond the Indian subcontinent (for an overview of diverging perspectives, see Bronkhorst & Deshpande 1999, Bryant & Patton 2005). In ISS, H.H. Hock advocates further research in the direction of the thesis of pre-historic convergence of Dravidian and Indo-European languages within the Indian linguistic area. The importance of substratum is recently more and more recognized, but the relevant substrata for Sanskrit are not restricted to Dravidian ones. In this light, the underlying Indo-European thought-constructs posited by Pinchard are probably too monolithic even if they remain undetermined in detail. It is to be noted that the two civilisations which provide the best illustrations for his philosophical Indo-European thesis are at the boundary of the Indo-European expansive 'wave' where they are in contact with various well attested and highly developed non-Indo-European civilisations. Recognizing Indo-European parallels and patterns does not imply the acceptance of

[15] 'Point ne doit nous surprendre, donc, que les témoignages d'un refus de l'écriture par les membres de la classe sacerdotale ou divinatoire dans les civilisations indo-européennes soient si nombreux, alors même que l'écriture y était souvent connue et utilisée dans d'autres contextes. Un tel refus ne fait que prendre acte d'une impossibilité congénitale, pour la sagesse, de se transmettre comme on transmet un livre. La sagesse n'est ce qu'elle est qu'autant qu'elle instaure *elle-même* son écart face à l'écriture.' (Pinchard 2009:306)

massive invasions of Aryan tribes, or in some other way massive displacements of genetic material. The basis is rather a 'memetic' expansion, rendered possible by the 'memory culture' referred to above. It is in any case recommendable to avoid the controversial period of the third millennium B.C. (which is studied in the context of the Indus or Sarasvatī Civilisation[16]) and to put the earlier limit of the (at least to a minimal extent tangible) history of Sanskrit to ca. 1500-1750 B.C.E. It is the period in which we find tribes that can be characterized as Vedic in the northwest of the Indian continent (Saptasindhu). From wherever they may have arrived there and whatever their genetic make-up, they start to spread throughout, first, the north of the Indian subcontinent, and later throughout the Indian subcontinent. Only after Sanskrit is transferred to writing is there a significant expansion of 'sanskritic' culture beyond South Asia, which brings us to our final point in this preface, Sanskrit as 'cosmopolitan' language.

C. The third recent publication which deserves a brief discussion in connection with the 'Ideology and Status of Sanskrit' is Sheldon Pollock's awe-inspiring *The Language of the Gods in the World of Men: Sanskrit, Culture, and Power in Premodern India* (2006), which deals with the establishment of 'cosmopolitan' Sanskrit throughout, mainly but not exclusively, South and South East Asia, and how this formation of the Sanskrit cosmopolis is the starting point for new processes of 'vernacularization' in which, however, Sanskrit remains a 'gold standard' of high culture. As it basically concerns a later period than Pinchard's book, there is only little chronological overlap (beginning of the first millennium). There is nevertheless unexpected mutual complementarity with Pinchard's book (which, as thesis, was finalized in 2005). Both deal with the 'language of the gods' but Pinchard studies it in the context of poetry and philosophy, with little attention to politics – about which, in the mainly pre-historical periods which interest

[16] Direct evidence for the use of Sanskrit or its immediate predecessors is here absent.

Pinchard, no direct information is available. Pollock, on the other hand, studies the instrumentality of a well-defined Sanskrit, accessible through various grammars, in the worlds of politics and religion. In two major parts of his book, Pollock studies two processes. In Part 1: 'The Sanskrit Cosmopolis' (pp. 39-280, chapters 1-7), Pollock deals with the adoption of Sanskrit (at the cost of early 'inscriptional' Prakrits) roughly in the first millennium Common Era and not only in India but also in large areas in Southeast and East Asia. Part 2: 'The Vernacular Millennium' (pp. 283-494, chapters 8-12), deals with a process which presupposes the preceding one: the adoption of vernaculars – or rather, one should say, heavily sanskritized vernaculars – at the cost of Sanskrit in the same areas, in the course of the second millennium. The first process is the formation of the Sanskrit cosmopolis. The second process is India's and Asia's vernacularization. At the end of each of these two parts, chapter 7 and chapters 11-12 respectively provide a comparative background by discussing processes that are similar and yet in important ways different from India's and Asia's turn to Sanskrit and their vernacularization: the Latinization and the subsequent vernacularization of Europe. These two Parts are followed by Part 3: 'Theory and Practice of Culture and Power' (pp. 497-580, chapters 13-14 and Epilogue) which reflects on theoretical issues in connection with the origin and disappearance of civilisations and on the regrettable absence of Indian data at the basis of current theorizations.

The central problematic of Pollock's important book is the relationship between culture and power, and between language and literature,[17] in South Asia and against the comparative background of European history of language and literature. Pollock's contention is that '[T]wo key inventions, the second a subspecies of the first, marked the commencement of the cosmopolitan era in the literary-cultural domain and would continue to mark its expansion: *kāvya,* or written literature, and *praśasti,* or inscriptional royal panegyric' (p. 12). This

---

[17] On the various literary cultures in South Asian history see now the important volume edited by Pollock, 2003.

is the starting point for a fascinating, richly documented exploration of one and a half millennium of literary production (in the form of poetical works and inscriptional panegyrics) in South Asia and beyond.[18] Pollock argues that the inscription and panegyric of Rudradāman found in Junāgaṛh of 150 C.E. is not just accidentally the oldest Sanskrit inscription that has been found – after around four centuries of inscriptions, from Aśoka onwards, in which no Sanskrit is used but what may be called in modern terminology a form of middle Indo-Aryan: Rudradāman's inscription constituted indeed the first beginning of a new employment of Sanskrit and a new domain for its political use. The analysis of the rapid spread of this new use of Sanskrit, the 'World Conquest and Regime of the Cosmopolitan Style' (title of chapter 3) and its establishment far beyond South Asia expands many ideas which were already clearly pronounced in Pollock's 'cosmopolis' article in ISS. For the analysis of its subsequent interaction with local languages and the 'creation of regional worlds,' Pollock concentrates, in Part 2, on the case of the emergence of Kannada literature. Pollock's achievements are remarkable both from the perspective of the exploration of primary sources and from the perspective of the theorization of civilisational processes and transregional cultural formations.[19] The book which identifies ruptures in South Asian history that have been entirely overlooked by generations of previous researchers can itself be regarded as a rupture and writing the history of Sanskrit literature should never be anymore as before.

In contrast with the solid and well-researched central part of Pollock's work, the beginning section presents a caricatural sketch of the condition of Sanskrit in the time before Rudradāman's 'turn to

[18] In the introduction of new terms in order to conceptualize the unique configuration of the conditions of Sanskrit, Pollock is not always sufficiently careful. The term, 'hyperglossia' (p. 50, 65, 118, 127, 262, 432), for instance, is not well demarcated vis-à-vis the well-established scientific terms 'diglossia' and 'bilingualism' and it is implicitly suggested to be applicable to North India although in Pollock's argument it is evidently based on the specific situation of Sanskrit in South India.

[19] G. Fussman (2008: 163) considers it the most important Indological work in the last 50 or even 100 years: 'un des plus grands livres, le plus grand livre peut-être, d'indianisme écrit dans les cinquante (cent?) dernières années.'

Sanskrit' (chapter 1, especially the section 'Precosmopolitan Sanskrit: Monopolization and Ritualization'; chapter 2 sections 1 and 2). For this sketch concerning the centuries before C.E., Pollock too conveniently uses evidence of later periods (especially from works in the school of Mīmāṁsā of the fourth and seventh century C.E.). Criticizing the easy acceptance by previous scholars of the political use of Sanskrit in inscriptions in the absence of evidence (before Rudradāman there is indeed no record of any Sanskrit inscription), Pollock is ready to overlook the abundant evidence in Pāṇini's grammar (4th century B.C.E.) for the emancipation of Sanskrit from the ritual domain. This enhances the contrast with Rudradāman's 'new beginning'.

Evidence and arguments presented in contributions in ISS (the contributions, from diverse theoretical perspectives, of Aklujkar, Kelly and Houben) may serve here as correctives. Indeed, in the sociolinguistic conditions which we can reconstruct for Pāṇini and the early Pāṇinīyans (for which Deshpande's studies, 1979, 1993, are still foundational), it is likely that Pāṇini's grammar was not an instrument for monopolization and ritual restriction of the *bhāṣā* 'language' but rather a confirmation of its secular domain which gave it a significant and unique tangibility that allowed it, in turn, to expand further and to become politically and culturally instrumental.

Neither Pāṇini nor his successors worked in a vacuum but presuppose a 'public' of users of the grammar. When Pāṇini's grammar was used for a statement from current usage (see my brief remark in Houben 2009b: 14), we should imagine a user of the language who wants to 'polish' a sentence the 'correctness' of which might have varied from fully 'Pāṇinian' to that of the usage found, for instance, in an inscription of Aśoka, *dhramacaraṇaṁ pi ca na bhoti aśilasa.*[20] The latter is regarded as a different language by us, but was not necessarily so considered by contemporaries (Cf. Houben 1996

[20] Cf. Bloch 1950: 100. *dhrama-* is to be seen as a scribal mistake at some point in the transmission between royal decree and incision in the rock. Parallel inscriptions read *dhaṁmacaraṇaṁ* and *dhaṁmacalanaṁ.*

for the non-perception of strict divisions of languages in sociolinguistic circumstances such as those apparently pertaining in ancient India). This user must have sufficient active and passive knowledge both of what we consider Sanskrit and of Aśokan dialects and must be well familiar with the procedures of Pāṇini's grammar[21] in order to take this sentence as a starting point, understand *bhū* as the root semantically and formally closest to *bhoti* and, answering the semantic and syntactic questions asked by the grammar with reference to the word and the preliminary sentence, to derive the 'polished' form *bhavati*; the same procedure is to be followed for other problematic words to arrive at the *saṁskṛta* version of the quoted line, *dharmacaraṇam api ca na bhavati aśīlasya* 'The very practice of religious law is impossible to someone without virtue.'

Although clapping is never done with a single hand, from the current perspective we perceive for over around two millennia a single 'Sanskrit' hand clapping. From the clapping itself we have to infer that there was, according to time and circumstances, another 'proto-Prakrit' or 'Prakrit' or 'vernacular' hand clapping of which we sometimes have no direct information at all, sometimes only very limited information, and only for later periods in the course of the second millennium C.E., when the regional languages such as Kannada are formed, somewhat detailed information. The unavoidable extrapolations to which this uneven distribution of the evidence continuously invites us is unavoidably informed by our understanding of linguistic processes in better documented areas and periods. Hence, we cannot afford to neglect either exploration of primary sources, or the reflection on fundamental theoretical issues connected to their interpretation.

The ISS volume was meant as a contribution towards these two dimensions of research in the social and sociolinguistic history of Sanskrit. The publisher Motilal Banarsidass is to be thanked for making it again available to students of Sanskrit, Sanskrit literature and their history.

---

[21] To us these requirements may seem to be difficult to meet, but for well-educated (*śiṣṭa*) users of grammar in Pāṇini's environment, they must have been by no means extravagant.

Three scholars, who were born in the first decade of the 20th century and died more than 90 years later at the turn of the same century (and of the second millennium), have contributed significantly to our understanding of the history of Sanskrit, including the social and sociolinguistic aspects of this history: M.B. Emeneau (1904-2005), S.M. Katre (1906-1998) and F.B.J. Kuiper (1907-2003). This new edition is dedicated to their memory.

REFERENCES

Aklujkar, Ashok N.

1996 "The early history of Sanskrit as supreme language." In: ISS: 59-85. Leiden: E.J. Brill.

2003 "A different sociolinguistics for Brahmins, Buddhists and Jains." In: *Contemporary Views on Vedic Civilization* (ed. by BhuDev Sharma): 54-69. [n.p.]: World Association for Vedic Studies.

2009 "Veda revelation according to Bhartṛhari." In: *Bhartṛhari: Language, Thought and Reality.* Proceedings of the International Seminar on Bhartṛhari, New Delhi, December 2003 (ed. by Mithilesh Chaturvedi): 1-97. Delhi: Motilal Barnasidass.

Bader, Françoise

1989 *La langue des dieux ou l'hermétisme des poètes indo-européens.* Pisa: Giardini.

Bloch, Jules

1950 *Les Inscriptions d'Aśoka, traduites et commentées.* Paris: Société d'édition "les belles lettres".

Bronkhorst, Johannes

1996 "Sanskrit and reality: the Buddhist contribution." In: ISS: 109-135.

1999 *Langage et Réalité: sur un épisode de la pensée indienne.* [Avec une préface de Ch. Malamoud]. (Bibliothèque de l'Ecole des Hautes Etudes, Section des Sciences Religieuses, vol. 105). Turnhout: Brepols.

Bronkhorst, Johannes and M.M. Deshpande (eds.)
1999 *Aryan and Non-Aryan in South Asia: Evidence, Interpretation and Ideology.* Cambridge, Mass.: Dept. of Sanskrit and Indian Studies, Harvard University.

Bryant, Edwin F. and Laury L. Patton (eds.)
2005 *The Indo-Aryan Controversy: Evidence and Inference in Indian History.* London: Routledge.

Caillat, Colette
1989 *Dialectes dans les Littératures Indo-Aryennes.* (Publications de l'Institut de la Civilisation Indienne, fasc. 55.) Paris: Collège de France, Institut de la Civilisation Indienne.

Cardona, George
1993 "The bhāṣika accentuation system." *Studien zur Indologie und Iranistik,* Band 18:1-40.

Chaubey, Braj Bihari
1975 *Bhāṣikasūtra of Maharṣi Kātyāyana with the commentaries of Mahāsvāmin and Anantabhaṭṭa.* Panjab University Indological Series, 4. Hoshiarpur: Vishveshvaranand Vishva Bandhu Institute of Sanskrit and Indological Studies, Panjab University.
1978 "Accent in the Śatapathabrāhmaṇa : the problem of change in its nature." *Vishveshvaranand Indological Journal* 16: 18-28.

Colas, Gérard
1998 Review of ISS. *Bulletin de l'École française de l'Extrême-Orient* 85: 468-470.

Deshpande, Madhav M.

1979 *Sociolinguistic Attitudes in India.* Ann Arbor: Karoma.

1993 *Sanskrit and Prakrit.* Delhi: Motilal Banarsidass.

2006 "Aryan origins: Brief History of the Linguistic Arguments." In: *India: Historical Beginnings and the Concept of the Aryan* (ed. by R. Thapar, J. M. Kenoyer, M. Deshpande, S. Ratnagar): 98-156. New Delhi: National Book Trust.

Fussman, Gérard

2008 Review of Pollock 2006. *Journal Asiatique* 296.1: 163-180.

Goldman, Robert P.

1997 Review of ISS. *The Journal of Asian Studies,* 56.4: 1126-1127.

Houben, Jan E.M.

1996 "Sociolinguistic attitudes reflected in the work of Bhartṛhari and some later grammarians." In: ISS: 157-193. Leiden: E.J. Brill.

2009a "Bhartṛhari as a 'cognitive linguist'." *Bhartṛhari: Language, Thought, Reality.* Proceedings of the International Seminar on Bhartṛhari, New Delhi, December 2003 (ed. by Mithilesh Chaturvedi): 523-543. Delhi: Motilal Banarsidass.

2009b "Pāṇini's grammar and its computerization : a construction grammar approach." Kulkarni and Huet 2009.

Forthc. "Yājñavalkya's accent and the bhāṣika: on the language of the Śatapatha-brāhmaṇa and its context." To appear in the Proceedings of the Fourth International Vedic Workshop, Austin, Texas, May 24-27, 2007.

ISS = *Ideology and Status of Sanskrit: Contributions to the History of the Sanskrit Langauge,* ed. by Jan E.M. Houben. (Brill's Indological Library, vol. 13.) Leiden : E.J. Brill.

Jamison, Stephanie

1997 Review of ISS. *The International Journal of Hindu Studies,* 1.2: 428-429.

Lewis, M. Paul (ed.)

2009 *Ethnologue: Languages of the World.* Sixteenth edition. Dallas, Tex.: SIL International. Online version: http://www.ethnologue.com/

Luján, Eugenio R.

1998 Review of ISS. *Word,* 49.2: 291-293.

Patyal, Hukum Chand

1997 Review of ISS. *Indian Linguistics: Journal of the Linguistic Society of India,* Vol. 58, no. 1-4 : 131-147.

Pinault, Georges-Jean

2002 "Tocharian and Indo-Iranian: Relations between two linguistic areas." In: *Indo-Iranian Languages and Peoples* (ed. by N. Sims-Williams): 243-284. Oxford: Oxford University Press.

Pinchard, Alexis

2005 "Les langues de sagesse dans la Grèce et l'Inde anciennes." Thése de Doctorat présentée par Alexis Pinchard sous la direction de M. Georges-Jean Pinault, directeur d'études. École Pratique des Hautes Études, section des sciences historiques et philologiques, Paris.

2009 *Les langues de sagesse dans la Grèce et l'Inde anciennes.* (École Pratique des Hautes Études, Sciences historiques et philologiques - III. Hautes Etudes du monde gréco-romain, 43.) Genève-Paris: Droz.

Pollock, Sheldon I. (ed.)

2003 *Literary Cultures in History : reconstructions from South Asia.* Berkeley: University of California Press

2006 *The Language of the Gods in the World of Men: Sanskrit, Culture, and Power in Premodern India.* Berkeley: University of California Press.

Polomé, Edgar C.

1999 Review of ISS. *Journal of Indo-European Studies* 27.1-2: 182.

Porzig, Walter

1925 "Das Rätsel im Rigveda: Ein Beitrag zum Kapitel 'Sondersprache'." In: *Germanica: Eduard Sievers zum 75. Geburtstage*: 646-660. Halle a/d Saale: Max Niemeyer.

Renou, Louis

1956 *Histoire de la Langue Sanskrite*. Lyon: Editions IAC.

1957 "Introduction générale" (translated from J. Wackernagel's "Einleitung", updated, annotated). J. Wackernagel, *Altindische Grammatik. Band I. Lautlehre*. New Edition. Göttingen: Vandenhoeck und Ruprecht.

Scharf, Peter

1998 Review of ISS. *Anthropological Linguistics* 40.1: 167-174.

Smith, Frederick M.

2002 Review of ISS. *Religious Studies Review* 28.4 (2002) : 392-393.

Squarcini, Federico

2002 Review of ISS. *Religioni e Societ'a* 42 (2002) : 142-145.

Thieme, Paul

1994 "On M. Mayrhofer's Etymologisches Wörterbuch des Altindoarischen". *Bulletin of the School of Oriental and African Studies* 57: 321-328.

Verpoorten, J.M.

1998 Review of ISS. *Bulletin d'Etudes Indiennes* 16: 321-324.

Wackernagel, Jakob

1896 *Altindische Grammatik. Band I. Lautlehre*. Göttingen: Vandenhoeck und Ruprecht. (Reprinted with new "Introduction générale" by Louis Renou, 1957.)

Watkins, Calvert

1994 "Language of gods and language of men: remarks on some Indo-European metalinguistic traditions." In : *Selected Writings* II: 456-472. Innsbruk: Institut für Sprachwissenschaft der Universität Innsbruck.

1995 *How to Kill a Dragon : Aspects of Indo-European Poetics.* New York: Oxford University Press.

Whitney, William Dwight

1888 *Sanskrit Grammar, including both the classical language and the older dialects of Veda and Brāhmaṇa.* 2nd edn. Leipzig: Breitkopf und Härtel. (Reprint Delhi: Motilal Banarsidass, 1977.)

Witzel, Michael

1987 "The localisation of Vedic texts and schools."

1989 "Tracing the Vedic dialects." In: *Dialectes dans les littératures indo-aryennes* (ed. by C. Caillat): 97-265. Paris: Institut de Civilisation Indienne.

1991 Notes on Vedic Dialects. (1) *Zinbun, Annals of the Institute for Research in Humanities, Kyoto University,* vol. 67: 31-70.

1997 "The development of the Vedic canon and its schools: the social and political milieu." In : *Inside the Texts – Beyond the Texts: new approaches to the study of the Vedas* (ed. by M. Witzel): 257-345 (esp. pp. 324-326 on bhāṣika-accent).

2005 Notes on Vedic Dialects. (2). In: *Indogermanica. Festschrift Gert Klingenschmitt. Indische, iranische und indogermanische Studien dem verehrten Jubilar dargebracht zu seinem fünfundsechstigsten Geburtstag* (ed. by G. Schweiger): 733-743. Taimering: Schweiger-VWT-Verlag.

CHAPTER ONE

INTRODUCTION: TOWARDS A SOCIAL HISTORY OF THE SANSKRIT LANGUAGE

Jan E.M. Houben

1. In early accounts of the development of the diverse but clearly related languages of Europe it was usual to trace them back to a single people or even a single person speaking a single language. Popular candidates for this role were the Thracians and the Scythians (this would link the European languages with the classical world) and Japhet, the third son of Noah (linking the European languages with the biblical world) (cf. Mallory 1989:9-14). With all the reconstructions and discussions the straight connection between people and language remained usually unquestioned, also when, at the end of the 18th and beginning of the 19th century, scholars started to include Sanskrit more and more often as one of the related languages. Thus, the French Jesuit Father Coerdoux, one of the first to make systematic comparisons between the words of the Greek, Latin and Sanskrit ("samscrouta") language, had stressed in a paper read in 1768 at the Parisian Académie des Inscriptions et Belles-Lettres, that one should see the "original relatedness of the Indians, Greeks and Latins" as the cause of the similarity between these languages (Benfey 1869:341; cf. Mansion 1931:18). In this framework, the origin of Sanskrit and its predecessor Vedic in the Indian subcontinent was intimately linked with massive and devastating invasions of 'Aryans' (*āryas*), more than a millenium B.C.E.

Nowadays, however, almost two centuries after the beginning of the intensive Western-style studies of Sanskrit and the Indo-European languages, and after a great amount of archeological research on the Indian subcontinent, the insight is gaining ground that, neither in the present nor in the past, languages, peoples and cultures can or should be postulated as entities with one-to-one correspondences. Earlier ideas associating the authors of the Rgvedic hymns with hordes of invading *āryas* destroying the earlier Indus-civilisation have become obsolete, and scholars are searching for entirely different models to account for the linguistic shifts which must have taken place in these periods (e.g. Kuiper 1967a, 1991; Renfrew 1987). Rather, the Ṛgvedic *āryas* should be seen as "a multitude of ethnic groups subscribing to a newly emerging ideology" (Erdosy 1995:3), for which Allchin proposes to use the term "acculturated Aryan" (Allchin 1995:43). Although there is still general agreement today about the "external origin of Indo-Aryan languages spoken today in South Asia" (Erdosy 1995:3), and about the movement of speakers of Indo-Aryan languages into South Asia in a distant past, "[s]uch movement, certainly is unlikely to have constituted an invasion or invasions, and it may not have involved conquest" (Allchin 1995:44). Consequently, in new models of the spread of Indo-Aryan languages in South Asia, processes of interactions and shifts in languages in situations of societal bilingualism have become more and more important (cf. Mallory 1989:258-259; Allchin 1995:44).

Linguists of the 19th century preferred to regard processes of language change and maintenance as entirely dependent on 'exceptionless' laws which made the language an organism having its proper nature and direction of evolution, and the social context not more than an important but external condition. What attracted the attention of scholars was, to cite the famous words of Sir William Jones in his paper presented in 1786 to the Royal Asiatic Society in Calcutta, "the wonderful structure" of the Sanskrit language, which is "more perfect than the Greek, more copious than the Latin, and more exquisitely refined than either." At present, however, the delicate and intimate relations between social conditions and language change and maintenance are both more appreciated and better understood on the basis of elaborate and detailed sociolinguistic studies of modern language situations and developments.

Special mention may here be made of Labov's theory of the social motivation of linguistic change (Labov 1965, 1972), which has given a new impulse to the formulation of models of linguistic change, and has provided the basis for a great number of well-documented socio-linguistic studies (Hock 1991b:646ff). While in earlier research 'the past' was studied in order to explain 'the present', Labov has argued and in fact demonstrated how 'the present' can be used to explain 'the past', i.e. how a better understanding of linguistic processes in present-day communities may help us to understand and reconstruct the past (cf. Labov 1994:9-27). According to Labov (1994:27), "The close examination of the present shows that much of the past is still with us. The study of history benefits from the continuity of the past as well as from analogies with the present."

The main non-linguistic factors taken into account in socio-linguistic studies on the relations and interactions between different languages in certain regions are usually limited to those of socio-economical and political power, vs. solidarity and affect (cf. Gibbons 1992:24). The fact that a language is spoken by an economically and politically powerful group should explain the adoption of that language by a group aspiring a higher status, or the conscious rejection of that language by a group opposing the dominant powerful group. In the work of Pierre Bourdieu, as far as it deals with language and power, the factor power is represented mainly by the state, and his examples usually concern the socio-linguistic conditions in France and Algeria (cf. Bourdieu 1991).

It can be said, therefore, that recent decades have seen considerable progress in the formulation of theories and concepts concerning processes of language change and processes in (mainly contemporaneous and relatively recent) social contexts, and that at the same time questions regarding linguistic origins and developments in the past have presented themselves much more than before in social and sociolinguistic terms. It is in this situation that the early but also the recent history of Sanskrit acquire special importance, because they present us not only with a series of urgent questions and problems, but also with an enormous amount of data concerning developments of more than 20 centuries and covering areas extending from the Indian subcontinent to Central Asia and the remote corners of East and Southeast Asia. On the one hand, the questions and problems concerning the history of Sanskrit are important in their own right and modern theoretical developments may be expected to contribute to new and more satisfactory answers, on the other hand, attempts to answer them may be expected not only to add an important historical dimension to modern theories on language in social context but also to contribute to their further critical development.

Thus, factors of socio-economical and political power, and factors of solidarity and affect, all have played roles in the history of Sanskrit the importance of which has not yet been fully assessed. As Pollock has convincingly argued, the intimate relation of the factor power with Sanskrit did not arise with the development of Indological studies of India and its languages (something which some of the critics of orientalism seem to suggest), but has its roots much further back in the pre-colonial past (Pollock 1993).

However, in order to account for the spread of Sanskrit in South Asia and beyond and its tenacity in its role of lingua franca of the cultural and political elite in the first millenium C.E., phenomena which transcend the time and space boundaries of states and polities, it may well be necessary to take other factors into account apart from or partly overlapping with the allpervading factors of power and social relations. Whatever the validity of Bourdieu's theories of state-related power for the situation in France and its colonies and for socio-linguistic relations in the modern Western nation-states, it may be doubted whether they can be applied directly to the situation in Asian countries, and, especially, whether they can account for the pre-colonial period in this area, when the 'nation-state' was not yet 'invented'.

2. It is against this background that the International Institute for Asian Studies (Leiden) organized a seminar on the "Ideology and Status of Sanskrit" in November 1994 for which scholars were invited to contribute papers concerning questions such as:

> What were the preconditions, and, subsequently, what were the effects of the formulation of a standard grammar of Sanskrit, and of elaborate theories and metaphysical ideologies around this grammar and the language? What was the interaction between grammar as standardized, reproducible knowledge and power? What was the scope and what were the limitations of the role played by Sanskrit in different social and cultural contexts? What was the role played by Buddhism and Jainism, movements which were to a considerable extent anti-Brahmanic in orientation, in the spread and standardization of Sanskrit? How did the pre-colonial socio-linguistic factors transform or remain or disappear in the colonial and modern period?

Further comments were given in the Introduction to the Abstracts of papers of the seminar:

> So far none of these questions has been satisfactorily answered, although several important beginnings have been made towards the methodical study of the familiar factors of power and solidarity and of possible additional factors. Apart from Pollock's work, mention may be made of Hock & Pandharipande (1976), Deshpande (1993a), van de Walle (1993), and, for the pre-history of Sanskrit, Kuiper (1967a, 1991). It is clear that the historical dimension is extremely significant for a critical assessment also of modern developments, especially in countries such as India with a strong traditionalist orientation. Moreover, because South and Southeast Asia offer such an immense wealth of social and linguistic data over a considerably long period of time, they form an ideal area for testing and developing descriptive and theoretical models for a more general understanding of language change and stability in a complex socio-economical and political context. It is no doubt too early to expect a detailed response from the 'past' to the results of modern synchronic sociolinguistics, not least because much basic philological work of editing and dating texts remains to be done. Nevertheless, already now it is possible and necessary to prepare the ground for a more profound 'cross-fertilization' of historical linguistics with sociolinguistics (cf. Romaine 1982).

The seminar brought together scholars and researchers in the field of South, Southeast and Central Asia, working from different perspectives and with different strategies and methods.[1] The focus was on Sanskrit as a language which has for many centuries played the role of 'high variety of speech' in numerous contexts and communities. Especially, the focus was on implicit and explicit ideologies which have developed around this language in the course of time, and on the status attributed to it, if possible against the background of early and recent socio-political developments as far as they can be reconstructed and observed. The present volume is an outcome of that seminar, although it does not have the character of a genuine 'Proceedings'.[2]

---

[1] A first report in IIAS-Newsletter 4 (spring issue) 1995:5-6 focused on the forum discussion at the end of the seminar.

[2] The papers read at the seminar appear here in an often considerably elaborated and/or revised form. An additional one (viz. P. Dundas' paper) has been incorporated to cover a generally felt lacuna in the discussion of the topic of the seminar. Six other papers presented at the seminar were either planned for publication elsewhere, or they fell outside

3. The much used (and misused) term 'ideology' calls for a few comments at this place. As pointed out recently by M. Silverstein in his contribution to the special issue of *Pragmatics* devoted to "Language Ideology" (vol. 2.3, 1992), the term 'ideology' was introduced by the French philosopher and nobleman A. Destutt de Tracy (1754-1836):

> Ideology was proposed as that special branch of zoölogy that recognizes the condition of humans, we animals who have ideas as the content of what we would call our minds. Central here is the fact that any ideas more developed than physiological sensations are dependent on such ideas' being clothed in signs, the organization of which by some systematic grammar allows the discursive expression of of a logical faculty of mind. Hence, for Destutt de Tracy, there is the general scientific field of ideology proper, the science of ideas, of which the subfield of grammar studies the signifying externalizations
> . . . Such a science would, for its propounder, also allow us to diagnose and understand "the causes of incertitude and [logical] error," thus presumably leading to an amelioration of the human condition vis-à-vis its natural mental faculties. (Silverstein 1992:311)

However, the term 'ideology', "proposed as a formation parallel to any of the other '-ologies' of a systematic scientific outlook" denotes nowadays "a part or aspect of Destutt de Tracy's very object of investigation, and in many appearances has the specifically 'pejorative' use . . . that presupposes we know certain ideas to be dubious, in error, and therefore suspect or at least suspicious, in the manner of 'mere' ideas as opposed to material, historical, indeed factual 'realities'" (Silverstein 1992:311f). In her introduction to the above-mentioned issue of *Pragmatics*, K. Woolard mentions, apart from the pejorative connotation, several other features which the notion of 'ideology' has in contemporary discourse, and observes that there are especially four often recurring features, none of which is universal to all usages.

(1) The first recurring feature is that ideology is taken as "conceptual or ideational, having to do with consciousness, beliefs, notions, or ideas." Ideology is here "the more intellectual and conceptual constituent of culture, the basic notions that the members of a society hold about a

---

the scope of the concept of this volume which was more strictly formulated than the invitaton for contributions to the seminar. Nevertheless, also these papers and the ensuing discussions have contributed substantially to the success of the seminar. Thanks are due to all contributors to the seminar and all participants for their enthusiastic participation.

fairly definite area such as honor, the division of labor (or we could propose, language) . . . " (Woolard 1992:237).
(2) According to a second recurring feature such an ideology consisting of a set of beliefs is viewed as "derived from, rooted in, reflective of, or responsive to the experience or interests of a particular social position, although they may be represented as universally true" (idem).
(3) According to a third feature, an ideology is always a matter of "distortion, falsity, mystification, or rationalization" (Woolard 1992:238).
(4) The fourth feature, finally, makes ideology something which is intimately connected to social power and its legitimation, or even a "tool or property of dominant social groups."

Woolard sees two additional parameters on which different understandings of the notion 'ideology' differ: the degree to which ideology is a coherent system, and the degree to which it is conscious and explicit (idem).

It will not be difficult to argue that each of the above-mentioned interpretations of 'ideology' may have its relevance in an analysis of the situation of Sanskrit in different periods and areas. In the quotation from Erdosy (1995:3) given above, reference was made to an 'ideology' of the Ṛgvedic Aryans. Although scholars disagree whether language-differences played a role in this Ṛgvedic 'ideology' (the texts do not clearly refer to people with 'un-Aryan' speech) they certainly started to do so in the 'Aryan ideology' and 'Brahminical ideology' of subsequent periods (e.g. Deshpande 1993a:53-107). The association of Sanskrit with certain social classes or status groups makes the links between ideology and dominant (in some situations also subversive) groups relevant. Even the more traditional understanding of ideology as a rather neutral concept of a 'set of beliefs' has its value simply because so much explicit statements and reflections on Sanskrit are available in the literature. At the same time it is exciting to explore the consequences of applying more critically refined concepts such as that of 'ideology' as a strategy in a context of lived relations (as John D. Kelly does in his contribution to this volume). For the sake of conceptual clarity, however, I would suggest to use another term to discuss aspects of the inescapably lived relations—and at the same time briefly explain another crucial word in the title of the book and the seminar: the term 'status', which, if we attribute it to Sanskrit ("the status of Sanskrit") may refer to the role this language plays in systems of social status. (For other terminological proposals see Briggs 1992 and Kelly in this volume.)

It is important to note that language ideology is not just an epiphenomenon to language and its use, but a factor actually affecting its structure. Thus, one of the strands in the feminist attack on the generic uses of "he," is an ideology "that the divisions and structures of language should—and in the best circumstances do—transparantly fit the divisions and structures of the 'real world'" (Woolard 1992:241f, referring to studies of M. Silverstein and Alan Rumsey).

Whatever the various meanings and uses of the terms 'ideology' and 'status', as far as Sanskrit is concerned they divert the attention from its 'wonderful structure' (cf. Sir William Jones quoted above) which has attracted so much attention of scholars since the beginning of the 19th century, and emphasize instead its use and place in a social context. Indeed, it can be said that in spite of competing understandings of the term 'ideology', in almost all uses it highlights the social dimensions of thought. [3]

4. Having briefly discussed some general aspects of the notion of 'ideology', and, incidentally, of the notion of 'status' as well, it is now time for an introductory discussion of Sanskrit and especially its history, so that the reader has a preliminary framework in which to place the topics of the papers in this volume. Before I present my "brief annotated chronological table," however, I would like to enumerate the most important presently available sources for the history of Sanskrit. Although the number of publications containing relevant material for a history of Sanskrit is exceedingly high (to be included are not only all studies of the grammar, style and vocabulary of Sanskrit in different periods and context, but also any contribution to dating and localizing a text or group of texts and to contextualizing it socially), and while there is also a good number of "Histories of Sanskrit Literature" (Keith 1928,

---

[3] I do not subscribe to Woolard's statement that "in spite of competing understandings of the term, in almost all its uses it highlights the social *origins* of thought" (1992:237, emphasis mine). Her next statement, however, remains valid: "The label ideology calls attention to the socially-situated and/or experientially-derived dimension of cognition or consciousness, simultaneously positioning our research within traditionally cultural and social theoretical realms."

Dasgupta 1947, and as a major segment of a history of Indian literature e.g. Winternitz 1907-22, and Gonda's *History of Indian Literature* starting with Gonda 1975), there are very few publications comprehensively dealing with the entire subject of "the history of the Sanskrit language," and, unavoidably when a subject requiring an encyclopedic treatment is dealt with in one or two hundred pages, those which do so hardly exceed the status of partly inspired and partly popularizing scholarly essays.

To the best of my knowledge, the most recent booklength discussion of this subject is Renou's *Histoire de la Langue Sanskrite* (1956b). For all its valuableness and insightfulness, and for all its richness in the information offered, it is still to be admitted, to quote Wezler's remark at the conclusion of the 1994 seminar, that it is "only a beginning." An earlier booklength discussion appeared also in French as the "Esquisse d'une Histoire de la Langue Sanscrite" (Mansion 1931), with its much more modest title giving nevertheless a good overview of the information available in its time. Grammars and general works on Sanskrit sometimes contain important contributions on the history of Sanskrit. In his elaborate "Introduction" (42 pp. + 82 pp. notes) to the second edition (1957) of Wackernagel's *Altindische Grammatik Bd. 1*, Louis Renou follows and greatly expands Wackernagel's original "Einleitung" (1896). Important material is further found in Renou and J. Filliozat's *l'Inde Classique* (1947a). Burrow's *The Sanskrit Language* contains a valuable chapter "Outlines of the History of Sanskrit" (1955, revised ed. 1973). Relevant for the history of Sanskrit is also van Buitenen's "Brief history of the languages of India" (Buitenen 1978).

Since language is not an independently evolving organism but rather, to the very core of its system, a social phenomenon, any history of a language will of necessity have to deal with its social conditions and functions: to a considerable extent it will have to be a *social* history. However, it should not just be a social history of the speakers and employers of Sanskrit, but should also deal with the linguistic developments and fluctuations, as well as with the sociolinguistic factors and processes associated or correlated with these.

The following chronological table will therefore (1) enumerate and briefly comment on some major social and political events (the earliest of them entirely hypothetical) which have been influential in the history of the Sanskrit language, or which are indicative of aspects of its situation; (2) mention some of the (postulated) major sociolinguistic processes taking place in the different periods. By extension and in accordance with the usage of some (Thieme 1994b and Wezler in note 73 to his contribution to this volume) though not all scholars (Mayrhofer 1986-), I will use the name "Sanskrit" here also for its earlier stages (various forms of Vedic). I will insert one or two references to each of the 17 papers presented in this volume at the appropriate points. This, together with the incidental references in the preceding sections of this introduction, should suffice to introduce the papers to the reader and contextualize them in this volume. After all, each paper has its own unity in subject matter and argument and often has a brief introduction and conclusion by the author, making any additional observations on their place and importance in the volume superfluous. It is left to the reader to discover and be inspired by the dynamics of the continuities and contrasts between the topics and arguments of the different authors.

The Social History of Sanskrit: a Brief Annotated Chronological Table

2000-1500 B.C.E.: The period after the hypothetical date of the end of the Harappan culture, and preceding the hypothetical date of the composition of the Ṛg-Veda, the oldest available text (in Vedic Sanskrit). Available data: archeological findings inthe north of the Indian subcontinent, including Pakistan, Afghanistan, parts in the former USSR to the north-west of these areas; in addition, the linguistic reconstructions and projections into the past on the basis of the Indo-Aryan, Dravidian, and other languages nowadays spoken in these and neighbouring areas. Statements on this period are theoretically and ideology sensitive; in spite of their hypothetical character they attract a lot of attention because of the importance of the cultural capital at stake (such as, the past and origin of Sanskrit, and of South Asian, Asian and European people). Crucial sociolinguistic processes projected into this period are: language contact and shift, bilingualism, convergence (cf. Mallory 1989, Allchin 1995, Hock present volume).

1500-500 B.C.E.: Period of (early and middle) Vedic texts. Fixation of some major Vedic rituals and ritual texts. (The performance of these rituals must have led to linguistic interactions to some extent similar to those in the 20th century studied by Deshpande present volume.) A pre-classical Sanskrit (Aklujkar present volume) or Brahminical koinè with traces of Vedic dialects (Witzel 1989) emerge and acquire a relatively dominant position.

5th-4th century B.C.E.: Lord Mahāvīra and the Buddha, living in or near the important political centre Magadha, teach not in the Brahminical koinè but in Prakritic languages (Middle-Indo-Aryan dialects). Roughly contemporaneous with these religious teachers, but living far away from them in the northwest, Pāṇini composes his grammar (Kelly present volume). Earliest roughly dated Brāhmī inscriptions (Prakritic) in Sri Lanka (Allchin 1995). Parallel with 'Sanskrit proper', Epic or Purāṇic Sanskrit, Buddhist Hybrid Sanskrit and other varieties start to develop (Aklujkar present volume).

3rd century B.C.E.: Emperor Aśoka. Brāhmī inscriptions (mainly in Prakritic languages, not in Sanskrit) on rock- and pillar edicts throughout Aśoka's empire.

2nd century B.C.E. - 5th century C.E.: Menander, most important king of the Indo-Greeks (2nd century C.E.), allegedly having philosophical discussions with the Buddhist monk Nāgasena (Milindapañha). Buddhist schools of thought, Sanskrit grammarians, Brahminical philosophical systems formulate views on the relation between language (in the course of time more and more often: Sanskrit) and reality (Bronkhorst present volume). Sanskrit fulfils the role of a religious-philosophical link-language (Aklujkar, Kelly, present volume). Jainas resist the drive for Sanskrit in religious-philosophical discourse even when it is already widely used in many Buddhist schools (Dundas present volume).

5th century C.E.: Bhartṛhari writes his Vākyapadīya, compendium on philosophical and semantic aspects of Pāṇinian grammar and records three current perspectives on the linguistic situation (apparently diglossic) of his time and milieu (Houben present volume).

4th - 13th century C.E.: Inscriptions in Sanskrit (instead of the previous mainly Prakritic inscriptons) expressing political power appear throughout the Indian subcontinent, and in regions as far off as Vietnam, Cambodia, and Indonesia. The sudden emergence, and eventually the equally sudden decline, of the 'Sanskrit Cosmopolis', which, because of the relative abundance of the available data, promises to offer a good basis for theorizing processes of transculturation, sanskritization, vernacularization (Pollock present volume).

7th century C.E.: The Chinese Buddhist pilgrim Yì jìng (I-tsing) stays in Bhoja (Sumatra) for six months in order to study Sanskrit, before continuing his journey to India (Radicchi present volume).

7th to 9th century C.E.: First wave of Sanskrit-Tibetan translating activities (Verhagen present volume).

10th century C.E.: Digambara Jain Prabhācandra provides a succinct critique (in Sanskrit) of the standard Sanskrit-centered worldview of the Brahmins (Dundas present volume).

10th century C.E.: Earliest recorded use of Indian metrics in the indigenous Khmer language (Terwiel present volume).

10th/11th century C.E.: Third Pariccheda dealing with Sanskrit compounds and appended to the Kārakasaṁgraha is probably composed on Java before it arrives on Bali where it has been preserved (Radicchi present volume).

10th - 13th century C.E.: Coḷas rule south India and produce many bilingual, Sanskrit-Tamil inscriptions (Menon, Pollock present volume).

11th century C.E.: Kashmirian Kṣemarāja comments on aspects of ('ungrammatical') language use in Tantric texts (Goudriaan present volume).

13th century C.E.: First sultanates in Delhi.

14th-15th century C.E.: A Pali inscripton, and later a text in Thai, point to the Pali text Vuttodaya (based on the Sanskrit Vṛttaratnākara of Kedāra Bhaṭṭa) as the most likely immediate source of Indian prosody in Thailand (Terwiel present volume).

17th century C.E.: Bilingual agreements between the Dutch and South Indian rulers (in Dutch and Telugu, Dutch and Tamil; Menon present volume).

17th-18th century C.E.: Production of 'manuals of spoken Sanskrit' to promote active use of Sanskrit (Wezler present volume).

18th century C.E.: The Tibetan scholar Si-tu "mahāpaṇḍita" searching for Sanskrit manuscripts in Tibet and Nepal, revising Buddhist canonical translations, translating Sanskrit grammatical texts into Tibetan (Verhagen present volume).

1784: Foundation of the Asiatic Society in Bengal.

1818: British victory over the Marathas.

19th - early 20th century: Emerging nationalism, Sanskrit (and sanskritized New-Indo-Aryan languages) become markers of Hindu-identity (van Bijlert, van der Burg, Bhate present volume). Rammohun Roy, Bankimchandra Chatterjee and Rabindranath Tagore (re-)construct a glorious past of the Hindu nation on the basis of Sanskrit literature (van Bijlert present volume). The Swamis Dayananda and Vivekananda, Shri Aurobindo, RSS promote the popularization of Skt language and literature (sanskritization), but more practical roles are assigned to (sanskritized) Hindi (van der Burg present volume). Study and status of Sanskrit in India are reinforced by the study of Sanskrit in Europe and U.S.A. (Bhate present volume).

Recent decades: Performances of traditional Hindu rituals with Sanskrit and Vedic formulas (mantras) by priests for lay people lead to complex processes of interaction between different languages and varieties of languages, especially to sanskritizations of vernaculars and vernacularizations of Sanskrit (Deshpande present volume, whose approach seems promising for the study and understanding not only of present-day sociolinguistic processes, but also of those of the past).

It will be one of the tasks laying ahead in the historiography of the Sanskrit language to precisely demarcate the periods (as well as areas of influence) and to identify the major cultural, social and sociolinguistic processes and factors at work within each period (within a certain area). The three chronologically overlapping sections over which the contributions have been divided[4] constitute therefore not more than a preliminary organization of the material. These three sections are:

Part 1: Origins and Creation of the 'Eternal Language'. This period includes the composition of the Ṛg-Veda, ca. 1500 B.C.E. One of its major landmarks is Pāṇini's grammar ca. 350 B.C.E. contributing greatly to establishing a recognizable and reproducible language. The ideological side of the creation of the 'eternal' language continues to the present day, but Bhartṛhari's work (5th century C.E.) would be a good point to demarcate the culmination of the earliest phase.

Part 2: Transculturation, Sanskritization, Vernacularization. This is Pollock's 'Sanskrit Cosmopolis' (defined for 300-1300 C.E.) plus some later centuries to accommodate late (not exclusively political) manifestations (e.g. in Tibet, 18th century, in Thai prosody mediated by the Pali language) when the Cosmopolis had already been replaced by other cultural formations in Cambodia, Vietnam, Indonesia. The processes of "transculturation, sanskritization, vernacularization" presuppose a linguistically well-established Sanskrit already widely acknowledged as a repository of 'cultural capital'.

Part 3: The Sanskrit Tradition: Continuity from the past or Construction from the present? The period of "constructing a tradition" starts in fact when the idea of an eternal Sanskrit language is first constructed, and continues to the present day. Earlier trends to attempt/pretend to continue an 'ageold tradition' when promoting Sanskrit (cf. Wezler present volume), acquire new dimensions when they combine with emerging forms of Indian nationalism during the period of colonization and after independence. With an increasing globalisation of South Asia, familiar processes of "transculturation, sanskritization, vernacularization" start to operate on an entirely different scale.

---

[4] Within each section the papers are in the chronological order of the main period discussed, except that in the second part they are ordered first according to geographic, next according to chronological considerations. It has been attempted to homogenize the style of the papers, but some variation was allowed in matters of their internal organization, preferences in (British or American) spelling, and the spelling of certain Sanskrit or Anglicized Sanskrit words.

Part One

Origins and Creation of the 'Eternal Language'

CHAPTER TWO

PRE-RGVEDIC CONVERGENCE BETWEEN INDO-ARYAN (SANSKRIT) AND DRAVIDIAN? A SURVEY OF THE ISSUES AND CONTROVERSIES*

Hans Henrich Hock

एतद्धस्तिदर्शन इव जात्यन्धाः (Śaṅkarācārya's bhāṣya on Chāndogya-Upaniṣad 5.18.1)

1. Introduction

South Asia is home to at least six distinct language families: Indo-Aryan, Eastern Iranian, Tibeto-Burman, Austro-Asiatic, Munda, and Dravidian, plus an 'unaffiliated' language in the extreme north, Burushaski.[1] (For a simplified view of where these languages are spoken today see Map I.) Indo-Aryan and Iranian are closely related to each other, and Munda is remotely related to Austro-Asiatic. For the remaining language families, outside genetic relationship is at best controversial. If they are related to each other, their relationship is so remote that any shared similarities must be secondary.

This paper grows out of continuing research on prehistoric and early historic South Asian convergence. Part of the research has been supported by a fall 1994 grant from the University of Illinois Research Board and by a spring 1995 sabbatical leave. I have profited from comments on an earlier version of this paper, read at the International Seminar on 'Ideology and Status of Sanskrit in India and Asia', International Institute for Asian Studies, Leiden (NL), and I would like to express my thanks to the organizer of the Seminar, Jan Houben. A related paper was read at the March 1995 Symposium on 'Language and prehistory in South Asia', University of Hawaii, at which I received valuable reactions from Murray Emeneau and Bh. Krishnamurti. Finally, I express my gratitude to Rahul Peter Das for sending me a copy of Hoffmann 1941. As usual, the responsibility for any mistakes in this paper rests with me.

[1] Nahali might constitute the remnant of yet another language family (Kuiper 1962, 1966 with references).

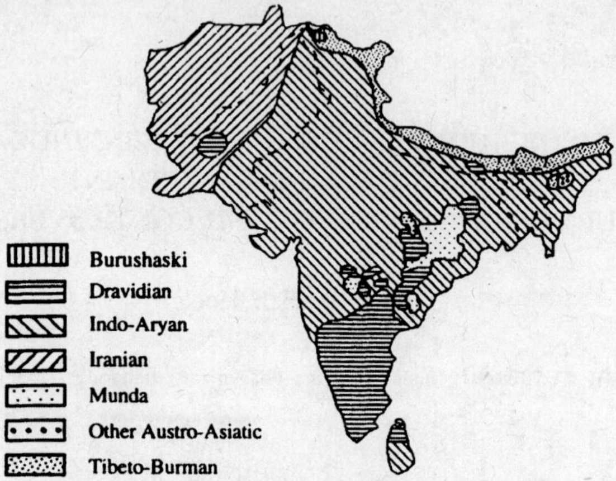

Map I: Simplified map of South Asian languages

Nevertheless, as is well known, over millenia of bi- and multilingual contact the languages have come to converge to a remarkable degree in their overall structure. (For a good synchronic discussion see Masica 1976.) Four features are commonly listed as characteristic of the South Asian Convergence Area.[2] These are:

These are:

I. An unmarked major constituent order Subject (S) — Object (O) — Verb (V), as in example (1);

II. A tendency to use non-finite absolutives, where modern European languages might use dependent clauses with finite verbs (2);

III. The marking of cited discourse by postposed quotative markers and a general absence of indirect disourse (3);

IV. A phonological contrast between dental and retroflex consonants (4).

---

[2] Another feature, which has recently been reintroduced into the literature by Abbi (1992), is lexical 'reduplication' or iteration (Skt. *āmreḍita*). Her study shows that this feature is interesting and relevant; but as Hock 1993b shows, its historical antecedents are not entirely clear: Non-verbal iteration is found to varying degrees in many early Indo-European languages, but verbal iteration (of the type Skt. *utplutyā_utplutya* ... 'continually jumping up') first appears in late Vedic. Unfortunately, the history of iteration in the non-Indo-Aryan languages of South Asia is not well understood.

(1) Hindi *maĩ* (S) *kitāb* (O) *paṛh rahā hū̃* (V) "I am reading a book."

(2) Skt. *tatra* ***gatvā*** (abs.) na mucyase "When you have gone there, you do not get free."

(3) Skt. *nakiḥ vaktā 'na dād'* ***iti*** (quot.) "Nobody will say, 'He shall not give.'"

(4) Skt. *pāta-* 'flight' : *pāṭa-* 'portion'

As is common in convergence areas,[3] the features I - IV do not necessarily cover the entire region: Kashmiri places finite verbs in second position in main and *ki/zi*-clauses, and SVO features are found in many Munda/Austro-Asiatic languages; Hindi-Urdu, Kashmiri, and many other Indo-Aryan languages, but also Dravidian Brahui mark direct discourse by preposed *ki*; Assamese lacks the contrast dental : retroflex. To judge by the evidence of Sanskrit, the absence of these features in some of the modern Indo-Aryan languages is secondary: On Kashmiri verb-second position see Hock 1982a. The use of *ki* as a direct discourse marker no doubt reflects Persian influence (see Hock 1982b, which however is in need of revision). And the absence of the dental : retroflex contrast in Assamese probably reflects contact with Tibeto-Burman.

The question of when South Asian convergence began and which group is responsible for it is highly interesting for anyone concerned with the early linguistic and ethnic history of South Asia. Attempts to answer the question, however, have given rise to considerable controversy.

As early as 1833, Pott considered the dental : retroflex contrast of Sanskrit to be at least partly due to the influence of the 'autochthonous' languages (78),[4] later specifying these as Dravidian (1836: 19, 453). Since Caldwell's similar claim (1856: 38), there has been a steady increase in the number of linguists subscribing to this view, and adding other features claimed to result from Dravidian 'substratum' influence, above all those in I - III.

The Dravidian substratum hypothesis is often supported by additional evidence, such as lexical borrowings from Dravidian into Indo-

[3] See e.g. Masica 1976 and Hock 1988a.

[4] However, on p. 175 he cited Middle Indo-Aryan as a possible source for certain unexpected Sanskrit retroflex consonants.

Aryan or the modern geographical distribution of Dravidian languages, facts which are considered to support the claim that Dravidian and Indo-Aryan were in contact in prehistoric times, in the extreme northwestern area first settled by the Indo-Aryans.

The most powerful arguments have been advanced by Emeneau 1954, 1956, 1980 and Kuiper 1967ab. As a result of these arguments, the essential correctness of the hypothesis is now widely accepted, including in Thomason & Kaufman 1988, a monograph on linguistic contact in general.

Most of the modern proponents of the hypothesis would subscribe to the following assumptions:

- All of the features I - IV can be reconstructed for Proto-Dravidian;
- The ancestors of the other languages lacked the features (or at least some of them);
- The SIMPLEST assumption is that the presence of the features in the other languages reflects the influence of Dravidian;
- The presence of features I - IV in non-Dravidian languages provides CUMULATIVE evidence for Dravidian influence;
- Since the features are found in the earliest attested stage of Indo-Aryan, (Ṛg-)Vedic Sanskrit, Dravidian substratum influence on Indo-Aryan must have begun prehistorically, in the second millenium BCE;
- The sociolinguistic setting for this influence was one of inequality: The conquering Indo-Aryans forced the indigenous Dravidians to learn their Sanskrit language; and as English has been influenced by the modern South Asian languages, the structure of Sanskrit was altered by transfer of Dravidian features.

Though widely accepted, the Dravidian substratum hypothesis has not remained unchallenged. Questions have been raised as to the cogency of the evidence which supposedly establishes a Dravidian presence in prehistoric northwest South Asia. Moreover, it has been claimed that features I - IV can be explained as the result of internal Indo-Aryan developments and/or as inheritance from Proto-Indo-European, thus making it unnecessary to assume Dravidian influence. The earliest scholar to have expressed such doubts seems to have been

Bühler 1864. See also Bloch 1925: 16, 29,[5] as well as Hock 1975, 1984, and the literature cited there.

Hock (1975, 1984) in addition argues that a prehistoric argument resting on circumstantial evidence, such as the Dravidian substratum hypothesis, must be established BEYOND A REASONABLE DOUBT. This claim states in bold terms a view underlying many of the arguments against the Dravidian substratum hypothesis: A cumulation of weak arguments does not necessarily add up to a strong case.

There are of course difficulties with the 'reasonable-doubt' argument, the most important being the question of 'How reasonable is reasonable?' Thomason & Kaufman (1988) for instance consider the 'reasonable-doubt' criterion overly restrictive and prefer to adhere to the notion 'simplicity'. However, historical linguistics furnishes ample evidence that what *ex post facto* may be the simplest argument is incorrect when the historical record is examined. (See for instance Hock 1991b:8 on a change of dissimilation which was later 'undone' by assimilation, giving the appearance of no change at all.) It may further be claimed that restrictive criteria (such as 'reasonable doubt') are heuristically useful: Like the neogrammarian hypothesis of absolute regularity in sound change, they force the investigator to examine the evidence more carefully (so as to offer more convincing arguments) than a less restrictive approach; and this, in turn, can lead to better insights into the nature of language change.

No matter which side of the two conflicting views may turn out to be correct, much of the controversy about the Dravidian substratum hypothesis is attributable to this difference in outlook.

There is another potential argument which, to my knowledge, has not been sufficiently examined in the literature. This is the question whether the concept 'substratum' is appropriate for the prehistoric contact (if there was any) between Dravidian and Indo-Aryan.

Nineteenth-century scholars like Pott and Caldwell would by and large be familiar only with the concept 'substratum' as an explanation for structural influence between languages. In the terminology of Thomason & Kaufman (1988), substratum influence results from the 'shift' of speakers from one language to another (usually from a lan-

[5] Bloch later changed his opinion; see e.g. 1929: 723-724, 1934: 53-54.

guage of lower prestige or power to one of higher prestige or power), with transfer of structural features from their native or primary language to the target language. Let us characterize this UNIDIRECTIONAL scenario as one of 'SUBVERSION'.

Although the word is somewhat loaded because of its use in current 'Critical Theory', it is useful to employ the term subversion as an abbreviation for 'substratum influence' and in the form Subversion, with initial capital (to distinguish it from the general phenomenon), as an abbreviation for such expressions as 'Dravidian substratum', 'Dravidian influence', and even short-hand for 'Dravidian substratum hypothesis'. Opponents of the hypothesis will be referred to as being 'ANTI-SUBVERSION'.

We now know that language contact can yield a variety of other results; see e.g. the discussion and references in Hock 1991b: Chapter 16. The most important among these for present purposes is 'CONVERGENCE', a mutual or BIDIRECTIONAL development through which languages in long-standing bilingual contact come to be more similar in their overall structure, while often retaining very distinct vocabularies. (The notion 'convergence' and 'convergence area', Germ. Sprachbund, was introduced by Jakobson 1931 and Trubetzkoy 1931. Emeneau has introduced and popularized an alternative term, 'linguistic area'. For historical/dynamic treatments of South Asian convergence, both 'global' and more localized, see e.g. Emeneau 1989, Gumperz & Wilson 1971, Krishnamurti 1991, Pandharipande 1982.)

In contrast to subversion, convergence crucially does not require shift from one language to another, but rather bilingualism (or multilingualism) over an extended period. Such continued bilingualism is best maintained in a situation of approximate social equality; but it can arise under other conditions as well, such as a 'social imperative' of maintaining ethnic, religious, etc. identity by preserving linguistic distinctiveness. Under such conditions there may occur multiple—and bidirectional—transfer and other modifications of linguistic structure, especially of features that make it easier to switch back and forth between the languages involved. As Gumperz and Wilson (1971) claim, given extended and intensive enough contact, convergence may ultimately result in languages with virtually identical grammars, but with very different lexica and morphology. (Maintaining different lexica and morphology makes it possible for speakers to believe that they are still meeting the 'social imperative' of speaking different languages; see Hock 1991b: Chapter 16).

In observable history, the interaction between South Asian languages seems to more typically involve convergence than subversion, at least between the 'literary' languages (and, to judge by the Nilgiri evidence discussed in Emeneau 1989, also between 'non-literary' languages among each other). We must therefore ask if the prehistoric sociolinguistic situation was sufficiently different to result in subversion rather than convergence.

In the remainder of this paper I examine in greater detail the major arguments that have been raised, or could be raised, in favor of one or another of the different views outlined so far. Although I have been partisan to some of the arguments and have definite views of my own, I will try to be fair in presenting the various arguments, discussing the assumptions (hidden or explicit) on which they are based, and evaluating their cogency and underlying assumptions. Even if some readers may disagree with my evaluation, I hope that they will find the presentation of arguments and assumptions stimulating for further research. As a last caveat I should mention that in order to keep the paper in manageable proportions, I have to forgo discussing many interesting arguments and details. For these I must ask the readers to pursue the discussion and references in the cited literature.

2. The major arguments for Subversion

Most proponents of Subversion would agree on the presence of the features I - IV above in the earliest Indo-Aryan, Ṛgvedic Sanskrit, as evidence for prehistoric Dravidian influence.

The most comprehensive discussion of the historical background for the features of retroflexion, absolutives, and quotatives is that of Kuiper 1967a (with 1967b). (In addition, Tikkanen provides an excellent survey of earlier and also more recent research.)

2.1. Absolutives

According to Kuiper, the use of absolutives is an inherited feature in Dravidian, but an innovation in Indo-Aryan, as well as Munda: In Dravidian, only absolutive (and other non-finite) constructions are possible for subordination. In Munda, the morphology of the absolutive differs between the northern and southern languages, and no such constructions are attested in the non-South Asian Austro-Asiatic languages. As regards the Indo-Aryan absolutives, Kuiper states that '(i)t is generally agreed that they are comparatively recent innovations', 'practically absent' in the two oldest books of the Ṛg-Veda (IV and VI). At the same time, the morphology of the type *kṛtvā́* 'having done' is quite archaic. Kuiper therefore claims that the formations 'must have emerged among lower social classes and must have been used in colloquial speech, long before they found acceptance in the highly traditional religious poetry'.

2.2. Quotative markers

Kuiper claims that Dravidian only permits direct discourse, followed by a word which means 'having said', e.g. Tamil *eṉṟu*. Only some of the Munda languages have quotative particles which, moreover, dialectally disagree in form; the structures therefore must be secondary. In Indo-Iranian, Iranian only shows Avestan *uiti* 'thus' + verb of speaking either preposed or inserted into the direct discourse, but not postposed. Postposed, and clearly quotative, *iti* is limited to Indo-Aryan. Its presence in the Ṛg-Veda is due to Dravidian influence.

2.3. SOV word order

There is a general consensus that Munda SOV is a South Asian 'areal' innovation, since non-Munda Austro-Asiatic languages have SVO and since certain features connected with SVO persist in Munda. The claim that Indo-Aryan SOV is due to Subversion is not as commonly made by

South Asianists as it is by Indo-Europeanists, such as Friedrich 1975, 1976, 1977, or Miller 1975. The argument is based on the observation that the earliest, Ṛgvedic language has a much smaller percentage of SOV structures (about 65%) than the later language of Vedic Prose (with about 95% SOV). This difference is taken to indicate a change toward the more strict SOV order of Dravidian.

2.4. *Retroflex*

Early scholars like Pott could simply assert that Indo-Aryan (Sanskrit) retroflex consonants reflect Dravidian influence, but as time progressed it became necessary to go beyond such blanket statements and to state precisely how this influence exerted itself. What was especially troubling was that, by and large, early Indo-Aryan retroflexion could be explained by purely internal developments, with parallels in other languages (see e.g. Konow 1906, Bloch 1925). Nevertheless, Konow (1906) and Bloch (1929) believed that Dravidian influence may have accelerated or aided in the propagation of these developments.

Emeneau (1956) and Kuiper (1967a) introduce a much stronger claim, which at the same time attempts to specify the manner in which Dravidian influence may have helped. They claim that prehistoric Dravidian/Indo-Aryan bilingualism led to the 'redistribution' of pre-Indo-Aryan allophones as retroflex phonemes, based on the presence of retroflex phonemes in Dravidian. Kuiper identifies these allophones as Indo-Iranian **š* and **ž*, the elements generally recognized as the 'triggers' for the development of Indo-Aryan retroflexion.[6]

[6] The precise manner in which Indo-Iranian **š* and **ž* gave rise to Indo-Aryan (Vedic Sanskrit) retroflexion, the conditions under which the development took place, and the extension of retroflexion beyond its original domain are still a matter of controversy. For earlier views and literature see Wackernagel 1896, especially pp. 164-177, and Debrunner's supplement of 1957. More recent literature is found, and referred to, in Kuiper 1967b, Hock 1975 (with 1974), Hock 1984 (with 1979, 1987), Kuiper 1991, see also Hock 1991a.

Another controversial issue is the question of the 'spontaneous retroflexion' of dentals, as in RV *atati* 'wanders' vs. later *aṭati*. This development, too, has been attributed to Subversion (e.g. Kuiper 1967a, Emeneau 1974); but alternative solutions have been proposed. Some retroflexes have been explained by sporadic internal developments (such as dissimilation), others as borrowings from 'Vedic Prakrits'; cf. the discussion and

2.5. Cumulativity of evidence and simplicity

According to Kuiper, the history of retroflexion, absolutives, and quotative marking provides CUMULATIVE evidence for Dravidian influence. As Thomason & Kaufman (1988) observe, the existence of such cumulative evidence is significant: Even if we can explain away one feature or another as possibly resulting from internal development or different outside influence, the totality of the evidence still points to just one language as source, namely Dravidian.

Emeneau (1971a) further argues that assuming Dravidian influence is the SIMPLEST explanation, since Dravidian is 'closely contiguous' to

---

references in Wackernagel 1896, Hoffmann 1941, Hock 1975, 1984, and 1991a, Vine 1987. If some of the developments should have been the result of contact, languages other than Dravidian might furnish alternative, or even more plausible sources: As argued in Hock 1984, it is 'difficult to see how [the substitution of retroflex consonants for dentals] could be attributed to the mistakes made by Dravidians trying to speak a Sanskrit with undifferentiated dentals' (cf. Emeneau 1974). Rather, just as in the case of modern-day contacts between Westerners and South Asians, I would expect speakers LACKING the contrast to make mistakes in trying to speak a language which has it. (Perhaps speakers of early forms of Munda, or of Tibeto-Burman, might be involved?)' Support for Tibeto-Burman provenience of some lexical items may be found in the fact that except where it has undergone South Asian influence, Tibeto-Burman has undifferentiated alveolars which could be nativized either as dentals or as retroflexes in languages like Indo-Aryan which already had a contrast dental : retroflex (whether that contrast was due to Subversion or not). That this is not just a thought experiment is suggested by the evidence in Witzel 1995 for river names ending in *-ta* or *-ṭa* (with apparent dental : retroflex variation) at the Himalayan border of Vedic Sanskrit, i.e., in an area where a Tibeto-Burmese presence is most likely. Interestingly, *kirāta*, the name of a non-Aryan people mentioned in the Ṛg-Veda and tentatively identified as Tibeto-Burman by Witzel, has a Pali variant with retroflex, *kirāṭa*.

Hock 1991a adds the further possibility that some 'spontaneous' changes of dental to retroflex may have resulted from inner-Indo-Aryan differences suggested by the Prātiśākhyas (such that a 'tooth-root' *t* of one variety of Vedic could be reinterpreted as postdental and therefore retroflex in another variety which had interdental *t*).

We should, I think, also consider the possibility that retroflexes replaced earlier dentals through sporadic analogical developments. Note in this regard Hoffmann's (1941) observation that most Sanskrit words with retroflex *-ṇḍ-* belong to one of two semantic categories, that of 'roundness' and that of 'breaking, crushing'. As Hoffmann correctly notes, this fact makes it possible that *-ṇḍ-* was secondarily extended to words belonging to one or the other of these categories.

Indo-Aryan and has all of these features. 'It hardly seems useful to take into account the possibility of another language, or language family, totally lost to the record, as the source.' This argument, too, has been adopted by Thomason & Kaufman, and cited as strong support for Dravidian subversion.

3. *Additional evidence for Subversion*

A number of other phenomena have been cited as supporting evidence, with varying degrees of agreement among different scholars. The following discussion centers on the most commonly cited arguments and/or on arguments that have been found relevant in Thomason & Kaufman's recent discussion of the issue.[7]

3.1. The evidence of Brahui

Most advocates of prehistoric Dravidian influence would agree on the significance of the presence of a Dravidian language, Brahui, in the extreme northwest of South Asia, close to the area of first settlement by Indo-Aryans in South Asia. The geographical isolation of Brahui, combined with the fact that most migrations have taken place from north(west) to south, is taken to establish that Brahui is a relic language, rather than a recent migrant to the area, and thus guarantees the presence of Dravidians in the area, at the time of Indo-Aryan arrival. The view is often considered supported by the fact that two other Dravidian languages, Kurukh and Malto, which with Brahui form the North Dravidian subfamily, are spoken fairly to the north, in eastern Central India, suggesting that Brahui was part of a Dravidian subfamily which extended over a vast portion of northern South Asia.

---

[7] Fuller discussion, including of somewhat antiquated arguments, can be found in Hock 1975 and 1984 (with references). For Emeneau's 1974 lexical-syntactic arguments regarding Skt. *api* : Drav. *-um*, see Hock 1975 and Gil 1994 (who apparently had not read Hock 1975).

3.2. Other geographical evidence

A second argument, accepted by Thomason & Kaufman (1988), rests on Southworth's attempt (1974) to establish a major east-west division of Indo-Aryan languages for the time of the Aśokan inscriptions (see Map II) and to link this division to more recent evidence that in his view suggests greater Dravidian influence in the west (closer to the area of first Indo-Aryan settlement).

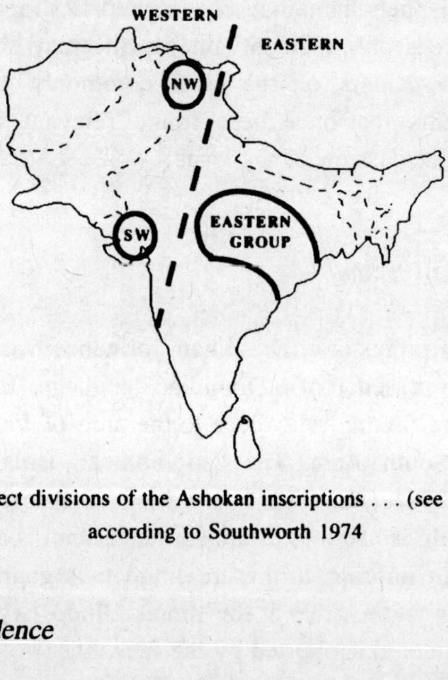

Map II: "Dialect divisions of the Ashokan inscriptions . . . (see Bloch 1950)," according to Southworth 1974

3.3. Lexical evidence

Further direct evidence for prehistoric contact is commonly said to be found in Dravidian lexical borrowings. Some scholars, such as Southworth (1979), Kuiper (1955), and Burrow (1955: 378-9, have compiled long lists of (Ṛg-)Vedic words which they believe to be of Dravidian origin (see also Kuiper 1991, 1992, dedicated to finding evidence for general non-Aryan, not just Dravidian, borrowing). Emeneau (1980) is more cautious, limiting to seven the number of what in his view are probable, or at least attractive, Dravidian borrowings in the Ṛg-Veda:

(5)			
	a. mayū́ra-	'peacock'	Tam. mayil, Mal. mayil
	b. budbudá-	'bubble'	Tel. buḍabuḍa 'with a bubbling noise', Tu. buḍubuḍu 'in drops'; non-redupl. Kan. buḍa, buḍu etc. (DED 3490)
	c. phála-	'fruit'	Ta. par̤u 'ripen', par̤am 'fruit', . . . Malt. páne 'ripen' (DED 3299)
	d. káṭuka-	'bitter, sharp'	Ta. kaṭu 'be sharp, hurt . . . ', . . . Br. kharēn 'bitter' (DED 952)
	e. kāṇá-	'one-eyed'	Drav. * kāṇ- 'see' (DED 1209) + neg. -a- = 'not seeing, blind'
	f. khála-	'thrashing floor'	Ta. kaḷam 'place, . . . thrashing floor', . . . Malt. qalu 'field in the mountains' (DED 1160)
	g. ulū́khala-	'mortar'	Ta. ulakkai 'pestle', Mal. ulakka, . . . Kod. oḷaka 'wooden pestle' (DED 580)

Of these lexical items, Emeneau considered a. and b. most persuasive; item a. because it is least likely to be inherited from Proto-Indo-European, is 'not further analyzable in Skt. terms', and has a closer phonetic resemblance to Dravidian than to Munda; b. because it has no reduplicated antecedents or even parallels in Indo-European etymological dictionaries, because as a type it is characteristically South Asian, and because it has its closest phonetic parallels in Dravidian. For the others, Emeneau believed that Dravidian origin is at least not any less attractive than competing etymologies.

3.4. The social setting

Explicit, or at least implicit, in the subversionist view of early Indo-Aryan/Dravidian contact is the assumption of unilateral influence of Dravidian on Indo-Aryan. (No mention is ever made of prehistoric Indo-Aryan influence on Dravidian.) Such a unilateral development requires the assumption that the prehistoric social relationship between Indo-Aryans and Dravidians was one of considerable inequality.

Dravidian speakers therefore were required to speak Indo-Aryan and, just as happened to English in modern South Asia, in shifting to Indo-Aryan they transfered structural features of their own language(s). This interpretation of Indo-Aryan/Dravidian interaction is aptly summarized by Emenau (1956: note 4):

> . . . it was to their [the Indo-Aryans'] advantage, political, economic, religious, to have subjects and proselytes. Absorption, not displacement is the chief mechanism in radical language changes of the kind we are considering.

This view is often considered supported by the belief that there was a great social chasm between Indo-Aryans and Dravidians, comparable to that between the British and the indigenous Indian population in recent colonial history. This belief, in turn, is considered supported by the claim that the Ṛgvedic Indo-Aryans make a clear ethnic distinction between themselves and the indigenous population, called *dāsas* or *dasyus*, frequently depicting the latter as 'infidels' (*adeva*), and characterizing them as 'black-skinned' in contrast to their own lighter hue. While not accepted by all Subversionists (Emeneau, for instance, does not), this view pervades much of the literature, not only on the linguistic, but also on the general prehistory of South Asia; see the following incomplete list of references: Zimmer 1879 (apparently the first propagator of the view); Macdonnell & Keith 1912: s.vv. *dāsa* and *várṇa*; Chatterji 1926: 7 (with the qualification that the Indo-Europeans were of "unknown racial characteristic (though it is not unlikely that they were Nordic originally [!])") and 32; Elizarenkova 1995: 36; Gonda 1975: 129; Hale 1986: 147 (see also 154); Kuiper 1991: 17 (vs. ibid. 3-4); Kulke & Rothermund 1990: 35; Mansion 1931: 6; Rau 1957: 16; Parpola 1988: 104-106, 120-121, 125; see also Deshpande 1979a: 260, 1993a: 216-127.

The claimed social chasm between Indo-Aryans and the indigenous population is significant in that it would provide support for the view that there was a unidirectional shift, from the Dravidian language of the socially 'inferior', suppressed population to the Indo-Aryan of the conquerors; and this shift, in turn, would motivate a unidirectional process of subversion.

4. *Anti-Subversion arguments*

While some scholars opposed to the Subversion hypothesis may have done so for ideological reasons (sometimes because of taking too literally the testimony of Sanskrit texts regarding linguistic purity), many others have done so for the simple reason that they felt the arguments raised by the pro-Subversion side to be lacking in cogency. This certainly has been the sentiment expressed in my earlier publications, especially Hock 1984.

It is important to note this point, since some Subversionists have misinterpreted the claim that the Subversion hypothesis lacks cogency as tantamount to a claim that most anti-Subversionists would not make, namely that they have 'disproved' the Subversion hypothesis. In principle, most anti-Subversionists leave the issue open for further discussion, with the burden being on the pro-Subversionists to improve their arguments or to find additional, and better, evidence.

Even Subversionists agree that one of the great difficulties in dealing with the linguistic prehistory and early history of South Asia is the fact that we have direct evidence from only one language family, Indo-Aryan; and even for this family the evidence is limited, because the early texts are composed in a language, Vedic Sanskrit, which is quite conservative and puristic. For other languages, we have to depend on evidence from much later periods. Moreover, the existence of language isolates such as Burushaski in the extreme northwest and perhaps also Nahali in Central India (see note 1), raises the possibility that there may have been languages other than Dravidian, Munda, and Tibeto-Burman which were encountered by the Indo-Aryans when they first entered South Asia.

Anti-Subversionists tend to be wary of using evidence such as the Aśokan or even present-day distribution of Dravidian (or Munda) languages, some 2000 to 3500 years after the fact, as support for prehistoric Subversion. The question, therefore, whether a Dravidian presence can be confidently established in the northwestern area of first Indo-Aryan settlement takes on special significance: If the arguments in favor of placing Dravidians in this area are weak, then alternative accounts for the Dravidian/Indo-Aryan structural similarities become more attractive.

For these and other reasons, the order of discussion in this section is different from that in sections 2 and 3.

4.1. The evidence of Brahui

While Brahui is now spoken in the extreme northwest, in a multilingual setting mainly with Iranian Balochi and Pashto, its presence in the area canno be traced back much farther than the sixteenth century.

To my knowledge, Bloch (1911, see also 1925, 1929) was the first to suggest that Brahui may have migrated to the area from farther south: According to their own traditions, the Brahuis (and all other present-day linguistic groups) are different from the original indigenous population and have migrated to the area.[8]

More significant, because better established, is the fact that according to their own tradition, the Kurukh and Malto, close linguistic relatives of Brahui, migrated to their present locations, via the Narmada valley, from a much more southern area in Karnataka; see the citations in Grierson 1903-1928, vol. 4: 406, Hahn 1911, Vesper 1971.[9] Several facts support this tradition: Bloch (1946) points out that the place names in present-day Kurukh and Malto territory are Munda, not Dravidian, in origin. Kuiper (1966) notes that Kurukh influence on Nahali, Kurku, and even Romany 'furnishes valuable linguistic evidence of an earlier settlement of Kurukhs in the Narmadā valley.' And Bhat (1971) shows that Koraga, a language spoken in South Karnataka has linguistic features that exclusively link it with the North Dravidian languages Brahui, Kurukh, and Malto. See Map III for these migrations and for the present-day location of the North Dravidian languages.

---

[8] The value of the tradition is weakened by the claim that the Brahuis came from Aleppo, in present-day Syria [!]; but this element may reflect a later 'Islamization' of an earlier tradition according to which the Brahuis are immigrants to the area.

[9] Their present positions result from migration from the area around Patna, in response to Muslim invasions.

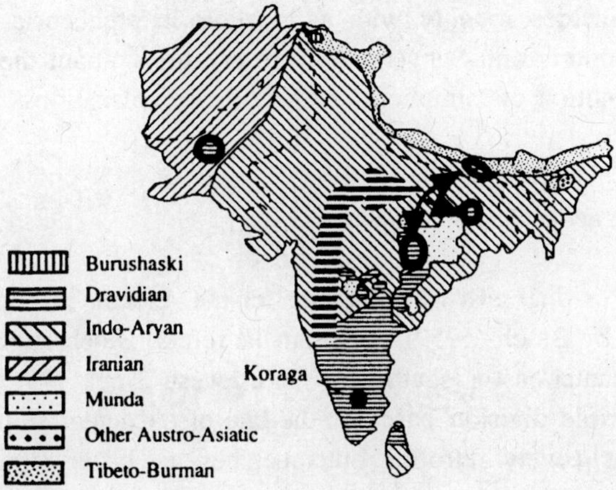

Map III: North Dravidian languages and migrations

The closest relatives of Brahui, thus, either migrated from the south or are now located there. This fact lends credence to the Brahuis' own tradition of foreign origin. As concluded in Hock 1975, 1984, we therefore cannot take the present location of Brahui as guaranteeing a Dravidian presence in the prehistoric northwest.[10]

In all fairness, it must be admitted that we cannot completely rule out such a presence either. It is certainly possible that there were Dravidians in the prehistoric northwest, that the language(s) of these Dravidians subsequently died out, or that the speakers moved further south to escape the Indo-Aryans, and that the present-day northwestern location of Brahui results from REMIGRATION NORTH. In fact, various Indo-Aryan languages and their speakers have likewise remigrated to the north, including Dumaki (close to present-day Shina), Gandhari Prakrit (medieval Khotan and farther east), and Parya in modern Uzbekistan (Comrie 1981). The most famous group is that of the Ḍom (or 'Gypsies') who via Central Asia spread all over Eurasia.

The evidence cited above combined with the possibility of remigration, however, casts doubt on the cogency of what might have appeared the simplest explanation, namely that the present-day location of

---

[10] Note that Emeneau (1962: 70, fn. 10), while preferring to consider Brahui an isolated relic, does admit the possibility that further work may show the language to have migrated from a more southerly position.

Brahui coincides roughly with its location in prehistoric times. This finding supports anti-Subversionist reservations about the cogency of the entire notion of 'simplicity' in historical explanations.

4.2. *Other geographical evidence*

Southworth's dual east-west division for the Aśokan inscriptions is not supported by Bloch (1950), to whom he refers. Bloch suggests a triple division: center/east : [south]west : northwest. Hock 1991a proposes a different triple division based on the fate of *r* + dental stop: northwest (almost exclusively retroflex outcome, beside cluster representations: Shahb. *tr* etc., Mans. *tr* etc.), center (north and south; dominant dental), and east (almost exlusively retroflex). A recent reexamination suggests that the central area must be divided: Southwestern Girnar (dominant dental) vs. north-central Kalsi (retroflex : dental ratio of 4 : 1). While the retroflex ratio of Kalsi is relatively high, it still is considerably lower than the near-absolute retroflex of the east. Given its proximity to the east, Kalsi may be considered a transition area between southwestern dental and eastern retroflex, with its relatively high retroflex ratio due to eastern influence. Under this assumption, Kalsi can be considered to be originally more closely affiliated with southwestern Girnar after all.

Significantly, retroflexion dominates in two geographically separate areas, not only in the east (which according to common wisdom has the greatest tendency toward retroflexion), but also in the northwest. This distribution does not conform to the one which Southworth claims to find in modern South Asia.[11]

---

[11] Southworth's modern retroflex distribution is based on text frequencies. The highest retroflex : dental ratios are found in Sindhi, Gujarati, Marathi and the Dravidian south, the lowest ratios in Panjabi, Hindi, the Bihari languages, and Bangla, with the remaining areas having an intermediate ratio. Unfortunately Southworth does not indicate the texts on which his statistics are based.

Examining versions of the 'Prodigal Son', representative of the different languages (and major subdialects) in Grierson 1903-1928, I arrive at rather different text frequencies and distributions: The highest retroflex : dental ratios (1 : 1-2.5) are found in a discontinuous Indo-Aryan area comprising Sindhi, Rajasthani, and Pahari dialects, and in Malayalam. Among the major languages, Kashmiri, Nepali, and Bangla have the lowest ratios (1 : 30 for

The distribution, however, agrees well with the modern Indo-Aryan outcome of *r* + dental stop discussed by Turner (1926 with 1921, 1924). In fact, as I became aware only after having examined (and reexamined) the Aśokan inscriptions, Turner connects the modern distribution to the Aśokan northwest : central : eastern distribution.

Perhaps surprisingly, the Indo-Aryan areas in which *r* + dental stop change to retroflex or dental respectively line up amazingly well with the Dravidian areas in which alveolar stops (mainly geminate) have turned into retroflex or dental respectively [12] (making allowances for some distributional irregularity in the transition area between dental and retroflex outcomes. See Map IV. [13] (The similarities become even greater if we consider that in northwestern Brahui, single alveolar *ṯ* merges with retroflex *ṭ*, not with the dental; cf. Emeneau 1971b.)

As I hope to show elsewhere, this alignment can be accounted for under the assumption that IAr. *r* + dental stop first changed to alveolar stop, whose fate then was the same as that of the Dravidian alveolar stop, namely merger with either dental or retroflex, [14] with similar choices being made by Indo-Aryan and Dravidian languages that are located in similar geographical locations, presumbably because of

---

Kashmiri, 1 : 9-15 for Nepali and Bangla). Intermediate ratios of 1 : 3-8 are found in most of South Asia, including the northwest and most of the Dravidian south. The northwest has a number of pockets with significantly lower retroflex ratios (beside Kashmir, note e.g. Burushaski with 1 : 33, Ormuri with 1 : 13.5, and Khowar with 1 : 58.5); there are similar pockets in the central area around Nahali (Gondi of Mandla with 1 : 13.5, Kurku with 1 : 34; see also Kuiper 1962: 255).

Whatever these geographical distributions may indicate about the history of South Asian languages, they do not support Southworth's grouping of Gujarati and Marathi with Sindhi and the entire Dravidian south, a grouping which is crucial for his claim that there was a strong prehistoric Dravidian presence in present-day western Indo-Aryan.

[12] See Subrahmanyam 1983, Zvelebil 1970.

[13] For most of Dravidian, only the geminate alveolar stop is considered; single alveolar stop commonly changes to an [r]-sound. The geographically easternmost Dravidian languages have assibilated outcomes of geminate alveolar stops; these are not included in Map IV.

[14] For a non-South Asian parallel in Norwegian/Swedish dialects see Steblin-Kamenskij 1965.

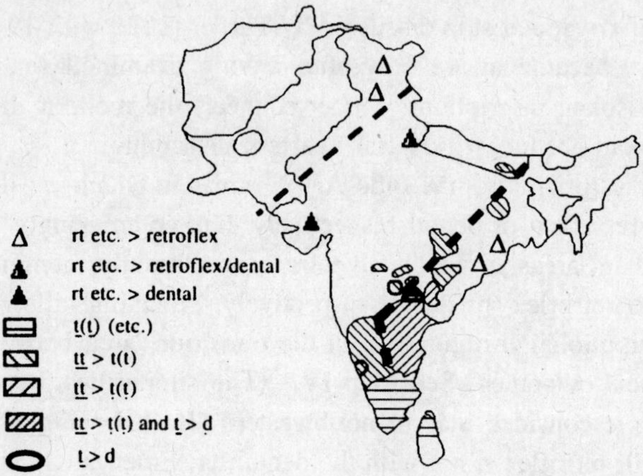

Map IV: Development of *r* + dental stop in the Aśokan inscriptions (indicated by different triangles) and the modern Indo-Aryan languages according to Turner, compared with the Dravidian development of alveolar stops

differences in bilingual communication in these different areas. (On the Indo-Aryan side, the vast central area corresponds more or less to the traditional 'madhyadeśa'.)

This scenario, if correct, raises significant questions regarding South Asian convergence and/or subversion; but these questions are of a much more complex—and interesting—nature than Southworth's account. Significantly, the simplest account again may turn out not to be the most accurate.

4.3. Lexical evidence

Anti-Subversionists tend to mistrust arguments based on 'mere' lexical similarities in different languages, since such similarities can be due to a variety of factors, only some of which require the assumption of direct contact. These factors are:

a. Inheritance from a common ancestor;
b. Borrowing, which may be
    i. direct (such as Engl. *saree* from Hindi *sāṛī*), or

ii. indirect (Engl. *sugar* from Skt.*śarkara* via Persian, Arabic, etc.),

iii. from a third source (Engl. *center* : Skt. *kendra*, both independent borrowings, ultimately from Gk. *kéntron*);

c. Independent onomatopoetic imitation (Engl. *cockadoodledo* : Skt. *kukkuṭ*, the rooster's crow);

d. Independent imitation of 'nursery words' (Engl. *papa* : Hindi *bāp* 'father');

e. Chance.

Of these factors, a. is not relevant in the discussion of Indo-Aryan/Dravidian contact; and with proper caution, it is possible to eliminate similarities of the type c. and d., which may reflect independent developments, rather than contact. Excepting fairly obvious cases, it is much more difficult to distinguish similarities attributable to factors b. and e.

Moreover, where similarities are likely to reflect borrowing, it is often difficult to determine the direction of borrowing, whether borrowing was direct (b.i.) or indirect (b.ii.), or whether both languages borrowed from a third source (b.iii). In this regard the etymologists' distinction between 'root' and 'motivated' etymologies is useful. While for root etymologies we cannot go farther than state the similarity, motivated etymologies often make it possible to determine the direction of borrowing. For instance, vernacular Hindi *šākajābar* is more likely a borrowing from Engl. *shock absorber*, than the other way around, since the English word can be derived from meaningful English elements (*shock* + *absorb* + the suffix *-er*), while the Hindi word is not internally motivated. Similarly, Skt. *śarkara* can be explained as a semantic specialization of *śarkara* 'grit, sand', i.e. as sugar in fine-ground form, while Engl. *sugar* cannot be internally explained.

Especially troublesome is the question of chance similarities: As the continuing controversy over remote linguistic relationship shows, there is no generally accepted answer to the question, 'What is the chance of similarities being accidental'. See e.g. Hock 1993a with references, as well as the long list of Tamil/English chance similarities (and other 'false friends') established in Southworth 1982. Note also the Dravidian/Indo-Aryan chance similarities in Hock 1984 and the Indo-Aryan/English ones in Hock 1993a.

The question of early Dravidian/Indo-Aryan lexical contact is further complicated by the fact that every Ṛgvedic word for which Dravidian origin has been proposed has been given at least one, often several alternative explanations, both in terms of direct inheritance from Proto-Indo-European or mediated inheritance through a Vedic Prakrit, and in terms of borrowings from non-Dravidian languages (especially Munda).

A non-partisan appraisal would have to be that, given the multiply different possible explanations, no explanation can be considered certain enough to be used as evidence for or against prehistoric Dravidian/Indo-Aryan contact. This is, in fact, the most general evaluation of such words in Mayrhofer II.

To illustrate the difficulties, let us examine three of the etymologies which Emeneau considered probable or at least plausible (see (5) above).[15]

Let us begin with (5a), *mayū́ra-* 'peacock'. While Tam., Mal. *mayil* looks fairly similar (especially since Ṛgvedic tends to have *r* for *l*), this form of the word is restricted to southernmost Dravidian, far from the northwest of the Ṛg-Veda. More widespread variants of the word contain a medial nasal, as in Tam. *maññai*, Parj. *mañjil/mañil*, Gad. *mañgil*, and yet further variants can be found (DEDR 4642). A possible explanation of the plethora of different forms lies along the lines of Krishnamurti (to appear): A primary root **may-* may have been extended by different suffixes, including *-il-* and/or *-nk-*, which subsequently fused with the root in different ways in different Dravidian languages.

But note that a similar root is found in Dravidian words for 'cat'; cf. Kol. *mai*, Kuwi S. *mrīyuli* (DEDR 4705), of which the latter word strongly resembles the dialectal Konda form of DEDR 4642 'peacock', *mrilu*. In this regard, note that Sanskrit *mārjāraka* means both 'cat' and 'peacock'. Still on the Dravidian side, we find another word for 'peacock' which looks like a metathesized form of Parj. *mañil* and some of the other forms in DEDR 4642; compare Tam. *ñamali, naviram*, Tu. *neyilu, navilu* etc. (DEDR 2902).

---

[15] For an evalution of Kuiper's (1991) much larger set of 'non-Aryan' words in the Veda, see Oberlies 1994.

Yet different, but phonetically similar forms are found elsewhere, including Munda *maraʔ*, and Eastern Iranian Saka *mur-āsa.*

What are we to make of this plethora of similar, and yet different, forms? And which of these forms, if any, should we relate to Vedic *mayū́ra-* ?

One possibility, first suggested to me by van Nooten (personal communication 1983), is that the word is onomatopoetic; see also Mayrhofer I: s.v.. Although, like Emeneau, I was at first sceptical, an extended stay at Jawaharlal Nehru University, famous for its peacocks, has convinced me that peacocks tend to sound like (angry) cats. An onomatopoetic explanation of the different words for 'peacock', then, makes it possible, not only to account for the various phonetic shapes (especially the element *may-*), but also the overlap with words for 'cat'.[16]

If the word, then, is accepted as onomatopoetic, it is entirely possible that the Dravidian, Indo-Aryan, Munda, and Saka words are independent creations and that even a number of the different Dravidian forms were created independently from each other.

If onomatopoeia is not accepted, the difficulty remains that the Dravidian forms most similar to the Ṛgvedic word are geographically the most distant, while geographically closer northern Dravidian forms are much less similar. Under the circumstances, the best approach would be to follow Mayrhofer (II-: s.v.) who considers the word 'Problematisch'. (Moreover, if we took this approach, we would not be able to explain the similarities between 'peacock' and 'cat' words.)

In either case, the word cannot be used with any degree of confidence to establish prehistoric Dravidian/Indo-Aryan contact..

As for ṚV *budbudá-* 'bubble', Emenau is correct in stating that it lacks direct Indo-European antecedents; but the word conforms to the pattern of early Indo-European intensive or iterative reduplication, which is of the form CVC-CVC (cf. e.g. Gk. *mor-mūr-ō* 'murmur' etc.); see Hoffmann 1956. This pattern markedly differs from the

---

[16] In fact, this explanation also opens the way to a different account for Skt. *mārjāra* 'cat', *mārjāraka* 'cat; peacock', not as primarily derived from *mṛj-* 'to stroke, clean' (as 'one who keeps cleaning him- or herself'), but with onomatopoetic *mār(j)-* (cf. the element *mVr-* of the Munda and Saka peacock words), plus perhaps folk-etymological, secondary influence of *mṛj-*.

(conservative) Dravidian one, which is of the type CVCV-CVCV, as in Emeneau's *buḍabuḍa*. Moreover, it is difficult to see why, if Dravidian is supposed to be the source for Indo-Aryan retroflexion, the Vedic word should have substituted dentals for the Dravidian retroflex stops.

Forms with the Dravidian type of reduplication do appear in late Vedic, and there is a post-Vedic *buḍabuḍa* 'bubblingly' (Harivaṁśa Pariśiṣṭa); but these are innovations, which may reflect later convergence with Dravidian.

The Ṛgvedic form, on the other hand, is too distant from the Dravidian type to be confidently explained as a borrowing. It is more likely an onomatopoetic creation, based on inherited Indo-European morphology, just as the Dravidian words are onomatopoetic and based on prevailing Dravidian morphology. Mayrhofer (II: s.v. *bud-budáyāśu-*) is certainly right in considering it unnecessary to attribute such similar onomatopoetic expressions to borrowing.

In addition to their problematic nature, most of the words that have been proposed as evidence for prehistoric Dravidian/Indo-Aryan contact are 'root etymologies'. A notable 'motivated etymology' is Emeneau's *kāṇá-* 'one-eyed' : Drav. **kāṇ-* 'see' (DED 1209) + neg. *-a-* = 'not seeing, blind', since its morphology is motivated only in Dravidian—if the etymology is correct. Mayrhofer (II: s.v.) evidently does not accept the etymology, but states that the word is perhaps explainable as a Vedic Prakritism, from earlier **karṇa* < PIE **kolno-*; cf. OIr. *coll* 'one-eyed'. [Note also Gk. (Hesych.) *kellás* 'one-eyed'.] While the Indo-European derivation may involve a root etymology (unless we derive the words from **kel-* 'prick'), there is perfect agreement in meaning; in contrast, the meaning of the 'motivated' Dravidian etymology is different (though relatable). Under the circumstances, Mayrhofer's evaluation that the etymology is uncertain may be the most appropriate. This word, too, thus cannot be relied on as evidence for prehistoric Dravidian/Indo-Aryan contact.

Now, Thomason & Kaufman (1988) are correct in noting that absence (or dearth) of unambiguous lexical borrowing does not prove absence of contact. As noted earlier, especially in convergence situations, lexical borrowing may be minimal.

What is more significant is the often-made observation (e.g. Tikkanen 1987: 296-297 with references) that a significant proportion of the putatively non-Aryan words in Indo-Aryan cannot be traced with confidence either to Dravidian or to Munda. Tikkanen takes this as supporting the view that the first prehistoric contact of Indo-Aryans with non-Aryans in South Asia cannot have been with Dravidians, but must have involved some unknown northwestern substratum which, in his view, is also responsible for the structural characteristics of early Indo-Aryan, including the dental : retroflex contrast.

For all we know—or do not know—about the linguistic situation in prehistoric northwestern South Asia, Tikkanen's assessment of the lexical situation could be correct. But postulating an unknown substratum to explain the structural characteristics of early Indo-Aryan is methodologically dubious, since by definition it is not open to verification or falsification.

Whatever one's evaluation of Tikkanen's hypothesis, one thing should be clear from the preceding discussion: The evidence of lexical borrowing does not provide any stronger support for prehistoric Dravidian/Indo-Aryan contact than the post-Vedic or modern distribution of languages or linguistic features. Arguments for prehistoric convergence or subversion therefore, by default, will have to be based solely on the structural evidence.

4.4. SOV order

Of the four structural features commonly cited as evidence for prehistoric Subversion, word order is the least probative. True, the later stage of Vedic Prose differs from the early Ṛg-Veda by having a much higher incidence of SOV (about 95% vs. 65%). But the common view that this presents a meaningful difference in chronology is not the only possible conclusion. Classical Sanskrit, in fact, furnishes good reasons for believing that the difference is one of genre or style (between didactic prose and hymnal poetry). Different classical genres tend to differ in terms of their word order preferences, such as 68% SOV in Kalidasa's dramatic dialogue vs. about 97% in the fables. Significantly, these differences are not associated with chronology, but only with genre and style. (See Hock 1994a for other differences in syntactic preferences between different Vedic and Classical genres.) If the difference between Vedic Prose and the Ṛg-Veda is due to genre, it can hardly be attributed to Dravidian influence.[17]

4.5. Absolutives

While it is true that the closest Indo-European relative of Indo-Aryan, early Old Iranian, does not present unambiguous evidence for absolutives, other early Indo-European languages do present parallels (see Hock 1984 with references). The closest parallel is found in Homeric Greek, with absolutives in *-on* (rare) or *-da/don/dēn* (more common); cf. (6).

(6) lûsai d'ouk edúnanto **parastadón** (Il. 15.22)
'They could not free (you) having come/coming closer.' = 'They could not come closer and free you.'

Significantly, the Greek absolutive is moribund and its formation is opaque, without precedent in the synchronic grammar of Greek. It is therefore more likely to be an inherited archaism than a recent innovation.

Now, as Kuiper (1967a) observed, the formation of the Vedic absolutive in *-tvā* likewise does not conform to the synchronically productive morphology and therefore is likely to be old. The question then is 'How old?' Kuiper claims that it postdates contact with Dravidian; but this is not the only possible conclusion.

In fact, the Subversion hypothesis leaves some important aspects of the formation of Indo-Aryan absolutives unaccounted for: There are two distinct and formally unrelated sets of variants for the (non-present) absolutive; one is the type *-tvā, -tvāya, -tvī,* the other is the type *-yă*. The exact historical reason for the variation is not clear, but it is associated with an eminently Indo-Aryan and general early Indo-European distinction, between simple and prefixed verbs (as in *kṛ-tvā* 'having done/made' vs. *saṁs-kṛ-tya* 'having made pure'). To judge by the historical record, this distinction did not exist in early Dravidian and

[17] Unless one could present independent evidence that all predominantly SOV genres, whether Vedic or Classical, are heavily influenced by Dravidians, while genres with less dominant SOV are not.

therefore cannot be attributed to Dravidian influence. Moreover, the very variation would be unexpected, if the formation of absolutives were due to Subversion: As is well known in historical linguistics, in contact-induced structural change, formal variation usually is abandoned; the introduction of variation in a contact-induced formation would be quite anomalous.[18]

Does this mean that the absolutive should be explained as part of the Indo-European heritage of Indo-Aryan? The absence of absolutives in Old Iranian and the fact that the Greek type in *-da/don/dēn* cannot be traced to the same Indo-European sources as Sanskrit *-tvā* etc. and *-yā* may suggest otherwise. However, it is a priori possible that Old Iranian innovated by losing an old absolutive construction; and it is well known that related languages can come to differ in their morphology, while maintaining syntactic similarity (and vice versa). Consider in this regard the difference in relative pronoun form between Hittite and Latin on one hand (*k^{w}i-/k^{w}o-*), and Indo-Iranian and Greek on the other (*yo-*), versus the great similarity in relative-clause syntax between these languages (at least in their earliest stages). It is therefore possible to speculate that the Old Indo-Aryan absolutives and/or their Greek counterparts represent early morphological 'renewals' of an inherited syntactic construction. (Note that the relatively rare Sanskrit 'present' absolutive in *-am* can in fact be derived from the same morphological source as the rare Homeric *-on*.)

A neutral assessment of the situation might well be that the feature of absolutive formation presents problems for both Subversionists and for anti-Subversionists. The Subversionist account has difficulty explaining the formal variation in the Old Indo-Aryan absolutive, while the anti-Subversionist account has to resort to speculation in order to explain the absolutive as an Indo-European inheritance.[19]

[18] It might be claimed that the variation already existed in Indo-Aryan prior to contact and that Subversion merely led to the new use of these varying forms as absolutives. However, this approach remains entirely speculative, unless it also accounts for the syntactic use of these forms prior to contact.

[19] Actually, Kuiper's claim that the absolutive, while highly archaic in form, must have been developed after Dravidian contact in popular Indo-Aryan and was only later admitted into the puristic poetic language is no less speculative.

Significantly however, under these circumstances the origin of absolutive formation is uncertain and the feature cannot be considered unambiguous evidence for prehistoric Subversion.[20, 21]

4.6. Quotative markers

Of the syntactic features commonly attributed to Subversion, the use of the quotative marker *iti* may be the best candidate.

Hock (1982b, 1984) argues that there is ample evidence for parallel structures in other early Indo-European languages. But the structures in Homeric Greek and Latin can at best be called 'quotatival'; they lack the formal and syntactic fixity of normal quotative markers. A genuine quotative is found in Hittite and other Anatolian languages (see most recently Fortson 1994), but the marker (*wa(r)*) has a different etymology from Skt. *iti*, and its position within the clause differs, too.

It is only in Avestan that we find markers that are relatable to *iti* and whose syntax is similar to that of Ṛgvedic *iti*. The particles are *uiti* and *iθa* (Younger Avestan also *iδa*), with the basic meaning 'thus', the same as of *iti*. Moreover, like Ṛgvedic *iti*, these particles can occur preposed, postposed, and inserted into cited discourse.

Hock takes this parallelism as evidence that *iti* has Indo-Iranian antecedents and thus need not be attributed to Subversion. But note that Avestan must have been a relatively eastern dialect of Old Iranian. The

[20] Tikkanen (1987) reaches a different conclusion. In his view, the past-tense or perfective value of the Vedic absolutive in *-tvā* etc. and *-yă̄* is not compatible with the temporally unmarked value of the early Dravidian absolutive and thus cannot be explained as the result of Dravidian subversion. Instead, Tikkanen invokes the unknown northwestern substratum of section 4.3 above as source for the absolutive. As I hope to have demonstrated in Hock 1992b, the Vedic absolutive may well have been temporally unmarked and comparable in this regard to the early Dravidian absolutive. In addition, note the comments at the end of section 4.3 above regarding the methodological questions raised by invoking an unknown substratum.

[21] Since Bloch 1929 it has often been argued that the use of absolutives as discourse linkers (of the type Skt. ... *uvāca* ... *(ity) uktvā* ... '... said ... (Thus) having spoken ...') reflects Dravidian influence. Recent publications (Hock 1994ab, Migron 1993) have shown independently that the use of such non-finite linkers has parallels in other Indo-European languages and thus may be part of the Indo-European heritage of Indo-Aryan.

possibility cannot be excluded that it was spoken in close proximity to Old Indo-Aryan and therefore could have participated in contact-induced changes of Indo-Aryan (whether these were due to subversion or convergence).

What may be relevant is that the 'free' syntax of Ṛgvedic *iti* (and its Avestan counterparts) gives way in post-Ṛgvedic to a relatively (though not absolutely) fixed syntax, with *iti* normally only occuring AFTER cited discourse. In this regard, post-Ṛgvedic Sanskrit comes to be more similar to what is generally considered the quotative syntax of the Dravidian languages. This post-Ṛgvedic change, however, creates certain difficulties for the Subversionist explanation of the Ṛgvedic quotative: How can we attribute to Dravidian influence the early 'free' use of *iti*, if only the later postposed one mirrors that of the Dravidian quotative?

There is a further reason for caution: As noted in Hock 1982b, the geographically more northern Dravidian languages (other than Brahui which has adopted the Persian preposed marker *ki*) have a much 'freer' syntax of quotative marking than the southern languages. If this syntax should preserve a feature of ancient northern Dravidian (or even of early Dravidian in general), the Ṛgvedic use of *iti* would be more similar to that of Dravidian after all.[22] (There is at least one aspect of Dravidian syntax in which it is fairly certain that the southern languages have innovated while the more northern languages have preserved the older pattern; this is the syntax of relative-correlative structures, for which see Hock 1988b.)

The problem is that in spite of Steever's excellent work (especially 1988), the prehistory and early history of Dravidian syntax is still quite poorly understood. Here as elsewhere, it may be hazardous to rely on

---

[22] Tikkanen (1988) takes what I have called the 'embracing' use of *iti* (of the type ... *uvāca* ... *iti* '... said "..." [unquote]) as evidence against Dravidian Subversion and in favor of his hypothesis of an unknown prehistoric northwestern substratum, since in his view parallel structures are hardly found in Dravidian, except for Kuvi. As far as I can tell, they are found in the Dravidian literary languages as well. (They may not occur as freely in literary texts as they do in Sanskrit, because they involve the syntactic process of 'extraposition' or 'epexegesis' which in Dravidian is a feature more of colloquial registers than of standard literature.)

relatively recent, even modern, evidence in trying to establish prehistoric Subversion.

4.7. Relative clauses, syntactic typology, and cumulativity

As I hope to have shown in §§4.4-6, the syntactic arguments for prehistoric Subversion are not particularly strong. Subversionists, however, feel that it is a mistake to examine each of the features separately; for the CUMULATIVE presence of the three features in early Indo-Aryan, as well as in Dravidian, cannot possibly be due to chance and must be explained as the result of Subversion.

Anti-Subversionists are not convinced that a cumulation of weak evidence adds up to a strong case. Moreover, Hock 1984 has claimed that the use of quotatives and absolutives (and other non-finite verbs) is a direct or indirect consequence of a wide-spread tendency for SOV languages to permit only one finite verb (marked for person, number, etc.) per sentence and that, therefore, the presence of SOV, absolutives, and quotatives 'should be treated more like a SINGLE feature than as cumulative evidence'.

The latter claim indirectly relates to a common assumption of Subversionists and also of certain Indo-Europeanists, that Dravidian and the Indo-European ancestor of Indo-Aryan had radically different syntactic TYPOLOGIES: Dravidian is said to be a 'rigid SOV' type, with only one finite verb permitted per sentence. All other verbs within the sentence must be non-finite (absolutives, relative participles, infinitives, or verbal nouns). By contrast, Indo-European is claimed to be a 'non-rigid SOV' type (or even SVO) which, significantly, permits more than one finite verb per sentence. As a consequence, in complex structures of relative and main clause, each clause has its own finite verb. The appearance of absolutives in Indo-Aryan, then, is considered a partial assimilation of the Indo-European type to the Dravidian 'finite-verb typology'.

There are several difficulties with this view. First, the quotative, commonly considered quintessentially Dravidian, is an obvious exception to the 'finite verb typology', since, as is well known, the cited discourse set off by quotative markers may have its own finite verbs.

Interestingly, this exceptional behavior has not been dealt with in traditional Dravidianist and Subversionist literature.

Dravidian offers widespread evidence for a second major exception to the 'finite-verb typology', namely the 'relative-correlative' construction, in which a relative clause (RC) containing a relative pronoun (RP) corresponds to a correlative (or main) clause (CC) containing a 'correlative pronoun' (CP), as in the Old Tamil example in (7a). Significantly, each of the two clauses contains its own finite verb (marked in boldface), contrary to the 'finite-verb typology' which would permit only ONE such verb for the entire sentence (and which would force the relative clause to have a non-finite relative participle). Structures of this type are entirely parallel to the relative-correlatives of Indo-Aryan, as in the Sanskrit example (7b), and other early Indo-European languages, as in (7c) from Hittite.

(7) a. [mi<u>nn</u>iṭai naṭunkuṅ kaṭaippeyal vāṭai ekkāl (RP) varuvat(u) **e<u>nr</u>i**]$_{RC}$ [akkāl (CP) **varuvar** en-k kātalōr-ē]$_{CC}$
"At what time you say the cold wind will come, at that time my lover will come" = "My lover will come at the time that you say the cold wind will come."

b. [apā́ṁ bílam ápihitaṁ yád (RP) **ā́sīd**]$_{RC}$ [vṛtrā́ṁ jaghanvā́m̐ ápa tád (CP) **vavāra**]$_{CC}$ (ṚV 1.32.11ab)
"What hollow of the waters was covered, slaying Vṛtra that he opened." = "Slaying Vṛtra, he opened the hollow of the waters that was covered."

c. [nu ku-it (RP) [(LU)]GAL-uš **te-ez-zi**]$_{RC}$ [nu a-pa-a-at (CP) **i-ya-mi**]$_{CC}$
"Now what the king says, that I (will) carry out."

Unlike the quotatives, the Dravidian relative-correlatives have been widely noted in Dravidianist literature and have repeatedly been attributed to the influence of various modern Indo-Aryan languages; see e.g. Nadkarni 1975 and Sridhar 1981.

A few Dravidianists (Ramasamy 1981, Lakshmi Bai 1985), however, have pointed out that the presence of relative-correlatives in Old Tamil and their wide distribution in the Dravidian languages make it unlikely that they result from Indo-Aryan influence, and that they must be indigenous to Dravidian. Curiously, Klaiman (1976) has attributed the early Indo-Aryan relative-correlatives to Dravidian influence. This, too, is unlikely because relative-correlatives are found in most of the other early Indo-European languages (see Hock 1992a with references). Rather, the syntactic similarities shared by Dravidian and early Indo-Aryan are quite certainly indigenous in both language groups and should not be explained as the result of subversion, or of convergence.

The entire issue of the Dravidian 'finite-verb typology' is reexamined in a brilliant pioneering study by Steever (1988). Steever, too, accepts the Dravidian relative-correlatives as indigenous. In addition he admits the difficulties posed by quotatives (and other structures) for the 'finite-verb typology' as usually formulated. His own, much more comprehensive and sophisticated account is further modified in Hock 1988b to explain certain peculiarites of Old Dravidian. Following Steever, Hock accepts the existence of a Dravidian 'finite-verb typology' (responsible for the widespread use of non-finite structures), but proposes that it needs to be MODIFIED to allow quotatives and relative clauses to have their own finite verbs. (The technical details of this modification need not concern us here.)

Hock 1989 demonstrates that in its broad outlines this 'modified finite-verb typology' also holds true for Sanskrit, and Hock 1992a attempts to show that the typology is characteristic of early Indo-European outside of India (and of other languages, including Turkish). If this claim is correct, then the syntactic similarities between Dravidian and early Indo-Aryan may simply reflect the fact that even prior to contact the two language groups were similar in their overall syntax, and there is no need for assuming either subversion or convergence.

Even if Subversionists do not want to accept the claim that the Indo-Aryan typology is inherited, they will have to seriously deal with the claim first adumbrated in Hock 1984 that SOV, absolutives (and other non-finite verbs), quotatives, and relative-correlatives are consequences of a SINGLE syntactic typology and thus cannot be interpreted as cumulative evidence for Subversion. While the claim of Hock 1984 can be accused of being motivated by anti-Subversionist sentiments, the unified typological account of these features in Steever 1988 is not open to such criticism.

4.8. *Retroflexion*

A common objection to attributing Indo-Aryan retroflexion to Subversion is that it can be explained in terms of purely internal developments, involving Proto-Indo-Iranian **š* and **ž* which change to pre-Indo-Aryan **ṣ* and **ẓ*. Subsequent developments, including assimilation of dentals to preceding retroflex sibilants and dissimilation of double sibilants, introduce retroflex stops. See the schematization in (8) based on Hock 1975 and 1979. Similar developments can be found in other Indo-European languages, most notably in Swedish and Norwegian dialects. Anti-Subversionist therefore will claim that it is unnecessary to invoke Dravidian influence.

(8)	(*liǵh-to- >)	*liždha- >	*liẓdha-	>	*liẓḍha- >	līḍha-	'licked'
cf.	(*wiǩ-to- >)	*wišta-		>		viṣṭa-	'entered'
	(*wiǩ-s >)	*wišš >	*wiṣṣ	>	*wiṭṣ >	viṭ	'people, clan' (N sg.)
	(*wiǩ-su >)	*wiššu >	*wiṣṣu	>	*wiṭṣu >	vikṣu	(id.) (L pl.)
						→ post-ṚV	viṭ-su

As noted earlier, Subversionists generally accept that Indo-Aryan retroflexion can by and large be accounted for by internal developments; but they believe that the crucial initial step, the change of Proto-Indo-Iranian **š* and **ž* to pre-Indo-Aryan **ṣ* and **ẓ*, was triggered by Subversion. They tend to point out that other Indo-European languages have retroflexion at a much later period; Indo-Aryan is the only early language with retroflexion (see e.g. Tikkanen 1987: 284). And they consider it unlikely that Indo-Aryan retroflexion could have arisen independently from Dravidian.

While it is true that Indo-Aryan retroflexion developed much earlier than retroflexion in other Indo-European languages, this does not mean that it can only be explained by Subversion. Different languages may exhibit similar developments at different rates and at different stages. (Gothic, for instance, virtually leveled out the effects of Verner's Law many centuries before the other Germanic languages; but this does not mean that the Gothic leveling resulted from some kind of subversion.)

The question whether it is likely that Indo-Aryan developed retroflexion independently from Dravidian is a more serious one. Unfortunately, it is impossible to determine the likelihood whether two similar phenomena might arise independently in languages that eventually share the same geographic area. As pointed out to me by Lyle Campbell (personal communication 1993), this is not impossible: In Brazil, Portuguese has come in contact with indigenous languages which, like Portuguese, have a pre-established, independently developed contrast between oral and nasal vowels. The Brazilian case, of course, merely establishes the possibility of chance similarity; it tells us nothing about its statistical likelihood; but recall the case of the Dravidian and Indo-Aryan relative-correlatives discussed in the preceding section, where again we find general structural similarities that result from independent inheritance, rather than subversion or convergence.

Following Bloch (1925), Hock 1975 and 1984 points to a number of differences between early Dravidian and Indo-Aryan retroflexion: Dravidian has a triple contrast (dental : alveolar : retroflex), while Indo-Aryan has a contrast only between dental and retroflex (plus post-dental, alveolar *r*). Dravidian permits word final retroflex (and alveolar) sonorants, early Indo-Aryan does not (except for the onomatopoetic nonce-form *bhāṇ* and artificial technical terms of indigenous grammar). Indo-Aryan has retroflex sibilants which are absent in Dravidian, while the latter has a retroflex approximant *r̤* which is absent in Indo-Aryan.[23] From the earliest times, Indo-Aryan has at least one initial retroflex consonant (in Skt. *ṣaṭ* '6' and derivatives), in Dravidian initial retroflex consonants are a late innovation.

These extensive differences would be difficult to explain if Indo-Aryan retroflexion resulted from Dravidian subversion and would favor independent development. It is interesting to note the parallel in Brazil: Although Portuguese and the indigenous languages both have an oral : nasal contrast (which we know is of independent origin), the

---

[23] Dravidian *r̤* is occasionally written *ẓ*, but Krishnamurti (1969: 318, n. 18) notes that there is no strong empirical evidence for this phonetic interpretation. Typologically, a system with a voiced obstruent not matched by a corresponding voiceless one is rare enough to require more than cursory justification. Note further that in the traditional Tamil alphabetical arrangement retroflex *r̤* holds the same position relative to retroflex *ḷ* as alveolar *r* to alveolar *l*.

contrast exhibits very different behavior in the two groups of languages: In the indigenous languages, nasal consonants tend to lose some of their nasalization next to oral vowels, a phenomenon not found in Portuguese.

Returning to South Asian retroflexion, note that at a later period some of the differences begin to disappear in most of Indo-Aryan and Dravidian (except the extreme south and northwest), as shown in Ramanujan & Masica's 1969 areal study of modern South Asian phonology. As argued in Hock 1984, in contrast to the prehistoric situation, there is now very robust evidence suggesting structural interaction. Interestingly, that interaction results in convergence, rather than subversion.

Pointing to the various difficulties outlined so far,[24] I confined myself in my earlier papers to arguing against the cogency of the Subversionist explanation of Indo-Aryan retroflexion. Tikkanen (1987, with references to earlier literature) has raised an alternative possibility, namely that retroflexion is an innovation of Dravidian and Indo-Aryan. Tikkanen's claim is based on the following observations: The Dravidian languages exhibit alternations such as those in the Tamil examples in (9) which show that some instances of alveolar and retroflex stops result from the assimilation of dentals to preceding alveolar or retroflex sonorants—very similar to the Indo-Aryan ones in (8),. although the details differ. Zvelebil (1970: 172 and 178-180) offers additional evidence which, to his mind, makes it possible to speculate that all Dravidian alveolar and retroflex stops arose through such developments.

(9)	koḻ 'kill'	+ -t- + -ēṉ	:	koṉṯēṉ	'I killed'
	āḷ 'rule'	+ -t- + -ēṉ	:	āṇṭēṉ	'I ruled'
cf.	kal 'stone'	+ tūṇ 'pillar'	. :	kaṯṯūṇ	'stone pillar'
	kaḷ 'booze'	+ tantāṉ 'gave'	:	kaṭṭantāṉ	'gave booze'

[24] Deshpande (1979a) claims that the Sanskrit dental : retroflex contrast developed in the post-Ṛgvedic period. However, as argued in Hock 1979, the highly patterned, rule-governed degeneralization of retroflex sandhi across word boundary, which can be observed in the Ṛg-Veda and constitutes an early phase of a change that gets virtually completed in the Classical period, presupposes that the retroflex/dental contrast has already come about, i.e. that the origination of this contrast predates the attested Ṛgvedic texts.

Tikkanen attributes the starting points for the innovations to two separate substrata (295) and claims that convergent developments between Indo-Aryan and Dravidian took place at a later time. On the Indo-Aryan side, he believes that the source for subversion was an unknown northwestern substratum, which in his view is also responsible for the large amount of early Indo-Aryan lexical items that can be traced neither to Proto-Indo-European nor to any of the known non-Indo-Aryan languages of South Asia. As for Dravidian, he entertains the idea that subversion is attributable to "some lost sub- or adstratum in the pre-Indo-Aryan period" (323).

Unfortunately, Tikkanen's proposal leaves unanswered the question as to what the relation was, if any, between the two separate substrata that gave rise to Indo-Aryan and Dravidian retroflexion. Is it likely that they had developed retroflexion independently? Methodologically, at least, invoking two separate substrata merely projects the issue of Dravidian/Indo-Aryan prehistoric relationship to an even more remote—and uncertain—period in prehistory.

A priori, an alternative account is possible, namely that the Dravidian and Indo-Aryan innovations resulted from CONVERGENCE (whether through direct or through mediated bilingual contact): If the Dravidian dental : alveolar : retroflex contrast did indeed originate through prehistoric developments which are remarkably similar to those that gave rise to the prehistoric Indo-Aryan dental : retroflex contrast, it would in my view become much more difficult to attribute these parallel developments to chance.

Note however that Zvelebil's proposal to derive all Dravidian alveolar and retroflex stops along the lines of (9) is quite speculative. (The eminent Dravidianists Emeneau and Krishnamurti are not willing to accept it at this point.) Any hypothesis based on Zvelebil's hypothesis must likewise be quite speculative. Moreover, the parallelism between Dravidian and early Indo-Aryan is not perfect: While Dravidian may have developed a triple contrast (dental : alveolar : retroflex), Indo-Aryan appears to have developed only a simple contrast (dental : retroflex), even though it had an alveolar sound, *r*, which could have triggered the development of an alveolar series. To become more acceptable, the hypothesis needs to be supported by stronger evidence and arguments.

Nevertheless, the possibility that Dravidian and Indo-Aryan retroflexion may result from joint—and convergent—developments raises interesting issues for further research and may revolutionize our thinking about the linguistic prehistory of South Asia.

4.9. The social situation

The issue of the prehistoric and early historic social relationship between Indo-Aryans and non-Indo-Aryans is not usually addressed in anti-Subversionist literature. Nevertheless, the Subversionist view that there was a deep social, or even racial', chasm between Indo-Aryans and the indigenous population, bears closer scrutiny.

Examination of the Ṛgvedic passages in which adjectives meaning 'black' or 'dark' are used in reference to human enemies suggests two spheres of usage. One is to the forts of the enemies, especially their 'womb', a term which may simply refer to their dark interior (ṚV 1:101:1b, 2:20:7ac, 4:16:13cd [25]). In two other passages in which the adjective refers to people[26] and which offer sufficient context for interpretation, [27] the adjective seems to be used in an ideological/metaphorical sense, contrasting the 'dark' world of the *dāsas* and *dasyus* with the light world of the *āryas* (ṚV 1:130:8 and ṚV 7:5:3ab beside

[25] Geldner translates the second of these passages as "die dasischen (Burgen), die die Schwarzen in ihrem Schoß bergen" ["the dasic forts which protect the black people in their womb"], but that is an arbitrary interpretation. In another hymn, ṚV 4:17:14, a passage of somewhat uncertain interpretation, the combination of 'dark' and 'womb/interior/abode' clearly has no 'racial' connotations: The first line talks about the wheel of the sun; the third and fourth lines refer to the dark bottom of a skin (*kṛṣṇá . . . tvacó budhné*) and a 'womb of darkness' (*rájaso ... yónau*), which Geldner himself plausibly interprets as referring to the dark interior of a tube or the like. — To get his 'racial' interpretation "Fünfzigtausend Schwarze warfst du nieder. Du zerschlissest die Burgen wie das Alter ein Gewand" ["You laid low fifty thousand black people. You tore up the forts like age (tears up) a garment."] for ṚV 4:16:13cd, Geldner has to assume 'attraction', i.e. inaccurate agreement, between *kṛṣṇā́* 'black' and *sahásrā* 'thousands'. This is not necessary if we interpret *kṛṣṇā́* as a sandhi form of *kṛṣṇā́ḥ* (fem.) and construe it as modifying *púro* (fem.) 'forts'.

[26] In ṚV 8:73:18ab, Geldner takes the adjective to refer to demonic enemies.

[27] Two passages do not offer enough context for interpretation (9:41:1c, 9:73:5d).

7:3:6cd). As far as I can tell, there is no unambiguous evidence for an awareness of color-related 'racial' differences in the Ṛg-Veda.[28]

'Racial' interpretations of this kind seem to be confined to western publications, beginning in the nineteenth century. I do not believe that the modern—and quite problematic—notion of 'race' is appropriate in the ancient world.

It is, I believe, similarly inappropriate to project the 'racially' and ethnically based ideology of modern colonial powers like the British into ancient and prehistoric times. True, those defeated in war often suffered a cruel fate, even extinction. At the same time, both 'civilized' empires (such as the Roman one) and 'barbarian' ones (such as that of the Huns) were truly multiethnic, multilingual, and multicultural. Wartime alliances might pit members of the same linguistic and ethnic group against each other (such as the Germanic allies of the Huns and of the Romans). As codified in Classical Sanskrit political theory, alliances often were made with the people who live on the other side of one's enemy (who might be ethnically closer to the enemy's party than one's own).

As acknowledged by Kuiper (1991), the Ṛg-Veda offers strong evidence which suggests a fluid situation of this type, in which ethnicity played a relatively minor role. First, one hymn mentions a *dāsa*, Balbūtha Tarukṣa, as the patron of a Vedic seer. Secondly, numerous passages refer in one breath to *dāsa* and *ārya* enemies (ṚV 6:22:10, 6:33:3, 6:60:6, 7:83:1, 8:51:9, 10:38:3, 10:69:6, 10:83:1, 10:102:3) and in one of these, both types of enemies are referred to as *ádeva* 'godless, infidel'.

Especially instructive is the famous 'Battle of the Ten Kings' (ṚV 7:18 with 7:33, 7:83 etc.; cf. also Kuiper 1991). If we examine the

---

[28] *Mutatis mutandis*, the situation is similar for Deshpande's (1993a) Mahābhāṣya passage which defines brahmins as light-complexioned and contrasts them with a person that is 'dark' (or 'black') and sits in the open market. There is nothing in the passage that forces us to view this difference as one of inherited skin color; it is entirely possible that the difference reflects occupational differences and prejudices between the upper-caste brahmin who is able to avoid the sun (by finding shelter inside, under a tree, or under an umbrella) and the lower-caste merchant who has to sit in the blazing sun of the open market. Similar class prejudices were a feature of European societies, before the idea caught on that having a nice tan is beautiful. And anybody who has been to South Asia knows that there they persist to the present day.

names of the 'Good Guys' and the 'Bad Guys' we find that both sides have people with 'Aryan' names, and both sides have people with 'non-Aryan' names, many of which might possibly be Munda; see (10). Note further that Bharata, here a 'Bad Guy', is a 'Good Guy' in ṚV 3.33.11,12 etc.; similarly Pūru in ṚV 5.17.1; the Bhṛgus everywhere else are 'Good Guys'. (Some names occur only here.) The most important perspective appears to be the feud between the seers Vasiṣṭha and Viśvāmitra, and both of these are 'Aryans'.

(10)	'Good guys'	'Bad guys'
	Sudās	**Pūru**
	Vasiṣṭha	**Bharata**
	SṚÑJAYA-s (?)	**Bhṛgu**-s
	Paktha-s	**Matsya**-s (or indigenous totem, Skt. calque ?)
	Alina-s	ŚIMYU
	etc.	Kavaṣa
		etc.

(Probable Indo-Aryan names are in **bold**; possible Munda names, in SMALL CAPS.)

The picture that emerges from this evidence is rather different from the one commonly drawn: While there clearly was hostility and warfare between Indo-Aryans and their opponents, the *dāsa*s and *dasyu*s, there was no social and political chasm comparable to that between the British colonialists and the South Asian people(s). Whatever ethnic and linguistic differences there may have been, they did not prevent *ārya*s and *dāsa*s/*dasyu*s from making shifting alliances with each other, requiring them to interact bi- or multilingually as near-equals.

Under the circumstances, if there was in fact Dravidian/Indo-Aryan contact, the results are more likely to have been bidirectional convergence than unilateral Subversion.

5. Summary and conclusions

The goal of this paper has been to present in some detail the major arguments of those who advocate prehistoric subversion of Indo-Aryan by Dravidian and those who oppose this position, and to evaluate the cogency and underlying assumptions of their conflicting arguments.

Subversionists operate with the assumption of unidirectional Dravidian influence on Indo-Aryan, affecting four major structural features. Three of these are syntactic (SOV order, absolutives, and quotative marking); one is phonological (the contrast dental : retroflex). The presence of these four different features in Indo-Aryan is considered to provide CUMULATIVE evidence for subversion, and since the features appear in the earliest Indo-Aryan text, the Ṛg-Veda, the assumption is that Subversion took place prehistorically. The unidirectional nature of the influence is taken to reflect a forced shift of Dravidian speakers to Indo-Aryan, with attendant transfer of structural features. The Dravidian presence in prehistoric northwest South Asia, required for subversion to take place, is considered supported by Dravidian borrowings in Ṛgvedic, the modern presence of the Dravidian language Brahui in the extreme northwest, and the distribution of dental vs. retroflex sounds in Middle Indo-Aryan and modern South Asia. Finally, it has been claimed that the Dravidian Subversion hypothesis is the SIMPLEST account for the situation.

Anti-Subversionists question the cogency of the arguments for a prehistoric Dravidian presence in northwest South Asia: The geographical arguments are problematic since they are based on the distribution of languages or features some 2000 to 3500 years after the fact, further complicated by the fact that there have been migrations from south to north (both of Indo-Aryans and of Dravidians) which may obscure the original geographical distribution. The evidence of borrowings is limited and controversial; in fact a significant proportion of putative early borrowings from non-Indo-Aryan languages cannot be traced with confidence to Dravidian (or to Munda). The syntactic feature of SOV can hardly be of Dravidian origin, and there are various problems connected with claiming Dravidian origin for absolutives and quotative marking. The claim that these syntactic features provide CUMULATIVE evidence for Subversion meets with the counterclaim that they are consequences of a SINGLE syntactic typology. Retroflexion is more problematic; but the early Dravidian and Indo-Aryan phonological systems of retroflex (and alveolar) sounds differ too much to be explainable by Subversion. It is only later that the systems become more similar—through convergent developments. Overall, then, the Subversionist hypothesis is not established beyond a REASON-

ABLE DOUBT. Finally, as shown especially in §§ 4.1 and 4.2, the claim that Subversion is the SIMPLEST account meets with the objection that the simplest explanation is not alway the most accurate one.

While many of the objections to the Subversion hypothesis cast doubt on its cogency, they do not 'disprove' it. Rather, they should be considered challenges for Subversionists to improve their arguments or to find additional, and better, evidence. On the other side, Subversionists tend to find many of the alternative accounts proposed by anti-Subversionists to be rather speculative; but the reverse is true, too (see e.g. note 19). Most important, Subversionists tend to consider the 'reasonable doubt' criterion overly restrictive; but anti-Subversionists have problems with the 'cumulativity' criterion and consider 'simplicity' to be of dubious value.

To some extent, then, the two aproaches have reached a 'stand-off' position. Given the limited nature of the available evidence and the conflicting evaluative criteria the two approaches subscribe to, this is perhaps inevitable. But it is also unfortunate, for the issue of the linguistic prehistory of South Asia clearly is important and resolving the question of prehistoric Indo-Aryan/non-Indo-Aryan contact would be interesting for anyone concerned with South Asian prehistory.

In this regard, a few of the observations in § 4.1-9 may suggest possible new avenues for research. One of these is Tikkanen's claim (1987 with 1988) that the structural similarities between Dravidian and Indo-Aryan are due to an unknown prehistoric northwestern substratum, which is also responsible for the large number of non-Dravidian (and non-Munda) borrowings in early Indo-Aryan. As noted, this claim is methodologically problematic, since it can be neither verified nor falsified. But as shown by his 1988 publication, Tikkanen has been doing research on modern northwestern languages, including Burushaski, with the goal of identifying the prehistoric northwestern substratum or substrata. Whatever the outcome of the research, it is bound to lead to an improved understanding of this very interesting, and also very under-researched, area in the extreme northwest of South Asia.

A second set of observations may be even more significant. As noted in § 4.9, the testimony of the Ṛg-Veda suggests that the early relation between Indo-Aryans and non-Indo-Aryans was not as unequal as generally assumed, but may rather have constituted an extended relationship of shifting alliances with each other, requiring bi- or multilingual interaction as near-equals. Under such conditions, we would expect CONVERGENCE, rather than subversion. Convergence does in fact seem to be the dominant Dravidian/Indo-Aryan relationship in historical times; see e.g. the convergent developments as regards retroflexion (§ 4.8), as well as Krishnamurti's suggestion (1991) that the famous Middle Indo-Aryan 'two-mora' conspiracy may have been a development shared with Dravidian.

In fact, the Dravidian dental : alveolar : retroflex contrast and the Indo-Aryan dental : retroflex contrast might very well be attributed to prehistoric convergence—if the hypothesis that these contrasts arose through a JOINT innovation (§ 4.8) can be supported by additional arguments. One of the most exciting—and potentially fruitful—avenues for further research therefore would seem to lie in further pursuing this 'Convergence Hypothesis' regarding the origination of Indo-Aryan and Dravidian retroflexion (and alveolarization).

CHAPTER THREE

THE EARLY HISTORY OF SANSKRIT AS SUPREME LANGUAGE*

Ashok Aklujkar

1.1 It is generally agreed that for a very long period Sanskrit has not been a living language in the full sense of the term [1] and (yet) there has been an equally long period in which various Indian vernaculars have

---

* When the core of this paper was read at the Seminar out of which the present volume of studies arose, it carried the title "Some musings on historical research concerning the status and ideology of Sanskrit." In view of the fact that the available time made it impossible to carry out the original intention of critically surveying all relevant and accessible research and the paper actually presented dealt with only one problem, albeit very central, the title has now been made specific.

Although only the status of Sanskrit has been explicitly discussed here, there are references in many sections of the paper to the ideological elements which determined this status.

I thank Professor Madhav M. Deshpande for helping me in the process of bringing precision to the thoughts expressed in this paper. Without the background of his publications and of the sporadic but many discussions we were able to hold over the last several years, the inadequacies of the present endeavour would have been much more numerous. I also wish to thank heartily Dr. Jan E.M. Houben for 'forcing' me into a situation in which I could not any longer postpone giving written expression to my thoughts on the sociolinguistic history of early India and for being a very patient editor. Further, it is my pleasure to acknowledge the help Dr. Gary Tubb (Columbia University) and Ms. Michele Desmarais (University of British Columbia) provided by identifying typographical errors and suggesting improvements of diction.

[1] Deshpande (1979a:3-14) points out that Sanskrit has been losing ground as a mother tongue, father tongue, or first spoken language for a long time. I probably would not go as far back in time as he seems to in locating the cessation of Sanskrit as a vernacular spoken by classes other than the Brahmin. Furthermore, I feel that the possibility of Sanskrit's being a standard dialect spoken by the higher classes but understood by other classes should have been entertained by him as applicable to a longer period (cf. Keith 1928:xxvi-xxvii; Hock & Pandharipande 1976:115-18). However, even with such disagreements, the period in which Sanskrit had a relatively restricted domain of usage would be very long.

been evaluated against it explicitly or implicitly. It has, until recently,[2] served as a frame for positioning other Indian languages, current as well as classical, and has regained prominence in India, probably several times, after receiving setbacks.[3]

The phenomenon briefly described above is intriguing. It appears all the more intriguing if it is recalled that Sanskrit has principally been associated with Brahmins through most of the known periods of Indian history. Brahmins have always been a minority in society—and not a minority espousing a philosophy of equality, or seeking unity, with others at that. What did the Brahmins do to put 'their' language at the top again and again, in a diverse and large country like India over nearly three millenia? How did they raise it to a high position the first time and how did they restore it to that position when it encountered an indifferent or hostile situation? While earlier studies have given expression, directly and indirectly, to the presiding role of Sanskrit, there has been, I believe, no adequate explanation of that role or a study which takes up that role as its historical concern. To be sure, many relevant observations and pieces of historical evidence are available in Deshpande 1979a, 1979b, 1987, 1993a, Hock & Pandharipande 1976 and Cardona 1990. However, the major concern of these studies is not the issue specified here. Especially, Deshpande, the most prolific writer at present on the sociolinguistics of ancient and early medieval northern India, has been primarily interested in broader issues and has studied sociolinguistic attitudes toward several related languages, not just Sanskrit.[4]

---

[2] That the situation has dramatically changed from the last quarter of the nineteenth century to the end of the twentieth century will be evident if one compares the present English-dominated situation in India with the one reflected in Bhandarkar 1877:2-3.

[3] Deshpande (1979a:28-29, 34-35, 36, 55, 58-59) provides evidence of the high standing enjoyed by Sanskrit in the days in which Ardha-māgadhī was thought of as the most distinguished language by the Jainas and in the days of Rāja-śekhara, Vāk-pati, Uddyotana-sūri, etc. He also draws attention to the process of Sanskritization in which emulating Sanskrit is an important component. Cf. also Emeneau in Deshpande 1979a:ix and 1993a:1.

[4] (a) Those observations of Deshpande which directly relate to the theme of this essay will be discussed primarily in section 4.1-4 and secondarily in the notes. The views of Hock & Pandharipande and Cardona will be mentioned in the notes as occasion demands.

(b) My differences from Deshpande concerning his sociolinguistic reconstruction of the early periods of Indian history and his use of relevant data are many. They are, to a sig-

1.2 One can read in several publications how the features of Sanskrit as a language are attractive and what great literature it contains. We need not doubt that the linguistic features and the appeal of literature, when they became a part of public consciousness, contributed to the continuation of an exalted position. But they cannot be accepted as direct causes of the first assumption of eminence by Sanskrit or of re-assumption of eminence by Sanskrit after a long period of hostile or indifferent environment. Our common experience is that most speakers find the features of their own language attractive (although they may not always be aware of them) but are not attracted to another language because of its features, unless they are sharp independent observers (who constitute a small group in any society) or there exist cultural or social mechanisms which bring the features to their attention. The mechanisms, in turn, are unlikely to be present unless the language concerned has begun to carry a special value. As for the development of great literature, history suggests that it usually *follows* the advantageous standing a language enjoys.

1.3 As I am not aware of any research in which the precise question I am raising has been raised and answered with a sustained focus, I am not in a position to present current thinking in the field with individual attribution or much detail. The impression I get, however, is that most scholarship assumes an early political-economic advantage for Sanskrit.[5] The prevailing understanding seems to be that Sanskrit first attained the influential standing it did because, at an ancient time, it came to India as the language, or as a close descendant of the language, of victors. It is usually held that the Aryans entered northwestern India in a distant past and, from there, managed to spread to the south and the east of the Indian subcontinent. As they spread, their language Sanskrit, or its ancestor, spread and assumed importance as the language of the

---

nificant extent, also fundamental in that they concern his inclinations as a historian and his presuppositions regarding what Indology has established as facts of Indian history. For this reason, I have treated them in a separate study to which I shall refer here as 'Aklujkar forthcoming a'. The concluding sections of that same study should be read for the larger Indological implications of the position put forward in the present paper.

[5] The explanation is rarely put in such stark terms, but this is what it essentially amounts to.

masters.[6] The cultural institutions, particularly the religious ones, of the Aryans were either imposed on the new lands or took root in them. The social class of Brahmins, being most important in the management of religious life, attained much influence. As Sanskrit was preserved and propagated by the Brahmins, it continued to assume a position of prestige and influence.

1.4 I have, in the present state of my knowledge, no quarrel with the *essentials* of this understanding. The strength of political (including military) and economic factors must be acknowledged, as it is a matter of experience in many sociocultural developments and as we have other cases in human history in which not only elevations and demotions, but even complete replacements of languages took place because of political and/or economic domination (just as sometimes political and economic domination came about because of linguistic realities). Similarly, I do not oppose the attribution of a special role to the Brahmins in the preservation and promotion of Sanskrit.

At the same time, however, I should clarify that I have formed no definite views regarding when and how the situation of early advantage for Sanskrit briefly specified above can be said to have come into being. My mind is still open to more than one model of positioning the language families and to more than one view of the original homelands of their speakers.[7] It is only the evidence pointing to a movement of the Sanskrit-speaking people(s) to the eastern and southern parts of the Indian subcontinent during the historical period that I find adequately strong. Secondly, I should draw attention to the following:[8]

(a) The meaning of the crucial word Ārya figuring in the historical reconstruction just given has changed over the approximately 150 years in which the Aryan thesis or hypothesis has been in vogue. From 'a ra-

[6] "It is clear that the Aryan invaders succeeded in imposing their speech on many of the earlier inhabitants of the country . . . " Keith 1928:xxvi.

[7] Kak 1994 contains a good reflection of what current research holds or would indicate as likely positioning and likely homelands.

[8] (a) There can be difference of opinion, on the part of individual scholars, regarding each of the changes I have summarized. What I am attempting to capture, as one must from time to time in any field of research, is the cumulative effect the superior part of relevant scholarship has left on my mind.

(b) I have summarized only the changes that have implications for the issue under discussion.

cial group in the anthropological or physical sense of 'race', 'Caucasian or largely Caucasian', through 'speakers of an (ultimately) Indo-European dialect[9] or complex of dialects', it seems now to be moving in the direction of 'a specific culture group mostly speaking an Indo-European complex of dialects and, in the earliest period, probably belonging predominantly to (what we can loosely call) the Caucasian or Caucasoid race'.[10]

---

[9] As the distinction between dialect and language is immaterial for our present purpose and cannot strictly or consistently be made in any case, I shall generally ignore it.

[10] (a) The literature indicating the semantic change summarized here is vast and of uneven quality. To draw attention only to the publications which refer to primary sources and which I have come across with less than a sustained bibliographic search, I mention: Wakankar 1993:27, Devendraswarup 1993:33-39, Mehendale 1993:43, Pathak 1993:86-99, Danda 1993:103-04, Gupta 1993:163.

(b) The following statement of Kuiper (1991:5-8) is especially close to the last meaning: "'Aryans' were in general those who maintained the world order by means of sacrifices and gifts. In this dual world these 'Aryans' were on the side of light vs. darkness, of Devas vs. Asuras, etc. 'Aryan' referred to a cultural community, including some Dāsas. . . . the Rigvedic society consisted of several different ethnic components, who all participated in the same cultural life. I fully agree with Southworth's words (1974:204f.): "the equation of IA speakers with 'Aryan' (i.e. the original intruders and their direct descendants) is not supported by historical evidence."" Cf. Kuiper 1991:96.

(c) Of the three elements I have brought together in the last meaning, the first two seem to have been most widely accepted or presumed. Acceptance or presumption of the third, the racial element, depends on a scholar's view regarding the original home of the Āryas and the place and time to be assigned to the earliest occurrences of the term Ārya.

(d) As physical anthropology now considers 'race', in the sense of 'a group of human beings marked by external features such as a certain size of the head or a particular shape of the nose', to be a concept of highly restricted applicability (Walimbe 1993:109-10, Gupta 1993:153-56), my use of the specification 'Caucasian' is only for the sake of approximation and convenience.

(e) I have not come across much explicit discussion regarding what to include in Ārya when it is taken, *in its earliest occurrences*, as a term primarily standing for the member of a specific cultural community. Kuiper's statement quoted in (b) has few companions in the limited amount of reading I have managed to do. Probably, acceptance of a specific social arrangement (*varṇa* system or its predecessor) should be added to the details given by Kuiper of Aryan culture.

(f) Traditional Indian understanding of Ārya is most commonly 'a responsible member of a society divided into four *varṇas* or four specific social classes, *kulīna*, born of a good family, gentleman, *sabhya*, cultured, respectable'. In political-economic contexts, this common meaning acquires the specific connotation of 'free person'. Early Tamil literature

(b) The expressions employed to speak of the coming of the Aryans have also undergone a significant change. Words like 'invasion' and 'aggression' have increasingly been replaced by 'migration', 'arrival', 'agricultural diffusion', etc., playing down but not eschewing the possibility of conflict, violence, and armed confrontation.

(c) Several respectable scholars are, further, suggesting that, while the Aryans moved into India at some pre-historic time, they were largely a domiciled community living in a linguistic area (i.e., in an area where languages belonging to several language families were spoken near each other and had begun to share certain features) and having racial and cultural diversity by the time our historical records such as the Rg-veda were composed or began to be collected as anthologies. In other words, just as it need not be assumed that the Aryans came to India in one single wave, it need not be assumed that the Indo-Aryans of the earlier waves were identical with the Vedic Aryans.

Despite these changes, one can accept the essentials of the explanation given in section 1.3, for all that the explanation needs is that the Aryans be seen as different from the other contemporary inhabitants of India, whoever they might have been, that the Aryans be thought of as the original possessors of Sanskrit or its source, and that the Aryans be viewed as successful in moving from the northwest in sufficiently large numbers to the eastern and the southern areas of India.

2.1 As I have already indicated, however, I do not think that the explanation given in section 1.3 is the full explanation. But before I specify what additions and changes are needed in it, I should clarify that I do not view my account as exhaustive. I should also clarify that I am aware that the causes for Sanskrit's high standing in different periods of Indian history would be different and that even the nature, degree, and

---

provides evidence of 'northern' as an additional meaning. See Annamalai 1993:73-74, Ramakrishnarao 1993:78-79, A.M. Shastri 1993:134.

(g) Because of the difference in the traditional Indian understanding of 'Ārya' and the meaning given to 'Aryan' by early Western scholars, some scholars have even suggested that 'Ārya' and 'Aryan' should not be used as synonyms; cf. Wakankar 1993:27, Shastree 1993:117.

(h) Determinants of the meaning of 'Ārya' and also determined by it are the meanings of words like 'Dāsa/Dasyu', 'Mleccha' and 'Barbara'.

geographical spread of its high standing would differ from period to period. I do not aim at capturing all the causal and temporal variety. However, I shall attempt to identify what, I feel, are causes that continued through most of the early periods.

2.2 The time span with which I shall be concerned is roughly the one which extends from the composition of the Veda to the composition of the early texts of systematic philosophy and *kāvya,* and the geographical area I have principally in mind is north India in the older sense of the term, that is, the northern part of the Indian subcontinent. Of the long time span I keep in view, the following would be the major divisions, if one were to follow the vicissitudes of Sanskrit as they have generally been seen in the scholarship on the subject:

(a) the period of Early Vedic represented by most of the Ṛg-veda, some parts of the Atharva-veda and many of the scattered *ṛcs* preserved in other Vedic texts, to which the appellation Vedic Sanskrit most fittingly applies and in which explicit recognition of any known language other than the language of the texts is yet to be detected;[11]

(b) the period of much of the Atharva-veda, the Yajur-veda saṁhitās, the early Brāhmaṇas (including the Āraṇyakas and Early Upaniṣads) in which we have the immediate predecessor of most of Sanskrit proper[12] and in which a recognition of the existence of other languages is found, but again, as in the Ṛg-veda, without any specific names (see note 11);

---

[11] I do not wish to imply that the content of the second 'which'-clause is any kind of innate or genuine characteristic of the period concerned. I have included it only to indicate that, in this period, the status of Sanskrit or of a relatively distant predecessor of (Classical) Sanskrit cannot be discussed in relation to any other identified or named language. It is more than likely that significantly distinct dialects, the early forms of Prakrits (Hock & Pandharipande 1976:109-13) and the early members of some non-Indo-European language families (e.g., the Dravidian and Munda) existed in the vicinity of Vedic Sanskrit and interacted with it, directly or indirectly. But we do not know what they specifically were or could have been.

[12] I use this term to indicate that we have not yet arrived at the language which is commonly called Classical Sanskrit and is taught nowadays at the beginning of one's Sanskrit study. My intention is not to suggest that there is a sharp break between Vedic Sanskrit and Sanskrit. As I shall indicate below in note 18, it is doubtful if, historically, we would be justified even in using the name 'Sanskrit' for the language of the periods (a)-(d). There is no definite evidence that its users in those periods gave it that appellation. See notes toward the end of Wezler's article in this volume for further discussion of this point. [Wezler's contribution, esp. note 73, Ed.]

(c) the period of the Middle Upaniṣads, early sūtra and Vedāṅga texts in which Sanskrit proper has almost fully emerged and the separation of contemporary Sanskrit from Vedic Sanskrit is either clearly presupposed or openly acknowledged;
(d) probably largely overlapping with the preceding, the period of early Epic or Purāṇic Sanskrit[13] (much of which is accessible to us only in a form mingled with the later Epic or Purāṇic Sanskrit) and of Śramanic movements and the early phases of Jainism and Buddhism, in which languages related to but different from early Sanskrit exist and are used for literary and religio-philosophical purposes;
(e) the period of Sanskrit proper co-existing with Epic or Purāṇic Sanskrit, Buddhist Hybrid Sanskrit and possibly other vernacular varieties, in which Sanskrit has largely ceased to be a language of all-purpose communication, in which the competing canonical languages, Pāli and Ardha-māgadhī, are probably undergoing the same fate, in which all three languages, but especially Sanskrit, have many centres of study even in South India, and in which Sanskrit and Pāli begin to establish their presence in East and Southeast Asia; and
(f) the period of classical Sanskrit, in which the language almost always conforms to the model provided by Pāṇinian grammar, in which even the Buddhists and the Jainas switch to the use of Sanskrit (without giving up the use of other dialects and languages) for serious religio-philosophical purposes, and in which Sanskrit is used for the pan-Indian content of practically all the śāstras.[14]

2.3 The prevailing understanding outlined in section 1.3 could conceivably be adequate to explain the ascendency of Sanskrit in periods (a) and (b). The language could have initially got an upper hand because of political (or military) and economic factors.[15] I also see no rea-

---

[13] Hock & Pandharipande 1976:120 contains a good summary of arguments that have been advanced to assign an early date to Epic Sanskrit.

[14] (a) I do not wish to imply that any other periodizations or subperiodizations are not possible. I have tried to combine in the above scheme considerations of (i) grammatical features, (ii) relationship with other languages, and (iii) spheres of use.

(b) At present, I accept the dates most scholars would tend to assign to the periods mentioned. But I do not consider them incontestable. Only *relative* chronology has generally been well argued for by the historians of the fields concerned.

[15] Far-reaching conclusions have been drawn on the basis of very few pieces of evidence in the case of the early Vedic people. Especially the historians seeking to erect a gen-

son not to accept that the general direction of the spread of Indo-Aryan culture has been to the south and the east. However, the explanation summarized in section 1.3 cannot be adequate for the periods following (a) and (b), that is, for the periods in which Sanskrit proper emerges. An increasing awareness of the difference between Vedic Sanskrit and (what we normally call) Sanskrit implies that Vedic Sanskrit would become, more and more, a domain of those who were charged, in the Aryan society, with the responsibility of preserving the older language and the religious activity going with it, that is, a domain of the Brahmins. Similarly, an increasing awareness of the difference between Vedic Sanskrit and the spoken contemporary dialects also implies that that dialect which was closest to Vedic Sanskrit, namely Sanskrit, would increasingly come to be associated with the Brahmins. This is, in fact, what happened as the available evidence tells us. Now, the Brahmins were a small minority, not inclined to seeking alliances on the basis of an egalitarian social philosophy. They had no direct political or economic power for any significant lengths of time. Therefore, the continuation of Sanskrit as a dominant language in the later periods cannot truly be explained on the assumption of political and/or economic might alone.

2.4 One way of getting over the difficulty I have pointed out would be to reject the very assumption that Sanskrit was dominant in all of the subsequent periods. This is, in fact, what some historians have done with respect to the periods designated (c) and (d) by me. They have preferred to see Sanskrit as making a come-back in period (e), after beginning to slip from its commanding position in period (c), roughly corresponding to the time almost immediately preceding that of the Mauryas, and after being almost entirely displaced in period (d), roughly corresponding to the time of the middle and late Mauryan emperors. However, as I shall point out in the sequel publication mentioned in note 4(b), namely in Aklujkar forthc. a: §2.35-38, this view is not justified, unless one chooses not to distinguish between the high

---

eral model for the study of ancient India have frequently ignored the highly tentative nature of many of the specific conclusions. While reading much of their research, one wonders if, starving from a lack of explicit historical records, they were not pushing problems to solutions more to meet their psychological need than to do justice to the evidence.

value attached to a language and its being in active use at the popular level in all walks of life.

2.5 As parts of a fuller explanation, we should, I believe, admit the following elements as obtaining in the periods concerned:

Element 1: Efforts were made to ensure that Sanskrit remained nearer to the language of the Veda.[16] The sustained proximity helped it reap

---

[16] (a) Evidence of this intention, as well as of the kindred intention that deviant forms *(apaśabda)* should not be used, is furnished by the discussion at the beginning of Patañjali's Mahābhāṣya.

Śata-patha Brāhmaṇa 10.5.1.3, mentioned in Hock & Pandharipande 1976:128, following Armand Minard 1932:58, suggests a close relationship between *vāc* and Vedic expression in the form of *ṛc, yajus* and *sāman*. It also speaks of *saṁskāra* ('perfecting') of *vāc*. This may be considered an indirect evidence of the desire to ensure proximity of Sanskrit to Vedic Sanskrit.

Note also that Bharata (Nāṭya-śāstra 17.2, G.O.S. edition) characterizes Prakrit as *nānāvasthāntarātmaka* but not Sanskrit.

One element in the concept of *saṁskāra*, to be mentioned in section 2.8, could have been preservation in the received form. Abhinava-gupta, on the Nāṭya-śāstra verse just referred to, explains the characterization, *saṁskāra-guṇa-varjita*, of Prakrit with: *saṁskṛtam eva saṁskāra-guṇena yatnena parirakṣā-rūpeṇa varjitaṁ prākṛtam.*

(b) Since sacrificial ritual worship was a prominent part of early Brahmanical (see note 33 for my understanding of this term) religion and since Vedic compositions were used in that worship, it can be said to have occurred naturally to the practitioners of Brahmanism that their language for religious (and serious, intellectual) communication should remain close to the Vedic language.

(c) That the efforts made to maintain closeness were extensive and continuous is evident from the early Indian linguistic literature.

(d) The fact that Sanskrit was a language of the higher classes (Keith 1928:xxvi-xxvii, 4-5) and not a living language, in the full sense of the term, for most of the centuries assumed here must have helped the conservation process (Bhandarkar 1877:35-36). In the later of these centuries, the very prestige acquired by Sanskrit must have contributed to its conservation, encouraging more and more people to excel in imbibing its established form. Still, it seems safe to say that the positive efforts to conserve deserve greater credit for the linguistic stability of Sanskrit, given the magnitude of Sanskrit linguistic literature, the value attached to *saṁskāra* of language (section 2.8) and the general robustness of educational institutions in early India (section 3.4).

(e) The observation made by more than one scholar that the nature of Sanskrit has not essentially (i.e., mainly in syntax and morphological categories) changed for nearly twenty-five hundred years (especially between 300-1200 C.E. as Keith (1928:xxvi) observes) and the difficulty researchers feel in determining whether the statements of the three sages of the Pāṇinian grammatical tradition reflect linguistic change occurring between their life-the benefits of the prestige that went with the Veda. A tradition of seeking association with the Veda for respectability had come into existence at a much earlier date than historians of ancient Indian culture have so far observed. Even the Buddhists and the Jainas, contrary to the perception prevalent at present, have extended the 'tipping of the hat' type of acknowledgement to the Veda in the ancient periods of their history.[17]

---

times (Sarangi 1979:110-102, Japanese numbering) indirectly support the observation made here.

(f) The remarks made here should not be interpreted as precluding the possibility that there were dialects, varied vernacular as well as vernacular-affected realizations and mutually differing style registers of Sanskrit. The effort made to conserve and promote a specific form of Sanskrit and the impressive success achieved by that effort, to which I have referred, must still be seen in unrigid and relative terms. Depending upon the intended function, various degrees of movement away from the Vedic model must have been deemed acceptable even by the conservatives. Also, since the area involved is large, the time concerned is long, and many different dialects must already have been in existence before preference for a particular dialect or form assumed the proportions of a policy, the success of the conservation effort must have been varied and complex. In general, the process seems to have been this: As the domain of Sanskrit usage shrank, the promoted conservative or standard form of it partly occupied the space previously occupied by its other forms (the remainder of the space went to new vernaculars or languages), both because it had wider intelligibility as one containing the largest number of common elements and because it enjoyed greater prestige.

(g) The conservation policy I mention here is also responsible, in part, for misleading some researchers into thinking that Sanskrit was never a vernacular or a 'true' vernacular. The response given to such researchers by Keith (1928:16-17 fn. 3) is as valid today as it was when he aimed it at G. Grierson (1904:481): "On this view standard English would not be a vernacular . . . [This view] rests largely on a failure to realize the true point at issue, on a confusion between the earlier period when Sanskrit was far more close to the speech of the lower classes and later times, or on the fallacious view that the only speech which deserves the style of a vernacular must be the language of the lower classes of the population."

[17] (a) The tendency in Brahmanism or Hinduism to extend a 'tipping of the hat' type of acknowledgement to the Veda has been discussed by Halbfass (1991:1-22). His source for the basic observation is Renou 1960:2: "un simple 'coup de chapeau' donné en passant à une idole dont on entend ne plus s'encombrer par la suite," corresponding to Renou 1965:2: "Even in the most orthodox domains, the reverence to the Vedas has come to be a simple 'raising of the hat', in passing, to an idol by which one no longer intends to be encumbered later on."

(b) For the evidence which leads me to extend Renou's and Halbfass's observation to Buddhism and Jainism, as reflected in the older parts of the Pāli and Ardha-māgadhī canons respectively, see: (i) Aklujkar forthcoming b. (ii) Wezler 1993:500 note 35: " . . . the Jains

2.6 Element 2: A transition from *daivī vāc* as a descriptive or non-assertive phrase to *vāc daivī* or *saṁskṛtā vāc daivī* as an asserting or predicating phrase came about without the ancient Indians becoming aware of it, or was brought about without making the ancient Indians aware of it.[18]

---

are of the opinion that the Veda has by and large been falsified by the Brahmins." Thus, the Brahmins are blamed, not the Vedas. (iii) In the comprehensive collections of early passages speaking of disagreements between the Brahmins, Buddhists and Jainas available in Mālavaṇiyā 1983, significantly, there is no passage expressing Buddhist or Jaina opposition to the Veda.

(c) What the point in (b) implies is this: The Jaina and Buddhist opposition to certain claims and practices of the Brahmins has been mistakenly extended by some modern researchers and adherents of these religions to include a rejection of the Veda. In the later period, exclusivism is generally stronger particularly among the philosophers, and we do come across a few Jaina and Buddhist authors who specifically reject the Veda. But even their statements do not suggest that the *average* Jaina or Buddhist held a negative view of the Veda.

(d) Although absence of opposition to the Veda is common to the early Buddhists and the Jainas, one gets the impression that, on the whole, the early Buddhists had a closer and more positive relationship with the Vedic-Sanskritic tradition than the Jainas.

[18] (a) I entertain the second possibility, indicating a deliberate strategy on the part of some ancient Indian thinkers, particularly the Brahmin thinkers, for two reasons: (i) The language we refer to as Sanskrit has not been referred to with that name by Brahmanical authors for many centuries after its difference from Vedic Sanskrit must have been felt by them. One suspects, although one cannot conclusively so prove, that a pattern exists in this silence. A cultural etiquette or convention seems to have been established, according to which *saṁskāra* is to be emphasized as a praiseworthy and beneficial feature of speech but a language as such having that feature is not to be specified. (ii) The Brahmins, in collaboration with the other social classes, particularly the Kṣatriyas, seem to have adopted a similar strategy of not emphasizing difference in, what we would call, racial and religious spheres of life (cf. Deshpande 1979b:21-22, following Suniti Kumar Chatterji 1962).

(b) As an explication of (i) in (a), I add the following:

In the very act of compiling the first version of the Ṛg-veda anthology, there could have been an awareness of the difference between the language of the compositions and the language of the compilers. The creation of the Pada-pāṭha also indicates that the language of the compositions was being felt as distant. The latest date, which is still quite ancient, that can be assigned to Brahmanical authors' awareness of the difference between the language of the Veda and their contemporary language would be that of the oldest Vedāṅgas, particularly the Nirukta and Pāṇini's Aṣṭādhyāyī.

As far as the evidence available at present goes, the earliest Brahmanical authors who can be said with certainty to use Saṁskṛta as a noun having a language as its referent do not seem to be much earlier than the beginning of the Christian Era: *dvi-vidhaṁ hi smṛtaṁ pāṭhyaṁ saṁskṛtaṁ prākṛtaṁ tathā / ... evaṁ tu saṁskṛtaṁ pāṭhyaṁ mayā proktaṁ samāsataḥ*

/ prākṛtasya tu pāṭhyasya saṁpravakṣyāmi lakṣaṇam // Bharata, Nāṭya-śāstra 14.5, 17.1. Cf. Srimannarayana Murti 1994:58.

In Kāli-dāsa's Kumāra-saṁbhava 7.90, although *saṁskṛta* is not used and an explicit juxtaposition of Sanskrit and Prakrit is not found, one may say, on the strength of the context, that Sanskrit as a distinct or distinguishable language is meant: *dvidhā prayuktena ca vāṅmayena sarasvatī tan mithunaṁ nunāva / saṁskāra-pūtena varaṁ vareṇyaṁ vadhūṁ sukha-grāhya-nibandhanena //*

(The chronologically next explicit Brahmanical references to Sanskrit as a distinct language of which I am aware are: *saṁskṛtaṁ prākṛtaṁ cānyad apabhraṁśa iti tridhā //* Bhāmaha (assuming he was not a Buddhist author), Kāvyālaṁkāra 1.16; cf. 1.28 *tad etad vāṅmayaṁ bhūyaḥ saṁskṛtaṁ prākṛtaṁ tathā / apabhraṁśaś ca miśraṁ cety āhur āryāś caturvidham // saṁskṛtaṁ nāma daivīvāg anvākhyātā maharṣibhiḥ / tad-bhavas tat-samo deśīty anekaḥ prākṛta-kramaḥ //*. Daṇḍin, Kāvyādarśa 1.32-33. Both Bhāmaha and Daṇḍin are usually placed in the seventh century C.E.)

Prior to these, what we have in Brahmanical writings are phrases in which *saṁskṛta* is used as an adjective: *vācaṁ codāhariṣyāmi mānuṣīm iha saṁskṛtām/ yadi vācaṁ pradāsyāmi dvi-jātir iva saṁskṛtām / rāvaṇaṁ manyamānā māṁ sītā bhītā bhaviṣyati // avaśyam eva vaktavyaṁ mānuṣaṁ vākyam arthavat / mayā sāntvayituṁ śakyā nānyatheyam aninditā //* Rāmāyaṇa 5.28.17-19. Here, *saṁskṛtā vāc* stands in all probability for what we call Sanskrit language. However, it is not referred to with the proper noun Saṁskṛta. Furthermore, one cannot be certain that it is contrasted with another *human* language or group of languages. Although the Rāmāyaṇa commentators (whose glosses have been kindly made available to me by Dr. Houben) read a 'Sanskrit : Prakrit' contrast in the passage, taking *mānuṣī/mānuṣa* as standing for Prakrit as the speech of ordinary men and women, there is no unambiguous support for this interpretation in the wording of the passage itself. The wording does not rule out, for example, the possibility that the contrast intended by Vālmīki was that of cultured speech of men (which could be but does not have to be Sanskrit) and the uncultured speech of Vānaras (which the Rāmāyaṇa listeners and readers would naturally take to be Hanūmat's language but which would not be intelligible to Sītā).

(The earlier sections of Houben's article and the notes toward the end in Wezler's article in this volume should be seen for references to earlier interpretations of this important Rāmāyaṇa passage.)

It may even be that Sanskrit was used *as the name of a specific language* first by non-Brahmanical authors (Gandhi 1927:Intro. pp. 73-74, quotes Sthānāṅga-sūtra, Anuyoga-dvāra-sūtra, and Bṛhat-kalpa-bhāṣya passages speaking of Sakkata or Sakkaya as distinct from Pāgata or Pāyaya) and there was initial reluctance, if not resistence, on the part of Brahmanical authors to adopt that divisive usage (cf. section 2.7). The absence in Pāṇini's Aṣṭādhyāyī of the name of the language the Aṣṭādhyāyī mainly describes *may* be due to such reluctance. That this main object language is distinct from Chandas is evident. Also significant in this context could be the fact that the Buddha is represented as knowing Chandas, not Saṁskṛta, as a language of the Brahmins. There is no reason why Culla-vagga 5.33 and Vinaya-piṭaka 2.139.1ff should be seen as reporting the historical situation incorrectly in this regard.

This prestige-bestowing development seems to have taken place in the following stages: (a) the rise of the concept of a Speech or Language Principle (viz., the very basic undifferentiated language which lies at the root of all individual languages including those of nonhuman beings) as a mark of living beings—as something invested in them by God or gods, as divine; (b) identification of the essence or original form of the Veda corpus with the Language Principle and of the Veda corpus itself with the closest possible realisation of the Language Principle; (c) thinking of the linguistic expression that the Veda corpus is as divine by a sort of 'next of kin' logic; (d) seeing Sanskrit as continuation of the Vedic linguistic expression; (e) transfer of the epithet 'divine' to Sanskrit.

Pieces of evidence supporting the stages summarized above are available in the literature beginning with the later hymns of the Ṛgveda. Because they are scattered in a large and diverse body of literature, it is not possible to refer to them here. Until they can be systematically presented for each stage in a separate publication, the following should be viewed as adequate justification of the assertion made:

For stage (a), the references and citations collected in the books and articles on the Vedic concept of *vāc* offer indirect but significant evidence.[19] Some of these books and articles are: Madhav Krishna Sarma

---

An implication of the preceding would be that, when the Brahmanical tradition first entertained the possibility of there being a joint or transition point in the continuum I have mentioned in the last paragraph of section 2.6, it thought of Chandas as marking that joint or transition point. It initially divided the continuum in terms of (i) what was thought of as its handed-down part and as close to the handed-down part and (ii) what was thought of as contemporary or evolving. Usage suggesting that (i) was further divisible into two along the indicated lines, that the latter of these could be called Sanskrit, and that, consequently, the meaning of Chandas is narrower, must be deemed late. An interpretation of Pāṇini's usage of Chandas and Bhāṣā along these lines, toward which I was slowly moving for different reasons, has been suggested by Rau (1985:104) on the basis of his study of Vedic citations in Patañjali's Mahābhāṣya.

[19] (a) Deshpande (1979a:1-3) has taken certain Ṛgvedic *vāc* passages as statements glorifying, specifically, the Aryan language. Srimannarayana Murti (1994:59-60, 63) takes *vāc* in the Ṛgveda as standing for Vedic speech only. In Aklujkar forthcoming a: §2.4-8, it is pointed out that the intent attributed by Deshpande to the specific passages is not justified and that Murti's restriction of the meaning of *vāc*, besides not being based on any positive evidence, is contradicted by some of the Ṛgvedic phrases cited by Murti himself.

1943, Śiva-nārāyaṇa Śāstrī 1972, Daivarāta 1971, Rāma-deva Tripāṭhī 1976.

Particularly valuable as early explicit evidence of stage (b) is the oft-quoted passage *sākṣāt-kṛta-dharmāṇa ṛṣayo babhūvuḥ* in Yāska's Nirukta 1.20 as understood and applied by Bhartṛ-hari in his Trikāṇḍī-vṛtti 1.5.

The separation between stages (a), (b), and (c) is largely conceptual, not chronological. The notions involved seem to have arisen at about the same time and probably had a defining influence on each other. It does not seem to be a coincidence that the *ṛc-s* which speak of *vāc* in a *philosophical way* mainly appear in *maṇḍalas* that must post-date formation of the nucleus of the Ṛg-veda anthology. One would expect that an anthology would not be undertaken unless some cultural (particularly, religious) value was seen in the undertaking and that a justification of the anthology would not be articulated unless it was already in existence (in some form). Further, it would be simplistic to assume that the whole of the present Ṛg-veda shows no signs of its coming into being as an anthology. It need not be the case that, in the final form of the anthology, no reflection is found of the values, goals, principles, etc. of the anthology makers.[20]

The *chronological* transition relevant to our present purpose then should be thought of as occurring between the first three stages and the fourth stage. One piece of evidence supporting it is this: Bhartṛ-hari (1.182 and Vṛtti thereto, Vṛtti 1.183) speaks of *daivī vāc* in a context in which it must refer to the language approved by the Pāṇinian grammarians—to what we call Sanskrit, as well as to the language that existed in an age free from contamination and corruption—in a golden age. Thus, a continuity is implied between Sanskrit, on the one hand, and the Veda language and/or the Language Principle, on the other, and

(b) Hock & Pandharipande (1976:123) take Ṛgveda 10.71 to be a hymn about *vāc* as a personification of ritually correct speech. I do not see why one must restrict the concept of *vāc* in this way in the context of the hymn. The references to *yajña* found in the hymn do not seem to have been made with the intention of specifically qualifying *vāc*.

[20] In passages such as Ṛgveda 10.90.9, a reflection of the anthology makers' estimation of the constituents of the Veda is found. *Ṛc*, etc. are said to come into existence out of the primeval sacrifice.

the adjective 'divine' is used in such a way as to connote its applicability throughout.[21]

2.7 Element 3: The disinclination to separate Sanskrit from the Language Principle and, what we would call, Vedic Sanskrit is matched, at the other end, by the disinclination, on the part of authors of early Sanskrit linguistic works, to indicate that, when they discuss what seem to be Prakrit[22] words to us, they have in mind *languages* related to Sanskrit but different from it. Their assumption appears to be that of a linguistic continuum, extending from what we call Sanskrit to what we call Prakrit.[23] Nowhere does one get the sense that they felt any urgency to

---

[21] (a) If efforts were made to contain the degree of separation between (what we call) the language of the Veda and Sanskrit proper (element 1, section 2.5) and if the distinction between the two languages or language phases did not receive articulation or emphasis in the ancient Brahmanical writings (note 17), the transfer of the epithet 'divine' through the stages I have outlined must have seemed natural.

(b) There is another way in which elements 1 and 2 may be thought of as working in conjunction. Both converge in using the Veda's prestige for the benefit of Sanskrit.

[22] For simplicity of statement, I shall generally use the term Prakrit as inclusive of Pāli. Most readers, I assume, will be able to figure out from the context if an exclusion of Pāli is warranted.

[23] (a) In effect, then, the Sanskrit grammarians assume one continuum covering the following of our intellectual constructs: *daivī vāc* 'Language Principle' and/or Vedic Sanskrit → Sanskrit proper → Prakrits. For them, all linguistic expression is located in this continuum. Different parts of the expression totality become manifest to us at different times. No part is newly created as such.

(b) Starting with different concerns (the meanings of *tad-bhava* and *nitya*), Kahrs (1992:241-45) has come to a conclusion that is surprisingly similar to the one I have drawn here. His article provides valuable independent confirmation.

(c) It may be thought that the perspective sketched here clashes with the occasional statements presupposing linguistic change through time that are found in the writings of early Sanskrit grammarians. This is not necessarily so. The statements are made in terms of specific expressions or words (e.g. *nyāṅkava* versus *naiyaṅkava*), not in terms of languages. Secondly, passage of time is not given as the ultimate or real cause of the changes. The cause is usually decrease in the level of spirituality, morality, intellectual ability, or articulatory ability. Nor are the changes dealt with as we would deal with them in a diachronic or historical grammar.

(d) The perspective I have delineated provides one possible explanation of (i) why ancient Indian composers or authors belonging to periods (a)-(c) mentioned in section 2.2 do not name the languages we know they could hardly have missed encountering and (ii) how the view, especially current in our times among the Arya Samaj scholars, according to which Sanskrit is the mother of all languages could have come into existence.

isolate Sanskrit as a language (see note 18). The capacity for absorbing deviation thus accorded to Sanskrit must have helped it in not being in open competition with other 'languages'.[24] The high linguistic ground it took must have meant that it had a long time to march ahead without other languages coming in its way.[25]

2.8 Element 4: The key expressions employed in stating or implying the higher standing of what we call Sanskrit are *saṁ + kṛ* and its derivatives. Not only is Saṁskṛta claimed to have undergone *saṁskāra*, the other languages are given a relatively low ranking in its favour because they lack *saṁskāra* (Deshpande 1979a:22).[26]

Now, at least from the days of Yāska, the Nirukta author, one component of the meaning of *saṁskāra* is clear: 'subjecting to, or being amenable to, or undergoing grammatical operation, having grammatical perspicuity'. However, it does not seem likely that Sanskrit would be placed on a higher rung simply because it had a grammar, that is, its forms were seen as derivable through certain operations, or because the forms had a certain transparency.[27] The presence of a grammar may make a language easy to study and thus perhaps widespread, but it is unlikely to bestow on it uncommon prestige, unless being widespread is (simplistically) equated with having prestige. Besides, it is doubtful if a grammar would facilitate the study of a language so much that even ordinary individuals would begin to respect it, as evidently was the case with Sanskrit.[28] Thirdly, we cannot be sure

---

(e) Superiority complex, xenophobia, and fear of becoming impure are the other possible explanations that I can think of for the phenomenon (i) mentioned in (d). Which one of them, if any, hold true in the case of the ancient Aryan or Brahmanical *linguistic* life must be determined through a separate investigation.

[24] In later centuries, we do have some evidence of competition and opposition, albeit rather limited.

[25] Deshpande (1979a:41-43 etc.) proposes early opposition to Sanskrit on the part of Jainas and Buddhists. I do not think such opposition existed in the earlier periods of those religions. See Aklujkar forthcoming a: §2.43-45.

[26] Cardona 1988:646-655 has much material useful in determining the meaning of *saṁskāra*.

[27] Actually, transparency is not felt unless good grammars are available for a language. Thus, the advantages which may accrue from being considered transparent are not ultimately different from the advantages which ensue from having grammars.

[28] The tendency seen in the vernaculars to sanskritize themselves is one of the strongest pieces of evidence in this respect; cf. Keith 1928:xxvii; Deshpande 1979a:34-35, 58.

that grammars were entirely missing for other old Indic languages when they were being composed for Sanskrit (Deshpande 1979a:105 note 1 end). And, finally, Prakrits are not said to lack transparency. In fact, the general assumption evident in literature is that they are easier to understand. Therefore, there must be something more to the concept of *saṁskāra,* as it relates to the question of Sanskrit's standing, than easy intelligibility and having evident grammatical features.

One additional constituent must be proper pronunciation, etc. That there was value attached to good qualities of speech in ancient India is abundantly clear from, among other pieces of evidence, certain adjectives employed in Vedic literature and the way the Buddha's speech is described.[29] If a certain kind of extra-mundane efficacy was associated with accurate and good pronunciation, then the presence of this type of *saṁskāra* would be even more valued.

To name only the earliest known explicit source, we have a confirmation of these two additional constituents in the second set of purposes which Patañjali (Mahābhāṣya, introductory part, MBh 1:2-3), assigns to Śabdānuśāsana: *te 'surāḥ ..., duṣṭaḥ śabdaḥ ..., yad adhītam ..., yas tu prayuṅkte ...* and *avidvāṁsaḥ ....*

Beyond this, a connotation must have existed to the effect that to be careful in speech—to attempt to use a language with *saṁskāra*—is to observe a certain discipline of the mind and body and that a person's subscribing to such a discipline is an indication of his good spiritual standing. The passage *yas tu prayuṅkte kuśalo viśeṣe śabdān yathāvad vyavahāra-kāle so 'nantam āpnoti jayaṁ paratra,* cited by Patañjali and referred to in the preceding paragraph, would not make sense if such a connotation is not assumed. The most explicit evidence is furnished, however, by the passages like Kālidāsa's *saṁskāravatyeva girā manīṣī tayā* [= Pārvatyā] *sa pūtaś ca vibhūṣitaś ca* (Kumāra-saṁbhava 1.28) and Bhartṛ-hari's *tasmād yaḥ śabda-saṁskāraḥ sā siddhiḥ paramāt-*

---

[29] (a) It is revealing that, in the famous Pāli passage (Culla-vagga 5.33, Vinaya-piṭaka 2.139.1ff) in which two monks request the Buddha permission to recast his words in Chandas, the adjectives *kalyāṇa-vācā* and *kalyāṇa-vāk-karaṇā* are applied to the monks.

(b) The terms for different types of faults of speech found in texts like the Mahābhāṣya (under Paspaśāhnika vārttika 18, MBh 1:13), the existence of Śikṣā texts, the numerous references in literary works to the hero's or heroine's excellence in speaking also suggest that good speech was not only valued, there was general awareness that it should be valued.

manaḥ / . . . vyavasthita-sādhu-bhāvena hi rūpeṇa saṁskriyamāṇe śabda-tattve 'pabhraṁśopaghātāpagamād āvir-bhūte dharma-viśeṣe niyato 'bhyudayaḥ (Trikāṇḍī 1.144, Vṛtti (VP I): pp. 201-02) and *sādhvī vāg bhūyasī yeṣu puruṣeṣu vyavasthitā / adhikaṁ vartate teṣu puṇyaṁ rūpaṁ prajā-pateḥ //* (Vṛtti 1.124-28 = kārikā 1.126).[30]

One last association of *saṁskāra,* which has not been pointed out so far in the research literature known to me, is with a highly pervasive principle of Vedic or Brahmanical thinking: To use a thing with knowledge of its genesis is superior to simply using it. Use must be, as far as possible, backed up by information about its 'how's and 'why's—the *ya evaṁ veda sa veda* principle articulated in a number of Brāhmaṇa and Upaniṣad texts. A *śāstra-pūrvaka prayoga* is preferable to a mere *prayoga.* The employment of a nonstandard linguistic form may not generate demerit, but it does not generate merit either. The capacity to achieve that exists only in a *saṁskṛta* or standard form, since its user, given the social realities of his time, will, in most cases, be an educated person and as such will know how the form came to be what it is or why it must have certain features. Thus, while Prakrit forms are not looked down upon in absolute terms and their easy intelligibility is acknowledged, the fact that they are only naturally acquired and are generally not backed up by a knowledge of their derivation[31] results in their being assigned a relatively low status.[32]

---

[30] (a) Note also *vāg-yogavido vicchidyāhaṁkāra-granthīn* in Vṛtti 1.143.

(b) Even a Ṛgvedic verse like *catvāri vāk parimitā padāni tāni vidur ye brāhmaṇā manīṣiṇaḥ* (Ṛgveda 1.164.45) seems to presuppose a relation between being resolute (*manīṣin),* spiritually advanced (Brāhmaṇa), and knowing *vāc* fully.

[31] It should be borne in mind here that we are talking about a period in which instruction in Prakrit grammar was not seen as necessary.

[32] (a) The last four constituents in the meaning-complex of *saṁskāra* apply also to the tradition of preserving the Veda. Correct pronunciation is highly valued. It is supposed to produce *puṇya* or a beneficial effect beyond the present world. Individuals who devote their lives to accurate preservation of the Veda are venerated as spiritually advanced. The preservation is to be backed, as far as possible, by a knowledge of how it is to be carried out (use of Śikṣās, Prātiśākhyas, grammars, etc.)

(b) In Abhinava-gupta's gloss on *saṁskāra-guṇa-varjita* as an adjective of Prakrit in Nāṭya-śāstra 17.2 (G.O.S. edition), we have an indirect and partial reflection of the parallelism between the Brahmanical adherence to Sanskrit, on the one hand, and to the Veda, on the other. Writes Abhinava: *saṁskṛtam eva saṁskāra-guṇena yatnena parirakṣā-rūpeṇa*

2.9 Element 5: For most of the specified time-span, a religious life which was a significantly different mixture of organized and unorganized religion from the one we nowadays normally imagine for that time-span prevailed. The well-demarcated religious thinking and living which the text-based Indological discussion of the three major religions of ancient India—of Brahmanism,[33] Jainism and Buddhism—usually presupposes was true only of relatively few individuals. While the three religions were not entirely unorganized, were not unconscious of the need to preserve their identities, and must have made efforts to propagate themselves, the average Indian lived a life that did not belong exclusively to (what we would call) one religious line of thinking. He took what can be described as a grocery cart approach. Even while following one teaching principally, he did not, in all likelihood, shun the holy men of other religions[34] or avoid completely the practices supposed to belong to another (in our terminology, religious) stratum—practices such as propitiating a local Yakṣa or making a donation to a local monument belonging to a heterodox religion if his prayer was answered. For most (ordinary) people, religious identity as Brahmanical, Jaina, or Bauddha was a matter of degree

---

varjitaṁ prākṛtam. Thus, *saṁskāra* and *parirakṣā* (conservation) are seen by Abhinava as the hallmarks of Sanskrit. They are hallmarks also of the oral preservation of the Veda.

(c) The parallelism I have pointed out in (a) and (b) constitutes one more way in which the fate of Sanskrit was tied to that of the Veda.

[33] (a) I use this term mainly because no other widely intelligible term roughly co-extensive with 'Hinduism' and yet not leading to the problems of 'Hinduism' is available. I do not wish to suggest that Brahmins were the sole authors, followers, or preservers of the religion or tradition recognized as Brahmanism, or that Brahmanism was only a religion, or that the ancient Indians viewed it as religion or as Brāhmaṇa-dharma, or that their understanding of what we include in Brahmanism would have been the same. I would have no objection if, in the present context, Brahmanism was replaced by 'Vedism' or 'Ancient Hinduism'.

(b) Throughout the essay, I try to be precise in my usage of 'Brāhmaṇa/Brahmin' on the one hand, and 'Brahmanism', 'Brahmanic', 'Brahmanical', etc. on the other, in accordance with what I have noted in (a). But there may be contexts in which I have not been or I cannot be precise.

[34] The reason was that holy men were viewed as stores of spiritual power or ascetic energy. Even a king was advised to maintain awareness of this consideration. In accordance with it, Kauṭilya (Artha-śāstra 1.19.29) advises the king to give priority to the affairs of temples, hermits and heretic ascetics over those of even the Śrotriyas, the most respected of the Brahmins occupied with their traditional duties.

rather than of exclusivistic self-definition—a matter of which part of the spectrum of religious life they mainly and usually occupied.

Or, perhaps, a better metaphor for Indian religious life in major divisions of the age with which we are concerned would be that of a cot made with cloth strips that run along the length and width criss-crossing each other. Generally, the practitioner took a linear approach, but he was always in close contact with the parallel and crossing paths, free to move to those other paths, if a need was felt. In other words, a composite culture in which organized exclusivistic religion 'existed and yet did not exist' had come into existence.[35]

3.1 Acceptance of the elements listed above is necessary to understand why honour was extended to Sanskrit so pervasively and why, although primarily associated with an openly non-egalitarian religious minority, Sanskrit continued to prevail over large areas for long periods and showed a remarkable ability to bounce back. Without the specified additional elements (and, perhaps, some other elements which might have escaped my thinking), we do not get a satisfactory explanation of the pre-eminence of Sanskrit.

3.2 My argument suggests that, during the periods (c) - (f) mentioned in section 2.2, it is not the political or economic backing which Sanskrit received that is as important for its spread and high standing as the culture, particularly the religious culture, in which Sanskrit found itself (and which it nurtured in return).

A further suggestion hidden in my argument is that the spread of Sanskrit in southern and eastern India is of a piece with the spread of Indian culture in Southeast Asia and in areas such as Tibet to the northeast of India. There, too, as respectable research has so far shown, we have no evidence of great or direct use of political or economic might.

---

[35] (a) Historical evidence supporting the point made in this paragraph is indirect but ample. Considerations of space do not allow its inclusion here.

(b) As we move ahead in time, exclusivistic tendencies are generally reflected strongly in the preserved literature. The causes may be increased urbanization, greater economic stake in religious establishments, spread of literacy, coming into being of larger academic institutions, etc.

The rulers and the state resources largely seem to have acted only as facilitators of a cultural process.[36]

The element of 'purity of speech' is present in the explanation I have offered. It is well-known that bodily and dietary purities were major concerns for most Indians (particularly the Brahmins). They were seen as determinants of spiritual purity and, through it, of social standing. Purity of speech linked to social standing thus has clear supporting parellels in Indian history.

3.3 The phenomenon of the pre-eminence of Sanskrit, to clarify my view further, became possible *positively*, because, at the time of its emergence, (a) the notion of the Veda as a text on which to base philosophical, social and political thinking, even if that thinking in fact happened to be new, had won wide acceptance, (b) the institution of attaching some kind of special power and sanctity to the Veda sound had already come into effect, (c) the followers of the Vedic way of life had already instituted certain educational mechanisms to maintain the purity of their language, and (d) the society had become accustomed to attaching value to knowledgeable, correct and clear speech as a mark of ennobling discipline and self-restraint.

The phenomenon became possible, *negatively*, that is, was not opposed effectively, (a) because a religious life not tending to be exclusivistic generally predominated, (b) because at least some socially influential thinkers saw some benefit in not explicating everything, that is, in retaining certain myths and de-emphasizing historical divisions,[37] and (c) because Śramaṇik religions like Jainism and Buddhism had relatively narrower philosophies—philosophies capable of drawing invariable commitment from only those who could be attracted to renunciation.[38]

---

[36] (a) The similarity pointed out here should be seen as lending further credence to my argumentation, especially because the time of the spread of Indian culture in Southeast Asia overlaps, to a significant extent, with the time with which we are concerned here.

(b) The spread of Pāli and Ardha-māgadhī also seems to have come about essentially in the same way as the one delineated in this paragraph.

[37] Note that I am not saying that the society had no sense of history.

[38] In contrast, the Brahmins had a framework explicitly recognizing most social needs -- all the *puruṣārthas* — of the largest number of persons in all age groups.

3.4 The processes and developments which probably helped Sanskrit in maintaining its pre-eminence once it came into being seem to be: (a) training[39] of a vast and astoundingly gifted body of *sūta* narrators[40] who constituted a very effective mechanism for reaching practically all levels of society, (b) creation of an educational network that seems unparalleled in the ancient world,[41] (c) development, mostly as a result of (b), of literature on practically all aspects of (ancient and medieval) life, and (d) constant cultivation of a class that mesmerized the ordinary man through its intellectual and linguistic achievements.[42]

3.5 The foregoing thoughts should not be viewed as excluding causes such as Brahmin-Kṣatriya collaboration,[43] utility as a language of religious life, usefulness as a link language,[44] advantages a frozen language has,[45] refusal to degrade the language by allowing its use for low-

---

[39] This could have been a largely informal activity accomplished mainly in the families.

[40] The sophistication of the *sūtas* can be gauged, among other things, from the massive literature that has been preserved in the form of the Mahābhārata and the Purāṇas, the intricate emboxing of stories that is achieved, and the countless family trees that are maintained without any serious mix-ups.

[41] Histories of education in India give one the impression that there was much geographical and social breadth and width to secular education in ancient and early medieval India. Although these histories rarely speak explicitly about sustained and vigourous commitment to education on the part of social and political institutions, the evidence they collect shows that such indeed must have generally been the case and that the modern view which sees all education as confined to and controlled by Brahmins does not hold good of India at least until about the end of the first millenium C.E. In this connection see particularly Altekar 1965:40-48, Mookerji 1969:50-69, 102-105, 151-155, 206-209, 245, 283, 331-332, 338-339, 343, 353, 363, 504-525, 545-546, 558-560, and Kane's History Dharmaśāstra II, 1:154-156, 363-370; III:164-165. In addition, especially for evidence of strong support for education, see Sankaranarayanan 1993 and 1994, and Vajreshwari 1958.

[42] The *varṇa* system, while it may give rise to other problems, increases the chances of a Brahmin individual to benefit from both genetic and environmental factors. It is evident that powers of memory and linguistic expression were cultivated by the Brahmins generation after generation to such an extent that they probably left the average ancient Indian in awe, as they do many a modern observer.

[43] I have pointed out the necessity of accepting this in Aklujkar forthcoming a:§3.8-9.

[44] Following Filliozat 1972, Hock & Pandharipande (1976:123-24) advocate this to account for the acceptance of Sanskrit by the heterodox sects and the so-called Sanskrit Renaissance of the early centuries C.E.

[45] (a) The implicit reference here is to convenience in teaching (variation need not be taken into account to the same extent as in the case of a constantly evolving language), not being overly burdened by local connotations, freedom to treat many more expressions as

level *vyavahāra*, repeated efforts to Sanskritize, etc.[46] Some of them are subsumed by the elements I have noted. Others are applicable only to the times in which Sanskrit had already assumed a leading role.

4.1 As mentioned toward the end of section 1.1, the scholar who has given the most information and the greatest number of observations on the ideology and status of Sanskrit so far is Professor Madhav M. Deshpande. What I have said above agrees with the views of this dedicated scholar to a certain extent but the areas and details of disagreement are far more numerous. There is an agreement of spirit in that we both accept that, in an investigation of the present kind, political, economic and religious factors should be accorded much importance and that a historian should not take statements in source texts at their face value. But beyond this, there are significant differences in how the types of factors mentioned are to be brought into the picture and what the details of the explanation of Sanskrit's prestigious position should be.[47]

There is a slim connection with my element 2 (section 2.6) in Deshpande's (1979a:1-2) reference to the claim made on behalf of the Aryan language (= Vedic language in the context concerned) that it was

---

synonymous than would be possible in a natural language, and potential for being understood over a wide area and/or a long period of time.

(b) Cf. " . . . the generally received standard of good and correct Sanskrit is the same as it was many centuries ago. There are certain models which modern writers and speakers have to conform to." (Bhandarkar 1877:35). "During this [= post-Mauryan] period, and up until modern times, . . . its [= Sanskrit's] survival without any appreciable change must be attributed to the fact that it was nobody's first language and every generation had to learn it from the same grammar books." (Deshpande 1979a:11)

(c) Deshpande (1979a:11) remarks: "It is an irony of history that the climax of classical Sanskrit literature is reached at a time when the Sanskrit language itself ceased to be anybody's first language." Perhaps it should be clarified that the situation briefly described by Deshpande, while appearing ironical, is not problematic. A language need not be a community's first or native language in order for literature to prosper in it. The second or artificially learned languages have some features which can foster literature in ways in which naturally learned languages either cannot or can only to a smaller extent.

[46] The implicit reference in most of the preceding list is to the causes and factors mentioned by participants in the Seminar which occasioned this paper.

[47] I have explicated and listed these details. Deshpande has mostly mentioned them in passing or implied them through the wording of his remarks. Section 4.3 explains why this difference exists in our presentations.

divine. Presumably, he too understands that the epithet *daivī vāc* which was originally applied to the Aryan or Vedic language came to be applied to Sanskrit in course of time. Thus, he should have no objection to my view that Sanskrit benefited (a) from being close and from being helped to remain close to the language of the Veda and (b) from absence of acknowledgement of its difference from the Vedic language. We both may then be understood as holding that the Vedic language, as a glorified or venerated entity, was involved in making Sanskrit 'more equal' among Indian languages.

However, the details I have given of the epithet transfer and the details Deshpande may provide will be significantly different. I hold (a) that the glorification in the Ṛgveda is primarily not an ethnic or communal glorification, (b) that efforts were consciously made to keep Sanskrit close to the Vedic language, (c) that the efforts were very probably informed by, what *we* may call, a theory of society management and (d) that Pāṇini is unlikely to have differed from Kātyāyana and Patañjali in regarding as divine and eternal the language he describes.[48] Deshpande has explicitly taken positions opposed to (a) and (d) and has not made any statements that would indicate that (b) and (c) would be acceptable to him. He seems to see the stages preceding the emergence of Sanskrit as *daivī vāc* as follows: (a) The Aryans declared their language to be eternal and divine out of ethnic pride or a feeling of superiority. (b) This language was preserved in the form of the Veda. (c) Sanskrit arose out of the Aryan or Vedic language. (d) The Sanskrit grammarians who succeeded Pāṇini appropriated the claim of eternality (and, presumably, divinity) which was originally made for the Aryan or Vedic language. In my reconstruction, the stages are: (a) Language in general was seen as eternal and divine, probably from as early a time as the relatively late Ṛgvedic and Atharva-vedic hymns. (b) The Veda was taken to be the most genuine or purest accessible representation of language. (c) Sanskrit, as closest to the language of the Veda and as a language to be kept as close as possible to the language of the Veda, was viewed as eternal and divine.

4.2 Further, Deshpande (1979a:6) sees loss of Sanskrit's prestigious position occurring, roughly, in the Mauryan period. He connects this

---

[48] For the last point, see Aklujkar forthcoming a: note 17.

phenomenon with the expansion of the concept of Ārya at the hands of Jainas and Buddhists and with competition between the Brahmins and Kṣatriyas.

I do not think that Sanskrit really lost much ground as a commanding language of culture around the 6th-2nd century B.C.E. period or that the Jainas and Buddhists were the initiators of any fundamental innovation in the use of the term 'Ārya'. While not denying that there were occurrences of Brahmin-Kṣatriya rivalry in Indian history and that this rivalry had a part to play in the mutual perceptions of Jainism and Buddhism, on the one hand, and Brahmanism, on the other, I do not accept that the rivalry determined language patronage on any wide scale or for a long period of time. In other words, I do not see as close a connection between the vicissitudes of Sanskrit and the histories of the Ārya notion and the Brahmin-Kṣatriya relationship as Deshpande sees. My argumentation in this regard is given at length in the publication Aklujkar forthc. a.

4.3 It is clear from section 4.1 that, of the five elements I have explained in section 2.5-9, none can really be said to figure in those of Deshpande's observations which can be considered to form part of his historical explanation of the status of Sanskrit. This is partly due to two reasons:

(a) The focus of Deshpande's writings is not the same as that of this essay. He is concerned with the broader issues of Indian sociolinguistic history. He does not explicitly raise the question, "How did Sanskrit come to occupy and hold the position of a supreme language?" Naturally, he does not try to answer it specifically or extensively.

(b) Deshpande decided to take only a certain kind of evidence into account. He (p. xiv) clarifies as follows the limitations of his 1979a publication, which is most relevant to the present essay: "It does not deal with nonlinguistic social and religious attitudes nor with the ritual and mystical aspects of linguistic thought in India, unless they are connected with sociolinguistic attitudes. Nor have I dealt with material in Indic texts which is of sociolinguistic interest but which is not related to sociolinguistic attitudes."

On the other hand, the question I set before myself has required that I consider nonlinguistic attitudes, religio-philosophical aspects of linguistic thought, and material of sociolinguistic interest not concerned with sociolinguistic attitudes. Accordingly, I have suggested that the views of the Veda, *saṁskāra,* and religious life as they were held by common men and the view of items to be emphasized in social discourse, as it was held by the intellectual leaders of the ancient Indian society, need to be brought into a discussion of why Sanskrit ruled the Indian linguistic waves.

4.4 Mere difference of writing orientation, however, does not explain the total absence of overlapping in the elements I have listed as responsible for the dominant position achieved and maintained by Sanskrit in periods (c)-(f) (section 2.2) and the specifics mentioned by Deshpande as determinants of Indian sociolinguistic history. The absence is due, I believe, also to a deeper difference of understanding. In the periods specified, the status of Sanskrit has such a profound relationship with the history of Indian society and the history of Indian languages that whatever one says with regard to the latter two must have some elements that bear also on the status of Sanskrit.[49] That any such elements existing in Deshpande's presentation have only a tangential relationship with the elements I have identified suggests that there indeed are deeper causes for my explanatory mapping not touching or barely touching his. For practical reasons, these causes will be pointed out in a separate publication (Aklujkar forthc. a). Suffice it to say here that they hold serious implications for the presuppositions of current Indology.

---

[49] (a) Consider, for example, the words: 'Aryan : Non-Aryan', 'Brahmanical : non-Brahmanical', 'orthodox : heterodox', 'traditional India : modern India', inclusivism, Sanskritization, bilingualism, code-switching, and *bhakti.* Each of these has a significant connection with how Sanskrit was viewed and stands for developments that have influenced the lives of large multitudes of people in very complex ways over hundreds of years. Each development, in turn, hides in its belly many other developments.

(b) As the results of Indological research frequently have very serious effects on the course of events in modern India, the issue addressed here has much indirect contemporary relevance as well.

CHAPTER FOUR

WHAT WAS SANSKRIT FOR? METADISCURSIVE STRATEGIES IN ANCIENT INDIA*

John D. Kelly

1. *Preliminaries*

1.1 Nāgārjuna, the astonishing leading intellect of Madhyamaka Buddhism, wrote his texts in elegant 'classical', i.e. Pāṇinian, Sanskrit. Not only did his texts follow the rules of Pāṇini's normative system, but Patañjali's Mahābhāṣya, the central commentary on Pāṇini, is said to have been the model for Nāgārjuna's prose style (Lindtner 1982:22), and his verses also followed metrical conventions, especially *anuṣṭubh* and *āryā*, common (though not exclusive) to Pāṇinian Sanskrit. And Nāgārjuna was perhaps not only a follower in matters of style, as Winternitz (1988:332) and others have argued. One set of problems here are specifically Buddhist. As is well known (and apparently was well known among the ancient Buddhists) the Buddha of the Cullavagga Vinaya instructed his followers not to adopt the ancient and refined Vedic metrical language (*chandas*) of the brāhmaṇa ritualists, but to understand and teach the truths he taught in whatever was the monk's own dialect. We will come back to this instruction below. In any case, it did not stop Buddhist councils that followed from standardizing a language, Pāli, as the vehicle of the Buddhist Tipiṭaka canon as they deliberated over what the Buddha had truly said, and how best to maintain and disseminate it. Nor did it stop this emergence of Buddhist texts in new genres of classical Sanskrit in the first and second centuries C.E.

Acknowledgments: Jan Houben, Gary Tubb, and Herman Tull each read all or part of this manuscript and gave me valuable advice. A version of this essay was read to the Asian Studies Department of the University of Hawaii at Manoa. Martha Kaplan has advised on every version and page. Thanks to all interlocutors, who share no blame.

I find the emergence of the Buddhist texts in classical Sanskrit interesting, but what truly intrigues me is that Nāgārjuna nowhere justified or situated his language choice. (Nowhere I can find, at any rate.) To this we might contrast the works of another Buddhist pioneer in classical Sanskrit genre and style, Aśvaghoṣa, whose works were landmarks in both Mahākāvya and drama.[1] Like Nāgārjuna, this Buddhist court-poet manipulated Sanskrit grammar masterfully. But where Nāgārjuna's paradoxes sought to point out unresolvable predicaments for thought and language generally, Aśvaghoṣa's poetic games and ironies transmitted much more self-consciousness about particular and socially-situated languages, genres and rhetorical tactics. Tradition reports that Nāgārjuna and Aśvaghoṣa were both brāhmaṇas, and that they both received good traditional educations. Might each, therefore, simply have been using his own language and—of course—be simply addressing his own community? Like all good simple explanations, this one raises new fundamental problems. Was there really a brāhmaṇa community, in Nāgārjuna's day or, for that matter, any day, that spoke the Pāṇinian prescribed language as its everyday vehicle for communication? (Academic blood has been shed over this question at least since an issue of the (British) Journal of the Royal Asiatic Society in 1904.) If there was such a community, was Madhyamaka Buddhism, and to raise the stakes, the Mahāyāna tradition in general, an intellectual offshoot from *that* community's history? To put the question impossibly, when we are talking about Buddhist Sanskrit, are we talking about Buddhists adopting the brāhmaṇa language, for their own purposes, within a history of schism, revision and change we can properly unify as a history of Buddhism, or are we talking about brāhmaṇas finding reasons to resort to their own versions of Buddhist arguments, within a Sanskrit universe of discourse? This last question is impossible because the real story is surely in some ways both and in some ways neither. The former possibility, that Buddhists turned to Sanskrit, is supported by the legend of King Kaniṣka's council, the legend that this king, not coincidentally of the first or second century C.E., directed his Buddhist Saṅgha to develop its interpretive literature in Sanskrit. To the latter possibility, we

[1] On Aśvaghoṣa's Sanskrit grammatical virtuosity, see Winternitz 1988: 249 ("faultless, even though it does not always comply strictly with the rules of Pāṇini") and Gerow 1978:249 ("consistent and utterly sophisticated use of standard literary devices").

have the abundance of references in Aśvaghoṣa's text to things non-Buddhist, especially including epic mythological and philosophical material, and also the existence of at least one well developed Nāgārjuna text, the Vaidalyaprakaraṇa, devoted directly to refutation of an orthodox school, Nyāya (whose sūtras were not yet even in final form, see Bronkhorst 1985a). So there are grounds for both perspectives, that the Buddhists turned to Sanskrit and that the brāhmaṇas picked up and remade Buddhism. To get farther here—a puzzle I have chosen somewhat arbitrarily as a starting point—we have to turn to some basic questions about community and language.

One could read Aśvaghoṣa as a kind of missionary, on mission to a brāhmaṇa, non-Buddhist readership. Such an approach would provide an explanation for why, in Aśvaghoṣa's epic poem the Buddhacarita, 'Life of the Buddha', the emergent Buddha considers and rejects a long series of *āstika* (Vedic orthodox) practices, claims and philosophies. But it strikes me as an unlikely explanation. And in any case, we should not doubt that the primary audience for most of Nāgārjuna's proper Sanskrit texts was Buddhist. Kalupahana (1986:81) argues that in the Madhyamaka-kārikās "his primary objective was to reject the substantialist or essentialist thought that emerged in the Buddhist philosophical tradition as a result of the speculations of the Sarvāstivādins and the Sautrāntikas." Lindtner (1982:27) argues similarly: these kārikās "are addressed to monks thoroughly conversant with the abhidharma of the most influential of all contemporary schools: Sarvāstivāda. . . . It would be misleading . . . to claim that Nāgārjuna also had non-Buddhists (Sāṃkhya, Vaiśeṣika) in mind."[2] Throughout Nāgārjuna's work, central terms in his lexicon, especially *dharma*, seem in sense much closer to Buddhist than *āstika*, especially Upaṇisadic or *dharmaśāstric*, antecedents.

In both cases, and especially in Nāgārjuna's (the history of poetics is less clear), the writers break with past practices. The texts mark an intellectual break in the Foucault/Bachelard sense. Why in Sanskrit? Let us remember Nāgārjuna's lack of explanation or situating of his so-called 'classical' Sanskrit. Whatever its context, and for all his excruci-

---

[2] ". . . though of course," Lindtner continues, "many of his arguments *also*—indirectly—apply to them."

atingly extremist concern to deliberate on what one can and cannot do with language and discourse in general, Nāgārjuna does not ponder the social nature or limits of this language in particular. His capacity to take Sanskrit for granted, while everything else is apparently at stake, is all the more remarkable when we consider questions of audience. Either, there already existed in Nāgārjuna's world a community of Sanskrit-ready Buddhists, capable of immediately confronting his paradoxical arguments, or Nāgārjuna was bringing one into being. To go further into this, we will have to move a bit backwards in time, and consider the story of King Kaniṣka's council and its Mahāvibhāṣā, a story of *mleccha* or barbarian descended Kings, converted to Buddhism, one of whom required that a great council of Buddhist scholars produce a great commentary in Sanskrit, a commentary announcing the very doctrines that Nāgārjuna apparently made it his purpose to overturn. But before plunging further into obscure, at least partly irresolvable history, we need some oversimplified theory.

1.2 This paper is an essay in the original sense of the term, an effort to organize my thinking on some connected questions and materials. Four questions, actually. What was Pāṇini's grammar for? Why did Buddhist texts in cultivated, Pāṇinian Sanskrit emerge? What was Sanskrit for? And, in general, what are grammatically codified, formally standardized languages for? Obviously we can't deal thoroughly with any of these questions in a single essay, and I am well aware that everything I propose might be wrong. I make no pretense to having definitive answers and do not seek final ones. If I may be allowed a Mahābhāṣya conceit, I make no pretense to being the *ācārya*, the teacher giving the final conclusions. It is my goal, instead, to be a useful *ācāryadeśīya.*[3] Thus, rather than trying only to work from and within points of cer-

[3] Patañjali's commentary often proceeds from questions posed by a student, *śiṣya*, to possible answers posed by an *ācāryadeśīya*, someone near the teacher, to the correct answer of the true teacher, the *ācārya*. Doomed by his limits, the *ācāryadeśiya* is fated to provide 'partial truths', *ekadeśin*, while the true *ācārya* can give the *siddhānta*, the final view (see, e.g., Sharma 1987:9). I am in fact from a discipline currently intrigued by 'partial truths' (cf. Clifford 1986), and I am aware of limits to my 'philological equipment'. Whether or not I share the flaws of the ancient and fictional *ācāryadeśīya*, it is a certainty that I do not aspire to deliver *siddhānta*. In Volosinov's terms (1983:43-44), I neither study nor seek to produce any completed monologic utterances, any discourse "that in principle precludes any active response."

tainty, holding off the speculative as much as possible, I want to work, very deliberately, from theory-laden questions. To use another metaphor, rather than seeking grounding in certainty like rocks in the historical stream, rather than seeking places to stand in order to reach as far as I can into the flowing water, I am willing to move around on treacherous rafts of theory, rafts of uncertain craftsmanship and suitability. I think that we also learn something precisely by seeing which of these are destroyed in the current. (And I would not propose that either method can replace the other.) At some points, and I will declare them, I take up theories precisely because I think that they won't float.

My title announces interest in 'metadiscursive strategies', a cumbersome phrasing. I take the concept from a recent paper by Charles Briggs (1992), an anthropological linguist. Briggs was contributing to efforts by linguists to address the phenomenon of discourse about discourse, statements about language use. This kind of language use can be found all over the place, including simple performatives (Austin's "I christen this ship . . . ") and simple, apparent self-contradictions ("I'm not talking to you any more"). Under the title 'language ideologies', however, linguists have been trying especially to specify what can be said about, as Silverstein (1992:320) puts it, 'nomically-calibrated' discourse about discourse, i.e., elaborate, communicated rules for kinds of skilled language practices. Briggs objected to the general terms used to describe this kind of discourse, 'language ideology' and 'linguistic ideology', for several reasons. The concept of 'linguistic ideology', invoking the concept of 'ideology', is in danger of the latter's connotation of rationalization, and secondariness to other things, while the discourse we are talking about is often fundamental to the shaping of its own object; 'linguistic ideology' also sounds more coherent and complete than the empirical cases necessarily are. It does not easily allow for attaching the discourse to specific situations and types of speakers, and it implies that this rule-type discourse about discourse is usually out to constitute a system of ideas about language as a system, whereas, what we more often find ethnographically and historically, is commentary on acts or types of speaking, singing, reciting, or writing, in short instructions for using language in particular skilled ways. Thus for 'linguistic' he substituted 'metadiscursive', and for ideology, following Foucault's kidnapping of military terminology, 'strategy'. The result is this thumping but extremely useful conception, 'metadiscursive strategies', in other words, arrangements of deliberate directions for skilled language use.

Now, sometime between 500 and 350 B.C.E., we are told (Cardona 1976:268), there came into being the rigorous, powerful grammar for Sanskrit that has ever since been associated with a single author or compiler, Pāṇini. It would be one thing to ask about Pāṇini's grammar for Sanskrit as linguistic ideology. Here our attention would be directed to comparative evaluation of propositions about language structure and function. What kind of linguistics was Pāṇini's? What are he claims and implicit premises in the grammar about language boundaries, origins, and rank? Some real and good questions lie down that road. But a different agenda of questions is raised if we approach Pāṇini's grammar as a 'metadiscursive strategy'. Then we take study of Pāṇini beyond the depiction of situated views of linguistic structure and function, toward questions about instrumentalities of discipline and operations of power that make such views consequential. Our studies change when we approach texts not as windows to distant world views but as tools made for use and used effectively (though not necessarily as originally intended) in distant places and times. We ask, then, not just what were the various views of language in ancient India, but also, what projects to direct language use both sought to accomplish, and did accomplish. Why would a vast tradition of knowledge develop, for which Pāṇini provided a synthesis, to direct people in the generation of proper Sanskrit, and in the evaluation of the propriety of proffered Sanskrit? What was this grammar for? And, is there a history of changing purposes to grammatical science? These are different questions than, how good a grammar is it?, or even, what kind?

In recent centuries many Indologists, philologists and linguists have addressed the question, how good is Pāṇini's grammar? Vivid evaluative judgments have staked out extremes, from the enthusiasm that was an important part of Europe's 'Oriental Renaissance' in the early nineteenth century (see Schwab 1984) to the denigration that flattered linguistic science later that century.[4] The more we learn about

---

[4] According to influential American linguist William Dwight Whitney, the insistence of generations of European philologists on the priority of Pāṇini amounted to something like a religious cult. "Such was . . . the spirit of the devotees of the native Hindu grammar a

discourse, knowledge and power (yes, let us flatter current theory), the clearer it becomes that insofar as these judgments evaluate Pāṇini's descriptive adequacy as well as his theoretical acumen and textual aesthetics, they have never fully addressed an important conundrum. Pāṇini's grammar provides an extreme example of what we might call a philographic double uncertainty principle: philological evaluation of the adequacy of any historically situated claim about language must consider not only the effects of the philological methods on the shaping of the data used to test the claim (the influence of the observers' methods on the data, raising problems as irreducible, though hardly identical, to those in physics), but also the effects of the claim itself and its reception on the discourse of its time. Despite this need, Indological philologists have done relatively little research into the social history of Sanskrit language in general, and *vyākaraṇa* ('grammar') discourse in particular—groundbreaking exceptions include Deshpande 1979a and Pollock 1985—and there is surely room for more, especially for research seeking to ferret out active agency and its effects.

2. What Are Languages For?

2.1 So let us build some rafts. As Christine Jourdan (1991) points out in a recent review article on pidgins and creoles, it is time for extensive reconsideration of the evolutionary premises in what we consider primitive, advanced, and normal or natural in language use. As Jourdan and others have argued, we are at a point of sea-change, especially, in what is presumed to be 'natural' in language. This is especially relevant, because what I have called classical Sanskrit, the standardized language that commentators in ancient India regulated by selective reference to Pāṇinian rules, this Sanskrit has often been characterized as something

---

generation ago . . . It is, of course, much to the credit of Pāṇini that he exercises such a bewildering fascination over the minds of those who involve themselves in the labyrinth of his rules—though the influence admits, I believe, of a natural explanation. I am fully persuaded that anyone who should master the Hindu grammatical science without losing his head, who should become thoroughly familiar with Pāṇini and escape being Pāṇini-bitten, would be able to make exposures of the weaknesses and shortcomings and needless obscurities of the grammar on a scale hitherto unknown." (1893: 197)

other than 'natural'. William Dwight Whitney, a late nineteenth century American linguist, was the most extreme in his denigration of so-called 'grammarians' Sanskrit', 'a peculiar dialect'. He wrote, "as soon as it took on the character of a learned dialect, it began to be stiffened into something a little unnatural; no dialect ever fell into the hands of grammarians without suffering from their pedantry" (quoted in Cardona 1976:239). Similar evaluations are often heard, that classical Sanskrit was 'static' or 'fettered'. Van Buitenen mixed metaphors:

> The spoken language continued its normal process of internal development; but Pāṇini's grammar froze for all time the cultivated language known as Sanskrit. The name of the language, one of the few not derived from a region or a people, states its own program: Saṃskṛta bhāṣā is the ritually perfected and intellectually cultivated language (1978:10)

When archaeologists track the relationship between humanity and plants, the rise of planned cultivation is usually portrayed as the opposite of static, stultifying, time-freezing or agency-fettering, but in philology the historic shift to the cultivation of linguistic form has been thought to have 'frozen for all time' the normal process. What model of nature underlies this perspective?

Once upon a time, around the time of the brothers Grimm, a science of the folk was established, especially in Germany, that contrasted folkways with civilization. The folk had their own language, in which the spirit or genius of their particular nation was unreflectively encoded. Civilization was then an arduous, ongoing and partially doomed process, through which reflective minds replaced the beautiful but limited world view of their original folk sensibility with an increasingly rational, cosmopolitan, universal and scientific understanding. The folk and their lore perhaps had their own historical unfolding, and some sought to portray literature as its higher expression, still with authentic roots. Textual authenticity and value then lay, precisely, beyond the limits of the deliberate, planned and rational. Sanskrit studies were of course a companion to this analytic tradition. In the nineteenth century Max Müller led the search for the earliest materials and thus the true Indian genius. He denigrated as 'disease of language' the consequences of emergent brāhmaṇa awareness of language in their practices, and what he saw as the enormous obfuscating muddles introduced into the Vedas by centuries of brāhmaṇa scholarship that followed.

Among the premises now in deep trouble, in this general scenario, is the starting point, the idea that the folk just arrive on the scene, whether Āryans, Germans, French, or whatever, with a shared, homogenous, and unreflective language and culture, a unity doomed before the corrosive powers of reason. This premise, that made pidgins and creoles unnatural, is now being reversed. There is nothing primordial about the existence of a homogenized language, with a unitary grammatical standard informing the practices of vast numbers of speakers far from direct interaction with each other. As Eugen Weber (1976) shows, it was only in the nineteenth century that French became the language of all of France, replacing a large number of other, mostly very local, now largely forgotten tongues, collectively called by the French 'patois'. While earlier state authorities had been concerned mainly to conduct all official and legal business in French, in post-revolutionary France political unity hinged on ideology as well as administration. It was not only the pressure and prestige of elite, urban, and cosmopolitan French public culture that enticed the unification, then. It was also deployment of state institutions, especially in education.

2.2 So, there are no natural languages. Pierre Bourdieu proposes a new, universal story through which to figure the history of languages:

> To speak of *the* language, without further specification, as linguists do, is tacitly to accept the *official* definition of the *official* language of a political unit. This language is the one which, within the territorial limits of that unit, imposes itself on the whole population as the only legitimate language . . . The official language is bound up with the state, both in its genesis and in its social uses . . . this state language becomes the theoretical norm against which all linguistic practices are objectively measured. (1991:45)

Bourdieu's new story is as generalized, and at least as extreme, as that of the German folklorists. What is natural here is not language, but power, what is inevitable is not civilization, but the nation-state. For those who know something of the tumultuous history of ancient India, points of recognition mix with points of clash, producing a sense of irony, a very definitely moving but crashing raft. Vedic language was surely official in ritual, obligatory on the formal occasions of *yajña*, which were sometimes in turn occasions of state or at least royal necessity. And

Sanskrit became a norm for linguistic measuring. The Sanskrit grammarians themselves, at least after Pāṇini, insisted that the purpose of their grammars was to enable students to recognize the *śiṣṭa*, the educated elite (see esp. Cardona 1988, and Deshpande 1993a). But the brāhmaṇas' style of formality or officialdom was nothing like nationalism or state power. Was it?

To begin with a vital point of dissonance, the ancient brāhmaṇas' aspirations for their language clearly diverge from those of the French state functionaries. The last thing the ancient brāhmaṇas expected or sought was everyone speaking proper Sanskrit. As is multiply attested, only the upper, twice-born castes were thought even capable of properly speaking the language, and only educated brāhmaṇas were eligible to be ritually official. Their 'nation' operated more like a private club than a folk with lore. But is the idea of 'nation' itself really useful here? Was something like an Āryan nation then getting constituted within a larger social field, as so many among those now asserting a 'Hindu' nationalism like to believe? Classical Sanskrit, in its codified, measurable, teachable form, was both standardized and standardizing, and, if we are to believe Bourdieu (1991:48), "only when the making of the 'nation', an entirely abstract group based on law, creates new usages and functions does it become indispensable to forge a *standard* language, impersonal and anonymous like the official uses it has to serve." For those who aren't sure that Bourdieu can, at least partially, put us on the right track here with this story of social organizing by performance standardization, consider the Buddhist Saṅgha. What the Buddhists standardized first, in their various canon writing councils, was not the Suttas delivering the philosophical and general moral teachings of the Buddha, but the Vinaya texts concerning his instructions on monastic discipline. Early (and later) Buddhist schisms are famous for their focus on the disciplinary structure for the Saṅgha, the society thereby made into a highly abstracted (idealized, 'imagined') as well as concrete community. Next, consider a different kind of cultural discipline. As discussed by Pollock in this volume, in centuries later than those I am discussing, prestigious Sanskrit arts clearly became the social vehicle of an efflorescing elite political culture, the virtually obligatory status markers and makers for the dominant classes in a South and Southeast Asian ecumene of new states. An emergent passion for inscribing Sanskrit onto buildings, monuments and other markers spread the literally sedimented form of the language across a vast new social space. But Pollock is surely correct to resist assimilation of this social history into European templates. This Asian ecumene was driven neither by a central empire nor by nation-state formation. Its form of dominating cultural self-assertion was far from the paradigmatic cultural assertions of nationalism of more recent centuries: not only did the prestige of Sanskrit resist relativization effectively, whereas cultural nationalists tend to nation-build by inventing or discovering parallel but distinct national arts and styles, but also, the Asian Sanskrit-invoking elites monumentalized their local social superiority by invoking this high culture, whereas the modern-period nationalisms have tended to promote images of "deep, horizontal comradeship" among the people of the nation (as Anderson has argued, 1991a:7). Images of shared *hindutva* 'Hinduness' in contemporary India are a clear instance of this properly nationalist kind of assertion, claim to a 'deep, horizontal comradeship' with no closer ancient analogue I know of than the Buddhist Saṅgha. And this analogy is clearly limited.[5]

Further, the earlier we go into Sanskrit history, the more problems emerge with Bourdieu's nation-state story of language standardization, and its emphasis on state regulation. One fact by itself is fatal for any linear story of Sanskrit as an emergent language of command for real emergent states in India: it was not the language of the Aśokan rock edicts. Aśoka, the Mauryan King of the Maghadan Empire, third century B.C.E., is generally credited as being the most successful statebuilder to his day in Indian history, though this reputation largely stems from the range of his stone-carvers. Tradition tells us that Sanskrit (though perhaps not Pāṇinian Sanskrit) was known at the Mauryan court; the Arthaśāstra is said to have been written there for one of Aśoka's predecessors (but see Trautmann 1971). Certainly, brāhmaṇas were known to Aśoka, as his edicts require respect for them. But his edicts were carved in stone not in Sanskrit but in Māgadhī and two or

[5] Striving to locate an ancient charter for democracy, Romila Thapar once wrote, "Central to the organization of the saṅgha was the emphasis on the equal status of every monk . . . But this insistence on equality did not apply to the world outside. It was almost as if the creation of a radical, egalitarian society within the monastery exhausted the drive toward such a society in the world outside" (1979:58).

three other so-called Prakrit dialects, and in Aramaic and Greek, the court languages of western colonists (Warder:1980:244).

2.3 So, the new form of the problem: in Ancient India, several languages, notably Pāli, Ardhamāgadhī and pre-eminently Sanskrit, were standardized with increasing precision and insistence, and not in the direct service of 'the state'. We need more stories than one about deliberate, collective standardization of language. How about two? If we want a next simplest theory, with which to build a new leaky raft, it is easy to find one: Benedict Anderson's much-debated version of the nationalism story, already referred to above. To Anderson, the nation and its language are not so intrinsically connected to the state, and the rise of nations and their national languages are conjoined on the one hand with necessary conditions he calls print capitalism (newspapers, novels, published grammars and so on) and entail on the other hand the collapse of a different kind of formal language, what Anderson calls 'sacred language' dependent on social hierarchy and a unifying and centralizing written script. The dawn of nationalism, he tells us, is the dusk of religion (Anderson 1991a:11), with nothing in between (not even, in his studies of language in Indonesia, any specifically colonial form of language organization; the Indonesia story Anderson tells goes straight from religious sacred-center orientations to nationalist self-recognitions, no means or space in between for a colonized subject position). He writes, "all of the great classical communities conceived of themselves as cosmically central, through the medium of a sacred language linked to a superterrestrial order of power" (Anderson 1991a:13). Again, we can launch our raft and begin a survey of the currents; again, I think, a doomed one. It is simple to assign religious address and service to each of the languages already mentioned: Buddhist Pāli, Jain Ardhamāgadhī, and for Sanskrit, the so-called Hindus. It is even easier to configure Sanskrit above all as a sacred language, given its enormous intertwining with Vedic language, text and ritual; it might also seem unproblematic to substitute the story of Vedic text formalization and memorization for Anderson's misplaced optimism about unitary, universal writing codes. But what about the Buddhist, and later Jain, writings in Sanskrit? And even without questions of heterodoxy or boundary transgression, what about the curious, crucial dimension of Pāṇini's grammar (one that Houben insisted upon in a gracious reading of a draft of this essay) that formalization of the more contemporary language, the one Pāṇini called *bhāṣā*, is generally given precedence there over the Vedic forms, the Vedic forms becoming exceptions accounted for, not founts of language order? How much of the history of Sanskrit can we truly tell as a story of service to the sacred? And where we can't tell it as service to the sacred, can we transform it into a story of service to nation or state? Or is there more driving language cultivation in ancient India than these two functions?

3. Back to the Buddhists: Kings and Schools

So now I am ready to begin, but I am running out of space. I have dwelt here on the questions because I hope to provoke better answers than my own. That said, we return first to the Buddhists and Sanskrit, then to the Pāṇinians and the Buddha's original injunction against *chandas*, the language of Vedic texts.

Working from secondary sources (I have consulted especially Thapar 1979, 1984, Nakamura 1989, and Warder 1980) and looking at the period from 500 B.C.E. to the second century C.E., it is not hard to develop a tale of two ends of the Gaṅgā. The Sarvāstivādin School of Buddhism, of the western end (and actually beyond it, into the headwaters of the Indus) are, in the first or early second century C.E. the triumphant producers of the Sanskrit-language Mahāvibhāṣā 'Great Commentary' commissioned by the Kuṣāṇa king Kaniṣka. We are told that this text production was sufficiently important that in its wake at least a major part of the Buddhist monastic community divided according to their reception of it, between the Vaibhāṣikas, who accepted the authority of these Vibhāṣās, and the Sautrāntikas, who accepted only the canonical Sūtras. We can recall, in turn, that Nāgārjuna's texts largely addressed the flaws of these schools, especially the Vaibhāṣikas. If his audience is precisely that already organized by its reception of a Sanskrit masterwork then the mystery of his language choice can resolve to the question of theirs.

The monastic strongholds of the Sarvāstivādins were after all in the land of Pāṇini, the northwest, the place where something like Pāṇini's Sanskrit was, at least at one time, as Deshpande puts it "a first language for a sizeable upper class" (1979a:4). But was this simply the Sarvāstivādin homeland? The first appearance of the Sarvāstivādins in Theravādin traditional histories is the story of their expulsion from the Mauryan monastic establishments at the earlier time of eastern power, Sthaviravādin/Theravādin doctrinal assertion, and (allegedly, but cf. Collins 1990) establishment of the Pāli canon, sometime around the third century B.C.E. The form of this story that connects king Aśoka, the great monk Moggaliputta Tissa, the expulsion of the Sarvāstivādins and the foundation of Pāli and its canon at a great council is suspiciously tidy, and we need not rely on it (for some compelling doubts see Bronkhorst 1993b): obviously the story does the work, useful for Theravādin history, of making the Sarvāstivādins look corrupt, deviant and secondary in their doctrinal work.

It seems to me most likely, neither that men of the monastic communities came exclusively from one region, nor that schools like the Sarvāstivādins should be imagined simply and wholly transplanted from one region to another, but rather, that what is most certain about this period is the emergence of a monastic ecumene devoted to transmission and evaluation of texts. Hock & Pandharipande (1976, 1978) rightly warn us against accepting the idea that the rise of Sanskrit is a story of traditionalist brāhmaṇas victorious over Prakrit heterodoxies, and suggest instead that Sanskrit filled a need for a link language in an expanding social world. In these circumstances, the early development of the *vyākaraṇa* 'grammar' and *nirukta* 'etymology' tools for language self consciousness—combined no doubt with the geographic spread of brāhmaṇas and the Vedic and epic texts themselves—might have made this learnable Sanskrit more capable of solving this ecumenical problem, creating the possibility of writing a text that could combine doctrinal or even dogmatic specificity with the capacity for wide-ranging broadcast and reception. After all, if we take tradition seriously, Nāgārjuna replies to the monks of the Indus headwaters from a monastery in Andhra.

In short, while it still might be possible to construe the story of Classical Sanskrit as something somewhat akin to national victory story—ironically, not the victory of traditional brāhmaṇas, but precisely, the victory of a Buddhist faction backed by *mleccha* royalty—it seems more plausible to investigate the function of link and of means to text production than to seek to resolve the metadiscursive projects toward exclusively religious and then state or national ends. But then, a new wrench in the works: if the useable powers of *vyākaraṇa* 'grammar' are one reason why the pendulum between canonical languages stopped swinging, and Sanskrit was thereafter hegemonic, can we possibly envision that this is what the crafters of the *vyākaraṇa* core intended?

I do not know of proof, but it seems likely that Patañjali's Mahābhāṣya commentary on Pāṇini historically preceded the collective, Sarvāstivādin Mahāvibhāṣā commentary on Buddhist doctrine (*abhidharma*). How then do we place Patañjali in relation to the decline of Mauryan power and the series of new conquering elites, Greek, Scythian and central Asian, coming to dominance in the Pāṇinian heartland? Consider the following juxtaposition, highly relevant to the idea of 'link language'. The earliest coins of the Kuṣāṇas (early first century C.E.) used Gāndhārī Prakrit to proclaim, as the Greeks' coins had, that the king was 'established in *dharma*' (Warder 1980:332)—and they apparently used this Gāndhārī language *before* they actually ruled in Gandhāra, which was then conquered by the next generation. And whereas (without better indication of Patañjali's time and place, we cannot say 'while') coins and texts strongly suggest that these outsider conquerors felt pressure to adopt, support and deploy local cultural institutions, Patañjali added a reference to *mleccha*s, 'barbarians', to the discussion of the purposes of *vyākaraṇa*. Kātyāyana's second Vārttika had given five uses for the study of words, all involving service to, study of and fidelity to Veda. It was Patañjali's Bhāṣyas that then added uses without direct link to Veda, and the first was *mlecchā mā bhūmety adhyeyaṃ vyākaraṇam:* "So that we should not become *mleccha*, grammar is to be studied" (Joshi & Roodbergen 1986, Bhāṣya #23 their enumeration. Cf. Cardona 1988). Did efforts to improve the tools for teaching brāhmaṇas not to speak and act like *mleccha*s enable *mleccha*s to adopt, as they pleased, the culture of the brāhmaṇas?

4. Support for Vedic chandas, *revisited*

4.1 To give the point a vivid, ironic face, let us wonder whether Pāṇini inadvertently caused the *kali yuga*, the fourth and worst era according to traditional Indian historiography. The cacophonous profusion of heterodoxy, the learned production and broadcast of contradictory views, not only outside but also within the clashing intellectual camps that were *āstika* and accepted Vedic authority—the intellectual world into which Bhartṛhari, in the fifth century C.E., is our extraordinary, partly inadvertent ethnographer—this *kali yuga* was enabled by the cultivated, learnable and increasingly productive language we call classical Sanskrit. If, in its unintended consequences, this is what the Vaiyākaraṇas did, what were they *trying* to do?

We know from the Arthaśāstra and elsewhere that grammar, etymology, phonetics and so on begin their intellectual lives as Vedāṅgas, limbs of the Veda, servants indeed of the central religious texts and their ritual system. Is there a break from this direct religious service—to, we shall term it, an intellectual mission that is not so much *vedāṅga* as merely *āstika*, not so much serving Veda and sacrifice as those merely defending or even merely accepting their authority? Bronkhorst has asked concerning Pāṇini's Vedic sūtras, whether they are to be taken as exclusively descriptive or also as tools for Vedic text composition (1991a:83). Remembering that the main target language of the Pāṇinian synthesis is a *saṁskṛtā bhāṣā* not as old as the Vedic language, might we wonder, indeed, whether at the hands of Pāṇini, Kātyāyana and Patañjali the science of grammar turned, increasingly, from the Vedāṅga service of recognizing, protecting, repairing (and perhaps producing) Vedic text, to the new service, recognizing, protecting, repairing (and thus producing) the *śiṣṭa* , the educated elite ?

4.2 In this light let us read two important, puzzling text passages. The first concerns Patañjali's style of linguistic and historical self-consciousness. As Hock & Pandharipande (1976, 1978) and others have shown, Patañjali did not explain divergences between Sanskrit usage and Pāṇini's rules as changes in Sanskrit language. However Patañjali was aware of historical change in social and especially pedagogical relationships, with consequences for the writing of *vyākaraṇa* texts. Notably, he provided an historical explanation why Kātyāyana wrote the Vārttika giving five reasons for study of Pāṇinian Sanskrit grammar:

> In olden days [*purākalpe*] it was like this: brahmins studied grammar after their (initiation-)ceremony. After they had learnt the different places of articulation, they were taught the Vedic words (Vaidika śabda). Nowadays, it is not like this. Having learnt the Veda (the students) are quick to say: "the Vedic words are known (to us) from the Veda, and the ordinary words from common speech. (So) grammar is useless. " To those students entertaining false notions the Āchārya 'teacher' teaches this science (of grammar) saying: "these are the uses, (therefore) grammar must be studied. " (Joshi & Roodbergen 1986 trans., Bhāṣya 44, their enumeration).

On the one hand, certainly by Patañjali's day, the possibility of using *vyākaraṇa* to produce new Vedic *chandas* is not envisioned, and fixed texts are received for memorization in a way less integrated with language education, Patañjali thinks, than in previous days. Vedic service and *vyākaraṇa* are diverging. On the other hand, as Deshpande (1993d) has shown, after Patañjali the social identity of the true *śiṣṭa* begins to slip into the past and approaches that of the mythic seer (*ṛṣi*). The possibility that contemporary *śiṣṭa* could exist independent of the prescriptive texts shrinks to insignificance. Training converges with competence, knowledge of prescriptive text with auspicious capacity, and pronouncement of previously unknown Veda becomes increasingly incongruous. Patañjali's text then both reflects and mediates a moment in these changes. In this passage and elsewhere, Patañjali's Mahābhāṣya teaches an acute strategic self-consciousness, commitment both to the unlimited, all-time felicity and propriety of the language of the *śiṣṭa*, and also the duty to teach not only correctly but also clearly, to meet the needs and challenges of increasingly needy and challenging students.

As *āstika* philosophical and technical systems effloresced, as Buddhists, Jains, and others also used and enriched the classical language, it certainly functioned as a 'link language' as described by Hock and Pandharipande. And I think it no accident of drift that, as Deshpande has argued, this Sanskrit had no 'first language' speakers after Patañjali's day. Put differently, despite the explosion in learned deployment, the language did not substantially creolize.[6] We are back to

[6] As is well known, there were trends of change in Sanskrit usage over time, e.g., an increasing resort to compounds. Further, enforcement of Pāṇinian rules via commentator exegesis was not uniform. But the stress on refinement and correctness, the overwhelming

the idea of the 'fettered' language, but now with clearer awareness why the 'fetters' were productive. What sort of link was Sanskrit pursued to provide? A link reaching up.

As we look backwards then, let us reconsider the figure of the original 'native speaker', as in the idea of Pāṇini privileging the 'native language' of his place, time, and status group. On the one hand, insofar as Pāṇini himself and earlier grammarians regarded the language they studied as that of the *śiṣṭa*, learned people, their authority was not 'folk' or 'natural'. But even granting this, the proposition that Pāṇini put the structure of the language of his peers ahead of the structure of the language of the Vedas is sufficiently extraordinary, and true, that we cannot leave it lying there. We need an account of this nativism.

Did Pāṇinian nativism spring from some kind of self-confidence? From a conscious, celebrating devotion to greatness? Or perhaps an unconscious confidence, blinded from full cognizance of the distance between Vedic and classical language, perhaps by commitment to a premise that it all was, after all, divine language? Pāṇinian nativism might also have been the opposite, a defensive self-assertion of a brāhmaṇa community threatened by heterodoxies from the east or conquerors from farther west, in short, a reactive initiative, perhaps even a self-sustaining and self-maintaining initiative, within the realm of the allowable, among conquered intellectuals. Or, it might have been a product of a simpler curiosity, inquiry built on but leaving behind the *vedāṅga* utilities: something like a scientific breakthrough after all, driven by its own problem-solving like Chomskians hammering away at English.

Sheer curiosity, or a struggle against disorder, or an absorbed self-consciousness? We needn't, and probably shouldn't, expect the productions of the lineage of *vyākaraṇa* intellectuals all to spring from one tidy motive or social situation—in fact, as above, we know at least that Patañjali was conscious of divergence in situation and purposes, and that he showed the most concern about *mleccha*s. We need not choose one image, not even, e.g., that of *vyākaraṇa* as a doomed, if ingenious, consolidating gesture, an effort to codify a working sense of

---

anxiety to live up to a felt Pāṇinian ideal, kept the language formal for everyone, and channeled creativity towards involution, elaboration, and increasing precision.

valuable proprieties, like a guild seeking a much tighter charter and rules in an expanding mercantile world, unwittingly creating explosive new demand for its ever-improving product. What seems clearest to me here is that the aftermath of the Pāṇinian cultivations, this distillation of precise language and the means to its analysis, was a classic case of the unintended consequences of intentional actions, one of the great interrupters and redirectors of ordinary cause and effect in history that so consoled Max Weber. Whatever were their motives, the Pāṇinians surely did not intend to create the means for everyone else to amplify and proliferate their entwined but divergent, innovative discourses. But that is what they did, when they discovered, mapped and disclosed the powers of language.

4.3 Let us exit, then, by way of the matter of the Buddha's injunction against putting his words into *chandas.* The most famous passage,[7] from the Cullavagga, the last part of the Vinaya 'basket' of the Tipiṭaka, is as follows (Horner, trans., 1952:191-92; translation amended thanks to Herman Tull):

> Now at that time Yamelu and Tekula were the names of two monks who were brothers, brāhmaṇas by birth, with lovely voices, with lovely enunciation. They approached the Lord; having approached, having greeted the Lord, they sat down at a respectful distance. As they were sitting down at a respectful distance, these monks spoke thus to the Lord: "At present, Lord, monks of various names, various clans, various social strata have gone forth from various families; these corrupt the teaching (vacana) of the Buddha with their own dialect. But we, Lord, chant the teaching of the Buddha in *chandas.*" The Lord Buddha rebuked them, saying, "How can you, foolish men, speak thus: "But we, Lord, chant the teaching of the Buddha in *chandas*?" It is not, foolish men, for pleasing those who are not (yet) pleased. . . ."
>
> And having rebuked them, having given reasoned talk, he addressed the monks, saying: "Monks, the speech of the Buddha should not be given in *chandas.* Whosoever should (so) give it, there is an offense of wrong-doing. I allow you, monks, to learn the teaching of the Buddha in your own dialect."

The Pāli word translated here as 'teaching', *vācana,* could also have been rendered, simply, 'word' or 'words'. "I allow you" (*anujanāmi*) might have more of an injunctive sense, also construable as "I

[7] There are also others; see Deshpande 1979a:115, and Edgerton 1953.

prescribe." The other crucial ambiguity here is, of course, *chandas*. It is usually taken as the name of a language, the Vedic language. In fact, Pāṇini's usage of *chandas* to refer to Vedic exceptions is often cited to justify that translation (cf. Thieme 1935:67f, Bronkhorst 1991a:81f). Yet in context here, addressing the lovely-voiced monks, *chandas* as metrical form, specifically for chanting, is also compelling: thus Horner construed *chandas* simply as "in metrical form." An injunction simply for prose?

The possibility of an original, *vedāṅga vyākaraṇa* that served in the cultivation of Vedic *chandas* allows for a middle way here. Were some of the Buddha's brāhmaṇa followers out to use Vedāṅga techniques to put the Buddha's teaching in the recognizable forms, meter and sound of Vedic hymns? Did they, as this dialogue suggests, even want such forms to be fixed, and like Veda, guarded from decay? In that case, the Buddha's response is not mainly against a *saṃskṛta*, cultivated language in general: it is against using *vedāṅga* for its other, perhaps even more basic purpose. The Buddha enjoined against his words being cast as if they were Veda. Or was it even simpler? Did the Buddha, simply, enjoin against his words being taught and remembered *as Veda*? The most difficult problem faced by this reading, that I can see, is that it would only be a minor offense. Was this Buddha, really, insisting on fidelity always to the language of the folk, here as remembered in a Pāli orthodoxy? Or was he simply insisting on keeping his teaching out of a growing Vedic canon?

Problems here that I cannot resolve start with how to socially locate this Pāli text: the Sri Lanka of later centuries, where the text was maintained at least? An Aśokan or at least Mauryan-period text-producing council? An actual memory of an actual lesson from an actual Buddha? On some path, I suggest, the possibility is raised of a confrontation between Veda cultivating *vedāṅgas*, and a Buddhist teaching determined to steer clear of that machinery. We need not thereby insist on a Buddha insisting on folklore, his wishes transgressed by elitist successors.

5. What Was Sanskrit For?

A recent sea-change in studies of language politics has led scholars—Benedict Anderson, Eugen Weber, Pierre Bourdieu and others—to suggest that national languages are top-down products of state and capitalist ideologies and institutional machineries (newspapers, school systems, etc.) and not bottom-up traditions of folk genius. Accepting the insight that systems of language propriety are taught, that *śiṣṭa* are never simply folk, scholars reconstructing the history of deliberate Sanskrit pedagogy (from its origins as *vedāṅga*, through the *vyākaraṇa* formalizations and Buddhist and other monastic curricula, into the multiple genres and venues of later *āstika* ascendance) might contribute much that will complicate current theorizing about language cultivation.

To finish, then, the argument made here: while the evidence could be worked toward saving Anderson's neat general map of religious language formalizations succeeded by nationalist ones, this is only possible if we find ways of construing the aims of the metadiscursive strategies of the likes of Pāṇini, Patañjali and Nāgārjuna as religious, nationalist, or religious-nationalist. Or if the story is of a transition from religious to national language, it is a very long transition. The link language image (Hock & Pandharipande 1976, 1978) explains the functional success of the classical language, but only after it is constituted as a pedagogical possibility, and its continuing 'frozen' formality is not only a concomitant of link function, nor a mere survival of its original career as maintainer of brāhmaṇa exclusivity, but also a key to its continuing, increasing power to express and sustain authority. It strikes me that to understand both the break from Vedāṅga to *āstika* intellectual disciplines, and the scarred, fractious history of great councils of so many Indic heterodoxies, we need a much better history of the pedagogical terrain, and especially the monastic terrain, than we now possess. In any case, that's where I plan to look next, in order to try to get these stories straight, with attention particularly to the possibility that there is more to this history of language cultivation than is imagined in reigning theories of linguistic ideology and language formalization.

CHAPTER FIVE

SANSKRIT AND REALITY: THE BUDDHIST CONTRIBUTION*

Johannes Bronkhorst

I.

Sanskrit plays a very special role in the traditional world view of Brahmanism. It is, to begin with, the language of the Veda. Since for many Brahmanical thinkers the Veda is uncreated and eternal, Sanskrit, too, is without beginning. Other languages are often looked upon as corruptions of Sanskrit which, being the source from which other languages have derived—better perhaps: degenerated—is the original language.[1]

But Sanskrit is more than just the original language. It is also the language which is closest to reality. The words and sentences of the Sanskrit language are believed to have some kind of inherent connection with the world we live in. This belief is no doubt linked to the belief in the efficacy of mantras, which, when correctly pronounced at appropriate occasions, are supposed to have various effects, from securing the success of a particular ritual act to curing a disease.[2] It also finds expression in the numerous etymological and related speculations which fill the Brāhmaṇas. The theme that seers have given names to things is no doubt connected with this same belief, because it provides something like a justification for it. We find it already in the Ṛgveda (e.g. 10.71.1).[3] We find it also in Yāska's Nirukta, as it seems.[4] Elsewhere the

---

* I thank Jan E.M. Houben for constructive criticism.

[1] See Bronkhorst 1993a.

[2] For mantras in general, see Alper 1989. This book contains, besides a number of valuable articles, an extremely useful Working Bibliography (pp. 327-443) and Bibliographical List (pp. 444-530).

[3] ṚV 10.71.1 reads, in the translation of Louis Renou (1956a: 71): "O Bṛhaspati, ce fut là le premier commencement de la Parole, quand ils (i.e. the first poet-seers, referred to by the

Nirukta refers to seers with direct insight into the nature of things.[5] It is no doubt this insight which allows the seers of the Brāhmaṇas to 'see' their hymns and 'find' rites.[6]

Perhaps the belief in the close connection between language and reality is not all that surprising. Psychologists from Jean Piaget onward have drawn attention to what they call the nominal realism in young children.[7] If young children in the modern West need time to separate words from things, perhaps certain other cultures, like that of Vedic India, allowed their members to hold on to the essential identity, or inseparability, of words and things right into adulthood.

Be this as it may. The truly amazing thing in India is that these etymological speculations of the Brāhmaṇas, and the presuppositions which underlie them, came to be rationalised in respectable branches of knowledge. The first one that comes to mind is, of course, the 'science of etymology' (*nirukta*), one of the six so-called 'limbs of the Veda' (*vedāṅga*). This 'science of etymology' claims to offer a method to find the meanings of unknown words. This method consists, essentially, in drawing other, similar, words into the picture whose meanings *are* known. The principle underlying all this can be stated briefly as follows: similar words must have similar meanings. Traditional 'grammar' (*vyākaraṇa*), which is another 'limb of the Veda', appears to be based on the same principle. Its own contribution consists in the attempt to identify the—or rather: a certain number of—constituent parts of words that have meaning, and to show how these constituent parts join up so as to produce the words and sentences of the Sanskrit language.[8]

The fundamental texts of the disciplines just mentioned do not refer to other languages than Sanskrit. They seem to have been composed in surroundings where the pre-eminent position of Sanskrit was taken for

---

word *dhīra* in the next stanza; J.B.) se mirent en branle, donnant une dénomination (*nāmadhéyaṃ dádhānāḥ*) (aux choses)." See further Renou 1955.

[4] See Bronkhorst, forthcoming a.

[5] Nirukta 1.20: *sākṣātkṛtadharmāṇa ṛṣayo babhūvuḥ*; Falk (1993: 241 = 1990: 108) translates "Persons who had direct insight into *dharma* turned into poets ('seers')."

[6] Oldenberg 1919: 223.

[7] See Piaget 1925. For more recent confirmations, see, e.g., Brook 1970; Scarlett and Press 1975; Williams 1977; Ball and Simpson 1977.

[8] Cf. Bronkhorst 1981, esp. p. 12.

granted. In an important sense, the Vedic tradition hung on to that position. Yet it became ever more difficult to ignore the existence of other languages. Another confrontation that it could not avoid, was the one with Buddhism, which presented India with an impressive number of ideas that did not fail to exert a profound influence on Brahmanism. This influence also concerned the relationship between language and reality. In the present paper I will try to draw attention to these ideas within Buddhism, and to the way they came to affect Brahmanism. Put in a nutshell, Buddhism appears to have led the way, from what we might call a belief in some kind of magical connection between language and reality, to a philosophically sophisticated theory about that same connection.

Let it be clear from the outset that Buddhism never had any special link with the Sanskrit language. Its original teachings were expressed in a language, or languages, different from Sanskrit, and certain Buddhist schools—prominent among them the Theravādins—have never used Sanskrit throughout their long history. Other schools did turn to Sanskrit at some point of their development, without however attributing to Sanskrit the special position which it occupied within Brahmanism.[9] Buddhist ideas about the relationship between language and reality, when they made their appearance, were therefore just that, ideas about the relationship between language and reality, and not ideas about the relationship between Sanskrit and reality in particular. For these ideas to become ideas about Sanskrit in particular, they had to undergo a special adaptation, to which I will turn later on in this lecture.

Before that, we have to consider the question how and why ideas about language and reality found their way into Buddhism at all. Buddhism is, first of all, a religion which teaches a path leading to the cessation of suffering and rebirth. Nothing in the early texts suggests that reflection on the relationship between language and reality was part of that path. For the origins of these ideas, we have to look at the special way the Buddhist message came to be handed down, and modified in the process. In their efforts to preserve the teaching of the Buddha, the early Buddhists were not content to memorise his own words. They also

---

[9] A certain distaste for non-aryan languages and for the speakers thereof is sometimes noticeable; see Lamotte 1970: XI, 1583 f., 1585-86 n. 3.

enumerated the elements contained in his teaching, and this led to the creation of lists of so-called *dharmas*, elaborately discussed in the canonical Abhidharma-Piṭakas and subsequent literature. This activity, whose only intention may have been to preserve the teaching of the Buddha, yet resulted in theoretical developments, which one could globally refer to as the *dharma*-theory. For reasons that cannot be discussed here at present, the *dharma*-theory came to assume an ontological dimension. The *dharmas* came to be looked upon as the only really existing 'elements of existence', which is, incidentally, the expression that is not infrequently used to translate the Buddhist term *dharma*. At this point Buddhism had become a philosophy—or at least it now included a philosophy—which possessed detailed lists of what there is. Things that do not figure in the lists of *dharmas* do not really exist, and this forced the Buddhist thinkers to deny the reality of all composite objects, which includes most objects of ordinary experience. This, in its turn, evoked the question why everyone seems to be subject to the same delusion: everybody believes that there are houses and chariots and the like in a world, which, in reality, does not contain any of these. The answer that the Buddhist thinkers proposed to this question is of particular interest to us in the present context. All these composite objects, which do not really exist, exist in name only; they are *prajñaptisat*.[10]

Probably the most charming passage in early Buddhist literature dealing with the problem here presented, occurs in the Pāli version of the 'Questions of King Milinda', the Milindapañha. The meeting of the Buddhist monk Nāgasena with the Indo-Greek king Menander as described in this text contains the following passages, in a slightly modified translation of T.W. Rhys Davids:[11]

> Now Milinda the king went up to where the venerable Nāgasena was, and addressed him with the greetings and compliments of friendship

[10] In the following remarks on the role of language in Buddhist thought, I follow to a large extent two articles by Paul M. Williams (1980, 1981). See further Harris 1991: 93 ff.; Lindtner 1992: 264 ff.

[11] Milindapañha (p. 25 f.); tr. Rhys Davids, 1890: 40 f. The Chinese version is to be found TI 1670, vol. 32, p. 696a l. 5 f.; p. 706a l. 9 f.; French translation by Demiéville (1924: 97 f.). Oetke (1988: 185 f.) has however shown, "dass an keiner Stelle der chinesischen Version . . . eine These ausgesprochen oder angedeutet wird, die mit der, dass ein Pudgala nicht existiert, äquivalent ist."

and courtesy, and took his seat respectfully apart. And Nāgasena reciprocated his courtesy, so that the heart of the king was propitiated. And Milinda began by asking "How is your Reverence known, and what, Sir, is your name?"

"I am known as Nāgasena, O king, and it is by that name that my brethren in the faith address me. But although parents, O king, give such a name as Nāgasena, or Sūrasena, or Vīrasena, or Sīhasena, yet this, Sire,—Nāgasena and so on—is only a generally understood term, a designation in common use. For no person is observed here."

[At this point king Milinda utters his scepticism with regard to the opinion expressed by Nāgasena, and questions the latter as to his relationship with the constituent parts. Nāgasena then answers as follows:]

"You, Sire, have been brought up in great luxury, as beseems your noble birth. If you were to walk this dry weather on the hot and sandy ground, trampling under foot the gritty, gravelly grains of the hard sand, your feet would hurt you. And as your body would be in pain, your mind would be disturbed, and you would experience a sense of bodily suffering. How then did you come, on foot, or in a chariot?"

"I did not come, Sir, on foot. I came in a carriage."

"Then if you came, Sire, in a carriage, explain to me what that is. Is it the pole that is the chariot?"

"I did not say that."

"Is it the axle that is the chariot?"

"Certainly not."

"Is it the wheels, or the framework, or the ropes, or the yoke, or the spokes of the wheels, or the goad, that are the chariot?"

And to all these he still answered no.

"Then is it all these parts of it that are the chariot?"

"No, Sir."

"But is there anything outside them that is the chariot?"

And still he answered no.

"Then thus, ask as I may, I can discover no chariot. Chariot is a mere empty sound. What then is the chariot you say you came in? It is a falsehood that your Majesty has spoken, an untruth! You are king over all India, a mighty monarch. Of whom then are you afraid that you speak untruth?" . . .

And Milinda the king replied to Nāgasena, and said: "I have spoken no untruth, reverend Sir. It is on account of its having all these things—the pole, and the axle, the wheels, and the framework, the ropes, the yoke, the spokes, and the goad—that it comes under the generally understood term, the designation in common use, of 'chariot'."

"Very good! Your Majesty has rightly grasped the meaning of 'chariot'. And just even so it is on account of having hair, nails, teeth, skin, flesh, nerves, bones, marrow, kidneys, heart, liver, abdomen, spleen, lungs, larger intestines, lower intestines, stomach, faeces, bile, phlegm, pus, blood, sweat, fat, tears, serum, saliva, mucus, oil that lubricates the joints, urine, brain, outward form, sensations, ideas, confections, and consciousness that I come under the generally understood term, the designation in common use, of 'Nāgasena'."

Many other Buddhist texts repeat, be it usually in a less attractive garb, the message which we learn from the Milindapañha: composite objects exist in name only. Already a passage in the Saṃyutta Nikāya states that "just as the word 'chariot' is used when the parts are put together, so there is the use of the conventional expression 'being' when the constituents of a person are present".[12] A hut, we read in the Śāriputrābhidharma, is nothing but a designation.[13] The Mahāvibhāṣā illustrates the category of nominal existence (*prajñaptisat*) by enumerating the objects "vase, cloth, chariot, army, forest, hut etc.".[14] The Abhidharmakośabhāṣya explains that a composite object is *prajñaptisat*, not *dravyasat*.[15]

For most Buddhists belonging to the mainstream,[16] the only things that really exist, not only in name, are the *dharmas*. The following extract from a passage of the Abhidharmakośabhāṣya expresses this clearly:[17]

---

[12] SN I.135: *yathā hi aṅgasambhārā hoti saddo ratho iti evaṃ khandesu santesu hoti satto ti sammuti.*

[13] TI 1548, vol. 28, p. 626c l. 11-12.

[14] TI 1545, vol. 27, p. 42b l. 1-2. Cp. the following statements from the same text, translated by La Vallée Poussin (1937: 166-67): "Le Bhadanta Vasumitra dit: 'Le nom qui désigne est *saṃvṛti* . . . '"; "Bhadanta dit: 'Parler d'être vivant (*sattva*), de cruche, de vêtement et autres choses, expressions (*vyavahāra*) produites par une pensée non-fausse, c'est *saṃvṛtisatya*; . . . '"; "Le Bhadanta Dharadatta dit: 'Le nom, de sa nature (*nāmasvabhāva*), est *saṃvṛti*; . . . '" Also the Vibhāṣā refers to the principle "Toutes choses sont vides et sans-soi"; see La Vallée Poussin 1937: 164.

[15] Abhidh-k-bh(P) p. 13 l. 24-25, on verse 1.20: *yadi rāśyarthaḥ skandhārthaḥ prajñaptisantaḥ skandhāḥ prāpnuvanti/ anekadravyasamūhatvāt rāśipudgalavat/*

[16] Following Harrison (1990: xviii n. 8; 1992: 77-78 n. 8) I use this term here to refer to what is often called Śrāvakayāna or Hīnayāna.

[17] Abhidh-k-bh(P) p. 334 l. 3-9, on verse 6.4: *yasminn avayavaśo bhinne na tadbuddhir bhavati tat saṃvṛtisat/ tad yathā ghaṭaḥ/ . . . / tatra cānyān apohya dharmān buddhyā tadbuddhir na bhavati tac cāpi saṃvṛtisad veditavyam/ tad yathāmbuḥ/ . . . / teṣv eva tu saṃvṛtisaṃjñā kṛt[ā] . . . / ato 'nyathā paramārthasatyam/ tatra bhinne 'pi tadbuddhir bhavaty eva/ anyadharmāpohe 'pi buddhyā tat paramārthasat/.*

> Where the idea of an object is no longer present when the object is broken into pieces, that object exists only relatively (*saṃvṛtisat*); an example is a vase. ... Where the idea of an object is no longer present when one removes the other *dharmas* mentally, that object, too, is to be looked upon as existing only relatively; an example is water. . . . To these objects a conventional name has been given. . . . In cases different from these there is absolute truth. Where the idea of an object is present even when the object is broken, or when one removes the other *dharmas* mentally, that object exists absolutely; an example is colour.

The older Saṃyuktābhidharmahṛdaya, from which the Abhidharmakośabhāṣya has borrowed extensively, has a similar passage, which, however, speaks of names rather than ideas: in case the name of an object is no longer present when it is analysed, that object exists relatively only.[18]

Here it is important to emphasise that reflections on the relationship between composite wholes and their parts are not marginal to Buddhist thought. Quite on the contrary, they are central to it, from an early date onward. The oldest parts of the Milindapañha may go back as far as the second century before our era. If the passage which I just read out to you belongs to the oldest kernel, which seems likely, it constitutes evidence that the concern with parts and wholes was already well established at that early date.

This date finds confirmation elsewhere. The school of thought which works out the *dharma*-theory in most rigorous detail is the one called Sarvāstivāda. From among the texts just mentioned the Mahāvibhāṣā, and to some extent also the Abhidharmakośabhāṣya, belong to this school. There is independent evidence to believe that the essential features of this school, too, were already in place in the middle of the second century before our era.[19] These essential features show that this school, too, had consciously rejected the existence of composite wholes at that time. Note here that followers of the Sarvāstivāda school of Buddhist thought continued to write detailed, and voluminous, treatises until beyond the middle of the first millennium of our era. The school led therefore a vigorous life for seven or eight centuries, and had plenty of opportunity to influence other thinkers, both Buddhists and non-Buddhists. We will come back to this in a while.

---

[18] TI 1552, vol. 28, p. 958b l. 8 f.; cf. Dessein 1994: I, 2, p. 802.

[19] Bronkhorst 1987: 71.

But the preoccupation with the relationship between parts and composite whole went on to characterise other developments within Buddhism as well. A particularly momentous development was the arising of what came to be known as Mahāyāna, to be distinguished from the mainstream (Śrāvakayāna or Hīnayāna), to which schools like the Sarvāstivāda belonged. Several theoretical developments came to be associated with the Mahāyāna. Recall that the non-existence of composite objects in Buddhism was assimilated to the rejection of the existence of the person. This is clear from the Milindapañha passage which I read to you, but also from other Buddhist texts. Other Buddhists, primarily those belonging to the Mahāyāna, went further. They, too, rejected the full existence of the person and of composite objects (*pudgalanairātmya*). But in addition to this, they claimed the essencelessness of the *dharmas* (*dharmanairātmya*). For them, the challenge to account for reality as we experience it became even greater than it had been, and continued to be, for the mainstream Buddhists. Not even the ultimate constituents of all there is, the *dharmas*, could now be accepted as really existing any more.

The non-existence of the *dharmas* is often mentioned in the early Prajñāpāramitā-Sūtras.[20] The *dharmas* are described as 'empty',[21] 'without own reality' (*asvabhāva*),[22] 'empty of own reality' (*svabhāvaśūnya*),[23] 'without self' (*nirātmaka*),[24] etc. We learn from at least one passage that 'self' (*ātman/pudgala*) and 'aggregate' (*piṇḍa*)—i.e., 'whole', 'composite entity'—are identical.[25] The 'self' is the 'aggregate'; the text considers both of them ultimately unreal.

---

[20] E.g. Suvikrāntavikrāmiparipṛcchā ch. 1, p. 9 l. 26, l. 30 f.; p. 10 l. 22.

[21] E.g. Aṣṭasāhasrikā ch. 18, p. 172 l. 15-20, p. 173 l. 3 f.

[22] E.g. Aṣṭasāhasrikā ch. 18, p. 173 l. 3; Suvikrāntavikrāmiparipṛcchā ch. 1, p. 10 l. 22.

[23] E.g. Prajñāpāramitāhṛdaya Sūtra (long version), p. 98 l. 13.

[24] Vajracchedikā Prajñāpāramitā 17, p. 85 l. 2 and 7; 28, p. 88 l. 9.

[25] Vajracchedikā Prajñāpāramitā 30-31, p. 89 l. 2-6: *bhagavān āha: piṇḍagrāhaś caiva subhūte avyavahāro 'nabhilāpyaḥ/ na sa dharmo nādharmaḥ/ sa ca bālapṛthagjanair udgṛhītaḥ/ tat kasya hetoḥ? yo hi kaścit subhūte evaṃ vadet: ātmadṛṣṭis tathāgatena bhāṣitā, sattvadṛṣṭir jīvadṛṣṭiḥ pudgaladṛṣṭis tathāgatena bhāṣitā, api nu sa subhūte samyag vadamāno vadet? subhūtir āha: no hīdaṃ bhagavan, no hīdaṃ sugata, na samyag vadamāno vadet/* ". . . One should neither speak of nor discuss the acceptance of aggregates (*piṇḍa*). The aggregate is neither a *dharma* nor a non-*dharma*. It is accepted by fools and stupid people. Why? He who says that the Tathāgata teaches the belief in the self (*ātman*), in a being (*sattva*), in the soul (*jīva*), in the person (*pudgala*), . . . he would not speak the truth."

In this vision of the world, then, neither composite objects nor constituents really exist. This includes the *dharmas*, the ultimate constituents for most of the main stream Buddhists. The texts identify the *dharmas* with empty space (*ākāśa*) which, for them, is non-existence (*abhāva*).[26] According to the Aṣṭasāhasrikā (ch. 13, p. 139 l. 10 f.) all dharmas are identical with empty space (*ākāśasama*); this is why one cannot count them, and why they have no measure (*pramāṇa*).

How does the Mahāyāna explain the phenomenal world? Here, too, it is language which plays an essential role. The 'Maitreya-chapter' of the Pañcaviṃśatisāhasrikā states that all things up to the Buddhadharmas are nothing but names.[27] Designations, moreover, depend upon the analytic imagination (*vikalpa*).[28] According to the commentary by Devaśarman on the Madhyamakakārikā, cited in the Prajñāpradīpa of Bhāvaviveka (Bhavya), the aim of the text commented upon is to destroy adherence to language and to the referents of language.[29] The Madhyamakāvatāra of Candrakīrti cites, under 6.68, a Sūtra in which the Buddha declares that absolutely everything is nothing but name (*prajñapti*); things do not really exist and it is the linguistic referent which logicians (*tārkika*) misconceive as being the real thing.[30] Elsewhere in the same chapter, Candrakīrti observes: "Its own being is inaccessible to words. Since the name (*abhidhāna*) aims at grasping the form of the 'objects of naming' (*prajñaptisat*), as long as there is naming, one does not speak of reality."[31] According to the Prasannapadā of the same author, "emptiness itself is defined as metaphorical naming. The wheel and the other parts of a chariot are the substrate of naming. This naming of the chariot on the substrate of its parts [signifies] its non-production as being in itself; and the non-production as being in itself is emptiness".[32] Saṃsāra, too, is nothing but a name

---

[26] See, e.g., Suvikrāntavikrāmiparipṛcchā ch. 4, p. 28 l. 1.

[27] Conze and Iida 1968: 234 (section II.6), 238 (section IV.39).

[28] Id. p. 238 (section IV.40): *vikalpa(ṃ?) pratītya abhilapanatā.*

[29] Cited by Williams (1980: 36 fn. 1): *de la dgag par bya ba ni gyis te/ brjod pa la mngon par zhen pa dang/ brjod par bya ba la mngon par zhen pa'o/*

[30] Madhyamakāvatāra p. 160 l. 9-12; tr. La Vallée Poussin 1910: 344-45. Williams (1980: 37 fn. 29) explains that *btags* represents *prajñapti.*

[31] Madhyamakāvatāra p. 139 l. 15-18; tr. La Vallée Poussin 1910: 328.

[32] Prasannapadā under verse 24.18, ed. Vaidya p. 246 (ed. La Vallée Poussin p. 504): *saiva śūnyatā upādāya prajñaptir iti vyavasthāpyate/ cakrādīny upādāya rathāṅgāni rathaḥ*

(*saṃjñāmātrakam*), according to the Prasannapadā under verse 11.2. According to a text cited in the Śikṣāsamuccaya of Śāntideva, everything is *vyavahāramātra, nāmadheyamātra, saṃketamātra, saṃvṛtimātra, prajñaptimātra*; that is to say, nothing but words.[33]

The *Mahāprajñāpāramitāśāstra attributed to Nāgārjuna contains a whole series of remarks about the relation between language and the world. The following one gives its position in a nutshell:[34] "The ignorant pursue names while what they seek is reality."

The above citations are from works belonging to the Madhyamaka school of Buddhist thought. Passages could also be cited from Vijñānavāda works, but this would take us too far afield.[35] Be it here noted that the Vijñānavāda frequently speaks of *vijñapti* 'phenomenon, percept'[36] rather than *prajñapti.*[37] The world is then described as *vijñaptimātra* 'nothing but percepts'. The connection between the two can be seen as follows. If things exist in name only, it is us who give those names. In other words, we create things, which are really nothing but our percepts.[38] D.T. Suzuki has indeed been able to show that *vijñaptimātra* and *prajñaptimātra* are often synonyms, at least in the Laṅkāvatāra Sūtra.[39]

I conclude this survey with a verse from the Mūlamadhyamakakārikā of Nāgārjuna, which appears to state that the false reality evoked by language is yet necessary in order to reach the highest aim. The verse reads: "Without relying on linguistic usage (*vyavahāra*), the

---

prajñapyate/ tasya yā svāṅgāny upādāya prajñaptiḥ sā svabhāvenānutpattiḥ yā ca svabhāvenānutpattiḥ sā śūnyatā/ Cf. May 1959: 239.

[33] Śikṣāsamuccaya (ed. Vaidya) p. 137 l. 12-13.

[34] Ramanan 1966: 73. The whole of chapter II of this book, "Concepts and conventional entities (Nāma and Lakṣaṇa)" (p. 70-88), is of interest in the present context.

[35] See, e.g., La Vallée Poussin 1910: 328; 1928-29: 554; 1933: 94; Lamotte 1935: 188, 190. On the continuity between the two schools, see Harris 1991.

[36] This is the interpretation proposed by B.C. Hall (1986), followed by R.P. Hayes (1988: 99-100).

[37] On the historical relation between *prajñaptimātra* and *vijñaptimātra*, see Schmithausen 1973: 171.

[38] Cp. Frauwallner 1956: 268-69.

[39] Suzuki 1930: 181.

highest truth (*paramārtha*) cannot be taught. Without obtaining the highest truth, nirvāṇa cannot be reached."[40]

All these passages are meant to show that the relationship between words and things in Buddhism, from at least the second century before our era onward, was intimately linked to another major concern of the Buddhist thinkers: the relationship between composite wholes and their parts. Composite wholes were not accepted to have real existence—this was the result of a particular interpretation of the doctrine of non-self, which we find already in the earliest Buddhist texts—and words were invoked to explain the universal belief in the existence of such non-existing entities. I wish to emphasise again that this complex of ideas was not marginal to Buddhist thought; it was not a set of ideas that someone may have had at some time, and which has left some traces in the texts. Quite on the contrary, these ideas pervade the Buddhist texts from a certain date onward, and belong apparently to the very essence of that which occupied Buddhist thinkers for a very long time.

II.

I will now turn to a completely different system of thought, to the Brahmanical school known by the name of Vaiśeṣika. In a recent article I have argued that this system of philosophy may have been created under the influence of Sarvāstivāda.[41] The reason I offered is that Vaiśeṣika is to a large extent based on four axioms, which can be looked upon as either straight borrowings of, or reactions against, axioms of the Sarvāstivādins. Two of these axioms are of special interest in the present context. Recall first that the Sarvāstivādins—like most other Buddhists—rejected the existence of composite wholes besides their ultimate constituents, the *dharmas*. Composite objects exist in name only. In Vaiśeṣika, on the other hand, composite objects are as real as their constituents, and exist alongside them. The vase is different from the two halves that it is composed of; together they constitute three entities. It goes without saying that the world as conceived by the

[40] MadhK(deJ) 24.10: *vyavahāram anāśritya paramārtho na deśyate/ paramārtham anāgamya nirvāṇaṃ nādhigamyate//* Candrakīrti's Prasannapadā explains *vyavahāra* as *abhidhānābhidheyajñānajñeyādilakṣaṇa*.

[41] Bronkhorst 1992b.

Vaiśeṣikas contains far more objects than the world of the Sarvāstivādins. The latter could make an inventory of all there is, by basing themselves on their lists of *dharmas*. These *dharmas*, they believed, had been made known by the omniscient Buddha. The Vaiśeṣikas, too, presented a list of categories which constituted, in their opinion, a list of all there is. The question is: how could the Vaiśeṣikas find out what filled their far more crowded world?

Their answer is directly relevant to the theme of this symposium. It is: the Sanskrit language. The Sanskrit language allowed them to find out what exists. I shall give some examples in a minute. Let me first, however, emphasise the parallelism and difference of this position as compared to that of the Sarvāstivādins. The Vaiśeṣikas accept the link between composite objects and words postulated by the Sarvāstivādins. But whereas the latter reject the real existence of composite objects, and assign no other role to words than that of explaining our common error, for the former composite objects are part of reality, and words are the key that gives access to that reality. This they explain by pointing out that names were given by seers who could perceive everything.[42] This in

---

[42] Vaiśeṣika Sūtra (ed. Jambuvijaya) 2.1.18-19: *saṃjñākarma tv asmadviśiṣṭānāṃ liṅgam/ pratyakṣapūrvakatvāt saṃjñākarmaṇaḥ/*. See also Wezler 1985a. The theme of seers who have given names to things is already present in the Ṛgveda and other early texts, as we have seen. Other texts take over the same theme. The Yuktidīpikā (ed. Pandeya, p. 5 l. 9 f.) ascribes the original function of naming things to the supreme seer (*paramarṣi*), who is, of course, Kapila. The Mahābhārata (12.262.8), probably inspired by the Nirukta passage cited earlier, states that the seer Kapila had an an insight into the nature of things (*pratyakṣadharma*); the MBh 1.11:11f. uses the same expression (here *pratyakṣadharman*) in connection with seers known as *yarvāṇas tarvāṇas* (so Cardona 1990: 7 and 16 n. 24). The Nyāya Bhāṣya uses the same expression as the Nirukta (*sākṣātkṛtadharman*) with reference to 'reliable persons' (*āpta*); see Franco 1994: 241. See further Ruegg 1994a, 1994b; also Bhartṛhari's VP 1.37-38; 3.1.46; Houben, forthcoming. Isaacson 1993, has drawn attention to the fact that yogic perception has played a role in Vaiśeṣika from an early date onward. The idea that poets have a special insight into the nature of things was to have a long life in India. Rājaśekhara, the author of the treatise on poetry called Kāvyamīmāṃsā (9th or 10th century C.E.), observes in chapter 12 (p. 62, l. 17 - p. 63, l. 1; tr. Granoff 1995: 364): "The true poetic eye, gained from propitiation of the goddess Sarasvatī, without need of external aids reveals things that have been directly experienced by the poet and things that the poet has never even experienced before, in a process that is beyond the range of human conception and cannot be described in words. For it is said that the goddess Sarasvatī reveals even to the sleeping poet both the theme of his poem and the language in which to express it. But others though awake are as if blind. For this reason it is said that really great poets are blind

its turn explains why the Vaiśeṣika texts frequently emphasise that this or that ontological situation justifies this or that current expression. The quality *pṛthaktva* (separateness), for example, explains that people speak of distinction. Sometimes the reasoning works in the opposite direction: the fact that the personal pronoun 'I' cannot be used in apposition with some such term as 'earth', proves that the soul is different from the body. Many further examples could be adduced to illustrate the parallelism between words and things from the Vaiśeṣika point of view, but they tend to be rather technical; I will not, therefore, harass you with more of them.[43] But I would like to add one more observation: even though the texts are not explicit about this, the conscious belief in the intimate connection between words and things may explain why the three most important (and perhaps oldest) categories of Vaiśeṣika – substance (*dravya*), quality (*guṇa*) and movement (*karman*) – correspond to the three main types of words: nouns, adjectives and verbs.

The Vaiśeṣikas do not, not at least in their early surviving texts, contrast Sanskrit with other languages. And indeed, one may wonder whether Sanskrit in particular is a vital ingredient of their belief in the correspondence between language and reality. This correspondence is usually conceived of as the relationship between names and what is named by them: nouns, adjectives and verbs, for example, name the different kinds of things that constitute objective reality. Different languages use different 'names'; this much is clear. But do these different 'names' correspond to different 'objects'? Jan Houben has recently drawn attention to the fact that early Indian thinkers—he speaks of Bhartṛhari in particular, but the grammarian Patañjali, too, can be included— did not show much appreciation for the variations of structure of different languages.[44] Different languages are often presented as collections of deviations of individual words. Seen in this way, reality

to things that have already been seen by others, but possess a kind of divine sight that enables them to perceive that which no one before them has ever seen. Even the Three-eyed God Śiva or Indra with his thousand eyes cannot see that which mortal poets see with their ordinary eyes. In the mirror that is the mind of poets the whole universe is reflected. Words and what they express vie with each other in their rush to be present to great minded poets. Poets explore with their words that which yogins see through the power of their religious accomplishments. And so the words of great poets are potentially infinite."

[43] See Bronkhorst 1992b: 99 f. for these and other examples.

[44] Houben 1993: 149 f.

corresponds to other languages as much as it corresponds to Sanskrit, precisely because they do not differ from it in a manner which would affect this correspondence. Having said this, it is of course important to add that for the Vaiśeṣikas there could be no doubt as to which language the original seers used while naming objects: this was of course Sanskrit.

One more question must here be addressed. How certain is it that Vaiśeṣika was indeed created under the influence of Sarvāstivāda Buddhism, and not, for example, under the influence of other schools, such as Sāṃkhya or the Jainas? This question has actually been raised in a recent publication, and at first sight it seems reasonable enough.[45] I would therefore like to use the present opportunity to add some reflections to the ones which I have presented in my earlier publication referred to above. These reflections do not, of course, exhaust the question. I will concentrate on the issue that has occupied us all along in this lecture, the question of the relationship between composite wholes and their parts. For reasons special to the history of Buddhism in India, this issue became of the greatest interest to the Buddhists. We find it back, in a different form, in Vaiśeṣika, but it is virtually absent in Sāṃkhya.[46] This as much as rules out Sāṃkhya. Jainism seems to side with Vaiśeṣika in some of its texts, but there is no indication that I know of suggesting that this issue was of any particular importance to them, as it was to the Buddhists and to the Vaiśeṣikas. To this I should add, that there is no evidence that Sāṃkhya and Jainism had developed any form of systematisation at the early date mentioned above for Sarvāstivāda (2nd cent. B.C.E.!). This development is, in Buddhism, linked to the *dharma*-theory and to the particular interpretation of the doctrine of non-self, neither of which have a parallel in Jainism. Moreover, hypotheses about the early development of Jainism are extremely precarious. Even their canonical texts—according to the Śvetāmbaras who, contrary to the Digambaras, believed that they had been preserved at all—were not written down until the fifth century of our era.[47] Having said that, I fully

---

[45] Houben 1995b: 733 n. 29.

[46] According to SK 10, the manifest (*vyakta*) has parts (*sāvayava*), whereas the non-manifest (*avyakta*) has not. SK 17 adds that aggregates exist for the sake of something else (*saṃghātaparārthatvāt*), and concludes from this that the *puruṣa* exists.

[47] On the late date of at least some Jaina canonical texts, see Bronkhorst 1995: 1039-40.

agree that the historical relationship between Vaiśeṣika and Jainism needs further exploration, and may yet throw new light on unresolved issues. I do not, however, expect that such research will produce reasons to think that Vaiśeṣika was more than marginally indebted to Jainism. And even if the Jaina tradition to the extent that the Vaiśeṣika Sūtra was (wholly or partly) composed by the Jaina schismatic Rohagupta were to be true,[48] this would only shift the problem, and one might still hold on to the view that the system was created under the influence of the Sarvāstivāda, this time by a schismatic Jaina. Of course, one cannot completely exclude the possibility that another Buddhist school, different from Sarvāstivāda, constituted the main influence on Vaiśeṣika.

There is one further argument, one that has a direct bearing on the theme of this paper. Vaiśeṣika postulates, or presupposes, a direct correspondence between words and things. So do Sarvāstivāda and other Buddhist schools, be it that for them the things in the world do not really exist. Neither Sāṃkhya nor Jainism entertained the idea of such a correspondence, so far as I am aware. They certainly did not emphasise the existence and importance of such a correspondence, as did the Buddhists. This is not surprising, for they had no need for such an assumption. The Buddhists of this time, on the other hand, needed this assumption very much, and indeed, their world view depended on it in a crucial manner. The same assumption resurfaces in Vaiśeṣika. Is it not reasonable to conclude that Vaiśeṣika stood under Buddhist influence?

III.

At this point we have to return for a minute to the Buddhist thinkers. We have seen that, from an early date onward, all of them agreed on the relationship between the phenomenal world and the words of language. I say on purpose 'the words of language', and not just 'language', for the interest of many of them appears to have been limited to words only. We believe in the existence of chariots, because there is a word for it. Combinations of words, primarily sentences, do not play a role in these reflections.

---

[48] See Leumann 1885: 116-123, and Mehta and Chandra 1972: 646 (s.v. Rohagutta), 664 (s.v. Vaisesiya). Cp. Schubring 1935: 13.

This changes with Nāgārjuna, the founder of the Madhyamaka school of Buddhist thought. Nāgārjuna no doubt believed, like his fellow-Buddhists, that the phenomenal world corresponds to the words of language, and is not ultimately real. But he went further. By analysing certain sentences, he could *prove* the unreality of the phenomenal world. No need to add that, while analysing these sentences, he started from the presupposition which he shared with his fellow-Buddhists, and perhaps with others as well, the presupposition namely that language and the phenomenal world somehow correspond to each other. Analysing sentences became in that way a form of analysing the phenomenal world.

Nāgārjuna's thought can be illustrated with the help of the statement: "A sound is produced." For Nāgārjuna, there must be a sound for it to be produced. But if the sound is already there, it does not have to come into existence. This is presented as an unresolvable contradiction.[49] Elsewhere Nāgārjuna analyses the (perhaps somewhat artificial) statement: "He travels the road that is being travelled." This is only possible, Nāgārjuna maintains, if there are two acts of travelling going on: this because the verb 'travel' occurs twice in the statement.[50] He concludes from this that neither travelling, nor traveller, nor indeed the road to be travelled exist.[51] These two simple examples allow us to see that Nāgārjuna takes the close correspondence between statements and phenomenal reality for granted. A more detailed study of Nāgārjuna's Mūlamadhyamakakārikā brings indeed to light, that something like the following presupposition underlies a number of its arguments: the words of a sentence must correspond, one by one, to the things that constitute the situation described by that sentence.[52] This is in itself not at all surprising, I repeat, for many of his contemporaries, among them prac-

---

[49] See e.g. MadhK(deJ) 7.17: *yadi kaścid anutpanno bhāvaḥ saṃvidyate kvacit/ utpadyeta sa kiṃ tasmin bhāva utpadyate 'sati//* "If something that has not come into existence exists somewhere, it may come into existence. Since no such thing exists, what is it that comes into existence?"

[50] MadhK(deJ) 2.5: *gamyamānasya gamane prasaktaṃ gamanadvayam/ yena tad gamyamānaṃ ca yac cātra gamanaṃ punaḥ//* "If one can travel the road that is being travelled, there would be two acts of traveling: the one by which the road is being travelled, and the traveling on it."

[51] MadhK(deJ) 2.25cd: *tasmād gatiś ca gantā ca gantavyaṃ ca na vidyate.*

[52] See Bronkhorst, forthcoming b.

tically all Buddhists, would agree that phenomenal reality corresponds to language. Nāgārjuna merely extends this belief, by including whole statements. Subsequently he shows that the belief in the precise correspondence between statements and phenomenal reality leads to unacceptable contradictions. He does not conclude from this that there may not, after all, be such precise correspondence between statements and phenomenal reality, as we perhaps would. Quite on the contrary, he sees this as a confirmation of his conviction that the phenomenal world does not really exist. But whereas for his predecessors phenomenal reality corresponds to the *words* of language, for Nāgārjuna and his followers phenomenal reality corresponds both to its *words* and its *sentences*.

IV.

With this in mind we turn to another Brahmanical thinker who, as it seems to me, has been profoundly influenced by Buddhist ideas.[53] This is Bhartṛhari, the linguistic thinker *par excellence* of classical India. Bhartṛhari stood, in fact, under the influence of both Vaiśeṣika and Buddhism, not to speak of several other currents of thought. The extent to which he is indebted to Vaiśeṣika is evident on almost every page of his Vākyapadīya. The Buddhist influence is less immediately obvious, but not any the less important, as it appears to me. I have drawn attention to Bhartṛhari's indebtedness to Buddhist thought in an earlier publication.[54] In the present lecture I will try to show how Bhartṛhari, at least where ideas concerning the relationship between language and phenomenal reality are concerned, remains closer to the Buddhists than to the Vaiśeṣikas. I will also point out how he adapts these essentially Buddhist ideas to his own vision of the world. We will see that Bhartṛhari accepts the close correspondence between language and phenomenal reality, that, like the Buddhists, he looks upon phenomenal reality as ultimately unreal, and that, like Nāgārjuna, he includes sen-

---

[53] For the argument here presented it is not important to know whether Bhartṛhari was directly acquainted with Nāgārjuna's works. Nāgārjuna's style of reasoning left a profound impression on Buddhist thought after him, so that Bhartṛhari may have undergone his influence indirectly. Some features of Bhartṛhari's thought suggest that he may have been acquainted with one or more Yogācāra thinkers; see note 81 below.

[54] Bronkhorst 1992a.

tences in the parts of language that correspond to the phenomenal world.

For Bhartṛhari the world, and each object in it, has two aspects: the one real, the other unreal. VP 3.1.32, for example, speaks of "the real and the unreal parts which are present in each thing."[55] The phenomenal world is unreal. It is the result of an (unreal) division of the undivided absolute:[56] "The Vedāntins base themselves on the truth of that object, in which seer, seen and seeing are not differentiated (*avikalpita*)." It seems likely that Bhartṛhari counted himself among these Vedāntins, or rather, Trayyantavedins, as he calls them. The essential reality of things, we read elsewhere in the Vākyapadīya, is beyond differentiation:[57] "With regard to things (*bhāva*), whose reality is beyond differentiation (*vikalpātīta*), the world is followed in linguistic expressions (*vyavahāra*) which are based on conventions (*saṃketa*)." Here it is stated that linguistic expressions correspond to the unreal divisions of reality. Another verse tells us more about the division here at stake:[58] "Heaven, earth, wind, sun, oceans, rivers, the directions, these are divisions of the reality belonging to the inner organ, [even though] they are situated outside it." Note that this verse does not prove that Bhartṛhari was an idealist, that he denied the existence of the outside world. It rather states that the divisions of the outside world are produced by the inner organ, and therefore by words, as we will see.

These few citations show already that, besides important differences, Bhartṛhari shared one idea with the Buddhists. Both they and he believed that the phenomenal world is not real, and owes its form to the influence of words. This idea had of course been an essential part of Buddhist thought since long before Bhartṛhari, as we have seen. It is, on the other hand, quite the opposite of the Vaiśeṣika position in the matter. We have already discussed the Vaiśeṣika conviction that words do not correspond to an unreal, but rather to the real world. Bhartṛhari ac-

---

[55] VP 3.1.32ab: *satyāsatyau tu yau bhāgau pratibhāvaṃ vyavasthitau*. Cf. Bronkhorst 1991b: 12 f.

[56] VP 3.3.72: *yatra draṣṭā ca dṛśyaṃ ca darśanaṃ cāvikalpitam/ tasyaivārthasya satyatvaṃ śritās trayyantavedinaḥ//*

[57] VP 3.6.25: *vikalpātītatattveṣu saṃketopanibandhanāḥ/ bhāveṣu vyavahārā ye lokas tatrānugamyate//*

[58] VP 3.7.41: *dyauḥ kṣamā vāyur ādityaḥ sāgarāḥ sarito diśaḥ/ antaḥkaraṇatattvasya bhāgā bahir avasthitāḥ//*

cepted the position of the Buddhists, but adapted it to his own requirements.

Those own requirements are those of a Brahmin, who has the highest regard for the Veda and for the language in which it is handed down. Sanskrit, Bhartṛhari informs us, is the divine language which, unfortunately, has been corrupted by incompetent speakers.[59] He even mentions an opinion according to which incorrect words are not expressive. Referring to some incorrect words, he states:[60] "Since they are not followed by the educated like correct synonyms, they are not directly expressive according to the traditional treatise." It is possible that Bhartṛhari did not share this point of view. His Vākyapadīya also contains the following verse:[61] "Some consider the incorrect word expressive by way of inference. Alternatively, there is no difference [between correct and incorrect words] as far as expressiveness is concerned, but there is a restriction with regard to merit and demerit."

Words separate things from each other:[62] "By force of the [fact that understanding has the form of words], every produced thing is distinguished [from other things]." "Words are the only basis of the true nature of things and of their use."[63] It follows that "those who know the nature of things see the power of words."[64] The fact that understanding has the form of words, referred to above, "is the external and internal *saṃjñā* of living beings. The consciousness in all kinds [of living beings] does not go beyond this measure."[65] Here it is to be noted that *saṃjñā* means both 'verbal conscience, ideation' and 'name'. The ex-

---

[59] VP 1.182ab: *daivī vāg vyatikīrṇeyam aśaktair abhidhātṛbhiḥ* "This divine speech has been muddled by incompetent speakers." The Mahābhāṣyadīpikā (Manuscript p. 7a l. 4; MBhD 1:16 l. 29 - 17 l. 1; ed. Abhyankar/Limaye p. 20 l. 1; ed. Swaminathan p. 24 l. 19-20) states the same in different words: *anye manyante/ iyaṃ daivī vāk/ sā tu puruṣāśakter ālasyād vā prakīrṇā/.*

[60] VP 1.178: *na śiṣṭair anugamyante paryāyā iva sādhavaḥ/ te yataḥ smṛtiśāstreṇa tasmāt sākṣād avācakāḥ//*

[61] VP 3.3.30: *asādhur anumānena vācakaḥ kaiścid iṣyate/ vācakatvāviśeṣe vā niyamaḥ puṇyapāpayoḥ//.* See the discussion by Houben (1992: 345 sq.), and VP 1.27 cited below.

[62] VP 1.133cd: *tadvaśād abhiniṣpannaṃ sarvaṃ vastu vibhajyate. tad-* refers back to *vāgrūpatā avabodhasya* in verse 132.

[63] VP 1.13ab: *arthapravṛttitattvānāṃ śabdā eva nibandhanam.*

[64] VP 1.171cd: *svabhāvajñais tu bhāvānāṃ dṛśyante śabdaśaktayaḥ.*

[65] VP 1.134: *saiṣā saṃsāriṇāṃ saṃjñā bahir antaś ca vartate/ tanmātrām avyatikrāntaṃ caitanyaṃ sarvajātiṣu//*

pression "the external and internal *saṃjñā* of living beings" may refer to them both. Bhartṛhari elaborates on the power of words in the following verses:[66] "The power residing in words is the basis of this whole universe. . . . Since the difference between *ṣaḍja* and other [musical notes] is perceived [only] when explained by words, all categories of objects are based on the measures of words." The creative power of language is exemplified by the illusion of a circle created by a firebrand turned round:[67] "It is observed in the case of a torch-wheel etc., that the form of an object is perceived on account of words (*śruti*), even though the basis [of the perception] is entirely different." "There is no cognition in the world that does not follow words. All knowledge appears as if permeated by words."[68] "It is from words that things proceed; [words] create the distinctions [in the phenomenal world]."[69] One might be tempted to think that this last line speaks about meanings rather than things; both are called *artha* in Sanskrit. Bhartṛhari speaks however about things in the objective world. This is particularly clear from a passage of his commentary on the Mahābhāṣya, often called Mahābhāṣyadīpikā, where the perception of words such as 'heaven', *apūrva*, and 'divinity' are presented as means to infer (*anumāna*) the existence of the corresponding objects:[70] "Just as the words 'heaven', *apūrva* and 'divinity', when perceived, are the means to infer the existence of objects never observed, . . . " The same three objects – 'heaven', *apūrva* and 'divinity' – are mentioned in the following, slightly obscure, verse of the Vākyapadīya:[71] "The sign of the thing denoted is, that

---

[66] VP 1.122-23: *śabdeṣv evāśritā śaktir viśvasyāsya nibandhanī/ ... ṣaḍjādibhedaḥ śabdena vyākhyāto rūpyate yataḥ/ tasmād arthavidhāḥ sarvāḥ śabdamātrāsu niśritāḥ//.* On the exact reading of this verse, see Bronkhorst 1988: 124.

[67] VP 1.142: *atyantam atathābhūte nimitte śrutyapāśrayāt/ dṛśyate 'lātacakrādau vastvākāranirūpaṇā//.* Tr. Houben.

[68] VP 1.131: *na so 'sti pratyayo loke yaḥ śabdānugamād ṛte/ anuviddham iva jñānaṃ sarvaṃ śabdena bhāsate//*

[69] VP 3.14.198ab: *śabdād arthāḥ pratāyante sa bhedānāṃ vidhāyakaḥ.*

[70] Mahābhāṣyadīpikā, Manuscript p. 11a l. 11; 'Critical edition' Āhnika I p. 28 l. 8-9; ed. Abhyankar-Limaye p. 33 l. 24 - p. 34 l. 1; ed. Swaminathan p. 40 l. 11: *tatra yathaiva svargāpūrvadevatāśabdā upalabhyamānā atyantāparidṛṣṭānām arthānām astitvānumānam ...* Bhavya's Madhyamakahṛdayakārikā 9.5 ascribes to a 'Mīmāṃsaka' the position according to which the existence of such objects is known from the Veda; see Kawasaki 1976: 6-7.

[71] VP 2.119: *asty arthaḥ sarvaśabdānām iti pratyāyyalakṣaṇam/ apūrvadevatāsvargaiḥ samam āhur gavādiṣu//*

there is an object corresponding to all words. In the case of words like 'cow', they say, it is similar to 'heaven', *apūrva* and 'divinity'."

It will be clear from these quotations, that the connection between language and phenomenal reality is close. And the language concerned is Sanskrit. But Bhartṛhari goes further. The fundamental unit of language is the sentence; this is equally true of the Vedic sentence.[72] This is important. It shows that Bhartṛhari does not merely postulate a correspondence between individual words and elements of the phenomenal world. The link between statements, in particular Vedic statements, and the phenomenal world is as important, or even more important. We'll return to this point in a minute. First we consider some of Bhartṛhari's observations with regard to the role of the Veda in the unfolding of phenomenal reality:[73] "Different sciences unfold, based on the primary and secondary limbs of that [Veda] which is the organising principle (*vidhātṛ*) of the worlds, [sciences] which are the causes of the mental traces (*saṃskāra*) of knowledge." The context of this verse leaves no doubt that it actually concerns the Veda, and that therefore the Veda is the organising principle, or perhaps one is entitled to translate: creator, of the worlds. A comparison with VP 3.14.198ab, cited above ("It is from words that things proceed; [words] create the distinctions [in the phenomenal world]"), and which, too, uses the verb *vi-dhā*, shows that the creation of the world is essentially a division, a differentiation, of the undivided absolute. Another verse explains the relationship between the Veda and the world in the following terms:[74] "Those who know the sacred tradition know that this [universe] is a transformation of the word. In the beginning this universe proceeds exclusively from Vedic verses."

The world having been created, or organised, by the Veda, tradition (*āgama / smṛti*) bases itself on the Veda:[75] "The texts of tradition (*smṛti*), which are multiform and have visible as well as invisible aims, have

---

[72] See Houben 1995c.

[73] VP 1.10: *vidhātus tasya lokānām aṅgopāṅganibandhanāḥ/ vidyābhedāḥ pratāyante jñānasaṃskārahetavaḥ//* Halbfass translates *vidhātṛ* 'organizing principle' (1991b: 5) or 'Organisationsprinzip' (1991a: 126).

[74] VP 1.124: *śabdasya pariṇāmo 'yam ity āmnāyavido viduḥ/ chandobhya eva prathamam etad viśvaṃ pravartate//*

[75] VP 1.7: *smṛtayo bahurūpāś ca dṛṣṭādṛṣṭaprayojanāḥ/ tam evāśritya liṅgebhyo vedavidbhiḥ prakalpitāḥ//.*

been arranged by knowers of the Veda on the basis of the [Veda] with the help of indicators." This implies, for Bhartṛhari, that the link between tradition and the world is close, too. The world follows the rules of the word:[76] "Even if [all] philosophies had disappeared, and there would not be other authors, the world would not deviate from the rules expressed by the Veda (*śruti*) and by the tradition (*smṛti*)." This implies, among other things, that the rules of behaviour are in a way inherent in the world:[77] "All duties (*itikartavyatā*) in the world are based on words; even a child knows them because of the mental impressions (*saṃskāra*) acquired earlier." The intuition (*pratibhā*) which is called "meaning of the sentence," and which makes us know our duties, can either be the result of verbal instruction, or it can be inborn:[78] "Whether the [intuition] is directly produced by the word or by the result of impulsions (*bhāvanā*), no one deviates from it where duties (*itikartavyatā*) are concerned." Even animals are guided by this intuition:[79] "Under the influence of that [intuition] even the animals act. . . . Who changes the sound of the male cuckoo in spring? How have animals learnt to build nests and the like? Who induces wild animals and birds to eat, love, hate, swim, and so on, activities well known among the descendants of each species?"

These verses have been interpreted to mean that the hereditary knowledge one finds among animals and in children is the result of the use of language in an earlier existence.[80] Nothing in the text supports this point of view. It is true that living beings are born with impulsions (*bhāvanā*) or mental traces (*saṃskāra*) which are linguistic by nature, but it would appear that these linguistic impulsions are not, or not al-

---

[76] VP 1.149: *astaṃ yāteṣu vādeṣu kartṛṣv anyeṣv asatsv api/ śrutismṛtyuditaṃ dharmaṃ lokọ na vyativartate//*

[77] VP 1.129: *itikartavyatā loke sarvā śabdavyapāśrayā/ yāṃ pūrvāhitasaṃskāro bālo 'pi pratipadyate//*

[78] VP 2.146: *sākṣāc chabdena janitāṃ bhāvanānugamena vā/ itikartavyatāyāṃ tāṃ na kaścid ativartate//*

[79] VP 2.147cd & 149-150: *samārambhāḥ pratāyante tiraścām api tadvaśāt// ... svaravṛttiṃ vikurute madhau puṃskokilasya kaḥ/ jantvādayaḥ kulāyādikaraṇe śikṣitāḥ katham// āhāraprītyapadveṣaplavanādikriyāsu kaḥ/ jātyanvayaprasiddhāsu prayoktā mṛgapakṣiṇām//*

[80] Biardeau 1964b: 317-18; Iyer 1977: 62.

ways, the results of instructions in an earlier life.[81] One could here repeat Bhartṛhari's question: What verbal impulsions would change the sound of the male cuckoo in spring? Bhartṛhari himself answers this question, and the others that accompany it, in the following verses:[82] "It comes from tradition (*āgama*) only, which follows the impulsions (*bhāvanā*). As for the tradition, it is different [for each individual] depending on the proximity or distance.[83] Six forms of intuition (*pratibhā*) are known, depending on whether they are produced by the own nature, the Vedic school, practice, Yoga, by the invisible (*adṛṣṭa*), or by a special [cause]." It follows that there is natural knowledge:[84] "Since knowledge is natural, the traditional religious and scientific treatises (*śāstra*) serve no purpose whatsoever." This also applies to morality:[85] "With regard to the two positions 'this is virtuous' or 'this is sinful', there is little use for religious and scientific treatises (*śāstra*) right down to the untouchables."

Bhartṛhari uses the word *bhavanā* 'impulsion' at several other occasions in the Vākyapadīya. The 'impulsion of the word' (*śabdabhāvanā*) is required to set the speech organs in motion, to emit an upward breath, and to make the points of articulation strike each other.[86] The impulsions, moreover, cause the imaginary divisions of the sentence which has, in reality, no parts:[87] "Although the meaning of the sentence is without divisions, the imagined divisions are based on *bhāvanā*."

---

[81] One is of course reminded of the *abhilāpavāsanā* of the Yogācāras, which is responsible for a number of percepts (*vijñapti*) besides the one of linguistic usage (*vyavahāravijñapti*). Cf. Lamotte 1973: 88-89, 108 (= Mahāyānasaṃgraha II, 2; II, 16).

[82] VP 2.151-52: *bhāvanānugatād etad āgamād eva jāyate/ āsattiviprakarṣābhyām āgamas tu viśiṣyate// svabhāvacaraṇābhyāsayogādṛṣṭopapāditām/ viśiṣṭopahitāṃ ceti pratibhāṃ ṣaḍvidhāṃ viduḥ//*. The reading *caraṇa* instead of *varaṇa* is here accepted, with Rau's hyparchetype **n** and the *Vṛtti*.

[83] The commentator Puṇyarāja explains: the tradition is sometimes acquired in this life, sometimes in another life.

[84] VP 1.150ab: *jñāne svābhāvike nārthaḥ śāstraiḥ kaścana vidyate.*

[85] VP 1.40: *idaṃ puṇyam idaṃ pāpam ity etasmin padadvaye/ ācaṇḍālamanuṣyāṇām alpaṃ śāstraprayojanam//*. This verse belongs to the Vṛtti according to Aklujkar 1971: 512.

[86] VP 1.130: *ādyaḥ karaṇavinyāsaḥ prāṇasyordhvaṃ samīraṇam/ sthānānām abhighātaś ca na vinā śabdabhāvanām//*

[87] VP 2.116: *avikalpitavākyārthe vikalpā bhāvanāśrayāḥ.*

The direct link between words and things explains the effects words can have on things:[88] "Just as it is observed that colours etc. have well-defined capacities with regard to certain things, in the same way one observes that words [have well-defined capacities] to remove snake poison etc. Just as they have a capacity to do this (to remove snake poison etc.) it should be understood that they also [have a capacity] to [produce] merit. Therefore, good people desiring elevation (*abhyudaya*), should use correct words." The capacity to produce merit belongs to correct words only:[89] "On the basis of traditional knowledge [received] from the well-educated, correct words are established as a means towards merit. While there is no difference in expressing the meaning, incorrect words are the opposite (i.e., not a means towards merit)."

V.

The link between words and things having been established, the study of language, and of Sanskrit in particular, enables one to reach conclusions about the world. Bhartṛhari uses the words of Patañjali, who says in his Mahābhāṣya:[90] "We accept the word as authority. What the word says is authoritative for us." Exactly the same phrase can be found in the Śābara Bhāṣya,[91] but Bhartṛhari clearly gives it a wider interpretation. His Vākyapadīya observes:[92] "People accept the word as authority; they are followed [in this] by the religious and scientific treatises (*śāstra*)."

We return to Bhartṛhari's acceptance of the sentence as primary linguistic unit. This implies that the phenomenal world corresponds to statements, first of all Vedic statements. This explains that, according to Bhartṛhari, injunctions and other rules are somehow built into the phenomenal world. Individual words do not constitute injunctions, or

---

[88] VP 1.155-156: *rūpādayo yathā dṛṣṭāḥ pratyarthaṃ yataśaktayaḥ/ śabdās tathaiva dṛśyante viṣāpaharaṇādiṣu // yathaiṣāṃ tatra sāmarthyaṃ dharme 'py evaṃ pratīyatām/ sādhūnāṃ sādhubhis tasmād vācyam abhyudayārthinām//* tr. Houben.

[89] VP 1.27: *śiṣṭebhya āgamāt siddhāḥ sādhavo dharmasādhanam/ arthapratyāyanābhede viparītās tv asādhavaḥ//* tr. Houben.

[90] Mbh 1: 11.1-2; 366.12-13: *śabdapramāṇakā vayam/ yac chabda āha tad asmākaṃ pramāṇam/.*

[91] ŚābBh 3.1.36 (p. 184); cp. 6.1.3 (p. 183), 6.2.6 (p. 228), 10.5.73 (p. 431).

[92] VP 3.7.38cd: *śabdapramāṇako lokaḥ sa śāstreṇānugamyate.*

śāstras, or rules of behaviour for animals and men. And it is through its sentences that the Veda becomes what it is. If the world is created, or organised, in accordance with the Veda, Vedic sentences must be meant, not just individual Vedic words. Bhartṛhari follows therefore Nāgārjuna in extending the correspondence between language and phenomenal reality beyond mere words, so as to include sentences.

But here a new difficulty comes up. Nāgārjuna had brought to light the contradictions connected with such a procedure. How does Bhartṛhari deal with these difficulties? Some passages of the Vākyapadīya show that its author was very much aware of them, and that he offered solutions to them. According to one of these solutions, objects of words have metaphorical existence, which shows their form in past, present, and future. It is therefore a metaphorically existing sound which is produced.[93] The problem of the road to be travelled can be solved in a similar manner. Another solution can be found in the Jātisamuddeśa of the Vākyapadīya. Words, according to this section, always refer to universals (*jāti*). Universals, in their turn, play an active role in bringing about the manifestation of the objects to which they belong:[94] "Nothing comes into existence which has no universal; the universal urges the causes to manifest itself." Seen in this way, the word 'sound' in "The sound is produced" refers to the universal, and there is no contradiction, even on the assumption that words must necessarily refer to something existing. Bhartṛhari may have thought of a transitive phrase such as "He produces a sound," for one of his verses refers explicitly to the grammatical object (*karman*). The verse reads:[95] "The universal is also effective with regard to a grammatical object that is being produced; it urges the action to bring about the object in which it resides." In the Sādhanasamuddeśa again another solution is offered, on the assumption this time that words refer to individuals:[96] "On the assumption that the meaning of the word is the individual, it is established

---

[93] VP 3.3.39 ff. Cp. Bronkhorst 1992a: 67 f.

[94] VP 3.1.25: *na tad utpadyate kiṃcid yasya jātir na vidyate/ ātmābhivyaktaye jātiḥ kāraṇānāṃ prayojikā//.*

[95] VP 3.1.27: *nirvartyamānaṃ yat karma jātis tatrāpi sādhanam/ svāśrayasyābhiniṣpattyai sā kriyāyāḥ prayojikā//.* The translation of this verse in Bronkhorst 1991b: 14 has to be corrected.

[96] VP 3.7.7: *vyaktau padārthe śabdāder janyamānasya karmaṇaḥ/ sādhanatvaṃ tathā siddhaṃ buddhirūpaprakalpitam//.*

that the grammatical object which is being produced, for example sound, is the means (*sādhana*); this is done on the basis of mental form." It is clear that here, once again, Bhartṛhari addresses the problem raised by Nāgārjuna.[97]

VI.

We have to address one final, but very important, question. What reason is there to believe that Bhartṛhari borrowed his ideas on the role of language primarily from the Buddhists? There can be no doubt that several elements of his views have parallels in Brahmanical literature, too. Consider, for example, the idea of the Veda as creator, or organising principle, of the world. Halbfass (1991: 5) draws in this connection attention to the fact that the Manusmṛti, too, characterises the Veda as an organising and sustaining principle, and even as the real basis of the social and natural world.[98] He then adds: "It would be wrong to view such statements as merely metaphorical. The Veda is the foundation of language, of the fundamental distinctions and classifications in the world, and of those rituals which are meant to sustain the social and natural order." Certain Upaniṣadic passages, too, emphasise the role of language in the construction of the phenomenal world.[99] And already the Śata-

---

[97] According to Helārāja ad VP 3.1.27, the solution proposed in VP 3.7.7 is that of metaphorical existence, the same solution therefore as that of VP 3.3.39 f.

[98] See, e.g., Manu 1.21: *sarveṣāṃ tu sa nāmāni karmāṇi ca pṛthak pṛthak/ vedaśabdebhya evādau pṛthak saṃsthāś ca nirmame//*; also Manu 4.256ab: *vācy arthā niyatāḥ sarve vāṅmūlā vāgviniḥsṛtāḥ/* "All things (have their nature) determined by speech; speech is their root, and from speech they proceed" (tr. Bühler 1886: 168). See also Nāṭyaśāstra 15.3 (ed. tr. M. Ghosh): *vāṅmayānīha śāstrāṇi vāṅniṣṭhāni tathaiva ca/ tasmād vācaḥ paraṃ nāsti vāg ghi sarvasya kāraṇam//.*

[99] See, e.g., MaiUp 6.6: *athāvyāhṛtaṃ vā idam āsīt/ sa satyaṃ prajāpatis tapas taptvānuvyāharad bhūr bhuvaḥ svar iti/ eṣaivāsya prajāpateḥ sthaviṣṭhā tanūḥ/*, and MaiUp 6.22-23: *dve vāva brahmaṇī abhidhyeye śabdaś cāśabdaś ca/ atha śabdenaivāśabdam āviṣkriyate/ atha tatrom iti śabdaḥ/ ... evaṃ hy āha: dve brahmaṇī veditavye śabdabrahma paraṃ ca yat/ śabdabrahmaṇi niṣṇātaḥ paraṃ brahmādhigacchati// ... yaḥ śabdas tad om ity etad akṣaram/ yad asyāgraṃ tacchāntam aśabdam abhayam aśokam ānandaṃ tṛptaṃ sthiram acalam amṛtam acyutaṃ dhruvam ...*

patha Brāhmaṇa states: "Everything here is speech, for by speech everything here is obtained."[100]

Here it is important to remember that Bhartṛhari's thought does not belong to one single tradition. It is clear from his work that he was acquainted with, and made extensive use of, various schools of thought, be they Brahmanical, Buddhist, or even Jaina.[101] He used a variety of ideas in order to construe his own system of thought, which therefore contains traces of all of them, but all of them adjusted so as to fit into the resulting scheme. Any parallelism between Buddhist thought and more or less similar statements in the Brahmanical tradition, we may be sure, confirmed Bhartrhari in the idea that he presented an essentially Brahmanical system of thought. In one important way, therefore, it is nonsense to look for Bhartṛhari's 'true' source of an idea which is present in several of his known sources. Yet we should not forget that the belief in the close relationship between language and the phenomenal world is particularly prominent in, and essential to, Buddhist thought. As I said earlier, these ideas are not marginal here, but they belong to the very essence of that which occupied Buddhist thinkers for a very long time. Moreover, only the Buddhists had gone beyond some vague and general statements, and had incorporated these ideas into systems of thought, which Bhartṛhari could and did draw upon. It is in this sense that I conclude that Bhartṛhari is here, as in certain other respects, primarily indebted to the Buddhists of his time.

---

[100] ŚB 10.5.1.3: *vāg ghy evaitat sarvam/ vācā hy evaitat sarvam āptam.* Tr. Eggeling 1885: 365. Cf. ŚB 14.3.2.20.

[101] See Houben 1994a; Bronkhorst 1990; 1992a; 1993c.

CHAPTER SIX

JAIN ATTITUDES TOWARDS THE SANSKRIT LANGUAGE*

Paul Dundas

1. Introduction

Before offering some observations on the various ways in which the Jains have envisaged the nature of the Sanskrit language, it might be best to make clear at the outset what I intend not to discuss in this context.

Since the time of Albrecht Weber and Georg Bühler, scholars have been familiar with the fact that the Śvetāmbara Jains of western India from about the thirteenth century produced an extensive literature of narrative, chronicle and hagiography written in an idiosyncratic style of Sanskrit, which has come to be called 'Jain Sanskrit'. Bühler viewed this vernacularised form of the language—for that is essentially what it is—as quite simply grammatically incorrect, but later scholars, less inclined to privilege that Sanskrit written in precise conformity to Pāṇini's prescriptions, have preferred to see this dialect as merely one of a variety of non-standard Sanskrits. The words of Johannes Hertel bear repetition in this respect:

> There is no such thing as standard Sanskrit even from the kavi [i. e. belles lettristic] point of view, and much less so from the standpoint of the truly scientific philologist: but there is a language, spread over a huge area, and used, through more than 2000 years after Pāṇini, orally as well as in writing, for literary as well as for every-day life purposes, by millions and millions of speakers and writers, belonging to entirely different climates, and countries, and races, and more or less influenced, in all these cases, by the vernaculars of the respective speakers and writers. . . . What Weber and Bühler and others regarded to be the

* I would like to thank the British Academy for a grant which enabled me to carry out some of the research for this paper and Jan Houben for inviting me to write it.

> Sanskrit of the Jains, is in reality that variety of Sanskrit which was spoken and written in Gujarat, and this variety, of course, in which so huge a mass of literature has been composed, has as much claim to the attention of Indologists as any other variety of the language, and must not be regarded as inferior to the other varieties on the ground of its showing some features which other varieties do not share (Hertel 1922: 21 and 22 and cf. Deshpande 1993a: 38-40).

Although there is a great deal of material remaining to be published and analysed, the distinguishing characteristics of Jain Sanskrit and the influence upon it of elements of Old Gujarati morphology, syntax and vocabulary have been reasonably well documented. Attention has also been drawn to the ability of Jain authors in late medieval western India to switch linguistic codes, sometimes writing in classical Sanskrit, at other times employing a vernacularised idiom of the language, depending on the literary genre and the audience being addressed (see Salomon 1989: 284-6 and cf. Jain 1993). However, I would submit that, for all its interest, Jain Sanskrit is from a historical and geographical perspective largely a localised phenomenon and that it should therefore have no major bearing upon the broader subject at issue, namely the Jain reaction to the pervasive cultural role of the Sanskrit language throughout ancient and medieval Indian history.

I also do not intend to discuss the various Sanskrit grammars that were produced by the Jains from the fifth century C.E. The existence of such works is, of course, clearly indicative of Jainism's long standing ambivalence towards Sanskrit. While the manifold claims of the language as a medium of learned communication eventually could not be denied by the Jains and standards for the expert manipulation of it had to be inculcated, the normative grammar of Sanskrit by Pāṇini and, in particular, its massively authoritative commentary by Patañjali had become too closely associated with Jainism's ideological opponents, the brahman ritualists, to be readily accepted as a source of correct linguistic usage. As a result, various types of Sanskrit grammatical analysis were introduced by Jain monastic scholars as substitutes for or equivalents to the Pāṇinian system, with one legend suggesting that Mahāvīra himself had in his youth been responsible for the original introduction of this discipline. The earliest Jain grammar of Sanskrit, the Jainendravyākaraṇa of Pūjyapāda, which was apparently known to Bhartṛhari (see Houben 1994a: 11-19), even tried to condense further Pāṇini's already telegraphic rules. However, an adequate assessment of the techniques and achievements of the Jain grammarians cannot be given here, even were it felt to be relevant.[1]

2. Basic Jain Views on the Nature of Language

For Jainism, language (*bhāṣā*) is a modification (*paryāya*) of a particular variety of atomic matter, the technical designation for which is *bhāṣāvargaṇā*. If such an interpretation is not unique in traditional Indian linguistic speculation (see Jain 1986: 34 and Houben 1994a: 7-11), it has nonetheless served the Jains as a particularly important component of their rejection of brahman ideas about the eternal nature of the Veda and the Sanskrit language. The principal Jain scriptural source for the material nature of language is chapter eleven of the Prajñāpanā Sūtra, a text which is composed of answers provided by Mahāvīra to a wide variety of ontological and epistemological questions and which, although precise chronology is uncertain, must date from the early common era. According to this scripture, the embodied *jīva*, or life monad, receives, while in a state of immobility and through the agency of its body, speech atoms which are subsequently turned into actual articulated language. When these atoms are expelled by the body as speech, they subsequently pervade the universe (see Paṇṇavaṇāsuttam, introduction: 321 and cf. Jain 1986, introduction: 16-17 and also 33-36 and Sikdar 1987: 206-8).

Speech, then, is for the Jains most significantly material and the product of physical effort. Whether this speech is intended by the Prajñāpanā Sūtra to be understood as specifically Prākrit or spoken language in general appears to be regarded as uncertain by the 'Jain-Āgama Series' editors. As they point out, the Prajñāpanā Sūtra, in giv-

---

[1] The NKC of the tenth century Digambara Jain Prabhācandra neatly points the distinction between rival grammatical systems. The Mīmāṃsā/grammarian *pūrvapakṣa* of the section dealing with the ability of non-Sanskrit dialects to convey sense quotes Pāṇini 3.2.1 as an example of a rule which can generate a wide range of correct forms. In his response, however, Prabhācandra quotes a rule from the Jainendravyākaraṇa to justify the correctness of a form rejected by the Pāṇinīya grammarians. See NKC: 760 and 766. For some general information about the Jain grammarians of Sanskrit, see Scharfe 1977: 168-9.

ing a breakdown of the constituent components of speech as a grammatical entity, includes the dual number along with the singular and plural, thus reiterating the normative Sanskrit model, because apart from a few fossilised remainders the dual is lacking in Prākrit. On the other hand, the scripture omits reference to the dual when dealing with the rather different topic of the ability of words to express number (see Paṇṇavaṇāsuttam, introduction: 326).[2]

Later Jain philosophers were to attempt to bolster and expand the few early scriptural statements about language. So the twelfth century logician Vādideva Sūri defended the materiality of speech against accusations of its apparent non-tangibility, arguing that the minuteness of *bhāṣāvargaṇā*, the substance out of which it is constructed, did not mean that spoken language lacked the capacity to be touched physically and that in fact this quality might be latent in the sound-substance. Sound can be deemed to be material because, in the same way as form, it is an object of sense perceptions (PraNTA: 298-301). No doubt arguments of this sort cannot be said to show Vādideva and other Jain thinkers in the most persuasive light. Nonetheless, the concomitant Jain argument (PraNTA: 286-93) that, through its being produced from causes such as activity of the palate and then subsequently decaying and, in addition, because of its manifest lack of any genuinely identifiable permanent attributes, speech was necessarily non-eternal, constituted a major challenge to a central ideological tenet of the brahman ritualists that language was some kind of eternal, abstract universal, of which Sanskrit was the sole authoritative manifestation.

3. *A Jain Root Language?*

One of the most striking features of Jainism is the wide range of languages in which its literature has been composed, including a variety of Prākrits, Sanskrit, Apabhraṃśa, Hindi, Rajasthani, Gujarati, Marathi, Tamil and Kannada. Indeed, scholarship has barely been able to accommodate this breadth of material and the overall picture of Jain litera-

---

[2] However, vernacular Sanskrit does tend to lack the dual number, as Deshpande (1993a: 29-30) points out.

ture, particularly with regard to the north Indian vernaculars, is at present very much incomplete. But did the Jains believe that there was some kind of primal speech from which this linguistic diversity flowed? More specifically, could Ardhamāgadhī, the Prākrit in which the Jain scriptural corpus is composed, which is the vehicle for the preaching of the *tīrthaṅkaras* and is, according to the Bhagavatī Sūtra (Deleu 1970:108), even spoken by the gods in heaven, be considered as constituting an original language equivalent to Sanskrit as envisaged by brahman tradition?

The canonical *locus classicus* (Aupapātika Sūtra: 178-9) for the Śvetāmbara description of Mahāvīra's preaching portrays him as addressing an audience comprising humans and gods, Āryans and non-Āryans (later tradition would include animals as well) "in speech conforming to all languages, in tones extending over a league, in the Ardhamāgadhī language" (. . . *savvabhāsāṇugamaṇīe sarassaie joyaṇaṇīhāriṇā sareṇaṃ Addhamāgahāe bhāsāe* . . .) which "transformed itself into the individual languages of all that audience" (*tesiṃ savvesiṃ āriya-m-aṇāriyāṇaṃ appaṇo sabhāsāe pariṇāmeṇaṃ pariṇamai* . . .). One other passage in the sūtra describes him conversing with king Kūṇika in Ardhamāgadhī. Beyond this, nothing further is said in any early Śvetāmbara source.

The Digambara Jain approach is more complex. There is agreement that a 'divine sound' (*divyadhvani*) flows from the body of the *tīrthaṅkara* when he is preaching, but a whole range of disparate views came into play in the course of Digambara history as to whether this emerges from his mouth or is constituted by syllables or not. The *divyadhvani* is also sometimes described as containing within itself all tongues, most specifically the 18 major and 170 minor languages of India. One source, the Mahāpurāṇa, states that it is naturally one language, while another, the Darśanaprābhṛta, claims that it half consists of Ardhamāgadhī and half of all other languages. A medieval commentator on the Darśanaprābhṛta goes so far as to claim that the gods receive the *divyadhvani* in the form of Sanskrit (for a full range of Digambara views on this subject, see Jainendra Siddhāntakoṣa: 429-432).

Attention has recently been drawn to a Theravāda Buddhist commentarial source which asserts that a child which has not been exposed to any initial linguistic input would naturally speak Māgadhī and it has been concluded, largely on the basis of descriptions of Mahāvīra's preaching in the Aupapātika Sūtra, that the Jains envisaged Ardhamāgadhī in similar manner as a *mūlabhāsā* or 'root language' (see Bronkhorst 1993a: 399-401, Norman 1991: 88 and cf. Deshpande 1994: 99). However, it is perhaps more likely that the Aupapātika Sūtra passage is actually referring to the universal applicability of the Jain doctrine, and if the much richer Digambara sources, which sometimes state that Mahāvīra's preaching was non-verbal, be taken into account, it then becomes virtually impossible to be confident about the existence of a pan-Jain view about some sort of root language from which all other forms of speech develop.[3]

Such a standpoint would, in fact, fly in the face of the fundamental Jain ontological principle that reality has to be understood as involving origin, stability and decay, rather than permanence alone, and Jainism, as befits a realist religion, has generally regarded the multiplicity of languages as no more than a reflex of the variety to be found in the living world. Since language is a means of revealing the self, of which all living being are embodiments, it can therefore be found in every creature, even in animals, albeit in non-syllabic form (see Jain 1986: 12-14, drawing particularly on the Prajñāpanā Sūtra).

4. Sanskrit As Not Superior To Prākrit

In the Mahābhāṣya, Patañjali had drawn attention to the existence of what he saw as debased linguistic forms, such as *gāvī*, 'cow', being employed instead of the standard Sanskrit *go*. This is, of course, invaluable historical evidence for the embattled position of Sanskrit as a spoken language around the second century BCE and for the fact that it increasingly came under pressure from a variety of Indo-Aryan vernaculars (see Deshpande 1993: 25-27). From the ideological point of view, however, Patañjali's strictures on the inadequacies of Prākrit proved a major and continual reference point for later defenders of

[3] From a stylistic point of view, the *Aupapātika Sūtra* can be held to date from around the early common era and hardly has any major chronological priority to Digambara views about the *divyadhvani*.

brahman hegemony and the centrality of Sanskrit, most notably the Mīmāṃsakas (see Granoff 1991: 26-28).

The standard brahman position was that while Prākrit words such as *gāvī* might actually convey meaning in a restricted communicative context, this meaning derives solely from a memory of the correct Sanskrit form *go.* The conventional value of vernacular usage only comes about on the basis of an original, prior grammatical authority which establishes general principles of correctness for words. This linguistic correctness can be judged quite simply on the basis of the direct experience of those utilising Sanskrit. An appeal to the validity of general usage to justify Prākrit would render the manifold general and specific rules of grammar worthless. It is grammar which provides the background for a direct understanding of whether a linguistic utterance is correct or not and proper linguistic usage therefore means employing Sanskrit which, by definition, conforms to the prescriptions laid down by Pāṇini and his commentators.

The tenth century Digambara Jain Prabhācandra provides in his Nyāyakumudacandra (NKC, pp. 757-67) a succinct critique of this Sanskrit-centred standpoint, although as a participant in *śāstra* and its conventions he was obliged to use Sanskrit to express it. Prabhācandra's overall position signals an unwillingness to accede to brahman demands that Sanskrit be viewed as an ideological institution and he instead invokes actual linguistic behaviour. Prabhācandra claims that those who employ vernacular forms like *gāvī* specifically abandon Sanskrit words in a transactional context, even if they are Sanskrit speakers. Prākrit words are not understood on the basis of initial recall of Sanskrit words and subsequent grasp of a statement's sense, because when there are no suitable Sanskrit knowers present in a particular situation, there could then logically be no meaning grasped from vernacular dialects (*bhāṣā*)[4]. But it cannot possibly be the case that those

[4] NKC: 762: *yat tāvad uktam, "gavādayaḥ śabdā eva sādhavaḥ, teṣām eva vācakatvopapatteḥ" ityādi, tad avicāritaramaṇīyam, yato lokavyavahārasamadhigamyo hi vācyavācakabhāvaḥ. lokaś ca gāvyādiśabdair eva vyavaharan pratīyate. saṃskṛtavedino hi samskṛtān śabdān parityajya vyavahārakāle gāvyādiśabdair eva vyavaharantaḥ pratīyante . . . na khalu prākṛtaśabdebhyaḥ*

"prathamaṃ saṃskṛtaśabdasmaraṇaṃ tato 'rthapratītiḥ" iti vyavadhānenārthapratyayo 'nubhūyate, saṃskṛtaśabdavat tebhyo 'pi sākṣād eva arthapratyayapratīteḥ, anyathā yatra saṃskṛtajñā na santi tatra bhāṣāśabdebhyo 'rthapratyayo na syāt. tato gavādiśabdavat śab-

who have not been exposed to Sanskrit are therefore incapable of making sensible linguistic statements. Furthermore, the claim that it is only the grammatically untutored who use Prākrit can be refuted by reference to the fact that there actually are individuals competent in Sanskrit who nonetheless also employ Prākrit forms. Prākrit for Prabhācandra is simply a linguistic fact of life.[5]

Prabhācandra further asserts that the various qualities which supposedly make Sanskrit a language different from and superior to all others (ability to convey religious values, use by distinguished men and so on) can also be found in Prākrit, and the standard brahman defence that traditional usage through generations validates Sanskrit's supremacy is deemed by the Jain to be an inadequate argument on the grounds that it would justify various equally time-honoured but nonetheless socially unsound customs followed by barbarians, such as that of a widow marrying her eldest son[6]. The primacy of Prākrit is asserted by Prabhācandra not just by a simple appeal to the traditional etymology which would derive the term from *prakṛti*, 'nature'. In addition, he adduces the term *saṃskāra*, literally 'putting together', which can signify 'rite of passage' and 'ornament'—in other words the application of an attribute or quality or object to a preexisting entity—as evidence for the fact that *saṃskṛta* (Sanskrit), grammatically an adjectival designation connected with *saṃskāra*, is merely a secondary transformation (*vikāra*) of a natural linguistic base.[7]

Yet, frequently referred to though the *prakṛti*/Prākrit connection and the consequent secondary nature of Sanskrit might be (e.g. von Hinüber 1994: 82), these attitudes to language status cannot be said to have received unanimous assent even within the Jain community. At the be-

---

dāntarasmṛtinirapekṣatayaiva sadā teṣām arthāvabodhakatvapratīter vācakatvam evopapannam.

[5] NKC: 763: *nanu cāsaṃskṛtamatibhiḥ saha saṃskrtaśabdena gavādinā vyavahāraḥ kartuṃ na śakyate, lakṣaṇaparijñānābhāvāt teṣāṃ saṃskṛtaśabdaparijñānānupapatteḥ. ataḥ bahutvād asaṃskṛtamatīnām aśaktipramādaprabhavo 'pi apabhraṣṭavyavahāraḥ parāṃ rūḍhim āgataḥ, yena śakto vijñātaśabdasvarūpo 'pi janas tenaiva vyavaharati . . .*

[6] NKC: 765.

[7] NKC: 764: *saṃskṛtaśabdasvarūpasya tu prakṛtitvam anupapannaṃ vikāratvāt. sato hi vastuno guṇāntarādhānaṃ saṃskāraḥ sa vikārarūpatayā kathaṃ prakṛtitvaṃ pratipadyeta.* Cf. Dundas 1991: 171-2 for some of these arguments being linked with Jain rejection of any innate authority in the brahman caste.

ginning of what is the most authoritative Jain grammar of Prākrit, Hemacandra (eleventh century) asserts that *prakṛti* is in actuality the Sanskrit language and that Prākrit is what arises in it and derives from it (*prakṛtiḥ Saṃskṛtam. tatra bhavaṃ tata āgataṃ vā Prākṛtam*) (Hemacandra:1; quoted by Pischel 1981:1). If this standpoint may not be unconnected to Hemacandra's position as court paṇḍit to the Caulukyas and to the fact that his Prākrit grammar is the eighth and final chapter, effectively a kind of appendix, of a largescale Sanskrit grammar, it nonetheless does show how one of the most prominent of all medieval Jains was not at all unwilling to accept the primacy of the Sanskrit language.

5. Prākrit and Sanskrit in Jain Literature

Although the historical origins of Ardhamāgadhī unquestionably lie in the vernacular(s) employed in preaching by Mahāvīra and his disciples, it quickly became a scriptural language restricted to the writings of the Śvetāmbara *āgama*. The early Jain insistence on a particular type of Prākrit as the vehicle for religious teachings, which was at the outset a means of distinguishing their authoritative texts from those of the brahmans, was reinforced by the production during the first six centuries or so of the common era of an extensive exegetical literature consisting of verse *niryukti*s and *bhāṣya*s and prose *cūrṇi*s also written in Prākrit, some of the earliest of which antedate the major Jain sectarian fission. It is noteworthy that while the Digambaras insisted for sectarian purposes that the scriptural corpus had been irretrievably lost, they still accepted that it had been composed in Ardhamāgadhī, and early common era teachers who can be regarded as aligning themselves with a self-aware Digambara sect, such as Kundakunda, Vaṭṭakera and the author / redactors of the huge scriptural texts, the Ṣaṭkhaṇḍāgama and the Kaṣāyaprābhṛta, continued to employ Prākrit, in this case a variety that has come to be designated 'Jain Śaurasenī'. In addition, a variant of the Mahārāṣṭrī Prākrit dialect which from around the second century CE had proved highly attractive to urban litterateurs and imitators of rural poetic modes, was employed by Jain writers to produce major works of belles lettres, such as Saṅghadāsa's Vasudevahiṇḍi, an account of the deeds of Kṛṣṇa's father, and Vimala Sūri's Paumacariya, the earliest Jain version of the Rāma story. This dialect also penetrated some of the later texts of the Śvetāmbara scriptural canon.

One can view the exclusive cultivation of Prākrit by Jainism during the first eight centuries or so of its existence as signalling a conscious ideological, anti-brahmanical stance or, alternatively and more realistically, interpret this as reflecting the religion's participation in a broader cultural milieu in which Prākrit, taking the term in a generic sense, was for some time a literary vehicle nearly equal in prestige to Sanskrit. However, this linguistic exclusivity, whatever motivated it, could not remain totally impervious to the growing sophistication and refinement of Sanskrit as a pan-Indian intellectual medium and by around the fourth or fifth century CE (or possibly earlier) we find the monk Umāsvāti producing what appears to have been the first significant Jain work in Sanskrit, the Tattvārthasūtra, a systemisation of Jain teaching utilising the genre of aphoristic *sūtra*, which was clearly intended to be read on equal terms with similar summarising collections by influential brahmans such as Patañjali, Jaimini and Kaṇāda.[8] From this moment on, Sanskrit plays an increasingly important role within Jainism which, while remaining a practical spiritual, ritual and ethical path, also began to transform itself gradually into a branch of learning.

It is sometimes suggested that the widespread conversion in the early common era of brahmans to Jainism (Umāsvāti was probably in origin a Hindu; see Ohira 1982: 53) was responsible for the increased utilisation of Sanskrit by the Jain community. This is not an entirely convincing argument, for brahman conversion must surely have been prevalent long before Umāsvāti and, in fact, Jain tradition unanimously accepts that all Mahāvīra's disciples were brahmans. Indeed, it might conceivably be argued that it was the willingness on the part of the Jains to countenance a form of Sanskrit – Prākrit bilingualism, thus provid-

[8] For a study of the Tattvārthasūtra, see Ohira 1982. Ohira's latish dating is in part influenced by her view that the Sanskrit *bhāṣya* on the Tattvārthasūtra was also written by Umāsvāti. Zydenbos 1983: 9-12 argues that the root-text and *bhāṣya* are not by the same author. Bronkhorst 1985b: 178-9 subscribes to the same view and argues that the Tattvārthasūtra was composed "in all probability between 150 and 350 A. D." I leave aside here the question of the relative chronology of the Tattvārthasūtra and another important early Jain work in Sanskrit, Mallavādin's Nayacakra.

ing a much wider range of intellectual usage and reference, which may have acted as a positive lure to many scholarly converts from the brahman caste. At this stage, a provisional conclusion—albeit one difficult to prove—might be that the well documented Jain connection from around the second century BCE with the north-western city of Mathurā which was located in the region of Āryāvarta, the heartland of traditional brahman users of Sanskrit, may have effected some kind of gradual shift in Jain linguistic usage (see Deshpande 1993a: 30-31, referring to Damsteegt), which subsequently percolated into more outlying areas of Jain activity in the west and south.

Nonetheless, that Jain tradition was unwilling to see Sanskrit as in some way 'triumphing' over the community's ancient linguistic custom can be seen in the hagiography of one of the two most famous brahman converts to Jainism, Haribhadra. This great scholar was, we are told, compelled to become a Jain monk because of his failure, despite all his Sanskrit learning, to grasp the purport of a Prākrit verse (see Dundas 1992: 11). Of still more interest in appreciating the complexities involved in the introduction of Sanskrit into Jainism is the case of the other great brahman convert, the logician Siddhasena Divākara (c. fifth/sixth century), the first major figure to utilise the resources of both Sanskrit and Prākrit in his writings. Inspection of the contents of Sidhasena's works suggests that his choice of language was determined by his intended audience.

Thus, the *Nyāyāvatāra,* which is written in Sanskrit and is the first Jain treatise devoted to logic, is presumably aimed at convincing the wider Indian academic and sectarian world of Siddhasena's coreligionists' claims in this field. Similarly, the Sanskrit Dvātriṃśikā, an early example of the doxographical genre of which the Jains were pioneers and which also includes a royal panegyric for which in medieval India Sanskrit was the sole appropriate medium, seems also to have been aimed at a broader, possibly courtly audience. Siddhasena's Sanmaitakka, on the other hand, is largely devoted to specifically Jain issues of epistemology and its use of Prākrit surely implies that the work was intended for 'internal consumption' only. Broadly speaking, Prākrit continued to have an inward-directed, parochial function for Jain writers and its use may well have been intended to provide an aura of antiquity for a particular poetic, narrative or intra-Jain polemical work.

Unfortunately, this generalisation by no means has a thoroughgoing explanatory value for the entire course of Jain literary and scholarly history. The question would have to be asked, for example, as to why so many medieval texts designed to guide the laity in their daily duties (*śrāvakācāra*) and which would have been of minimal interest in the wider cultural world were written in Sanskrit.[9]

Phyllis Granoff's masterly studies of the medieval hagiographies of Siddhasena Divākara (Granoff 1989, 1990 and especially 1991) suggest that Jain tradition saw his spiritual development from arrogant brahman scholar who had associations with the royal court to pious Jain devotee submissively acknowledging the authority of the ascetic community, as being connected with tensions involved in the relative claims of Sanskrit and Prākrit as languages of religion and communication. It would be redundant to reiterate Granoff's data and arguments here and, instead, I would like to draw attention to the implications of one small, if reasonably well known (e. g. Deshpande 1979a: 55-56), episode in the hagiographies.

According to the version found in the thirteenth century Sanskrit Prabhāvakacarita of the Śvetāmbara Prabhācandra (8.108-116), Siddhasena's engrained attachment to brahmanical learning led him, "being without regard for Prākrit, even though it had been enunciated

---

[9] The most famous of the *śrāvakācāra* works, Hemacandra's Yogaśāstra, was presumably written in Sanskrit because directed towards the court circle of Kumārapāla Caulukya. As noted below, Jain writers may have used Sanskrit in the later medieval period due to the fact that Prākrit was less easy of access for much of their audience. However, an extremely large part of Jain story literature, at least among the Śvetāmbaras, continued to be written in Prākrit, possibly because of the prestigious model of Prākrit canonical and commentarial narrative. Note that exemplary narratives in Sanskrit and Prākrit alike are still read out by monks when preaching today, but of necessity they have to be followed by a vernacular translation or summary. See Cort 1993: 203.

The medieval Jains, in particular those of western India, increasingly utilised what became a third poetic language along with Sanskrit and Prākrit, namely Apabhraṃśa. This subject is too large and uncertain to be more than alluded to briefly now. Although Apabhraṃśa was an artificial and standardised language, albeit continually influenced by living vernaculars, the wide range of popular metres employed by it meant that the language was a highly effective medium of religious proselytisation. Through being sung in popular gatherings, Jain Apabhraṃśa narratives and epics, and subsequently Old Gujarati and Rajasthani hymns and stories, must have played a much greater part in the perpetuation of Jain culture in the late medieval period than either Sanskrit or Prākrit. See Bhayani 1989.

by the omniscient ones" (*prākṛte kevalajñānibhāṣite 'pi nirādaraḥ*), to propose to the Jain community that the scriptures (*siddhānta*) be translated into the Sanskrit language. The response of the senior Jain monks was emphatically negative: "For we have heard through the tradition of the ancients that there were formerly fourteen Sanskrit Pūrva scriptures. These, which could only be mastered by the application of intense intellect, disappeared in the course of time. Today there exists a corpus of eleven scriptures which has been enunciated by (Mahāvīra's disciple) Sudharman. He made it on this occasion (*iha*) Prākrit to help people such as children, women, the confused and fools. How could you be disrespectful towards this?"

All Jain sectarian groups accept that there was once a body of texts, now lost, called the Pūrvas, which was preached by all the *tīrthaṅkaras*, mastered by their disciples and forms the basis for the surviving Prākrit scriptures (see Dundas 1992: 59-60). No early information survives about the language in which the Pūrvas were supposed to have been written and Prabhācandra appears to be the first writer to assert that they were composed in Sanskrit rather than Prākrit. This claim is hardly widespread in late medieval Jain tradition but it is noteworthy that it was reiterated by the famous Śvetāmbara teacher, Hīravijaya Sūri (late sixteenth century), in response to a specific question about the language of the Pūrvas (Hīrapraśnottarāṇi: 34 a and cf. Kapadia 1941: 89-90). As Prabhācandra presents the situation, Prākrit is deemed to be more accessible and 'popular' and thus Sudharman's redaction of the scriptures in that language is indicative of the compassion of the ancient teachers. At the same time, Prākrit is really only suitable for the intellectually inadequate, while authentic Jainism, as it were, is located at a linguistic point of origin which involves Sanskrit. The existence of the scriptures in a vernacular is in the last resort brought about by temporal decay.

The hagiographers of Siddhasena Divākara were writing nearly a millennium after their subject's lifetime and no version of the Jain scriptures in Sanskrit was ever produced. Yet there is some evidence dating from around Siddhasena's period that the hagiographical references to a proposed translation of the *āgama* were not merely a narrative device and that this in fact was an issue that did genuinely exercise early medieval Jain teachers.

The relevant source is the *cūrṇi*, or Prākrit commentary, on verse 88 of the Prākrit *niryukti* commentary on the Daśavaikālika Śūtra, its author being Agastyasiṃha who most likely flourished in the fifth century. The context introduced by the *niryukti* is *nāṇāyāra* (Sanskrit *jñānācāra*), the eight actions appropriate to the gaining of knowledge. The sixth of these relates to syllables or phonemes (*vaṃjaṇa*), the seventh to meaning (*attha*) and the eighth to both syllables and meaning. According to Agastyasimha:

> A sūtra comes about through syllables. Suppose one makes that sūtra [composed in] Prākrit Sanskrit, as for example *dharmo maṅgalam utkṛṣṭam* (i.e. instead of the original Prākrit *dhammo maṃgalam ukkaṭṭham*, "*dharma* is the best auspicious word" Daśavaikālika Sūtra 1.1). Alternatively, one can (completely) alter the phonemes (of the Prākrit sūtra) while maintaining the same sense (e.g. by substituting the expression *puṇṇaṁ kallāṇaṁ ukkosaṁ dayāsaṃvaraṇijjarā*). But this (i. e. translating into Sanskrit or altering the phonemes) should not be done. Why? Because a disagreement (*visaṃvāta*) with regard to syllables will lead to a disagreement about meaning. When there is loss of meaning, there is loss of correct behaviour; when loss of correct behaviour, absence of (the possibility of) deliverance, and when there is absence of deliverance, then ascetic initiation (*dikkhā*) becomes pointless. Therefore one should not alter the syllables of scripture.

Agastyasiṃha then goes on to show how a completely different and unsatisfactory Sanskrit meaning, or set of disconnected meanings, could be constructed out of an otherwise intelligible piece of scriptural Prākrit and also how failure to maintain both the meaning and wording of a piece of scripture can lead to complete gibberish[10].

---

[10] Daśavaikālika Cūrṇi, p. 53: *vaṃjaṇe tti dāraṃ. vaṃjanam akkharaṃ, tehiṃ vaṃjaṇehiṃ nipphaṇṇaṃ suttaṃ taṃ suttaṃ pāgataṃ sakkayaṃ kareti, jahā "dharmo maṅgalam utkṛṣṭam" evamādi. tasseva vā atthassa aṇṇāṇi vaṃjaṇāṇi kareti, jahā "puṇṇaṃ kallāṇam ukkosaṃ dayā saṃvaraṇijjarā." evaṃ ṇa kātavvaṃ. kiṃ kāraṇaṃ? vaṃjaṇavisaṃvāte atthavisaṃvāte, atthaviṇāse caraṇaviṇāse, caraṇaviṇāse mokkhābhāvo, mokkhābhāve ṇiratthā dikkhā, ato vaṃjaṇaṃ ṇa kātavvaṃ.*

attho tti dāraṃ. tesu ceva vaṃjaṇesu aṇṇaṃ atthaṃ vikappeti. jahā "āvaṃtī keyā vaṃtī logaṃsi vipparāmasati" [=Ācārāṅga Sūtra 1.5.1.1] *etassa atthaṃ visaṃvāeti, "āvaṃtī" deso tattha "keyā" rajjū "vaṃtī" kūve paḍitā taṃ logo "vipparāmasati" maggati, eriso atthavisaṃvāto ṇa kātavvo.*

ubhae tti dāraṃ. jattha suttaṃ pi attho vi viṇassati taṃ ubhayaṃ. jahā, "dhammo jaṃgalasukkamho ahiṃsā pavvatamastake, devā vi tassa ṇassaṃti jassa dhamme sadā matī, ahākaḍehiṃ raṃdheṃti kaṭṭhehiṃ rahakāriṇo.," evamādisutatthavisaṃvāto.

In Agastyasiṃha we find an apparently staunch, and possibly representative, advocate of the primacy of Ardhamāgadhī Prākrit as sole scriptural language. Translation into Sanskrit is reprehensible not because of any connections that language might have with the brahman caste, but rather because the phonetic and semantic confusion which might arise would lead to chaos in Jain ascetic institutions. Such a standpoint may reflect controversies which took place in the community prior to the final redaction of the scriptures some time in the fifth century. As noted above, the early exegetical literature on the Ardhamāgadhī scriptures was composed in Prākrit. The prose *cūrṇi* commentaries, however, which date from around the fifth to eighth centuries, show increasing signs of Sanskritisation, with Sanskrit frequently being used to gloss Prākrit expressions and Sanskrit forms and verses scattered throughout.[11] The production in the eighth century by Haribhadra of largescale Sanskrit commentaries upon a few selected canonical texts marks an important watershed and from this moment on all major exegesis on the Jain scriptures is in Sanskrit.[12]

Agastyasiṃha's admittedly brief remarks make clear that Ardhamāgadhī could not always have been regarded as a transparently intelligible language and it seems that, as the medieval period lengthened, Prākrit as a whole increasingly became difficult for many to understand. Some writers suggest that Ardhamāgadhī had reached a state of such obscurity that it was essential to study it in tandem with Sanskrit exegesis. According to the main hagiography, written in the thirteenth century, of the great eleventh century Sanskrit exegete, Abhayadeva Sūri, the Ardhamāgadhī sūtras with their recherché vocabulary were

---

This argument was followed by the tenth-eleventh century Municandra Sūri in his commentary on Haribhadra, Dharmabinduprakaraṇa, 1.69 (p. 29). For a similar version given in the Niśīthacūrṇipīṭhikā, see *ibidem*, footnote 2.

[11] A possible feature of this Sanskritisation may have been the widespread use in Jain manuscripts of the unhistoric glide 't' (*ta-śruti*). There is no doubt that from the linguistic point of view this is quite simply an erroneous scribal practice (see Bhayani 1992), but it may be that the intention behind it was to give Prākrit a Sanskrit-like appearance.

[12] Williams wishes to argue for the existence of two Haribhadras, the earlier dating from the beginning of the sixth century, the later from the middle of the eighth. His argument derives not so much from the greater use of Sanskrit erudition by the latter Haribhadra, although that is a factor, as from the more standardized Prākrit he employs compared to his predecessor. See Williams 1963: 4-7.

linguistically untilled or barren ground which had to be infused with meaning by Abhayadeva's Sanskrit commentary (see Dundas, forthcoming b).[13]

Post-canonical works composed in Ardhamāgadhī are extremely rare, with the possibly eighth century Pañcasūtraka, a short treatise on the lay and ascetic life which has remained popular within the Jain community to this day, being the most notable. Attempts were occasionally made to produce pseudo-canonical scriptures in Ardhamāgadhī but without any real understanding of the nature of the language. The Aṅgacūliyā, which may date from around the end of the sixteenth century, a time of intra-sectarian conflict within the Śvetāmbara community, takes the form of a discussion between Mahāvīra's disciples Sudharman and Jambū on the subject of correct ascetic behaviour and was no doubt intended as a warning to dissident monastic elements. The apocryphal nature of the Aṅgacūliyā can be seen from the fact that it is manifestly a reworking of a slightly earlier work, the Āyāravihi, which was composed in Prākrit interspersed with Sanskrit. The 'author' of the Aṅgacūliyā knew that the ancient scriptures were written in Prākrit but proved unequal to the task of completely prākritising his original, inadvertently leaving intact within the 'scripture' some Sanskrit verses and a chunk of Sanskrit prose (see Sen 1941).

We should, of course, not exaggerate the extent to which Ardhamāgadhī had become unintelligible to the Jain community, or at least to trained monastic specialists within it. In all likelihood, a problem more immediate than the language's archaic nature must have been the accusations voiced in the Moghul period of the general indeterminate meaning of the Jain scriptures and the possible multiple interpretations of their teachings which could ensue. Semantic polyvalency was

---

[13] The eleventh century Jineśvara Sūri claimed that in his time there were many who could not read Prākrit poetry (Gāhārayaṇakosa, verse 21) and it may be significant that his largescale Prākrit *kāvya*, the Līlāvaīkahā, survives only in the form of a thirteenth century Sanskrit abridgement by Jinaratna. In sharp contrast to Sanskrit which, irrespective of the actual moment when it was no longer spoken as "mother tongue", never ceased to be the most prestigious vehicle of oral and literary communication in traditional India, Prākrit, for all its vernacular origins, had become by this time a truly dead language, an artificial poetic medium developing only through the introduction into it of regional (*deśī*) vocabulary. Indeed, composing an extended work in Prākrit may have been a more significant indicator to a lay audience of a monastic author's learning than his knowledge of Sanskrit

acknowledged as being a significant feature of Prākrit and one of the main functions of traditional Jain scriptural exegesis was to demonstrate and also delimit the range of meanings and contexts which could be generated by an Ardhamāgadhī expression (see Dundas, forthcoming b). Towards the end of the seventeenth century, the Śvetāmbara scholar-monk Samayasundara produced in response to criticisms of the Jain scriptures an extraordinary work, the *Arthalakṣī*, which demonstrates how eight lac (800 000) meanings could be derived, with the aid of unusual word breaks and esoteric glosses culled from eight lexica, from the syllables of the Sanskrit expression *rājāno dadate saukhyam* ("kings bestow wellbeing") (see Vrat 1994: 180-181). If Ardhamāgadhī was at times of indeterminate meaning, then Sanskrit could be shown to be no different in this respect.

It is difficult to gauge how widespread a familiarity there was with Sanskrit within the Jain community during the later medieval period. The production by Jain monks until the eighteenth century of examples, utilising Jain themes, of the most prestigious of all Sanskrit literary genres, the *mahākāvya* or court epic, shows that there was a learned audience capable of appreciating the virtuosity entailed in such writing (see Vrat 1994). But perhaps still more indicative of the manner in which the Jain community envisaged Sanskrit is an anthology of stories, the Bharaṭakadvātriṃśikā, satirising the Śaiva clerics and monks who were a prominent feature of rural Gujarat in the fifteenth and sixteenth centuries and significant competitors with the Jains for popular support. The uneducated buffoonery of the Śaivas is highlighted most clearly in several narratives which describe their hapless attempts to use Sanskrit (Bharaṭakadvātriṃśikā, 20, 26, 28 and 32).[14] There are no pious lay or monastic heroes in any of these stories to provide religious edification of the sort invariably found in Jain narrative literature. Their lively style and content instead suggest a lay audience familiar

[14] According to its editor, Hertel, the Bharaṭakadvātriṃśikā was probably written in the mid-fifteenth century by the monk, Munisundara. Bharaṭakadvātriṃśikā 26 is representative of the anti-Śaiva mockery found in the collection. Some Śaiva ascetics trapped by a flood resolve to send a letter asking for help from a royal minister who is their patron. The leader of the ascetics decides that such a learned man deserves to be addressed in Sanskrit but, on writing the letter, he can only produce broken Gujarati in a Sanskrit phonetic framework. Thus the minister learnt the stupidity of his guru.

with the Sanskrit language as a medium for humour and entertainment, but which was at the same time unwilling to accept the pretensions of those who would attempt to use Sanskrit, maladroitly in the case of the Śaivas, as a badge of intellectual and religious status.

6. Prākrit and Sanskrit in Jain Ritual

It should occasion no real surprise that the Jains were assiduous cultivators of Sanskrit as a literary language. However, that a tradition whose ancient liturgical texts were exclusively couched in Prākrit was at times prepared to countenance the use of Sanskrit in ritual performance deserves some passing mention.

The central Jain mantra, the *Pañcanamaskāra*, whose earliest occurrence in complete form dates from around the beginning of the common era, and the various statements of homage, confession and observance found in the Āvaśyaka Sūtra provide a body of Prākrit ritual utterance which lies at the heart of Jain practice (see Dundas 1992: 70-72 and 145-49). In the field of *mantraśāstra* especially, the Jains evolved a wide range of Prākrit mantric utterances, for the most part based on the *Pañcanamaskāra*, which was utilised during important ceremonial occasions. Vādideva Sūri argued as part of his rejection of brahman claims for the non-created nature of the Veda that Prākrit mantras yielded results despite not being composed in Vedic Sanskrit and were in actuality all the more powerful through having been formulated and deployed by morally upright Jain ascetics (see Dundas, forthcoming a). However, a sizeable number of Sanskrit mantras also occur throughout medieval Jainism (see Namaskār Svādhyāy) and there seems no reason to doubt that the Jains became increasingly prepared to utilise the ritual language of a common South Asian religiosity.

One of the most influential ritual handbooks in Jainism is the Nirvāṇakalikā which contains instructions about important matters such as image installation and teacher consecration. Although in actuality it most likely dates from around the eighth century, the Nirvāṇakalikā is attributed by Jain tradition to the ancient teacher

Pādalipta and is thus believed to be located near the very beginning of the common era. No inconsistency seems to have been felt in the fact that what must on this basis be adjudged the oldest of all Jain ritual manuals is written in Sanskrit, rather than Prākrit.

Another manual, the Vidhimārgaprapā, by the fourteenth century Jinaprabha Sūri provides important evidence for the conduct of ritual, at least at an idealised level, in late medieval Jainism. Jinaprabha, whose linguistic catholicity extended to composing a devotional hymn in Persian, was aware of the necessity for occasional variations in the use of language in ritual. The Vidhimārgaprapā is largely written in Prākrit but, in his description of the procedures for image installation (pp. 97-104), Jinaprabha uses Sanskrit on the grounds that the majority of mantras used in that particular ceremony are in that language (Vidhimārgaprapā p. 97: *so ya sakkayabhāsābaddhamaṃtabahulo tti sakkayabhāsāe ceva lihijjai*). Similarly, in another work, the Devapūjāvidhi, which describes image worship (see Vidhimārgaprapā, pp. 121-27), Jinaprabha suddenly switches from Prākrit to Sanskrit because the bulk of metrical compositions used while bathing the image are also in Sanskrit (p. 123: *sā sakkayabhāsābaddhagīikavva-ajjiyāvittabahula tti sakkayabhāsāe ceva lihijjai*). No implication is made by Jinaprabha that one language is more 'sanctified' than the other. What is at issue is nothing more than ritual convention and practicality established over centuries.[15]

7. *Concluding Remarks*

No doubt the observations made in this short paper have seemed to relate as much to Jain attitudes to Prākrit as to Sanskrit. However, this is surely excusable inasmuch as only through gaining some clear sense of the function of Prākrit within Jainism can it be possible to delineate the

---

[15] The earliest layer of the liturgy for the important ritual of image worship (*caityavandana*) is in Prākrit, but the text subsequently incorporated some Sanskrit verses. According to one medieval description of the ritual given by Śānti Sūri (eleventh cent.) in his Ceiyavaṃdaṇamahābhāsa, verse 498, at the time of uttering the prescribed hymn of praise to the *tīrthaṅkaras*, a male participant should enunciate the *Pañcanamaskāra* mantra in Sanskrit.

two main stances which Jains have adopted towards Sanskrit thoughout their history. As an ideological institution supporting the dubious moral and ritual claims of the brahman caste, Sanskrit could only be re-acted against, with its supposed non-created nature and ability to 'neutralise' sacrificial violence being denied. On the other hand, as the lingua france of *śāstra* and general literary culture, that same language could be enthusiastically utilised by the Jains without any danger of compromising their sectarian identity and socio-religious values. Linguistic usage is thus merely one example, albeit a crucial one, of the many areas in which the Jains variously redefined, rejected or accommodated themselves to the encircling Indian cultural world (cf. Cort, forthcoming).

CHAPTER SEVEN

SOCIOLINGUISTIC ATTITUDES REFLECTED IN THE WORK OF BHARTṚHARI AND SOME LATER GRAMMARIANS[*]

Jan E.M. Houben

1. Introduction

In this paper I will first discuss some aspects of the sociolinguistic context in which the Sanskrit grammarians, and especially Bhartṛhari, the grammarian-philosopher of ca. the 5th century C.E., were working, and next study in the light of this context the statements Bhartṛhari and some of his interpreters made regarding Sanskrit and its relation to non-Sanskrit. Although, as someone with a philological training, I believe that one should let the texts speak for themselves as much as possible, I also agree with Popper that all knowledge is theory-impregnated.[1] At some point it is always necessary to reflect on the scope and limits of the theories with which we approach a text. Acts and utterances to which our texts refer are understood in a social and sociolinguistic

---

[*] This paper is an outcome of the research on "Theoretical and Sociolinguistic Attitudes of Bhartṛhari and later Sanskrit Grammarians" which I carried out in 1993-1994 as a research fellow of the International Institute for Asian Studies (IIAS, Leiden). Thanks are due to the IIAS for the excellent support provided in various ways, and to the Netherlands Organization for Scientific Research (NWO) for financial assistance on several occasions. I am greatly indebted to my teachers in Bhartṛhari-studies, Professor A. Aklujkar and Professor J. Bronkhorst, and to Pt. V.B. Bhagavat and Professor G.B. Palsule for the discussions which I could have on some difficult passages during my short stays in Pune in 1993-94. Finally, I thank the participants of the seminar "Ideology and Status of Sanskrit" for their reactions to my presentation, and Professor A. Wezler for his detailed comments on an earlier version of this paper.

[1] Popper 1972:104-105: "Since all knowledge is theory-impregnated, it is all built on sand; but its foundations can be improved by critically digging deeper; and by not taking any alleged 'data' for granted."

context. This context is to be reconstructed on the basis of (1) the incomplete and often problematic data available for the period; and (2) unavoidably, either intuitively or methodicaly, some theories and concepts are brought in to organize the data and to predict aspects of the situation about which no direct information is available.

A concept which has received considerable attention in sociolinguistic research, and which seems to be also extremely relevant to the sociolinguistic situation in ancient South Asia, is the concept of 'diglossia' (cf. Krishnamurti 1986:xvii-xxii, 287ff; for modern South Asia: D'Souza 1988). I will discuss previous contributions to the subject of 'diglossia in ancient South Asia', and suggest a strategy to further improve our picture of the situation. This will be my main concern in sections 2 and 3. The next part of my paper (section 4), will deal with the *attitudes* reflected in Bhartṛhari's work concerning the linguistic situation as it emerged in the discussion in the first part. Subsequently, the variations in the attitudes of some later grammarians (mainly commentators on Bhartṛhari's Vākyapadīya and on Patañjali's Mahābhāṣya) on the issues raised by Bhartṛhari will be briefly discussed (section 5). I will present these variations as varying ways of 'naturalizing' the arbitrariness of the standard language. The main points arrived at in this paper will be briefly summarized in section 6.

2. Sanskrit and Diglossia in ancient South Asia

2.1 According to what has become known in linguistics as the Uniformitarian Principle,

> knowledge of processes that operated in the past can be inferred by observing ongoing processes in the present (Christie 1983:ix, cited in Labov 1994:21).

The application of sociolinguistic concepts to the distant past implies the acceptance of this principle. It implies, moreover, that we assume that processes observed in one cultural area can serve as a basis for understanding processes in a different one. This means that we are not postulating a South Asian culture which was essentially different from e.g. Western culture—we are not in search of the essence of Indian culture and thought—but we assume that there is continuity, that generally speaking similar factors apply to both South Asian and Western people, their societies and the languages spoken in these societies. Since we are dealing with a past which we try to reconstruct on the basis of limited data, the Uniformitarian Principle can be not much more than a working hypothesis: we cannot be sure beforehand that similar factors were indeed at work in the past as in the present. However, in our reconstruction we accept new factors only if familiar factors prove to be insufficient.

2.2 The concept of 'diglossia' has attracted a lot of attention in sociolinguistic studies in the last few decades. A recent bibliography on Diglossia gives more than 2900 entries for the three decades between 1960-1990 (Fernández 1993). The classical formulation of the concept is the one by Charles A. Ferguson (Ferguson 1959:336). According to Ferguson, diglossia is

> a relatively stable language situation in which, in addition to the primary dialects of the language (which may include a standard or regional standards), there is a very divergent, highly codified (often grammatically more complex) superposed variety, the vehicle of a large and respected body of written literature, either of an earlier period or in another speech community, which is learned largely by formal education and is used for most written and formal spoken purposes but is not used by any sector of the community for ordinary conversation. (Ferguson 1959:336)

The defining languages on the basis of which Ferguson formulates his concept are Arabic, Swiss German, Haitian Creole and Greek, each with distinct high and low varieties. The situation of diglossia is to be distinguished from the more common situation in which there is a standard variety which is commonly used even in informal contexts by a sector of the community for which the standard is at the same time the mother tongue. The attention attracted by 'diglossia' is perhaps to be understood against the background of the ideology—current since the 19th century—according to which the best and most stable and 'natural' situation is that of a single nation, one people, and one language in one state. Diglossia, however, is defined as a stable situation in which this one language has a high variety which is no-one's mother tongue. A considerable number of the publications (mainly articles) to which the bibliography refers concerns attempts to identify new cases of 'diglossia', apart from the four defining languages.

2.3 Also the relationship between Old Indo-Aryan or Vedic and classical Sanskrit and other Indian languages (mainly Middle Indo-Aryan or the Prakrits) has been identified as 'diglossic'. Since the nineteenth century Sanskritists have struggled with the question of what the precise status of Sanskrit was, whether, for instance, the language described by Pāṇini was a truly spoken one; whether it could be considered a living language even if it was spoken in restricted contexts [2]; what the precise relationship was between Vedic and classical Sanskrit on the one hand and the Prakrits on the other, etc.[3] The first to present the data collected by earlier generations of Sanskritists in the framework of the concept of diglossia were Hock and Pandharipande (1976). They mention three arguments for a diglossic relationship, from Vedic times onwards: (1) the occurrence of hypersanskritized forms: forms which were already Sanskrit were made 'even more sanskritic' to avoid any resemblance with Prakritism; (2) the classical drama, in which "Sanskrit is spoken mainly by the educated, upper-class male protagonists, while various types of Prākrits are used by most women and by males of lower rank and education" (1976:113); (3) explicit statements of Sanskrit authors. Hock and Pandharipande refer to statements of the grammarian Patañjali and to those in the Nāṭyaśāstra, in which a distinction is made between the language of the learned and the language of common people (1976:114f).

Diglossia as understood in these statements applies to the relationship between Sanskritic and Prakritic traditions, or between Old and Middle Indo-Aryan languages/dialects. This relationship they consider to be not only bidialectal but also diglossic in accordance with Fergu-

---

[2] Rapson's contribution and the discussion in the 1904 issue of the JRAS were the culmination of several earlier discussions. Doubts concerning the status of Sanskrit as an actively spoken language often derive from the consideration that Sanskrit is mainly an artificial construction of brahmins or grammarians, and are closely related with ideas about what properties a 'real' language should have. Cf. also Winternitz 1981:36-39 + footnotes; Renou 1956b:82 + footnote. Cardona 1976:238-239 reviews the discussion concerning the status of the language described by Pāṇini. Some scholars admit that Sanskrit was spoken to a very limited degree, but seem to underestimate its importance for and dynamic interaction with the colloquial (cf. Joshi & Roodbergen 1986:134-135 and 1991:13-15, and discussion below in section 3.8).

[3] This is a topic of discussion since Pott explained features of Vedic Sanskrit by assuming Prakritic influence: cf. Pott 1833 and Hock's contribution to this volume.

son's 1959 definition (Hock & Pandharipande 1976:107, 113). However, the relationship between on the one hand Sanskrit and Indo-Aryan languages and on the other hand non-Indo-Aryan they label as 'bilingual'.

2.4 Another relevant publication is Gina M. Lee's "Diglossia in Ancient India" (Lee 1986) in which the author focuses on two of the three arguments mentioned by Hock & Pandharipande to consider the relationship between Sanskrit and Prakrit diglossic, namely the argument of the classical Sanskrit drama in which some characters use Prakrit; and the argument of the hyper-sanskritisms. She concludes that only the second argument provides strong evidence for diglossia, and studies a number of cases of hyper-sanskritisms to confirm the strength of this argument. A hyper-sanskritisms, as understood by her, is a hypercorrection, i.e., a "morphological change which originates as an attempt to avoid using forms which contain phonological patterns found in a low prestige dialect."[4] Her reason to doubt the value of the drama as evidence for diglossia is that it was written for and viewed by a very limited educated audience.

2.5 The third and last relevant publication to which I would like to refer here is Madhav Deshpande's "Conceptions of Diglossia in the Writings of the Sanskrit Grammarians," (Deshpande 1991; superseding Deshpande 1986) which deals with the attitudes of the Sanskrit grammarians concerning the linguistic situation of their time. Some of the points brought forward by Deshpande are (1) that Kātyāyana "seems to be asserting the need of speaking proper Sanskrit at all times" (Deshpande 1991:31); (2) that Patañjali gives us a "concrete instance of diglossic variation" if he tells us the story of two sages who used correct Sanskrit forms during sacrificial performances, but degenerate forms outside the ritual context (idem); (3) that according to Patañjali, for

---

[4] Lee 1986:155; in her understanding of the term, it is irrelevant whether the resulting form is considered prescriptively/etymologically correct or incorrect, as she is mainly interested in "the social forces behind such modifications." To mention only one of the instances of hypersanskritisms she collected on the basis of Bloomfield & Edgerton 1932 and Mayrhofer 1956: *utsuka* 'anxiously desirous' from **ucchuka*, Old-Indian *icchu* 'wishing, desiring': though the sequence *-cch-* does occur in Sanskrit, it is also often the Prākrit reflex of Sanskrit *-ts-*; the only reason to change **ucchuka* to *utsuka* must therefore be that the former 'sounds' Prākritic.

each correct Sanskrit word there are many degenerate forms (idem:37); at the same time, Patañjali admits that both correct Sanskrit forms and degenerate or Apabhraṁśa forms are capable of communicating the same message (Deshpande 1991:33). The main area in which Old and Middle Indo-Aryan are strong is the northern part of the Indian subcontinent.

On the one hand, Deshpande says that "[f]rom Kātyāyana onwards, the existence of diglossia emerges as a very significant factor in the minds of the Sanskrit grammarians" (Deshpande 1991:29), and explains that diglossia here refers to the "linguistic situation from the conservative point of view of the Sanskrit grammarians, who refused to ascribe to the Prakrit vernaculars the status of separate languages" (Deshpande 1991:30). On the other hand, Deshpande is hesitant to characterize the situation of Sanskrit in the post-Vedic period of Patañjali and later grammarians as "true diglossia, in the original narrow sense of various layers within Sanskrit usage itself" (Deshpande 1991:35).[5] After all, Ferguson defined the concept for two varieties of one and the same language: a primary dialect and a divergent, superposed variety. According to Deshpande, however, Sanskrit had become very much "removed from the linguistic behavior of the masses" and "restricted to a highly contextualized domain" (idem). As early as in Patañjali's time the spoken use of Sanskrit was, in Deshpande's view, almost entirely restricted to the sacrificial context. Even the élite spoke a form of Apabhraṁśa or Prakrit at home (Deshpande 1991:36).

Deshpande's argument seems to imply that if we acknowledge Prakrit and Apabhraṁśa as languages different from Sanskrit we can no more speak of a diglossic situation. Thus, relationships between Indo-Aryan languages which Hock & Pandharipande would be ready to con-

---

[5] Elsewhere, however, Deshpande comes close to admitting different layers within Sanskrit usage: Deshpande 1993a:17-32, esp. 31: "This allows us to understand how Sanskrit grammarians [in Deshpande's preceding discussion especially Kātyāyana and Patañjali, JH] took care of linguistic change, even when they did not openly admit the fact of change. . . Some of [the usages] were part of the contemporary *śiṣṭa* usage, while others were viewed as being substandard and were rejected. This provides us a way of analyzing different strands in the usage of Sanskrit ranging from the historically Pāṇinian Sanskrit to the rejected vernacular Sanskrit."

sider as diglossic, would fall outside the scope of diglossia as understood by Deshpande.

2.6 A point which emerges from the previously discussed attempts to apply the concept of diglossia to the sociolinguistic situation in ancient South Asia is that the concept itself is not without problems. Nor did Ferguson present his 1959 definition as the final word on the topic. Indeed, a considerable number of the publications in Fernández' Bibliography on Diglossia to which I referred above is devoted to proposing amendments or even complete revisions of Ferguson's preliminary definition. One relatively minor point on which Ferguson's definition does not suit the ancient South Asian situation is his stipulation that the superposed variety should be the vehicle of a large and respected body of written literature. The superposed variety in early South Asia, however, was not the vehicle of *written* literature but mainly of fixed *orally* transmitted texts. More important problems arise because Ferguson, as he himself has pointed out (Ferguson 1959:325 n 2), uses the terms 'language', 'dialect', 'variety' and 'superposed variety' without precise definition.

Quite a different definition of and approach to diglossia was adopted by Joshua A. Fishman, who emphasizes the distribution of social functions attributed to the high and low standard language respectively. In Fishman's functional approach it is of secondary importance whether the high standard language is genetically related to the low standard language or not. Fishman has been criticized for trivializing the concept of diglossia because his functional approach would make even different registers of one language the basis of a diglossic situation.[6] However, in his 1985 formulation Fishman requires that the so-called superposed variety in a diglossic society is the variety that is no one's mother tongue, is learned later in socialization under the influence of one or another formal institution outside the home, and is not equally accessible to everyone (Fishman 1985:39). This requirement precludes that the presence of different registers which can easily be adopted and mutually understood without any problem by all speakers of a community forms a basis for considering that community diglossic.

---

[6] Cf. Lee 1986:161-162, n 2; d'Souza 1988:29-30; Moag 1986:350: there would be oversimplification, diglossia would obtain wherever two languages or varieties are involved.

Fishman distinguishes between diglossia which he understands as a characteristic of society, and bilingualism, which refers to an individual who has full command over two languages. Fishman distinguishes moreover four different types of diglossia, along two parameters: the high variety may or may not be a classical language; and the high and low variety may or may not be genetically related.

A similar result could be reached from a different direction by amending certain aspects in Ferguson's definition. This was done by Bruce C. Johnson (1986) who, starting with Ferguson's 1959 article, relaxed the requirement that the two languages or varieties involved in the diglossia are related from a purely linguistic point of view. Instead, what is crucial according to Johnson is whether a speech community *considers* them to be related. While Ferguson speaks of a 'very divergent' variety which is superposed on the primary dialects of the language, Johnson adds that the high and low varieties are "not necessarily mutually intelligible, but the language distance between them is relatively slight and/or members of the community consider them to be varieties of one language" (Johnson 1986:337-338). Johnson further distinguishes three types of diglossia: (a) 'classical diglossia' typified by Arabic and Greek; (b) 'creole diglossia', for instance Haitian Creole; (c) 'border diglossia' as in the case of Swiss German.

2.7 In the absence of full terminological clarity it seems expedient to shift our attention from the partly problematic terminology and definitions to the available data concerning Sanskrit and study them in more detail in comparison with those of Ferguson's defining languages which are most closely parallel. Both according to Fishman's parameters and according to Johnson's revision of Ferguson's definition we then arrive at the two examples of 'classical' diglossia, viz. Arabic and Greek. The classical diglossia of these two languages and Latin were the subject of an article by Versteegh, who paid special attention to the Greek of the post-classical period (Ferguson's starting point being the diglossia of modern Greek). In Versteegh's article, the three abstract notions 'latinitas', 'hellenismos' and ''arabiyya' are juxtaposed in order to suggest a "model to evaluate the grammarian's attitude towards such notions as standard language, corruption of speech, dialect and colloquial language" (Versteegh 1986:425; cf. Householder 1989:143-146). Below I will argue that several of Versteegh's observations concerning especially post-classical Greek also apply to Sanskrit at least from Pāṇini's time onward and including the time of Bhartṛhari (5th century CE). Next, I will take a closer look at some statements of Bhartṛhari and later grammarians on the relation between Sanskrit and non-Sanskrit.

3. *Classical diglossia of Sanskrit, Greek, Arabic and Latin*

3.1 According to Versteegh "the three speech communities, Greek, Arabic and Latin, had a similar linguistic make-up and, consequently, the three grammatical traditions took a similar view of the development of their language and the actual linguistic situation in which they flourished" (Versteegh 1986:425)

In the concluding section of his article, Versteegh distances himself from a view expressed by Steinthal in his history of classical Greek grammar. According to Steinthal, the old Greek language was dead towards the beginning of the 3rd century A.D. From then on, in Steinthal's view, this language has "no life, no development, it is no longer a living organ for the spirit (Geist)" (Steinthal 1890-91, cited in Versteegh 1986:442). Versteegh thinks that Steinthal is "wrong in assuming that the standard language was dead," for:

> In the first place, the grammarians themselves certainly regarded this language as something living, something that was the symbol of their unified culture. In the second place, it is precisely typical of this kind of speech community that the 'dead' standard continues to exercize its influence on the spoken varieties. Most contemporary scholars have only eyes for the interference of the colloquial that is found in written texts, but much more important, perhaps, is the interference of the standard language in the colloquial. In a diglottic community, nobody escapes this influence, which determines the development of the language. Only the standard language, the high variety of this diglossia as Ferguson (1959) calls it, can fulfil the demand of a common language that unites the people in a way no spoken mother tongue can, since the spoken varieties act within this kind of community as a centrifugal, decentralizing force. In this respect, the Latin, Greek, and Arabic situations are very much alike. In all three cases, the failure to recognize the importance of the spoken use of the standard has led to an erroneous view of the development of the language. (Versteegh 1986:442)

3.2 What is being said here with regard to the grammarians of Latin, Greek, and Arabic and their situations seems to fit the situation of Sanskrit grammarians in early South Asia remarkably well. The first point, which deserves to be discussed at some length, is that also the Sanskrit grammarians regard the language described by them (at least as far as the *bhāṣā* is concerned) as a language which is generally known and actually used, (although for 'correct' usage reference is made to a restricted circle of speakers). This is clear both from explicit statements and by the examples used by Patañjali and Bhartṛhari. Since the importance of the spoken use of the language in the period from Patañjali onwards is sometimes played down,[7] it will not be out of place to review some indications for this active, spoken use of Sanskrit in the literature.

Although Versteegh speaks of the grammarian's Greek as a 'living' language in opposition to others who consider it a 'dead' language, it should be realized that the 'living-or-dead' terminology suits the metaphor of language as a biological organism—a popular metaphor among European linguists up to the 19th century, severely criticized by, among others, Whitney and Saussure—but is out of place if language is considered to be first of all a social phenomenon. Following the careful discussion by Deshpande, it would seem preferable to speak of "grammar-independent usage"[8] (1993a:31) instead of 'living Sanskrit' as the linguistic object of the Sanskrit grammarians.

3.2.1 Here, I will first briefly review some indications in other than grammatical texts. Most of these indications were referred to by Renou (1956b:89-94).[9] Next, I will turn to some well-known indications in early grammatical works and add a few indications found in the work of Bhartṛhari. If we leave out of consideration Vedic prescriptions concerning language use in the ritual (which sometimes presupposes an active mastery of Sanskrit or its predecessor), we may first distinguish between (A) descriptive passages (describing linguistic usage, either of characters in a story, or apparently or allegedly of actual people or his-

---

[7] Cf. the discussions referred to in note 2, and Deshpande 1991:35f, referred to in section 2.5 above.

[8] I.e. usage not primarily based on the intentional study of grammar books.

[9] It is not my aim to add many new instances to those mentioned by Renou, but the references are more precise and the organization and contents of my discussion is entirely different from Renou's.

torical personalities), (B) prescriptive passages (exhorting people to use certain forms or a certain language), and (C) passages implying the active or receptive knowledge of Sanskrit among certain circles of speakers.

(A) Descriptions in epic and narrative texts provide only very indirect evidence on account of a strong element of fiction in these texts. Thus, the Rāmāyaṇa, containing what are often considered to be the first references to Sanskrit as a language name (although *saṁskṛta* in the relevant passage is clearly adjectival with *vāc*), distinguishes between a *saṁskṛta* speech of (normal) people (*mānuṣīm . . . saṁskṛtām*) and a *saṁskṛta* speech (corresponding to what we call 'Sanskrit'?) of the 'twice-born' (the three highest classes).[10]

From such epic descriptions may be distinguished those statements which can make a somewhat stronger claim to reflect actual reality. Rājaśekhara (11th century CE), in his Kāvyamīmāṁsā, includes an encyclopedic section on the 'ethnic and linguistic geography' of India which, in broad outlines, goes well with indications from other sources (as argued by Deshpande 1993a:83-107; cf. Deshpande 1979a:28-33). Rājaśekhara informs us which people are more interested in Sanskrit, which in Prakrit and which in Apabhraṁśa or Paiśācī; which styles (use of nominal forms vs. verbs, long vs. short compounds, etc.) are preferred in different areas; the character of Sanskrit recitation in different regions (Kāvya-mīmāṁsā, especially chapter 7 on usages regarding language and pronunciation, and 17 on the colour of complexion of various people). Rājaśekhara also informs us that the king Śātavāhana made his entire harem speak Prakrit. That Prakrit was particularly

---

[10] Hanuman thinking about the speech to use when addressing Sītā held captivated on Laṅkā by Rāvaṇa:

. . . *vācaṁ codāhariṣyāmi mānuṣīm iha saṁskṛtām / yadi vācaṁ pradāsyāmi dvijātir iva saṁskṛtām rāvaṇaṁ manyamānā māṁ sītā bhītā bhaviṣyati* (Rāmāyaṇa 5.28.17-18).

That this is a reference to two varieties of speech is also the interpretation of later commentators, cf. Govindarāja's comments in which he contrasts a local *mānuṣa* language of men (*atra vākyasya mānuṣatvaṁ kosaladeśavartimanuṣyasaṁbandhitvaṁ vivakṣitaṁ / tādṛgvākyasyaiva devīparicitatvāt*) and the *gīrvāṇabhāṣā*, Rāmāyaṇa, Krishnacharya's ed. vol. 2:112-113. A different interpretation of this Rāmāyaṇa-passage has been proposed by Aklujkar (present volume, p. 71, note 18).

popular in the Śātavāhana kingdom can also be inferred from other (e.g. epigraphical) sources.

According to the author of the Jaina work Upamitibhavaprapañcākathā, Sanskrit is "dear to people who are proud of their knowledge," and he informs us that the well-educated despise other languages, but that he himself will use in his work a simple Sanskrit which is "suitable to all people" (*sarvajanocitā*) (Renou 1956b:91 [11]).

The Kashmirian poet Bilhaṇa (11th-12th century CE), in the autobiographical 18th chapter of his Vikramāṅkadevacarita, affirms that everywhere in the capital city of his native area in the Himalayan hills, even the women speak both Sanskrit and Prakrit as if these were their mother tongues.[12] Another author from Kashmir, Kalhaṇa (12th century), refers to a king who speaks only the "Apabhraṁśa of drunken people" instead of the "divine language" (Rājataraṅgiṇī 5.206). Apparently, he presupposes that the norm for kings is to speak Sanskrit.

Of special interest and value are the testimonies of Chinese Buddhist pilgrims who seem to be aware only of the Sanskrit language as the language of instruction and discussion in the world of Indian Buddhism.[13]

(B) Of quite a different nature are the prescriptive passages, which are to be interpreted in accordance with their status as statements presupposing a certain starting position and aiming at the 'idéal'.[14] If the Garuḍa Purāṇa exhorts people of the three highest classes to avoid (listening to) Prakrit (which is placed on one line with language dealing

[11] For further bibliographical of this text which was not availbable to me see Winternitz 1988:505 n 1.

[12] Vikramāṅkadevacarita 18.6: . . . *yatra strīṇām api kim aparaṁ janmabhāṣāvad eva pratyāvāsaṁ vilasati vacaḥ saṁskṛtaṁ prākṛtaṁ ca.* Bilhaṇa's statement can be taken as an indication that fluency in Sanskrit was possible for the women in his time, or at least that it was imaginable in a poetic but nevertheless realistic description of his native place. On the realism of Bilhaṇa's description cf. Winternitz 1922:86 [1985:94]: "Here he describes his native land, particularly his native village Khonamukha, in a manner so true to nature that Bühler, who visited the place, has expressed his admiration at the exactness of the description." At the same time, it is clear that this situation, even taking into account that it was stated with some exaggeration, was something quite extraordinary.

[13] Renou 1956b:91 n 1; cf.especially the information provided by Yì jìng (I-tsing) on 'the method of learning' in Buddhist India: Takakusu 1896:167-185.

[14] Cf. Pollock 1985, for the importance of theory ('how things should be' according to prescriptive works) for understanding historical practice, and vice versa.

with materialistic subjects, false reasoning (of heretics), and language of Mlecchas), it presupposes a practice in which both Sanskrit and Prakrit are actively used.[15] (If Sanskrit was not already used in several contexts one would expect an exhortation to use and listen to Sanskrit rather than an exhortation to avoid Prakrit.) A statement like the one in Kāmasūtra 1.4, "by having one's conversations in the assemblies neither too much in Sanskrit nor too much in the local language a person should become highly esteemed in the world" (*nātyantaṁ saṁskṛtenaiva nātyantaṁ deśabhāṣayā / kathāṁ goṣṭhīṣu kathayaṁl loke bahumato bhavet*), presupposes a practice in which some people do make excessive use of Sanskrit while others restrict themselves more to the local language. Mention may also be made of works teaching 'spoken Sanskrit' (cf. Salomon 1982; Wezler in the present volume), which can be seen as attempts to expand the sphere of Sanskrit. The existence of this literature confirms that Sanskrit and approximations of Sanskrit were used in restricted contexts and in small circles.

A special type of prescriptions is that of works on poetics and dramaturgy advising on the use of language by the different characters of a literary work. The Nāṭyaśāstra (ca. 2nd-3rd century CE? Kane 1971:43-47; De 1960:18) presupposes at least a receptive knowledge of simple Sanskrit on a large scale when it prescribes Sanskrit as an important (but not the only) language to be employed in dramas.[16] The same applies several centuries later when the poetician Bhāmaha (8th century), defining a clear literary work (viz. one that is partly or entirely in Sanskrit), said that it should have a meaning which is understood by people from the wise to the women and children (*āvidvadaṅganābālapratītārtham*) (Kāvyālaṅkāra 2.3).

---

[15] Garuḍa Purāṇa 1.98.17-18: . . . *lokāyataṁ kutarkaś ca prākṛtamlecchabhāṣitam / na śrotavyaṁ dvijenaitad adho nayati taṁ dvijam /*

[16] Cf. Nāṭyaśāstra chapter 14 and 17.25ff. It is not clear from which edition of this still not satisfactorily edited text Renou (1956b:90) cited the expression *gūḍhaśabdārthahīnaṁ janapadasukhabhogyam* (other editions have *budhajanasukhabhogyam*, Nāṭyaśāstra 16.129). Grierson, however, emphasized that it was nevertheless only Prakrit which was easily understood by all, as "all the comic portions of a drama, even the speeches of the Vidūṣaka, who was necessarily a Brāhmaṇ by caste, had to be written in Prakrit. If they had been in Sanskrit they would not have raised a laugh" (Grierson 1904:473).

(C) Passages which imply in a more indirect way the active or receptive knowledge of Sanskrit in certain circles of speakers (beyond the circle of brahmins in a ritual context) are for instance Caraka 3 (Vimānasthāna) where chapter 8 suggests not only that physicians gave their pupils instruction in Sanskrit but also that their controversies were mainly in Sanskrit. The Arthaśāstra (ca. 3rd - 4th century C.E., cf. Trautmann 1971), in the section on 'royal decrees' (2.10), clearly presupposes that these messages for officers within the country and to political leaders of other countries are written in Sanskrit, especially since it includes *apaśabda* 'incorrect or substandard words' (together with e.g. *akānti* 'absence of charm', and *punarukta* 'repetitiousness') in the list of major shortcomings in writing that should be avoided.[17]

3.2.2 Turning now to the indications provided by early grammarians, we may mention first of all the distinction made by Pāṇini between *chandas* and *bhāṣā*, which seems to refer to the distinction between the language of Vedic texts and the language of (well-educated) people in daily life (apparently including a body of pre-Pāṇinian 'secular' literature to which P 4.3.87-88 refer but which is entirely lost). Some of the sūtras in Pāṇini's grammar make only sense if they refer to an active, spoken use of the language (e.g. Renou 1956b:67; Thieme 1985). From Pāṇini's rule 8.2.83 *pratyabhivāde'śūdre*, prescribing a certain way of "responding to a respectful greeting, except in the case of a Śūdra.", one would infer that Sanskrit speakers responded not only to the greetings of people of the three highest classes, but also to those of the fourth and lowest class, the Śūdra (whose greeting was no doubt understood by the Sankrit speaker, although it is not clear to what extent it was grammatically 'correct').

Patañjali, as well as his predecessor Kātyāyana, frequently refer to the linguistic usage of the well-educated as the standard to determine

---

[17] According to the Arthaśāstra one speaks of an *apaśabda* if gender, number, tense or case are used wrongly. Patañjali's Mahābhāṣya, however, cites as examples of *apaśabdas* (*apabhraṁśas*) words which can be found in Jaina Ardhamāgadhī texts (MBh 1:5.21-22; cf. Deshpande 1979a:9), so that, from a modern perspective, Patañjali is referring to Prakrit forms. The Arthaśāstra shows remarkably little awareness of differences in language or dialect, but in chapter 13 it is emphasized that a king should adopt a similar character, dress *and language* as the subjects in a newly acquired country (Arthaśāstra 13.5.7; I am grateful to Prof. H. Bakker who drew my attention to this passage).

the correctness of forms and their semantic range. The most important words used in this context are *loka* 'world, worldly or daily usage'; *laukika* 'belonging to the world, to worldly or daily usage' (versus, or sometimes including linguistic usage which is *vaidika* 'belonging to the Vedas'); *prayoga* 'usage', 'employment (of a form)'; occasionally *vyavahāra* 'usage', 'verbal usage'. Verbal usage in the world (*loka*) includes not only correct usage but also incorrect usage (cf. MBh 1:259.13-14 on Vārttika 13 on P 1.3.1). The standard of correct usage is the usage (*prayoga*) of the well-educated (*śiṣṭa*). I will mention here a few well-known passages. First, in the introductory section of the Mahābhāṣya we find the following statement of Kātyāyana:

> *siddhe śabdārthasaṁbandhe lokato 'rthaprayukte śabdaprayoge śāstreṇa dharmaniyamaḥ.*
>
> When [it is assumed that] the *saṁbandha* 'relation' between *śabda* 'word' and *artha* 'meaning' is *siddha* 'established', on account of [the usage in] everyday life, [and] when [it is assumed that] the use of words is occasioned by the thing-meant, the science [of grammar] [provides] a restriction [on the use of words] for the sake of merit.[18]

Here we are especially interested in the word *lokato* 'on account of [the usage in] everyday life'. The whole statement amounts to an acknowledgement that people in daily life know how to express the things and meanings intended by them in words, but need the help of grammar to be able to restrict themselves to grammatically correct words. This is also what emerges from Patañjali's elaborate discussion of this statement of Kātyāyana (cf. Joshi & Roodbergen 1986:esp. 115-119 on *lokato*).

Patañjali also informs us what he considers to be the entire area in which words are used. This area includes "the earth with its seven continents, the three worlds, the four Vedas" (MBh 1:9.20-23). Subsequently, he mentions some forms which are used only in some areas and contrasts them with the forms used by the Aryans. Elsewhere, Patañjali

---

[18] This is followed by the phrase, *yathā laukikavaidikeṣu*, which seems to compare grammar, the *śāstra* ('science' or 'system') which deals with the use of words, with other *śāstras* that deal with matters pertaining to daily life or the Veda. Patañjali supplies: *kṛtānteṣu*, which the commentator Kaiyaṭa interprets as *siddhānteṣu*. Joshi-Roodbergen translate the phrase as: "Like in (the case of precepts) found in *loka* 'non-ritual literature' and in the Veda" (Joshi-Roodbergen 1986:120).

points out that short *a* with open pronunciation occurs neither in *loka* 'daily life, daily language', nor in the Veda (MBh 1:15.14-15). Similarly, he points out that short *e* and *o* occur neither in *loka* nor in the Veda, the latter with the exception of a few Sāmaveda traditions(MBh 1:22.23-24).

A nore explicit reference to 'verbal usage' is occasionally made with tne word *vyavahāra*, which at one place is used in conjunction with *loka*, viz. in Patañjali's comments on Vārttika 6 on P 5.3.67. The sūtra prescribes the affixes *kalpa*, *deśya*, and *deśīya* after a nominal stem (or even after a verbal stem) to denote 'not quite fully'. This gives for instance forms like *guḍakalpā drākṣāḥ* 'grapes which [in sweetness] are almost like molasses', and *paṭukalpaḥ* 'not quite fully skillful', 'sort of skillful'. One of the problems discussed by Kātyāyana and Patañjali is that in the case of an object which is clearly known (for instance molasses) one can know whether something (molasses or grapes) is really molasses to the fullest degree, or whether it is not quite fully molasses. A quality, however, is not in the same way clearly known as an object, so how can one decide whether someone is, for instance, fully skillful, and another almost fully skillful? The answer is that one has to acquire knowledge of the semantic range of 'skillful' versus 'sort of skillful' from observing daily usage[19]:

> Having observed the usage from daily life, [one acquires] clear knowledge of the quality. For example. It is said "This Brahmin is skillful" if he accomplishes his things in an easy way. It is said "This Brahmin is sort of skillful" if he does not accomplish [his things] in such an [easy] way. (MBh 2.420.13-15)

Of interest is also a passage where Patañjali discusses the question: who are the *śiṣṭas*, 'well-educated', to whom he frequently refers as the normative speakers of Sanskrit? Part of this oft-quoted discussion goes as follows[20]:

---

[19] *lokato vyavahāraṁ dṛṣṭvā guṇasya nirjñānam / tad yathā / paṭur ayaṁ brāhmaṇa ity ucyate yo laghunopāyenārthān sādhayati / paṭukalpo 'yam ity ucyate yo na tathā sādhayati /*

[20] *evaṁ tarhi nivāsata ācāratas ca / sa cācāra āryāvarta eva / kaḥ punar āryāvartaḥ / prāg ādarśāt pratyak kālakavanād dakṣiṇena himavantam uttareṇa pāriyātram / etasminn āryanivāse ye brāhmaṇāḥ kumbhīdhānyā alolupā agṛhyamāṇakāraṇāḥ kiṁ cid antareṇa kasyāś cid vidyāyāḥ pāragās tatrabhavantaḥ śiṣṭāḥ /*

The translation follows Deshpande's rendering (1993a:28) with minor adaptations.

> "Then [we will define *śiṣṭas*] by their way of life and place of residence. That particular way of life is found only in the region of Āryāvarta."
> "Which area is Āryāvarta?"
> "[It lies] to the east of the Ādarśa region, to the west of the Kālaka forest, to the south of the Himālayas and to the north of the Vindhya mountains. Those selfless Brāhmaṇas who live in this Āryavarta, the land of the Āryas, who just store a basketful of grain, and have attained the highest wisdom in some branch of learning for its own sake, they are the *śiṣṭas* 'the normative speakers of Sanskrit'." (MBh 3:174.)

Although here the brahmins of a certain region are identified as the normative speakers of Sanskrit, this does not mean that they are held to be the only speakers of Sanskrit, as becomes clear, for instance, from the anecdote in which a grammarian is outwitted by a charioteer (of mixed descent) in a discussion on grammatical derivations (MBh 1:488.18ff).

A passage which is often connected with an alleged historical development in Sanskrit usage between Pāṇini and Patañjali is the discussion on the question whether or not there are 'unemployed forms'. In this context Patañjali mentions 2nd plural perfective forms like *ūṣa* and *cakra* as 'unemployed forms' and says that instead people use the corresponding past passive participles *uṣitāḥ* (*kva yūyam uṣitāḥ* 'where did you (pl.) live?'), and *kṛtavantaḥ* (*kiṁ yūyaṁ kṛtavantaḥ* 'what did you (pl.) do?') (MBh 1:8.22-9.13).

3.2.3 Finally, I mention a few places in the Mahābhāṣya-Dīpikā, generally ascribed to Bhartṛhari, where reference is made to verbal usage in daily life. First, in a discussion of the precise implication of the word *nitya* 'permanent' in the statement that *śabda, artha,* and their relation are *nitya*, Bhartṛhari remarks [21]: "When it is said that *śabda, artha,* and their relation are *nitya*, this is understood to be an explanation of words that are frequently used by people down to cowherds etc., not of other ones."

A more particular reference to verbal usage is made in the sixth Āhnika of the MBhD. Although Bhartṛhari suggests that he is spelling out the thought of Patañjali, he claims without explicit basis in Patañjali's statements that the form *priyaviśvāya* (besides *viśvapriyāya*, both

[21] MBhD 1:21.18-20: *nitye śabdārthasambandha ity ucyamāne abhīkṣṇyaṁ yaḥ śabdaḥ prayujyate* [JH → *ye śabdāḥ prayujyante* ?] *āgopālādibhyas* [JH → *āgopālādibhis* with AL 25.21; MS: *āgopālāditis*] *teṣām idam anvākhyānam anyeṣāṁ na.*

meaning 'loving everything or everyone' or 'to whom everything / everyone is dear') is used in daily life[22]: "And in daily life the use of this word *priyaviśvāya* is observed."

Bhartṛhari also explicitly states that grammar follows existing usage[23]: "since the science of grammar is dependent upon usage, there are only persons (viz., the different grammarians) who record the usages well known in the world; there are no persons who [newly] establish connections [between words and meanings]." This view he contrasts with another view—about which he is less enthusiastic—according to wich grammarians would create words in the sense of a certain meaning.

3.2.4 There is, therefore, sufficient evidence that the Sanskrit grammarians themselves regarded the language described by them as one which is, at least in certain circles, generally known and actually used. There was, in their view, 'grammar-independent usage' of the language they described and discussed. References from other sources than the grammarians suggest that there was at least some basis for their view. This situation corresponds to that of the Greek grammarians who, according to Versteegh, regarded their language as 'something living'—although in the present article we have rejected the 'living-or-dead' terminology, a corollary of the outdated metaphor of language as a biological organism, as misleading.

3.3 The second point mentioned by Versteegh (see section 2.1) is that "it is precisely typical of this kind of speech community that the 'dead' standard continues to exercize its influence on the spoken varieties." Also in the case of Sanskrit it seems natural to accept that there was an important influence which it continued to have, even or especially in its somewhat fossilized form, on the vernaculars. There are obvious reasons why it is impossible to have direct access to this influence: there are no direct records of the vernaculars, and even to the extent we have reflections of the vernaculars in Middle Indo-Aryan and 'mixed' or 'hybrid' sources, it is difficult to separate sanskritizations of the vernacular from vernacularizations of Sanskrit. Nevertheless, it is worth

---

[22] *loke cāyaṁ śabdo dṛṣṭaprayogaḥ priyaviśvāyeti* (MBhD 6a:23.6).

[23] *prayogatantratvāt śāstrasya, lokaprasiddhaprayogāṇāṁ smartāraḥ kevalaṁ bhavanti, nābhisaṁbanddhāraḥ* (MBhD 6b:36.4-5) [emend ms *-saṁbaṁdhadvāra* with AL 260.7 to *-saṁbanddhāra* rather than to the *-saṁbandhāra* of the editors of MBhD 6b].

mentioning that developments in the direction of the norm of Sanskrit may be detected in the so-called 'Buddhist Hybrid Sanskrit' (cf. von Hinüber 1989). Moreover, the great number of Sanskritic words in the Dravidian languages in South India can be taken as evidence for the influence of Sanskrit on the vernaculars. Besides, there is this parallel kind of evidence which points quite convincingly to the active use of Sanskrit, viz. the already mentioned hyper-sanskritisms (above, section 2.4) within what is accepted or supposed to be correct Sanskrit.

3.4 Also the third point mentioned by Versteegh seems to apply to Sanskrit: as a standard language it functions as the common language, while the more commonly spoken varieties act as a centrifugal, decentralizing force. This is illustrated by the divergent *deśī*-languages, and it is also reflected in Patañjali's statement that for each correct word there are many degenerate forms. It may have been a factor contributing to the gradually increasing use of Sanskrit in the Buddhist and Jaina tradition after an initial period in which other languages were preferred. Even if the usefulness of Sanskrit have not been the initial motivation to adopt Sanskrit in the firt place, it may have reinforced the new situation once it had arisen.

A point which deserves further study (and one emphasized by Pollock in his contribution to the present volume) is that Sanskrit is different from the languages compared by Versteegh in that its spread is neither connected with a single religion (as in the case of Arabic), nor with a well-defined political unit (Greek since Alexander the Great, Latin in the Roman empire).

3.5 Some additional points of interest are the following: First, Versteegh suggests that there is an intimate connection between the diglossic language situation and the increase in the number of new speakers of Greek after the conquests of Alexander the Great. According to Versteegh, "the diglossia commonly accepted for the later and the modern period [ref. to modern Greek as one of the defining languages of Ferguson, J.H.] was already present right after the Alexandrian conquests" (Versteegh 1986:443). This diglossia was an inherent feature of the expansion of the Attic dialect of Greek accross the new empire (accross the *oikoumenè*) (Versteegh 1986:443). Although the precise conditions under which it happens are not known to us, Old Indo-Aryan and Sanskrit in particular have also expanded their domain to considerable numbers of new speakers in different periods of the history. If we skip for now the early prehistoric periods in which Indo-Aryan spread to large numbers of new speakers who first became bilingual and later on gave up their original language (following the model proposed by Allchin, 1995:330), we see that especially in the time when the use of Sanskrit increased among the Buddhists and Jainas (early centuries of this millennium) there must have been a considerable expansion of the number of Sanskrit users. Testimonies of Chinese Buddhist pilgrims show that Sanskrit was widely used, not only in a great number of texts but apparently also in discussions. The background and precise circumstances of the shift of the Buddhists and Jainas to Sanskrit (especially the Buddhists seem to have made it accessible to large numbers of new speakers) and its importance for the development of this language as a 'lingua franca' at least in the sphere of intellectual and religious discussions have not yet received sufficient attention.

3.6 Second, while there must indeed have been some basis in reality for the grammarians' references to the usage of the high standard, in the sense that there was a limited number of people who employed the superposed variety in various contexts, it is to be expected that the picture presented by the grammarians is greatly unbalanced in that the common colloquial is almost entirely neglected. According to Versteegh, "it is typical of diglottic speech communities that grammarians who are confronted with a high and a low variety tend to disregard completely the colloquial and to concentrate exclusively on the standard variety. One might even say that for grammarians working in such a speech community the colloquial does not exist." (Versteegh 1986:436, cf. 446 n 9). In order to be able to make a knowledgable use of the evidence provided by the grammarians, it is important to be well aware of this tendency of the grammarian's perspective to distort the data in a certain direction. This point can also be illustrated by the situation of the defining languages of Ferguson, who states that

> In all the defining languages the speakers regard H as superior to L in a number of respects. Sometimes the feeling is so strong that H alone is regarded as real and L is reported 'not to exist'. . . Very often, educated Arabs will maintain that they never use L at all, in spite of the fact that direct observation shows that they use it constantly in all ordinary conversation. Similarly, educated speakers of Haitian Creole frequently deny its existence, insisting that they always speak French. This attitude

> cannot be called a deliberate attempt to deceive the questioner, but seems almost a self-deception. (Ferguson 1959:329-330)

It is likewise to be expected that the references of Sanskrit grammarians to the usage of correct Sanskrit are not without basis, but that, on the other hand, these references reflect a very selective perception of the linguistic situation.

3.7 Third, there are important implications for 'historical developments' in languages and varieties involved in a situation of 'classical diglossia'. It is perhaps expedient to quote briefly some of the observations of Versteegh with regard to the period in the development of Greek which is usually called koiné-Greek or post-classical Greek (from the time of Alexander the Great onward):

> It is thus possible to distinguish various levels in post-Classical texts, not as discrete varieties of the language but as more or less successful approximations of the standard of High Attic. . . . [T]he post-Classical period is thus characterized by the existence of a linguistic continuum between the lowest form of popular speech—be it mother tongue or second language—and High Attic literary language. . . . The Greek continuum was, thus, alive in the sense that there was a large amount of mobility along the scale, while the extreme ends of the scale did not change their structure. . . . Apart from the degree of knowledge of the standard language, there is another factor that determined the nature of written texts in the post-Classical period, namely that of the attitudes within the community towards the required correctness of written texts. . . At the beginning, there had been a leniency *vis-à-vis* the use of colloquialisms in writing . . . In the course of the centuries it became . . . fashionable, on the one hand, to avoid colloquialisms, and on the other hand, to imitate the literary models of Classical Attic culture. . . . This means that the structure of the written language cannot be used for a chronology of the development of the language: the changes in written texts only reflect the changes in the attitude towards the standard norm and not the changes in the language itself. (428-429). In a diglottic community, the standard language—the high variety—is not only used in written speech, but also in formal oral contexts. In spite of the fact that the colloquial is everyone's mother tongue, the social elite tend to use a colloquial mixed with elements and phrases from the high variety, or even an approximate version of the high variety. As long as this spoken form of the standard language was not identifiable with the 'real' colloquial, as long as it did not violate the rules of the language, most grammarians felt that it was not unreasonable to use it in their analysis of the language. In this way they believed they could meet the requirement of empirical observation that had become of paramount

> importance in every branch of Greek scholarship: they did observe the living language, at least in their own eyes. (436)

In spite of the fact that the historical (socio-political) circumstances of Sanskrit were quite different from those of Hellenic Greek, much of what is said by Versteegh would seem to apply to Sanskrit as well. If we think carefully through the implications of the classical diglossia of Sanskrit we have to arrive at the conclusion that it is misleading to ask for a historical development in the language, at least if the development is understood as a linear process which leads from one stage to the next and to subsequent stages. Indeed, as long as there is a generally accepted standard which is sufficiently defined by grammars and/or a collection of (classical) texts or a 'canon', it is possible for later generations to 'return' to archaic usages which had become obsolete for some time. As long as the standard remains valid and available, shifts in the usages of the normative speakers cannot lead to distinct and stable stages in a linear development. At the most, one can speak of trends within the standard or varying deviations from the standard. Some of these trends, such as the preference for past passive participles instead of verbal forms for the past tense (end of section 3.2.2), proved to be quite persistent in the literature from Patañjali and the epics onwards. It is true that such trends should not be mistaken as indications for a spoken use of the language by 'native speakers' (Joshi & Roodbergen 1986:135), but they do point to an active use of the language by speakers preferring the easier participle-forms to the verbal forms.

3.8 On the basis of these parallels and in accordance with the Uniformitarian Principle, I would like to propose to consider the language situation of Sanskrit and its relation with non-Sanskrit roughly characterizable as a situation of classical diglossia. The value of this approach may be illustrated with reference to a recent evaluation of the position of Sanskrit in which no use is made of the concept of diglossia. Joshi and Roodbergen (1991:14) contrast "a spoken language learnt at home as one's native tongue" with "a spoken language learnt at school, but not necessarily used at home also." Comparing Pāṇinian and post-Pāṇinian Sanskrit with Latin in Europe throughout the Middle Ages, they consider Sanskrit "a language forcefully kept alive by an equally forceful institution, the school":

> This must also have been the language which Pāṇini, naturally basing himself upon the usage of the *śiṣṭas*, codified and fixed once for all, to be transmitted, again, by the school. We therefore are in complete agreement with J. Wackernagel (1896, Einleitung, p. xxii), who nearly 100 years ago expressed the view that already in Vedic times Sanskrit was not a natural language any more, but a caste language transmitted by the school ("keine naturwüchsige Sprache . . . sondern eine schulmässig vererbte Standessprache"). (Joshi & Roodbergen 1991:14-15).

Joshi and Roodbergen rightly emphasize that the system of education [24] is an important factor in the continuation of Sanskrit, as it is in the continuation of other high varieties in a diglossic situation. One may doubt, however, to what extent one can justifiably contrast a 'natural' language spoken at home and a 'language forcefully kept alive' in Pāṇini's time, if the high variety was to be called *saṁskṛta* 'polished' (the 'polishing' must take place on the basis of a 'natural' language learned at home) in subsequent periods. [25] It is likely that there was more continuity and mutual understandability of the different varieties than Joshi and Roodbergen are ready to admit. When only the contrast is emphasized (following Wackernagel's judgment of 1896), the dynamic relation between the two, indications for which have been pointed out in the preceding sections, disappear entirely out of the picture and we are left with an unsatisfactory model for evaluating descriptions and statements of Pāṇini and later grammarians in the context of early South Asian languages and social relations.

An important point concerning the 'classical diglossia' which here pertains is that, from the point of view of the grammarians and other Sanskrit authors, the main contrast is that between correct Sanskrit and non-Sanskrit. In between there are various degrees of correctness of

---

[24] The terms 'institution' and 'school may be somewhat misleading: the Brahminical system of education, to a considerable extent taking place in a private sphere, had little to do with public institutions and schools as we know them in our society. Moreover, once Buddhism and Jainism start to use Sanskrit on a larger scale, it is no longer entirely dependent on the Brahminical system of education.

[25] The terminology is as much objectionable as the 'dead-or-alive' terminology which we rejected in section 3.2. Once language is primarily seen as a social phenomenon, there is little reason to consider the variety preferably spoken in the private sphere as more 'natural' than the variety preferably spoken in the public and ritual sphere.

Sanskrit. Contrasts important to modern linguistics like that between Indo-Aryan, Dravidian and other language families in South Asia were rarely made and apparently rarely perceived.[26] Centuries of mutual influence between Sanskrit (Old Indo-Aryan) and local languages (cf. section 3.3 and, elsewhere in this volume, Hock on the importance of convergence) have also reduced the contrasts between languages which seem to have quite diverging genetic backgrounds. One may therefore wonder to what extent it is useful for someone dealing with Sanskrit in the Indian linguistic area to stick to Ferguson's requirement for diglossia that it should obtain between varieties of one language or between genetically related varieties. What seems crucial in the case of Sanskrit is that the languages or varieties are *felt* to be related, but that nevertheless the high variety is not for everyone equally accessible. This would justify an approach like that of Fishman or a modified model based on Ferguson (section 2.6). The diglossia would then not depend on a question like: "are these different languages or rather different varieties of one single language?" a question often extremely difficult to answer on purely linguistic grounds in a situation of long-standing language-contacts, and irrelevant when speaking subjects do consider the varieties and languages related, probably partly mutually understandable, and experience nevertheless a certain distance between the two. Even though we have to be careful in taking the grammarians' testimony seriously because their perception of the linguistic reality is likely to be significantly distorted, we need not go to the other extreme and say that diglossia exists *only* in the perception of the grammarians, something Deshpande seems to have suggested when contrasting their view with

---

[26] Dravidian as a local or deśī-language was of course recognized, e.g. in the VP Vṛtti on VP 1.153 (VP I:210.1). The term *mleccha* 'foreign, foreigner' has been used also with regard to language by Patañjali and in Mīmāṁsā, but it may very well refer to someone speaking an Indo-Aryan language (though not Sanskrit), e.g. in the well-known passage in the MBh (Paspaśāḥnika) on the purposes of grammar (MBh 1:2.7-9). Here, *apaśabda* is even explicitly characterized as *mleccha* (*mleccho ha vā eṣa yad apaśabdaḥ | mlecchā mā bhūmety adhyeyaṁ vyākaraṇam*).

the modern perception that Sanskrit and Prakrit are indeed different languages.[27]

4. Bhartṛhari on the relation between Sanskrit and non-Sanskrit

4.1 The ground is now prepared for a closer study of the statements in Bhartṛhari's work concerning the relation between Sanskrit and non-Sanskrit. The most elaborate passage occurs at the end of the first book (VP 1.175-183). In the first part of this passage (VP 1.175-180), Bhartṛhari defines 'degenerate' (*apabhraṁśa* 'substandard' or 'incorrect') forms.

175. *śabdaḥ saṁskārahīno yo gaur iti prayuyukṣyate |*
tam apabhraṁśam icchanti viśiṣṭārthaniveśinam ||
176. *asvagoṇyādayaḥ śabdāḥ sādhavo viṣayāntare |*
nimittabhedāt sarvatra sādhutvaṁ ca vyavasthitam ||
177. *te sādhuṣv anumānena pratyayotpattihetavaḥ |*
tādātmyam upagamyeva śabdārthasya prakāśakāḥ ||
178. *na śiṣṭair anugamyante paryāyā iva sādhavaḥ |*
te yataḥ smṛtiśāstreṇa tasmāt sākṣād avācakāḥ ||
179. *aṁbvaṁbv iti yathā bālaḥ śikṣamāṇo 'pabhāṣate |*
avyaktaṁ tadvidāṁ tena vyaktau bhavati niścayaḥ ||
180. *evaṁ sādhau prayoktavye yo 'pabhraṁśaḥ prayujyate |*
tena sādhuvyavahitaḥ kaś cid artho 'bhidhīyate ||

175. The word, lacking correct formation, which was intended to be employed as [the word] *gauḥ* 'cow', is considered a substandard word (*apabhraṁśa*) with regard to [that] specific meaning.
176. The words *asva, goṇī* etc. (while they are incorrect if they are intended as *aśva* 'horse', and *gauḥ* 'cow') are correct in another field (namely, if used to express 'having no wealth' and 'receptacle' respectively). And it is on the basis of the different grounds [to employ the words] that [their] correctness is determined.
177. They (words such as *asva, goṇī* etc. which are incorrect if intended as *aśva* 'horse', and *gauḥ* 'cow') are the causes of the production of a cognition with regard to the [corresponding] correct words; becoming as if identical [with it] they reveal the meaning of the correct word.

---

[27] The fluency of the boundary between language and (related) dialect becomes clear in Bourdieu 1991 (e.g. p. 45-49), who points out the importance of non-linguistic, external factors, especially political ones.

178. As they are not accepted as correct synonyms by the well-educated,[28] they are according to the traditional composed text (*smṛti-śāstra*) not directly significative.

179. Just as a child which is learning pronounces incorrectly an indistinct *aṁbu, aṁbu*[29]—through this those who know it get a clear idea of the [corresponding] distinct term—

180. like that the incorrect word, employed instead of the correct one to be employed, expresses, through the intervention of a correct word, one meaning or the other.

It is seen that there are three factors which decide that a word is an incorrect one (*apabhraṁśa*): (1) that the formation of the word is not correct (*saṁskārahīna*); and (2) that there was a wish to pronounce the word correctly (*prayuyukṣyate*); and this (3) with regard to a certain intended meaning (*viśiṣṭārthaniveśin*). If such an incorrect word is pronounced, the one who hears it infers first which correct word was intended by the speaker, and understands the meaning from this inferred word. However, in its incorrect form the word may be similar to a word which would be correct in a different context. So from an incorrect word one meaning or the other may be understood through inference. In this situation, Sanskrit is the target, and the degree of realization, indeed, the degree of the capacity to realize the target, is variable.

From the example of the child pronouncing the word for 'mother' (or 'water'?) incorrectly, one would infer that, in Bhartṛhari's perception, the distinction correct - incorrect pertains also to children's speech and the understanding of it. Since the utterance of the child is considered an incorrect realization of the standard, it follows that some conti-

---

[28] As briefly pointed out elsewhere (Houben 1995a: 238 n 372), it can be agreed with Deshpande 1993d that in VP 1.29, 43, 172, perhaps 27 and 158, the expression *śiṣṭas* seems to refer to the authors of traditonal grammatical texts; but in 3.13.21, 3.14.79 they can hardly be such authors, but are rather contemporary 'well-educated' persons (to whom special faculties are ascribed in 3.13.21).

[29] The readings in the kārikā vary from *aṁbvaṁbviti* to *aṁbāṁbeti*. According to the later commentator Vṛṣabhadeva (VP I:232.13f) the reference is to the children's pronounciation of *ambā, ambā* 'mother, mother'. One would here rather expect the vocative *amba, amba* (for the form, cf. P 7.3.107, Wackernagel 1896:6, Debrunner & Wackernagel 1930:121-123). With the objectively strong reading *aṁbvaṁbviti* adopted by Rau it may still be the literal quotation of the incorrect pronounciation for *ambā* or *amba*, although one might also interpret the statement as a reference to an incorrect pronounciation of the word *ambu* 'water'.

nuity is assumed between the speech of the child and the finally correct way of speaking. Children do not first learn one language at home and a different one 'at school'.

4.2 Next, Bhartṛhari discusses a different situation, in which speakers of substandard forms no more attempt to use the standard forms. The reference to this situation is followed by a few statements on the status of Sanskrit, which seem to represent different and even competing viewpoints (VP 1.181-183):

181. *pāramparyād apabhraṁśā viguṇeṣv abhidhātṛṣu /*
prasiddhim āgatā yena teṣāṁ sādhur avācakaḥ //
182. *daivī vāg vyatikīrṇeyam aśaktair abhidhātṛbhiḥ /*
anityadarśināṁ tv asmin vāde buddhiviparyayaḥ //
183. *ubhayeṣām avicchedād anyaśabdavivakṣayā /*
yo 'nyaḥ prayujyate śabdo na so 'rthasyābhidhāyakaḥ //

A straightforward translation would be:

181. Among those who do not speak correctly, the incorrect words have by force of tradition gained general acceptance, so that for them the correct word is not expressive.
182. Divine speech is nowadays (*iyam*) mixed up by incompetent speakers. But those who propound the impermanent have with regard to this doctrine an opposite view.[30]
183. Because there is no interruption for both groups, if one word is used with the intention to use another, then this word does not express the (intended) meaning.

In an article devoted to Bhartṛhari's perspectivism, i.e. his tendency to accept the validity of different perspectives (Houben forthc.), I pointed out that

> The usual interpretation, as explained for instance in Iyer's "Bhartṛhari on Apabhraṁśa" (Iyer 1964; cf. Iyer 1969:59-60), is that in this passage Bhartṛhari sets forth his view of the 'divine speech' which has become corrupted and that he refutes an opposite view according to which the corrupt forms precede the correct form which are the work

[30] Though the word *viparyaya* may mean 'misapprehension, error, mistake', its basic and neutral meaning 'opposite' is more likely here. At other places in the verses where Bhartṛhari uses the word it usually means 'opposite, change, shift' (e.g. VP 1.75; 2.306, 389, 436; 3.6.8, 19; 3.7.120 etc.), only in the specific context of VP 3.3.52 and 59 it refers to an epistemological distortion in the relation between language, thought and reality. Monier-Williams' Sanskrit-English dictionary mentions the compound *buddhivbiparyaya* explicitly in the sense 'opposite opinion' s.v. *viparyaya*.

> of grammarians (cf. also Tripathi 1986:86-88; Sharma 1977:236-237[30a]). Moreover, even if a period in which the 'divine speech' is not corrupted is not accepted, it is to be admitted that only the correct word is directly expressive of a meaning (Iyer 1964:246).

This usual interpretation, however, gives an inaccurate picture of what Bhartṛhari said in these verses. As I argued in the above mentioned article, the statements in the VP 1.182-183 should be taken as references to either two or three different views or perspectives, to none of which Bhartṛhari is exlusively committed. What I will try to do at this place is to contextualize the three perspectives which I identified in the mentioned article (cf. also Houben 1994a:3-7), and to try to understand them in the light of the concept of 'classical diglossia'.

4.3 Perspective A: The first perspective is stated in the first line of 1.182 as follows: "Divine speech is nowadays (*iyam*) mixed up by incompetent speakers." On the basis of this statement and the discussion in the other verses from 1.175 onwards, keeping in mind, moreover, the concept of diglossia and its general applicability in early South Asia (section 3.8), we may say the following with regard to this perspective: (1) There is a clear recognition of the high standard (VP 1.175-180), this standard is even deified (VP 1.182ab). (2) There is a recognition of the existence of substandard forms (VP 1.175-180). (3) There is no reference to a discrete low variety or a distinct 'language' apart from the generally accepted standard. There are only imperfectly realized 'correct' words. The closest one comes to accepting such a discrete variety is when the substandard forms are accepted as having become well-established in some communities (VP 1.181). (4) The almost total neglect (in the many verses devoted to perspective A) of the (or *a*) low variety (which must have been used quite widely) as a discrete variety is typical for the *perception* of a situation of diglossia by speakers of the high variety (above, section 3.6). (5) The omnipresence of the high standard, and added to this its 'deification' in the first line of 1.182, can be understood as a 'naturalization' of the standard (to the notion of 'naturalization' I will return below).

4.4 Perspective B is the opposite of perspective A. This is all we get about the contents of this view from the second line of VP 1.182, which attributes this view to "those who propound the impermanent." The

---

[30a] Also Kumar 1989 finally sticks to this interpretation.

Vṛtti, the oldest commentary on the VP, provides some further information on this view[31]:

> But those who propound the impermanent, who do not accept that correct words lead to *dharma* 'merit', (and who) consider the established fixity of correct forms to be similar to the conventions among wrestlers, say that the collection of correct [here: Prakrit (!)] words is *prākṛta* in the sense of 'being in the *prakṛti*, i.e. in the basis'. But later on a changed form [namely, Sanskrit] has been established, which was arrived at through accentuation and phonological and morphological modification (*svara-saṁskāra*) by persons with impaired understanding.

The view as stated here, comparable with some partly parallel statements in the MBhD (1:16.28-19) and in a passage in the work of the Jaina author Namisādhu, seems to be most suitable to a Jaina or, somewhat less likely, to a Buddhist context (cf. Houben 1994a:3-7; Bronkhorst 1993a). The Jainas, as well known, cherished a different Indo-Aryan language as the language of their scriptures, viz. the prakritic Ardhamāgadhī. Also the Buddhists (at least most of the early schools) cherished other languages (or varieties) than Sanskrit, but they did not use the term *prākṛta* to refer to their language as the Jainas did. On the other hand, the Buddhists would suit the label "those who propound the impermanent" (used in the verse) better than the Jainas (the latter hold that real entities must have both permanent and impermanent aspects, Tattvārthasūtra 5.29). In any case, the second perspective seems to imply that not Sanskrit is the basis of Prakrit (the latter being an imperfect form of the former), but that Prakrit is the basis of Sanskrit (the latter being an artificial modification of the former). What I call conveniently 'Prakrit' here following the Vṛtti's *prākṛta*, may include all kinds of spoken and written prakritic languages and varieties (for which cf. von Hinüber 1986), perhaps including those we would consider non-Indo-aryan. The 'cherishing of a language variety' by the Jainas and Buddhists did not lead to such detailed well-established systematic

---

[31] *anityavādinas tu ye sādhūnāṁ dharmahetutvaṁ na pratipadyante, mallasamayādi-sadṛśīṁ sādhuvyavasthāṁ manyante, te prakṛtau bhavaṁ prākṛtaṁ sādhūnāṁ śabdānāṁ samūham ācakṣate / vikāras tu paścād vyavasthāpitaḥ, yaḥ saṁbhinnabhuddhibhiḥ puruṣaiḥ svarasaṁskārādibhir nirṇīyate iti.* (VP I:234.2-5)

regulations as the cherishing and cultivation of Sanskrit by—mainly—Brahminical authors.

In spite of the difficulties in interpreting this perspective and in identifying those who propounded it, the following remarks can be made: (1) There is a recognition of the high standard, which, however, is not 'deified' or 'naturalized' as in perspective A. (2) The high standard is considered to be based on rather arbitrary conventions of persons who are not very much esteemed. (3) The so-called substandard forms of perspective A (the Prakrit forms) are considered to be 'correct' and basic to the 'modified' forms (the Sanskrit forms). (4) The view, which suits other early references to Prakrit, is only referred to but not explicitly rejected by Bhartṛhari.

4.5 Perspective C. The statement in the last verse (VP 1.183) is not a new elaboration of perspective A (as was held by other scholars), but it implies a relativization of the opposition between the two perspectives mentioned in verse 1.182. It is not clear whether Bhartṛhari refers here to an existing view (as suggested in the Vṛtti), or whether he states an observation of his own on the opposition. For convenience's sake we will speak of a 'third perspective', although it is not clear by which persons it was held in the form it was stated by Bhartṛhari.

Elsewhere (Houben forthc.) I explained that 'groups' in the expression "no interruption for both groups" (*ubhayeṣām avicchedād*) in 1.183 may refer either to the two groups of thinkers, viz. those who propound the permanent and those who propound the impermanent, or to the two groups of linguistic forms, Sanskrit and Prakrit. In either case, 'no interruption' seems to imply that there is no interruption in the tradition of words. What is said, therefore, amounts to the following:

If someone wants to pronounce a Sanskrit word and uses instead a Prakrit one, the word is not directly expressive of the intended meaning. Moreover—and this implication was neglected by most later interpreters of this verse—if someone wants to pronounce a Prakrit word and uses instead a Sanskrit one,[32] this word is not directly expressive of

[32] One may think of various reasons a Sanskrit speaker experienced difficulties when attempting to speak correct Prakrit words. His background may have been in one local language while he tries to speak in another local language. Or some of the Prakrits were already so much cultivated that they had become distant from the mother tongue of potential speakers.

the intended meaning either. Both the Sanskrit and the Prakrit forms have a continuous tradition.

The Vṛtti on this verse attributes this view to a group of thinkers who denied the occurrence of 'cosmic cycles'—a description which would suit the Mīmāṁsakas, whose view on correct and substandard forms would also be, at least partly, in accordance with the statement in the Vṛtti (cf. ŚBh on MīS 1.3.10, 24-29). The opposite view, held by the Naiyāyikas among others, is that the world originates at the beginning and disappears at the end of countless time-cycles. On crucial moments Bhartṛhari seems to remain non-committal to these two opposed views (Houben forthc.).

Here we will not attempt to arrive at a precise identification of those holding the view, as this is greatly hindered, first, by our lack of knowledge of the precise Mīmāṁsā-sources which were available in Bhartṛhari's time; second, by the divergence between the explanation in the Vṛtti and what seems to be Bhartṛhari's intention in this verse. Before turning to this divergence, we will summarize our conclusions so far.

4.6 What we find reflected in VP 1.181-183 if we contextualize it in a mainly Sanskritic milieu in the 4th or 5th century (North) India, is: (1) one single language situation which may be roughly characterized as 'classical diglossia'; (2) three different perspectives on this language situation.

Perspective A (VP 1.175-181, 182ab) is the perspective of the Sanskrit grammarians and the well-educated élite, according to which the entire linguistic field can be described with the opposition correct-incorrect, and which tends to 'naturalize' or even to 'deify' the cultivated standard language.

Perpsective B (VP 1.182cd) is the 'subversive' perspective of those who cultivate a variety which contains forms considered substandard in perspective A. The naturalization and deification of the standard according to perspective A is rejected. Perspective B seems to be parallel with perspective A in that both accept that Sanskrit forms are somehow more cultivated and regulated, while the Prakrit forms are less cultivated and regulated. However, the increased cultivation and regulation, c.q. the absence of these, are valuated quite differently.

Perspective C as stated in 1.183 implies a recognition as well as a relativization of the two opposed perspectives A and B.

If we apply Bhartṛhari's non-committal attitude as attested elsewhere to this situation, we would expect him to consider perspectives A and C quite acceptable, and perspective B, though less interesting for him as a Sanskrit grammarian, as a viewpoint to be recognized.

5. Later grammarians on the relation between Sanskrit and non-Sanskrit

5.1 We will now briefly discuss some variations in perspective A, as they can be found in the statements of grammarians after Bhartṛhari (commentators on the VP and on the MBh). As I pointed out above, there is a subtle yet not unimportant difference between the Vṛtti and the statements in the VP-verses regarding the capacity of the substandard words to express a meaning.[33] In the Vṛtti on 183 we find a strong denial that generally accepted 'substandard' words can ever be *vācaka*, 'directly expressive of meaning'[34]:

> Here, the generally accepted (*rūḍhaḥ*) word and the not generally accepted (*na rūḍhaḥ*) word which is applied to meanings while another word is intended, as in the case of the talk of children, neither of these two is expressive of the meaning (*arthasya na vācakau bhavataḥ*). But in their case there is either understanding of the meaning through the medium of the (corresponding) correct word, or there arises merely an idea (of the intention) on account of the habit of careless people like from the winking of the eye etc.

---

[33] On the basis of this and some other indications which I plan to discuss in a separate article I think that the ancient Vṛtti on books 1 and 2 of the VP is not from the hand of Bhartṛhari but was written by someone closely related to him (e.g. his pupil). If one wants to maintain nevertheless the traditional view that the Vṛtti is written by Bhartṛhari it will be necessary to account for the diverging trends in the verses and the Vṛtti in one way or the other, for instance by assuming that it was Bhartṛhari's attitude itself which evolved over time.

[34] *tatrānyaśabdavivakṣayā bālapralāpavad artheṣu prayujyamāno yaḥ śabdo rūḍho yaś ca na rūḍhas tāv ubhāv apy arthasya na vācakau bhavataḥ / tatra tu sādhuvyavahitā vā bhavaty arthapratipattir abhyāsād vā pramattānām akṣinikocādivat saṁpratyayamātraṁ jāyate //* (VP I:235.3-5).

This denial of the capacity of generally accepted substandard words to express meaning directly has no support in the kārikā commented upon. It is, moreover, in disaccord with other statements in the VP: not only does VP 1.181 (discussed above) suggest that direct expressiveness of the 'generally accepted substandard word' is acknowledged, there are two other statements which do the same in most explicit terms: VP 1.27cd[35] says: "While there is no difference [between correct and substandard words] in expressing the meaning, substandard words are the opposite (i.e., not a means towards merit (*dharma*))." And according to VP 3.3.30cd[36]: "Or, while there is no difference [between correct and substandard words] in being expressive, a restriction is made concerning merit and demerit." With these statements, Bhartṛhari is on the same line as his predecessor Patañjali who remarked in the MBh[37]: "While the understanding of meaning is similar through a correct and a substandard word, there is a restriction regarding *dharma* (i.e. merit and demerit)" (MBh 1:8.21) Also in the MBhD, the commentary on the MBh attributed to Bhartṛhari, it is accepted that as far as the expression of meaning is concerned, the substandard word is not different from the correct word, the only difference being that the latter leads in addition to *abhyudaya* 'elevation'.[38]

The idea is, therefore, that both the word which meets the grammatical standard and the one which is substandard are equal in their capacity to express a meaning. The difference between the two is that the grammatically correct form leads in addition to 'merit' or 'elevation', whereas the substandard form does not do so. If the rules of grammar are followed one is restricted to the use of correct forms only and avoids an involuntary use of substandard forms.

The Vṛtti, however, not only holds that only the use of the correct high standard form leads to 'merit', it also holds that it is only and exclusively the correct high standard form which is *directly* expressive of meaning. The 'incorrect' substandard forms are not directly expressive of meaning, but they make something known in an inferior way, "like

---

[35] *arthapratyāyanābhede viparītās tv asādhavaḥ.*

[36] *vācakatvāviśeṣe vā niyamaḥ puṇyapāpayoḥ.*

[37] *samānāyām arthagatau śabdena cāpaśabdena ca dharmaniyamaḥ kriyate.*

[38] Cf. MBhD 1:26.13-14; 27.4-6. At the same time, the MBhD mentions a view according to which incorrect words do not express their meaning: MBhD 1:10.14-15.

from the winking of the eye etc." The Vṛtti is rather persistent in its refusal to recognize direct expressiveness of substandard forms, as is clear from its comments on VP 1.181 and VP 1.27, where clear starting points in the verse for the acceptance of direct expressiveness are entirely neglected.

5.2 For an understanding of the difference between the Vṛtti and Bhartṛhari I would like to have recourse to the notion of 'naturalization' as it has been used in writings on power and ideology, as for instance in Bourdieu's *Outline of a theory of practice*: "every established order tends to produce (to very different degrees with different means) the naturalization of its own arbitrariness" (Bourdieu 1977:164; cf. also Briggs 1992). This notion can be applied fruitfully to attempts to justify the well-established arbitrariness of linguistic signs (cf. Saussure 1916:100ff) as well. In this light, (a) the thesis that grammatically correct words lead to merit and that substandard forms do not; (b) the thesis that, even if substandard forms have become well-established in certain circles, only grammatically correct words express their meaning directly unlike these substandard forms; (c) the deification of the high standard language which was perfect in the distant past and which has become contaminated in the present; can all be seen as attempts to naturalize the arbitrariness of the high standard language. From this point of view, Bhartṛhari would naturalize the arbitrariness of Sanskrit in accordance with his predecessor Patañjali (reflected in perspective A), but he also relativizes it to some extent by mentioning the opposite view (perspective B) without refuting it. The Vṛtti, however, is much more committed to this naturalization which had already become traditional (at least in certain circles) in Bhartṛhari's time. While Bhartṛhari accepts thesis (a) and (c), leaving some room for their relativization, the author of the Vṛtti is less ready to relativize these two, and is moreover convinced of thesis (b) which has no support from Bhartṛhari.

5.3 Also later grammarians show a variation in the degree and way the Sanskrit language is naturalized. Their own view can usually be inferred only indirectly, as their works are mostly commentaries and explanations of the older, authoritative grammarians (Pāṇini, Patañjali, Bhartṛhari).

Helārāja, a Kashmiri author from ca. the 10th century CE, wrote a commentary on the third book of the VP which is the oldest available commentary on this voluminous book. Commenting on VP 3.3.30cd (discussed above), Helārāja avoids the straightforward interpretation which would accept equal capacity to express meaning in the grammatically correct and the substandard form, and interprets the passage in accordance with the Vṛtti (which Helārāja holds to be the work of Bhartṛhari, the author of the verses). Helārāja also cites the passage in the MBh which says that both forms are equal in expressing their meaning, but he finds a way to interpret it as a statement that the substandard form expresses its meaning in an inferior way (cf. discussion of this kārikā in Houben 1995a:241-242).

Among the later grammarians in the Pāṇinian tradition, Kaiyaṭa (early 11th century?) is in accordance with the interpretation of the Vṛtti and Helārāja in his interpretation of MBh 1:8.21: "While the understanding of meaning is similar through a correct and a substandard word . . . " (see above, note 36) when he suggests that substandard words do convey some meaning when they have become well-established in some circles, but that they are not directly expressive like the correct words; but he also refers to a view of 'others' who hold that substandard words may be equally expressive as the correct words (Kaiyaṭa in Paspaśāhnika, MBh (S): 1:58.9-14). The reason why in the first and apparently preferred view of Kaiyaṭa the expressive capacity of the substandard word is different from that of the grammatically correct one is spelled out by Nāgeśa (18th century): in the case of the former a 'confusion of expressive power' (*śaktibhrama*) has occurred: through wrong usage a form like *gāvī* has become associated with the meaning 'cow', although only the word *go* was originally furnished with the power to express the idea 'cow'.

According to Nāgeśa's own view, however, as expressed in his Vaiyākaraṇasiddhānta-mañjūṣā, the established grammarians' view of Patañjali and Bhartṛhari is that substandard words may be equally expressive as correct words.[39] In this respect he is on the same line as the grammarian Kauṇḍabhaṭṭa (17th century), author of the Vai-

[39] Vaiyākaraṇasiddhānta-mañjūṣā, Sabhāpati-edition, p. 54: *sā ca śaktiḥ sādhuṣv ivāpabhraṁśeṣv api, śaktigrāhakaśiromaṇer vya[va]hārasya tulyatvāt.*

yākaraṇabhūṣaṇa, an important work on semantics and philosophy of language. In the section devoted to *śakti* 'expressive power (of words and other linguistic forms)', Kauṇḍabhaṭṭa refers to the above cited verses of the VP, and explains that Sanskrit and non-Sanskrit words are equally able to express their meaning [40]: "Just like Sanskrit, each word of the common language is everywhere in the same way directly expressive (*śakta*)." Nevertheless, only the Sanskrit words lead in addition to merit. It is important to note that in Kauṇḍabhaṭṭa's interpretation the 'common language' *bhāṣā*, corresponding to Bhartṛhari's *apabhraṁśa* 'degenerate or substandard language' of VP 1.175-183, refers also to contemporary local languages, as he speaks in the same passage of "the language of Mahārāṣṭra etc." (*mahārāṣṭrādibhāṣā*). [41] This no doubt implies that he considers the discussion of the ancients to be applicable to his own time (probably the first half of the 17th century), in which both Sanskrit and old-Marathi ('language of Mahārāṣṭra') were strong in the area neighbouring his native Ikkeri (cf. Deshpande 1992b:74).

6. Conclusion

The main points arrived at in the preceding discussion are the following.

(1) For evaluating the socio-linguistic position of Sanskrit in ancient South Asia, at least in the northern part of the Indian subcontinent where Sanskrit and its Indo-Aryan (and non-Indo-Aryan) predecessors

---

[40] *saṁskṛtavad bhāṣāyāḥ sarvatraikatvena pratyekaṁ śabdāḥ śaktā eva*, Vaiyākaraṇa-bhūṣaṇa-sāra, Śaktinirṇaya, 218.7-8. The view that only Sanskrit words are directly expressive and non-Sanskrit words not he attributes to the Naiyāyikas, the philosophers of the Nyāya-system. According to Kauṇḍabhaṭṭa's interpretation, "those who propound the impermanent" in VP 1.182 would refer to the Naiyāyikas, which means that he apparently neglected the Vṛtti-explanation about the *prākṛta*-language because the Naiyāyikas have not the slightest affinity with this view.

[41] The views of Kaiyaṭa, Kauṇḍabhaṭṭa and Nāgeśa on the capacity of non-Sanskrit words to express meaning have also been discussed by Sharma (1977:239-249), who considers the view that only Sanskrit words are directly expressive as the final viewpoint of Bhartṛhari and Patañjali, and attempts to interpret the crucial passages (VP 1.175-183, MBh 1:8.21) accordingly. The VP-Vṛtti he considers to be from the hand of Bhartṛhari.

had been strong since early times, the concept of diglossia provides a good starting point, in any case a much better one than the contrast between a 'living' language and a 'dead' or 'artificial' one. A functional approach like that of Fishman or Ferguson's model as adapted by Johnson seems most suitable in the South-Asian linguistic area with long-standing convergence-relations. More specifically, the situation of Sanskrit can be considered to be a case of 'classical diglossia' and a better understanding of this situation can be expected to result from more detailed studies of the position of Sanskrit (in different historical and areal contexts) in comparison with other cases of 'classical diglossia'.

(2) Statements of Bhartṛhari on the relation between Sanskrit and non-Sanskrit, especially VP 1.181-183, have often been interpreted (apparently since the ancient Vṛtti) as asserting the divine status of Sanskrit and the exclusive expressiveness of Sanskrit words. These verses, however, present three perspectives on the linguistic situation of Sanskrit as known to Bhartṛhari, in modern terms characterizable as a case of 'classical diglossia'. Two of the three perspectives must have been quite acceptable to Bhartṛhari. About the third one he was less enthusiastic, though he does not argue against it.

(3) Variations in the views of grammarians since Bhartṛhari on the relation between Sanskrit and non-Sanskrit can be seen as varying ways and degrees of 'naturalizing' the arbitrariness of the high standard language.

Part Two

Transculturation, Sanskritization, Vernacularization

CHAPTER EIGHT

THE SANSKRIT COSMOPOLIS, 300 - 1300: TRANSCULTURATION, VERNACULARIZATION, AND THE QUESTION OF IDEOLOGY

Sheldon Pollock

I.

The 'Sanskrit Cosmopolis' is the name I want to suggest for what may be the most complicated—and as a totality least studied—transregional cultural formation in the premodern world. While 'cosmopolis' might imply a number of things to different readers, it is on the 'polis' or political dimension that I want to concentrate. For one defining feature of the Sanskrit cosmopolis is that Sanskrit became the premiere instrument of political expression in the polities that comprised it, those of most of South and much of Southeast Asia. In part because of its geographical and temporal magnitude, in part because it constitutes something of a historical anomaly, this cultural formation has never been historicized or theorized as a whole, and any attempt to do so is likely to disappoint specialists of the particular formations among which its study has always been parceled out; even the dates I have given for framing the limits of its origin and dissolution may be disputed. But disagreement is inevitable in trying to make sense of this complex, and perplexing, chapter in the history of language and political-cultural power.

A number of factors, discussed in what follows, make Sanskrit's cosmopolitan career remarkable. First, the historical career of Sanskrit: Only slowly and reluctantly, it appears, did Sanskrit emerge as a public political language—such as we can characterize this from inscriptions—from the sacerdotal environment in which it was most at home. It emerges dramatically as such a language in the polities of the subcontinent after the beginning of the common era, something that happens almost simultaneously in Southeast Asia, and in very similar ways, especially with reference to Sanskrit's complicated contests with regional languages. In the end, for the most part by the fourteenth century, Sanskrit lost these contests, and lost them everywhere, but before that happened it was to be found as the paramount linguistic medium by which ruling elites expressed their power from Puruṣapura (Peshawar) in Gandhāra in the northwest of the subcontinent to as far east as Pāṇḍuraṅga in Annam (south Vietnam) and Prambanan in central Java. There are important holes in the cosmopolis—in Sri Lanka, for example, for all of its history, and in Burma for much, Sanskrit is not used to articulate political will—that are almost as hard to explain as the presence of the cosmopolis itself.

Second, the conditions of possibility for Sanskrit's diffusion as a language of politics: No organized political power such as the Roman imperium, or coherent, scripture-based religious idea-system such as Islam, was at work here. Sanskrit's spread was effected by traditional intellectuals and religious professionals, often following in the train of scattered groups of traders and adventurers, and carrying with them disparate and decidedly uncanonized texts of a wide variety of competing religious orders, Śaiva, Buddhist, Vaiṣṇava, and others. Third, its social domain: There is little to suggest—the very fact that we have to ask the question is counterevidence—that Sanskrit was an everyday medium of communication in South let alone Southeast Asia, or that ever functioned as a language-of-trade, a bridge-, link-, or koiné language or lingua franca (except among those traditional intellectuals) like other imperial or cosmopolitan languages such as Greek, Latin, Arabic, Persian, Chinese. Fourth, and related to this, its political work: We have little direct evidence that Sanskrit actually functioned as a language of practical imperium—the medium of chancellery communication or revenue accounting, for example—certainly not in Southeast Asia, almost certainly not in peninsular India or the Deccan (even for north India hard evidence is suspiciously scanty). What work then did Sanskrit do in much of the Sanskrit cosmopolis? One hypothesis I want to explore is that Sanskrit articulated politics not as material power—the power embodied in languages-of-state for purposes of boundary regulation or taxation, for example, for which so-called vernacular idioms typically remained the vehicle—but politics as aesthetic power. To some degree the Sanskrit 'cosmopolis' I shall describe consists precisely in this common aesthetics of political culture, a kind of poetry of politics.

The spread of Sanskrit in the first millennium as a strikingly homogeneous expressive mode of political power, helped create a new kind of vast zone of cultural interaction, what some might name an ecumene. Constituted by no imperial power or church but in large part by a communicative system and its political aesthetic, the Sanskrit ecumene is characterized by a transregionally shared set of assumptions about the basics of power, or at least about the ways in which power is reproduced at the level of representation in language, and Sanskrit's unique suitability for this task. For the thousand-year period between roughly 300 - 1300 C.E., in the repertory of cultural forms in the package of empire, Sanskrit becomes the key item.

What I want to do here, first, is to chart in concrete detail the historical route whereby Sanskrit achieved this status. For this I will look rather briefly at Sanskrit's emergence as a public language of politics around the beginning of the common era; then in greater detail at its diffusion in southern India; and, again briefly, at what happens in two specific domains in Southeast Asia, Khmer country up to the end of Angkor, and early Java. All this is only a preliminary sketch for a reconstruction of the internal political-cultural histories of the polities that make up the Sanskrit cosmopolis—the shared traits that are developed, the nature of its local inflections, and the very variable conditions for its dissolution—which I will not have the space to provide here. I want instead to think aloud about what is important in the Sanskrit cosmopolis for both cultural and political theory. These are the themes, all closely related, of my subtitle: transculturation, vernacularization, and ideology.

Let me characterize briefly what concerns me here, by formulating some research questions: (a) How did the transculturation process at work in the Sanskrit cosmopolis function, that is, what induced people to abandon local cultures, and eventually to re-assert them? Can comparative analysis with other processes of transculturation in antiquity (Romanization, for example) or modernity (American globalization) reveal anything about the specificities of the Sanskrit case? (b) Can we make any valid generalization about the relationships between Sanskrit and vernacular culture especially in terms of political language? What significance should we attach to the later displacement of Sanskrit by vernacular political-cultural production? Can we usefully identify *domains of discourse*—for example, between the performative, 'workly', or expressive domain of language on the one hand, and constative, documentary, or contentual on the other[1]—to get a clearer sense of the work of Sanskrit in the Sanskrit cosmopolis? (c) Finally, can we theorize this process without risking mechanical functionalism and anachronism ('legitimation' being a causal explanation that illustrates both problems)? In a subset of this question I would include others: What role if any are we to attribute to the notion of ideology in its strong formulation (a discourse of false necessity that by systematic distortion naturalizes and reproduces relations of unequal power)? Are there not presuppositions—and unwarranted universalizations of our particulars—about power, conflict, agency, that we have already accepted when we look for 'ideological' effects? Doesn't any operational definition ("I shall take as ideology . . . ") produce immediate closure, inhibiting the production of new theory about society and culture from the empirical matrix? And surely new theorization is precisely what we would require to account for a premodern cultural formation of unprecedented character, and indeed, the reason why we bother to study it at all. This would be the case even if contemporary social theory were unanimous and coherent; it is *a fortiori* so given the disorder, even vacuum, that many have found at its core (e.g., Abercrombie et al. 1990:230).

Although my understanding of this whole complicated process compels me at present to bracket the explanatory role of ideology (in its strong acceptation) in the construction of the Sanskrit cosmopolis, my method points to a critique of the study of 'ideology' in its weak formulation as a history of the *idéal*, of ideas, representations, and arguments—of what texts have *said about* Sanskrit. For my part I want instead to try to capture *practices*, and then ask what sort of social explanation—discourse of power or whatever—may account for these practices. In the past I have always tried to acknowledge what I would call the reality of the normative and the normativity of the 'actual', that is, to acknowledge not only that the actual has theoretical and normative

---

[1] The dichotomies are those of Heidegger, Austin, and Lotman respectively, though I may not always use them in the senses they intended.

consequences, but that the *idéal*, the normative, the theoretical, has actual consequences (for example, the traditionalization of reality, the turning of texts into reals).[2] But I think Indology has too often neglected practice, especially social practice, however limited our ability to recover it may be. Sanskritists have what historians call 'bad data'—except of course for inscriptions and literary texts, where we are among the richest in the world—and it is instructive to reflect on what, in the historical reality of Sanskrit as a practice, can account for such impoverished data. My hypothesis about the work of Sanskrit in the Sanskrit cosmopolis offers some suggestions. At all events, neglect of practices is problematic on epistemological grounds, too. For in the end, what the *idéal*, or even ideology, really *means*—since meaning is always historical—lies in what people *have done* with it, and therefore not in their shared beliefs so much as in the forms in which life is organized (Giddens 1981:68).

II.

When and how—from what earlier location, and under what circumstances—does Sanskrit enter the domain of 'public' political discourse in South Asia? To be sure, the answer to this question depends to some extent on our understanding of its terms. There may be an association of great antiquity between kingly power and Sanskrit in South Asia, though the earliest materials (from the vedic *saṁhitās* and *brāhmaṇas*) come to us in what has long been constituted as a liturgical corpus and is accordingly hard to dissociate from that context; whereas the 'epic' materials, whose political imagination I have always sought to foreground, are, precisely, imaginary. The term 'public' gestures toward the question of writing, and thus the third century B.C.E. forms something of a historiographical limit for my inquiry. 'Sanskrit' is another term not without potential ambiguity. But I will not here address the idea of 'vernacular Sanskrits' or even such phenomenon as so-called Epigraphical Hybrid Sanskrit, which may be thought to throw into

---

[2] A useful distinction between traditional and traditionalistic is made by Brian Stock (1990:38): "Traditional action is substantive. It consists of the habitual pursuit of inherited forms of conduct"—Bourdieu's *doxa*—"which are taken to be society's norm. Traditionalistic action, by contrast, is the self-conscious affirmation of traditional norms"—my *realization* of texts.

question what we really mean by the name (Salomon 1989; Damsteegt 1978). Even given long pre-existent relations of Sanskrit and political power, the potentially deceptive shadow cast by the rise of writing, or the range of linguistic phenomena that may find inclusion under the name 'Sanskrit', I think we can locate an important break in the history of Sanskrit and public political expression—just as there will be an important break in the history of regional languages and public political expression, marking the end of the cosmopolis—where the sociality of Sanskrit seems to change radically, and where the writing of texts in standard Sanskrit (a category wholly intelligible and 'emic' in early South Asia) becomes obligatory in the public expression of royal power.

The crucial period is of course the interval between the two great imperial formations, the Maurya and the Gupta, when some of the key innovations occurred in the domain of language practices that were to mark the entire following millennium. This is illustrated in the well-known developments in two of the principal formations occupying this interval, the Sātavāhanas and the Kṣatrapas.

The Sātavāhanas took control of a major part of peninsular South India, and some parts of Central India, in the period following the collapse of Maurya hegemony. Their rule lasted from the last quarter of the third century B.C.E. to about the middle of the third century C.E. From the multitude of inscriptional and numismatic evidence available to us now (Mirashi 1981), something very striking emerges: Although this was a decidedly *vaidika* dynasty, as evidenced both by their continual performance of *śrauta* rites and by explicit self-identification (e.g., *ekabahmaṇa*, Mirashi 1981:13, 35), there is no evidence for their use of Sanskrit in any non-liturgical context; I do not know of a single literary work in Sanskrit associated with the court, or indeed, found in the entire space-time world of the Sātavāhanas—nearly half a millennium and most of Deccan and much of peninsular India.[3] Everything we know

[3] The presence at this court, near its end, of the grammarian Śarvavarman, however legendary, is instructive: his *Kātantra*, the first post-Paninian grammar (after the Buddhist Kumāralāta), eliminates all *vaidika* rules from the grammatical system, and thus may be thought to prepare the way for the expansion of a desacralized use of the language that I suggest was in the offing. I discuss below the one Sanskrit text produced in the Sātavāhana world, the *Yugapurāna*.

about the Sātavāhana dynasty and their world seems to suggest that Sanskrit was avoided—apparently rigorously avoided—outside liturgical, and their related scholastic, contexts.

Whether or not such avoidance pertains to the entire South Asian world before this period (though I believe one can argue it largely does) ultimately has little historiographical bearing on the discontinuity that marks the start of the Sanskrit cosmopolis. For the fact is—let me repeat it, though it is long familiar—that political inscriptions, that is, public texts in standard Sanskrit and expressing royal power, explode into prominence from the third-fourth century on, whereas not a single example is found anywhere in India before the second century C.E., or some three to four hundred years since public writing makes its appearance in the subcontinent. Indeed, there are no Sanskrit inscriptions at all anywhere, from Peshwar to Tamil Nadu, except for a few exiguous (generally two-line) records commemorating liturgical, *vaidika* or quasi-*vaidika,* rites: the founding of a temple enclosure (EI 16:27, ca. 50 B.C.E.), say, or the establishment of a sacrificial post memorial (*yūpa*) (ASI A/R 1910-11:40ff.; perhaps early first century C.E.). This holds equally well for the decidedly 'brahmanical' dynasty that had succeeded the Mauryas to the north, the Śuṅgas, of whom we have, so far as I can see, only one late inscription in Sanskrit (the Ayodhyā stone inscription of the *dviraśvamedhayājin* Dhanadeva, which commemorates the construction of a tomb, first century C.E.; EI 20:57). An additional important body of hard evidence indicating language practices outside such *vaidika* contexts mentioned above are the so-called hero-stones (in Kannada *vīragal*s; *pāḷio*s in the north), which celebrate local heroes fallen in a cattle raid, defense of a village, and the like (Settar and Sontheimer 1982). So far as I can tell, few are written in Sanskrit—so few in fact that in the mass of regional-language examples they constitute a statistical zero.[4]

The first public political text in Sanskrit of importance is indubitably the celebrated inscription of the Kṣatrapa king, Rudradāman.[5] The text

---

[4] Two instances are the well-known stone pillar inscription of the time of Bhānugupta (510 C.E.), which resembles a hero-stone, and a sixth-century *satī* stone (*Bulletin of the Deccan College Research Institute* 9 [1948]).

[5] To judge from Sātavāhana records there may have been something of a tradition of composing such *gadyakāvya praśasti*s in Prakrit (Sircar 1965-83:Vol. 1:203-5), but this is rare.

of this inscription has been known for more than a century and a half, from the time James Prinsep first published it in 1838. What I want to highlight, however, is the fact that in all the hundred and fifty years since Prinsep—a period that has witnessed an intensive hunt for inscriptions throughout South Asia, issuing in forty-two volumes of *Epigraphia Indica*, eight volumes of *Corpus Inscriptionum Indicarum*, and countless other reports of inscriptional finds from archaeological investigations around the subcontinent—nothing has been discovered to diminish the cultural-historical significance of the Kṣatrapa break.

An additional hint about Kṣatrapa innovation and Sātavāhana traditionalism may be offered by a contemporary brahmanical text, the Yugapurāṇa. The only work to refer "in any detail to the Indo-Scythian incursions" according to John Mitchiner (1986), in his new (and imperfect) 'critical' edition, the Yugapurāṇa was likely to have been composed in Ujjain not much after the arrival of the Śakas, ca. 25 B.C.E. For the author of this Sanskrit text issuing from the cultural sphere of the Sātavāhanas, the conflict with the Śakas brings about the apocalyptic *yugānta* (this text provides in fact the first account of the *yuga* theory): For "all four social orders will adopt the same behavior ... and outcastes will perform Vedic sacrifice with holy mantras" (vss. 50 and 53).[6] Only those regions will survive that are *dharmapriya*, namely, the regions of the Sātavāhana empire. This text is composed, uncharacteristically for the Sātavāhanas, in Sanskrit because, I would suggest, it has or seeks vedic-purāṇic authority. For most other textual production at this period—to repeat the striking paradox—the brahmanical Sātavāhanas insistently employed Prakrit for their public records, while their adversaries, the outsider Śakas, had begun to use Sanskrit.[7]

Now, although I am concentrating here on public political texts in Sanskrit, the transformation to which I am pointing manifests itself profoundly in other dimensions of imperial culture. The most important of these for me—to which I will return in this paper—is the development of what around this time came to be termed *kāvya*. Others be-

---

As for verse inscriptions, none exists in Prakrit, or, as we shall see, in any of the regional languages for many centuries.

[6] Verse 53: *tretāgniṁ vṛṣalā loke hoṣyanti laghuvikriyāḥ / oṁkāraprathitair mantraiḥ yugānte samupasthite //*

[7] Cf. Mirashi 1981:66: "The Sātavāhanas were themselves followers of the Vedic religion. They performed several Vedic sacrifices, but they got their description [sic] incised not in Sanskrit but in Prakrit. All their other inscriptions also are in Prakrit. On the other hand, most of the inscriptions of the Śakas are composed in fairly correct Sanskrit . . . This contrast in the attitudes of the indigenous Hindus and the foreign Śakas is certainly noteworthy."

fore me have directly linked to the great political-cultural transformation at the beginning of the common era the actual origins of *kāvya*, and though I would not go so far, I do not think their arguments have been fully answered yet (Lévi 1904; Sircar 1939).[8] Like the vedic prehistory of Sanskrit and kingly power, there is a long prehistory to classical *kāvya*. Indeed, it derives a measure of its very power from its echoes of this prehistory. But the existence of what the next thousand years of cultural tradition will identify as *kāvya* is exceedingly difficult to demonstrate for much before this period. A stray reference in Pāṇini, a few citations in Patañjali (who never uses the term itself) prove precious little, even if we could securely date these references; the total absence of any *kāvya* texts (or memory of such texts) itself is rather more instructive. And in fact Sanskrit tradition itself has recorded its awareness that newness had entered the world somewhere in this period: Aśvaghoṣa, the Buddhist poet of the second century, like all subsequent ethnohistorical accounts of Sanskrit literary history (Pollock 1995), famously awards this novelty to Vālmīki (*vālmīkir ādau ca sasarja padyam*, "Vālmīki created the first verse-poem," *Buddhacarita* 1.43, echoing of course the poem itself), and everything in the monumental text of Vālmīki's work resists dating much before the common era.[9] For the moment, however, my main concern is with the less contested evidence of the epigraphical record, whose political-cultural significance I want to interpret somewhat differently from earlier scholars.

The appropriation of Sanskrit for public political purposes at the end of the first century C.E., is an event symptomatic or causative of a radical transformation of the historical sociology of Sanskrit, comparable, and no doubt related, to the Buddhist appropriation of Sanskrit—and what Brough called a "quite definite translation in Sanskrit" of much of the 'canon' (1954:362, 367)—after half a millennium of rejection. In this process newly settled immigrants from the northwest seem to par-

---

[8] Inscriptional evidence published since these essays only tends to confirm their view. The earliest securely datable evidence of Sanskrit *kāvya* is from the time of Śoḍāsa, son of Rājūvula, the Kuśāna king ruling in Mathurā ca. 50 B.C.E., the Mora step-well inscription (EI 24:195ff.). The second earliest metrical inscription in Sanskrit of which I am aware is found at the end of the Khānākherā stone inscription of Śrīdharavarman (ca. 279 C.E.), who by the way describes himself as a Śaka appointed as *mahādaṇḍanāyaka* (EI 16:230ff.).

[9] I elaborate on these questions for Sanskrit, and think about the proposition "literature begins" more broadly in Pollock forthcoming.

ticipate centrally. Years ago Louis Renou may have been right to argue that "les souverains étrangers ont consacré la vogue du sanskrit littéraire plutôt qu'ils ne l'ont suscitée" (Renou 1947a:244); more recently, Gérard Fussman urges us to avoid any mechanistic model and to view the factor of political change as mere concomittance (and "concomittance n'est pas causalité," 1980b:425). Yet the synchrony of the two events is striking, and others may be right to locate in them an "innovating force."[10] What is historically important is not so much that newcomers from Iran and central Asia should begin to participate in the prestige economy of Sanskrit—other groups had long sought and found incorporation in Indian cultural communities—but rather that Śakas, Kuśānas and the Buddhist poets and intellectuals they patronized begin to turn Sanskrit into an instrument of polity and the mastery of Sanskrit into a source of personal charisma.[11]

There seems to be something new here, and we must try to understand what it is. When Fussman, for example, remarks on "le prestige que la civilisation indienne du Madhyadeśa a pu avoir chez les chefs de tribu du Swāt" (1980a:9), we might be inclined to assume that these tribal chiefs just pick up Indian civilization as if it were lying there already full-formed. What the epigraphic record (thin though it admittedly is) suggests happened instead is that they help *create* this civiliza-

---

[10] Damsteegt 1989:306. It is odd that his argument is not carried further, and in fact is relegated to a footnote. Here as in his monograph (1978) a certain muddle remains. He rightly points out that in Mathurā, as elsewhere, "the inscriptions of the pre-Kṣatrapa age [which includes 'Hindu', that is, 'Brahmanic', inscriptions] are all composed in MIA"; "Sanskritization appears only after the arrival of the Kṣatrapas." He then goes on to say, on the same page, that the turn to Sanskrit "is due, not to the fact that [some EHS] records are connected with the court, but to the fact that they are under the influence of Brahmanic culture" (p. 302). The question that remains central is how and why for the first time a publicly inscribed Sanskrit unconnected with liturgical purposes comes into being.

[11] Rudradāman celebrates his own proficiency in all the brahmanical *vidyās*, sciences, including grammar itself (see below, p. 236). At the same time—and this is contradictory—these Western Kṣatrapas seem not to have been highly brahmanized: they appear not to have adopted a gotra affiliation for another century, there is no indication of special patronage of brahmans, and their administration seems largely to have relied on non-brahmans, Pahlavas, Ābhiras, etc. (Pingree 1978:4). The Sanskritizing tendency of the Śakas seems to be evident from their earliest documents. Fussman has noted how Sanskrit has 'infiltrated' the middle-Indic of their early records, and remarks on their "learned or pretentious borrowings" from Sanskrit (1980a:9).

tion by employing Sanskrit in a hitherto unprecedented way. They make political poetry in a language that had not been used that way before—for the publicly inscribed celebration of a historical ruler—and that from that point on for a thousand years will be made only in that language. We may thus wish to rethink the received account that imagines a "*resurgence* of Brahmanism" leading to a "*re*-assertion of Sanskrit" as the language of literature and administration after the Maurya period (Norman 1988:17-18, italics added; cf. Kulke & Rothermund 1990:85), and consider instead the possibility that a new cultural formation, a Sanskrit cosmopolitan formation, was on the point of being invented.

Whatever the cogency of my account of the origins of the Sanskrit cosmopolis—the quest for origins always has something chimerical about it—its subsequent history can be traced with reasonable exactitude. After the Kṣatrapa/Kuśāna innovations and the creation or confirmation of Sanskrit as the paramount instrument of political expression, Prakrit will forever be banished from the realm of public political poetry, throughout the subcontinent and beyond. The last sign of Prakrit used in inscriptions in the North, apart from the Kharosthi documents from Central Asia (where Prakrit is found well into the fourth century) and the mere engraving of Prakrit poetry (which enjoyed, for example, a brief fashion in Bhoja's Dhārā), is in the hybrid Kuśāna records; there is nothing at all in the North after about 320 C.E. In the upper Deccan, the last Prakrit inscription of the Vākāṭakas, who ruled over what is now eastern Maharashtra and southern Madhya Pradesh, is found in the Bāsim plates of Vindhyaśakti II, ca. 355 C.E. (CII 5:vi.), the earliest of the Vākāṭaka copper-plate grants. In fact, it is the only Prakrit record of this dynasty that has been found, though given the nature of the literary production of members of this family—Pravarasena II (Setubandha, ca. 400), Sarvasena of the Vatsagulma branch of the line (the lost Harivijaya, ca. 330 C.E.),[12] and others whose works are included in the Māhārāṣṭrī anthology Gāhāsattasaī (Mirashi CII 5:lvii)—there is every reason to suppose that their earlier records were in Prakrit.

[12] The fragments preserved by Bhoja have recently been edited in Kulkarni 1991.

The Bāsim plates themselves are an instructive finale to this historical transformation in the Upper Deccan, and are an early instance of a defining feature of the newly created Sanskrit cosmopolis that we shall encounter repeatedly throughout southern India and Southeast Asia: the cultural division of labor between Sanskrit and regional languages, for which, though 'diglossia' may be (marginally) appropriate in the case of Prakrit, I would suggest the term *hyperglossia.*[13]

'Diglossia' conventionally points to the prevalence of split norms, with restricted mutual intelligibility, between literary and colloquial usage in a *single* language; modern Tamil and Bengali are often cited as examples (cf. Shapiro and Schiffman 1983: 164, though they provide no census of features taken to constitute *a language*); the Prakrits were viewed as different *bhāṣā*s, and grammaticalized as such, from at least some centuries after the common era. That term, as well as 'bilingualism', is inadequate for capturing the extreme compartmentalization of usage—and the fact that it is society-wide—let alone difference in cultural opportunity, which are in evidence in the case of Sanskrit and such regional languages as I consider here (Kannada, Khmer, Javanese). This difference lies not merely in internal split (di-) but extreme superposition (hyper-) of different languages. The tension between, say, Sanskrit and Kannada, in the face of this superposition marks the entire history of the latter.

In the Bāsim plates the genealogical portion (if not quite yet a *praśasti* yet still rhetorical) is written in Sanskrit, the 'business' portion, concerning a grant of land to (n.b.) brahmans, is in Prakrit, the record ending with a benedictory phrase in Sanskrit (*siddhir astu*). The record shows clearly that Prakrit and Sanskrit could (and perhaps always did) inhabit the same cultural space before the complete victory of the latter. The prominence of Prakrit in inscriptional discourse, accordingly, does not represent some sort of ignorance of Sanskrit, a common confusion,[14] nor even, I think, a mere rejection of Sanskrit, on the assumption

---

[13] The earliest instance of this division in the realm of Prakrit is the Mora step-well inscription (see note 8). This opens with the documentary or dating portion of the record in Prakrit, followed by a passage in Sanskrit poetry commemorating the construction of a *śailam . . . gṛham* of the *vṛṣṇīnāṁ pañcavīrāṇām*. Other more or less contemporaneous documents found at the same site, including identifications of images of the gods, are in quasi-Prakrit (EI 24:201, 204, 205). (Incidentally and by contrast, those inscriptions in the same place that are associated with the Śakas are quite evidently in Sanskrit, EI 24:206, 207.)

[14] Cf. for example Mirashi (1981:177) on the Sātavāhanas: "Even if we grant that the rules of the Dharmasūtras were observed in practical life and the members of the three higher castes lived with their gurus and studied the Vedas for some time, their knowledge of San-

that there was some invariable correlation between Prakrit and Buddhism and Sanskrit and Brahmanism.[15] The two idioms simply had, from far earlier on, very separate discursive spheres, which, as this Vākāṭaka record shows, had begun to intersect in new ways by the early fourth century.

Whereas Prakrit continues here to execute documentary functions, Sanskrit has emerged from its sacral domain with a very different kind of public work to do. In a real sense, of course, given the nature of these public uses, one could well argue that Sanskrit never did emerge from the domain of the liturgical, but rather extended that domain, since wherever a choice of codes was available it was the public function of Sanskrit to articulate the non-quotidian, the expressive, the 'literary' (by which, however, I in no way mean something discursively irrelevant; see below, p. 239 and n. 48), and not the documentary. As we shall see, Sanskrit comes to monopolize all such 'workly' and ideational functions of inscriptional, and by extension literary, discourse, and reduces regional languages—Tamil, Kannada, Khmer, and old Javanese, to name only those I will discuss—to an apparently subaltern status and function in the poetry of polity.

III.

An exemplary case of the institution of a Sanskrit political-cultural idiom is offered in the epigraphical record of the Pallava dynasty. Here we can follow in a detailed and continuous fashion the long-term developments of language and royal power in a multilingual environment. These are the earliest epigraphically attested rulers to hold sway over the northern regions of Tamil Nadu from their base in the ancient

---

skrit must have been very meager" (though for some reason he thinks the description of Sātakarni by Gautamī Balaśrī was "first written in Sanskrit and then converted into Prakrit," 178). Sircar argued that Prakrit hybrids as we find them in epigraphy are evidence of an "intermediate stage in the popularity of Sanskrit and the decline of Prakrit" (1965-83: Vol. 1:430 n. 2), as if a half-realized Sanskrit were somehow a half-popular Sanskrit.

[15] This has the status of an *idée reçu*; for one statement see Sircar in EI 34:197-98 (though here he is speaking specifically of Nagarjunakonda). Contrast the evidence from the Pallava and Ikṣvāku materials I cite in what follows. And this is to say nothing of Southeast Asia, where, while in Śrīvijaya the earliest inscription is in Old Malay and Buddhist (JASB 1935:61), Buddhist inscriptions in Sanskrit are found in Cambodia (e.g., Vat Prey Vier 664 C.E.)

city of Kāñcī. The dynasty issued charters from about 300 C.E. until 950 C.E., their dominions being largely absorbed by Coḷa Āditya I around 910-15 C.E. Their inscriptions have recently been collected in chronological order by the late T.V. Mahalingam (1988).[16]

The very first record is a stone inscription of Siṁhavarman (I) from the end of the third century C.E. (= EI 32:87-90). It is in Prakrit, if a somewhat unusual form of Prakrit ("in no way absolutely pure Prakrit," as Pischel put it, showing phonological preservations of Sanskrit forms and certain other "gross irregularities against Prakrit" [1981:9]). There is no *praśasti* portion, but only a brief identification of the king. The document records a *dakṣiṇa* to one [Jīvasi]vasami for his performance of *santisathiyāyaṇa* (*śāntisvastyāyaṇa*) rites. The second record (= EI 6:84-8) is about a decade later. This time a copper-plate,[17] but again in Prakrit and without any *praśasti* portion, it was issued by the *yuvamahārājo bhāradāyasagotto palavāṇaṁ sivakhaṁdavammo,* in assigning a *bramadeya.* It is striking, however, that the legend on the seal is in a somewhat different alphabet from that of the grant itself, and renders the name of the king in the Sanskrit form *śivaska* [*ndavarmmaṇaḥ*?] in contrast to the *sivakhaṁdavammo* of the plate itself. Around 338 C.E. the third extant Pallava record, a land-grant on copper-plates (= EI 1.1), was issued by the *aggiṭṭhomavājapeyasa*-[sic]*medhayājī* king, *sivakhaṁdavamo*, still in Prakrit and still lacking anything resembling a *praśasti.* Again the seal of these plates bears the

---

16 Additional Pallava inscriptions have been discovered since Mahalingam's work was completed about 1977. These are promised in a supplement volume. There is a rather large number of inaccuracies in the work, though it is not always clear whether these are simple reproductions of inaccuracies in the records themselves or new ones introduced here.

17 There are notable linguistic and discursive implications of material form of early Indian epigraphs. Copper-plate grants (a fashion that seems to be invented no earlier than the third century C.E.) were issued from the centers of royal power, and reflected linguistic and discursive interests and decisions of such power; and they were composed by intellectuals attached to the court (and sometimes actually signed by the king himself). Stone inscriptions, by contrast (from the third century B.C.E. on) were sometimes composed by individuals absent from the court, and did not always therefore reflect its linguistic and discursive interests. These implications of material form tend to diminish in later periods; and of course there are numerous exceptions from the earliest period. See also Ramesh 1984:xx n. 1.

name of the king in Sanskrit: *śivaskanda [varmaṇaḥ]* [18]; in Sanskrit, too, is the benediction at the end: *svasti gobr[ā]h[m]aṇalekhakavācaka-śrotṛbhya iti.* All this, to my mind, lends additional weight to what is suggested by the peculiar Prakrit of these early grants, and what I argued above: an insistence on avoiding Sanskrit in the documentary *laukika* mode, however imperfectly such avoidance is done at the linguistic level, however brahmanical the context (the gift of a *dakṣiṇa*, *brahmadeya*, and the like), however *vaidika* the grantor (*aggiṭṭhomavājapeyassamedhayājī*, etc.).

By the fourth generation after Śivaskandavarman (ca. 330-350 C.E.), however, the inscriptional style of the Pallavas changes dramatically and permanently. Records from the reign of Vijayaskandavarman (ca. 400-436 C.E.) and after are in textbook Sanskrit, and from the beginning show the elements of what, at that moment, is in the process of becoming the standard *praśasti* style: the fixing of genealogical succession, the catalogue of kingly traits of the dynasty, the eulogy of the ruling lord, following which is the documentary account of the gift that the record inscribes, and its conditions and imprecations against violating them. (A number of these elements seem to appear first in the records of the Kadambas, but the epigraphical remains of this dynasty are too scanty to permit inferences about borrowing.). Typical is the following record of Vijayaskandavarman (III), where what I would identify as the interpretative or expressive function of the *praśasti*, to which I will often return, begins to grow clear (Mahalingam No. 5 = EI 15:249-252):

> The genealogy is traced back to the fourth generation (as expected, in view of *śrāddha* ritual); the great grandfather or dynast is credited with performing the *aśvamedha* sacrifice; the grandfather is praised for his command of the three kingly powers (*utsāhaprabhu śaktisampannasya*) and for his "seizing kingship by his own heroic effort" (*svavīryādhigatarājyasya*) [*pace* Mahalingam 1988:35]; his father has won glory in countless battles and subjected the circle of kings to his will. Vijayaskandavarman himself is described as "a man of character adorned with suitable conduct, a man true to his word,

[18] This is also the case in an apparently contemporaneous charter of one Jayavarman (Kistna district, Tamil Nadu). The grant itself is in Prakrit, whereas the seal reads *bṛhatphalāyanasagotrasya mahārājaśrījayavarmmaṇaḥ* (Within the grant, too, the name of the gotra, and the name Maheśvara, are in Sanskrit, lines 3-4). The Sanskrit is also written in a different set of characters from the Prakrit. EI 6:315-319.

whose stores of merit increase daily by reason of his gifts of cows, gold, land; a man who rejoices in obedience to gods and brahmans, who has determined the true meanings of all the *śāstras.*" The *praśasti* is followed by the details of a gift of a village to a brahman, and the standard imprecations against infringement on the gift.

The Pallava public text, for prose *praśasti*s at least, attains its final form by this point: a *gadyakāvya*-style genealogy, followed by the grant specifics, followed by the imprecations and date. All that will be added later are introductory invocations of the gods (*maṅgalācaraṇa*s) in verse. These do not appear in the Pallava records until the reign of Siṁhavarman III, ca. mid-sixth century, in a copper-plate "*praśasti* composed by Medhāvin, who is skilled in all *śāstra*s, wise as Bṛhaspati" (vs. 9).[19] Simultaneously with the first appearance of the metrical *praśasti* comes the first appearance in Pallava records of Tamil. Here we find again the division of linguistic labor mentioned earlier, and to which I shall return in greater detail later in the paper: Sanskrit is henceforth used to interpret, supplement, reveal reality; whereas for documenting reality, so to speak, in the pragmatic portions of the grant, non-Sanskrit is, with increasing necessity, required.

After an invocation to Jinendra, Munīndra, Devendra, the genealogy of the Pallavas begins, starting with Brahmā. Siṁhavarman is born among the Pallava kings, "those whose lotus feet are awakened by the light of the sun-like jewels on the heads of rival kings." Then comes Siṁhaviṣṇu, "who could defeat the Lion[-form] of Viṣṇu [*jitasiṁhaviṣṇuḥ*], or by his power conquer Indra with his bow [*balena jiṣṇur dhanuṣāpi jiṣṇum*], who ornamented his brilliant clan [*bhrājiṣṇuvaṁśaṁ svam alaṁkariṣṇuḥ*] and could destroy the bold in battle [*nirākariṣṇus samareṣu dhṛṣṇūn*]. Did he not have all the *kṣātra* virtues—truthfulness, generosity [or: non-abandoning of truth], discipline—such as no other possessed, he who took the land of the Coḷas, she who wore a veil of palmtree groves, and a belt jingling [. . . ?]. It was he who gave the village of Śramaṇāsrama to the ascetic Vajranandi, a man filled with countless eminent virtues," who was devoted to the worship of Jinendra, Jainendra, Munīndra. Then follows the Tamil portion of the grant: King Siṁhaviṣṇu communicates an order to the nāṭṭār of the Perunagara-nāḍu, a subdivision of the Keṇkuṉṟa-kôṭṭam, informing him of the grant of the village Amancerkkahi and another 16 1/2 *paṭṭi* of land in the Dāmar village to Vajranandi. The previous rights of ownership are made over to the donnee, the old tenants are

[19] The beginning is damaged, and the Sanskrit portion is imperfectly edited in Mahalingam 1988:89. The edition in *Transactions of the Archaeological Society of South India* 1958 is unavailable to me.

to be removed. The actual account of the granting of the land is given, the precise boundaries are named.

The point to which I want to call attention here will be banal for anyone who has read a single medieval Indian charter from southern India. But it is in part the very expectability, especially the division of linguistic labor that has become common-sense, that I want to underscore. For the entire 600-year duration of the Pallava dynasty, there exists not a single inscription in which Tamil does any work beyond recording the everyday—to record a remission of taxes, the boundaries of a land-grant, the receipt of goods, the transaction of a village council, the sale of land, the construction or renovation of a shrine, the death of a soldier. These, moreover, are all functions usually denied to Sanskrit from an early date; and while counterexamples may be found among earlier Pallava records where Sanskrit is used to *document* the everyday world (i.e., in the 'business' portion of the grant), it is important to stress that none exists where everyday local language is permitted to *interpret* the world (i.e., in the 'poetic' part of the grant).[20] This will not change until a new power with a new cultural politics comes to rule in the late tenth century(see below).

Elsewhere in southern India the relationship between Sanskrit and Prakrit, and Sanskrit and local language, as we can read this off the epigraphical record, is virtually identical to what we find in the case of the Pallavas of Tamil Nadu for most of the first millennium. Let me briefly survey the state of affairs in the lower Deccan, the region to the west and north of Tamil Nadu (the present-day states of Karnataka and Andhra Pradesh). As we saw, in the middle of the fourth century the Vākāṭaka dynasty ceased to produce records in Prakrit and adopted Sanskrit exclusively. The same is true of the Pallavas, who adopt Sanskrit totally by the end of the same century. This is also the case with the Kadambas of northwestern Karnataka, the first historically recorded dynasty of that region. Whereas Mayūraśarman ca. 330-360 C.E. (thus virtually contemporaneous with the Pallava Śivaskandavarman)[21] is still writing

---

[20] One marginal exception to the documentary restriction of Tamil in Pallava grants is the striking account of the election of a new king, Nandivarman II, after the death of Parameśvara II in ca. 730 C.E. (Mahalinga No. 93).

[21] Contrast *Annual Report of the Mysore Archaeological Department*, for the year 1929:56, which argues for a date of 258 C.E., but on very shaky grounds. See also the pillar inscription

in Prakrit, the Tāḷagunda stone pillar inscription of the time of his great-great-grandson Śāntivarman (undated, ca. 455-470 C.E.),[22] is composed in wonderful literary Sanskrit. Prakrit not only disappeared throughout the subcontinent in the rush toward public Sanskritization, but it disappeared everywhere almost simultaneously.

The situation of the Ikṣvākus, the ruling family of southeast Andhra that succeeded the Sātavāhana dynasty in about 225 C.E., and were themselves followed by the Pallavas ca. 300, may be a little asynchronous, but is otherwise telling. The first 40 of their 76 extant records are in Prakrit. Most of these come from Buddhist sites in Nagarjunakonda, though a number celebrate the *vaidika* achievements of the dynasty (e.g., EI 31:63, Caṁtamula is the performer of the *agihota, agiṭhoma, asamedha* sacrifices, the donor of *gosatasahasa*, etc.; this epigraph adorned a pillar at a *stūpa*). The three Sanskrit epigraphs come from the third generation, the time of King Ehavala Śāntamūla; epigraphically these are said to belong to the "third or fourth century," so the language change may in fact be synchronous with Pallava developments. The Sanskrit items record the foundation of a temple of Śiva (EI 33:149), another temple foundation and endowment (EI 34:19), and the installation of a *śailamay ī pratimā* of the *saṁyaksaṁbuddha* (EI 35:12-13). All the remaining records are in Prakrit (Srinivasan and Sankaranarayanan 1979). Note again that not all Prakrit inscriptions are Buddhist in character, and not all Buddhist inscriptions are Prakrit.

The status of Kannada, for its part, exactly parallels that of Tamil in the Pallava records. In the epigraphs of the Gangas, one of the oldest attested dynasty in southwestern Karnataka, having ruled from the fourth-ninth centuries, Kannada is not used until the time of Avinīta in the sixth century, when again its function is documentary (Ramesh 1984:104).[23] But the record for the Gangas and Kadambas is thin for the

---

of (probably) Mayūraśarman, in Prakrit, with a closing Sanskrit benediction, EC 7:252. According to G.S. Gai, the second extant record of the dynasty, the Chandravelli Kadamba inscription (Sircar 1965-83:Vol. 1:473), is not in fact in Prakrit, having only been mistranscribed as such; his forthcoming edition of Kadamba inscriptions will give the (virtually correct) Sanskrit text (personal communication, Dec. 1994).

[22] The Pillar inscription has a lively description of Mayūraśarman who goes to pursue his vedic studies in the Pallava capital Kāñcīpuram; it emphasizes his Sanskritic character, which for some scholars has made the use of Prakrit in his records unintelligible (cf. *Annual Report of the Mysore Archaeological Department*, p. 57 n. 4).

[23] The Kadamba family may have used Kannada—once—for documentary purposes from a somewhat earlier date, if we accept a mid-fifth century date of the Halmiḍi record (*Mysore Archaeological Report* 1936:72ff.); G. S. Gai gives good reason not to, however (*Journal of the Epigraphical Society of India* 17 [1991]); Maṅgaleśa's Bādāmi cave inscription (ca.

early period, and we can begin to follow the cultural politics of language in the Deccan kingdoms clearly only from the Bādāmi (Vātāpi) Cāḷukyas onward. And here we notice trends that confirm a general pattern emerging. As in the case of the Pallavas, the percentages of inscriptions that are wholly or partially in Kannada relative to those that are wholly in Sanskrit gradually rise, from 30% (30 out of 89) among the Bādāmi Cāḷukyas, ca. 543-757 C.E., to something like 90% (205 out of 230) among the Kalyāni Cāḷukyas, ca. 960-1200 C.E., the real turning point occurring in the world of the Rāṣṭrakūṭas.

Here we can chart this shift in linguistic practices of the polity in some detail. Their first documents appear a little before 741 C.E. For the period between 741 and 819, 37 records are extant, of which 30 are in Sanskrit (81%), 7 in Kannada/Telugu (between 786 C.E. and 794 C.E., the wife of Dhruva, Śilamahādev ī issues 5 records in Kannada, which I am not counting here). Contrast with this the later developments: Between ca. 819 and 974, out of 94 records available today, 14 are in Sanskrit (15%), and 80 in Kannada. In the 33 year reign of Krishna II (881-914), who succeeded Amoghavarṣa, only 3 out of 41 records are in Sanskrit; in the reign of Krishna III, ca. 939-967, 180 records have been discovered, of which perhaps 10 are in Sanskrit (less than 6%).

In all these inscriptions, for something like the first 500 years, Kannada remains unwaveringly documentary (this holds for the first *versified* Kannada inscriptions of the Gangas, which begin in the eighth century [Ramesh 1984:254, 274; cf. xxxvi]). There appears not to be a single expressive record until the time of Krishna III of the Rāṣṭrakūṭa dynasty (after 939 C.E.),[24] that is, within a few generations of the first

575-580 C.E.) would be the next earliest (IA 10:60). Note that the Halmiḍi inscription commences with a *maṅgalācaraṇa* to Acyuta in Sanskrit; Maṅgaleśa's is plain, documentary prose.

[24] The undated (stone) inscription is published in EI 19:289 (1927-28). The editor of the record is, oddly, silent about its importance as the first Kannada *praśasti* (which is what the text calls itself, line 36), as he is about its unusual find-spot, Jabalpur in Madhya Pradesh—one of the rare Kannada inscriptions found outside of the Kannada-speaking region. Although this may be the first instance of public royal poetry, there are a few (very few) cases of inscribed Kannada verses from a little earlier, e.g., that of ca. 700 C.E. in IA 10:61 (a *vīragal*, in commemoration, n.b., of a brahman); several Jaina epigraphical verses not issuing for a royal court are found at Śravaṇabeḷgoḷa, EC 2 (revised ed. 1975): Ko 91,92), though their date is uncertain. A similar structure of cosmopolitan and regional language literary production occurs in Andhra; cf. Nagaraju forthcoming.

extant text of Kannada literature (the Kavirājamārgam, at the court of the Rāṣṭrakūṭa king Amoghavarṣa, ca. 850 C.E.).

It is surely an arresting fact that Sanskrit's competitor languages are so long disallowed any but a documentary function in the public domain of royal *praśasti* discourse, even in the case of those languages that clearly possessed substantial literary histories of their own, such as Tamil. I know of no study of the problem of language and polity in the successor formation to the Pallavas, that of the Coḷas, especially with regard to the question of when Tamil comes to be used for *praśasti* purposes, but a pass through the material indicates that Tamil is not, in fact, used for composing anything comparable to Sanskrit *praśasti*s until the ornate historiographical records of Rājendra Coḷa, ca. 1025 C.E. (SII 1:95-99 or SII 2.1:105-9), or better, those of Rājādhirāja, ca. 1046 (SII 3.1:51-8), that is to say, about the same time as what most scholars identify as the epoch of Kamban and something of a new era of Tamil literature (see below).[25]

What generalizations can we make on the basis of all this epigraphical evidence? First, the transregional use of Sanskrit for public political texts in South India was instituted by no specific event of political or religious revolution, but instead by some far less obvious process of cultural imitation and borrowing, which I will consider more particularly at the end of this paper. Second, the development of Sanskrit seems to have been at the expense of local literary traditions—indeed, there obtained an inverse relation of cultural power with vernacular languages—and it accordingly receded as local literary language was re-asserted; and third, the cosmopolitan character that is generated by these transregional developments is not just a shared language but a shared language *practice* that points, among other things, toward something we might call the aestheticization of the political. Henceforth and for a millennium, if political will was to be expressed in a public text it would be expressed in Sanskrit. Indeed, a uniform idiom

---

[25] According to K. G. Krishnan, "Rājarāja I [985-1014] . . . was the first king in the Tamil country to use a preamble in verse [sc., in Tamil] detailing the achievements and the glory of the king's rule" (*Journal of Indian History, Golden Jubilee Volume*, ed. T. K. Ravindran [Trivandrum: U. of Kerala, 1973:109]). Although I have not done a detailed study of the matter, the Pandyas seem to use Tamil for expressive purposes a little earlier; see for example the undated (10th century?) plates printed in SII 3:441ff.

and aesthetics of politics, one remarkably homogeneous in diction, form, and theme—I have only been able to hint at this here—comes to characterize all of the subcontinent.

The elements of the Sanskrit cosmopolis as a political-cultural idiom are put in place in southern India in a matter of decades. Again, no 'Sanskrit' political formation had conquered the Deccan and peninsular India during this period; no religious revolution had occurred, no new revelation was produced in Sanskrit. The creation of a linguistically homogeneous, and conceptually almost standardized form of discourse seems to have just happened. And in a form of premodern globalization—or shall we say, early Westernization—much of the world to the east experiences a similar transculturation.

IV.

A little before the beginning of the common era, during one of the great axial moments in cross-cultural contact and exchange that saw the explosion of trade between South Asia and the Roman Empire, people of the subcontinent developed relationships of a new complexity and intensity with the regions to the east. These relationships and the migrations that were likely to have been associated with them were, as noted earlier, the efforts of small groups of traders, adventurers, religious professionals. There is no evidence that large-scale state initiatives were ever at issue, or that anything remotely resembling 'colonization' took place. No ties of political subservience ensued, no material dependency or exploitation; no demographically meaningful settlements of the subjects of any Indian polity; no military conquest (cf. Tarling 1992:I:281-82). Yet from about the fifth century on, or at more or less the same time as the cultural transformation described earlier was taking place on the subcontinent, Sanskrit inscriptions appear with an almost breath-taking simultaneity and with increasing frequency in what are now the nations of Burma, Thailand, Cambodia, Laos, Vietnam, Malaysia, and Indonesia (Sumatra, Borneo, and Java).[26] And while the fashion for Sanskrit epigraphs dies out rather quickly in Burma, some-

[26] Dated inscriptions do not begin to appear until about the seventh century. Earlier dates are established by paleography, whose calculations—in contrast to the precision claimed for records of the subcontinent—vary rather widely in terms both of dating and provenance of scripts. See further on this below.

what more slowly in Thailand and Champa (south Vietnam), they continue to be produced for centuries elsewhere: the last dated Sanskrit inscription in Cambodia, for instance, appears to be 1293 C.E. (BEFEO 25:393), a little before the abandonment of Angkor and the disappearance of public writing in Sanskrit. In Java, where the history of public and private Sanskrit is very different, royal texts in Sanskrit cease to be produced in any number after the ninth century, though they are occasionally composed as late as 1447 C.E. (de Casparis 1991:30).

In large parts of the region, then, for nearly a thousand years, the altogether exogenous code of Sanskrit with its incomparably complex mode of literary expression comes to be used in the Mon-Khmer- and Malayo-Polynesian-speaking worlds of Southeast Asia for the production of important and in some sense defining forms of political culture—a curious development, no doubt. And given the manner in which it occurred—without the enforcement of a military power or the pressure of an imperial administrative or legal apparatus—it has few obvious precedents. I want to chart very briefly the career of public Sanskrit in two areas, Khmer country and Java, concentrating on its relationship to pre-existing linguistic codes. I also want to point to a very significant difference in terms of the politics of vernacular culture that these two cases present.

In Khmer country, the history of Sanskrit begins with some undated records from what are supposed to belong to the so-called Funan polity, the first of the centralized polities that expressed their political will in Sanskrit.

> Paleography is typically the argument used in dating, though Coedès thought he found confirmation in Chinese annals (BEFEO 31:8). It might be worth re-opening the questions both of the dating of these early records, and the vector of Indian contact. At least according to my reading of the inscriptions, the assumption of Pallava or east-coast Indian influence (Bhattacharya 1991:2) has hidden what may be the more important provenance: the Kadamban and later Cāḷukyan controlled regions of the western coast. Note for one thing that the dating systems of our records, from some of the earliest examples on, is in the Śaka year. The My-son Stele Inscription of Śambhuvarman from south Annam, for example, ends in a dating formula that we never find once among the Pallavas (who dated exclusively in regnal years), but rather among the Cāḷukyas: *-uttareṣu caturṣu varṣaśateṣu śakānāṁ vyatīteṣu* etc. (upper limit Śaka 499 = 577 C.E.). The Cāḷukyas and they alone at this time, date in the Śaka year, almost invariably from their first record on (EI 27:4-9 , the Bādāmi rock inscription of Chalikyo Vallabheśvara or Pu-

lakeśin I, *śakavarṣeṣu catuśśateṣu pañcaṣaṣṭiyuıeṣu* = Śaka 465 = 543 C.E.).[27] Their records moreover typically include some (or as in the case of the celebrated Aihoḷe record of Pulakeśin II, all) verse, as is found in the Southeast Asian texts; the Pallavas never use verse. Nagaraju 1984 argues on strictly paleographic grounds for a west-coast Indian provenance (see also Sircar 1965-83:Vol. 1:509n.).

Arguments for very early dating that are based on paleography, like Chhabra's mid-fifth century date of the Prosat Pram Loven Stone inscription of Guṇavarman, (Sircar 1965-83, vol. 1:511 = BEFEO 31.1), are vitiated by the fact that this form of Grantha was still in use at the beginning of the sixth century (Kumāraviṣṇu III) and even later (Mahalingam 1988 finds comparability between the Uruvupalli grant and a record of the *eighth century*; cf. his remarks on the chart no. 6 preceding the list of inscriptions); Sarkar also notes that the 'Pallava-Grantha' script found in Javanese inscriptions does not change much in the centuries between 400 and 750 C.E. (1971:2). Furthermore, the first *dated* records, of the early seventh century (Coedès 5:17, 613 C.E.; 5:20, 624 C.E.), show little of the discursive maturity of these putatively mid-fifth century texts. And last, although not impossible it would be improbable to find on the periphery of the Sanskrit world a form of textual complexity in inscriptions that had just become available at the center; this makes a third-century dated for the Vo-cahn inscription (Jacques in de Casparis 1991:10, and Bhattacharya 1991:6.) unlikely in the extreme.

The epigraphical habit in Sanskrit grows continuously in Khmer country from this early date onward, experiencing special efflorescence in the Angkor period. Of the approximately 200 *dated* Cambodian inscriptions in Sanskrit, only 20% (some 40) predate Angkor; for 225 or so *undated* Sanskrit inscriptions, only 35% (75-80) precede the founding of Angkor. And as the habit grows, so grow the complexity and indeed the importance of the inscriptions.

In general, the history of Cambodian inscriptional discourse follows that of continental South Asia closely. Early inscriptions in Sanskrit, up to the time of the founding of the Angkor dynasty in the early ninth century, are short if still fundamentally literary gestures. This is largely the case in the subcontinent, although longer *praśasti* texts become common already from an earlier period in the north (beginning of the fourth century), though not in the south. The Pallavas are still writing largely documentary instead of expressive records prior to about the seventh century (Medhāvin's text and a few others excepted), when

---

[27] Sircar argued that the spread of the Śaka dating system was co-extensive with the spread of Cāḷukya power (1965:259, 264; cf. also 1965-83:II:692-93; cf. also Nagaraju 1984:72).

things begin to change markedly, the innovating force likely being the Bādāmi Cāḷukyas and their Rāṣṭrakūṭa successors. Here political poetry, of which the Aihoḷe inscription of Ravikīrti is only the most famous of a number of examples, reaches a point of dazzling complexity (especially in the records of Govinda III and Amoghavarṣa). Detailing the temporal and stylistic connection between Cāḷukyan/Rāṣṭrakūṭa and Angkor poetry requires more space than I have here. What in short can be said straightway, however, is that between the 9th-13th centuries a very similar fascination with publicly displaying the most sophisticated forms of royal poetry seizes the minds of royal elites in Khmer country exactly as it had in India.

These early Cambodian records are thoroughly infused with the idiom, intelligence, and political imagination of the Sanskrit subcontinent. There is no question that local inflections are present from the beginning, for example, a Sanskritized Buddhism conjoined with royal eulogy (as in the Ta Prohm Stone record of Rudravarman [Sircar no. 83 = BEFEO 31.8], see below), such as is rarely found in the subcontinent, and especially a foregrounded presence of women related to specific kinship structures in the region.[28] But in general Angkoran inscriptional discourse is thoroughly comparable to what one finds in India, in terms of substance, form, and performative character. It is again the self-presentation of royal elites, composed in a Sanskrit that deploys, and increasingly so over the following centuries, all the rhetorical and formal resources of the most complex and sophisticated poetry, not to speak of a virtually perfect orthography and grammar whose mastery

[28] Women are prominent from the very first verse of the first record, the Neak Ta Dambang Dek Stone inscription of the time of Jayavarman, to the very last, of 1293 (BEFEO 25:393), which contains a *praśasti* of Śrīśrīndramukyamahiṣī. (A good example is the Mebon Inscription [BEFEO 25:309ff.]: it begins with a eulogy first of Sarasvatī, then of the maternal aunt of Balāditya (vs. 10), her daughter, Mahendradevī, vs. 11-12. Consider these two verses: "When the clan was gone and joined with the gods, a girl, a second Lakṣmī to benefit the world, a noble coral tree of fame, took birth from the milk ocean of that clan [*pace* Finot]. Her name was Mahendradevī, a lordly daughter of kings, her fame was constantly sung by the celestial nymphs. Mahendravarman married her and thereby made his lordship complete.") It is thus puzzling to read in the new *Cambridge History of Southeast Asia*, "Our ability precisely to define the role of women in early Southeast Asian society is clouded by the epigraphic records . . . initiated by an élite who were emulating Indic culture. True to the Indian epics and religions that promoted male superiority and female dependency, there are infrequent references to women. . . ." (Tarling 1992:190).

shows no slackening up to the very moment of its disappearance. And it is publicly performed, so to put it, displayed in places of great symbolic importance, on pillars in royal or aristocratic temple precincts. The Ta Prohm Stone inscription, a fragment of what must have been a very fine piece of poetry, is rather typical of these first inscriptions.[29] It is one that is good to think with for figuring out what Sanskrit is deployed in Khmer country to do: make untestable, imaginary, persuasive—literary—claims about the world.

> Two striking *maṅgalācaraṇa* s to the Buddha are followed by eleven verses to king Rudravarman, e.g.: "He who by reason of his own superiority, does not consider any virtue too small. Like a crown upon the heads of the worlds he <...> to stand — As if offering to view all the virtues of kings assembled in a single place the Creator made this singular being on earth, King Rudravarman [*pace* Coedès]. All goodly deeds this king has done in his quest for ultimate *dharma*. . . ."

This purpose is one that vernacular language texts are never allowed to execute. The fate of non-Sanskrit is one of the two additional features of the textual culture of Khmer country that I want to discuss in relation to inscriptional Sanskrit, and is one already familiar to us. The other is the nature and extent of Sanskrit literary culture itself beyond the domain of public poetry, something to me at least puzzling.

Precisely as we have seen to be the case in much of South Asian cultural history before the last quarter of the first millennium C.E., regional language inscriptional production in Khmer is eschewed in any capacity other than the documentary-contractual. Dated inscriptions in Khmer come to be published almost at the same time as dated inscriptions in Sanskrit (early seventh century), whereas undated Khmer inscriptions appear scarcely a century after undated Sanskrit inscriptions, if that. Nearly half of all inscriptions are solely in Khmer, one third are in Sanskrit alone, and a quarter utilize both languages. One invariable feature of them all is the linguistic hyperglossia we encountered in India: Sanskrit is rarely used to make purely documentary statements, Khmer is never used to make expressive, workly statements. Moreover, the two languages had a very unequal relationship with each other.

---

[29] The record is probably to be dated to the mid-sixth century. Perhaps I misunderstand when Jacques asserts that "no such composition [? i.e., ornate *praśastis*] at all has been found before the reign of Yaśovarman I" (in de Casparis 1991:9).

Whereas Sanskrit is, linguistically, utterly uninfluenced by Khmer—except for personal names, Khmer words never appear in Sanskrit—Khmer (indeed, like Kannada, for example) is massively invaded by Sanskrit at least at the lexical level, and from the earliest period (Pou in de Casparis 1991:12ff.; cf. also Bhattacharya 1991:6). Not only does this indicate that vernacular literacy was mediated by Sanskrit literacy (as was probably the case for most of India),[30] but also that there was a relationship of asymmetrical cultural authority between them.

The presence of public Sanskrit in Khmer country during this thousand year period raises a number of complex questions about transculturation even more starkly than for southern India. Who, exactly, are the agents of this transculturation is one of the more fascinating of them.

> Khmer kings sometimes allude to an Indian ancestry: in the first inscription of Yaśovarman (889 C.E.), for example, one ancestor is said to be "a Brahman who knew the vedas and vedāṅgas and had achieved success in Āryadeśa (*vedavedāṅgavid āryadeśe / labdhodayaḥ* [Majumdar 1953, No. 60, pp. 74ff. vs. 5]). There was, moreover, undoubtedly some circulation of intellectuals back and forth to the subcontinent, especially in the case of Śrīvijaya and the Buddhist university at Nālandā in Bodh Gayā, eastern Bihar; the Plaosan (central Java) temple inscription of ca. 800 C.E. refers to the "constant flow of people from Gurjaradeśa" (Sarkar 1971:No. 10, 48), while Coḷas (along with Khmers and others) are mentioned to be in Java (Van Naerssen 1977:43 and n. 95). Indian brahmans were occasionally imported, as for example for the lustration of the Khmer domain in the ninth century (Coedès IC 4:42 vs. 14; noted by Wolters 1982:91).

Whatever else may be the case, we know that Sanskrit culture was completely indigenized. Khmer princes could and did write royal *praśasti*s in the Angkoran domain—at least they are identified as the authors (Sūryakumāra, as composer of the Ta Prohm Inscription of Jayavarman VII [1186 C.E.; Majumdar 1953, No. 177], is the king's son, as is Vīrakumāra, composer of the Pra Khan inscription [No. 178]). The growth of a class of Khmer brahmans is perfectly reasonable (de Casparis in Tarling 1992:287), for precisely such a development occurred in Java and Bali.

---

[30] A good parallel is found in Latin. In Germany in the twelfth and thirteenth centuries, for example, "notwithstanding the extensive production of poetic and prose works in the vernacular, we have no positive evidence of even basic literacy without the study of Latin" (Palmer 1993:7).

Why Sanskrit was used at all is a no less vexing question, and while I return to it at the end of this paper in a more theoretical vein, it is worth reviewing scholarly opinion. Southeast Asian scholarship, for its part, seems noticeably uninterested in the question.[31] O.W. Wolters, for example, who has written the most interesting account of Southeast Asia as a cultural region, and who asks large questions, never wonders about the language practices of Angkor documents, never asks why or for whom Khmer people are writing in Sanskrit.[32] One recent view expresses skepticism about Coedès belief that Sanskrit was the "official language of the royal chancellery," for which there seems to be no evidence; on the contrary, everything points to the use of Khmer for everyday pragmatic functions. But from this we are led to the opposite pole: The Sanskrit of the Khmer inscriptions had only one audience, the gods, since the élite that knew Sanskrit was too small to account for their use, and since they are found only on temple sites:

"The overwhelming majority of Sanskrit poem inscriptions of the ancient Khmer territory are prayers to the divinities of Indian origin, which explains the use of this language. They have been cut in stone in order to remind the gods of a king or a commoner who has made religious foundations or endowments. ... In actual fact concrete data given in those poems are comparatively scanty. ... The essential fact ... is that without exception all these inscriptions were placed in temples or sacred areas, which implies that they are concerned directly either with the gods (if they are in Sanskrit) or with the administration of gods' properties (if they are in Khmer); and that is precisely confirmed by the reading of these texts" (Jacques 1986:328; cf.1991:12).

We do however find inscriptional discourse that is not exclusively "concerned directly either with the gods or with the administration of gods' properties." An important (undated) family poem found in Coedès V:238, in the editor's words, "ne relate aucune fondation, aucune donation, et semble avoir simplement pour objet de préciser l'étendue du domaine de la famille." Moreover, the inscriptional poems

[31] In their book on Java, van Naerssen and de Jongh do not mention the language question once.

[32] He asks, however, why the Vietnamese in the fourteenth century are writing in Chinese (they are appropriating the foe's language "to defend ... [an] independent status in the face of Chinese imperial pretensions," 1982:74).

have nothing like the form of prayer (though the category has no simple definition in Sanskrit traditions), except in the initial *maṅgalācaraṇa*s, and if these made them prayers all Sanskrit literature would be prayer.

The Khmer inscriptions evidently have got some other, political-cultural, work to do. They make claims about political power of particular kings, and are directed to those for whom such knowledge is pertinent, the royal élites. They are the "you" whom the *praśastikāra* typically invokes in the opening *maṅgala*s of such texts to receive the benefits of the prayer (cf. e.g., Coedès V:47, V:239.10a; V:251.11; 13; 15; 19). The fact that they are found at temples need only signify that the temple construction was also occasion for the narrativization of kingly being. The discourse of the *praśasti*s is of a piece with that found in a copper-plate and other kinds of inscriptions in India, which are clearly not addressed to 'gods'. That these were texts of importance for the polity itself—not metaphysical messages—is indicated by the family inscriptions studied by Michael Vickery (1985).

> Vickery identifies a serious jockeying for position within the Angkoran bureaucracy at work in the Sanskrit inscriptions of the period of Sūryavarman I. These are "historical genealogical inscriptions set up by hereditary official families for the purpose of recording their claims to property and rank throughout the previous two hundred years from the reign of Jayavarman II. . . . It is as though these families were intensely preoccupied with their prerogatives and property and with the establishment of formal claims to them. As the Russian historian, Sedov, put it, 'one senses a tendency on the part of the authors to use any pretext at all, even the most insignificant, to erect a stele listing the properties of their families'" (Vickery 1985:232). That these inscriptions were considerably more than prayerful messages to the gods, that what they communicated (challenges to rival elites, according to Vickery) was meant to be read and to be taken seriously, is further suggested by the repetition of the same record in various scripts on the same stele (Majumdar 60, 61) or by the painstaking care with which stele were sometimes faked (see the case already signaled by Coedès, K. 834, Vol. 5:244ff.). That they were made in Sanskrit renders them all the more arresting, and raises yet more questions about listening or reading publics, and the uses of these texts. There is no reason to believe that the aesthetics and politics of the royal inscriptions were taken any less seriously.

Agents and audiences aside, the language practice, and the linguistic asymmetry between Sanskrit and Old Khmer, are clear: political poetry in Cambodia is Sanskrit poetry, never Old Khmer. We might want to formulate this more strongly: Textualized literature up to the end of

Angkor is Sanskrit literature; there is no evidence for non-Sanskrit *literate* literary production before the *seventeenth* century.[33] It should go without saying that stating this fact does not deny literary imagination to a people, but brings to consciousness the cultural, and indeed political, conditions under which the literization of literature—the privilege of expressive, workly, non-documentary inscription—becomes possible in history. The character of Khmer language-usage in texts that are preserved to us, and the later historical development of Khmer literature combine to suggest strongly that the latter could not come into existence, as a literized entity, until Sanskrit literary culture came to an end in the fourteenth century.[34]

But—and here I come to something that mystifies me in Cambodia—political poetry is *all the Sanskrit in Cambodia that there is.* There is no literary habit of Sanskrit beyond this, no new, *non-epigraphic* texts in the language. The Khmer world produced a Sanskrit literary culture that mastered and mastered fully a complete grammar, lexicon, metric, mythography. To read the well-known Mebon or Pre Rup inscriptions of Rājendravarman from the late tenth century (BEFEO 34:770ff.) is to realize that the entire canon of Sanskrit poetry was studied, from the Mahābhārata and Rāmāyaṇa to the Raghuvaṁśa and Sūryaśataka, along with the canon of shastric texts from the Kāmasūtra to the Suśruta. Yet this mastery appears to have been deployed in the production of not a single line of Sanskrit literature other than the pub-

---

[33] This was disputed by Coedès, who believed in vast quantities of old Khmer literature destroyed in "the one long series of disastrous wars" that is the history of Cambodia (cited by Zoetmulder 1972:17). Zoetmulder rightly doubts "the very existence [of old Khmer and Cham literature] through the entire period of close relations with Indian culture," pointing to the preservation of Javanese literature in precisely the conditions that Coedès thought accounted for the absence of Khmer literature (ibid.). The first epigraphic text in Khmer verse is dated 1701, though a manuscript work in Khmer verse (indeed, the oldest extant), the *Lpoek Aṅgar Vatt*, the 'Poem of Angkor Vat', is dated 1620 (Khing 1990:24-59). The lone shred of early 'Khmer' verse in inscriptions I know of is a four-line strophe in mixed Sanskrit-Khmer dated Śaka 896 = 974 C.E., engraved on the wall of a Buddhist cave; it functions as the *śāsana* for the foundation of the sanctuary, the *maṅgala* being in Sanskrit (JA 1914:637-44 = Coedès nos. 173, 174).

[34] Compare the history of the gradual literization of Vietnamese after its emancipation from Chinese cultural hegemony beginning the fourteenth-fifteenth centuries (Wolters 1982:72ff.; cf. above n. 32).

lic poetry of the *praśasti.*[35] Occasional reference is made to other kinds of textual production in this world (a twelfth-century Cham king "supported his accession to the throne by writing a Sanskrit treatise" said to resemble a *smṛti*; the tenth-century Khmer king Yaśovarman is purported to have composed a new commentary on the Mahābhāṣya).[36] But none of this original production, if it ever existed, is extant, and never entered into any kind of local tradition of reproduction or memory.

Sanskrit was thus *exclusively* the cosmopolitan language of elite self-presentation, in both senses of the word: Only Sanskrit was used for this purpose, and it appears to have been used for no other. Why and how that mode of self-presentation had become desirable in the first place, and why it related as it did to local modes—the issues of transculturation, vernacularization, and ideology—are critical if complicated questions, to which I return below. Potential answers become even more elusive when we try to account for the very different career of Sanskrit in the other case-study I want briefly to introduce, that of Java.

In Java, the history of Sanskrit runs a very different course from what we saw to be the case in Khmer country. There are, all told, only something like 250 inscriptions. They begin to appear, as elsewhere in Southeast Asia, in the early fifth century, but continue to be produced in any number only through the ninth, when the first inscriptions in Old Javanese come to be written. As in the case of Khmer inscriptions, these are all royal documents; there is no 'epigraphical habit' that extended outside the kraton.

There is no doubt that these documents from old Java have much in common with the materials we have been examining. They include (and are often self-described as) copper-plate grants (*tāmrapraśasti*), *jayapatras* (here, 'edicts'), and *praśastis*. Many formal features in these different genres are shared with the mainland examples (freehold grants, for example, record the date, the king's name and virtues, the

[35] Jacques seems to argue for their existence (in de Casparis 1991:5), but on what grounds? Of what Sanskrit texts beside the one or two dubious instances I mention have we any secure knowledge?

[36] For the first, see Wolters 1982:44; for the second, Phnom Sandak Stele Inscription, Majumdar no. 73b, p. 155 verse 13 (though I don't derive that sense from this verse).

specifications of the grant, and end with imprecations), and much of their political-aesthetic idiom.

Instructive here is the Ligor Inscription from the Malay Peninsula (775 C.E.; Chhabra 1965:26ff.). The record decidedly foregrounds the language and the formal structures of Sanskrit poetry: It deploys all four kinds of metric (*samavṛtta, ardhasama -, viṣama -, jāti)*; *alaṁkāras* in profusion, rare grammatical forms. It begins without *maṅgala*, directly praising the king Śrīmahārāja Śailendravaṁśaprabhu, "a sun to destroy the darkness that is his foes," moonlike, Kāma-like, handsome. His fame outshines that of other kings; he is the support of his own virtues and of other virtuous men. "Those whose hopes had been destroyed by the ring of flaming fire of poverty he restored to their state of well-being; as springtime is to mango trees so the king is to the virtuous. . . . "

But there are some features that to my mind distinguish Javanese Sanskrit inscriptions from anything else. For one thing, the bureaucratic jargon of the documents deploys a large number of official titles the majority of which are non-Sanskritic (Sarkar 1971:xix). A more elusive difference is the general aesthetic: From the very first record, the undated commemorations of the footprints of King Pūrṇavarman and his elephant, or the fifth, a verse inscribed on rock in praise of a near-by stream (which, with its clear cool water is as purifying as the Gaṅgā), a certain local genius can be glimpsed through the Sanskrit inscriptions that to some degree sets them apart from others (I have found nothing comparable in Khmer epigraphs). The stone inscription of Sañjaya (732 C.E.), for example (after a standard opening with date, reference to the establishment of a liṅgam by the king, two verses to Śiva, one to Svayaṁbhu, one to Śrīpati), contains a striking *māhātmya* of "the incomparable island of Java (*dvīpavaraṁ yavākhyam atulam*), rich in grain and goldmines, won by the gods with sacred mantras. Soon enough though we return to an almost-familiar idiom:

There was a goodly king who protects the earth according to *dharma* and ruled over his subjects affectionately like a father over his son, and his name was Sanna. He died in the course of time, and the world was helpless and grief-stricken. But there had arisen from him, like another Mt. Meru, Sañjaya, the color of gold, with large arms and thighs, and tall, being "elevated by having his feet upon the kings who were the 'principal mountains' (*kulācala-*) situated on the earth." Respected by the learned, understanding the finest points of *śāstra*; like Raghu he defeated numerous neighboring kings [metrically corrupt]; he rules now according to *nyāya*. And so long as he rules people can sleep on the king's highway without fear of robbers; they gain *dharma*, *artha*, and *kāma*. "Surely the Kali Age is weeping ceaselessly, for there is no place here to take the impress of its limbs."

The first use of Old Javanese in public documents of which I am aware is 804 C.E. (BEFEO 46:24ff.), or at least 400 years after the earliest records; after that date, and very quickly, Old Javanese becomes increasingly and then exclusively the language used in official texts. The inscriptional materials in Old Javanese are virtually without exception documentary and not workly texts (something like 90% of them are *sīmas*, or legal transfers of tax rights usually to religious institutions). What is striking is how quickly, relative to what we find in mainland Southeast Asia or in India itself, Old Javanese begins to crowd out—or maybe better put, encompass—Sanskrit. Sanskrit was used seriously only through the middle of the ninth century, after which time it seems to have come to an end as a major form of public expression. Concomitantly, however—to turn directly to the fate of vernacular literary culture—we find from about the tenth century on an efflorescence of belles-lettres in Old Javanese unlike anything else in all of Southeast Asia. As in Khmer country there is little evidence of original textual as opposed to epigraphic composition in Sanskrit (many Sanskrit verses are transmitted in Old Javanese literary texts, however, which cannot always be traced).[37]

If Sanskrit had disappeared from the inscriptional domain, it lived on in an amazing way in the literary. As is well known from the work of Gonda and especially Zoetmulder, the impact here is profound; the latter remarks that "Sanskrit was so much part of that new culture which [the Javanese] wanted to make their own and to which they wanted to adapt themselves" that they adopted language even where their own was adequate (1972:9, 12), to the point that upwards of 40% of the Old Javanese lexicon is derived from Sanskrit.[38] Thematically, all these Old

---

[37] According to Zoetmulder (1974:16) "We have no direct proof that new books in Java were written in Sanskrit"; *āgama* and other ritual texts may be an exception (and those later tantric and magical materials composed in what has been called 'archipelago Sanskrit') though even here it is not clear whether most of this material was not imported.

[38] Indeed, Sanskritization has returned, like the repressed, in the present. Among the three sociolinguistic levels of modern Javanese, *ngoko*, *krama*, and *krama inggil*, the last is a "consciously archaizing Sanskritic sublanguage" emerging under the socially hierarchizing pressures generated by Dutch colonialism (Anderson 1991:131ff; 205ff; note the words for 'horse' in the three levels: *jaran*, *kapal*, *turangga*).

Javanese texts developed via a systematic adaptation, sometimes translation, of Sanskrit works over a six-hundred year period from the ninth or tenth century These include the epics (the so-called *parwa* literature, containing interspersed Sanskrit *pratīkas*), *purāṇas*, lexicons, grammars, didactic works; and especially the genre of *kakawin* (= *kāvya*) (Zoetmulder 1974:22-24; 68; 89). The whole linguistic and cultural development of *kakawin* literature—the highly Sanskritized idiom (perhaps as much as a third of the lexical items are *tatsamas*), the complex forms of Sanskrit versification, and in many cases the close appropriation of narratives from Sanskrit originals—bears the closest comparison with what is taking place in regions like Karnataka and Andhra at precisely the same time.

Thus we have several commonalities but also some important and puzzling differences. As elsewhere in Southeast Asia, Sanskrit in Java is the first vehicle for literized royal self-expression. The public texts in Sanskrit evince substantial learning and the language is largely untouched by the local idiom. Strikingly, but precisely what we saw to be the case in Cambodia, there appears to have been no Sanskrit textual production in Java beyond inscriptional poetry. On the other hand, and unlike virtually every other region where the vernacular is quickly literized under the influence of Sanskrit,[39] Javanese is absent from public inscription for almost half a millennium, but when Javanese does begin to be used for public records, these are exclusively documentary, just as elsewhere. Much sooner than elsewhere the habit of Sanskrit inscriptions becomes obsolete, and then a dynamic Sanskritizing literature in Old-Javanese, without parallel in Southeast Asia, but remarkably similar to what is found around the same time in much of southern India, begins to be produced. Sanskrit begins to die in Java the moment old Javanese begins to live, as five hundred years later in Cambodia, Khmer literature comes into being once Sanskrit has vanished.

And more generally, while there is all manner of variation throughout the Sanskrit cosmopolis as a whole, a significant uniformity invests it with a kind of unity. A traveler around the year 1000 one would have seen, from the plain of Kedu in central Java to the basin of Tonlé Sap in

[39] Perhaps considerably earlier than the concrete evidence indicates, as de Casparis argues from the tendency to overuse the *virāma* (in imitation of the clear word-boundary style of Indonesian) in the Dinoyo grant of 760 C.E. (de Casparis 1975:31).

Cambodia, from Gaṅgaikoṇḍacoḷapuram in Tamil Nadu to Patan in Gujarat and beyond, imperial formations that had many features in common. The material and social ones I have ignored here: their largely hierarchized societies, administered by a corps of functionaries, scribes, tax collectors, living in grand agrarian cities geometrically planned in orientation to the cardinal points and set within imaginary geographies that with their local mountains, rivers, and springs recapitulated the geography of India,[40] urban structures "freighted with cosmic symbolism, helping one to visualize the order of things" (generalizing Lombard's eloquent description of Java, 1990:11). It is their common political-cultural, especially literary-cultural, features I have emphasized: the existence of cultural and political élites assiduously mastering the intricate codes and protocols of Sanskrit poetry, and the publication of their works throughout these cities, in varying degrees of density and grandeur—stately public poems in Sanskrit engraved on the ubiquitous copper-plates recording gifts and donations, or on stone pillars looming up from gigantic architectural wonders.

There was thus, I think, a certain concrete reality to the 'Sanskrit cosmopolis', one that does not exist only in the retrospective gaze of the historian. For a millennium, and across half the world, élites participated in a peculiar supralocal ecumene. This was a form of shared life very different from that produced by common subjecthood or fealty to a central power, even by shared religious liturgy or credo. It was instead a symbolic network created in the first instance by the presence of a similar kind of discourse in a similar language deploying a similar idiom and style to make similar kinds of claims about the nature and aesthetics of polity—about kingly virtue and learning; the *dharma* of rule; the universality of dominion. A network, accordingly, wherein the élite shared "a broadly based communality of outlook," and could perceive "ubiquitous signs of its beliefs."[41]

---

[40] Cf. Groslier for Cambodia: "Toute la toponymie khmère ancienne, au moins sous sa forme sanscrite, montre cette volonté de reconstituer au Cambodge la géographie sacré des Indes, aves ses montagnes, ses fleuves, ses sources saintes, etc." (BEFEO 1977:179). The same is true of Java, and for much of India itself.

[41] This apt description of the Sanskrit cosmopolis is how Wolters characterizes Southeast Asia (1982:43); more on which below.

V.

The point of the admittedly dry exercise I have just undertaken—tracing the historical trajectory along which Sanskrit with its specific idiom and aestheticization of politics (if that is the right way to formulate it) traveled in the thousand-year period between about 300 and 1300 C.E. throughout South and Southeast Asia—is to make social-theoretical sense of it. How are we to render this process intellectually useful and not just ideographically diverting? Can we determine the conditions that enabled this language, and with it a large meaning-system, to spread in the peculiar ways it did and with such vast translocality, to become the means by which a whole world gave voice to a political vision? How are we to grasp the power of such cultural forms, their attraction for local people, their careers, their hegemony over or compromise with the vernacular, especially in relation to questions of social identity and political formation as these come to be embodied in cultural—and above all, in literary—expression?

I say "peculiar ways" because how these developments took place seems to be without obvious parallel. Let me restate them. First is the fact that, in much of South let alone Southeast Asia, Sanskrit nowhere approached a language of everyday life—not the language of the market, the army, the kitchen, of childhood, friendship, or love.[42] Furthermore, none of the conditions obtains in the Sanskrit cosmopolis for what Benedict Anderson (the only scholar who has thought both politically and differentially about translocal languages before and after modernity) calls "classical communities linked by sacred languages" (1983). Unlike all other such communities, which "conceived of themselves as cosmically central," the Sanskrit cosmopolis had no unambiguous real center (as opposed to a mythic and—as we have seen—infi-

[42] One even has doubts, for Southeast Asia, about Sanskrit as a language of *popular* religious propagation. I don't think there is any more textual evidence to suggest the development of a *sermo humilis* or *evangelicus* for Sanskrit than there is a *sermo militaris* or *rusticus*. To query the social location and depth of the spread of Sanskrit is not of course to minimize the importance of religious professionals in its spread. There are celebrated Chinese pilgrim accounts of Sanskrit in Śrīvijaya—no one disputes the propagation of Sanskrit in scholastic circles (though paradoxically it was precisely Śrīvijaya that for much of its history eschewed Sanskrit for public discourse). In northeast Asia, where we have vastly more evidence, the propagation of Mahāyāna during these centuries (and by these same pilgrims) was taking place in regional languages.

nitely reproducible one). No developed conception of an 'immense community' is found, as in Christendom, Ummah Islam, and the Middle Kingdom. There is no fixity—'unsubstitutability' or 'non-arbitrariness'—of Sanskrit's written sign, as in Latin, Arabic, Chinese, which Anderson believes helps constitute such a community. The scripts used for Sanskrit changed over time, with regional varieties present from a very early period. And we have already discounted from the beginning such standard conditions of cultural transformation as those associated with imperial subjugation or its bureaucratic inducements.

What I want to stress is that all of this holds equally true for the 'Indian' no less than for the Southeast Asian side of this world—indeed, it is not clear what except the later nomenclature distinguishes these regions (on which more below). The career of Sanskrit in Java , for example, is to a striking degree homomorphic with its career in Karnataka or Kerala; its history in Cambodia, where Sanskrit occupied the total linguistic space of political and literate literary discourse (though not 'business' discourse) for a millennium, is the same only more so, and puts the entire question into greater relief. How do we understand the processes by which whole social strata willingly abandon their linguistic routines and doxa, and submit, altogether voluntarily, to a new culture, especially one so mercilessly disciplined as that of Sanskrit; and those other processes by which the local is re-asserted? These are very large questions—the problems of transculturation, vernacularization, and ideology in my title—which I can hope, not to answer but only to pose in some useful way in concluding this paper. And I can do so at this point only by a kind of negative dialectic, without offering a final grand theory (for which real history is usually too messy anyway). There are two distinct analytical issues I want first to address—(a) the historiographical mis-en-scène within which the whole question is currently placed, and (b) the social theory available to us, now, to make sense of it—before considering (c) some alternative formulations.

(a) The history of the treatment of these questions especially in Southeast Asia studies is instructive, and for a newcomer to the field falls rather easily into two major phases of research. The first was the colonial-European and Indian-chauvinist stage, which sought, in the European case, an antecedent to its own contemporary imperial project, and, in the Indian case, the consolation of its own great 'colonial' past in the face of a humiliating colonized present. One of the typical Indian voices here is that of R. C. Majumdar, who conceived of the growth of the Sanskrit cosmopolis as colonization by a master race—the "Indian colonists" confronting "local people [who] were almost semi-savages," and "how all these were changed and Indian social and religious ideas were deeply implanted in the soil"—for it is almost "a universal law, that when an inferior civilization comes in contact with a superior one, it gradually tends to be merged into the latter" (1944:23). The source of such thinking, and probably of the specific construction, is European. The French art-historian Alfred Foucher, for example, had argued in the 1930s that "En résumé, il ne s'agit pas ici d'une simple influence mais dans toute la force du terme, d'une véritable colonisation" (cited Chakravarti 1978-80:viii). For their part, French orientalists evidently viewed what they saw as premodern colonization by Indians as a forerunner of their own civilizing mission—Coedès in fact speaks of the "civilizing activity of India" (1968:xvi)—and Lombard is probably right to see, among the Dutch, an anti-Islamic undercurrent in the linkage between Dutch and early 'aryan' colonization, punctuated by a somber Muslim interlude (1990:12).

The second phase of research was inaugurated by decolonization in the region after WW II, which, predictably, stimulated a quest for the local, the indigenous, the autochthonous. The object of study was no longer to be what was brought into the region—"Southeast Asia as a receptacle for external influences"—but the continuity and specificity of 'native' culture itself, "the cultural distinctiveness of Southeast Asia both as a whole and in its parts" (Reid 1990:1). The emphasis was on recuperating some kind of cultural authenticity, indeed, culture itself, apart from the Sanskrit cosmopolitan species. This approach achieves a sophisticated formulation in the work of O. W. Wolters (1982), whose sustained argument, echoed by many writers since, is that 'Indianization' did not introduce "an entirely new chapter in the region's history," but "brought ancient and persisting indigenous beliefs into sharper focus."[43]

[43] Indianization for example made possible "a heightened perception of the [already existent] overlord's superior prowess" via his ascetic (= heroic) achievement and therefore relationship with Śiva (Wolters 1982:10-11); it did not create a new form of political power.

Much of this (often masterful) analysis is open to criticism, not least for what strikes the non-Southeast Asianist as its defensive indigenism. Indeed, the very concepts 'indigenism' and 'autochthonism' are empty ones for those who take cultures to be, not things, but processes, and who accordingly consider 'the indigenous' either only as the moment on a timeline prior to the particular transformation one is studying and illegitimately generalized, or as the point prior to which it is impossible to historicize—but not anything essential to the ethnos. The kinds of transculturation processes at work in the Sanskrit cosmopolis, I will argue below, are ongoing and permanent; they mark all culture.

This is not to claim that cultural flows from the subcontinent encountered an empty space, let alone that nothing local came to be added to the translocal cultural flows that were received; on the other hand, for the key conceptions that Wolters cites such as 'universal' sovereignty and intimate relationship or identity with the supreme god, which empowered Southeast Asian polities in the historical period, there is a lot of Indian, and no Southeast Asian, evidence. Of crucial importance is the fact that the symbology of imperial sovereignty was never expressed, as we have seen, in any language other than Sanskrit, and it is not probative (because non-falsifiable) to say that Sanskrit could have been expressing non-Sanskrit notions ('prehistoric features'; Wolters 1982:15, 91ff.). It is notable, too, that so much of Wolter's interpretation of Southeast Asian kingship—when presumably he is arguing within the framework of prehistorical, 'indigenous' continuity—is derived from Sanskrit materials.

Much of this historical revisionism is also marked by an essentialization of 'India', as if the cultural worlds of the subcontinent were themselves some singular stable entity and not at the same time involved in a dynamic process of self-fashioning. There seems to be no awareness of the fact that the 'Indianization' of Southeast Asia was not dissimilar from the 'Indianization' of India; the peculiar local responses to this process cannot mark off the region from India, which itself was responding in similar ways. It is thus ironic that much of Wolter's characterization, which he thinks should be able to contribute to a "genuinely Southeast Asian history" (1982:44), actually applies just as well to India itself.[44]

> Similar arguments can be raised in response to Denys Lombard's recent assessment. Although he sees a 'Southeast Asian culture' (in the singular) arising in this period—"si la notion d' 'Asie du Sud-est' a bien aujourd'hui de solides fondementes géo-historiques, c'est que le coeur de Java a battu pendant près d'un millénaire au même rythme que celui d'Angkor et de Pagan, puis de Sukhotai"—he does not want to grant any role to transcultural processes in constructing this. He asserts, for instance, that Sanskrit as used in Java "refers to realities that are properly Javanese" (1990:13-14). This suggests a philosophy of reality that sees it as constituted prior to language, rather than seeing 'reality' as constructed by language and discourse; and a cultural logic that posits a primordial 'Javaneseness' over which Sanskrit is laid, rather than seeing historical Javanese culture as never a unitary thing but a constant process, of which Sanskrit is part. Precisely the same can be said of India, for there is no singular 'Indian culture' to exert 'Indianization', whereas India itself is 'Indianized' just as Java is 'Indianized'. To be sure, understanding the Sanskrit texts of Java means placing them in a Javanese social world. This is true of every text everywhere; there is no Sanskrit text in 'India' that does not need, in some non-trivial sense, to be placed in a 'cadre local' to be understood (1990:14). The authors of the *kakawin* s may stand in the same relation to Sanskrit as Corneille and Racine to Greek and Latin authors, but this applies equally well to Kamban, Pampa, Nannaya, Eḻuttacchan, Sāraḷādās, Tulsidās. What does his analogy really tell us about cultural models, transculturation, and the social identities constituted by literature?

(b) Analysis of the cultural transformation of especially Southeast Asia is typically underpinned by a functionalism that seems not only anachronistic but conceptually flawed. The weak functionalism (e.g., Filliozat 1977:405) that explains the role of Sanskrit in much of the cosmopolis but especially in Southeast Asia as driven by *practical* interregional communication needs (i.e., beyond what pertains to scholastic environments) I have already questioned. If there was anything approaching an everyday Southeast Asian koiné influenced by a South Asian language, that language was likely to have been Tamil.[45]

---

[44] I now find that Hermann Kulke makes a similar argument, not for quite the same methodological reasons but to sustain his hypothesis that South India and Southeast Asia stood in a relationship not of primacy and imitation but of 'cultural convergence', both of them responding to the same local social-political needs in the same ways (1990:22ff., 26).

[45] Consider the number of Tamil words in Malay, which came about through trade and commerce, cited by Filliozat himself (1977:401f.; some of what are taken to be Tamil words sedimented in Southeast Asian languages could, of course, be old Kannada [*mala* for *malai*,

A stronger and more refined functionalism holds that the idea-system of which Sanskrit was the vehicle was needed for political 'legitimation'. We find this notion coupled with a kind of post-Independence indigenist revisionism in Paul Wheatly's assessment a generation ago: Southeast Asians were "relatively advanced" at the beginning of the common era, and "came to realize the value of Indian concepts as a means of legitimizing their political status, and possibly, of stratifying their subjects. To achieve this end they summoned to their courts brahmans skilled in protocol and ritual" leading to "the whole exceedingly complex ceremonial of Indian court life" (1961:186). This explanatory framework remains intact in Hermann Kulke's recent analysis:

"At a certain stage of this development Brahmins 'came hither' [to mainland Southeast Asia] in order to legitimize the new status and wealth of these chiefs. Obviously there existed a tremendous need of additional legitimation which obviously no other traditional institution was able to provide fully . . . Brahmins appear to have been invited particularly as a sort of 'extra' legitimators of a new and more advanced type of authority which was not sanctioned by the traditional societies of South-East Asia . . . Obviously in both [South India and Southeast Asia] there had existed the same or at least similar socio-political needs for a new type of legitimation" (Kulke 1990:20-12, 30; cf. 22).

There is nothing obvious to me about this statement at all, for there is no reason to accept legitimation theory in the first place, though it is ubiquitous in the literature especially on the question of the transculturation of the Sanskrit cosmopolis.[46]

The fact is that the theoretical basis for this entire explanatory structure has been exploded by contemporary social theory. A serious cri-

---

etc.]). The actual koiné of the region was probably largely old Malay itself (Tarling 1992:I:114).

[46] Functionalist legitimation theory undergirds the entire conceptual framework of the new *Cambridge History of Southeast Asia*: "Indian cultural symbols" allowed Cham leaders to "mobilize local populations"; "aspiring leaders" in central Java "had somehow to acquire a superior legitimacy that would distinguish them from the others and enable them to prevail"; early Khmer leaders "learned to justify their authority by placing it in a universal context of devotion that could fully absorb the religious aspirations and compel the loyalty of their followers" (Tarling 1992:254, 205-6; 157ff.). This is *a fortiori* the case in earlier scholarship (van Naerssen and de Jongh 1977:41 *et passim*).

tique of functionalism is offered perhaps most effectively by the sociologist Anthony Giddens, who argues with far greater subtlety than selective quotation can suggest that "Social systems . . . have no 'needs' . . . Not even the most deeply sedimented institutional features of societies come about, persist, or disappear, because those societies need them to do so. They come about *historically*, as a result of concrete conditions that have in every case to be directly analyzed; the same holds for their persistence or their dissolution" (1981:18). Less ready to hand is a critique of legitimation per se, but Giddens again provides some of the conceptual resources to help in developing one.

For now, let me just offer the following points: (1) Legitimation theory derives from historical problems of post-Napoleonic constitutional monarchies, from which Weber first introduced it. Transferring it to the domain of Asian premodernity inhibits rather than advances thought. (2) 'Legitimation' implies a model of consensual rational choice that is largely belied by experience. (3) It rests on a conspiracy theory of politics: 'legitimation' suggests a knowledgeability on the part of rulers that is unavailable to the people, who are therefore cultural dopes and dupes, being persuaded to believe in ideas opposed to their interests. (4) Or it depends on an anachronistic model of consensus building that underestimates, potentially, the sanctioning of action by force and violence. (5) (The following points derive from Giddens) What area of 'normative commitment' is being addressed by 'legitimation'? There are large areas of routinized social life that are not 'directly motivated'. (6) Moreover, "those in subordinate positions . . . may frequently be much less closely caught within the embrace of consensual ideologies than many writers . . . assume" (Giddens 1981:67); hence the argument of Abercrombie et al. (1980, 1990) that legitimation (or ideology) is largely a matter of building *ruling class* consensus. Add to all this the recent critique of ideology from the sociologist of peasant Southeast Asia, James Scott. Again, although they are too nuanced to reproduce here, he offers powerful theoretical and historical reasons to conclude that the entire concept of legitimation, hegemony, ideology, in the ways we have always understood them—as discourses that reproduce domination—are "simply irrelevant" for domination in agrarian societies (1990:70-107).

If the theoretical foundations for making sense of the Sanskrit cosmopolis seem to be shaky, can we appeal to any comprehensive historiography of large, translocal cultural transformations in premodernity? Has any historical or sociological structure to the process been suggested that might be usefully subjected to cross-regional analysis, and that—by revealing similar processes with different outcomes—might escape the functionalism and the economism underlying most other explanations? Alas, little work exists on the meaning of cultural transformation in premodernity, even in the case of great imperial or quasi-imperial movements such as Hellenization or Romanization. Let us just consider the latter, a not insignificant process in human history. The historian Ramsay MacMullen is one of the few to consider what the 'choice' to Romanize signified. (He himself points out that "there seems to have been no scholarly attention paid to anything but the symptoms" of Romanization, and virtually nothing on the motives for cultural change [1990:63 and n. 33].) What made Romanization a choice for, say, the Gauls? Rather predictably he concludes it was the desire to possess the prestige of the people who conquered them, and to participate in their political culture (what Tacitus already called their *honoris aemulatio*, 'ambition for promotion').

In some ways the case of Sanskrit is similar, in others very different. A most signal difference was that there was no conqueror's prestige, for there was no conquest. There was similarly no bureaucratic compulsion to Sanskritize, as there often was to Latinize in view of the role of Roman law in the administration of the provinces. Nor was there anything comparable, I think, to the cultural power exerted by the 'center' in a center-periphery world-system relationship. As I have said, there was no concrete center; moreover, the progressive cultural conquest of Sanskrit on its eastern periphery—for obscure reasons the Sanskrit cosmopolis never expanded westwards[47]—was of little interest to the mainland, if we are to judge from the paucity of serious reference in Sanskrit texts to the world to the east. As for interaction with local culture, whereas within the cultural sphere of Latin and Greek, virtually all literization (*Verschriftlichung*) was denied to local languages, in the case of Sanskrit, literization of local languages typically begins simultaneously with the introduction of Sanskrit. But as we have seen, for centuries (half a millennium in the case of Javanese—and Kannada, Telugu, Marathi—and for a full millennium in the case of Khmer), local language *literacy* seems to have been confined to the realm of the communicative and excluded from the domain of the expressive, the

---

[47] Perhaps for the same reason that the Latinate world never expanded eastwards: that space was occupied by Hellenism, and prestige cultures seem to map out spheres of influence that do not overlap.

'literary', indeed, in an important sense, the political: that was a sphere reserved exclusively for Sanskrit.

(c) In a new historiographical mis-en-scène, therefore, and with no historical sociology and little positive social theory to help us, how are we to make sense of the conditions of possibility of the Sanskrit cosmopolis? Naturally, no monocausal explanation will be adequate to so complex a history. But let me cut into the problem via the political-cultural dimension that has been my focus throughout. In this domain one possible analysis is that Sanskrit became a key feature in a widely shared, highly imitative repertory of culture in what might be called the empire-system of premodernity. (In this I am not too far from Bourdieu's notion of 'field of cultural production' [1994], which is one theoretical aid.) As in the system of nation-states of modernity, where the structure of the system produces a number of cultural effects whose explanation derives from the objective relations constituting the field—the selection and standardization of one dialect to represent the nation, for example—so the empire-system consisted in a relatively stable field of highly imitative behavior. In fact, there seems to be a definite imitation of an imperial form successively reproduced both *horizontally* in time (by peer polity emulation or some such process) and *vertically* (by historical imagination): in Achaeminid (and Sasanian), Hellenic (and Byzantine), Roman (and Carolingian and Ottonian), Guptan, Angkoran, Coḷa embodiments. This imperial culture and self-understanding had a particular package of items. One of these was a language of cosmopolitan stature.

This had to be a language of transethnic attraction; a language capable of making *translocal* claims (not local claims—that was a matter of *deśabhāṣā*); one powerful not so much because of its numinous qualities (something scarcely evident in the epigraphs we actually possess), but because of its aesthetic qualities, its ability somehow to make reality more real. (By this I want to refer both to the Heideggerian *Werkhaftes des Werkes*, its "disclosure of a particular being, disclosing what and how it is" ["eine Eröffnung des Seienden . . . was und wie es ist," 1960:30], as well as to the *constitutive* feature of representation, which *creates* the being *by* disclosing it, as fame is created by being named in poetry.) These aesthetic qualities, moreover, are authenticated by the language's possessing a tradition of literary texts that embody and realize them.

Furthermore, this had to be a language dignified and stabilized by grammar. Only in such a language could the fame of the ruler be expected to receive permanent, indeed eternal, expression. But this is only a part of the story. The conceptual affinities between the order of Sanskrit poetry, the order of Sanskrit grammar, and the moral, social, and political order are profound indeed. They are embedded, for example, in a millennial-long cultural trope that we can trace from Rudradāman in second century Gujarat, "he who won wide fame by his theoretical and practical mastery and retention of the great knowledges, grammar and the rest" (*śabdārtha-*[. . .]*vidyānāṁ mahatīnāṁ pāraṇadhāraṇavijñānaprayogāvāptavipulakīrti-*), to Bhoja in tenth century Dhārā, "he who was wise in all aspects of language use" (*niḥśeṣavāṅmayavid-*). Sañjaya in eighth century Java, "he who understood the finest points of the shastras" (*śāstrasūkṣmārthavedi-*), and Sūryavarman in eleventh-century Angkor, "he whose mind itself seemed truly a mobile body, with the [*Great*] *Commentary* [of Patañjali] and the rest [of the grammatical treatises] for its feet, [the two kinds of] poetry [prose/verse] for its hands, the six systems of philosophy for its senses, *dharmaśāstra* for its head" (bhāṣyādicaraṇā kāvyapāṇiḥ ṣaḍdarśanendriyā | yanmatiḥ dharmaśāstrādimastakā jaṅgamāyate [sic leg.]).

In 800 C.E. in Europe this language was Latin, a basic component in the *imaginaire politique* that sought to recreate the Roman empire at the Carolingian court, where the language was subjected to profound regrammaticalization (as witnesses *De litteris colendibus*); a similar undertaking was made during the 'Ottonian renaissance' two centuries later, where the *translatio imperii* necessitated a revivification of Latin. In both cases regional language text production was discouraged in favor of an imperial-language textuality wholly alien to the everyday lives of the court. Similarly, from ca. 1000 C.E. on in West Asia this language was New Persian, whose earliest great literary production sought to link the new political formations with an imagined Iranian imperial past. It was adopted by ruling elites in Sistān, Ghazni, or Delhi regardless of what they may have spoken in their kitchens. In South and Southeast Asia for a full thousand years before this point, this language was Sanskrit. Sanskrit performed the imperial function of spanning space and time, and thus enabled one to say things with lasting and pervasive power.

> One intriguing difference between the career of Sanskrit as a cosmopolitan or imperial language and that of Latin is that not only did Sanskrit mediate the literization of local languages wherever it went, and almost immediately, but it rendered them securely authorized languages of record from the very start. There was self-evidently, as I have said, a division of linguistic labor and apparently a division of cultural power, but the fact that local language could be the idiom for the expression of contractual truths, and permanently so (since these contractual arrangements were typically made for "as long as the sun and moon shall shine in the heavens") differentiates Sanskrit from Latin. As M. Irvine points out, "The movement to authorize the vernacular in the age of Alfred and Athelstan had no parallel in the Carolingian world, and French and German became languages of record slowly ... For Alcuin and his successors, only Latin texts participated in Christian *sapientia*, and only Latin was considered authoritative as a language of record for history and laws" (1994:331-32). In the Latin world the vernacular, unsystematized by grammar, was viewed as unstable and changeable in the way Latin was not, and hence unsuitable for the expression of perduring truth, which a language of record must be capable of expressing. How, from this perspective, the authorization of vernaculars in South and Southeast Asian is to be understood merits serious reflection.

More than this, Sanskrit enabled one to say things—the aesthetic qualities I just referred to—that were not yet sayable in any of the other languages (Tamil importantly excepted). This brings us to consider more deeply the role of the literary in all this. Sanskrit in the inscriptional discourse of the Deccan, in South India, and in Southeast Asia has semantic prerogatives that are unusually clear. Sanskrit alone is permitted to be the language of the figure of sense—of simile, metaphor, above all *śleṣa* or paronomasia; it alone the language of the figure of sound, and the language of metrics (Sanskrit metrics being one of the great treasures and cultural exports of Indian antiquity*). These functions separate the object of Sanskrit discourse from the world of the everyday, not only for the obvious reason that the everyday world does not contain (except randomly or below the threshold of conscious creation) the figures of sense and sound and metric, but because the everyday world—of village boundaries, freehold conditions, tax exemptions, endowment requirements—is not the place for the activities with

* Editor's note: cf. Terwiel's contribution to the present volume.

which these functions of language are associated: the interpretative, the ambiguous, the polysemic, the imaginative, the persuasive, the captivating. This is not to say that inscriptional discourse does not make deadly serious claims about material and other realities: about territory, succession, royal prerogatives, relations of political dominance.[48] But as its very form shows—which becomes increasingly complex and learned over time (the influence of Bāṇa, for example, grows with almost equal force in the Deccan and Cambodia)—this is not its sole or even main purpose: that purpose is to make the real somehow superreal by poetry. Given its role in enhancing reality, Sanskrit is with increasing regularity both in South India and in Southeast Asia excluded from expressing the everyday, whereas the everyday, which must be univocal, is more and more frequently expressed only in non-Sanskrit. It is here that the analysis of the 'workly' aspect of a text that Heidegger spoke of, along with its 'documentary' opposite that Dominick LaCapra introduces (with useful complication, 1983:30), may be supplemented by materials from outside European modernity. Our public poets did not want these two realms confused, they usually (and as time passed invariably) segregated them by a differentiation of codes, with two different kinds of truth, operative in two different kinds of worlds.

For these reasons we have to begin to realize that these epigraphs are as important for their performative or symbolic meanings, their workly character, as for their informational or discursive or documentary functions. The French who edited the Cambodian inscriptions, like Indologists elsewhere working with such records, never cease to complain of what they saw as the sheer inanity of *praśasti* texts. "Aussi pauvres en faits qu'ils sont riches en propos sans intérêt," "interminable panégyrique," says Finot in discussing the epigraphical remains of Angkor itself (BEFEO 25:289) or the massive public poem on the stele at Mebon (ibid:309). Without interest and interminable to whom? Someone took care beyond imagining to compose the 218 complex punning verses of Mebon or the 198 of PreRup—indeed, if we are to follow Jacques, to compose it according to the dimensions of a stone surface that had already been selected! (in de Casparis 1991:7-8)—en-

---

[48] E.g., Vickery 1985 (discussed above, pp. 220), and, for a small but telling instance from the medieval Deccan—the Kalyāni Cāḷukyas read the Aihoḷe inscription to construct themselves a past—Pollock 1996.

grave it and erect it in a visible spot in a grand temple complex. What else must be present for us to take these poems seriously as cultural statements of significance? And when will we begin to see that among the facts that are important in these texts is their textuality itself; that the creation of the fame and virtue of the king through a celebration of his virtue and fame is what this textuality is meant to do; that the metaphors of the texts are metaphors people lived by, and the education and cultural virtuosity they evince is a whole way of being?[49]

All this, however, prompts an equally important question that has not yet been asked: When and why does it eventually—sooner in Karnataka and Java, later in Cambodia—become necessary to do this celebrating in a local idiom, and thus for the court to demand the production of vernacular as opposed to cosmopolitan literature? Can we make any arguments about a relationship of the development of local literary—more generally, cultural—autarchy and social and political autarchy?

Kannada, by all evidence, develops a literature concurrently with the development of a Kannada-nadu polity, under the Cāḷukyas of Bādāmi and more significantly under their successor, the Rāṣṭrakūṭas. It is no coincidence, but an indication of a new relationship of vernacular poetry and polity, that the first major discursive work on old Kannada literature, the Kavirājamārgam, which strives consciously to *territorialize* this literature (1.36ff.), emerges from within the center of. the Rāṣṭrakūṭa court in the mid-ninth century; the important literature at north Karnataka courts for the next three centuries will be Kannada. Tamil literature experiences a new surge of creativity, with new kinds of literary genres (often far more Sanskritized than previously) during the consolidation of the later Coḷa domain under Rājarāja (985-1014) and his immediate successors; crucial to place in this context, I think, is Kamban's *Rāmāvatāram.* Much the same thing occurs among the Veṅgi Cāḷukyas in the twelfth century, when a new brahmanized form of Telugu poetry, perfected by Nannaya, comes into existence. Something of the same argument could be made for Java. Although the his-

[49] "The veneer of Indian literary allusions in their inscriptions is no more than a metaphorizing of their situations and heroes and a comment on the quality of their scribes' education," says Wolters in a well-known article on Khmer 'Hinduism' (Wolters 1979:427-42, esp. 440). Since when are metaphors, or the education of the ruling elites, devoid of sociocultural significance?

torical record and the dating of texts are problematic, there appears to be some concomitance between the development of old Javanese literature and the growth of a new (mixed agricultural/maritime) regional polity in eastern Java—Kaḍiri, Singhasari, Majapahit—from the 10th century on (similarly, in the architectural idiom, the cosmic cosmopolitanism of Borobudur or Prambanam gives way to a new 'autochthonism').[50] And one might wish to make a similar case for the emergence of a literized regional culture happening at around the same time—with Alfred, 871-99 C.E.—a world away in England. Somewhere in all this complicated material, among these radical shifts in cultural politics, lies the basis for an important new theorization of a politics of vernacular culture in the polities of premodernity. To work towards this theorization, however, will mean rethinking the subalternity of vernacularization, on the one hand, and of the problem of ideology on the other. A brief word on both.

A dominant assumption in both Western and South Asian scholarship holds that vernacular culture somehow necessarily expresses subaltern consciousness. Gramsci, for example, believed that "the vernaculars are written down when the people regain importance" (Gramsci 1991:168). This is, unfortunately, untrue for both Europe itself and South Asia. I have already alluded to the example of Alfred's vernacular politics (directly and consciously juxtaposed to the old imperial model of Charlemagne, Irvine 1994:417). As for South Asia, it is largely an illusion, albeit one widely shared, that the literization—for some, indeed, the *invention*—of regional languages was due to subaltern *bhakta*s. This is false not only for South India (in Karnataka, for example, old Kannada literature is courtly, suffused with Sanskrit, and unintelligible to those ignorant of Sanskrit); but also in the north, where some of the earliest regional-language texts are composed by courtly Muslims (e.g., the verses of Mas'ud Sa'd Salman, ca. 1100, of the Yamini Kingdom of Lahore). The relationships between language, literature, and social power in South Asia are not going to be unpacked

---

[50] Cf. Zoetmulder 1974:26; van Naerssen and de Jongh 1977:60ff.: "Contrary to the abundance of manuscripts originating from East Java, very few—if any—could be attributed to the pre-*pralaya* period [before Airlangga]" in Central Java. They go on to caution against believing that "literature was absent in the early Central Javanese period," but the evidence they cite applies to *Sanskrit* literature.

by any simple formula transferred from Europe, especially one that is itself shaky.

This pertains all the more so to the even murkier question of ideology' in the strong sense (of Bourdieu, Giddens, and others), as systematically distorted communication. The notion that the Sanskrit poems of polity were produced to secure a consensus of false necessity in a contingent set of power relations—in addition to or instead of relying on techniques of coercion—is, as I have tried to suggest, a mere assumption, and an exogenous, anachronistic, unfounded one at that; I have already noted the view that even in the domain of Western capitalism, where the concept is native, this assessment of ideology has been seriously challenged (Abercrombie et al. 1980, 1990; their view that 'ideology' serves to produce coherence in the *dominant* class itself may in fact be pertinent to our materials, too). We cannot simply read off automatically from the choice to express political will in Sanskrit any particular social consequences (e.g., hierarchization, hegemony; the production of false belief), let alone any singular material cause ('theocratic hydraulic'/agrarian mode of production). To put this more generally: We may readily accept that "*linguistic relations are always relations of symbolic power* through which relations of force between the speakers and their respective groups are actualized in a transfigured form" (Bourdieu & Wacquant 1992:142); but what we cannot assume is the nature, directionality, effect, and negativity of this 'power'. It needs to be worked out through historical analysis of concrete cases.

Even a simpler view of ideology as cultural domination cannot pass unexamined. The argument can be made that cultural colonization and its response, indigenism, are phenomena of modern imperialism not easily retrofitted onto the premodern world; from this perspective, the appropriation of Sanskrit by elites in southern India and Southeast Asia might more easily be understood as autonomous cultural choice. Just as we realize the nonsense of speaking of superior or inferior cultures, or of the 'gift of civilization' [51]—true ideological constructions of progressivist modernity—so we cannot easily make a moral adjudication of cultural domination. We cannot know with any sense of certitude

[51] The idea underwrites the work of Coedès 1968 (cf. also Wheatley, Sanskrit represents "a recognizably superior cultural pattern" 1961:188; note also Brunt 1990:268 for Latin in western Europe).

whether the Sanskrit transculturation of Indian and Southeast Asian elites was a 'bad' thing or not (at least not with the certitude of MacMullen, who refers to the Romanization of Gallic elites as "a sort of decapitation of the conquered culture," 1990:62). To be sure, if transculturation processes empowered people to speak in some ways, it disabled them from speaking in others, and a growing sense of that disability may be one condition of re-vernacularization. But there lurks in this assessment an antihistorical and essentialized view of 'culture' as the homogenous and monopolized capital of a singular ethnos. The fact is, however, that the cultural materials being transferred are *already hybrid themselves*; and like the transmitter the receiver culture too is something always in process and not a thing with an essence. 'Transculturation', accordingly, turns out to be something of a misnomer, since it is the real and permanent condition of all cultural life, with 'the vernacular' and vernacularization themselves being, not something 'authentic' but just another unstable stage in a sequence of changes. The Sanskrit poetry and poetic sciences transferred to Southeast Asia were themselves created by 'transcultured' poets like the Daṇḍin of Tamil Nadu or Bhāravi (of Kannada Nadu?), just as the Roman literary culture transferred to Gallic elites was in fact created by non-Romans: the Greek Andronicus and the Oscans Naevius and Ennius. Indeed, as the Sanskrit cosmopolis shows so strikingly, there exist no cultural agents who are not always-already transcultured.

A useful corrective to the shortcomings of theorizing premodern cultural flows might be found in recent thinking about the cultural processes of the 'global ecumene' of modernity. The anthropologist Ulf Hannerz, for example, usefully details the different interpretations of cultural change here, where the influence of the center ('radical diffusionism') has been variously understood to bring about homogenization (the cocacolonization of the world) or its opposite, a new and anxious celebration, or even creation, of the local. He rightly points out that translocal processes can add new materials for transformation by local cultures, and that there exists a kind of dialectic between micro and macro processes (Hannerz 1989).

But Hannerz's view requires the expansion provided by deep historicization. For such an undertaking, the Sanskrit cosmopolis is a crucial case, since it displays to us the vast historical processes wherein the real condition of culture becomes visible, as the constant appropriation and localization of ever new translocal flows. Here, too, moreover, we can glimpse a time before—and perhaps the beginnings of the moment when—various nationalisms equated language community and political community, and modernity created the true *ideological* representations of culture: the illusory and dangerous notions of the authentic, the autochthonous, the indigenous, the native.

CHAPTER NINE

THE USE OF SANSKRIT IN SOUTH INDIAN BILINGUAL ROYAL INSCRIPTIONS: SOCIAL, POLITICAL AND RELIGIOUS IMPLICATIONS

A.G. Menon

1. *Introduction*

The pioneering research of Kuiper on the genesis of a linguistic area (1967) and the combined work of Emeneau and Burrow on the Dravidian borrowings from Indo-Aryan (1962) made a substantial contribution to the continuing discussion regarding one of the most vital aspects of the Indian cultural history, namely acculturation. [1] The study of Indo-Aryan loanwords in Tamil and Tamil loanwords in Indo-Aryan is made possible by the availability of old texts in Indo-Aryan as well as in Tamil. The publication of the dissertation of S.Vaidyanathan: *Indo-Aryan Loanwords in Old Tamil* in 1971 did not provide a definite solution to questions like whether a word like *mayūra* is related to Old Tamil *mayil* or *maññai* 'peacock'. [2] The discussions centering around dental/alveolar and retroflex consonants or the structural similarities have led to speculations regarding contacts between speakers of Indo-Aryan and Dravidian languages in the pre-historic past. As for the well-documented historic past of the Dravidian languages, here one comes across not only the scattered use of Indo-Aryan loanwords, but also an intentional use of an Indo-Aryan language hand

[1] Kuiper, F.BJ. (1967); Emeneau, M.B. and Burrow, T. (1962). All three authors have dealt with the etymological origin of many individual words in their numerous publications.

[2] Cf. the questions raised in Hock's contribution to the seminar [present volume, p. 38f, Ed.]. Vaidyanathan's research is primarily based on the Old Tamil literature known as the Sangam literature.

in hand with a Dravidian language. In this context we shall turn our attention to the use of the Sanskrit language in the earlier Tamil inscriptions. Historically, the practice of inscriptions reflects a transformation from the occasional use of a few Indo-Aryan loanwords towards the use of the Sanskrit language in royal proclamations. Such a transformation could not have taken place in a vacuum. The cultural significance and the symbolism of using two languages side by side demands a close examination of the available data. I shall try to analyse the use of Sanskrit in the bilingual inscriptions belonging to the Pallava and Coḷa periods in the South Indian history.

2. *Nature of the inscriptions*

Royal grants are of two kinds: i) those made by the king himself; and ii) those made by his minister (*sandhivigrahādhikārin*) for him. The direct grants from the kings always contain several clauses which are well described in the Indian law-books, and are legally necessary to their validity; these are : a) the donor's genealogy; b) the description of the nature of the grant, the people or person on whom it is conferred, the objects for which it is made, and its conditions and date; c) imprecations on violators of the grant; d) (rarely) attestations of witnesses where the grant is not autographed (Burnell 1878:108).

Giving the names of three or more generations of the donor complies with the legal requirements of identification. It can deal with the names of the kings with the years they reigned and mention also some of their battle victories.[3] From the 11th century, with predominant Brahminical influence, long mythical genealogies came into use which were intended to connect the Dravidian princes of South India with the two great mythical races of the north, and the kings of Ayodhya (Burnell 1878:109).[4]

[3] See Mahalingam (1988: lxxv) for the long list of predecessors of the donor.

[4] See also the genealogical description in the Tamil Rāmāyaṇa of Kampan, Menon & Schokker 1992:611.

3.1 Language of the inscriptions

The early Pallavas had Prakrit as their court language which was replaced by Sanskrit during the middle Pallava period. In the later Pallava period, inscriptions written in Tamil with an admixture of Sanskrit and Prakrit loans either assimilated or unassimilated, are found (Panneerselvam 1968). This is in accordance with the development observed in inscriptions throughout India: "In India our earliest inscriptions are in Prakrit, then we have Saṁskrit, and still later inscriptions are usually bilingual, in both Saṁskrit and the local language" (Sastri 1974:222).

According to Subrahmanian the early Pallavas belong to a period before 600 C.E. and the imperial or later Pallavas belong to a period after 600 C.E (Subrahmanian et al. 1979:68). The earlier of the early Pallavas issued their charters in Prakrit and the later of the early Pallavas issued their charters in Sanskrit. The use of Prakrit and Sanskrit as the language of their charters, according to Subrahmanian, was the result of their association with the Śātavāhanas.[5]

The use of Prakrit is predominant in Jainism and the use of Sanskrit is predominant in the Brahmanical religions. From the history of the Pallavas we know that some of the Pallava rulers were Jains. The use of Prakrit and later Sanskrit in the bilingual Pallava inscriptions may reflect the religious background of the monarchs. Mahalingam notes that only a few Pallava inscriptions give sufficient information about the Jains in the Pallava kingdom though much information is available from the literary and other contemporary epigraphs. He mentions a few inscriptions endowing gifts to the Jains (Mahalingam 1988: cxxix).

---

[5] See Subrahmanian et al. 1979:67. "Those who believe in the Andhra origin advance the view that since the early charters of the Pallavas are in Prakrit or in Sanskrit, and since their patronage of Sanskrit is more conspicuous than their affection for Tamil a non-Tamil origin has to be conceded and in view of their early subordination to the Satavahanas their Andhra origin gets confirmed."

The Coḷas ruled south India from the tenth to the close of the thirteenth century.[6] During their strong centralised rule the Sanskrit language and culture manifested itself in the numerous inscriptions and in some literary works. Many of the bilingual inscriptions of this period start with Sanskrit and end with Tamil. The formula-type of construction of the text and above all, the literary style of the long *praśasti*s of the kings and chieftains are some of the conspicuous aspects of the royal inscriptions.

From the study of the Tamil *praśasti*s belonging to the Coḷas, Pāṇḍyas and the kings of Vijayanagara the length, the literary quality and the change in the contents—from mythical and fictitious to retelling of the ancestral victories and the victories of the concerned king—of the eulogy are evident. Not only the language of the *praśasti*s gradually changed from Sanskrit to Tamil, but also the mythical origin and the references to gods and goddesses have undergone gradual change (Sastri 1964:144).

With the rise of the imperial Coḷa power in the south, the form of the inscriptions changed as if a new literary stream had entered into the south. The *praśasti*s in the inscriptions reflecting the political might of the Coḷa empire were formulated in a new poetic style by professional court poets. The *praśasti*s themselves have assumed the place of a new wave of literature. In this context, one is remembered of the dry prose of the earlier inscriptions. As Sastri, the great historian of South India, rightly points out "the difference is more noticeable in Tamil, the language of the people, than in Sanskrit, the language of learning" (Sastri 1937:511). And further:

> With the rise of the Cola power, there ensues a broadening of the channels of literature and a more copious flow of literary effort, the expression of a fresh energy released by the realisation, for the first time, of an imperial state in South India. The direct connection between the growth of the Cola

---

[6] See the following notes of K. A. Nilakanta Sastri in "Sanskrit Learning in the Cola Empire," Sastri 1974:135:

"From the tenth century to the close of the thirteenth they [the Coḷas, AGM] ruled south India with rare distinction and bestowed on the country the benefits of a strong unified and enlightened administration." "In the consciousness of the people of the Cola empire, in fact, there was ever present a vivid sense of the debt they owed to the Sanskrit language and culture, and this comes out clearly in the numerous inscriptions of the age and in some striking literary references."

> empire, a new political fact, and the birth of the new literature, becomes clear if we compare the highly ornate and poetic praśastis of the Cola inscriptions with the meagre and arid prose of the inscriptions of an earlier time. The difference is more noticeable in Tamil, the language of the people, than in Sanskrit, the language of learning. All the praśastis of the Cola kings from the time of Rajaraja I, with few exceptions, may be classed among the best specimens of the literature of the age; the stately diction, the easily flow of the verse, and the animated narration of historical incidents mark them out as a class by themselves in the literature of Tamil. (Sastri 1937:511)

Besides Tamil, Sanskrit formed an important literary language in the Tamil country. Apart from influencing the contents of the Tamil literary works, a number of Sanskrit texts arose also from the south. The Cola inscriptions show the importance given to the Vedic schools.[7]

South Indian historians have drawn our attention to a number of significant endeavours of the Coḷa monarchs in the field of language. Their inscriptions mention about their personal interest in the growth and spread of the knowledge in the Sanskrit language.

> . . . from the introductory verses in the Sanskrit lexicon Nānārthārṇavasaṁkṣepa, we learn that a village of Śaiva Brahmins learned in Sanskrit lore was established in the Coḷa country by Kulottunga I. . . . A more important instance of royal patronage of Sanskrit learning belongs to a much earlier period. It is this. Madhava, the son of Venkatarya and Sundari, lived in a village on the south bank of the Kaveri, and composed an extensive bhasya on the Rg-veda. (Sastri 1937:551)

In the time of the later Coḷas, the language of the Tamil *praśasti*s developed into the style of pure Tamil. But in the time of the Pāṇḍyas, i.e. before the Coḷas, *praśasti*s were composed with many Sanskrit words intermingled with the Tamil words. In the period of the Coḷas and Nayakas the Tamil *praśasti*s were composed in the spoken (colloquial) language. A

---

[7] Mahalingam 1967:144: "Besides Tamil, Sanskrit formed an important literary language in the Tamil country through the centuries right down to modern times. Not only did Sanskrit literature and thought exert a continuous influence on the form and content of Tamil literary works as on those of all other Indian languages, but there came up a considerable volume of original writing in the Sanskrit language by authors from the Tamil country . . . . The foundation of the Cola and Vijayanagar empires was significantly marked by a fillip to Vedic studies."

parallelism can be observed between the colloquial nature of the language of the *praśasti*s and the literary language of the Tamils. Many colloquial words have found their way into the Tamil *praśasti*s. cf. *reṭṭa* for *iraṭṭai*, *cōḷa* for *cōḻa*, *kuṭutta* for *koṭutta* etc. (Suppiramanian 1983:97-98). After the Pallavas and during the rule of the Tamil dynasties the Grantha characters were used to write the Sanskrit words in the middle of the Tamil inscriptions, e.g. *cinkatanam*, *cimmacanam* and *cimhasanam* (Suppiramanian 1983:98).

3.2 The Script

We are thus dealing with inscriptions which are both bilingual and digraphic, Sanskrit in Grantha and Tamil in Tamil script. Special scripts are used for special purposes. Just as the use of Nāgarī script in the early inscriptions of the Pallavas reflects their orientation towards Aryan culture, the use of the Sanskrit language along with the use of the Tamil language in their inscriptions is a confirmation of their origin as against the culture of the Tamils.

According to Burnell:

> The development of the early stages of the Grantha character is very difficult to trace, for the reason that the N. Indian civilization, when it got as far down in the peninsula as the Tamil country, found there a people already in possession of the art of writing, and apparently a cultivated language. Thus Sanskrit did not regulate the Tamil phonetic system, nor did it become more to the people than a foreign learned language; it thus remained almost exclusively in the knowledge of the Brahmins, and the Grantha alphabet is nothing more than the character the Tamil Brahmins used and still use, for writing their sacred books in a dead language. (Burnell 1878:39).

4.1 Bilingual Pallava inscription and the functional aspects of languages

The Chirrur copper plates of Nṛpatunga (9th century) were first noticed by Robert Sewell. N. Ramesan (1972:1-77) has studied these inscriptions and included them in his published doctoral dissertation. Nagaswamy (1978:34f) has pointed out a number of mistakes in the readings and published a revised reading of the Tamil portion. There are seven copper plates. The first part is written in Sanskrit with Grantha script (first three plates) and the second part is in Tamil written in the Tamil script (the remaining four plates). The Sanskrit portion gives the genealogy of the Pallava rulers beginning with their mythical origin and explains the reason of the grant of land to some Brahmins at the request of one Paranjaya. The Pallava king granted the village Chirrur and renamed it as "Pṛthvīmādevīmaṅgalam" coinciding with the name of the wife (Pṛthvīmādevi) of the person who requested the grant. The name of the executor of the grant, one Dramiḷādhirājā is also mentioned in the Sanskrit portion. The Tamil portion concentrates on the details regarding the boundaries, tax exemption, the rights, the irrigation canals and the names of the Brahmins who are the beneficiaries. There seems to exist a functional difference in the use of the two languages. The nature of the language of the Tamil portion of this inscription which belongs to the ninth century, is predominantly literary with the intermingling of Sanskrit words written in Grantha characters. It is interesting to note the contents of the Sanskrit and the Tamil portions for an evaluation of the two languages.[8]

4.2 Persons involved in a royal charter

The following persons are involved in the above bilingual inscription: (a) the one who requested the grant; (b) the king who granted the grant; (c) the

[8] See Nagaswamy 1978:30-43.

minister who executed the grant; (d) the Brahmins who received the grant; (e) the poet (Kumāra) who composed the *praśasti*; and (f) the scribe who inscribed the whole text on copper plates. On the other side of the communication line we meet the villagers and the village officers who are involved in the collection of taxes. The comparatively high number of Sanskrit words in the Grantha characters found within the Tamil portion of the inscription deals mostly with proper names. The pragmatic message of the inscription is conveyed in Tamil.

5.1 Bilingual Coḷa inscriptions

Another bilingual copper-plate grant engraved on ten sides of six plates belonging to the later Coḷa period, according to Burgess, is written in Grantha characters.[9] The first three plates are in Sanskrit, and the rest is in Tamil. As in the previous inscription, the Sanskrit part deals with the mythological genealogy of the king, battle victories, the titles as destroyer of enemies and as a true devotee and worshipper of the lotus feet of the god Bhoganātha. Worship and devotion and the recognition of the grace of Viṣṇu as the lord of the great world are the subjects of the Sanskrit portion, according to which the aim of the grant is "the purification of all his [i.e. the king's] sins." The Tamil portion written in Grantha explains the boundaries of the land which is given as gift to a number of Brahmins. The 36 shares of the land are divided among twenty Brahmins. These Brahmins include those who officiated at sacrifices, taught the Vedas, and functioned as priests.

The grant of Rājendra Coḷa Parakesarivarman consists of twenty-one plates and is inscribed in the Coḷa Grantha characters.[10] The inscription belongs to the first half of the eleventh century. The first five plates are in Sanskrit and the remaining sixteen in Tamil. As in the previous cases the Sanskrit portion describes the *vamśāvali* (genealogy) of the Coḷas. The

---

9 This copper-plate grant can be found in Burgess 1886 (inscription nr. 25, p. 181).

10 Burgess 1886 (inscription nr. 29, p. 204).

village Anaimangalam is donated to the Bauddha Vihāra (monastery) of Cūḍāmaṇivarman in Nagapattinam. The Vihāra was built in the twenty-first year of Rājarāja. Rājarāja dedicated the village Anaimangalam to Lord Buddha—residing in this Vihara. His son Rājendra Coḷa confirmed the grant after his father's death and caused it to be engraved on copper-plates (Sastri 1937:224). The name of the author of the Sanskrit portion is Nandanarayana and the names of the engravers, five in numbers, are also mentioned at the end of the Sanskrit portion. The executor of this grant is the minister Tillayali. The long Sanskrit portion is intended to portray the long legendary genealogy and the solar origin of the Coḷa dynasty. This inscription includes in the Sanskrit portion twelve fictitious names of ancestors starting from the Sun: a mythical origin in a mythical or godly language. K.A.N.Sastri mentions a beautiful story of a Coḷa king who acts like Rāma, and thus came to the South:

> He came to the south to catch a Rakshasa who had assumed the form of an antelope. He went to the south with his army. He killed the Rakshasa and walked along the banks of the river Kaveri, "the river which brings to the earth, in the guise of water, the nectar obtained by the gods after churning the ocean of milk." (Sastri 1937:140)

In order to understand the use of a language for conveying a specific message, let us look at the contents of the Sanskrit and the Tamil texts of a bilingual inscription. From the earlier inscriptions it appears that the two main languages of the bilingual inscriptions have their own domains. Below are given three examples (in translation) from the Sanskrit and the Tamil portion of a bilingual inscription:

From the Sanskrit portion:

> As long as the holy moon-crested (Śiva) sports with his own Devi on Mount Kailasa; as long as on the milky ocean Hari prolongs his meditative sleep on the serpent-bed; as long as the sun, the sole lamp of all worlds, dispels the gross darkness so long may this Coḷa family shield from evil the whole round world. (Burgess 1886:216)

The ancestral line starts from Manu, Ikṣvāku, Mandhatri, Mucukuṇḍa, Valabha and Sibi. Next:

> As the full moon on the ocean of that family was born Coḷa, a treasury of the seven arts. . . .

> In that family arose Rājēndra, a very Bṛihaspati (Ravikula) the beacon of the solar race (Suraguru), repelling the host of enemies. . . .
> He, the light of the family of Manu, while yet a boy played sportively in battle with Vīra Pāṇḍya, as a lion's cub with a huge elephant wild with passion and confident of his strength. (Burgess 1886:217)

From the Tamil portion:

> We Kōnerinamaikoṇḍāṉ on the ninety-second day of the twenty-first year of our reign while sitting in the maṇḍapam to the south of Rājāśraya the palace to the south of Tañjāvūr executed for the inhabitants of Paṭṭaṇakkūurram division of the fertile country of Kshatriyaśikhāmaṇi-vaḷanāḍu, to the Brāhmin free-holders of lands, to the low caste people of Dēvadanappaḷḷi and to the townsmen of Veṭṭapperṟūr in the division of Kaṇimurrūṭṭu by the king of the Kiḍāra country to maintain the charity of the Sūḷāmaṇipadma-vihāra (Chūḍāmaṇipadma-vihāra) built by Sūḷāmāmpadma (Chūḍāmaṇivarman) in Nāgapaṭṭaṉam, situated in the Paṭṭaṉakkūṟṟu division of the fertile country of Kshatriyaśikhāmaṇi-vaḷanāḍu. Half of the above mentioned land and produce shall be in the enjoyment of this temple and the other half shall cover the several expenses and other taxes incurred in money or paddy by this village. Thus for the exemption from taxation and for the exchange of the lands from the former owners to the temple we issue this order. (Burgess 1886:218f)

5.2 Analysis of the inscriptions

Sacral origin of their dynasty seems to be an important reason for mentioning the names of Hindu gods as their ancestors. Burnell mentions an inscription of a Coḷa prince (a grant by Kulottunga in the 23rd year of his reign, i.e. 1087, from Pittapur) of the 11th century, which begins with Hari, Brahmā, Atri, Soma etc. It mentions also sixty *cakravartins* who reigned at Ayodhya in an uninterrupted succession (Burnell 1878:109). Burnell characterises this kind of *praśasti* as a "fictitious genealogy and most extravagant selflaudation" (Burnell 1878:109). Moreover, in the view of Burnell,

> The Vijayanagara style is purely conventional bombast, and in bad verse for the most part. The succession of kings is carelessly given, and often sacrificed to the exigencies of metre. Fictitious conquests are mentioned in

> detail, and the king's character and actions are made to correspond exactly with the ideal of a Hindu sovereign according to Alankarasastra and astrological imaginations (cf. the description of Rāma, Buddha etc.). . . . In all of them the king's panegyric is extravagant, and spun out with childish conceits. (Burnell 1878:110)

The conventional idea of a Hindu king rendered necessary the ascription of all kinds of fictitious conquests and qualities (Burnell 1878:111). The first part of this type of inscription will also show the religion of the reigning king.

While discussing the Brāhmī inscriptions (2nd century B.C.E. to fourth century C.E.)[11] from South India, T.V. Mahalingam notes that the language of these inscriptions is different from the Tamil language of the classical Tamil literature (Sangam) and that it contains a good proportion of Prakrit words. One of the possible reasons for the deviation is that it is related to the Buddhist and Jain monks using a hybrid dialect (Mahalingam 1967:157). Inscriptions are intended to be read and their contents is to be understood by those who see them. As such the script and language employed should be such as could be easily read and understood by the people of the locality. Therefore, even inscriptions should be incised only in the local language, if the official language was different and it was not understood in the area (Mahalingam 1967:156).

The predominantly fictive and mythological information gleaned from the Sanskrit portion with the predominantly legal nature of the Tamil portion in the bilingual inscriptions can be seen as a division godly vs. worldly. Tamil religious literature is full of parallel divisions, e.g. King vs. God, and palace vs. temple. The bilingual inscriptions reflect this parallelism through the use of two languages: one which is mystical and understandable for a few and the other worldly and understandable to many.

---

[11] According to Allchin 1995:176, 336, writing in Brāhmī script appears in Sri Lanka as early as 450 B.C.E.

5.3 From Bilingualism to Diglossia

An inscription (1014 C.E.) of Rājarāja I, father of Rājendra whose inscription we have mentioned above, deals in the first three lines with the victories of the king.[12] It is a long monolingual (Tamil) inscription describing an endowment for an annual temple festival and other ceremonies. The Tamil *praśasti* in this inscription is short and limits itself to the victories on earth as against the mythological and fictive nature of the later bilingual Coḷa inscriptions. The language of the *praśasti* is literary Tamil while the later endowment part contains many words from the colloquial language: a clear indication of diglossia.

The fictive nature continued and the role of Sanskrit is taken over by Tamil in the literary texts relating to the genealogy of kings. In a 12th cent. Tamil text known as Kalinkattupparani, composed to praise the victory of the Coḷa king Kulottunga I, the function of the Sanskrit portion of the bilingual inscriptions is taken over by literary Tamil. The tenth chapter tracing the ancestry of Kulottunga I describes him as an incarnation of Rāma and Kṛṣṇa. The 12th cent. Tamil Rāmāyaṇa of Kampan connects the Coḷas with Rāma and Suriyavamsa.[13]

6. Bilingual agreements in the colonial period

For a better understanding of the status and function of Sanskrit in the bilingual inscriptions mentioned above, we may now turn to another inscription from the same area as mentioned in one of the Coḷa inscriptions. About six centuries later the balance of power has changed and the colonial rulers started exerting their influence over South India. The language of the colonial ruler is no longer Sanskrit, but a language related to Sanskrit. On the one hand these rulers were, for their activities in the south, respon-

---

[12] See Sastri 1935:201 and Hultzsch 1917:1-14.

[13] Cf. Kalingattupparani and Kamparamayanam.

sible to their superiors in their home country, and on the other hand they had the responsibility of making their intentions clear to the local people. As a result of this double responsibility they were forced to maintain a functional bilingualism. In June 1658 C.E. the Dutch East India Company took over the city Jaffna(patnam) on the north of Ceylon (Srilanka) from the Portuguese. A month later they captured Nagapattinam, on the east coast of Tamilnadu. The Dutch Admiral Rijklof van Goens was responsible for this mission. The Nayak of Tanjore was first unwilling to negotiate with the Dutch. However, they reached an agreement and this agreement was inscribed on a silverplate in Telugu, dated 15 September 1658.[14] A corresponding Dutch version on paper is also available. In 1676 the then Maratta prince Ekoji after ending his conflicts with the company came to an agreement and this agreement, as the previous one in Telugu, had a Dutch and a Tamil version.[15] The actors are now different; but the place of execution and the object involved are the same. Instead of a Coḷa king donating a village to a Buddhist monastery, a Maratta prince is forced to 'donate' the rights of trade to the Dutch East India Company. The Telugu inscription like the Sanskrit-Tamil bilingual inscriptions of the Colas, demarks the areas and the number of villages in Nagapattinam, where the Dutch are allowed to come and conduct trade. They also mention the various tax exemptions similar to the ones found in the Coḷa royal grants.

Like the Sanskrit words written in Grantha characters in the Tamil portion of the Sanskrit-Tamil bilingual inscriptions, the Dutch words are written in Grantha characters in the Tamil inscription corresponding to the Dutch version of the Dutch-Tamil bilingual agreements. The language is predominantly colloquial. Similar to the *praśasti*s which praise the Cola kings in the Sanskrit-Tamil inscriptions, the Dutch are mentioned with all titles:

---

[14] Heeres 1931:127f gives the text in Dutch corresponding to the Telugu text of one of the Silver plate inscriptions.

[15] See Heeres 1934:34-39 for the Dutch version of the contract, and for the Tamil version Sastri 1974:111-126. The village given as endowment to the Buddhist Vihāra in the earlier Rājarāja/Rājendra copper plates ('Leiden plates') are mentioned again in this silver plate.

> the Honourable Dutch Company . . . represented by Signor Peter Verwer. Senior captain, Signor Thomas van Rhee, the junior captain, and other members of the council at Nagapattinam, acting on behalf of Signor Admiral Maharaja Rijklof van Goens, Lieutenant General of India, Malangarai Member of council, and Governor of Ceylon, the Coramandel coast, Salakkari and the Madura coast . . . " (Sastri 1974:124).

Another important similarity with the Sanskrit-Tamil inscriptions is the protection given to the *dēvadāya* (village given to the temple), *brahmadāya* (village given to the Brahmins), *mānya* ('free' village) and *maḍappuram* (village providing food etc. to the temple) (Sastri 1974:125). The seventh point in the Dutch-Tamil inscription specifically mentions that the villages given to Gods or temples and Brahmins will remain as before.[16]

7. *Conclusion*

The presence of Sanskrit and Tamil, and subsequently literary and spoken Tamil, in South Indian inscriptions (later also Dutch and Tamil in Dutch-Tamil bilingual agreements) brings us to questions relating to the status of Sanskrit, in general, and the status of the language of the king/god and the royal élite as against the language of the people; in particular. It is necessary to place this problem in a broader perspective of the functioning of the society and not to regard it as an isolated instance of diglossia or bilingualism. The use of Prakrit and later Sanskrit by the Pallava monarch is a continuation reflecting their origin. However, the same is not true for the Coḷas. In the period of the Pallavas and the Coḷas, the Tamil Bhakti literature developed into a social movement. On the one hand we see the literary Tamil of these poets, and on the other hand the bilingual inscriptions in

---

[16] Thus, these inscriptions are valuable not only from the point of view of the history of the continuation of the style of the eulogy but also for the history of the continuation of the importance given to the religious values. In this respect an interesting comparison could be made on the basis of the contents of the Leiden Copper Plates and the later Dutch and Tamil records of the seventeenth century.

Sanskrit and Tamil—both literary and colloquial. The Sanskrit of the bilingual inscriptions is a sacral, religious and royal language; it is mainly used to communicate a mythologial background, whereas the pragmatic message of the documents is very precisely conveyed in the local language.

CHAPTER TEN

SPEECH OF THE GURUS: INSTANCES OF TREATMENT OF SANSKRIT IN TANTRIC LITERATURE

Teun Goudriaan

I.

The linguistic study of Tantric literature is still in its infancy. The lack of adequate documentation in this field of Sanskrit philology has its consequences for contemporary projects; for instance, for the huge lexicographical project "Encyclopaedic Dictionary of Sanskrit on Historical Principles" started up at Poona in 1948 by the initiative of S.M. Katre, and the first fascicle of which came out in 1976 (Ghatage 1976). A preliminary list of sources on p. LXXVI of Vol. I reveals that many Tantras have been included, while some other, partly important texts, are unfortunately not represented. Among these sources are the Svacchanda and Netra Tantras, the Prapañcasāra and Yoginīhṛdaya, and several Tantras of magical orientation. All of those mentioned by name have been published before 1976; we do not speak now of unpublished texts, or of those published in the meantime such as the Kulālikāmnāya. Tantric Sanskrit is therefore incompletely represented in this most important lexicographical project[1].

Can we really speak (as is sometimes done) of a 'Tantric Sanskrit' on a par with 'Epic Sanskrit' or 'Buddhist Hybrid Sanskrit'? It is true that the Sanskrit used in Tantric literature is often of a peculiar kind; but do these 'irregularities' coincide, are they structured, in a degree sufficient

[1] Recently, an initiative to remedy this deplorable lack of data at least for the doctrinally and ritually important terminology has been launched in a joint French-Austrian effort "Dictionnaire des Termes Techniques de la Littérature Tantrique" directed by Gerhard Oberhammer and André Padoux.

to enable us to characterize the language of these texts as 'Tantric Sanskrit'?

This would not be, in my opinion, a realistic position. Many Tantric texts have been written down as a direct reflection of the oral teaching of gifted formulators: *gurus*, *nāthas* or *siddhas*. They were people of very different background and greatly different education and linguistic training. Among them must have been a substantial number of well-instructed Brahmans who had been fascinated by, and initiated into, traditions of Tantric-yogic doctrine and practice. We should not forget that by no means all Tantras have been written in 'irregular' or 'bad' Sanskrit. Some of them, especially of the secondary works and commentaries, betray a sufficient mastership of the rules of correct language and of stylistic variation. The term 'Tantric Sanskrit', even if continued to be used, is therefore perhaps only a catcher for a great variety of symptoms.

II.

In the light of the preceding, we should not be surprised to find that different opinions (or, if one prefers, ideologies) exist about the status and use of Sanskrit in the teaching and transmission of Tantric truths. Such discussions are, however, not frequent and they have not yet been collected and studied adequately.

In any case, quite divergent motivations occur for the use of ungrammatical or non-standard (rather than 'substandard') language. We can expect the formulation of such motivations mainly in the commentaries, if they exist, because the original Tantras[2] usually do not bother to go into such questions: they are presented as of divine origin, and supernatural inspiration does not subject itself to critical discourse. Commentators may be a little less scrupulous. But even one and the same commentator may give different explanations. For instance, Kṣemarāja (11th century), a famous representative of Kashmir Śaivism and an accomplished master of Sanskrit prose writing, when confronted with an irregular *sandhi* in Svacchanda Tantra (SvT) 11.95: *māyā-aharmukha*, explains that this is *chāndasa*, a term I would like to interpret here as "a feature of inspired metrical speech on a par with the

[2] On this term, see Goudriaan & Gupta 1981:4.

Veda." He thereby implies that such a feature should be reverenced and scrupulously maintained. But while commenting on an earlier passage of the same text (SvT 4.234d), *yāvaśaktitaḥ,* "as far as (the level of) Śakti," he remarked *yāvacchabde talopa aiśvaraḥ* "the dropping of the unvoiced dental in the word *yāvat* is (a special feature) of Īśvara's speech" (as usual, Śiva is the speaker in this Tantra). Of course, these explanations do not seem to be discrepant with each other, but we would have been grateful to Kṣemarāja for a little more explanation.

The Piṅgalāmata is one of the anonymous texts which have something, however short, to say about the nature of Āgamic speech (the Piṅgalāmata considers itself as an Āgama). We consulted an old Nepalese manuscript (National Archives 3-376/113 of 1174 C.E.). After a question of the interlocutor, Piṅgalā, who wants to know whether or not Āgama is recognizable by certain characteristics, Śiva explains (Piṅ 1.6f.) that Āgama has come down from his, Śiva's, mouth by oral instruction from generation to generation (of teachers and hearers), and is perfected by the characteristic of *chandas*, which here again denotes metrically bound speech exceeding, like the Vedas, the limits of grammatical regulation:

> *śivavaktrāmbujāyātaṃ pāramparyakrameṇa tu /*
> *chandolakṣaṇasaṃsiddham āgamety abhidhīyate //*

The Vedic association is often found elsewhere in the Tantras, e.g. in the Kulārṇava, KulT 2.10: the *kuladharma* is the essence of the ocean of the Veda, churned with the churning stick of wisdom. But by no means all Tantras are as friendly towards the Vedic tradition.

We can perhaps imagine that, at the time of instruction by the *guru*, critical remarks made by pedantic, argument-loving pupils about defects of language in Āgama or Tantra were not appreciated. Such a situation is without doubt referred to in the Ṣaṭsāhasra Saṃhitā, ṢSS 3.16 (Schoterman 1982:94):

> *gurudevāgnibhakte ca kathanīyaṃ na durjane /*
> *padārthasyākṣarārthasya carcācarcaṃ na kārayet //*
> One should recite a text to a person who is devoted to his Guru, God and the fires; not to a man of evil disposition; one should not allow endless analytical reasoning about the meaning of words or syllables.

Similar admonition is given by the commentator Subhagānanda on Tantrarāja Tantra, TRT 25.11 *garbhanyāseṣṭasiddhikṛt.* He explains that this should be interpreted as *garbhanyāse iṣṭasiddhikṛt* "(the *yantra*) will procure a desired result on the occasion of the (ritual) deposit of a germ." And he adds: *āgamānāṃ sandhir divyatvād asmābhir na vicāraṇīyaḥ* "we should not ask ourselves questions about the sandhi in the Āgamas, because they are divine in nature."

Modern interpreters have tended not to bother themselves about such restrictions. Pandit H.P. Shastri, when commenting upon the highly incorrect language of the Nityāhnikatilaka, [3] remarked that a text of this nature must have been written by a representant of the Nātha sect or one of its close associates, who all came forth (in the Pandit's opinion) from the lowest strata of society. In this case, applying the argument of 'lack of instruction' is not so controversial, because the Nityāhnikatilaka is a secondary— although admittedly old—text, of the *paddhati* type, and its author is known by name (Muñjaka or Muktaka). But what to say of the perhaps still more incorrect and anonymous Kaulajñānanirṇaya? Its editor, Prabodh Chandra Bagchi (Calcutta 1934), in his Preface, took a more cautious standpoint. He gave two possible motives for writing texts in such ungrammatical language.

First motive: the teaching "should be accessible to all initiates [or pupils, TG] even without any preparation in grammar" (Bagchi 1934:V). This does not seem a very plausible argument, although the primacy of the didactic purpose must be acknowledged. [4] It can be stated, however, that the many nonstandard features and strange stylistic set-up of several Tantras including the Kaulajñānanirṇaya do not exactly serve to facilitate instruction.

The second motive for using incorrect language presented by P.Ch. Bagchi (1934:V) is more or less a continuation of the didactic argument just mentioned. He refers to a passage from the Vimalaprabhā, a commentary on the Buddhist Kālacakratantra, which he quotes in full. It may suffice to translate here the gist of it:

> . . . and in order to destroy the predilection for cultivated expression of those propagators of such expression . . . (the Author applies) sometimes transgression of metrical codes, sometimes neglect of the caesura in metrical speech, sometimes omission of case-endings, sometimes deletion of consonant or vowel, sometimes (again.in metrical speech) replacement of a long vowel by a short one and the reverse, sometimes

---

[3] Shastri 1905:LXIV.

[4] See Śivadharmottara Purāṇa., ch. 2, referred to by Hazra 1963:179f.

> the use of a locative instead of an ablative, or of a genitive instead of a dative. . . . Therefore, also in the commentary I feel obliged to write with a view to destroy the conceit (of certain people) because of (their) cultured use of language, having recourse to the meaning (rather than the form of words).[5]

So, in this view, the real intention of 'bad grammar' is not to instruct the uncultured (as Bagchi wrongly interpreted also this passage), but to destroy the attitude of overcultured snobbery among the initiates.

Another dimension is added to the problem by the sometimes very strange language of the mantras which occur in Āgamic literature (not to speak of the monosyllabic *bījas*). Occasionally, they are in a pseudo-vedic style, for instance the mantras in the sacred literature of the non-Tantric Vaikhānasa community. I quote Colas 1994:297: " . . . certes les nombreuses incorrections grammaticales qui emplissent les mantras vaikhānasa, allant jusqu'à rendre ceux-ci inintelligibles sembleraient contredire . . . la signification que le principe leur accorde . . . " Thus, the mantras seem at first sight to be ununderstandable and therefore devoid of sense. Colas gives two counter-arguments against this seeming senselessness of the mantras: 1. The exegete (teacher) can and should press a meaning upon the mantra in question with the help of grammar and etymology (perhaps rather say: he should reveal its hidden meaning). 2. As a component of the ritual discourse (to which the mantra forms, in Colas' terminology, a "meta-discourse"), any mantra takes part of the finality of that ritual (Colas does not subscribe to the theory of the 'meaninglessness' of ritual). We cannot pursue the discussion about the mantras here.

Resuming the question, it could be said that deviation of linguistic standard, characteristic for a substantial part of Tantric literature, may indeed be partially caused by incomplete instruction in grammatical details. But we should add, that the transgression of rules has certainly often been cultivated on purpose for reasons as given above.

There is another point which can lead us to a more subtle approach to the problem. In many texts, it is not so much a constant practice of in-

---

[5] *teṣāṃ ca suśabdavādināṃ suśabdagrahavināśāya....kvacid vṛtte apaśabdaḥ / kvacid vṛtte yatibhaṅgaḥ / kvacid avibhaktikaṃ padam / kvacid varṇasvaralopaḥ / kvacid vṛtte dīrgho hrasvaḥ, hrasvo 'pi dīrghaḥ / kvacit pañcamyarthe saptamī, caturthyarthe ṣaṣṭhī..../....evaṃ ṭīkāyām api suśabdābhimānanāśāya likhitavyaṃ mayā arthaśaraṇatām āśritya.*

The passage has been treated in more detail in Newman 1988:124f.

correctness, but rather a complicated and highly varied shifting between correct and incorrect formations; a procedure which suggests a sovereign freedom from grammatical niceties without breaking thereby (this should be made quite clear) the adherence to the revered speech of gods and gurus. As an instance we quote the alternation between Kulālikāmnāya (KulĀ) 8.80a *prajvalan dṛśyate bhūtaiḥ* and 9.64c *jvalanto dṛśyate bhūtaiḥ*. Such freedom of alternation was noticed already by Leen van Daalen for Epic Sanskrit (van Daalen 1980:130f, 282). The speech reflected in several Tantras suggests the divine freedom from petty formality, implying thereby a lesson in emancipation, in playfulness, in leaving behind one's shortsighted prejudices.

III.

Keeping ourselves on the level of petty grammatical rule-stating, can we postulate, with V.V. Dvivedi,[6] a historical development of ever-deteriorating knowledge of the rules of grammar? This seems generalizing too much, although it is probably true to a certain extent, depending on circumstances.

There are indeed instances of deterioration, for instance if we compare certain passages occurring in respectively SvT, Tantrasadbhāva, KulĀ, and (worst of all) Manthānabhairava. But there are of course several younger Tantras of fairly correct language, among them KulT, TRT, or Mahānirvāṇa. Some authors of secondary works and commentaries, for instance Bhāskararāya (17th century) were great Sanskrit scholars. Another point: in the textual history of old Tantras we may find attempts by scribes to polish away the incorrect features of the older tradition. Such attempts are frequent in the history of the KulĀ. Thus, in the pāda quoted above, KulĀ 9.64c *jvalanto dṛśyate bhūtaiḥ*, we find instead of *jvalanto*: *jvalan sa* in two of the younger manuscripts, and *jvalan vai* in a third one. On the other hand, early palm leaf mss. of this text sometimes contain quite wild readings. I would therefore rather speak of an undulating process of deterioration and restoration; or of "wear and tear" and "polishing" within the manuscript tradition.

---

[6] Dvivedi in Bhattacharya & Dvivedi 1978, Sanskrit Upodghāta p. 90; against Winternitz.

Hardly necessary to say that, in the scarcity of critical editions, one can commit severe mistakes on the linguistic character of a text.

IV.

The reflection on 'Tantric Sanskrit' can, as we saw, hardly be separated from the ideology of its divine origin. "This book on the Goddess," says Kulālikāmnāya (KulĀ 25.221) is "adorned by divine speech," *divya-bhāṣāvibhūṣitam.* The language of Āgama and Tantra is believed to be a direct successor to the primeval, non-discursive stage of sound which embodied the pure wisdom of Brahman consciousness, a "wave of wisdom," *jñānaugha* (BY 2.36 a.o.); or "ocean of wisdom," *jñānasāgara* (KulĀ 25.221). This view has been laid down in lapidary form in Śiva Sūtra (ŚivS) 1.4 *jñānādhiṣṭhānaṃ mātṛkā* "the Womb of Speech is the repository of wisdom" ("repository": the commentator Bhāskara explains *adhiṣṭhānam* by *ādhāraḥ*). According to the much younger Kāmadhenu Tantra (KāmT 8.2ff.), the Mātṛkā is the real essence of all deities and other beings. She is the Mother of all Veda-based science and can be worshipped in the form of 50 beautiful young women. Also all mantras have the form of young women. Without these letters which constitute the Mātṛkā, says the text, the cosmos is like a dead body. Other views on the worship of the Mātṛkā exist, but the deep reverence to the Source of speech is everywhere the same. Her effusion into the world of articulated speech is inevitably realized in the form of Sanskrit, as is proved by the dialogues between Śiva and Devī held in that language. This dialogue set the pattern for the *guru-śiṣya* relationship in teaching. Abhinavagupta, in his commentary Tattvaviveka on Parātriṃśikā vs. 1 explains this as a self-reflection of the cosmic *aham*, who is "of Bhairava nature, untainted by division of his Energy into 'own' and 'not-own'" (TViv p. 6: *svaparaśaktyavibhāgamayo bhairavātmā*). We cannot pursue this subject now; this would lead us too far into theological speculation.

Since origin and nature of the Āgamic texts are divine, they should be treated with the utmost reverence. Śiva's wisdom should be cherished as a "woman of good family," while the other so-called 'revealed' literature (Vedas, *śāstras* and Purāṇas) is to be compared with women of easy virtue, says the Jñānasaṃkalanī Tantra (JST 1.7):

vedaśāstrapurāṇāni sāmānyagaṇikā iva /
yā punaḥ śāmbhavi vidyā guptā kulavadhūr iva //

Something similar is said in the Kulārṇava (KulT 3.4). The quotation is a well-known one.

As this Lady of Speech is of divine beauty, it is important that the revealed Truth should be expressed 'in style', so to say; that means, in any case, in metrically bound form, if possible made attractive by pregnant formulation, but also secretive by procedures of mystification. Thus, the Ṣaṭsāhasra Saṃhitā (ṢSS 3.45f.), knows of sixteen different ways to hand down the teachings in a disguised way.[7]

The reverence for Sanskrit as the medium of instruction into divine revelation also appears from the ritualization of text recitation by the guru or another specialist. We find such instructions e.g. in the Piṅgalāmata (Piṅ 1.11f.) and in the Tantrāloka (e.g. TĀl 28.394). Manuscripts should be treated with reverence, says the Ṣaṭsāhasra Saṃhitā (ṢSS 3.28), and the same text, in 3.98, ordains that before recitation one should worship first the *(guru)krama,* then the manuscript, then the Yoginīs and virgins (who guard the tradition). The importance of worship of the Āgama is also stressed by the Kulālikāmnāya (KulĀ 25.221 *āgame pūjite sarvaṃ pūjitam*).[8] On the other hand, Sanskrit seems not to have been obligatory in commentation, cf. TĀl 28.405 *bhāṣā . . . yad yad eti śiṣyasya sambodhopāyatvaṃ tathaiva gurur āśrayed vyākhyām* "language etc., whatever is conducive to the pupil's understanding, that the guru should apply while commenting." Jayaratha, *ad loc.*, holds that six *bhāṣā*s are possible as means of instruction dependent upon the initiate's knowledge; the first alternative is Sanskrit.

V.

We have seen that divine speech of Āgama and Tantra, although far from clearly characterized, tends to possess some peculiar features, among which are a relative freedom from the commands of grammar;

---

[7] Schoterman 1982:115. - For stylistic devices in the Kulālikāmnāya, see Goudriaan & Schoterman 1988:93ff.

[8] Compare the reverence for the book in Buddhist tradition as described by G. Schopen 1975.

but one sometimes also observes a predilection for pregnant, mystifying formulation different from ordinary speech (not to speak of the ubiquity of 'meaningless' mantras and bījas). This latter feature implies that this revealed speech (itself a manifestation of the Goddess) is able to enhance its divine character by a concealment of hidden truth. Such concealment itself is a hallmark of divinity: *parokṣakāmā hi devatāḥ,* this Upaniṣadic dictum would occasionally also be applicable to Āgamic style. Revelation of such concealed truth is possible by at least three methods, viz. 1. etymology; 2. exegesis (applied to difficult passages in the Tantras as well as to quotations from the Veda[9]); 3. restatement (as in KulĀ 25.156f.).

Only of the first method: etymology, or (as one might call it) *parokṣanirūpaṇam,* I shall give a few instances. First, a case from a text bordering on both Vedic and post-Vedic, or even Tantric, formulation: Maitrāyaṇīya Upaniṣad 2.6, where the subject is the Ātman: *sa vā eṣo 'sya hṛdantara akṛtārtho 'manyata: arthān aśnānīti / ataḥ khānīmāni bhittvoditaḥ pañcabhī raśmibhir viṣayān attīti / ātmeti hośanti* (MaiUp 2.6-7, p. 101) "That same one, unsatisfied within his heart, thought: 'I will eat the objects.' Then, breaking through the orifices of this body, he has emerged with five rays and eats the objects of the senses. Because of this, they call him Ātman." The text implies or suggests by etymological procedure that there is an inherent, secret connection between *ātman* and *atti*; the connection was missed by van Buitenen in his translation on p. 128.[10] Such etymologies are, as we know, a conspicuous feature also in older Vedic literature, especially the Brāhmaṇas. We might, with Peter Verhagen, speak of "hermeneutic etymology,"* which is of course different from linguistic etymology. We have to do with a pointer to truth hidden within doubly meaningful sound.

In the Tantras, etymologies are very unevenly distributed. They always concern important, pivotal terms. For instance, according to the Piṅgalāmata, Āgama is so called because *ājñā* 'authorization', that is: *vastu,* 'reality', perhaps 'mastery of reality', is reached by it, *gamyate,* on all sides, *samantāt: Ājñā vastu samantāc ca gamyatety āgamo mataḥ*

---

[9] For a famous instance of the latter, see Padoux 1990:167.

[10] The MaiUp. reverts to the theme in 6.10 and 6.31; cf. also BĀUp. 4.4.24.

* Editor's note: In Verhagen's oral presentation and discussion of his paper at the seminar "Ideology and Status of Sanskrit," Leiden, November 1994. Cf. also Verhagen 1994:11.

(Piṅ 1.4). Note the 'wrong sandhi' after *gamyate*. The text proceeds with similar explanations of *jñāna* and *tantra*.[11]

Still more 'mystical' are the etymologies in the Kulārṇava, e.g. in KulT 17.7, where four explanations are given of the word *guru*: 1. *gu = andhakāra, ru = nirodhaka*; 2. *ga = siddhida, ra = pāpasya dāhaka, u = Viṣṇu* (association of *ra* with 'burning' is understandable, because this syllable is connected with Agni; *u* symbolizes Viṣṇu in the speculation on *Oṃ*). 3. *ga = jñānasampatti, ra = jñānaprakāśaka, u = Śiva* (thus, Śiva is referred to as the origin of all wisdom with whom the Guru is identical); 4. *guhyāgamatattvabodhanāt, rudrādidevarūpatvāt* (Guru,) "because he reveals the hidden realities of Āgama, and because he incarnates the gods, in the first place Rudra." In the last instance, the etymological procedure consists of revealing the introductory function of the syllables in question; we might call this *pratīkadīpanam*. The whole 17th chapter of the Kulārṇava is a collection of such etymologies.

The Kulālikāmnāya knows of the same procedure, e.g. in KulĀ 6.81 it gives a (well-known) explanation of *mudrā*: *mocanād drāvaṇād yasmān, mudrākhyāḥ śaktayaḥ smṛtāḥ* "it is taught that the Energies are called *mudrās* because they afford emancipation and the end of stagnation." Other interesting cases which we shall not discuss now are found in the same text, KulĀ 25.84f. Also commentators apply such methods, e.g. Kṣemarāja on SvT. 6.3 *praṇava*.

From the above instances it appears that such etymological procedure is especially apt to bring to the surface the pregnancy of the texts with hidden symbolical meaning, not their devious ways of expression. In the milieu influenced by Tantric thought, the Sanskrit language operates not so much as a means to maintain status by conformity to acknowledged grammatical codes. Rather, it serves to distinguish the divine from the ordinary, to guide the aspirant by its inner nature of spirituality.

[11] A different view on the meaning of Āgama is formulated in TĀl 35.1f.

CHAPTER ELEVEN

TIBETAN EXPERTISE IN SANSKRIT GRAMMAR: IDEOLOGY, STATUS AND OTHER EXTRA-LINGUISTIC FACTORS*

Pieter C. Verhagen

1. *Introduction*

The majority of Buddhist literature that reached Tibet in the context of the dissemination of Buddhism from the 7th century onwards was written in some form of Sanskrit—either approaching the norm of classical Sanskrit, or more or less hybrid Prakrit-Sanskrit. At the present moment I will not be dealing with the ideological and other considerations involved in the conscious adoption of Sanskrit as *the* vehicular language of the later, Mahāyāna Buddhist scriptures before these entered Tibet, but with the status and role Sanskrit acquired in Buddhist Tibet.

Evidently the most natural way for Tibetans to access the discipline of Sanskrit grammar was via the indigenous Indic systems of grammar. After some early beginnings of, particularly phonological, linguistic description in the Prātiśākhyas and semantic c.q. etymological investigation in the Nirukta, the basis, and in many respects the *summum* of indigenous Sanskrit grammar is of course Pāṇini's Aṣṭādhyāyī (5th century BC). In spite of the Brahmanical background of *vyākaraṇa*, the occupation with the grammar of Sanskrit in the Buddhist circles that

* The present article is the second in a series of articles devoted to Tibetan Expertise in Sanskrit Grammar. (The first article in this series is Verhagen forthcoming a.) It is in part a summary representation of the paper actually read at the IIAS-seminar "Ideology and Status of Sanskrit in South and Southeast Asia". The parts corresponding to materials that I have published elsewhere or that are forthcoming, have been summarized here. The research for this article has been made possible by a fellowship of the Royal Netherlands Academy of Arts and Sciences.

the Tibetans came into contact with, and subsequently in the Tibetan circles as well, need not amaze us.

Sanskrit grammatical studies were by no means the prerogative of a Brahmanical elite. In all but the most early periods of the history of indigenous grammar in India, Buddhist scholars have played a role of considerable importance, as exemplified by the correlation between the Buddhist *Cāndra* grammar (5th century CE) and the important Pāṇinian commentary Kāśikā-vṛtti, and, secondly, by the introduction of the topical re-ordering of the *sūtras* by the Buddhist grammars Kātantra (before ca. 400 CE) and (within the Pāṇinian school) Rūpāvatāra (10th/11th century), which was later adopted by the so-called Kaumudī commentaries, the most popular methods of tuition in Pāṇinian grammar from the sixteenth century onwards[1].

In the present paper I will discuss some salient points in the background and the context of the tradition of Sanskrit linguistics in the Tibetan scholarly world. For convenience's sake I will broadly distinguish three types of factors that have in some way contributed to the genesis and development of Sanskrit linguistic studies in Tibet, namely:

(1) historical and political factors;
(2) scientific factors;
(3) religious factors.

2. *Historical and political factors*[2]

The dissemination of Buddhism in Tibet involved the transmission of a vast complex of Indic cultural elements encircling the nucleus of the *Buddha-dharma*. This immensely complex system of dogmas, philosophical and metaphysical notions, related cults and practices, forms of social organisation, artistic expressions etc., subsumed under the term 'Buddhism', had an extremely important literary component. The introduction into the Tibetan tradition of a vast corpus of Indic literature,

---

[1] Cf. Scharfe 1977: 174-175.

[2] This first section is a brief summary of my sketch of the history of 'royal' patronage of Sanskrit studies in Tibet, published earlier as the introductory section in my contribution to the Heesterman Festschrift, Verhagen 1992: 375-378.

mainly belonging to the so-called Mahāyāna and Tantrayāna forms of Buddhism and predominantly written in Sanskrit, often Buddhist Hybrid Sanskrit, necessitated the production of Tibetan translations of these texts. As mentioned above, the Tibetans adopted the Indic indigenous traditions for their tuition in Sanskrit grammar, and a considerable corpus of forty-seven texts on the subject of Sanskrit grammar was incorporated into the second Buddhist canon, the so-called Bstan-'gyur.[3]

During the first period of dissemination of Buddhism in Tibet, mid seventh to mid ninth century CE, entailing the first wave of Sanskrit-Tibetan translating activities, the royal dynasty of Yar-luṅ, the first clan to exercise sovereign power over all of Tibet and a considerable number of adjacent regions, extended their patronage to the translation efforts, thus contributing decisively to their ultimate success. Moreover, it has been shown that the periods during which the vast majority of the Tibetan canonical translations of Sanskrit grammatical treatises and related materials were made, scil. the 13th -14th and the 17th century, correspond precisely to periods in Tibetan history of dominance of one centralised authority, *in casu* the *Sa-skya-pa* and *Dge-lugs-pa* sects respectively, that were the dominating powers of the time, in religious as well as in profane, political matters. These dominant sects also functioned as patrons of the translating activities and consequently also of Sanskrit studies, which in the context of the orientation on Indian sources of Buddhism could rightfully be called the key to orthodoxy for the Tibetans.[4] It has been suggested that more profane considerations may also have played a role in the 'royal' c.q. 'princely' patronage of Sanskrit studies, e.g. matters of prestige and status.[5]

---

[3] For a detailed description of these texts and their translations, cf. Verhagen (1994: 46-165, 231-322).

[4] Cf. Verhagen 1992: 375-378, 1994: 201-205.

[5] Cf. Verhagen 1992: 378, 1994: 205-206.

3. *Scientific factors*

An approximation of what we in the West would call scientific interest and precision has always been a hallmark of the Tibetan scholarly world. Particularly the translators have been described as early Indologists or Indologists avant-la-lettre; one might venture the nomenclature palaeo-Indologists. Their primary aim was the precise and faithful rendering of the Buddhist classical literature into Tibetan.

A critical attitude regarding the work of the translators is evident from the earliest period onwards, for instance, in the 'royal' period we find the first codification of terminology and techniques of translation (in particular in the Sanskrit-Tibetan lexicon Mahāvyutpatti and its partial commentary Sgra-sbyor-bam-po-gñis-pa[6]), the institution of central translation committees [7] responsible for the updating of earlier translations to the contemporaneous orthography and standardized lexicon, and for the checking of new translations for conforming to this orthography and lexicon, and we find that edicts regulating the translating techniques and procedures are issued by two Tibetan kings (on which more below).

In the 'classical' period [8] we see that a great number of translations were still being revised, before and after the compilation of the Tibetan canon(s). Investigation and direct consultation of Sanskrit originals by Tibetan scholars continued even in later centuries, when most of the Buddhist canon had long since been translated into Tibetan, and when an extensive accompanying literature had been written in Tibetan. Even in the 'post-classical' period we find that forms of textual criticism and philological investigation of the Sanskrit materials are being continued by the elite of the Tibetan scholars. Two striking examples will be dealt with presently, one from the 16th and one from the 18th century CE.

---

[6] Both preserved in the Tibetan *Bstan-'gyur* canon; cf. e.g. Snellgrove 1987: 441-443.

[7] Cf. e.g. Simonsson 1957: 259-260.

[8] The periodization of Sanskrit studies in Tibet in a 'pre-classical' (mid 7th-mid 9th cent.), a 'classical' (11th-14th cent.) and a 'post-classical' period (16th-18th cent.), as proposed in Verhagen 1994: 203-217.

3.1. Skyogs-ston Lo-tsā-ba Rin-chen-bkra-śis (ca. 1495-after 1577)

In a forthcoming article Leonard van der Kuijp (Harvard) investigates some important materials pertaining to the linguistic activities of Skyogs-ston Lo-tsā-ba, one of the major disciples of the famous grammarian Zha-lu Chos-skyoṅ-bzaṅ-po (1441-1528). Among these he describes a unique document providing evidence for the fact that textual criticism was still being applied to the translated literature, even at that time. This document is a four-folio Tibetan manuscript, acquired by Van der Kuijp in Nepal, the ultimate provenance of which is unknown. It bears the title Sgra'i-ñer-mkho-gal-che-ba'i-skor-'ga'-zhig "Some necessary and important linguistical [notes]," and is, according to the colophon, a "copy of a hand-written manuscript by Skyogs-ston."[9]

The text consists of a collection of notes that Skyogs-ston made while studying the Tibetan versions of specific canonical materials, namely the first three[10] of the popular Kriyātantra collection of texts known as the Pañcarakṣā. It is evident from these notes that Skyogs-ston not only consulted the Tibetan translation(s), but, in cases where there was reason to assume that due to the original translator(s), reviser(s) or scribes some error had corrupted the Tibetan transmission, he would go back to the Sanskrit originals.

It appears that Skyogs-ston used several Sanskrit manuscripts for this purpose: two, perhaps three of Mahā-pratisāra-vidyā, two of Mahā-sāhasra-pramardana-sūtra, and at least one of Mahā-mayūrī-vidyā.[11] As an example, the first entry on the Mahā-pratisāra-vidyā-rājñī observes that in a specific phrase in the beginning of the text the canonical translation has *bden-pa-daṅ* 'and real/true', where two Sanskrit manuscripts available to Skyogs-ston have the term *vivikta* 'separate', 'solitary'. On

---

[9] *k [a] ṭ [a] cchu-skyogs-ston-karma-lo-tsa'i-legs-par-bśad-pa-phyag-bris-ma-las-ṅos-bśus* [= *(b) zhus* ?], f. 4r, Van der Kuijp forthc.: author's ms p. 6.

[10] Scil. Mahā-sāhasra-pramardana-sūtra (Stoṅ-chen-rab-'joms-kyi-mdo), Mahā-mayūrī-vidyā-rājñī (Rigs-sṅags-kyi-rgyal-mo-rma-bya-chen-mo) and Ārya-mahā-pratisāra-vidyā-rājñī ('Phags-pa-rigs-sṅags-kyi-rgyal-mo-so-sor-'braṅ-ba-chen-mo), Peking *Bka'-'gyur* Suzuki repr. (1955-1961) title nos. 177-179, Derge *Bka'-'gyur* Tohoku cat. (1953) title nos. 558, 559 & 561.

[11] Van der Kuijp forthc.: author's ms. p. 7.

the basis of the Sanskrit reading he proposes the emendation *dben-pa-daṅ* 'and separate/solitary'.[12]

3.2. Si-tu Paṇ-chen Chos-kyi-'byuṅ-gnas (1699/1700-1774)

A second excellent example of the latter-day Tibetan occupation with Indic sources and linguistics is to be found in the works of Si-tu *mahāpaṇḍita*, by far the most outstanding Tibetan linguist of his century. Within Tibetan literature proper he is best known for his extensive commentary on the two basic treatises of Tibetan grammar, which is universally accepted as the most important commentary in this field; a kind of Summa Grammatica one might say. He was also responsible for the redaction of a blockprint edition of the Tibetan canon. Moreover, he spent a considerable part of his career revising the translations of many of the linguistic treatises in the canon (grammatical and lexicographical materials esp.), and making a number of new translations. In his works he often scorns particular earlier translations and translators for their lack of accuracy.

His autobiography (based on his personal diary) shows his untiring search for Sanskrit manuscripts in all regions of central and eastern Tibet, as well as during his sojourns in Nepal. It should be borne in mind that at the time some major monastic institutions in Central Tibet were veritable treasure-houses of Sanskrit manuscripts. The Bihari scholar Rāhul Sāṅkṛtyāyana described (and photographed) several hundreds of Sanskrit manuscripts he encountered in six monasteries[13] in Central Tibet when he visited Tibet in the thirties of this century.

The most remarkable sign of the purely scientific nature of Si-tu's interest in these matters is perhaps his translation of a chapter dealing with the morphology of Vedic Sanskrit (Vaidika-prakriyā from

---

[12] *so-'braṅ* [supralinear note: *hor-par-] -mdo'i-gleṅ-gzhir / byams-pa'i-stobs-daṅ-zhes-pa'i-'og-na / bden-pa-daṅ-zhes-pa-'dug-ste / rgya-dpe-gñis-na / bi-bikta-zhes-pa-snaṅ-de : dben-pa-daṅ-zhes-par-'gyur : bas : bod-dpe-yi-ge-nor-bar-snaṅ /*, f. 1v1-2, Van der Kuijp forthc.: author's ms. p. 8.

[13] Kun-bde-gliṅ (in Lhasa) and Sa-skya, Ṅor, Zha-lu, Spos-khaṅ and Rta-nag-thub-bstan monasteries (in Gtsaṅ), Sāṅkṛtyāyana 1935, 1937, 1938.

Rāmacandra's Prakriyā-kaumudī).[14] In the canonical Tibetan translation of this grammar this chapter is omitted. Here and elsewhere, Si-tu takes the translators to task for this omission and other weaknesses in this translation. Si-tu filled this lacuna by making a separate translation of this chapter, now included in his collected works.

For the reading of the Buddhist literature available in Sanskrit, knowledge of the grammatical peculiarities of Vedic Sanskrit was of course not required. His translation, and hence his making accessible to the Tibetans this very specific segment of Indic grammatical lore, seems to have served no direct, practical purpose in this Tibetan Buddhist context. Granted, rare instances of Buddhist commentators evoking Pāṇinian Vedic rules to explain specific hybrid Sanskrit forms are known, but they are too marginal to be of any consequence here.[15] The main motive seems to have been pure curiosity and an attempt at completeness.

A matter dealt with quite extensively in the Indo-Tibetan exegesis of the Tantristic lore, is that of the correct pronunciation of the Sanskrit terms in *mantras*. Here scientific and religious factors or motives are inseparable. The efficacy of the *mantra* depends on—inter alia—the full and correct pronunciation or recitation or its reproduction in writing. As a result, some knowledge of Sanskrit phonology was necessary in connection with the multitude of *mantras* that play a central role in Tantristic and—to a degree—in Mahāyāna Buddhism. This led to the development of a genre of manual in the Tibetan Tantristic literature, viz. the so-called 'pronunciation-manuals' (*klog-thabs*). These manuals instructed the Tibetan adepts in the main points of the pronunciation of Sanskrit, often, understandably, giving particular attention to the aspects that were alien to Tibetan, and therefore most problematic for the Tibetans.[16]

---

[14] For a more detailed treatment, cf. the forthcoming second volume of my *History of Sanskrit Grammatical Literature in Tibet.*

[15] E.g. Candrakīrti's commentary on Āryadeva's Catuḥśataka quotes the Vedic rule P. 7.1.39, and a *vārttika* to this rule, to account for certain hybrid Sanskrit forms in a verse from the Samādhirājasūtra, cf. Tillemans 1990-2: 118, Bronkhorst 1993a: 404-406, Lang 1993: 440-442.

[16] On the Tibetan linguistic exegesis of *mantras*, cf. Verhagen 1990, 1993 and the forthcoming second volume of my *History of Sanskrit Grammatical Literature in Tibet.*

A second instance where the scientific and religious backgrounds meet, can be found in the formation of Tibetan indigenous grammar. This is primarily modelled on Indic linguistic description. However, it is more than a mere—attempted—clone of Indic *vyākaraṇa.* It consists of an amalgam of heterogeneous elements, terms and techniques derived from the Mahāyāna philosophical speculation on language and the Tantristic exegesis relating to *mantra*s (being explicitly Buddhist sources) on the one hand, and the traditions of indigenous Sanskrit grammar on the other.[17]

4. *Religious factors*

This brings us to the third set of elements that played a role in the reception of Indic linguistics in Tibet, viz. factors of a religious nature. We find that to a large extent religious factors have determined the development of Tibetan indigenous grammatical science. Due to the predominance of Mahāyāna and Tantrayāna Buddhism in Tibet, many language-oriented and linguistically-based ideas stemming from these forms of Buddhism have found their way into the Tibetan linguistic description: from exoteric, philosophical Buddhism notably the derivational model of the three *vyañjana-*, *nāma-* and *pada-kāya* (a set of notions already found in the Abhidharmakośa). From Tantristic Buddhism we find that especially elements (models and terms) pertaining to phonology have been derived, particularly the terminology and models used in connection with the exegesis of the Sanskrit *mantra*s used in Tantrism.

To the Tibetan Buddhist traditions evidently the translations—when made by competent translators, adhering strictly to the original text and to the conventions for translation technique and terminology—are, as exposés of the Buddhist doctrine, just as valid as the Indic originals. Here, clearly, the correct interpretation of the Sanskrit originals constituted the key to orthodoxy.

The intention to attempt to create translations that are faithful, precise, consistent and complete renderings of the original is explicitly included in the early eighth- and ninth-century royal edicts concerning

[17] Cf. Miller 1966, Simonsson 1982 and 1986, Verhagen 1995 and forthcoming.

the procedure of translating the teachings of the Buddha. Since recently we are in the fortunate circumstances that two versions of this edict, or perhaps more precisely, two consecutive edicts, are now available. The best-known version of the edict is that included in the Tibetan canon, as an introductory section in a ninth-century commentary on the Sanskrit-Tibetan translation-lexicon.[18] This edict dates from the year 814 CE, and was a decree by king Khri-lde-sroṅ-btsan Sad-na-legs (799-815).[19] The ongoing Austrian-Italian project investigating the important manuscript library of the monastery of Ta-pho (Spiti, Himachal Pradesh) has—among its many important findings—resulted in the discovery of an earlier, shorter edict[20] on the same topic, in this case dating from 783 or 795 CE, and being a decree issued by Sad-na-legs's father and predecessor Khri-sroṅ-lde-btsan (755-797).

These two edicts constitute extremely important documents regarding the translation techniques and conventions prevalent in the Tibetan traditions in the earliest period. The earliest edict is much simpler and shorter than the second. In fact, when comparing the two, it becomes evident that the second confirms all of the contents of the earlier one—here and there making stylistic changes—and that it adds quite a few expatiations, mainly on specific details and dilemmas encountered in the practice of translating. As such, the second edict, being at least some twenty years later than the first, gives evidence of the accumulation of experience with the problems involved in standardization of translation techniques in this interval of two (or three) decades between the two edicts.[21]

The first, earlier edict simply states:

> As regards the method of translating the excellent Dharma, one should make [i.e. translate] it into good, satisfactory Tibetan without violating [i.e. changing] the meaning, and, without altering the order[22] of the

---

[18] Sgra-sbyor-bam-po-gñis-pa, ed. Ishikawa 1990: 1-5; transl. & study: Simonsson 1957: 238-262, partial transl. Snellgrove 1987: 442-443.

[19] Cf. Uray 1990, Panglung 1994: 161.

[20] Edition & study: Panglung 1994.

[21] Cf. Panglung 1994: 164, 171-172.

[22] Tib. *go-rims*, here translated as 'order', could also mean 'system', 'structure' i.c. system of structural-syntactic relations.

> Sanskrit terms; one should translate producing a [firm] connection [i.e. harmony?] between meaning and word-form.[23]

The second edict has a passage virtually word-identical to this.[24] This, however, is followed by a rather lengthy excursus on several details in the translation-technique and -norms, that are only to be found in the later edict. In a preceding passage, the second edict had already insisted on the translation-terminology having to be in accordance with both the basic doctrines of Buddhism as well as the rules of grammar (*vyākaraṇa*).[25] In the following sections the edict specifies a number of important points in the translation process: matters such as word-order, syntactic structure and levels of meaning (distinguishing a literal, overt sense and an implicit / implied sense) are dealt with first.

By way of example, a passage reads:

> If a good, satisfactory [translation] and a [better] understanding results from altering [the order of the terms], in the case of a metrical [text], whether in a four- or six-line [meter], one may translate altering [the order of the terms] whenever [or: in so far as] [this results in] a good, satisfactory [translation], [but only] within the confines of the single verse.[26]

Then, in a lengthy passage[27] adducing also a number of examples, the second edict refers to the problems in translating that result from the frequent occurrence of polysemy and homonymy in Sanskrit. It stresses the deciding role of context[28] in resolving the ambiguity resulting from polysemy. It also admits the use of loan-words under certain conditions, instead of making a Tibetan translation for each and

---

[23] *dam-pa'ï-chos-bsgyur-ba'ï-lugs-nï-don-daṅ / myï-'gal-la-bod-skad-la-bde-bar-bya-ba-daṅ / rgya-gar-skad-go-rims-las-myï-bsnor-bar / don-daṅ-tshïg-tu-'breld-bar-byos-la-sgyurd-cïg /*, Panglung 1994: 164.

[24] Ed. Ishikawa 1990: 2: *dam-pa'i-chos-bsgyur-ba'i-lugs-ni ... ma-bsnor-bar-sgyur-cig /*, cf. Simonsson 1957:247-248, Snellgrove 1987: 442.

[25] Ed. Ishikawa 1990:1-2: *chos-kyi-gzhuṅ . . . kyaṅ-bcos /*, Simonsson 1957: 243, Snellgrove 1987:442.

[26] Ed. Ishikawa 1990:2: *bsnor-na-bde-zhiṅ-go-ba-bskyed-pa-zhig-yod-na / tshigs-bcad-la-ni-rtsa-ba-bzhi-pa'am / drug-pa'aṅ-ruṅ-ste / tshigs-su-bcad-pa-gcig-gi-naṅ-na-gaṅ-bde-ba-bsnor-zhiṅ-sgyur-cig /*, cf. Simonsson 1957: 248, Snellgrove 1987: 442.

[27] Ed. Ishikawa (1990: 2-3): *skad-gcig-la-miṅ-du-mar-'dren-pa-ni ... rgya-gar-skad-so-na-zhog-cig /*, Simonsson 1957: 250-252.

[28] Ed. Ishikawa 1990:2: *ltag-'og-daṅ-bstun-la-gar-sñegs-pa-bzhin-du-miṅ-thogs-śig*, Simonsson 1957: 250.

every Sanskrit term. As an extreme example of polysemy, the text mentions the Sanskrit noun *go* that can variously mean 'direction' (*phyogs*), 'earth' (*sa*), 'light' (*'od*), *vajra* (*rdo-rje*), 'cow' (*ba-laṅ*), 'sky' (*mtho-ris*) etc.[29].

The use of loan-words [30] is explicitly allowed for the names of countries, persons, flowers, trees etc. In case a loan-word is used, a generic indication of the category of meaning should be added before the term, e.g. *rtswa-ku-śa*, 'the grass Kuśa', an example given supra in this text.

Finally, a few remarks about a passage speaking of the translation of the esoteric, mystical literature of Tantrism. This paragraph [31] is found in both edicts, with some significant variations—especially in the latter half—but with generally similar contents. Due to its conciseness and opacity, this passage is open to considerable divergence of interpretation, and it has in fact been quite diversely interpreted by scholars such as Simonsson, Snellgrove and Scherrer-Schaub.

In any case, all interpretations that I have seen, agree that this part of the edict amounts to the application of a number of severe restrictions on the translation of Tantristic texts. It is evident that the translation of this esoteric literature is far more restricted than that of the exoteric Buddhist scriptures. Translation of a Tantristic text is only allowed with specific permission, presumably of the central committee of translators. The translator must proceed particularly scrupulously and conscientiously when translating such a text, and his translation must be submitted to the central authorities for approval.

These elaborate precautions are due in this case, because of the particular, secret and esoteric nature of the Tantristic literature. As the [Tapho] edict has it:

> As to the Tantras of the Mantra[-yāna], the basic texts themselves state that they are to be kept secret. Therefore it is not allowed to teach and

---

[29] Similar enumerations of the many meanings of the stem *go* can be found throughout Indic lexicographical literature, e.g. Abhidhāna Viśvalocanā verse 267-268 (ed. Jamspal 1992), as well as in Buddhist exegetical literature, e.g. in the Abhisamayālaṃkāra commentaries by Ārya Vimuktisena (6th cent.) and Dharmamitra (8-9th cent.), cf. Ruegg 1977: 291.

[30] Ed. Ishikawa 1990:3: *yul-daṅ- / ... rgya-gar-skad-so-na-zhog-cig*, Simonsson 1957:253-254.

[31] Ed. Ishikawa 1990:4: */ gsaṅ-sṅags-kyi-rgyud-rnams ... bsgyur-du-mi-gnaṅ-ṅo //*, cf. Simonsson 1957: 260-262, Snellgrove 1987: 443, Verhagen 1993: 322-324.

> explain them to unfit persons, because it will cause harm if encoded terms are misunderstood.[32]

It should be mentioned here that the Sanskrit *mantras* are generally left untranslated in the Tibetan traditions. In some rare instances one finds translations of whole *mantras* or parts of *mantras*, but always in an exegetical context. Usually, be it in a written form in one of the many Tantristic scriptures or in the context of the visual arts, or in a spoken / recited form, when applied in the ritual liturgy, we find that the Indic *mantras* are not translated. In writing they are merely transliterated in Tibetan script.

Consequently, in my opinion it is quite likely that among the Tibetan Buddhist scholars linguistic awareness has—at least partly—developed under the influence of these untranslated Sanskrit—or rather Indic—formulas, and that their interest in Sanskrit linguistic matters is to a great extent motivated by the striving for perfection and continuity in the execution of rituals and other practices involving the use of *mantras*. Perhaps this correlation between the maintaining of purity of the ritual and its formulas, and the development of linguistic sciences, is in some ways comparable to the early origins of *vyākaraṇa* in India, where the development of the Prātiśākhya, Nirukta and Nighaṇṭu literatures served the same purpose of maintaining correctness of the ritual formulas and hence purity and efficacy of the ritual, in this case of the Vedic ritual, of course.[33]

5. Conclusion

Summing up, the extensive translation activities of the Tibetan scholars, and their enduring interest in the Sanskrit language and its literature have led to the position of Indic linguistics as an important field of study among the Tibetan Buddhist scholars. We have seen how various historical, scientific and religious factors have determined the periodization and the contents and nature of these studies.

---

[32] *sṅags-kyi-rgyud-rnams-ni-gzhuṅ-gis-kyaṅ- / gsaṅ-bar-bya-ba-yin-te / snod-du-ma-gyurd-pa-la-bśad-ci-bs [t] and-t [u] -yaṅ- / myi-ruṅ-bas / ldem-po- [da] g-las-log-par-go-na-skyon-yod-pas /*, Panglung 1994:170.

[33] Cf. e.g. Renou 1947b.

It is evident that the Indo-Tibetan literature stores a wealth of materials on Indic linguistic topics, investigation of which will surely shed much light on the Tibetan translation-techniques, an important tool for our interpretation of the Indo-Tibetan literature which is in fact one of the major literary sources for the study of later Buddhism.

CHAPTER TWELVE

MORE ON THE KĀRAKASAṂGRAHA, A SANSKRIT GRAMMATICAL TEXT FROM BALI

Anna Radicchi

1. Introduction

The Kārakasaṃgraha is one of the "Sanskrit Texts from Bali," edited by S. Lévi as far back as 1933. Since then, the text has not been seriously looked at or analyzed further except for passing mentions relative to "Sanskrit in Indonesia."[1]

J.A. Schoterman briefly reexamined the Kārakasaṃgraha in the context of "An Introduction to Old Javanese Sanskrit Dictionaries and Grammars," an article which appeared in *Bijdragen tot de Taal, Land-en Volkenkunde* (BTLV) in 1981. He went back to the Balinese manuscripts (*lontar*s) containing the short treatise: in some of them the Kārakasaṃgraha appears as a Prathamapariccheda, 'first chapter', given separately or already put together with a Dvitīyapariccheda, 'second chapter', on *samāsa*s ('compounds'), and then with a Tṛtīyapariccheda, 'third chapter', again on *samāsa*s.

Among the manuscripts containing the Kārakasaṃgraha, those in which the Kārakasaṃgraha is the first of three *parricchedas*,[2] clearly document the last stage in the tradition of this text, which was finally assembled together with two other parts, all three of them making up two fundamental chapters of Sanskrit grammar, the one on *kāraka*s, the

---

[1] See mainly J Gonda 1973: 183 and Notes 209-210.

[2] I was able to see two of this type of *lontar*s, entitled *Aji Krakah*, preserved at the Gedong Kirtya of Singaraja in Bali: IIIc 1138/16 and IIIb 1578/43; in addition *Aji Krakah* IIIc 92, presented at the Kantor Bali Penelitian Bahasa in Denpasar. A search among manuscripts in Indonesia and The Netherlands would almost certainly bring to light other ones for collation; such a search has not been carried out here, as it is not directly pertinent to the study in question, limited to the Kārakasaṃgraha.

other on *samāsas*. The third *pariccheda* is an appendix on particular *samāsas*, especially useful for *kakawin* literature.

On a different occasion[3] I tried to demonstrate that the Kārakasaṃgraha belongs to the Indian grammatical school of Kātantra (KT). This point which is generally mentioned—and rightly so, given that Kātantra and Mahātantra were already read in Lévi's edition at the end of one of the two manuscripts used—had never been explicitly accepted and certainly never definitively demonstrated.

2. *The Kārakasaṃgraha and texts of the Kātantra school*

2.1 A comparison between the Kārakasaṃgraha and texts of the Kātantra school is to be set in the historical period of Durgasiṃha's commentary (perhaps the 8th century C.E.) divulged in Europe by J. Eggeling's meritorious edition of 1874-1878. At that point the Kātantra school already had a long tradition: Durgasiṃha commented on the southern recension of the Kātantra's *sūtrapāṭha*, already differentiated from a northern Kashmirian recension; Durgasiṃha's commentary also ably levelled material from different periods and sources.

The *kārakapāda* (KT 2.4) has been considered part of the original nucleus going back to Śarvavarman;[4] but today this seems a rather improbable assumption. The *samāsapāda* in *ślokas* (KT 2.5), which follows the *kārakapāda*, and is in Lüders' opinion an addition dating back to the 6th century,[5] fuses naturally with the previous *pāda*, which already contains elements of versification.

In the period following Durgasiṃha, the Kātantra developed into a school abounding in commentaries on Durgasiṃha's *vṛtti*, sub-commentaries, new commentaries by other authors, *pariśiṣṭas* and annotations on the *pariśiṣṭas*. The school flourished in Bengal in the 15th century, and scholars collecting manuscripts discovered it still flourishing there by the end of the last century.[6]

---

[3] 34th ICANAS, 22-28 August 1993. Only a sketchy summary appeared in the *Abstracts* of my paper "Indian Grammatical Traditions in Indonesia."

[4] B. Liebich 1919; cf. particularly: 9-11.

[5] H. Lüders 1940: 679.

[6] The various grammatical schools, compelled to leave the other provinces following the second revival of the school of Pāṇini under the leadership of Mahārāṣṭra Brāhmans like

The success of Durgasiṃha's commentary and of the recension of the *sūtrapāṭha* it definitively contributed to fix was probably immediate. Vardhamāna, the author of the first commentary, the Kātantravistara, on Durgasiṃha's *vṛtti*, may have had a patron in Karṇadeva, probably the same one who ruled over Gujarat in 1088 C.E. Trilocanadāsa, on whose commentary, the Kātantravṛttipañjikā, an extensive tradition of Bengalese manuscripts exists, seems to have been close to Vardhamāna.[7]

The various parts into which the original grammar of the Kātantra had divided Pāṇini's material soon began to enlarge along their own lines. The *kāraka*s are the frequent topic of special monographs. All grammatical systems sooner or later elaborated the chapter of *kāraka*s which lent itself, more than other chapters, to going beyond the field of grammar and becoming a subject of speculation and logic. The Kātantra, the oldest of all non-Pāṇinian grammatical systems, was probably the first to elaborate the chapter on *kāraka*s.[8] The Kārakasaṃgraha of the Balinese *lontar*s appears to be a document of this early elaboration, and should first be compared to the *sūtrapāṭha* commented on by Durgasiṃha.

2.2 The following are, briefly, the main points of this comparison. First of all, the way the material is laid out. Of the three ancient Indian grammars reformulating Pāṇini's *sūtra*s—all three orthodoxically respecting them—the Cāndravyākaraṇa, the Jainendra and the Kātantra, only the latter places the two sections corresponding to the Aṣṭādhyāyī-sections on *kāraka*s and *vibhakti*s, one after the other, first KT 2.4.8-16 corresponding to P 1.4.23-55, followed by KT 2.4.17-42 corresponding to P 2.3.

The Jainendra keeps the two sections separate, adhering more closely to Pāṇini: P 1.4.23-55 on *kāraka*s is followed in JV 1.2.108-125,[9] then P

Bhaṭṭojī Dīkṣita and Nāgojī Bhaṭṭa, had taken refuge in Bengal, says Haraprasāda Çāstrī 1900: II. Cf. also R. Mitra 1877: 3.

[7] Cf. S.K. Belvalkar 1976: 74.

[8] The catalogues present numerous titles. See no. 380, 57, 42 and 48 in Haraprasāda Çāstrī 1900. J Eggeling 1889: 208 quotes the entire text of one *Shaṭkāraka*, whose beginning is the same as that of no. 380 in Haraprasāda Çāstrī 1900. It is interesting to compare its fourteen couplets to our Kārakasaṃgraha, to understand how the latter is closer in form and chronology to the text commented on by Durgasiṃha.

[9] The numbering is that of the edition of the *sūtrapāṭha* commented on by Abhayanandin.

2.3 on *vibhaktis* in JV 1.4.1-77. The Cāndravyākaraṇa combines the two Pāṇinian sections in CV 2.1.43-98, traversing all the norms in parallel and rearranging them according to the progressive order of the *vibhaktis*, from the second to the seventh, putting *prathamā* and *ṣaṣṭhī* at the end. Thus the arrangement of the material in the Kātantra is unambiguous and unique.

Another characteristic of the Kātantra is that of etymologizing on the basis of the *dhātu* (verbal root) *kṛ*, in which the first section of the *kārakas* ends up, with KT 2.4.12-15: *yena kriyate tat karaṇam, yat kriyate tat karma, yaḥ karoti sa kartā, kārayati yaḥ sa hetuś ca.*

After that, KT 2.4.17-42, corresponding to P 2.3, deals with the *vibhaktis*. The discussion starts with *prathamā*; next KT 2.4.19 lists the *kārakas* according to the progressive order of the remaining *vibhaktis* from 2 to 7: *śeṣāḥ karmakaraṇasaṃpradānāpādānasvāmyādyadhikaraṇesu.* Afterwards, the treatment will not respect this order: first comes *pañcamī* (KT 2.4.20), followed by *dvitīyā*, then *caturthī, tṛtīyā, saptamī* and finally *ṣaṣṭhī*.

The grammatical theory contained in the Kārakasaṃgraha is presented according to the presentation scheme of KT 2.4.8-42. There is a first passage of 5 *ślokas* on *kārakas*, [10] which follows the 2 introductory *ślokas*, and this broadly corresponds to KT 2.4.8-16. It immediately takes from the Kātantra the etymologization on the *dhātu kṛ*. Scholars have noted that the hemistich read in Lévi as *yatkṛtaṃ karma tat proktaṃ sa karttā yaḥ karoti vā* is easily compared to KT 2.4.13, 14. The Kārakasaṃgraha then continues to go deeper into *kartṛ* and *karma* on its own. Which *vibhaktis* have the function of agent? Three *vibhaktis*, it responds, *tṛtīyā, prathamā* and *ṣaṣṭhī*. As regards *karma*, which takes

---

[10] We quote them as they are given in Lévi's edition, only noting that *apadāne' pi* in the fourth *śloka* is to be corrected as *apādāne' pi*:

karma karttā tayor yogaṃ yo vetti sa vicakṣaṇaḥ I
yat kṛtaṃ karma tat proktaṃ sa karttā yaḥ karoti vā II
tṛtīyā prathamā ṣaṣṭhī tisraḥ kartṛtvajātayaḥ I
pañcamī saptamī tābhyāṃ ṛte tat karma śabdyate II
sadvitīyā tṛtīyā ca pañcamī ṣaṣṭhikā tathā I
vibhaktayaś catasras tāḥ karaṇaṃ samprakāśitāḥ II
tṛtīyakā caturthī ca ṣaṣṭhī tisro vibhaktayaḥ I
sampradāne samuddiṣṭās tv apadāne' pi pañcamī II
vibhaktī dve'dhikaraṇaṃ ṣaṣṭhikā saptamī tathā I
tat sarvaṃ yuktitaś cintyaṃ śeṣe ṣaṣṭhī tu manyate II

place in a point of time and space starting from a limit, once *saptamī* and *pañcamī* have clarified point and limit, they are no longer needed to express it. The following 3 *śloka*s complete the review of the *kāraka*s, giving them in the order of the corresponding *vibhakti*s. There are four *vibhakti*s made to express the *karaṇa*: *tṛtīyā* and *dvitīyā, pañcamī* and *ṣaṣṭhikā*. It appears that nothing of what Pāṇini teaches in 2.3.18-27 is left out. Three *vibhakti*s are designated for *sampradāna*: *tṛtīyakā*, *caturthī* and *ṣaṣṭhī*. For *apādāna* there is *pañcamī*. Two *vibhakti*s are *adhikaraṇa*: *ṣaṣṭhikā* and *saptamī*. Here also in the joint functioning of *ṣaṣṭhikā* and *saptamī* we seem to note respect for P 2.3.36-41. "All this must be adequately reflected upon," concludes the last hemistich in this first passage, "for the rest there is *ṣaṣṭhī*, one thinks (according to P 2.3.50 *ṣaṣṭhī śeṣe*)." These last three *śloka*s, which find no literal correspondence in the Kātantra, correspond in the function to KT 2.4.19, making up a more articulate link than KT 2.4.19 to the second passage on *vibhakti*s.

It is certainly the second passage of 11 *śloka*s in Lévi's edition, which takes complete advantage of P 2.3 and evokes compelling comparison with KT 2.4.17-42. This second passage is a text mixing theory and exemplification, both occupying entire lines. The theory, some carelessness in Lévi's edition apart, is accurately handed down and prevalently technical. In comparison, the exemplificative lines appear confused. It is as if two separate hands had joined. The technical one presents a type of specialized grammatical discourse, while the other illustrative hand, kept separate within distinct lines, is negligent.

S. Lévi hints in passing (1933: XXXII) at a collection of texts of the type on which bilingual exercises (93-107) are based, to which the exemplification in the Kārakasaṃgraha would refer. We, however, would prefer to recall the section on *vyākaraṇa* in the Agnipurāṇa, which must have been compiled more or less at the time of our Kārakasaṃgraha; there, in the *śloka*s of the *adhyāya* dedicated to *kāraka*s [11] exemplification spontaneously intermingles with theory. In any case, here we are interested in, and limit our discussion to, the technical hand.

2.3 With the *śloka* on *tṛtīyakam*, after those on *prathamā* and *dvitīyā*, begins the clear identification of fragments from the *sūtrapāṭha*s of the Kātantra and the Aṣṭādhyāyī, used in constructing the various lines.

---

[11] *Adhyāya* 354 in the Ānandāśrama edition.

The *śloka* on *tṛtīyakam* seems almost entirely constructed on the text of the Kātantra. The *śloka* reads:

kartṛtvaṁ sahayogyaṁ ca karaṇaṁ deśakālayoḥ /
viśeṣaṇaṁ ca hetvarthaṁ kutsite'ṅ ge tṛtīyakam //[12]

Leaving aside *sahayogyam* (*tṛtīyā sahayoge*, KT 2.4.29), *viśeṣaṇam* (*viśeṣaṇe*, KT 2.4.32), *hetvartham* (*hetvarthe*, KT 2.4.30), and finally *kutsite'ṅge*, identical to KT 2. 4.31, what remains is *kartṛtvam karaṇam tṛtīyakam* and *deśakālayoḥ*. Pāṇini, with 2.3.18 *kartṛkaraṇayos tṛtīyā*, provides for *kartṛtvam karaṇam tṛtīyakam*. Regarding *deśakālayoḥ*, we think instrumental case with names of time and places is contemplated therein (classic examples: *māsenādhito granthaḥ*, 'text studied in a month'; *krośenādhitaḥ*, 'studied for the space of a *krośa*'), which Pāṇini had taken into consideration in the *dvitīyā* section (P 2.3.5-6). Here the Kārakasaṃgraha goes beyond the Kātantra, which has no corresponding shifting of the rule.

Another half *śloka* in the Kārakasaṃgraha which is unequivocally built on the basis of material from the Kātantra is the one dealing with *saptamī*:

bhāve'dhikaraṇaṃ [13] *kāle deśe nirdhāraṇe yathā* /

This is clearly based on *kālabhāvayoḥ saptamī* (KT 2.4.34) and *nirdhāraṇe ca* (KT 2. 4.36). What remains of the half *śloka*, besides the term for the *kāraka*, is *deśe*. P 2.3.36, *saptamyadhikaraṇe ca*, provides verification of this use, since it 'draws', with *ca*, from the preceding *sūtra* uses of *saptamī* with words having the sense of 'far' or 'near'.

In contrast, the *śloka* for *ṣaṣṭhikā* in the Kārakasaṃgraha is entirely built with Pāṇinian material. Key terms from the Aṣṭādhyāyī are met there, from the specific section on *ṣaṣṭhī* in 2.3, and from *sūtras* of the same *pāda*, referring to *ṣaṣṭhī*, in the *tṛtīyā, pañcamī, saptamī* sections. The verse reads:

śeṣādhikaraṇaṃ deśaṃ sampradāne ca karmaṇi /
nirdhāraṇaṃ ca karaṇe hetau kartari ṣaṣṭhikā //

---

[12] The text of the fourth *pada* has been reconstructed; Lévi could not decipher it and had to content himself with the reading *sūcitaṃ ge tṛtīyakam*, which evidently has no meaning. The correction to *kutsite'ṅge tṛtīyakam* is legitimated by the *lontars* cited in note 2. The name of the *vibhakti*, which oscillates between *tṛtīyā* and *tṛtīyakā* according to the metre, just as *ṣaṣṭhī* alternates with *ṣaṣṭhikā*, here appears in the neuter.

[13] Reading *bhave* and *nirdhāraṇe*, instead of *bhave'dhikaraṇaṃ* in Lévi's edition.

From P 2.3.50f come *śeṣa-* (P 2.3.50), *karaṇe* (P 2.3.51), *karmaṇi* (P 2.3.52f), *sampradāne* (P 2.3.61), *-adhikaraṇam* (P 2.3.64 and 68), *kartari* (P 2.3.71). Outside the *ṣaṣṭhī* section, but referring to uses of *ṣaṣṭhī*, compare: P 2.3.26 *ṣaṣṭhī hetuprayoge*; P 2.3.41 *yataś ca nirdhāraṇam*; and finally P 2.3.30 and 34-35 for *deśam*.

It is true that *hetau* in the Kārakasaṃgraha may also go back to *ṣaṣṭhī hetuprayoge*, which opens the *ṣaṣṭhī* section in the Kātantra. However, *ṣaṣṭhī hetuprayoge* is also a *sūtra* (P 2.3.26) in the middle of the Pāṇinian section on *tṛtīyā*. Here the transfer from one section to another had already appeared in the Kātantra, before the Kārakasaṃgraha. *Karmaṇi* returns in KT 2.4.38 and is important because it continues as *anuvṛtti*; but the importance of the same *karmaṇi* in P2.3.52 as *anuvṛtti* for the following *sūtras* is even greater.In conclusion:the *śloka* cannot be read without Pāṇini. It is mainly constructed using Pāṇinian material. However, here and there the material employed is found in the Kātantra.

Also the hemistich for *pañcamī*:

> *apādānaṃ*[14] *ca karaṇaṃ deśaṃ hetos tu pañcamī* /

recalls not so much the Kātantra but rather Pāṇini's section on *pañcamī*, which after the initial *apādāne pañcamī* (P2.3.28) has *karaṇe* (P 2.3. 33), and then (P 2.3.34-35) contemplates uses for *deśa*. *Hetos* also goes back to P 2.3.23-24 for a use of *pañcamī* prescribed in the *tṛtīyā* section.

Finally, the line on *caturthī*:

> *sampradānaṁ tadarthaṃ ca caturthī karmaṇi smṛtā* /

If on the one hand it recalls KT 2.4.27 with the expression *tādarthye* which is already a mahābhāṣyan advance on Pāṇini, on the other hand it contains the expression *karmaṇi* which is the *karmaṇi* of P 2.3.14 and of P 2.3.17.

Concluding, the hand composing the lines above certainly used all the material in the Aṣṭādhyāyī 2.3. However, section 2.4.17-42 of the Kātantra's southern recension was also already there at its disposal. All the formulations can be explained collating material from the two texts.

Compared to the Kātantra, the Kārakasaṃgraha is more advanced on the way the Kaumudīs will follow. We deduce this first of all from the

---

[14] Instead of *apadānam* in Lévi's edition.

reordering of the *vibhaktis* according to the series numbers from one to seven. This order had already appeared in KT 2.4.19, but was subsequently given up. Secondly, from the internal reordering which shifts Pāṇini's scattered norms under the individual *vibhaktis*. The Kārakasaṃgraha is more punctual than the Kātantra also with regard to this last point.

3. Lévi's edition and the original Indian treatise

S. Lévi gave only the Sanskrit part of his two manuscripts. This is false from the point of view of the Balinese *lontars* which contain the Kārakasaṃgraha accompanied by a commentary in Old Javanese. And it also clearly sounds false that *iti samāsaḥ samāptaḥ*, "thus the section on compounds has been completed," which concludes the colophon of the second manuscript and is reproduced by Lévi, while the text edited by Lévi does not include the treatment of *samāsas*.

However, Lévi's edition as presented contains the basis, apparently original, of the brief Indian treatise called Kārakasaṃgraha: it seems identifiable in the first five *ślokas* of the theory of the *kārakas* that begin to arrange the material on the model of the *sūtrapāṭha* commented upon by Durgasiṃha and in the theoretical lines of the second passage which, beginning with the one for *tṛtīyakam*, become more technical and seem to preserve a text that has remained substantially sealed and intact.

We would not include the two introductory *ślokas* and the lines which give the exemplification in what we consider the original still legible base. Doubts also remain on the link between the first five *ślokas* and the other eleven, articulated with a *yuktitaś cintyam* that seems to have become a convenient, repetitive linking device.

Adherence to the text commented on by Durgasiṃha who, according to prevailing if not unanimous opinion, could have lived in the 8th century C.E., and on the other hand that distance in time which a re-elaboration such as the one presented seems to demand, suggest that our document was compiled around the 10th century. Kaumudī-type evolution also suggests this date. Most probably it entered Java shortly after it started circulating in India.

4. *Historical conditions in India and Indonesia*

Looking at the Indian sub-continent of that period, one feels inclined to focus on the Bengal area and on what is now Bihar with Nālandā. One may be more or less caught in the net of references woven by H. Bh. Sarkar 1973, with the pride of the propagator of the ideals of the Greater India Society, in an article stressing Bengal's influence on Indonesian civilization.

It is however certain that with the inscription found at Kĕlurak,[15] dated at 782 C.E., we acquire absolute certainty of the religious-cultural links between the Śailendras of Java and Bengal, since verse seven of the inscription explicitly states that the head of the Śailendra King Indra was purified with the dust of the lotus-feet of the *guru* of the land of Gauḍī. Moreover, the epigraphic evidence of the so-called Pre-Nāgarī script[16] found in Java beginning from the foundation charter of Kalasan dated 778 C.E. leads to Northern India.

Then there is the Nālandā copper-plate of Devapāladeva,[17] which advises that in the 39th year of his reign (about 860 C.E.)[18] this King Pāla granted five villages to support a monastery built at Nālandā by Bālaputradeva of Suvarṇadvīpa. The latter was a son of Queen Tārā, who was in turn the daughter of a Dharmasetu (=Varmasetu) of the lunar race, married to the mighty king who was the son of the renowned ruler of Yavabhūmi, the jewel of the Śailendra dynasty.

There were thus close links between the Śailendras of Java-Sumatra in the second half of the IX century and the Pālas of Bengal, the liberal protectors of Nālandā, joined by a common faith, Mahāyāna Buddhism which in that period irradiated from Nālandā. However, there was a continuous flow of people from the Gurjaradeśā as well, testified to by the Pre-Nāgarī inscription from the Caṇḍi Plaosan,[19] this also issued by one of the Śailendra kings.

---

[15] Last re-edited by H. Bh. Sarkar 1971, I: 41-48.

[16] Of fundamental importance remains F.D.K. Bosch 1928; cf. pp. 8-13 on palaeography.

[17] Hiranandra Sastri, after publishing this document in *Epigraphia Indica* XVII 1924: 310-327, gave text and translation together, with a synopsis, 1942.

[18] C. 849, according to H.B. Sarkar 1985: 219.

[19] See J. G. de Casparis 1956: 175 ff.

By the first half of the 10th century, the political and religious panorama in Java changes. In central Java, the grandiose Prambanan complex with stories from the Rāmāyaṇa faces the *stūpa* of Borobudur. Śivaism and Hinduism had gained ground against Buddhism. It was never a religious conflict, but rather a process of syncretism in which from time to time one component dominated the other.

The inscription of Pereng,[20] dated 863, is Śivaist: it is the first document of Hinduism's revival, almost a counterpart in Java to the religious and philosophical movement which accompanied the thought and activity of the great philosopher Śaṇkara on the Indian sub-continent.

With Sindok, the centre of political power moves definitively east. And it is during Sindok's reign, at the latest, that the Javanese Rāmāyaṇa is written. We have arrived at the period of the flowering of the *kakawin* genre in Java. It flourishes at the time in which Hindu texts command true respect, and it is a product of the Javanese courts: the court of Sindok, of the preceding Śailendra kings, then Dharmavaṃśa, Airlangga at the beginning of the 11th century, and finally the sovereigns of Kediri. We do not look beyond 1222, the year of the attack of the adventurer Angrok on the throne of Kediri. At that point our Kārakasaṃgraha must have already entered Java.

5.1 Sanskrit studies in multicultural Java

The *kakawin* genre, this poetry in Old Javanese, is certainly familiar with the pedantic, nearly scholastic reproduction of Indian verses, their translation and paraphrasing, but it has also been able to go beyond all that. While using elaborate metrical forms based on the Indian ones, although expressed in refined *alaṃkāras* of Indian origin and following the *rasas* and *bhāvas* of Indian aesthetics, when free creativity prevailed, *kakawin* literature spoke the native language.

Yogīśvara, the mythical author of the Javanese Rāmāyaṇa, was not believed to have known Sanskrit.[21] This is precisely the misunder-

---

[20] See N.J. Krom 1931: 165, and also G. Coedès 1964: 203.

[21] See, however, C. Hooykaas 1955:33: "Perhaps it will be possible one day to make acceptable that he mastered his considerable knowledge of Sanskrit in India itself, where he learned many Rāmāyaṇa's . . . "

standing that has engaged scholars in what we think were substantially sterile debates on the architectural structures and images which enriched Java during the golden age of Hinduization: Was it a continuation of Indian art on Indonesian soil or a native flowering?[22]

It seems this question should be put in terms of language. What language did the images and texts speak? there is no doubt, they spoke Javanese. In Old Javanese, it is the *kakawin* literature, produced by a cultural élite in the courts, imbued with the Indian culture. Thus, there was biculturalism or rather multiculturalism.

Indian culture has been one of the great cultures Java has come into contact with and has assimilated in the ways and aspects most congenial to it. Modern Javanese preserves a strong Indian lexical imprint; there is a very low percentage, as is well known, of terms from Indo-Aryan languages in respect to the number of Sanskrit terms. But a part of the lexicon has Arab or Chinese origins, and through the languages of modern colonizations, expressions conveying values and objects from the classical Latin or Greek world are also present. At the base of this lexical treasure of varying origins is that multiculturalism, including the composite historical and prehistoric native background, which makes Java so fascinating. Multiculturalism has asserted itself and has gradually been enriched throughout history and must not be lost sight of at the historical level we are interested in.

In Java, one cannot speak of a culturally dominant group of Indian origin superimposing its language, neither of an Archistratum or Kultursprache from which the Javanese would have taken their abstract and cultured vocabulary. The Sanskrit invading the courts in the period of *kakawin* production is the Sanskrit of administrative and judicial jargon, the Sanskrit in which documents and epigraphs are written, the Sanskrit of untranslatable philosophical and religious terms, but it is also the Sanskrit of proper and common nouns. It is an imposing treasure, nearly half of the total lexicon. However, creativity was not creativity in an adopted language but the creativity of a multicultural élite expressing itself in its own standard language—incidentally, in a situation of diglossia with the local spoken language—drawing fully on a foreign culture borne by another standard foreign language. Foreign language and culture, which were no longer foreign, had become an

---

[22] Cf. on this, in detail, A. Radicchi 1992, particularly: 24-27.

integral part of life and communication. This means 'multiculturalism' in its most profound sense.

It is difficult to believe that the élitist community that produced *kakawin* literature would be satisfied with anything less than up-to-date texts of grammatical trends coming from India. The fact that direct contact with the Indian world continued in this period cannot be doubted, in spite of relative scarcity of supporting documents. Here we can mention Dīpaṅkara born in east Bengal in 980, who studied for twelve years in Suvarṇadvīpa under the celebrated Buddhist scholar Dharmakīrti and whom a Nepalese manuscript shows during his visit to Yavadvīpa, probably in the first quarter of the 11th century.[23] This is how our Kārakasaṃgraha may have reached Java, brought by some cultured traveller coming from a study centre where the work was read as a text of one of the grammatical schools in vogue in India.

The lexicon must have constituted an essential part of Javanese cultural intercourse with Sanskrit. The reference to King Jitendra of the Śailendra dynasty, who in the Javanese Caṇḍakiraṇa is said to have been the promoter of the translation of the Amaramālā into the vernacular, is cause for reflection. It is also certain that the study of grammar and its norms was indispensable for the translating from Sanskrit into Old Javanese, but less indispensable for freely created production in Old Javanese, once the translations were acquired. It was inevitable that the diligent study of Sanskrit would gradually slacken, a fact that has been noted long ago.

In any case, one should not equivocate on the study of Sanskrit, as long as it was studied, in Java. From this point of view, we consider the presence of a specific, technical text like the Kārakasaṃgraha important evidence.

---

[23] Cf. H.B. Sarkar 1937: 596.

5.2 Yì jìng's testimony

It seems useful to go back again to an important source of information on the study of Sanskrit in Indonesia, the Record of Yì jìng (I-tsing), since the details the monk gives continue to be interpreted differently by different scholars.

Yì jìng says[24] that in the fortified city of Bhoja (corresponding to the present-day Palembang in Southern Sumatra) more than one thousand monks studied texts in Sanskrit and in Pāli, at the same time observing the rules and ceremonies of monastic life.

In 671 Yì jìng stopped at Bhoja, on his way to India, and remained there for six months to study Sanskrit; he stayed there again on his return to China, for a long period ending in 695, studying and translating Indian texts. Having had the experience of staying both in India and Sumatra, he advised monks to remain at Śrī Bhoja one or two years before going to India.

Yì jìng noted that monks in Sumatra investigated and studied all the subjects that existed just as in the Middle Kingdom (Madhya-deśa, India) and that the rules and ceremonies were not at all different. If there had been any differences in the way Sanskrit was studied, Yì jìng would certainly have noted them, especially considering the importance he gave to the study of *vyākaraṇa*, essential for the accuracy of a translation. In this respect, he was critical of the Chinese scholars who had preceded him.[25]

Two aspects of the study of Sanskrit carried out at Nālandā stand out in the pilgrim's account: it was traditional and scientific at the same time. The curriculum of *vyākaraṇa* studies he indicates in view of what we would today call a reading of Pāṇini at the historical level of the end of the 7th century is the same we would propose today—apart from the different stages of textual tradition: the Aṣṭādhyāyī, the Mahābhāṣya, Bhartṛhari's works and the Kāśikā. However, along with this and in addition to the indispensable equipment of Dhātupāṭha, Uṇādi, etc., Yì jìng mentions works for beginners: the Siddhirastu, where the alphabet was learned, and those chapters of the three Khilas that children began

[24] Cf. J. Takakusu 1896: xxx ff.

[25] J. Takakusu 1896: 168 ff.

to study at the age of ten, containing, among other matters, the *sups*, *tiṅs* and *lakāras*, i.e. the forms of noun and verb inflection obviously at that time already collected separately in practical handbooks. Study was based on memory, the traditional Indian method, and the Chinese traveller was amazed by the Indian ability to memorize.

We believe up-to-date Sanskrit grammatical trends continued to arrive at Nālandā and that Sanskrit continued to be studied there in the same way until the Muslim hordes swept away its libraries in about 1200. We also believe that this was the kind of Sanskrit study that flowed from the Indian sub-continent into Sumatra and Java.

There were certainly different conditions on the two islands. In Sumatra, there were monks who wanted to translate correctly Sanskrit works in an attitude of respect for the sacred religious texts. In Java, there was a court milieu which used Indian texts freely, but with scholarship and great intelligence.

5.3 The Kārakasaṁgraha and the second and third paricchedas *in Java and Bali*

Having entered Java, the Indian Kārakasaṃgraha was commented on and annotated in Old Javanese. From Java it reached Bali; it is impossible to say exactly when. With King Udāyana of Bali, at the end of the 10th century and the beginning of the 11th, links with Java became closer; the king had married the daughter of Sindok's grandson and Airlangga would be born in Bali.

The Kārakasaṃgraha had certainly arrived in Bali after 1500, along with numerous other Hindu texts which the island preserved in its archives and homes, when the vestiges of Indo-Javanese culture were disappearing in Java. The Kārakasaṁgraha must have been copied and recopied in Bali. The appearance of our present Kārakasaṃgraha is also the outcome of this constant work by Balinese copyists.

As a title, Krakah finally evolved into a common term, 'treatise', which no longer referred to the specific topic of grammar.[26] Like

[26] J.A. Schoterman (1981: 435-436) recalls the *lontars* of the Gedong Kirtya entitled *Aji Krakah*, which contain declensions; others entitled *Aji Krakah* or *Krakah Śāstra* contain *mantras*. Other *lontars* I have seen at the Fakultas Sastra of the Universitas Udayana in

Schoterman (1981: 436),[27] we think this represented a later development, as a result of the authority of the 'real' Aji Krakah.

It has been said above that, in what we imagine to be the last stage in the tradition of this text, the Kārakasaṃgraha appears as a first *pariccheda*, linked to two others on *samāsas*. However the three *paricchedas* are also found in separate Balinese *lontars*, each containing one of the three. They were probably joined in Java, before reaching Bali. This kind of compilation limited to the two important parts of grammar, *kārakas* and *samāsas*, is frequently met with in the grammatical literature of the Indian subcontinent, in all grammatical schools, not only that of the Kātantra.

The second *pariccheda* (Dvitīyapariccheda) opens with the well-known verse naming Pāṇini and listing the six classes of *samāsas*. This mention of Pāṇini interested H. Bh. Sarkar (1934: 110) and later J. Gonda (1973: 209-210, note 33), who read the verse in the manuscript catalogued by H. H. Juynboll 1911: 215 as no. 5075.

More than the mention of Pāṇini, what is interesting, even at a first cursory glance,[28] is the whole treatment of this second *pariccheda*, which has never been properly studied. Schoterman, clearly disoriented, noted (1981: 434-435) that in this second *pariccheda* the Skt. compounds are discussed in great detail, "with every type of conceivable compound being mentioned and explained in both Skt. and OJ [Old-Javanese]." A division of the compounds into six classes and twenty-eight sub-classes is, in effect, well-known in India, also found in small handy works. Chronologically closer to our text is perhaps the *samāsādhyāya* in the Agnipurāṇa.[29]

The Dvitīyapariccheda lists one sub-class of *karmadhāraya* less than the Agnipurāṇa, six instead of seven, and two more sub-classes of *dvandva*, four instead of two, with a consequent total of twenty-nine sub-classes. For the rest, the theory of the *samāsādhyāya* in the Agnipurāṇa, accompanied by an exemplification, in any case traditional,

---

Sanglah, Denpasar, entitled *Krakah Panini, Krakah Sari, Krakah Puja*, have nothing to do with our Kārakasaṃgraha. The *Krakah Sanggraha* of the Gedong Kirtya (IIIc 1293), later than S. Lévi's edition, is simply a copy of the Kārakasaṃgraha edited by Lévi.

[27] Responding to Hooykaas' sweeping statement (1964: 38) about the term *kāraka* used in Bali as a generic name for grammatical/linguistic/philological treatises.

[28] Cf. *lontars* mentioned in note 2.

[29] *Adhyāya* 355 in the Ānandāśrama edition.

which often coincides with that of the Dvitīyaparicცheda, is comparable passage by passage. Actually, it seems to constitute the simple base to which further elaborations found in the Dvitīyapariccheda were attached.

The *vyākaraṇasāra* in the Agnipurāṇa, also judging from the sequence of subjects, still seems like material from the Kātantra school. Of this opinion is also the Veṅkateśvara edition of the Agnipurāṇa, which reads before *adhyāya* 349: *atha kaumāravyākaraṇam.* In his study of the Agnipurāṇa S.D. Gyani (1964: 28) arrives at 1000 or 1100 C.E. as the end of that process of development of the Agnipurāṇa from its original to its extant form, which began about 700 or 800 C.E.

It is most probable that the Dvitīyapariccheda had an Indian original; a Sanskrit text is still distinguishable in the *lontar*s, even if it would be difficult to reconstruct *śloka*s there. The Indian original may have entered Java at about the same time or even together with the Kārakasaṃgraha.

The third *pariccheda* deals with particular *samāsa*s. Among them are two which had already been dealt with in the second *pariccheda*, the *nañsamāsa*, already given as a sub-class of *tatpuruṣa*, and the *sahapūrva*, analyzed among the *bahuvrīhi*s. This already gives us an idea of the subsidiary character of the third *pariccheda* , which served as a supplement to the general typological division provided by the second *pariccheda*. The compounds considered occupy a regular place in Sanskrit grammar and usage; less regular is the *viparīta*, with inverted members, which was widely used in *kakawin* literature. This compound is accurately exemplified. Moreover, there is abundant exemplification throughout the whole treatment: the examples are analyzed in Sanskrit, and further explained again in Old Javanese. Regarding this third *pariccheda*, it is difficult to imagine an original coming from India. It seems to respond to an indigenous interest in analysis and understanding. In actual fact, neither *śloka*s nor a coherent Sanskrit text are distinguishable there.

The *pariccheda* concludes with an *iti samāsānta*, which signifies the end of the treatment of the *samāsa*s, and then *iti Aji Krakah*, which means that the treatise called Krakah has come to an end as well, i.e. the compilation of the three *pariccheda*s is now a fait accompli.

We believe the model of the compilation to be Indian, like the basic texts of the Kārakasaṃgraha and of the Dvitīyaparicched a; but the supplement consisting of the Tṛtīyaparicched a may have been put together in Java. Perhaps here we are face to face with a concrete approach to Sanskrit and to the study of its grammar in Java in the 10th or 11th century.

6. *Conclusion*

In the direct, constant cultural relations that linked Indonesia to India, not only did literary and philosophical texts play a role, but grammar texts as well, which, at least partly, accompanied trends in religion, taste and philosophy, coming from India. The appropriation of the products of Indian culture in that process of acculturation which reached its peak in Java in the period of *kakawin* production also regarded grammar texts. *Vyākaraṇa* is all too frequently considered a specialised study, removed from its cultural context.

Then Hinduism, which was becoming extinct in Java, took refuge in Bali. Concerning the tradition of Kārakasaṃgraha, we might limit ourselves to mentioning the part played by Balinese copyists.

And yet that *lontar* preserved at the Gedong Kirtya (IIIc 1293), which copies the Kārakasaṃgraha edited by S. Lévi, provides food for thought. We do not see why, as a document on the history of Sanskrit in Indonesia, it should not be taken into consideration along with certain Balinese hymns or *mantras*,[30] written in a more or less correct but in any case still legible Sanskrit. They surprise us, like a wave of Indonesian Hinduization sweeping once more across the island of Bali, where it has been almost miraculously preserved, in a form of its own, up to the present.

---

[30] Regarding this literature, we owe much to C. Hooykaas. Cf. mainly T. Goudriaan and C. Hooykaas 1971.

Manuscripts referred to:

Aji Krakah, Gedong Kirtya (Singaraja): IIIc 1138/16
Aji Krakah, Gedong Kirtya (Singaraja): IIIb 1578/43
Aji Krakah, Kantor Bali Penelitian Bahasa (Denpasar): IIIc 92
Krakah sanggraha, Gedong Kirtya (Singaraja): IIIc 1293

Other Sources: see General Bibliography

CHAPTER THIRTEEN

THE INTRODUCTION OF INDIAN PROSODY AMONG THE THAIS

B.J. Terwiel

1. *Introduction*

There are two scholars who independently from one another have taken the trouble to trace the origin of Indian metre in Thai literature. They come to diametrically opposite conclusions, one decided that a Sanskrit tradition via Cambodia was responsible, the other that it came via Sri Lanka and the Pali language. While these two suggestions taken together correspond neatly with the characterisation by Schweisguth (1951:13-14) of the two main external influences on Thai literature (a marked dependency on inspiration from Sanskrit literature on the one hand and the deep influence of Theravada Buddhism on the other) the two views indicate that the matter deserves consideration.

2. *Prosody in Thailand through a Sanskrit tradition via Cambodia ?*

The first to attempt to trace the introduction of prosody in Thailand was the late Klaus Rosenberg. In his overview of Thai *chan* (P: *chanda*) epic poetry he begins by summarising the arguments that would count against his hypothesis, namely those that would appear to favour the Pali tradition. He mentions particularly the role the Vuttodaya may have played, because the standard Thai textbooks on metric poetry, from the earliest transmitted seventeenth-century Chindāmanī onwards, base themselves explicitly on this work (Rosenberg 1976:16-17). The Vuttodaya was written in the twelfth century C.E. in Sri Lanka by the Buddhist monk and grammarian Sangharakkhita and it is the standard Pali textbook on Indian metre. It constitutes an almost word-for-word translation of one of the four most important Sanskrit texts on prosody, namely Kedāra Bhaṭṭa's *Vṛttaratnākara.*

Rosenberg notes that while it is true that the author of the Chindāmanī cites this Pali text and while it is also established that in the fourteenth century there was a monk from Martaban who came to the Thai capital, Sukhothai and used Indian metres in a laudation to the Thai king,[1] these two indications do not suffice to determine that a Sri Lankan connection via Buddhism and the Pali language was responsible for the Thais obtaining their metrical tradition. Instead he opts in favour of a Cambodian link via the Sanskrit tradition.

2.1 His argumentation rests upon two considerations. Firstly he points out that, when we disregard a few verses in the *Mahāchāt kham luang,* three of the four oldest pieces of Thai *chan*-poetry that can be dated to the Ayutthaya period belong to a Brahmanistic-Hinduistic tradition and cannot be counted as Buddhist literature.

The plot of the first of these poems *Anirut kham chan* (Ani-ruddha's poem) is indeed directly derived from the Kṛṣṇa legend which was widely known in Southeast Asia as an episode in the Harivaṁśa.

Another of these poems, entitled *Suea Kho kham chan* deals with the story of the Tiger and the Bull who, as result of their good deeds are changed into two handsome princes, Phahonwichai and Khawi. The plot revolves mainly around the chivalrous and adventurous life of these two princes until they each gain a kingdom. The beginning of the *Suea Kho kham chan* seems to be inspired by a theme out of the Buddhist literary tradition, namely from the Bahalagāvī-Jātaka, but most of the following scenes are identified by Rosenberg (1976:133-134) as coming out of Indian kāvya-poetry.

The poem entitled *Dutsadi Sangwoei kham chan* is a kind of prayer which apparently was intended for recitation by court Brahmans when a new white elephant was ceremoniously received at the court. The discovery of a white elephant, a former king's rebirth, is widely interpreted, not only by the court astrologers but also by the general Thai populace, as a divine approval of the ruling monarch.[2] Rosenberg

[1] Both the role of the Vuttodaya and the theme of the Buddhist monk from Martaban will be discussed in some detail below.

[2] On 13 November 1835 G.B. Bradley on board the brig Ariel had been irritated with a company of Thai singers who shared his journey to Chantaburi near the southeasternmost

draws attention to the fact that the vocabulary of the *Dutsadi Sangwoei kham chan* is for more than ninety per cent Cambodian, mixed with some Sanskrit words. He regards this text as representing the first stage of the Thai poet's wholesale take-over of Cambodian metric poetry

The fourth Ayutthayan piece of epic poetry is called *Samuthakhōt kham chan.* The content of this poem is a mixture of *Anirut kham chan* and the first of the Paññāsajātakas (the story of Samuddaghosa). The author of the *Samuthakhōt kham chan* is generally believed to be the same as that of the *Suea Kho kham chan.* Rosenberg, however, rejects this on the ground that in the introductory paragraph of the *Samuthakhōt kham chan* the Buddha is praised, while the opening phrases of the *Suea Kho kham chan* Brahma and Siva are mentioned. In Rosenberg's view, this identifies the author of the *Samuthakhōt kham chan* as a Buddhist and that of the *Suea Kho kham chan* as a Brahmanist (Rosenberg 1976:126).

It would seem from this remark, that Rosenberg has not fully appreciated the role of the court Brahmans in Thailand. The Thai court Brahmans have functioned in the predominantly Buddhist Thai setting not long after Ayutthaya gained preeminence among the Thai cities. They may originally have come from Cambodia, but some trace their ancestry to India.[3] They tend Hindu shrines and are distinguished by their way of dressing. The Thai court Brahman is someone who traditionally has maintained access to works which derive from the ritual, scientific, and esotheric Brahmanic tradition so that he can apply this knowledge to calculate the most auspicious moment for conducting state ceremonies and perform them. When a Thai court Brahman invokes deities that clearly belong to the Hindu pantheon he does not violate the Buddhist beliefs of the general public, simply because the Buddhist

---

port of Siam. He writes in his unpublished diary: "the singers ... I am informed are now practising with a view to sing to the White Elephant at Chantaboon. They sing many times a day, of which I have already become heartily sick. This is to be in worship probably of some, one or more, of the departed spirits of the Siamese sovereigns which according to the superstitions of this people enter into or become white elephants." The white elephant has inspired many European authors to write on this subject. Probably the best overview of the subject is in Quaritch Wales (1931).

[3] In 1822 Crawfurd interviewed one of these Brahmans, who claimed to be the fifth generation of an immigrant from the Island Ramesiran (Crawfurd 1828:119).

religion does not draw a clear line between Hindu and Buddhist concepts of the inhabitants of the heavens.[4] Indeed, the Brahman in Thailand has been recorded to recite his Hinduistic invocations in the Pali language (Gerini 1976:38).[5]

Therefore the difference in the invocations of the two poems may not be interpreted as representing incompatible or contrasting points of view. Instead, the difference in invocation neatly reflects the different themes. The *Samuthakhōt kham chan* being named after a Jātaka and starting off with a theme that reminds of a Jātaka warrants opening verses praising the Buddha, while the *Suea Kho kham chan* has no connection with a Buddhist tale.

The first argument by Rosenberg rests therefore upon his observation that this small group of works, all of them probably written during the seventeenth century, show a prominent Brahmanic-Hinduistic and relatively little Buddhistic content and that the main themes of the stories of these four texts were probably introduced to the Thais, like much other Indian material, via Cambodia. While one may regard his juxtaposition of the Brahmanic-Hinduistic tradition and Buddhism in the Thai cultural setting with some scepticism, Rosenberg might well be right in his opinion that stories from the Indian tradition entered Thailand via Cambodia. That three of the four seventeenth-century poems are based on such Indian themes simply demonstrates the popularity of that genre in Thai literary circles during the seventeenth century. It ought to be kept in mind, however, that accepting the direction from which the poems' *content* may have arrived in Thailand does not address the matter of the metrical *form* of these poems. Moreover, there is conclusive evidence that the adoption of Indian metre in Thai preceded the seventeenth century by some two hundred years, so that the matter of which genres were popular during the seventeenth century has little bearing on the question.

2.3 Rosenberg's second argument for a Khmer-Sanskrit origin of Thai metrics rests upon his observation that all but one of what he rec-

---

[4] This is clearly demonstrated in the *Samuthakhōt kham chan* itself. After the opening verses in honor of the Buddha, the author continues with a veneration of Brahmā, Śiva and Viṣṇu.

[5] In Cambodia with the fall of Angkor in the fourteenth century Sanskrit ceased to be the official language and Pali supplanted it in various domains. See Pou (1989).

ognises as the eight metric forms used in *chan* poetry in Thailand during the Ayutthayan period (in their Sanskrit names *śloka, vasantatilaka, indravajra, mālinī, śārdūlavikrīḍita, sragdharā* and *āryā*) can be demonstrated to have been used at an early stage in Cambodia. The one metre used in Thailand but not in Cambodia can be identified as the 12-syllable *toṭaka.*

In order to compare the Cambodian and Thai traditions adequately a singling out of only those metres which the two traditions have in common seems insufficient. An overview of the use of Indian metrics in Cambodian inscripts is given in Table 1, which is based upon the work of Mahesh Kumar Sharan, who has listed 148 inscriptions written in Cambodia between the fifth and the beginning of the thirteenth centuries C.E. and who has been able to identify almost every line of Sanskrit poetry in them (Sharan 1974). He has found no less than 21 different metres.

Sharan draws attention to two characteristics of the Cambodian inscriptions. First the authors demonstrate a full mastery of Sanskrit with its complex rhetorical and literary conventions. In addition it is remarkable that Khmer and Sanskrit are frequently used together in the same inscriptions, whereby Sanskrit is used for sacred subjects, such as panegyrics, royal genealogies and dates, whilst Khmer is reserved for the more mundane topics, such as listing measures of land and names of donated slaves. A similar mixture of Sanskrit and vernacular language has been noted for South Indian epigraphy. The first remark may be taken as a measure of the remarkable cosmopolitan role that the Sanskrit language played in large tracts of Southeast Asia whereby the élite in the towns of Champa, Cambodia and various islands of the Indonesian archipelago shared this vernacular.* The second indicates not only the high status but also the religious function of that medium.

Editor's note: cf. Pollock's contribution in this volume.

Table 1 Indian metres used in the Sanskrit verses in Ancient Cambodian Inscriptions in order of popularity

Metre	Number of Inscr	Number of lines
śloka	81	2093
vasantatilaka	46	249
upajāti	38	403
indravajrā	21	81
upendravajrā	4	6
Mixture of upajāti, indravajrā and upendravajrā	2	225
śardūlavikrīḍita	31	112
sragdharā	21	41
āryā	20	46
mālinī	18	36
anuṣṭubh	17	275
vaṁśastha	8	34
mandākrāntā	5	7
pṛthvī	3	3
aupacchandasika	2	6
vaitālīya	2	3
triṣṭubh	2	3
vṛtta	1	4
rathoddhatā	1	1
puṣpitāgrā	1	1
svāgatā	1	1
saṁvṛtta	1	1
Unidentified	12	68

From Table 1 it is clear that there are eleven regularly used metres in old Cambodian inscriptions, namely the *śloka*, the complex of three related eleven-syllable metres *upajāti, indravajrā* and *upendravajrā*, the *anuṣṭubh*, the *vasantatilaka*, the *śārdūlavikrīḍita*, the *āryā*, the *sragdharā*, the *mālinī* and the *vaṁśastha*.

Rosenberg's finding that the Thais have seven metres in common with the Khmer tradition can thus be rephrased: almost all of the eight metres in older Thai epic poetry can be found among the 21 Indian metres on record for Ancient Cambodia. Unexplained remains why the Thais have not taken over the *upajāti, anuṣṭubh* or *vaṁśastha*, which were all popular in Cambodia. Also unexplained remains the fact that one of the favourite Thai metric forms, the *toṭaka*, does not occur in the Khmer tradition at all.[6]

The parallels that Rosenberg notes between the metres used in Thailand and in Cambodia are thus not as striking as he apparently found them to be. They are quite adequately explained by the circumstance that both indigenized metric traditions can eventually be traced to one of the classical textbooks on Indian metrics. Most of the metres used by the Thais can also be found, for example in old-Javanese *kakawins* and these parallels are unlikely to have been caused by direct contact between the Thais and the Javanese (Teeuw 1990:188).[7]

One important finding in Rosenberg's work is that Indian metres in early Cambodian inscriptions were not only used when they were writing in the Sanskrit language, but as early as the tenth century C.E. such metre can be found in an inscription which, although it contains a number of Sanskrit loan words, must be classified as having been written in the Cambodian language, so that he has established a date for the indigenization of Indian metre in Khmer.[8]

On the whole, however, the evidence which has persuaded Rosenberg to conclude that the introduction of Indian prosody in Thai culture must be traced to Cambodian literary practices does not withstand scrutiny. He is probably right when he traces the likely inspiration of some poetic forms of Thai literature, such as the verses known by the Thais as *kāp*, to the Cambodian tradition. The intensive interaction between the Ayutthayan and Cambodian court is beyond doubt and it has left many traces. In this interaction, the Cambodian civilization, which has been recognized as an Indianized centre since approximately the first century C.E., has functioned as the donor and inspiror. It would be wrong, however, to depict Thai poetic practices as *wholly* coming from the Khmer. Some features, such as reduplication and elaborate

---

[6] For details on the *toṭaka*, see Table 2.

[7] Not only the Javanese, but also the Balinese poets use such metres. See Rubinstein (1988:302-303). There exists a list of 105 Balinese *Kekawin* metres which are all eventually derived from one of the classical Sanskrit texts on prosody. The similarities between the Thai Chindāmanī and the Balinese Swarawyañjana Tutur are also evidence of the strength of the Sanskrit prosodic tradition which underlies both.

[8] Rosenberg (1976:19), referring to Inscription No.173 of the Coedès Inventory.

expressions[9] have been reported for a great variety of Southeast Asian languages and without supporting evidence it seems not warranted to assume a unilinear flow between Khmer and Thai practices.[10] Diadic word play, the use of inner rhyme, a regular distribution of words with particular tones, alliterative practices and other poetic devices are part and parcel of chanted Tai language forms.[11] Some of these practices are a recognisable stratum in the Thai interpretation of the *chanda*.

3. Prosody introduced through the Pāli tradition

The second scholar who has given extensive thought to the history of Thai *chan* poetry is Thomas Hudak, who apparently is unaware of Rosenberg's earlier research on this topic. In contrast to Rosenberg, Hudak is firmly of the opinion that the Thais obtained their metrics via their exposure to the Pali tradition (Hudak 1985:107; 1990). He bases this opinion upon three arguments. In the first place the better Thai versification textbooks and literary anthologies reveal that the source was the Vuttodaya. Secondly, he notes that the oldest *chan* poetry that has survived is firmly part of the Theravada Buddhist tradition. The third argument rests upon an overview of the major role the Pali language has played in Thai history (Hudak 1990:45).

While these arguments partly contradict the evidence collected by Rosenberg each of them deserves closer examination.

3.1 The role of the Vuttodaya.

All Thai literary anthologies and versification textbooks mentioned by Hudak go back to one and the same source, namely the seventeenth-century Chindāmanī.[12] In this text there are direct citations from the

---

[9] Some examples of elaborate expressions in Thai are: *ap nam ap tha* ('to bathe'), *pu ya ta yai* ('grandparents'), *mo lok mo laek* ('muddy').

[10] A short bibliography of Southeast Asian reduplication can be found in Theraphan (1979:259-260).

[11] See, for example, Compton (1979) and Hartmann (1984).

[12] A critical study of the text was found in Chanthit (1962).

Vuttodaya. These citations cover not only the definition of 'heavy' (Pali: *garu*) and 'light' (Pali *lahu*) syllables, but also those passages describing the six standard metres in older Thai epic poetry, in their Pali names: *indavajirā, toṭaka, vasantatilaka, mālinī, saddūlavikkīlita* and *saddharā*. See Table 2.

Table 2: The parts of the Chindāmanī that are based upon the Vuttodaya

Explanation of *Lagu* and *Garu* and the *Ganas* (— — — = Magana, - - - = Nagana, — - - = Bhagana, - — — = Yagana etc.) corresponding with Ch. 1, Vuttodaya. The mnemonic device in Thai (*rao kin taengmo...*) is apparently inspired by the Sanskrit example on p. 3 of the Vuttodaya.

This is followed by six metrical forms:

1. Intharawichien, chan 11 (a chanda with 11 syllables)
   (Vuttodaya, ch 3, 18: indavajirā, 2 Taganas, 1 Jagana, 2 Gurus: — — - / — — - / - — - / — / —)

2. Todok, chan 12 (a chanda with 12 syllables)
   (Vuttodaya, ch 3, 31: toṭaka, 4 Saganas: - - — /- - — /- - — /- - —)

3. Wasantadilok, chan 14 (a chanda with 14 syllables)
   (Vuttodaya, ch 3, 47: vasantatilaka, 1 Tagana, 1 Bhagana, 2 Jaganas, 2 Gurus: - - — / — - - / - — - / - — - / — / —)

4. Mālinī chan 15 (a chanda with 15 syllables)
   (Vuttodaya, ch 3, 50: mālinī, 2 Naganas, 1 Magana, 2 Yaganas, with a pause after the eighth syllable: - - - / - - - / — — , — / - — — / - — —)

5. Satthunlawikilit, chan 19 (a chanda with 19 syllables)
   (Vuttodaya, ch 3, 58: saddūlavikkīlita, 1 Magana, 1 Sagana, 1 Jagana, 1 Sagana, 2 Taganas, and a Guru, with a pause after the twelfth syllable: — — — / - - — / - — - / - - — / , — — - / — — -/ —)

6. Sattharā, chan 21 (a chanda with 21 syllables)
   (Vuttodaya, ch 3, 60: saddharā, 1 Magana, 1 Ragana, 1 Bhagana, 1 Nagana, 3 Yaganas, with pauses after every seventh syllable: — — — / — - — / — , - - / - - - / - — , — / - — — / - — —)

It ought to be noted that the Vuttodaya was already known and the six metres chosen by Phra Horāthibodī were in use long before he composed the Chindāmanī some time during the reign of King Narai

(1657-88).[13] This is clear both from the few pieces of early literature that have survived, but also from the extracts of older poetry given in the Chindāmanī itself.

3.2 The oldest Thai chan text

Rosenberg has classified four texts that have survived from the seventeenth century and which were wholly written in metrical form as constituting the oldest layer of *chan* poetry. He glosses over the much older *Mahāchāt kham luang* because it 'merely' contains a few verses. Hudak, citing as his authority the noted Thai literary historian Plueang na Nakhon, judges the few metrical verses of the *Mahāchāt kham luang* to be the first recorded appearance of *chan* poetry (Hudak 1990:16).[14] If we define *chan* poetry as the Indian metrical tradition as applied to the Thai language, the instances in the *Mahāchāt kham luang* form indeed an important piece of evidence. While the *Mahāchāt kham luang* was not transmitted in its original form, the parts which were transmited in metre (found in the Mahāvana-kaṇḍa and the Maddi-kaṇḍa) are generally regarded to belong to the oldest layer, which is attributed to the later part of the reign of King Trailokanāt (1448-88).

The metres used in the *Mahāchāt kham luang* are the *wasantadilok* (Pali: *vasantatilaka*) and the *mālinī*, two of the six metres which were later selected out of the Vuttodaya by the author of the Chindāmanī.

Also relevant in the debate of a Pali or Sanskrit origin of the Thai *chan* tradition is the fact that the *Mahāchāt kham luang* is based upon a translation of the Vessantara Jātaka which describes the one-before-last birth of the Buddha, a topic in Thailand invariably connected with the Pali tradition.

---

[13] There is a possibility that the text was written not long before Phra Narai's reign. This could explain a mildly puzzling sentence at the end of the first section of the Cindāmanī in which the author says: "Phra Horāthibodī who originally lived in Sukhothai wrote this at the time when King Narai was Lord of Lopburi." This could be taken to allude to a time before Narai's reign, but usually Thai historians think it refers to Narai's habit to reside for lengthy periods at the town of Lopburi.

[14] Some thoughts on the symbolic value of the first composition of the *Mahāchāt kham luang* in 1482 can be found in Charnvit (1976:140).

When we include texts in the Pali language, the use of Indian metre in the *Mahāchāt kham luang* is not the oldest on record in the Thai region. This honour goes, as Rosenberg acknowḷedged, to a Buddhist monk who lived in the mid-14th century. While Ṙosenberg mentions that this monk came from Martaban, it should also be noted that this monk either originated and was educated in Sri Lanka or at least had close links with the Sri Lankan Pali tradition. He is known to us only by his title of Mahāsāmi Saṁgharāja. Upon invitation by the king of Sukhothai he successfully established a branch of his nikāya.[15] His pupils Anomadassi and Sumana who had studied among the Sihalabhikkhus in Martaban, Lower Burma, had a major influence upon the history of Thai Buddhism.[16]

It was this Mahāsāmi Saṁgharāja who in 1361 composed an inscription in Pali, eulogising the king of Sukhothai, in which he makes use of the *vatta, indavajirā* and *upajāti* metres. Of these three, only the *indavajirā* is one of the metres used in classical Thai epic poetry and taught in the Chindāmanī. The *upajāti* is a mixed form of *indavajirā* and *upindavajirā*. The *upajāti* and *vatta* metres are mentioned in the Vuttodaya, but not in the Chindāmanī.

3.3 The strength of the Pali tradition in the Thai region

Sri Lankan influence upon the Buddhist textual tradition continued after the episode of the Mahāsāmi Saṁgharāja particularly in the Lanna Kingdom of northern Thailand during the fifteenth century. Thus it has been recorded that in 1424 a considerable number of Lanna and Khmer Buddhist monks went to Sri Lanka, lived in Mahāsāmi Vanaratana's monastery and were reordained on a river. A third strain of differently ordained monks was thus introduced, competing successfully with the two other nikāyas of Theravāda Buddhism that were already estab-

[15] He may have been identical with the famous monk Anumati, also known as Udumbara Mahāthera, or Mahāsvāmi Udumbarapuppha from Martaban. See Griswold and Prasert (1973:119-121).

[16] The role of Sumana is described, for example in the Jīnakālamani while Anomadassi assisted Prince Līdaya in the writing of the Traiphumikathā.

lished in the North.[17] These intimate contacts with Sri Lanka must have contributed to the remarkable growth and flourishing of Pali studies in Mainland Southeast Asia, particularly in Northern Thailand.

A sign of the power of this movement was the calling of a general meeting to revise the Tipitaka in the year 1477, which is regarded by the Thais as the Eighth Buddhist Council. In addition a large number of literary works in the Pali language were created, including works that are generally regarded of great historical and literary merit. Among the better known compositions are indigenous histories such as the Cḥāmadevīvaṁsa and the Sihinganidāna (maybe early 15th century) by Bodhirangsi, a Pali grammar: Sadatthabhedacintāpādakkamayoja by Dhammasenāpati, the Jīnakālamanī (a history of Buddhism) written by Rattanapañña in 1516, Mangaladīpanī in 1524, a commentary on the Mangala Sutta (Suttanipāta 11, 4) by Sirimangala and many other works (Coedès 1915; Likhit 1980 and Hudak 1990: 47-48).

These are the considerations that lead to the suggestion that Hudak is probably right in suggesting that it was likely that the Pali language (by way of the Vuttodaya or one of its commentaries) was the vehicle with which the Thais learned about Indian prosody. This implies that this knowledge of Indian metre was thus twice adopted in mainland Southeast Asia, once during the first millennium via the Sanskrit language in Cambodia and a second time, in the fourteenth century to Thailand via the Pali language, carried by Buddhist monks from Sri Lanka.

The oldest Sanskrit document in the Cambodian region, but often attributed to the Funan period, is the famous Vô-cạnh inscription inscription from the second half of the third century C.E. The oldest inscription from Cambodia proper dates from the fifth century and four out of the five verses therein are in the *śārdūlavikrīḍita* metre. There is ample evidence that the region intensively took part in cultural developments that originated from various parts of the Indian subcontinent and that this included the literary tradition, complete with its poetic

[17] Theravāda Buddhism was firmly established in the region during the Mon period, prior to the Thai invasion of the region. In the year 1369 the Sīhalabhikkhus, a separate nikāya with its own ordination tradition, was established by the same Sumanathera (who had been invited by King Mahādharmarāja in 1361, mentioned above. Its northern Thai headquarters weren established just outside the Chiangmai city walls in the monastery now called Wat Suandok (Saeng 1980:87-99).

traditions (Sharan 1974:47). For example, in an inscription dated at the end of the sixth century during the reign of Bhavavarman II mention is made of a complete copy of the Mahābhārata, the Rāmāyaṇa and at least one of the Purāṇas (Briggs 1951:43). We may safely assume that Sanskrit epic poetry was well established at that time, which according to the scheme of state formation proposed by Hermann Kulke (1986) would fall in the second, or regional phase of state formation.

While in this paper the likelihood of an independent and separate introduction of Indian metre in Cambodia and Thailand is argued, it is relevant to note that the adoption of Indian metre also occurred in China. Between 488 and 550 C.E. Shen Yüeh and his followers, under influence of Sanskrit metrical traditions, invented a highly original and effective form of tonal prosody. The authors of a recent study on this subject see various parallels between what happened in China during the fifth and sixth centuries and in Thailand many centuries later, such as the adoption of an equivalent of 'light' and 'heavy' syllables (Mair and Mei 1991).[18] One remarkable parallel between the introduction of Indian metrics in China and that which seems to have occurred eight hundred years later in Thailand not noted in that article is that the *toṭaka* was a popular metre both in China and in Thailand, while in Cambodia it apparently was not used. The fact that both in early China and much later in Thailand the Indian metrical system was introduced by Buddhist monks may have played a role, for the *toṭaka* consists of a group of four anapests which lends itself particularly well to the recitation of sutras.

---

[18] I thank Prof Dr. M. Friedrich of the Department of Chinese, Hamburg University for pointing out this introduction of Sanskrit prosody into China and making available this article.

4. *Prosody in a social setting*

The export of Indian metrics to various Asian cultures therefore seems to have taken place at least on three different occasions, once to China, once to Cambodia and most recently to Thailand.[19] In each case prosody was first practised in Sanskrit or Pali before it was transferred to the local language. Indian prosody was transferred to the Chinese language during the fifth and sixth century. As we have seen above, the earliest recorded use of Indian metrics in the indigenous Khmer language dates from the middle of the tenth century. Finally, the oldest recorded adaptation of Indian metres to the Thai language dates from the late fifteenth century. In every case the Indic prosodic formulae must have posed a major challenge to the local poet, but at the same time it seems also to have been a source of inspiration. New rules had to be invented in order to force differing types of languages to fit a series of metrical corsets that had been devised for Sanskrit.

A crucial aspect of the adoption of Indian prosody in Thai literature was the reinterpretation of what constitutes a *lahu* and a *garu* syllable, leaving future poets with the need to adopt a multitude of foreign loan words. This explains the rather artificial and sometimes abstruse character of Thai epic poetry.

The learning of prosody in a Thai historical context has been assessed by Rosenberg as being a typically royal accomplishment, one that was practised by the Thai king and his intimate circle only. He sees it as part of palace education, of the skills to be acquired by princes and princesses (1976:22-23). Rosenberg has been led to this opinion because the works that are written with the help of these prosodic rules that have survived the destruction of Ayutthaya in 1767 were written by the king and by a few very high-ranking individuals who apparently belonged to the intimate royal circle. This would imply that the Chindāmanī, which is intended to teach the various forms of writing poetry including these prosodic forms, should be regarded as a text only used in the court.

---

[19] The history of the introduction of Indian metrics in Java is not wholly clear, it is possible that Java received its texts directly from India but Funan may have played a role.

It is possible, however, to see the role of the metric forms of the poetic tradition in Thai history in a somewhat broader sense. While it is true that the few surviving pieces of classical Thai poetry are ascribed to royalty or to those close to the king, this does not necessarily mean that only that limited élite group had access to this tradition and practised it.

There can be no doubt that the Chindāmanī is basically intended to teach poetics, only this overriding purpose would explain the opening section which provides a long list of words of Pali origin, words without which the rules of prosody cannot be followed. If Rosenberg were right, the Chindāmanī would be a book intended for princes and princesses. However, Phra Horāthibodī himself reveals in various places in the Chindāmanī that he wrote it as a textbook for the educated person, for poets ("If you learn this list you can become a *nakprāt* (a wise educated person)," but most frequently he identifies his reading public as the future scribe ("If you internalise these rules you can become a good scribe (*samian*).")[20]

If we accept that the Chindāmanī is intended among others to teach poetics to future clerks, we must considerably broaden the category of those who learnt prosody beyond the king and his entourage. It would appear that at least during a large part of the Ayutthaya period the learning of poetics was considered an intrinsic part of the make-up of all administrators and that the Chindāmanī must be seen as the textbook for those who had ambitions to join those ranks.

According to Kenneth Hall (1976:12-13), state administrators during the classical period of Southeast Asian statecraft are characterised by their ability to participate in various state ceremonies, by their being schooled in ritual and by their capability to be appointed in a great variety of positions, unlike modern administrators who are schooled for a particular task.

The learning of an elaborate form of speech, replete with words that in the case of the Thais often were of Pali or Sanskrit origin can be seen as belonging to that ritual referred to by Kenneth Hall, part of the baggage of Southeast Asian administrators at the time. Only those who were familiar with the elaborate expressions were deemed fit to handle

---

[20] Wyatt (1969:22) says: "The book abounds in such statements as 'Once you know this, you can become a clerk and enjoy an easy life'."

and transmit the royal wish, not just the chief executives but also their scribes. This elaborate form of speech developed as a device to set apart and ritualise the business of government.

The ritual role of Southeast Asian courtiers can hardly be overstated. It would be an interesting exercise to attempt to correlate the introduction of prosody in Thailand with a major change in the administration generally attributed to the fifteenth-century King Trailokanāt. It was in his rule that the old relatively simple hierarchical system was transplanted with a much more elaborate administration along Cambodian lines. This seems to have heralded also a change in the concept of the king itself, as head of this much more intricate court. More so than before, the Thai king became set apart from ordinary beings and equipped with godly attributes. Under strong influence from Cambodia, Thai royalty also developed a royal etiquette that is reminiscent of the devarāja cult, but in doing so it did so selectively, not taking over various Hindu features of this cult.

The acceptance of prosodic rules appears to fit in well with a highly formalised social system where the use of foreign words and intricate forms of speech is a marker to distinguish a well-educated person. In such a system the mastery of poetry developed to become the tool with which a promising student could draw attention to his gifts. The training in the rules of verbal etiquette is essential in a society where the ability to speak euphoniously has "always been" a highly valued social skill (Hudak 1986:195). The growth of an elaborate form of language, relying on a multitude of foreign loan words fits well in such a hierarchical system. The use of such a difficult verbal and written code may be regarded as a part of a ritualisation process: that which emanates from the highest ruler via his court ought to be exceptionally well-phrased and elegant. The use of a multitude of abstruse expressions which can only be understood by a privileged class would not diminish its effectiveness. On the contrary, in a hierarchical society the transmission of a thought in a complex phraseology can add substantially to its effectiveness and persuasive force.

The knowledge of poetic language was thus part of being a scribe, a courtier or a member of the royal family. Only those who mastered the difficult art of Thai poetry and who could demonstrate that they had internalised the most elegant form of expression were worthy to carry and transmit the royal command. Eventually a full command of this form of speech was regarded as a necessity for those who wish to act on the king's behest.

5. Conclusions

In this article two different views on the origin of Indian metrics in Thailand have been scrutinised and it has been shown that this poetic tradition most probably has the twelfth-century Vuttodaya as its source of inspiration. The Pali language, rather than Sanskrit was the medium in which this tradition was introduced. During the fourteenth century prosody was found in a Pali inscription and as early as the fifteenth century in a Thai text based upon the Vessantara Jātaka.

This introduction is the latest of a series of introductions of Indian metrics and their subsequent adoption to a local, non-Indian language. During the first millennium the Chinese and Cambodians but also the Javanese (and at some undetermined time later the Balinese) all adapted Indian prosody to compose new forms of literature each of these directly or indirectly inspired by Sanskrit textbooks on prosody.

The development of an elaborate hierarchical system, together with a ritualisation of the bureaucracy have been singled out as being of particular relevance for the Thai adoption of prosodic rules. While this aspect apparently did not play a role in the case of the Chinese adaptation of Indian prosody, it may well have played a role in the other Southeast Asian regions.

Part Three

The Sanskrit Tradition:

Continuity from the past
or
Construction from the present ?

CHAPTER FOURTEEN

DO YOU SPEAK SANSKRIT? ON A CLASS OF SANSKRIT TEXTS COMPOSED IN THE LATE MIDDLE AGES

A. Wezler

1. In 1960 appeared—as No. 4 of The Maharaja Sayajirao University Oriental Series of the Oriental Institute, Baroda—a booklet of only 38 + 86 pages entitled *Gīrvāṇapadamañjarī and Gīrvāṇavāṅmañjarī.* According to the information given on the reverse of the title page it is "reprinted from the Journal of the Oriental Institute."[1] The editor of these two short Sanskrit texts, and author of the "Introduction"—which is in fact only appended to the texts themselves—is Umakant Premanand Shah. In publishing them, however, he but took up, and carried out, a suggestion of P. K. (=Parashuram Krishna) Gode's, as is quite frankly stated by Shah himself.[2] It is hence Gode to whom the credit goes for having first drawn attention to these texts and for having recognized their importance, though mainly in terms of their cultural and historical significance only.

Of the two texts the first one, the *Gīrvāṇapadamañjarī* (GPM), was composed by Varadarāja, the well-known author of the Madhya-, Laghu- and Sāra-Siddhāntakaumudī, i.e. "a medium, short and supershort version"—to use Cardona's (1976:287) apt rendering—of the Siddhāntakaumudī of the famous grammarian Bhaṭṭoji Dīkṣita, who was also his guru.[3] Varadarāja "may be assigned to ca. 1600-1650

---

[1] Viz. the "Text" as "Supplement" to JOI Baroda VII (1957-1958) and the "Introduction" as "Supplement" to JOI Baroda VIII (1958-1959) and IX (1959-1960), respectively. Note that these supplements are not (normally) bound together with the journal in one volume.

[2] Shah 1960:4 ; cf. also Gode 1956:170.

[3] Cf. Gode 1941 [1954], in particular 195f [324f].

A.D."[4] As usual, i.e. as in most other cases in the history of Indian literature, practically nothing is known about the author's life, etc.[5]

The second text, viz. the *Gīrvāṇavāṅmañjarī* (GVM), was in its turn composed by a certain Dhuṇḍirāja (alias Ḍhuṇḍirāja)—one of the 35 authors of this name listed in the New Catalogus Catalogorum.[6] His date is also discussed by Gode who assigns this work to ca. 1702-1704. Shah flatly states that "the GVM is an imitation of the GPM,"[7] but "as a literary composition" he regards it as superior to the latter.[8] The GPM is quite aptly described in the India Office MSS Catalogue[9] as "being courses of elementary conversational questions and answers on everyday occurrences, on literary, devotional and other subjects."

As far as I can see, the publication of these two previously unedited texts has almost totally been ignored by Sanskrit scholars.[10] That is to say, the GPM and the GVM have drowned in the growing, and indeed really terrifying, mass of new books appearing year after year. Yet I for one don't at all think that they in fact deserve this fate; but my own earlier attempt at drawing attention to them[11] has evidently not been successful. As for the GVM, however, the situation has changed for the better, though only quite recently; for Madhav M. Deshpande's book of 1993 on *Sanskrit & Prakrit Sociolinguistic Issues* contains a chapter "On Vernacular Sanskrit: The Gīrvāṇavāṅmañjarī of Dhuṇḍirāja Kavi," published in his book for the first time. Yet I shall have to refer to his findings not before the third part of the present paper.

According to Shah (1960:1) both texts were "composed with a view to teach Sanskrit by Direct Method . . . in the form of dialogues (*ukti-pratyuktibhiḥ*)."[12] He feels "reminded of the *Ukti-Vyakti-Prakaraṇa* of Pandit Dāmodara" of Vārāṇasī also insofar as in both, the GPM and the

---

[4] Quoted from Shah 1960:4; cf. Cardona 1976:286 (the reference to "Gode 1950" is not clear to me).

[5] For the little that is known cf. Gode 1941.

[6] Viz. Vol. VIII, 10ff., i.e. s.v. Ḍhuṇḍhi°/Dhuṇḍirāja.

[7] Shah 1960:5; but cf. Gode 1941:189 n. 7 [1954:317 n. 3].

[8] Shah 1960:5; for the reasons cf. also Gode 1941.

[9] 1904: 1574, Ms. No. 4108.

[10] I know of just one review, viz. by V. S. Agravala, published in JOI, Baroda X (1961-1962) 327f.; but the article of R. Salomon (1982) is another of the very few exceptions.

[11] Cf. Wezler 1985.

[12] See p. 5.

GVM, too, "the scene is laid in Banaras," and hence assumes that "all three texts preserve for us the direct method of teaching Sanskrit in Banaras, the great centre of Hindu culture and Sanskrit learning." "Both the texts," he says a little later (1960:7), "are written in a simple language, the main object being to acquaint a student with Sanskrit composition," but in the sentence next but one he contends that they "are originally meant for teaching Sanskrit," and at the end of his "Introduction"(1960:86) he states by way of summary that "the GVM and the GPM are, on a very modest scale, works meant for those who wish to obtain proficiency in reading, writing and speaking in Sanskrit." Already Rajendralal Mitra had described the GPM as "an elementary grammar of Sanskrit language, in the form of a dialogue interspersed with moral tales"[13] and Gode, on his part, had, apparently elaborating the notion "elementary grammar," classified it as "a Sanskrit conversational grammar," meant "to enable junior students of Sanskrit to pick up the language quickly without frightening them with dry grammatical forms."[14]

Shah's own description of the character, or rather purpose, of the two texts is slightly self-contradictory and—especially when taken together with those of Rajendralal Mitra and Gode—puzzling to such an extent that it seems imperative to do what we could, or perhaps even ought to, have done right at the beginning, viz. look for relevant statements by the authors, Varadarāja and Dhuṇḍirāja, themselves. The usual bow to Gaṇeśa apart, the first sentence of the GPM reads as follows:

> *kevalavaidikānāṃ vyavahārārthaṃ katipayasaṃskṛtapadāni mayā vilikhyante*[15]
>
> I am going to write some words (i.e. a few lines/a short text) in Sanskrit for the *vyavahāra* of people who are only *vaidika* s (i.e. know, or are supposed to know—but not necessarily also understand—those Vedic

[13] Cf. Gode 1941:195 [1954:324].

[14] Ibidem.

[15] One of the MSS. used by Shah for his edition omits this phrase; cf. Shah 1960 ("Text"):1.

mantras which are obligatory for the performance of religious ceremonies like the upanayana, marriage, etc.).[16]

This is evidently a much clearer statement: The specific 'target group' is named and the aim to be achieved by the work is given with equal clarity; for *vyavahāra* cannot but be used here in the sense of 'communicative activity' the emphasis lying—rightly, as of old in India[17]—on the verbal aspect. Varadarāja's intention is hence expressly to provide a means for the active use of the Sanskrit language by brahmins who have some knowledge only of the Vedic form of Old Indian. It should be noted, though in passing only, that the expression *saṃskṛta* seems to be used here in exactly the same manner as in the West, viz. to denote the 'classical' form of this language as opposed to and insofar as it is to be distinguished from the older Vedic Sanskrit.

This introductory statement of the GPM is echoed, as it were, in its concluding verse[18] which reads

kṛtā varadabhaṭṭena gīrvāṇapadamañjari /
gaṇeśaprī taye caiva vaidikaprī taye bhavet //

(in which the addition of God Gaṇeśa among those the author wants to delight by his work may be taken to express his hope that it will spread over a large area to be studied by many without tears).[19]

Dhuṇḍirāja's statement of his aim is much more detailed; for apart from the first half of the first verse, in the *śārdūlavikrīḍita* metre, all the *ārambhaślokas* without exception are meant to reveal the purpose of his GVM. For they read thus:[20]

kāśīsthena hi dhuṇḍirājakavinā gīrvāṇavāṅmañjarī
bālānāṃ sukhabodhanāya racitā saṃśodhanīyā budhaiḥ /
kevalaṃ vaidikānāṃ tu śabdābdhim atidustaram /
svalpāyāsena santartuṃ nirmitā taraṇir dṛḍhā //
śabdaliṅgavibhaktyādi kartṛkarmakriyāvyayam /

---

[16] As was pointed out to me by Ashok Aklujkar, *vaidika* brahmins are not *śrotriyas*, and can, at this point of time, not any longer be considered as "well-versed in the Vedas" (as V. S. Apte (1957) characterises them).

[17] Cf. Wezler 1994. —Note, however, that Varadarāja himself professes that he "writes."

[18] Shah 1960 ("Text"): 18.

[19] Cf., however, Gode 1941:196 [1954:325] who asks whether "it is possible to suppose that *Gaṇeśa* was the name of VR's father and *Durgā* the name of VR's grandmother."

[20] Shah 1960 ("Text"):19.

nānāpadārthasaṃjñārtham anayā budhyate 'khilam //
For[21] the poet/writer Dhuṇḍirāja, who lives in Vārāṇasī, has composed the GVM—which is to be/can be corrected by the learned—for the easy understanding of beginners.

But [thus] a firm (i.e. reliable) boat has been made by which (those who are) only *vaidika* (brahmins) are able with little effort to successfully[22] cross over the ocean of words that [otherwise] is extremely difficult to cross.

Nouns, [their] gender, case endings, etc., [the *kārakas*] agent, direct object, [the] verbs and indeclinables become fully intelligible by this [GVM] so that various matters (*padārtha* s) become clear.

Which *padārthas* the author has in mind he explains in the last two of his introductory verses:

prātar ārabhya viduṣā kartavyaṃ karma yad bhavet /
uktam āsāyaparyantam asti yat kramaśo 'khilam //
uktipratyuktibhiḥ kiñcit strīpuṁbhyāṃ vā vinodataḥ /[23]
gṛhakṛtyavidhau sarvaṃ vakṣyamāṇam udīryate //
The duties to be observed by an educated man (i.e. a brahmin), starting from the morning right till the evening, are completely taught in accordance with the sequence [of their performance], part of it in dialogues, and [what is done] by husband and wife as a diversion / when amusing themselves. Whatever calls for instruction[24] regarding the rules about household matters is stated [in the GVM].

This shows that Dhuṇḍirāja is not only much more explicit than Varadarāja, but that he also pursues a second didactic aim: In addition to leading 'beginners' to an easy understanding of, nay to mastery of Sanskrit, the 'language of the gods'[25]—which necessarily includes its active use—he wishes to instruct as regards the daily duties of a brahmin and similar household matters, and significantly, he even touches on the topic of love-making, i.e. the GVM ends, as Shah (1960:5) remarks, "in the climax of *śṛṅgāra*, with the happy union of the Brāhmaṇa householder and his wife—a romantic end (for a Brāhmaṇa on a *parva*-day) in a work which is professed to have been composed as a primer of Sanskrit for *bālas* (*bālānāṃ sukhabodhāya* [sic !]);" the exclamation

---

[21] The particle *hi* does not, however, seem to have a real semantic function here.

[22] Cf. the preverb *sam*-.

[23] *-da-* is an emendation (by the editor) of *-di-* attested in all the MSS.

[24] In later Sanskrit, e.g. Navyanyāya texts, the passive participle of the future is often used in a sense similar to that of the gerund.

[25] This is after all the literary meaning of *gīrvāṇavāṇī* / *-vāc* .

mark Shah puts at the end of this sentence is a clear signal of his indignation, flowing from the well-known 'modern', i.e. Victorian, Indian prudishness; one has the impression that he is undecided only insofar as he does not know what is worse, sex between a brahmanical husband and his wife at the end of a *parvan*-day—i.e. a day of full moon or new moon on which a particular ritual has to be performed by the couple throughout their lives which includes inviting saṃnyāsins and (other) brāhmaṇas for dinner,[26] and a day further on which one should give up sexual intercourse as well as oil and meat according to the Śāstra[27]—or the fact that sexual intercourse is at all referred to in a text meant for boys. In reality, however, Shah's indignation is not justified, at least not in the latter case; for clearly, the expression *bāla* is not used here to denote a male person who is biologically not yet mature, but a *vaidika*, i.e. a man of uncertain age who has learned by heart at least a number of Vedic mantras and knows how to perform certain important rituals. And it is this special 'target group' which the GVM has in common with the GPM—a remarkable fact to which we shall have to return later.

2. Shah (1960:3) correctly observes that "manuscripts of both works are not rare" and that "they seem to have been popular in Northern and Western India within a century of their composition"; but *he fails to note that there are also more works of this type.* Two of these other works[28] I should like to present here, viz. texts manuscripts of which happened to arrest my attention more than 20 years ago when they were put on my desk (I was working at that time for the "Nepal-German Manuscript Preservation Project" in the National Archives of Nepal at Kathmandu). Already at that time it occurred to me that they should be made accessible to scholars, perhaps even in critical editions, and I hope that the 'Introduction into Spoken Sanskrit', the publication of which I announced long ago and which will contain these texts, too, will now definitely appear in the near future.

---

[26] Cf. e.g. Gonda 1980:179, 244 and 349.

[27] Cf. History Dharmaśāstra V, 1:221. Note that Apte (1957) knows a compound *parvagāmin*, "one who has sexual intercourse with his wife at particular times or occasions when such intercourse is prohibited by the śāstras."

[28] For still others see Madhav M. Deshpande 1993a:37f.

The first of these two works bears, according to the colophons, the title Saṃskṛtatattvabodhinī (STB); it was composed by a certain Vāmadeva Miśra about whom I have been unable so far to find any information.[29] It is basically a story about a brahmin, Devadattaśarman, and his extraordinarily gifted son, Gopībhaṭṭaśarman, who is also his pupil. They live in Viśālā, i.e. Ujjayinī or the modern Besāḍ in Bihar.[30] One day the father takes his son to the 'royal assembly' (*rājasabhā*) where the young man gives so convincing and astonishing evidence of his Sanskrit erudition that the king spontaneously decides to entrust his father with the education of his own son, prince Candradhvajavarman. Out of deep respect for the learned brahmin the prince then comes every day—except, of course, those days on which teaching is prohibited[31]—to the house of Devadattaśarman. The narration of the education the prince is given is interrupted, as it were, by a detailed description of the invitation of brahmins and svāmins to Devadattaśarman's place—on the occasion of a *parvan*-day: An account is given of the preparations of the arrival and reception of the guests, of the meal with its many courses and of the conversation between the svāmins and their host. After the departure of the ascetics one of the brahmanical neighbours, Mahādevabhaṭṭa, starts a conversation mainly with his host's son which, however, before long assumes the character of a veritable examination; that part of the 'curriculum' which Gopībhaṭṭaśarman still has to cover is outlined and finally he is given the opportunity to show his extraordinary capacities as an extempore poet (*samasyāpūraṇa* etc.) The observation that he is not yet married quite naturally leads to the discussion of the suitability of a brahmin girl from Pāṭaliputra as bride. The arrival of prince Candradhvaja who comes for his daily class prompts the brahmanical guests who had stayed behind to take leave in

[29] Dr. S. Ramaratnam, Head of the Department of Sanskrit, Vivekananda College, Madras, was kind enough to check the entries under "Vāmadeva Miśra" in the manuscript of the relevant, yet still unpublished volume of "New Catalogus Catalogorum," but could not find a Saṃskṛtatattvabodhinī among the texts written by various Vāmadeva Miśras. —Internal evidence in the STB seems to point to the 18th or 19th century as the date of its composition.

[30] Quite oddly, in the body of the text itself the city clearly referred to is Vārāṇasī! I don't know how to explain this striking contradiction. Did Vāmadeva Miśra—like the author of a roman à clef—want to veil the identity of persons he mentions?

[31] Cf. e.g. Balbir 1990: especially 50ff.

their turn. The reader is informed about the subjects the prince is being taught—evidently for quite some years now—which reach from the Prakriyākaumudī down to the Kaṇādaśāstra. Then the guru declares his education to be complete. When the king has convinced himself, through his own questioning, in fact examining, of his son, that the brahmin has surpassed the hopes set on him as a de-facto *rājopādhyāya*, he secretly orders various gifts to be fetched and then to be presented to him by the prince. This *gurudakṣiṇā* consists in various animals (an elephant, horses, cows), jewellery, gold, coins, a house and land, clothes, and even Gopībhaṭṭa is given some presents. The return of father and son to their place hence becomes a veritable procession, accompanied as they are by the prince and his retinue. "Rescued from the ocean of poverty," as they now were thanks to the generosity of the king, Devadattaśarman and Gopībhaṭṭaśarman henceforth lived happily.

In his introductory verse Vāmadeva Miśra also discloses his aim in composing the STB, viz. by stating

> *vināpi kurve bahubhiḥ prayāsair*
> *gī rvāṇanipuṇān kiśorān* //
> I shall make youngsters familiar with/proficient in the language of the gods (i.e. Sanskrit) without much effort.

Quite evidently his expression *kiśora* is used here as a synonym of *bāla* which is quite common in the text itself. Since it is first of all Gopībhaṭṭa who is referred to by it, there cannot be any doubt that *bāla* denotes a young man, not yet married, but a husband-to-be.

No similar statement is found in the verses at the beginning of the second text I should now like to deal with briefly. The text is entitled Varasaṃskṛtamañjarī in the second of the three *ārambhaślokas*, but only Saṃskṛtamañjarī (SM)[32] in the colophons. The author calls himself "son of Makarandasūri" (*Śrīmakarandasūrisūnu*)[33] and declares that he has been entreated—to compose his work—by his beloved one.[34] He

[32] In one of the MSS. this title is also given to the GPM; cf. Shah 1960:3 n. 2.

[33] According to what he tells about himself, and his descent, in the concluding verses, his name was Śivaśarman, he was the youngest of three sons, and a *muni*. It seems that the SM was composed by him during the reign of the eldest son of Pṛthivīnārāyaṇa Śāha—who conquered Kathmandu —viz. Pratāpa Surendra, i.e. Siṃha, Śāha (1775-1777).

[34] *dayitayā hṛdayasthitayā kayācid api vijñapito muditānanaḥ* /
vikasitaṃ kusumais tribhir uttamaiḥ puraharasya pure puragopure //

further says that the work consists of three parts,[35] i.e. "flowers" (*kusuma*), and that he resides near the gate "of the city of the 'destroyer of strongholds'"—which could be a periphrasis for Vārāṇasī (*puraharasya pure puragopure*), but most probably refers to Deopatan (now a part of Kathmandu).

But in the body of the text itself, viz. at the very outset of the prose text preceded by the three verses just mentioned, a relevant statement is found; significantly however it forms an integral part of the story itself. A young man, a 'poet' (*kavi*), whose name is to be disclosed only later, is again and again requested by his *priyatamā*—while he is sitting with her at a window on the upper story of a temple—to teach her 'the language of the gods' (*gīrvāṇavāṇī*); willing to comply with her wish he asks her the name of her father and similar matters, pretending that he does not already know the answers. She answers in Sanskrit, and in the course of this conversation tells him that she has learned "the Amarakośa, etc., from her father," together with the youngest of her brothers, and that she should like her husband to teach her brother the *Vyākaraṇaśāstra*. What she actually says is: *tasya buddhiḥ samīcīnā vartate / tasmai vyākaraṇaśāstraṃ tvayā paṭhyatāṃ*, "he is very intelligent, thou shouldst teach him grammar," whereupon he replies: *re mūrkhe, tvayā ity ekavacanam asmāsu kimarthaṃ prayuṅkṣe*, "you stupid girl, why do you use the singular 'thou' with reference to us (i.e. me)?" She apologizes and admits that she does not know how many numbers there are and when which of them has to be used. What then follows is Sanskrit morphology presented as dryly as imaginable; the case affixes are enumerated as they have metalinguistically been named by Pāṇini, i.e. together with their 'markers' (*anubandhas*); paradigmata of the nominal and pronominal declensions are given, some of the cardinal numbers are taught, etc., etc. In short, as the young lady herself states at the beginning of the second 'chapter' ("flower"), she is taught the "knowledge of the case endings" (*vibhaktijñāna*), "of the genders" (*liṅgajñāna*) and "of the numbers" (*vacanajñāna*), and in some detail at that (*vistareṇa*). It is, however, this second chapter which really makes up for the hard task of reading practically only paradigmata of Sanskrit declensions. For this is not just, as indicated by its title,[36] a chapter on the

[35] The third part deals with the daily duties of people.

[36] Viz. *Śṛṅgārarasasaṃgraha*.

śṛṅgārarasa—and hence an elaboration, so to say, of the concluding part of the GVM—, but in fact an highly amusing and funny dialogue in which growing erotic tension is built up, only that its finding relief is tactfully not described by the author. Much of the charm of this chapter—which leads the readers into the house or rather bedroom of the couple—I feel, ultimately lies in the character of the young wife who is, at least within the Indian context, remarkably self-assured and frank, and with an unusual lack of shyness.[37]

Thus after having listened to the almost endless series of paradigmata of declensions, etc., she resumes the topic of the use of the singular with reference to her husband and argues that he himself has stated that the singular is used to denote what is numerically one, i.e. a single entity. His reply is that with reference to one's husband the singular should not be used. She asks on which authority this is based, and he then quotes a *śruti* passage[38] to the effect that the singular should not be used with reference to a *guru* or to oneself. But she does not regard her case to be lost and objects that he is after all her husband and not her *guru*, whereupon she is informed by him about the various meanings the substantive *guru* has in Sanskrit—with the help of two verses quoted from a Nītiśāstra which are then explained to her word by word. The husband is so pleased by her eagerness to learn and the manner in which she apologizes for her lack of knowledge that he declares his love for her, assures her that his only happiness is she and declares that on that day there will be no class. "Play [a game] with us! Do you know [to play] or not?" She confesses that as a young girl she had secretly watched her parents playing and therefore has some knowledge of the rules. Before they actually start playing, they discuss which stake each of them is to make. He promises to give her 50 coins with which he could have jewellery

---

[37] If one takes into consideration works like the Kumārasambhava and the—Nepalese—Svasthānīvratakathā, one wonders whether and, if so, to what extent, the author of the SM could have been influenced by *religious* erotic literature. —As is well-known, "one of the most basic forms of presentation of a narrative in ancient Indian literature is to have one person telling a story to another" (Warder 1974:117)—and to make this an event within another story (on the literary device of the 'frame story' cf. Witzel 1987); no work, however, has been done as far as I know on the role of females, especially of female narrators or instructors.

[38] Viz. *ekavacanaṃ na prayuñjīta gurau cātmani*, which I have not yet been able to identify; besides, I am not at all certain whether this is really a quote from a *śruti* text.

made for her in case he loses, and suggests that if she loses she should "give" him every day two additional *rati*s.

The game the young couple plays is evidently similar to or identical with backgammon or tric-trac.[39] She wins and gets the 50 coins, but the game is continued. She catches him attempting to cheat, but in the end she loses nevertheless. When he demands her stake, and wants to kiss her, she confesses, or pretends, to be hindered by bashfulness to comply with his wish. This provokes a lesson about *lajjā*, most eloquently given her by the husband, culminating in his request that while staying with him in the *antaḥpura* she should abandon all bashfulness and behave like a *veśyā*. She admits that he is right, but says that for her, born and brought up in a 'great family' as she is, it is simply impossible to do that; even talking about such behaviour is improper. The husband then quotes the following verse from the Mahānāṭaka:[40]

> *kāryeṣu mantrī karaṇeṣu dāsī*
> *dharmeṣu patnī kṣamayā dharitrī* /
> *sneheṣu mātā śayaneṣu veśyā*
> *śayyāsakh ī lakṣmaṇa sā priyā me* //

in which the various roles an Indian wife ideally should fulfil—in the view of the Indian macho—are clearly stated. The detailed explanation of this verse is followed by quoting another relevant one, from the Rasaviveka,[41] viz.

> *sārāsāraṃ na jānāti surate yāpi sundarī* /
> *nāyakānāṃ tayā sārdhaṃ śunī maithunam ucyate* //
> Sexual intercourse of lovers with a beautiful [young lady] who does not know the good and the bad side in love-making is called intercourse with a she-dog.

This, too, is explained word by word, and thus she is finally persuaded to do what he wishes her to do, but only after more of such coquettish, and by no means only verbal, foreplay. And again she proves a most worthy partner of her husband, full of self-confidence: e.g. she says that she is strong enough to throw him down on the bed in her turn, she ridicules him for being himself not free from bashfulness, she tries to em-

[39] Cf. P. Thieme 1961, 1977, and quite recently 1994a. Cf. in addition Syed 1994.

[40] Viz. 5.9; the problem of the variants is something I don't want to address now.

[41] In spite of my endeavours I have not been able to procure a copy of this text (edited by T.K.V. N. Sudarśanācārya, Tirupati 1956) and hence have not managed to identify the quotation.

barrass him in that she refuses to take such a position that her feet are directed towards him—which would indeed not be in accordance with the rules of the Śāstra although these, of course, refer to quite different a situation— and in that she asks him to do what he wants to do standing at the head of the bed, etc. All this makes for good reading and is in fact so amusing that the third chapter, devoted to a description of the daily religious duties of a brahmin and similar subjects, cannot but compare rather badly with the preceding one; therefore, and not only because time and space are limited, I deem it legitimate to break off my presentation of the SM here, in order to turn now to a number of problems posed by all the four texts, the GPM, the GVM, the STB and the SM; for it cannot be disputed that the latter two belong to the same class as the first two, although questions like that of relative chronology and hence that of their relation to each other have still to be answered.

3. The significance of this class of texts for our knowledge of the cultural history, especially of the way of life of brahmins in Northern and Western India, was already recognized by Gode,[42] and the relevant testimony of the GPM and GVM has been used and discussed in great detail by Shah in his "Introduction." With regard to the STB it has to be emphasized that much information can be gathered also about the 'system of education' of the times when this text was composed, the usual 'curriculum' of a brahmin or a prince, i.e. which works or parts of works they were expected to study and in which sequence. The history of traditional Indian education has great gaps and not only in this regard.

It should not, however, be forgotten that texts like the GPM, etc., cannot by any means be classed as documentary reports; on the contrary, they are quite evidently literary fiction, although of widely unequal a quality. Yet it is no less evident that their authors wish to draw a basically and virtually 'realistic' and colourful picture, and that they by and large also know from their own experience and/or observation what they are talking about. It is precisely this conspicuous endeavour to describe elements of every day life—of members of the class of

[42] Cf. Gode 1941 and especially 1956:161-171. The fact that the GVM has some importance also as regards political history seems rather a coincidence.

brahmins—, by which these texts clearly and remarkably stand out against most of the known Sanskrit literature.[43]

Nevertheless there are, of course, also features which have a long 'prehistory' in Indian literature, e.g. the—aesthetically highly problematic—'device' of merely enumerating names of trees[44] or vegetables or fruits or dishes, etc.[45] The 'originality' of texts like the GPM, etc., can hence at best be styled a relative one, especially as the description of a normal day, i.e. a day conforming to the norms of the Dharmaśāstra valid for brahmins, cannot be dislinked from the didactic goal the authors evidently have set themselves. I do not mean so much the 'secondary' aim of (most probably) impressing these norms by describing their being, so to say, naturally obeyed by brahmanical householders; what I have in mind is rather the 'primary' didactic aim of 'teaching Sanskrit' by using this language itself in describing that which is best known to the pupils-to-be, viz. everyday life as they themselves led. In the case of the STB and even more so of the SM it is less clear precisely of whom the 'target group' consists. The contents of the narrative parts of the STB, it should be noted, do not warrant the conclusion that it was written with the aim of teaching Sanskrit to brahmin ladies who have a more or less limited previous knowledge of the language. On the contrary, the conclusion which really suggests itself—if the outline of Sanskrit morphology is taken into consideration, too—is that the author had in view members of his own class in general who do not any longer speak Sanskrit *svabhāvena daivānugraheṇa vā*, to modify a phrase of Patañjali's, the Mahābhāṣyakāra,[46] or who have learnt or picked it up as children from their fathers and other male adult

---

[43] Cf. Wezler 1985. —Cf. also E. Auerbach's remarkable observations about Petronius' "Cena Trimalchionis," viz. that his realistic manner of representation comes closer to our modern one than anything else in classical literature (1988:33ff.).

[44] Cf. in this connection Rau's apt remark (1957:53) that "ancient India did not know a romanticism of the forest ("Waldromantik")" which is true to some extent even for the Epics, i.e. the descriptions e.g. of a forest that are practically but enumerations of tree names. On the other hand, in terms of an 'emic' interpretation one would have to take into consideration that enumeration is an elementary form of gathering information, of making sure of one's own knowledge and of memorizing it. As for the *Varṇakas* see Shah 1960:56, et passim.

[45] For their explanation see Shah 1960:56ff; cf. 12ff. (who, however, calls this chapter 'Food and Drinks'—just like Mr. Om Prakash in the first edition of his book (1987)).

[46] Viz. MBh 3:174.10ff.

relatives, but who have at best only a rudimentary knowledge of the language—and are in this regard similar to the *vaidikas* of the GPM and GVM Yet, also with reference to the 'primary' didactic aim it is interesting to note that means and aim overlap to a very large extent: the active use of Sanskrit as a means of conversation is demonstrated with a view to guiding the members of the 'target group' to follow this example and to speak the language themselves. This not only seems to be the common central purpose of all the four texts under discussion, but also a trait which clearly distinguishes them from grammatical works in the proper sense of the word.[47] For this very reason I cannot agree with Gode[48] who calls the GVM a "grammatical work": That there is a close and multifaceted relation to the *Vyākaraṇaśāstra* cannot be disputed, but texts like the GPM, etc., are to be classed— not as 'grammar textbooks', but rather—as 'conversation textbooks' or 'manuals of spoken Sanskrit'. In view of this their specific character they, however, differ from bilingual phrase-books, which are also attested within a wider area which was exposed to Indian cultural influence[49] or from bilingual manuals for teaching Sanskrit to speakers of vernaculars like the Ukti-Vyakti-Prakaraṇa or the Lekhapaddhati which were carefully examined by R. Salomon 12 years ago.[50] On the other hand, they would clearly deserve to be studied more closely by scholars specialized in or at least familiar with language teaching methods and the research carried out on this subject. It is hardly necessary to state that the problem is an almost universal one, viz. of leading students or people in general to an active use of a language that they are learning or have already learnt; but it would, no doubt, be interesting to analyse the solution(s) the Indians or perhaps I should say: the brahmins, have found.[51]

Yet there is another question one cannot help asking oneself, especially in connection with the subject of this Seminar: Of what kind was

[47] I am referring, of course, to those which are in fact meant to teach Sanskrit, in contradistinction to earlier works like Pāṇini's Aṣṭādhyāyī. Cf. also fn. 53 below.

[48] Gode 1956:169.

[49] I have in view e.g. Kumamoto 1988, or a text which my friend Dr. Ch. Cüppers has published, the first part of which is a kind of Tibetan-Newari Dictionary and the second a corresponding phrase book, i.e. Cüppers 1992.

[50] Cf. Salomon 1982.

[51] An interesting and highly informative picture of "The Pandits and their Manner of Teaching" has been drawn by Dr. J. R. Ballantyne (1866-67).

the knowledge of Sanskrit at the time when these texts were composed? And why did the authors deem it at all necessary, or at least desirable, to produce such 'Sanskrit conversation textbooks'? It is by far more difficult to answer these questions than to ask them. For even in those cases where a text can be dated with a high degree of certainty and precision and where it is possible to determine the city in which its author lived and worked, our knowledge of the contemporary situation, cultural, political, sociolinguistic, etc., is unfortunately such that we cannot deduce a plausible explanation for the composition of texts like the GPM. That is to say, I am not fully convinced that Shah is right in assuming that what he calls "a great revival" of literary activity and Sanskrit learning at Kāśī in the 16th century is alone, or even basically, responsible for the appearance of texts like those under discussion. I also do not want to dispute the existence of "a periodic Sanskritizing language reformism among the orthodox elements of Hindu society" that Salomon (1982:15) finds "vividly attested for medieval times . . . in the UVP." But should we not go at least one step further and wonder why brahmins regarded such a 'revival' at all as necessary? In this connection it is also important to note that—with the exception of a portion of the GVM[52]—all four 'textbooks' attest an ideal world of brahmanical life, not in the least affected by political events, e.g. the fact that political power is in the hands of Muslims or other *mlecchas*, etc. But this latter observation perhaps gives a clue for finding an answer to the questions just mentioned: The appearance of these 'Sanskrit conversational textbooks', of these works of "Sanskrit instructional literature," to use Salomon's term for this genre, might well have been provoked by the fact, or the feeling, that traditional Sanskrit learning was endangered in brahmanical circles, real pandits apart, or that it had become too bookish, too much a language of the Veda and the Śāstra only,[53] and was not any longer a living means of communication among the brahmins; after all brahmins are according to their self-understanding gods on earth, though of a special kind,[54] who not only have a special *adhikāra* with re-

[52] Viz. that dealt with in detail by Gode 1956.

[53] In this connection it should also be noted that according to its concluding verse Varadarāja's Sārasiddhāntakaumudī ed. . . . by G. V. Devasthali 1968:224 has been composed *vedavedapraveśāya* (only this is quoted by Gode 1941:191 [1954:320]) as also *sarvaśāstrapraveśāya*.

[54] I.e. different from the *kṣatriyas*; see e.g. Manusmṛti 1.92; 2.135; 9.245, 313ff.

gard to the *gīrvāṇavāṇī* but whose specific 'weapon' also is speech, i.e. Sanskrit.[55] Do we hence have to reckon with the possibility that not only the strict observation of traditional custom or the transmission of Vedic or Śāstric texts was regarded by members of the highest *varṇa* as a central element of their self-identity, but also the active use of that language which had become 'theirs' in a very singular sense? And that the contemporary political etc. conditions were of importance only insofar as they were essentially responsible for a general 'climate' which was either in favour or against expressing this self-identity?

Be that as it may, one cannot help wondering whether the authors of these texts were sufficiently qualified for the task they set themselves, i.e. how good their own knowledge of Sanskrit actually was.[56] Now, in the case of the texts under discussion the situation is clearly different from that of the UVP: It is perhaps true that the Sanskrit used in the GPM, etc., may be called 'popular', too,[57] but the question whether it is "an artificial 'Easy Sanskrit', invented and propagated"[58] by their authors, which Salomon has to address, does not arise because strange verbs and odd constructions like those found in the UVP, in no small a number at that, are practically absent. Nevertheless, it suffices to read one page of any of these texts in order to see that the language in which they are composed cannot be classified as pure 'classical' Sanskrit either. Quite evidently this is due, at least to a very large extent, to the influence exercised on this Sanskrit by the NIA languages, i.e. mother-tongues, of the authors; the influence, however, becomes apparent first of all in the sphere of semantics and of the choice of words. Let me give just two examples: the participle *vijñapita* is used, in the third *ārambhaśloka* of the SM, as we have already seen, in the sense of 'entreated', and this is decidedly nearer to the meaning the historically related verbs have in Old Awadhī, Gujarātī and Marāṭhī than to that of

[55] Cf. e.g. Manusmṛti 11.33.

[56] I agree with Shah (1960:7) that the authors of the GPM and GVM are not to be expected to have made any morphological mistakes and that it is hence methodically correct to accept the grammatically correct forms or even restore them by emendation wherever necessary.

[57] Cf. Salomon 1982:16; see however p. 4.

[58] Quoted from Salomon 1928:18.

Skt. *vijñapayati.*[59] Again, the comparatively frequent use of the root *mil,* and deratives,[60] is equally a vernacularism.

That is to say, though in a different manner, these texts, too, testify to a 'peculiar Sanskrit'[61] just like the UVP, but the results of the interferences between certain NIA languages and Sanskrit is markedly different. Hence the language of the GPM, etc., also calls for a thorough and comprehensive examination; and the results it will certainly yield in abundance will draw the attention of scholars—who seem to have been particularly fascinated by the perhaps indeed more spectacular interferences, e.g. between Tamil, or other Dravidian languages, or Newārī and Sanskrit[62]—to the less conspicuous, but no less interesting interference between the Sanskrit of the late middle ages and various NIA languages, or rather their old(er) forms. The study of the language of these texts will thus ultimately contribute to throwing some light on a phase in the development of Sanskrit of which very little is known so far,[63] i.e. the last centuries before British Civil Servants became more and more interested in the 'sacred' language of the brahmins.

In fact, Madhav M. Deshpande has already carried out such a study, and a detailed and penetrating one at that, though with regard to the GVM only, viz. in his latest book (1993a). Our thanks are due to him also for drawing our attention to J. Hertel's half-forgotten essay of 1922 "On the Literature of the Śvetāmbaras of Gujarat" and the highly impressive—and in my view fully justified—plea Hertel makes for an entirely unbiased study of the various types of Sanskrit as they are actually attested not only in texts, but also in speech. I do agree with both, Hertel and Deshpande, in most of what they say; nevertheless, I should like to add on my part a few remarks which are, however, critical in their regard only to some extent.

I don't find Deshpande's term 'vernacular Sanskrit' really appropriate: what is meant is a variety of non-standard Sanskrit which is admittedly heavily influenced by a vernacular, or by vernaculars, i.e. "a lan-

---

[59] Cf. Turner 1966: § 11705.

[60] Turner 1966:582 and § 10133ff.

[61] Quoted from Salomon 1982:14.

[62] Cf. e.g. Schrader 1928, or the paper on the grammar of the Svayambhūpurāṇa by my friend B. Kölver, to be published in the Festschrift for Manfred Taube.

[63] It is not covered by Renou 1956b.

guage/languages widely spoken in a country or region,"[64] "a language/languages or a dialect/dialects native to a region or country,"[65] but it does not itself have this character. Hertel's proposal to call it 'popular Sanskrit' is equally unconvincing: we are not in a position to prove that it was "enjoyed or liked by a lot of people" or even "approved of or held by most people" or else that it "aimed at the needs or tastes of ordinary people."[66] I should even go so far as to wonder whether Hertel is right in assuming a continuous tradition of "a popular and colloquial spoken Sanskrit," although I admit that the evidence given by Deshpande speaks in favour of this assumption, i.e. to be more precise, the assumption that brahmins who happened to meet at traditional centres of Sanskrit learning like Vārāṇasī or at places of pilgrimage used Sanskrit as means of communication (among themselves), and that this sub-species of the "language of the gods," strongly influenced by various vernaculars as it was, may be regarded as continuation of 'spoken Sanskrit,'[67] the *bhāṣā* of former times. Nevertheless to me it rather seems necessary to first study much more comprehensively and thoroughly all the relevant material[68] and data before a final conclusion can be drawn. The peculiar Sanskrit used by the authors of texts like the GVM, etc., i.e. the extent to which it is influenced by their first language, or perhaps we could say, their mother tongue, could after all also be explained by presuming that they just did not generally, or hardly ever, use Sanskrit in conversation about everyday matters, but only in connection with Śāstric discussions. It is at this point that I should like to draw attention to a statement found in the Vṛtti on Bhartṛhari's Vākyapadīya I 14, which reads thus: *sarvo hi prāyeṇa svasyāṃ vidyāyāṃ*

[64] Quoted from Collins Cobuild English Language Dictionary, London 1990.

[65] Quoted from The New Penguin English Dictionary, London 1986.

[66] Cf. n. 64.

[67] As kindly pointed out to me by Thomas Oberlies, Sukumar Sen 1957, contains a chapter (36-51) on "Spoken Sanskrit," yet his peculiar conception of the language which he gives this label quite clearly calls for a critical reexamination—as also his theory about the nature and development of Buddhist Hybrid Sanskrit. —Halāyudha Miśras's Sekaśubhodayā, edited by Sen, however, deserves full attention, at least as regards the interference between Sanskrit and NIA (cf. also Sen 1928). As for the type of language used in the texts under discussion in the present article, mention should also be made of Edgerton 1926/27.

[68] According to another of Ashok Aklujkar's useful comments this should include Jambhaladatta's version of the Vetālapañcaviṃśati and the Śukasaptati, two texts which could very well have served, if not even been composed, as a kind of accompanying reader.

vyākaraṇam anugacchati, apabhraṃśaprayogeṇa ca niyatam apatrapate, "for everybody usually follows grammar in his field of learning and is certainly ashamed by the use of (i.e. if he by negligence uses) an incorrect word(form)."[69] By *sarva* the author of the Vṛtti most probably refers to a particular group of people only, i.e. the brahmins, or even a particular elite of them; in any case this statement not only testifies to diglossia and not only to a clear functional differentiation between correct Sanskrit (i.e. a Sanskrit that is in conformity with Pāṇinīyan grammar) and a vernacular—at a particular point of time in history—; but it testifies equally, at least implicitly, to a much more liberal, if not even indifferent, attitude toward the type of Sanskrit which is written or spoken when other subjects than one's own *vidyā* are dealt with.

Quite recently I read again Kumārasambhava 3.3

> *ājñāpaya jñātaviśeṣa puṃsāṃ lokeṣu yat te karaṇīyam asti* |
> *anugrahaṃ saṃsmaraṇapravṛttam icchāmi saṃvardhitam ājñayā te* ||

where Kāma addressing Indra says: "O you who discern the special qualifications of men, command what you desire to be done for you in the [three] worlds. I should like this favour, shown by your remembrance [of me], to be enhanced by [the bestowing of] a command." [70] What occurred to me once more in reading this, was that Sanskrit has not only been, as Hertel states,[71] "also the language of the courts and of diplomacy," but that it is, and in no small measure, a 'courteous' language in the etymological sense of the word; yet this is but another feature of the 'language of the gods', which has still to be studied; [72] and I need not add that it ought to be studied precisely because of its signifi-

[69] That is to say, I by and large agree with M. Biardeau's (1964a: 51) rendering of this passage.

[70] The translation is that of M. R. Kale 1967.

[71] As quoted by M. M. Deshpande 1993a:38. —In passing I note that the second paragraph quoted by Deshpande from Hertel (1922) contains an irritating misprint: instead of "that in this country" read "that in his country"; what Bilhaṇa describes in the last canto of his Vikramāṅkadevacarita is Śrīnagar, and Kashmir.

[72] With the *locus classicus* of the idea of a peculiar common responsibility of *kṣatriyas* and *brāhmaṇas* for the other living beings and 'the world'—which in my view forms the basis of the Indian ideology of the relation of the upper two *varṇas*—, viz. GautDhS 1.8.1f., I shall deal at some length in an essay still under preparation.

cance for the "Ideology and Status of Sanskrit in South and Southeast Asia."[73]

Ceterum censeo terram Tibetanam
in veterem dignitatem ac libertatem
esse vindicandam.

---

[73] As for the designation, I should like to note that P. Thieme very recently (1994b:323) has expressed his sad feeling about M. Mayrhofer's "throwing aside the name 'Sanskrit'"; indeed, one could very well consider using 'Sanskrit' as the designation for Vedic as well as all the various forms of standard and non-standard 'classical' Sanskrit.

Though scholars of Indo-European studies will, I am afraid, hesitate to follow Thieme or me, Indologists, especially those among them who attended this Seminar, or now read the present Volume, will accept this proposal much more readily because the Indian grammarians, and not only they, did not after all regard 'Vedic Sanskrit' and 'Classical Sanskrit' as two different languages, but distinguished only between 'Vedic' and *laukika* words. Hence the notion of a linguistic continuum to which Ashok Aklujkar rightly draws our attention (see his contribution to this volume) also covers these two varieties of 'correct speech', and not only 'Sanskrit' and the *apabhraṃśas*.

Finally, regarding the question where *saṃskṛta* is first attested as designation of a language— and the verse from the Rāmāyaṇa (Rāmāyaṇa 5.28.17-18) quoted by Sheldon Pollock in the discussion of Aklujkar's paper—, I should like to add that this whole issue including this passage has already been discussed by E. W. Hopkins 1902:83ff. (cf. Hinüber 1986:19), who in his turn refers to Jacobi 1893:112-119.

CHAPTER FIFTEEN

SANSKRIT AND HINDU NATIONAL IDENTITY IN NINETEENTH CENTURY BENGAL

Victor A. van Bijlert

1. Since 1983 a number of good historical and sociological studies have been devoted to the rise of national identities (cf Hobsbawm 1992:4-5; Anderson 1993:XII). These works, written by western scholars, are mainly dealing with this subject in its western manifestations, covering the period from the Renaissance up to the present. In other words, the period of transition from European *ancient regimes* to the building of the modern nation state.

Does this mean that the construction of modern national identity and concomitant nationalism are a uniquely European phenomenon? This is not so, as Benedict Anderson in his justly famous book *Imagined Communities* (Anderson 1993) has shown, for he devotes a good part of the book to nationalisms as they sprang up in such diverse non-western areas as the Spanish American colonies (chapter 4), British Malaya, the Philippines (chapter 7), Vietnam and China (chapter 9). Strangely enough, he is casting only a cursory glance at India.

This does not have to worry us since in recent years a number of good studies have been written on Indian national identity-formation and nationalism by Indian social historians. In this respect among the most useful and sophisticated authors are Partha Chatterjee (Chatterjee 1993a and a), Sudipta Kaviraj (Kaviraj 1993), and Gyanendra Pandey (Pandey 1990), all belonging to the Subaltern Studies group, as well as Tapan Raychaudhuri (Raychaudhuri 1988) and Ashis Nandy (Nandy 1994) who do not belong to this group.

Modern nation building in India started in the 19th century and is complexely and problematically linked to the British colonization project. The creation of a national Indian identity for nineteenth century Bengali intellectuals, who were by all accounts the first to enunciate it, assumed the form of anticolonialism rather than striving to reach an independent nation state India. In the words of Sudipta Kaviraj:

> Alien rule is a kind of *a priori* of their thinking, a deeply hated limit which they . . . are not able to transcend. . . . These authors remain within these limits not because they like British rule. In some ways their rejection of a colonizing western rationalist civilization often goes deeper and is more fundamental than that of later nationalists; but they simply do not see the end of colonial subjection as a historically feasible project. For them the epochal historical question . . . was: how did a civilization with such varied resources become subject to colonialism? (Kaviraj 1993, 6-7)

The anticolonial consciousness which Kaviraj sees emerging among the Bengali intellectuals is "a merely oppositional attitude towards colonialism, and if we gather up all its historical characteristics it is more a cultural critique, a resentment against ignominy rather than a political-economic rejection of its civilizing pretensions" (Kaviraj 1993:12).

Thus, the site for such critique is not to be found in the arena of political activism, but in the consciousness of the sensitive intelligentsia (Chatterjee 1993b:6-9). The consciousness of the receptive intellectual responds to the outward world which seems to have slipped from its control due to the mounting cultural forces of colonialism with its organizational power, drive for efficiency, and hegemony of technological advantages. The only response left to the seemingly powerless intellectual is the retreat into an inner space of high culture and vernacular language, an area of relative freedom and independence apparently left untouched by western influence with its rational and civilizing pretensions.

Within this inner domain the intellectual is in control. Here is freedom to create and interpret, here the capital of cultural resources can be freely invested to be spent later by distributing the cultural production through the printing press. In society the texts that are being produced begin to work in the consciousness of the readers, in other words, a public, an audience.[1] It goes without saying that initially this cultural

[1] The problematic of the cyclical movement of cultural production between its producers and its consumers is one the themes of the discipline of 'cultural studies'. On cultural studies see: Giddens et al., 1994; During (ed.) 1993, and Grossberg et. al. (eds.) 1992. These anthologies which only constitute a mere fraction of what is written about cultural studies, gives a good impression of the problematic, variety and width of the subject.

capital was the exclusive possession of the indigenous learned ones, subaltern though they were vis-a-vis the British. In other words, this cultural capital rested with those who had the necessary education, as well as the necessary financial means, for intellectual pursuits. The cultural capital was, as is the case with every form of capital, in the hands of an elite.[2]

For the urban Hindu upper and middle class intellectuals [3] the greatest and most obvious cultural capital accumulated over many centuries was the overwhelming mass of Sanskrit literature. It is my contention that this came to be utilized as one of the major legitimizing sources of Indian national identity constructed as Hindu identity. The other source was the increasing adaptation of the vernacular Bengali to modern uses, making Bengali prose one of the great vehicles for print capitalism.[4] Whereas the immediate impact of Bengali cultural production (in a Hindu mode) reached as far as the linguistic area, the impact of Sanskrit was 'all-Indian' so to say even if its direct accessibility was limited to an intellectual elite. The remarkable antithesis between a Hindu identity based on Sanskrit, with pan-Indian pretensions, and a localized identity based on Bengali was never fully resolved.

It is clear that the whole mass of Sanskrit literature in its entirety could not be used as a legitimizing source of nationhood. After all, the cultural critique of colonial modernity was itself a mode of modernity. The answer to the western challenge had to be proportional to its impact. Hence rational choices were made, those Sanskrit texts were selected that seemed best suited to the project of cultural and religious modernization and the raising of national consciousness. The texts thus selected from the beginning of the nineteenth century onwards gradually turned into a canon, not exactly in the religious sense of the word, but rather in a cultural sense.[5] With hindsight it can be argued that the choice for Sanskrit texts had thrown a dark shadow on the future, for it

---

[2] On the concept of 'cultural capital' and its possession by elites, see Bourdieu 1993:1-2; 83-84.

[3] I use the term 'intellectual' here rather generally in the sense of a person who has had acccess to traditional and modern education and who writes.

[4] On print capitalism, see: Anderson 1993:39-46.

[5] I use the word canon here rather in the sense of Steiner 1989:32-39; 62-66; 83-87; 214-219.

almost inevitably had to estrange most non-Hindus for whom, after all, Sanskrit could not have much emotional and evocative value.

2. What were the reasons and motivations for the Bengali Hindu intellectuals to use Sanskrit texts as an ideological basis for nation building? In what follows we will take up for examination writings by Rammohun Roy, Bankimchandra Chatterjee and Rabindranath Tagore, three famous and influential Bengali authors whose writing career spans almost a century. They all wrote on Hindu religion and the Indian nation.

As to Indian culture and the nation, the following motivations and assumptions can be extracted from many Bengali and English texts of that period: (a) gaining respect and self-respect, (b) the antiquity of Sanskrit, (c) the classical character of Sanskrit literature, (d) apparent universal extension of Sanskrit over a cultural area more or less coterminous with the geographical landmass of South-Asia, (e) Sanskrit was regarded as the ancestor of all the North-Indian vernaculars, (f) Sanskrit narrative texts were the source of most local mythologies; Sanskrit texts were thought to have provided the models for regional vernacular literature from the middle ages onwards.

Let us take a closer look at the issue of respect. It is an established fact that towards the end of the eighteenth and the beginning of the nineteenth century, Protestant Christian missionaries in India made many disdainful comments on what they regarded as the utterly damaging influence of Hinduism on the population. Hinduism according to them was inhumanly cruel, morally degrading, superstitious and to top it all, blatantly polytheistic.[6] For example Rev. Ward in 1818 remarked that,

> . . . the authors of the Hindu mythology have taken care, that the quarrels and revels of the gods and goddesses shall be held up to the imitation of the whole community. (Dutta 1992:31)

In 1854 McLeod Wylie stated:

> The old Government was intolerant, corrupt, and capricious, and the Hindu priests wherever Muhammadanism left them in power, taught the people to treat them as Gods, and then instructed them in the worship of deities, who were even more wicked than themselves. (Dutta 1992:30)

[6] For a booklength exposition and discussion of missionaries' views on Hinduism, see Dutta 1992.

While already in 1813 William Wilberforce maintained:

> . . . Are we so little aware of the vast superiority even of European laws and institutions, and far more of British institutions, over those of Asia, as not to be prepared to predict with confidence, that the Indian community which should have exchanged its dark and bloody superstitions for the genial influence of Christian light and truth, would have experienced such an increase of civil order and security, of social pleasures and domestic comforts, as to be desirous of preserving the blessings it should have aquired. (Stokes 1992:35)

Let us not forget that the gentlemen just quoted did not represent British conservatism, they were in their own ways liberals and followers and inheritors of Benthamite utilitarianism. The drift of the argument of these gentlemen was that if India was to become modern and enlightened, it should abandon its superstitious Hinduism.

The Hindu Bengali intellectuals, who were aware of these views felt compelled to answer such a challenge. Their answer lay in pointing out that Hinduism was not what these British observers had made it out to be, that Hinduism in its pristine glory as preserved in its best Sanskrit literature would satisfactorily invalidate these charges.

However, British intellectuals in India were not unanimous in their condemnation of all things Hindu. William Jones, for example, had been an admirer of Sanskrit literature as indeed of Persian literature. In a discourse on the institution of an Asiatic Society, held in Calcutta probably somewhere in 1784, Jones expresses the intellectual pleasure to be drived from the study of Asian culture (Works Sir W. Jones:1-4). On India, especially ancient India, Jones remarks in a lecture held in 1786:

> Let me here premise, that, in all these inquiries concerning the history of *India*, I shall confine my researches downwards to the *Mohammedan* conquests at the beginning of the *eleventh* century, but extend them upwards, as high as possible, to the earliest authentick records of the human species.
>
> India then, on its most enlarged scale, in which the ancients appear to have understood it, comprises an area of near *forty* degrees on each side, including a space almost as large as all *Europe* ...
>
> ...
>
> The *Hindus* themselves believe their own country, to which they give the vain epithets of *Medhyama* or *Central* , and *Punyabhumi*, or the *Land of Virtues*, to have been the portion of BHARAT, one of the *nine*

> brothers, whose father had the dominion of the whole earth. (Works Sir W. Jones:28-29)

In many ways Jones foreshadows the kind of glorious discourse on ancient India, interpreted as Hindu India, which proved so powerful an ideological weapon for the nineteenth century Bengali Hindu. Jones' judgment on contemporary Hindus was less favourable though, for in the same lecture he says: "... how degenerate and abased so ever the *Hindus* may now appear, ... in some early age they were splendid in arts and arms, happy in government, wise in legislation, and eminent in various knowledge" (Works Sir W. Jones:32). The great glory of the Hindus lies in a remote past of which we nowadays, according to Jones, only possess four things: "their *Languages* and *Letters* ... their *Philosophy* and *Religion*... actual remains of their old *Sculpture* and *Architecture*... the written memorials of their *Sciences* and *Arts*" (Works Sir W. Jones:32). Must we believe that Jones intentionally constructed this Hindu past with a view to legitimize and strengthen British domination of contemporary India? It is not entirely absurd to read such intentions behind Jones' remarks and indeed in many other of his writings on India. But one thing should not be forgotten: the information on India was gathered from indigenous informants, a debt of gratitude to whom Jones never tired of paying.

William Jones was not the only admirer of ancient Hindu India. Warren Hastings wrote in the introduction to the first translation of the Bhagavad Gita from Sanskrit into English, by Charles Wilkins and published in 1785:

> I hesitate not to pronounce the Geeta a performance of great originality; of a sublimity of conception, reasoning, and diction, almost unequalled; and a single exception, among all the known religions of mankind, of a theology accurately corresponding with that of the Christian dispensation, and most powerfully illustrating its fundamental doctrine. (Introduction, p. 10)

It is known that the translations that were made of Sanskrit literature in the beginning of the 19th century were read and admired in Europe. A good example of European admiration for Indian texts is Schopenhauer (1788-1860) who was an avid reader of Indian philosophical and religious literature. This can be seen from the references to Indian, mainly Sanskrit, texts in his works. He had the greatest admiration for the Upaniṣads which he initially had come to know through the Latin translation of Anquetil-Duperron of Dara Shikoh's Persian translation. Later he studied the Upaniṣads in the various English translations that started to appear in the nineteenth century, among which the translations made by Rammohun Roy. That Schopenhauer held the Upaniṣads in high esteem is clear from the following passage from his *Parerga und Paralipomena*, II, kapitel 16, section 184, where he discusses the translations of Anquetil-Duperron:

> . . . wie atmet doch der 'Oupnekhat' durchweg den heiligen Geist der Veden! . . . aus jeder Seite treten uns tiefe, ursprüngliche, erhabene Gedanken entgegen, während ein hoher und heiliger Ernst über dem Ganzen schwebt. . . . Es ist die belohnendeste und erhebendeste Lektüre, die (den Urtext ausgenommen) auf der Welt möglich ist: sie ist der Trost meines Lebens gewesen und wird der meines Sterbens sein.[7]

This quotation has since become a household word with almost every Hindu nationalist, and has acted as a great boost to their morale.[8] But let us return to nineteenth century Bengal itself.

3.1 Rammohun Roy, the well-known Hindu reformer and liberal philosopher of Bengal, tried to counter missionary critique by a project of Hindu reformation, whose mode was intellectually similar to the liberal utilitarianism of his western opponents. In a way he tried to turn the tables against them by showing the relative superiority of the Hindu scriptures. In order to make his point, he published between 1815 and 1819 five Upaniṣads, Īśa, Kena, Kaṭha, Māṇḍūkya and Muṇḍaka, along with a few small Vedāntic tracts and the Brahma Sūtra in Sanskrit with Bengali translations and lengthy introductions preceding the translations. Simultaneously he published these texts also in English translations without the Sanskrit text, but again with lengthy introductions. It is exciting to realize that Rammohun's translations contained the first printed editions of these texts.

In a letter written to John Digby sometime in 1816 or 1817, Rammohun gives the following reasons for publishing his translations of Hindu texts:

---

[7] Sämtliche Werke:469. *Parerga und Paralipomena* from which this passage is taken was originally published in 1851.

[8] One of the important Bengali intellectuals who literally and approvingly quoted these words by Schopenhauer is Bankimchandra. The latter did this in a lecture held in Calcutta in 1894. See: Bankim Racanavali III:169.

> I . . . have . . . found Hindoos in general more superstitious and miserable, both in performance of their religious rites and in their domestic concerns, than the rest of the known nations on the earth . . . I thereore, with a view of making them happy and comfortable both here and hereafter, not only employed verbal arguments against the absurdities of the idolatry[9] . . . but also translated their most revered theological work, namely, Vedant, into Bengali and Hindustani and also several chapters of the Ved, in order to convince them that the unity, of God, and the absurdity of idolatry are evidently pointed out by their own scriptures. (Correspondence Roy:19-20)

It is noteworthy that Rammohun to some extent shares the criticism of the missionaries, but does not reject Hinduism for it. On the contrary, he tries to reconstruct - or should we say 'invent' - a more humane Hindu tradition based on the Vedānta and the Upaniṣads. Note also the fact that he implicitly refers to the Hindus as a nation, even though this word may not have signified exactly the same thing as approximately sixty years later.[10]

About the relative superiority of Hinduism over other world religions, Rammohun once remarked:

> The Hindus seem to have made greater progress in sacred learning than the Jews, at least when the Upanishads were written. . . If religion consists of the blessings of self-knowledge and of improved notions of God and his attributes and a system of morality holds a subordinate place, I certainly prefer the Vedas. (in Dobson Collet 1988:98)

In a nutshell we already have in Rammohun's words the notion of a Hindu nation whose original national language was Sanskrit, and whose ideology should be derived from Sanskrit sources. Of course in modern times it would not be possible to reinstall Sanskrit itself as a national language. The modern national language of the nation should be the vernacular Bengali, purified and Sanskritized. This was very much Rammohun's view. He tried to popularize the use of Bengali not only through his religious and philosophical writings, but also by pub-

---

[9] Rammohun uses often such words which nowadays we would no longer use to describe those religious practices. From the point of view of the Upaniṣads and the Advaita Vedānta, however, he was not entirely unjustified in calling certain aspects of the image worship of his day by the rather pejorative name of idolatry. The word is of Greek origin, and in fact means no more than just 'worship of images'.

[10] On the problematic term 'nation' and its several meanings, see Hobsbawm 1992:14-23.

lishing a small Bengali grammar in 1833, called *Gauḍīya Byākaraṇ* (in Rāmmohan Racanāvali:365-412).

That Rammohun regarded ancient, that is to say pre-islamic, India as possibly a Hindu nation, could be inferred from his "Appeal to the King in Council" from 1823. There he consistently refers to England as the 'British nation', from which it seems his concept of the 'nation' approached that of the 'nation state'. About India he says:

> The greater part of Hindustan having been for several centuries subject to Muhammadan Rule, the civil and religious rights of its original inhabitants were constantly trampled upon, and from the habitual oppression of the conquerors, a great body of their subjects in the southern Peninsula (Dukhin), afterwards called Marhattahs, and another body in the western parts now styled Sikhs, were at last driven to revolt. . . (Rāmmohan Racanāvali:508)

Rammohun does not explicitly say here that the original inhabitants of 'Hindustan' were Hindus, but the Muslims at least are regarded as conquerors, and they trampled on the religious rights of the original inhabitants. The geographical expanse of Hindustan seems to include South India and the Punjab. In a tract called "The Rights of Hindoos over Ancestral Property" 1830 Rammohun is more explicit about what India comprises: "India, like other large empires, is divided into several extensive provinces, principally inhabited by Hindus and Mussalmans." Provinces like Dukhun, the Deccan that is, and Telinga which is presentday Andhra Pradesh, are mentioned, as well as the fact that their languages are not based on Sanskrit, unlike, by implication, the Northern languages (Rāmmohan Racanāvali:544).

The picture which emerges from Rammohun stray remarks show the motivations and assumptions for nascent Hindu nationalism I mentioned before: (a) gaining respect and self-respect, (b) antiquity of Sanskrit, (c) the classical character of Sanskrit literature, (d) apparent universal extension of Sanskrit over the geographical landmass of South-Asia, (e) Sanskrit as the ancestor of all the North-Indian vernaculars.

3.2 Rammohun represented the oldest and at the same time the more radically liberal trend within this nationalistic discourse. Because of his social activism and his liberal Hindu views he was subsequently regarded as one of the first Indian patriots. In March 1865 a lecture was given entitled "Bengalis as they are, and as they ought to be," at the

Young Men's Literary Association, Presidency College.[11] In it the speaker says among other things:

> India, my country, illustrious for her original civilisation, is now lost; and I wait for the restoration.
>
> Now, Gentlemen, who is the man, that is to restore her to her former seat, who is that faithful patriot that intends to coronate her once more with her own crown of original glory? Where is that patriot, of illustrious fame, the Raja Ram Mohun Roy whose labors wrought so much for the social, intellectual and moral promotion of our countrymen? [p. 1 of the tract]

> Rajah [sic] Rammohun Roy stands perhaps the only example we can hold up for our admiration, and if I may be permitted to say so, for our imitation. Was he ever afraid of? - did he ever shrink from proclaiming what he considered to be the truth, to his benighted countrymen? Did he ever regard the scoffs, the persecutions, and animadversions which were heaped on him, by his unreasonable and misguided antagonists? [p. 24]

The lecture contains numerous exhortations towards greater feelings of love for the country and patriotism. The speaker tells his audience for example wherein lies the true greatness of a country:

> The true greatness and happiness of a country consist in wisdom; in that comprehensive and enlarged wisdom, which includes education, knowledge, religion, virtue, freedom; with every influence which advances and every institution which supports them. The idea of such greatness and of such happiness can have no adequate nourishment but in civilized society and it is only the best even in that society who are true to the idea. [p. 28]

Civilized society is formed by humans. In order to build up a good society, everyone has to build character. The best means to character building are sound ethics which ought to be grounded in some noble concept of religion:

> Character is the first thing that man should have in himself, a man without character is beast. In order to form a good character, you must form some good principles, and in order to form principles, you must have a religion. . . . You must know your God and the knowledge of God is the sole and whole object of education. I do not ask you to be a follower of Christ or Krishna, Allah or Zoroaster . . . you must have a will of your

---

[11] *Bengalis as they are, and as they ought to be*, A Discourse read at the Young Men's Literary Association, Presidency College, by U.N.T. [agore added in ink], Calcutta March 1st 1865. The text is available in the India Office Library, London.

> own, a free will; – then choose a God and follow his precepts. It is the inner man who is to be faithful, not the mouth. [p. 21]

The urge toward patriotism and nationalism in this lecture remain rather secular. There is no explicit glorification of a Hindu past, not even in the mild form of Rammohun. The fact that the latter is held up as an admirable example of Indian patriotism does however suggest that Rammohun's ideas are largely endorsed by the author of the lecture.

4. A rather similar urgent concern with patriotism but in a more explicit Hindu pitch—but these terms are problematic I should warn—is represented by the famous Bengali novelist and essay-writer Bankimchandra Chatterjee (1838-1894). [12] Bankim wrote more than half a century after Rammohun and but a decade after the author of the lecture quoted above. Bankim wrote most of his works in Bengali but was also an able author in English.

In a number of rather lengthy Bengali treatises Bankim has unfolded his constructions of a modern Hinduism adapted to the present needs of the country. In them he constructs a Hinduism that could serve as an ideology for national reconstruction. [13] The best known are his *Kṛṣṇacaritra*, a biography of Krishna based on the epical and purāṇic stories, but written with modern methods of textual criticism in order to separate the mythological embellishment from the plausible facts; a long philosophical dialogue *Dharmatattva* published in 1888, in which he elaborates his thesis that Hindu religion is Hindu culture; and a Bengali translation of the Bhagavad Gītā with commentaries, published posthumously in 1902. In English he wrote several articles on Hinduism and his *Letters on Hinduism.* Especially in the Bengali treatises Bankim liberally quotes from the Vedas, the epics, the Purāṇas and the Mānava Dharma Śāstra. This constitutes his canon of Hinduism, with the Bhagavad Gītā as a special favourite.

What did he think about the knowledge of Sanskrit and its literature? In a speech delivered in 1894 he laments the lack of knowledge of Sanskrit among many educated Hindus:

> I had . . . occasion to inspect . . . a Vedic Tol . . . I found there were nine students only on the rolls . . . This appeared to me to be very disheart-

[12] For more biographical details, see Raychaudhuri 1988, chapter 3.

[13] For details see Chatterjee 1993a:54-84; and Raychaudhuri 1988:145-155.

> ening evidence of the slight interest taken by our educated young men in the Vedic studies. I do not mean to say that all educated Hindus should be Vedic scholars - practically this would be impossible, but I am strongly of opinion that all Hindus who are willing to go through a course of 'Higher Training', as we call it, ought to possess a certain amount of knowledge, even if only second-hand knowledge, of the great Vedic Literature of our country . . . (Bankim Racanavali III:149)

Obviously for Bankim too Sanskrit was the great national language of ancient Hindu India. In the next lecture Bankim expatiated on the content of the Vedic texts. Especially the Upaniṣads were favoured. He called the Upaniṣads 'the most interesting portion of the Vedic Literature' (Bankim Racanavali III:167). He had noticed that their popularity led to subsequent numerous imitations, so that the total number of known titles of Upaniṣads exceeds the hundred. But the India of the Vedas and the Upaniṣads, of Buddhism and the Bhakti movement, was the India of Hindus alone. There were those who tried to accommodate Muslims. But hear what he says about such initiatives:

> . . . Pandit Satyabrata Samasrami mentions even an Allopanishad, or the Upanishad of Allah, the shameless production of some sycophant of the Mussalman rulers of India. (Bankim Racanavali III:168)

Ancient India as a great Hindu nation had lost its independence in the course of the centuries. First to the Muslims, then to the British. This view Bankim elaborated in a Bengali article called *Bhāratvarṣer svādhīnatā evaṁ parādhīnatā*:

> Formerly India had been independent - now for many centuries it has been dependent. The presentday Indians recollect this with deepest anguish. . . For so long many have stood against us with sword in hand. What doubt is there that happiness lies in independence. Whoever would doubt this is absolutely wicked, the lowest of mankind, etc.

In the next paragraph Muslim rule and British rule are mentioned. There is a sudden shift from India to Bengal. Still, what is true of Bengal is true of the whole of India.

> The Bengalis who have studied English have, regarding this, learned two words 'Liberty' 'Independence', as their translation we have got *svādhīnatā* and *svatantratā*. In the minds of many there is the perception that these two words signify the same thing. It is the common conviction that they signify a situation in which a people rules itself. If a king is from a different country, then his subjects are dependent, and the realm is under foreign rule. For this reason, India that is presently under

> British rule is called dependent and under foreign rule. For this reason, Bengal that was ruled by the Mughals or ruled by Shiraj ud Daulah is called dependent and under foreign rule. (Bankim Racanāvali II:241)

Bankim compares the past of India with the present situation and concludes that independence and dependence are only important to the extent that they give more or less happiness to the people. He ends the article with the somewhat melancholy observation: "In presentday India the Brahmans and the Kshatriyas, that is, those of high rank, have fallen, the Shudras, that is, the ordinary people, have risen a little bit" (Bankim Racanāvali II:245).

More than through his prose writings, Bankim became the champion of nascent Hindu nationalism for the whole of Hindu India through his poem 'Vande Mātaram', 'I praise the Mother'. The poem occurs in Bankim's most celebrated Bengali novel '*Ānandamaṭh*'. Its main theme is the Sannyasi rebellion of 1772 near Purnea against the Muslims and the British. One of the leading characters, the Sannyasi Bhavananda, sings the song which begins with the words "Vande Mātaram." The poem is almost entirely in Sanskrit, and had for some time aquired the status of national anthem, but due to its place in the novel, a national anthem of Hindu India, or rather of a Hindu nation that was to be constructed or resurrected. The first words, Vande Mātaram, became a revolutionary slogan, an emblem of renascent Hindu national consciousness.[14]

The poem itself does not have a trace of Hindu revivalism nor does it show any anti-muslim mood. The poem is a hymn of praise of the mother, who is none other than the land of Bengal, and by extension mother India.

> *vande mātaram*
> *sujalāṁ suphalāṁ*
> *malayajaś ītalāṁ*
> *śasyaśyāmalāṁ*
> *mātaram*

---

[14] In the first decennia of the twentienth century there were at least two magazines in English devoted to revolutionay action in order to bring about Indian independence, that were called Bande Mataram. One of them was printed and published in Poona by Hari Raghunath Bhagavat. The other one was published from Geneva. Its editor was Madame Cama in Paris. Many issues of both Bande Matarams were proscribed by the British Government of India.

śubhra-jyotsnā-pulakita-yāminīm
phullakusumita-drumadalaśobhin īm,
suhāsin īm sumadhurabhāṣin īm
sukhadāṁ varadāṁ mātaram

I praise the Mother
whose waters are sweet, who abundantly bears fruits,
who is soothing as sandalwood,
who is green with corn,
the mother.

Whose nights cause thrills of delight because of the beauty of the moon,
who is resplendent with blossoming petals and flowering trees,
who smiles sweetly and speaks very tenderly,
the mother who gives happiness and grants [our] wishes.

While the first half of the poem contains praises of the physical beauty of the mother land, the second half stresses the need for the devotees of the mother to realize her in their hearts. In other words the mother as the idea of the nation has to come about through the conscious devotion of the people. We can hardly have a better example of what Anderson calls an imagined community. The second part, although mainly in Sanskrit, contains some lines in Bengali as well:

tumi vidyā tumi dharma
tumi hṛdi tumi marma
tvaṁ hi prāṅāḥ śarīre
bāhute tumi mā śakti
hṛdaye tumi mā bhakti
tomāri pratimā gaḍi
mandire mandire.[15]

You are knowledge, your are religion,
you are [our] heart, you are the core of [our] heart,
for you are the life-breath in [our] bodies.
In our arms you, mother, are our strength;
In our heart you, mother, are our devotion;
it is only your image we build
in every temple.

In the novel there is a remarkable explanatory scene just before the whole poem is sung. When Bhavananda is about to sing the hymn and

[15] The whole text of the poem is found in Bankim Racanāvali I:590.

starts to sing the lines "whose nights cause thrills of delight," the other character, Mahendra is made to say: "but this is a country, this is not the mother." Then Bhavananda answers:

> We do not recognize any other mother—*jananī janmabhūmiś ca svargād api garīyasī*, (*the mother and the place of birth are more important even than heaven*). But we say, only the place of birth is the mother, we do not have a mother, no father, no brothers, no relatives,—no wife, no sons, no room, no house, for us there is only she whose waters are sweet (*sujalā*), who abundantly bears fruit (*suphalā*), who is soothing through the winds carrying the fragrance of sandalwood (*malayaja samīraṇa-śītalā*), who is green with corn (*śasyaśyāmalā*). Then Mahendra understood and said, then sing again.
> (Bankim Racanāvali I:590)

Now Bhavananda sings the complete hymn Vande Mātaram.

In order to make the ideological and emotional energy of the concept of the nation enter the faculty of imagination of his readers, Bankim translated the familiar Bengali religious concept of divine mother, the Goddess Durga or Kali, into the land of birth as mother. The figure of Mahendra expresses the thoughts of the ordinary reader, who would initially object to regarding a piece of land as a sacred mother, for the emotional content a stretch of land evokes seems limited. Only when the land can be regarded as the visible manifestation of a divine principle, is it capable of striking a deeply devotional chord. The religious modality of imagining the nation informs the second part of the hymn, when it says: "In our heart you, mother, are our devotion; / it is only your image we build / in every temple." The nation is a jealous mistress, for Bhavananda exclaims her votaries have abandoned all other emotional ties for her.

5. The last author for examination is Rabindranath Tagore (1861-1941).[16] Strictly speaking Rabindranath is not only a literary figure of the nineteenth century as the major part of his literary career, covering in all more than sixty years, advanced well into the twentieth century. Still, his earlier writings on which initially rested his fame, formed very much part of nineteenth century Bengali elite culture. Tagore's rise to

---

[16] For more details on Rabindranath Tagore's life and literary work, see the excellent volumes in Bengali by Prasanta Kumar Pal (Pal [1982/3-90/1]); or the somewhat dated but still useful English biography Krishna Kripalani (1980).

literary and intellectual fame around the nineties of the last century heralded the transition from nineteenth century Bengali intellectual debates to the more pan-Indian twentieth century and its rise of politically active nationalism as advocated by the Indian National Congress.

In August 1901 Rabindranath published two Bengali articles in one of the leading Bengali magazines *Baṅgadarśan* on the concept of the nation. In the first one entitled *Nation ki?*, "What is a nation?," he summarized and discussed the famous tract by Ernest Renan on the invention of a nation, *Qu'est-ce qu'une nation?* In the second article called *Hindutva*, 'Hinduness', he used Renan's ideas for a discussion of the country, India.[17] As the original title suggests, Rabindranath rather explicitly constructed the nation India as a Hindu nation. In a reprint of the article four years later in a collection of essays called *Ātmaśakti*, he changed the title *Hindutva* into *Bhāratvarṣīya Samāj*, "Indian Society," so as to soften the somewhat communalist sounding reference to an exclusively Hindu India. The text of the article remained unchanged however.

Defining the essential characteristic of the concept of the nation in his first article, Rabindranath paraphrases Renan as follows:

> The nation is a living entity (*sattā*), a mental object. Two things have constructed the inner nature of this object. These two things are in fact one and the same. One of them is situated in the past, the other in the present. One is the wealth of public memories of the past, the other the mutual consent, the desire to dwell in the same place—the desire to preserve in a suitable way the whole of the inheritance one has received. . . . To a large extent we have been already created in the past by our forefathers. Past heroism, greatness, and glory, on these rests the national feeling. In the past a single public glory (*gaurav*), in the present a single public desire; unitedly having done great deeds in the past and the resolve to perform such great deeds once more: these are the profound basis of creating a people (*janasampradāy*) (Ravīndra-racanāvali, vol. 2:621)

It is clear that Rabindranath believed the Indian nation of the past to have been a Hindu nation. The evocation of past glory, heroism, and sacrifice of the forefathers, can hardly have escaped the readers as an incentive to nation building in the present.

---

[17] Both articles can be found in: *Ravīndra-racanāvali*, vol. 2:619-625. On p. 826-827 of the same volume there are some bibliographical notes on these articles.

In the second article Tagore explicitly speaks about the Hindu past of India. His greatest concern is with the concept of unity of a nation. He claims that the unity of the nation is based on the unifying principles underlying the coherence of society:

> . . . unity of the people's minds is not realized in all countries in one and the same sense. For this reason European unity and Hindu unity are not of the same kind, but saying this, it cannot be said also that there is not a single unity among the Hindus. (Ravīndra-racanāvali, vol. 2:622)

What separates Europe ideologically from India is Hindu culture. The latter has given to India a specific kind of social unity not found elsewhere. According to Rabindranath 'unity in diversity', is how one could characterize the underlying principle of Hindu civilization, whose important binding force is *dharma*, somewhat problematically translated by the European term 'religion':

> With respect to the great building work of civilisation—i.e. uniting the variegated - it has to be seen what the Hindus have made of it. . . .
>
> By giving shelter to so many different people, Hindu culture in various ways has deprived itself, and still it has not abandoned anyone. High and low, homogeneous (*savarṇa*) and not homogeneous (*asavarṇa*), all of them it has drawn close, to all of them it has given the shelter of religion (*dharma*), all of them it has forced on the path of duty, thus preventing them from laxness and degradation. (Ravīndra-racanāvali, vol. 2:622-623)

Ultimately for Rabindranath the unifying force behind Indian civilization was the Hindu dharma, the complex amalgam of Hindu culture and religion. To Rabindranath's mind the situation of his times were unsatisfactory due to a lack of energy among the Hindus. The solution he proposed consists in social/religious reform. Religion should not be backward looking, it should not be an unthinking emulation of the past, but rather be energized by the same spirit which informed the society-building of the forefathers. As he writes in the same article:

> For the protection of national self-interest everyone in the nation sacrifices personal self-interests. In the times when Hindu society was full of life, every part of society used to regard the self-interest of the integral body of society as its own ultimate self-interest. . . .
>
> Let us install as a living reality in our hearts that same ever-wakeful feeling of weal (*maṅgal*) [inherited] from our ancestors and apply it everywhere in society, only then will we again reach great Hindu civili-

> sation (*hindu-sabhyatā*). To give education to society, health, food, wealth and riches, this is our own work; this alone is our weal - this should not be regarded as trade, rather, not to hope for anything else in exchange for this [activity] but merit (puṇya) and well-being (*kalyāṇ*) is sacrifice (*yajña*), is the unification with God (Brahman) through work (*karmayog*), to always remember this is Hindu-ness (*hindutva*). (Ravīndra-racanāvali, vol. 2:625)

Lastly we may ask, what in Rabindranath's view was the role of Sanskrit in all this? In the period he wrote these articles, he also wrote a number of religious essays in which he tried to construct a more open, and very personal, version of the Brahmo spirituality and liberal theology he inherited from his father, Debendranath (1817-1905), who after the death of Rammohun Roy had been the second prophet of Brahmoism.[18] Rabindranath himself has all his life been connected with the Brahmo Samaj movement, and often saw himself as one of its voices. There is little doubt that the kind of religion Rabindranath had in mind in the article *Hindutva*, would be the liberal Hinduism he constructed elsewhere.

The main ingredient of this religion are the thoughts and poetical inspiration derived from the older classical Upaniṣads. In his religious writings, Rabindranath liberally quoted from the Upaniṣads, a habit he kept untill his death in 1941.[19] The religious essays and discourses composed between 1901 and 1907 are especially relevant to our present discussion since they immediately succeeded his nationalistic writings. Among the religious essays composed between 1901 and 1907 (and published in 1909 in a collection called *Dharma*) there are articles with titles like *Prācīn Bhārater Ekaḥ*, 'The One of Ancient India' (written in 1901), and *Dharmer Saral Ādarśa*, 'A Simple Ideal of Religion' (written in 1902).

They served to construct or reconstruct an ancient Indian religion on the basis of what Rabindranath believed the Upaniṣads had taught. Undoubtedly, the concept of this religion shows strong traits of a humanistic and humane approach to Indian life, and could be called progres-

[18] For more details on his life until 1858, see Autobiography Tagore.

[19] Although it should be added that most of his quotations occur in the collection of Upaniṣadic verses made by his father and published under the name *Brahmo Dharma* in 1849-50. We may legitimately assume Rabindranath used his father's selection as his guide to the content and the meaning of the Upaniṣads.

sive, but the impression that it is Hinduism and nothing else will not easily fade. For in none of the texts by Rabindranath so far mentioned do we find the slightest hint of Muslim India or of the Muslim past. The overwhelming impression of their discourse is that of a more liberal and explicitly humanistic version of Bankim's construction of Hinduism as a religion for national regeneration.[20] By choosing the Upaniṣads as his main source Rabindranath had brought his religious project fully into line with that of his great spiritual ancestor, Rammohun Roy, whom he immensely admired.

About the religious ideal of the Upaniṣads in ancient India, Rabindranath says the following in the article *Dharmer Saral Ādarśa*:

> Once a simple ideal of religion did exist in our India (*Bhāratvarṣa*). In the Upanishads we get acquainted with it. Therein the revelation of Brahman (God) is full, unbroken, it is not encumbered by the web of our conceptualisations. . . .
>
> The Upanishad has shown this world (*jagat - saṁsār*) full of diversity to be absorbed in the endless truth of Brahman, in the endless knowlegde of Brahman. The Upanishad did not conceptualise a particular world (*lok*), it did not erect special temples, it did not install particular forms [of the Gods] (*mūrti*) at some particular place - by only perceiving Him everywhere in a perfect way, it totally removed every manner of complexity, every manner of conceptualised unstableness. Where else is there such a great ideal of pure religious simplicity?
>
> . . . The Brahman of the Upanishad . . . is everywhere inside and outside; He is the most inner One, He is most far away. By His truth we are true, by His joy we have been revealed. (Ravīndra-racanāvali, vol. 7:462)

The exhortatory mode of this passage seems rather similar to what we found in the hymn *Vande Mātaram*. In Tagore's text the divinity encompasses the whole world, and thus India, but the idea of this divinity is Indian as it stems from, or is legitimized by, the Upaniṣads. The burden of the message is that 'we', i.e., the Indian public—but who is this public if not the educated Hindus?—should not forget the simple relig-

[20] In the course of the twentieth century however, Rabindranath's nationalism changed dramatically, from liberal 'Bankimite' to explicit opposition to rising militant nationalism and chauvinism, and caustic criticism of Hindu revivalism. See for instance his novels *Ghore Bāhire* (Home and the World) from 1916, *Gorā* from 1910, and his volume of essays in English, *Nationalism*, first published in 1917 and until today reprinted by Macmillan India.

ious ideal of the Upaniṣads, in other words, the heritage of the ancient Vedic seers. Bankim's hymn is more explicitly local. Not the whole universe pervaded by the Upaniṣadic deity, but the mother land, the place of birth, is the divinity that should inspire national feeling, nay more, total surrender and sacrifice. Bankim wrote his hymn almost entirely in Sanskrit, Rabindranath generously quoted from a particular Sanskrit literature.

6. And yet the overall impression remains the same. Ancient India was a glorious Hindu nation whose greatest cultural capital was the Sanskrit literature and the civilization connected with it. In order to regain self-respect as a Hindu nation, Hindus should go back to and reinterpret this cultural and civilizational capital. The dark sides of this cultural project emerged with the growing militancy and politicization of certain upper class Hindus. Borne onwards by the rising tides of early twentieth century Indian nationalism, they found in discourses such as the ones we have just shown, an almost impeccable legitimation for their communal political ends, even if they twisted and bent these discourses to near distortion of the original intentions.

CHAPTER SIXTEEN

THE PLACE OF SANSKRIT IN NEO-HINDU IDEOLOGIES: FROM RELIGIOUS REFORM TO NATIONAL AWAKENING*

Corstiaan J. G. van der Burg

1. Introduction

In a not so recent, but still extremely seminal paper on Neo-Hinduism as contrasted with surviving traditional Hinduism, Paul Hacker (1978:583) distinguishes several aspects which he views as typical of Neo-Hinduism. In his opinion, a major peculiarity of Neo-Hinduism—understood primarily as a mental attitude, distinct from traditional Hinduism—is that "the continuity with the past is broken." Although Hacker does not mention it explicitly, this characteristic of Neo-Hinduism could with good reason be related to the place and the role of Sanskrit.

At about the same time Agehananda Bharati (1970:269) gives vent to his annoyance with the "decisively anti-Sanskritic trend among the apologists of the Hindu Renaissance," a point of view he says to share with Staal.[1] Thus, according to Bharati: "Not only do speakers for the Renaissance not study Sanskrit, but they overtly or covertly discourage followers from doing so." In the same vein Bharati states that "apart from Dayananda Sarasvati . . . the founders of the Renäissance admired and absorbed the poetry of the medieval saints, together with their overt and covert hostility toward traditional, Sanskrit-based learning." (Bharati 1970:273)

* The author wishes to thank Frans H.P.M. Janssen, Utrecht, for his help in making available several primary sources.

[1] Staal 1963:273. It is, however, unclear to me which of Staal's arguments Bharaṭi is in agreement with. Most probably he refers to the 'heuristic usefulness' of the concept of Sanskritization, in spite of its limited applicability in the analysis of cultural processes.

Both quotations, and in particular the latter, seem to indicate undeniably that Hinduism's primordial association with its most natural and organic linguistic medium Sanskrit is absent in the case of Neo-Hinduism. However, we should not take such sweeping statements at face value. Far from contesting the opinions of these authorities on Neo-Hinduism, we may at least comment on their conclusions. For example, by considering the relationship of Neo-Hinduism with Sanskrit more from a historical point of view. Then we will see that there has indeed been a complex association between the two. For Neo-Hinduism is—in Hacker's own words—not a unified system of ideas (1978:583). Nor can we speak of one single-minded vast Neo-Hindu movement, because there are as many currents as there are ideas in what we might call Neo-Hinduism. Each of these has its special relationship with Sanskrit in varying degrees of intensity, as well as its own 'history' with Sanskrit, which is often coloured by the particular founder or leader of the movement. This relatedness with Sanskrit we can trace back in the lives and ideologies of many prominent exponents of Neo-Hinduism.

The main concern of this chapter is an attempt to gain an insight into the status of Sanskrit and the role it has played in the ideologies of some of the Neo-Hindu agents, as there is obviously a certain amount of controversy about it, judging by the quotes of Hacker and Bharati as opposed to our own findings. Our interest, therefore, is not what Neo-Hinduism has contributed in the linguistic field to the study of Sanskrit as such. It is rather the 'context' of Sanskrit we are interested in, not the 'text'. We will limit ourselves to those of the Neo-Hindu exponents who may be described as representing a form of Neo-Hinduism which has been generally accepted as such.

2. *Swami Dayananda Sarasvati (1824-1883)*

2.1 One of the Neo-Hindus of the first hour was the Kathiawari Brahman Swami Dayananda Sarasvati, the founder *malgré lui* of the reform movement Arya Samaj, the 'Society of the Nobles'. Nobody seemed to have been more preoccupied by Vedic and Sanskrit than he was. However, for the major part of his life his knowledge of Sanskrit seems to have been limited to Sanskrit grammar only (Jordens

1978:33). "In spite of himself," I said, because it appears that Dayanand had no urge to start a new religious movement.

Jordens, his biographer, tells us how Dayananda, as a *sannyasin*,[2] devoted his whole adult life up to the age of 36 to some study of *Vedānta*, *Yoga* and the search of the perfect *guru* who would show him the way to *moksha* (1978:32). But somehow—nobody seems to know why—he gave up his apparently fruitless search for liberation and started studying Sanskrit grammar under the guidance of Swami Virajanand Sarasvati, a then famous blind guru.

We must guess for the reasons for this sudden change. Jordens suggests a general answer: Dayananda became convinced that "the deepest secret of religion and *moksha* lay hidden in the Hindu scriptures." Dayananda found "how difficult they were, and how inadequate his own knowledge of Sanskrit was. The key to Sanskrit is grammar. So, if he wanted to unravel the teachings of the scriptures, he had to become a master of Sanskrit." (Jordens 1978:32)

"For three years," Kenneth W. Jones says (1976:31), "Dayananda studied with Virajanand, accepting not only a new theology but a set of goals which gave redirection to his life. When Dayananda left Virajanand in 1863, he gave as *gurudakshina* (a departing gift) the promise to reform Hinduism. Dayanand, the seeker of individual immortality, emerged a reformer challenging the present."

2.2 Surprisingly, in spite of his intentions to reach the total Indian society, in his first years of preaching Dayananda retained his *sannyasi* dress and directed his message mainly to the top layer of the Indian society, the Brahman community, to whom he spoke in Sanskrit.

Eventually, the contacts with anglicised Indians, in particular Brahmo Samaj leaders, whom he met in a visit of Calcutta, made him radically shift his reform techniques: no more *sannyasi* dress, no Sanskrit any more, but contemporary dress and Hindi. In this way he wanted to reach a different audience: no longer only his fellow Brahmans, but educated non-Brahmans (Jones 1976:34). Dayanand had been made to realise that the usefulness of Sanskrit as a means of communication was limited and depending on the education of the public he sought to reach.

[2] This and a number of other Sanskrit words are here given in their anglicized spelling in accordance with a great number of the primary and secondary sources on Neo-Hinduism

What Dayananda had in mind with the eventual establishment of the Arya Samaj was that he "wanted to bring together all Hindus who agreed on a couple of very broad issues: a dedication to religious and social reform, and a conviction that this reformation had to come through a revival of Vedic religion" (Jordens 1978:144). "Just as Dayananda's own goal lay far beyond the establishment of the Samaj, similarly the ultimate goal of the Aryas should lie far beyond their own group, beyond narrow creedal inhibitions: they should aim at the final establishment of the unity of dharma by striving to persuade all groups and sects to accept the Vedas" (Jordens 1978:145). Sanskrit fitted well in this framework, in a double role: as a means of communication and a means to reach *moksha.*

2.3 In the case of Dayananda and the Arya Samaj we see two processes at work. Initially it is elitist: An individual search for *moksha* and for knowledge of the scriptures necessitates the command of Sanskrit. Next, this personal quest is transformed into an attempt to create an elite community which was to be guided by the sacred scriptures. And this attempt ends up in a popular reform movement, attacking on the one hand hereditary brahmanical authority and, on the other, defending itself against non-Hindus. Although the status of Sanskrit remains in principle unchallenged, it has for all practical purposes been replaced by other languages, Hindi in particular, Sanskrit playing only a nominal role.

3. Aurobindo (1872-1950)

3.1 Aurobindo was an elitist. And he had a message. Not only for India but for the entire world. His relation to the West was ambiguous.

When we view Aurobindo's scholarship in connection with the indological work of Max Müller, Aurobindo's ambivalent attitude towards the West, and Western science in particular, will be revealed. Having been educated in Britain, as an anglicised Indian, he felt himself compelled to react against the 'materialistic' Europe, the same Europe which influenced him politically so much, and which had opened his eyes to India's magnificent past.

His reaction was twofold, at the least: First, there was an increasing spiritualization, in the sense that such a spiritualization was the *summum* of Indian culture and religion, a heritage granted to India and to be messaged to the whole world. Second, as a natural consequence of the former reaction: there was a distancing from the West, even an antithetical stance towards the West (Dijk 1981:180).

3.2 We will exemplify Aurobindo's relationship with the West by focusing on his reaction to Max Müller. Aurobindo's acquaintance with Max Müller dates from his years of study in Britain (1879-1892), in particular in London and Cambridge, where he, next to his university college studies, was trained for the Indian Civil Service (I.C.S.). Both studies were based on the ideals of British education, and even in the curriculum of the I.C.S. the Indian subjects were of secondary importance. No wonder: the curriculum was drafted on the basis of suggestions made by a commission chaired by the famous Thomas Babington Macaulay, well known for his contempt for Indian culture. Nevertheless, Sanskrit and Arabic were of course included in the curriculum, but they were given only half as much weight as Greek and Latin (Dijk 1981:179).[3] There was one exception to this Europe-oriented I.C.S. training scheme: A series of lectures, given for I.C.S. students by Max Müller in 1882 and published in print in 1883, was put on the list of compulsory literature for the students.

The booklet, entitled *India, What Can It Teach Us?* has inspired Aurobindo undoubtedly. For Max Müller wanted to explain that not only Europe has something to teach India, but that it can also learn something from India, in particular from ancient India, two- or three-thousand years ago. Being an acknowledged indological scholar, Max Müller must certainly have appealed to the patriotic feelings of the young Aurobindo when he writes: "We all come from the East—all that we value most has come from the East, and in going to the East . . . everybody . . . ought to feel that he is going to his 'old home' . . . " (Dijk 1981:175 and Müller 1883:29f).

Although it is unclear whether Max Müller points here to the Asian origin of all religions, or to his famous thesis of the family-relationship of Indo-Iranian with European languages, this much seems to be cer-

[3] Van Dijk refers also to Roy 1960:136.

tain, that Max Müller has been the first indologist whom Aurobindo became acquainted with, and whose ideas he discussed most, in later years.

Certainly Aurobindo must have felt confirmed in his ideas by Max Müller's statement that the real India was Hindu India and that only Hindu India was "the famous India which had to offer something to Europe (the 'West')," while the era of decay more or less coincided with Islamic rule. This India in decline had to 're-aryanise' itself in order to be able to aryanise the world (Dijk 1981:179).

3.3 In this connection it is relevant to see how Aurobindo reacted to Max Müller as a Sanskrit scholar and why he distanced himself later on from this aspect of Max Müller's scholarly expertise. Although it is difficult to say when and where Aurobindo learned Sanskrit (Dijk 1981:179), it is certain that before his Veda-studies in Pondicherry (after 1910) he had given his opinion on Max Müller's indological work. Already in Baroda he states that "the Europeans have seen in our Veda only the rude chants of a[n] . . . primitive pastoral race sung in honour of the forces of Nature" (Aurobindo Centenary 3:117 and Dijk 1981:179). This is, according to van Dijk, an allusion to Max Müller and his natural-mythological explanation of Vedic myths. In his Baroda period Aurobindo also remarked that Max Müller were "more a grammarian and philologist than a sound Sanskrit scholar," who was proficient in the Sanskrit language, "but . . . could not feel the language or realise the spirit behind the letter" (Dijk 1981:179).

Aurobindo himself had another purpose in mind: instead of raising scientific or generally cultural interest with his translation of the Upanishads, he wanted to present Europe with 'the religious message of India' as a reaction to Max Müller's translation in 'The Sacred Books of the East' (Aurobindo Centenary 12:53 and Dijk 1981:179). Aurobindo wanted Sanskrit scholars to be at the same time guru-like personalities. And this was regrettably not the case with people like Max Müller, because, as Aurobindo sourly remarks: "when we come to them for light, we find them playing marbles on the doorsteps of the outer court of the temple" (Aurobindo Centenary 12:478 and Dijk 1981: 180).

3.4 From that perspective we must view Aurobindo's later scholarly work on linguistics called "The Origins of Aryan Speech" (Aurobindo Centenary 10:551-581; 27:163-179) as an expression of his disappointment with the Western lack of spirituality and an attempt to present an alternative to Max Müller's linguistic discoveries.

4. Vivekananda (1863-1902)

4.1 "The orthodox pandit's approach to exegesis and to the use of the scripture converges with the Western indologist's to the extent that the primary text is taken as the basis from where both proceed," says Bharati (1970:285). However, "The agents of the Renaissance mistrust and dislike both, and they replace them by nontextual, generalized, impressionistic peroration of the type set fort by Vivekananda and the other scions of the Renaissance and its apologetic." Generally spoken, Bharati may be correct at this issue, but in detail, in particular in the case of Vivekananda, his remarks need more nuance.

4.2 Returning from a long stay in the USA and Europe—in particular England—Vivekananda held a speech in Madras in 1897 about the future of India (Works Vivekaṇanda 3:649). One of his major themes was the uplift of the masses, which he understood as primarily intellectual. His remarks on the role which Sanskrit could play in this connection are relevant for our argument, because they are somewhat more than mere verbalism. In short, his idea is to "bring out the gems of spirituality that are stored up in our books, and in the possession of a few only . . . . In one word, I want to make them popular. I want to bring out these ideas and let them be the common property of all, of every man in India, whether he knows the Sanskrit language or not." The great difficulty in the way—the Sanskrit language—cannot be removed until "the whole of our nation are good Sanskrit scholars." Realising the impracticability of such an enterprise, Vivekananda suggests that "the ideas should be taught in the language of the people; at the same time, Sanskrit education must go on along with it, because the very sound of Sanskrit words gives a prestige and a power and a strength to the race." The reason that in the past so many attempts to raise the lower classes failed, lies according to Vivekananda in the fact that Ramanuja, Caitanya and Kabir . . . [and the Buddha] "did not apply their energy to the spreading of the Sanskrit language among the masses. Knowledge came but the prestige was not there, culture was not there." Most revealing is the passage, quoted below, where he recommends sanskritization—in the literal sense of studying Sanskrit and getting acquainted with its culture—as a means to raise the condition of the masses. This was more than half a century before M.N. Srinivas defined sanskritization as a social phenomenon and introduced the concept to the scholarly world . . .[4]

In this passage, Vivekananda says:

> Teach the masses in the vernaculars, give them ideas; they will get information, but something more is necessary; give them culture. Until you give them that, there can be no permanence in the raised condition of the masses. There will be another caste created, having the advantage of the Sanskrit language, which will quickly get above the rest and rule them all the same. The only safety, I tell you men who belong to the lower castes, the only way to raise your condition is to study Sanskrit . . . The only way to bring about the levelling of caste is to appropriate the culture, the education which is the strength of the higher castes. That done, you have what you want.

Later on, he states: "The solution is not by bringing down the higher, but by raising the lower up to the level of the higher" (Works Vivekananda 3:652), and:

> Why do you not become Sanskrit scholars? Why do you not spend millions to bring Sanskrit education to all the castes of India? That is the question. The moment you do these things, you are equal to the Brahman. That is the secret of power in India. Sanskrit and prestige go together in India. (Works Vivekananda 3:654)

4.3 Whatever we may think of his philosophy and educative insights, we must admit that Vivekananda, being a well-educated Bengali of Kshattriya origin, adopts here a very sympathetic attitude to the people with a less favourable background. After a stay in the West where his message about the spiritual superiority of Hinduism and of India had been warmly received (much to his own surprise), his plans with his downtrodden fellow-citizens are more down to earth: Sanskrit, not as a medium or a spiritual message, but rather as a means to emancipation.

---

[4] Srinivas 1952, *passim*. Nowhere in Srinivas's books I found any references to Vivekananda's views of sanskritization. According to Staal 1963:261, "The term is used to mean a social process by which a lower caste attempts to raise its status and to rise to a higher position in the caste hierarchy."

5. The Rashtriya Swayamsevak Sangh

5.1 One of the results of Neo-Hindu activism is a process of politicization of religion, or rather the religionization of politics, as we will see. For example in the form of Hindu communalist (and Hindu nationalist) movements. In particular the militant anti-Muslim activist RSS (the *Rashtriya Swayamsevak Sangh*: the 'National Volunteer Corps'), founded in Nagpur in 1925 by K.B. Hedgewar, deserves our interest. "Hedgewar, like all revivalists, believed that the Hindu past possessed the conceptual tools with which to reconstruct society" write Anderson and Damle (1987:71), and: "Also like other revivalists, he [i.e. Hedgewar, CvdB] was convinced that only Hindu thought would motivate the population to achieve independence and to restructure society." In the early part of the twentieth century, Aurobindo stated the case in terms that the RSS was later to emphasize:

> If you try other and foreign methods we shall either gain our end of national awakening with tedious slowness, painfully and imperfectly, if at all. Why abandon the plain way which God and the Mother have marked out for you to choose faint and devious paths of your own treading? [5]

5.2 With respect to Sanskrit, the RSS passed in March 1958 a resolution concerning a national language policy, in which it is stated that:

> The RSS is of the firm view that no foreign language can ever be the right medium for administrative and other purposes of any free country. The continuance of English as the official language of Bharat is bound to perpetuate the mental slavery and the existing gulf between the people and the government. English can never enable us to develop our National Personality. . . . The RSS has looked upon all languages of Bharat as national. They have been equally sustained by Sanskrit—the Rashtra Bhasha par excellence. If now some difference has come to forefront it is due to a policy of deliberate neglect of Sanskrit that has been consistently followed. The [Akhila Bharatiya Pratinidhi, CvdB] Sabha considers the present situation detrimental to national unity and feels that the language policy be unequivocally restated and firmly implemented, thus dispelling all apprehensions of the people. Hindi, for

---

[5] "This passage," write Anderson and Damle (1987:99, note 6) "is taken from *Bhawani Mandir* which Aurobindo Ghose wrote during the first partition of Bengal. Quoted in Purani, *Sri Aurobindo*, p. 82."

> some time past, has evolved as the common language of inter-provincial communication. It should be used as such for all official purposes. The regional languages should be used in their respective areas. As development of all languages is possible only on the basis of Sanskrit, instruction of Sanskrit should be compulsorily imparted. (RSS Resolves:11)

5.3 Gradually, RSS nationalism is displaying almost religious features, not only by the veneration of the sacred language, but also by its service of India as a manifestation of the Mother Goddess. This may be illustrated with some citations from Anderson & Damle 1987:

> The corporate Hindu nation is identified as the 'living God'.[6] The primary goal of the RSS discipline is preparing the mind so that individuals will act in a detached manner for the well being of the divine object (the Hindu nation). The mental progression involves bursting through a set of circles of attachment. It has achieved its goal when the individual experiences a greater loyalty to the nation than to any other 'lower' form of attachment. (Anderson & Damle 1987:76)

> The metaphor of the Divine Mother is used to describe both the nation and the 'sacred' geography where the nation resides. Both are material emanations from the *shakti* [divine female power, CvdB]. The Goddess may have both benign and negative aspects (creator/sustainer and destroyer). The imagery which the RSS usually employs emphasizes the benign aspects of the Goddess. The metaphor offers RSS publicists emotionally-packed imagery to convey their message. The Mother image informs feelings for the homeland, that piece of earth which has nourished and sustained the people through history and is the true setting for the life of the people today . . . (Anderson & Damle 1987:77)

> The nation has a 'sacred' geography, encompassing an impressing amount of real estate. Golwarkar spoke of it as extending from Iran in the west to the Malay Peninsula in the east, from Tibet in the north to Sri Lanka in the south.[7] (Anderson & Damle 1987:77)

> Besides a "sacred" geography, the nation is said to possess a soul, referred to as *chiti* [*citti*, CvdB] by one prominent spokesman.[8] *Chiti* [*citti*, CvdB] is a kind of higher law that takes precedence over any political institutions or manmade rules.[9] It determines the social frame-

---

[6] Golwalkar 1966:24-25. Andersen & Damle 1987:101 note 30.

[7] Golwarkar 1966:84.

[8] Upadhyaya 1968:52.

[9] Upadhyaya 1968:54-55.

> work within which dharma is worked out. (Anderson & Damle 1987:77)

An important implication of the idea that the nation possesses a 'soul' is that the entire Indian cultural heritage must have a unity and common origin. Thus, the unity of the Indian cultural heritage has been emphasized with much vigour in Golwarkar's statement that:

> The same philosophy of life, the same goal, the same supremacy of the inner spirit over the outer gross things of matter, the same faith in rebirth, the same adoration of certain qualities of brahmacarya, sattya etc., the same holy *samskars* [rituals], in short the same life-blood flowed through all these limbs of our society. (Golwarkar 1966:102, cited after Andersen & Damle 1987:78.)

The idea of a common source finds expression in other statements of Golwarkar, e.g. "The people in the South were always considered to be as much Aryan as those in the North."[10] A unity and common source are also assumed for much of India's linguistic diversity: "the source of inspiration for all these Dravidian languages has been that queen of languages, the language of Gods—Sanskrit."[11]

5.4 In general, RSS nationalism—evidently a multifaceted phenomenon—derives its inspiration from a supposed glorious past, before the arrival of Islam, while on the other hand it is directed against all 'alien' elements in Indian society, notably the Muslim element. V.D. 'Veer' Savarkar's *Hindutva*, from 1923,[12] is said to refer to a people, united by a common country, blood, history, culture and language. Savarkar was also the first to use the term Hindu Rashtra, 'Hindu Nation', an oft-repeated notion in the ideology of Hindu communalism. In an atmosphere of mounting tension between Hindus and Muslims, the Hindus were said to constitute a 'nation', while the Muslims were only a 'community' (D'Cruz 1988:23). For these reasons, we see the position

---

[10] Golwarkar 1966:115, cited after Andersen & Damle 1987:79.

[11] Golwarkar 1966:112, cited after Andersen & Damle 1987:79.

[12] This tract, written in 1922 by the militant Hindu nationalist Vinayak Damodar Savarkar while he was in the Ratnagiri jail, was reproduced by hand and distributed among Maharashtrian nationalists (Andersen & Damle 1987:60 note 45). Andersen & Damle (*ibidem*) note that it was eventually published in English in the collected works of Savarkar: *Samagra Savarkar Wangmaya: Hindu Rashtra Darshan*, 6 vols. (Pune: Maharashtra Prantik Hindusabha, 1964), vol. 6:1-91.

and role of Sanskrit, and to a lesser degree of (highly sanskritized) Hindi, as a nation- or at least a Hindu identity-marker, unifying all Hindus.

6. Religion, language, nation

6.1 Now that we have seen that these voices about the close association between Neo-Hindu currents and the Sanskrit language turn out to be somewhat more than sheer verbalism, the question rises how we can account for this connection. Two facts are noticeable in this respect.

First, there is the obvious ease with which Sanskrit has been integrated in a unifying ideology serving a universal—or at least national—ethic of Hindu culture. Which kinds of Hinduism do we meet in the Neo-Hindu movements, in terms of structure and cultural substance? Are there kinds of Hinduism which are particularly suitable to such a large-scale 'democratic'—not to say profane—use of a sacred language like Sanskrit?

Second, from the cases we presented it can be concluded that there is a particularly close relationship between Neo-Hindus and nationalism. In fact this seems to be so much the case that Hacker came to speak of "religious nationalism" (Hacker 1978:584). The question which we are interested in here is: "What is the effect of this relationship upon the status and role of Sanskrit?"

With regard to the first observed fact, the question of a usable typology of Hindu religion arises. In an article on religious change Mark Holmström (1971:28) remarks that existing Hindu societies and Hindu history can only be understood by paying attention to the interplay of two radically different kinds of religion, associated with two kinds of morality and social relations. On the one hand, he discerns a religion which consecrates the existing social order, values of submission and hierarchy, and a relativist morality of closed groups. On the other hand, he meets with a devotional religion with values of choice and equality, and a tendency towards a universalist 'open' morality. In his opinion these two types of religion exist in unstable combination in every Hindu community, traditional as well as modern. They correspond to values of heteronomy and autonomy, which coexist in every social morality.

In broad terms Holmström refers to the views of Louis Dumont, who in a famous article on world renunciation in Indian religions distinguishes two types of religion: 'group religion' and 'religion of choice' (Dumont 1960:33-62). The latter is, according to Dumont, associated with—and on the whole even derived from—the thinking of the *sannyasin*, the renouncer who has broken all bonds with society in an attempt to reach *moksha*. In this way Dumont sees in Hinduism the polarity of 'social religion' and 'religion of choice' as an elaboration of the polarity in the ideas of the heteronomous 'man-in-the-world' *versus* the autonomous renouncer.

Apart from Holmström, others, like Richard Burghart and Timothy Fitzgerald, also elaborated and improved Dumont's typology. The main distinction they make is between religion as the ever-present moral order of the universe, a *dharma* to which all beings are subject, a religious outlook, stressing ritual order and hierarchy (type I); and a soteriological religion, a path of salvation (type II). Type I stands for the traditional 'mainstream' Hinduism, which is 'group-tied', simply meaning: embedded in the social relations of a group or a set of groups. It is not a 'World Religion' and not for export; it is neither a soteriology nor is it a system of meaning available for non-Hindus. Analytically speaking, it is the "centre of gravity, the context within which the other phenomena, the sectarian soteriologies, the potential 'religions' for export, are rooted" (Fitzgerald 1990:113).

The other kind of Hinduism, type II, comprises the ideologies which are generally centred around a personal soteriology. It is sectarian rather than caste-based, it inclines towards free choice of personal devotion instead of ascribed status and duties; it is 'other-worldly' rather than 'this-worldly', and it tends towards egalitarianism and individualism, rather than hierarchy. Authority lies not with the Brahmin, the traditional religious specialist, but with the ascetic who has achieved some personal realisation of transcendent deity (Fitzgerald 1990:113).

Historically, these two ideal types have been interwoven and dynamically related. Analytically however, they can be distinguished, and we must conclude that the major part of the Neo-Hindu 'movements' match more type II Hinduism, the 'religion of choice', than the 'group religion' of type I Hinduism. Ideally, the Neo-Hindu 'religion of choice' has no caste-barrier, no hierarchy, no hereditary authorities and it mediates salvation not only for the individual, but also for the community, the nation, or in some cases even for the universe. Thus, it will be perfectly understandable that the 'democratic' use of Sanskrit will fit well into the structure and ideology of these 'religions of choice'. This is in sharp contrast with the role Sanskrit plays in traditional 'group religion', where the use of Sanskrit is confined to those who have a hereditary prerogative over it.

6.3 With regard to the second question, about the role of Sanskrit in the relationship between Neo-Hindu movements and nationalism, we can add our own observations to Hacker's findings, which are quite helpful for our problem.

Hacker remarked that

> although nationalism is ultimately an importation from the West, it has a somewhat different meaning here than in the West. National pride in India is not primarily grounded in reminiscences of the political history or in political ideals but in the consciousness of the cultural, in particular religious, achievements of the native country (Hacker 1978:607).

This means that Hinduism has been made subservient to a nationalistic ideology. In other words, Indian nationalism is in particular characterised by its religious overtones. This is what we saw already.

Now, from what has been said follows logically, that Sanskrit as the religious language *par excellence* should *in principle* also be the language for the nation as a whole. This was the case with Vivekananda's plea in favour of a sanskritization of the nation, and with the RSS, as we observed.

Therefore, we fail to see how Sanskrit could answer to the image of religious discontinuity, which Hacker and Bharati had in mind. On the contrary, we would say.

6.4 Nevertheless, in two respects we can indeed speak of a "broken continuity with the past." First it is there, where the spread of Sanskrit knowledge has been 'democratized', instead of being reserved for a religious elite, as in the past. Second, in cases where its role has been taken over by Hindi for practical reasons, as in the case of Dayanand Sarasvati. In such cases Sanskrit has marked only a certain stage in the development of some Neo-Hindu movements, not an ultimate goal or major issue.

6.5 In the framework of our typology, we still see two processes at work in the Neo-Hindu use of Sanskrit: On the one hand, there is the creation of an elite, at home and abroad, based on an inclusivist and supracultural study of Sanskrit scriptures. Here, Sanskrit is the language of the universal religion.

On the other hand, at home only, there is a process of popularization and 'profanation' of Sanskrit and Sanskrit scriptures, sometimes used in Hindu identity-formation and in the creation of a 'Unity of Dharma'. Here Sanskrit plays the symbolic role which Hindi will never be able to play.

This much, I hope, will be clear: in either case Sanskrit is not seen as a luxury one can easily do without.

CHAPTER SEVENTEEN

POSITION OF SANSKRIT IN PUBLIC EDUCATION AND SCIENTIFIC RESEARCH IN MODERN INDIA

Saroja Bhate

1. India is one of the few countries in the world with an ancient, living tradition. Since this tradition is enrobed in Sanskrit, Sanskrit occupies an important place in the cultural life of India. Since the dawn of civilization in India, Sanskrit as a language had been one of the foremost topics of study.[1] It was, in fact, not only a part of the syllabi but also the medium of instruction during the ancient and medieval periods. Text-books of different subjects including grammar, logic and medicine were written in Sanskrit. Sanskrit thus formed an integral part of the curricula since early times. It has continued, to some extent, to be studied as one of the Indian languages in the Indian schools and Universities, whereas its use as a medium of instruction is confined to some traditional schools.

Although Sanskrit education has, thus, a history of more than 3000 years, the scope of the present paper is confined to the last and the present centuries. The story of the position of Sanskrit during this periods is a story of ups and downs in the political and social life in India. In order to understand the changing ideology of Sanskrit, it is necessary to record here a few milestones in the history of education in India from the beginning of the nineteenth century or from a little earlier time.

2.1 During the 17th and 18th centuries there were two types of schools in India: elementary schools started by the European traders for the education of their children, and the traditional, so-called Pāṭhaśālās and

[1] The Veda governed the life of the Indians and the words of the Veda reigned supreme. The study of the Sanskrit language in all its aspects became indispensable for the Indian Aryans in order to protect the words of the Veda.

the Madarsahs of Hindus and Muslims respectively. While the teaching in the elementary schools was confined to the 'three Rs' (viz. reading, writing and arithmetics), the Pāṭhaśālās and the Madarsahs provided teaching from different Śāstras including logic, law and grammar in Sanskrit and Arabic or Persian respectively. Education in the elementary school was not compulsory for those who wanted to study in the Pāṭhaśālās and Madarsahs. The general scenario of education in India towards the end of the 18th century looked very gloomy and depressing. The whole Indian society was in doldrums due to the foreign invasions and a feeling of sluggishness had swept all over the nation. In 1792 Charles Grant wrote in his pamphlet entitled "Observations on the state of Society among the Asiatic Subjects of Great Britain,":

> The Hindoos err because they are ignorant . . . The apathy with which the Hindoo views all persons and interests unconnected with himself is such as excites the indignation of Europeans. . . Patriotism is absolutely unknown in Hindoosthan.[2]

Causes of this downfall of Indian education are, according to the historians, the growing poverty of the country, indifference of the states to this problem and unworthy teachers. According to Grant the only solution to his problem was introduction of Western education in English.

As far as the Sanskrit education in the Pāṭhaśālās was concerned, the outdated and degenerate character of the syllabi, excessive emphasis on memory, the method of rote learning leading to more pedantry and automatism and, above all the rigid curricula which could not be adapted to the requirements of the period were responsible for the death of the age old system of learning.

2.2 In 1811 Lord Minto, the Governor General of India expressed in his minute a deep concern over the decay of Indian education. According to him this sad state of education was mainly due to the withdrawal of financial support by the princes and zameendars. The Charter Act of 1813 forced the East India Company to look into the problem of education in India. It also opened the gates of India for missionaries. Although the directors of the Company had already declared their policy of religious neutrality, the Evangelicals were to some extent successful

---

[2] Cited after Rawat 1970:133.

in their mission. Their mission served a two-fold purpose from the point of view of Indian education: (1) it started education of Indian languages and culture, and (2) it created a sense of emulation in the mind of the Indians who started private educational organizations.

The picture of Indian education towards the end of the 18th century is thus a picture of an Indian society without convictions and without a sense of direction. One should not, however, be blind to the silver lines of this dark cloud. For instance, although traditional Sanskrit learning started slowly dying, introduction of Indian Law in place of the British Law in India raised to importance traditional sanskrit Pandits who were required for the interpretation of the Indian Law. In 1781 Warren Hastings started in Calcutta a Madarsah in which he introduced study of Sanskrit along with other subjects.[3] In the Fort William College that was founded in Calcutta in 1800, Sanskrit, Arabic and Persian were taught along with other subjects. In 1818 Elphinstone who was appointed Governor of the Presidency of Bombay started a Sanskrit College in Poona (modern spelling: Pune). Sanskrit had always received encouragement from the Maratha rulers in this area, Shivaji in particular, who started the institution of Dakṣiṇā (honorarium) in the 17th century for encouraging Sanskrit scholarship. The scheme was continued by the Peshvas, the ministers of the Maratha rulers in Pune that was their headquarters. Elphinstone's Sanskrit College, the Dakṣiṇā Mahāvidyālaya, was started with the help of funding from the Peshvas. Sanskrit Pandits from all over the country used to come to Pune to demonstrate their feats of erudition and contest for the award of Dakṣiṇā. As a result quite a few Pāṭhaśālās were started in and around Pune in order to prepare experts to judge the scholarship of aspirant Pandits.

However, these efforts to revive oriental learning were far and few between. Although the Evangelical ideology contributed to this revival, the utilitarian ideology of some of the British and Indian reformists prevailed, and Sanskrit education could not flourish beyond a certain extent in the beginning of the 19th century.

---

[3] History tells us that Akbar had already introduced the study of Sanskrit in Madarsahs. Cf. Joshi 1979, vol. 9:375.

2.3 The history of education in India in the beginning of the 19th century is marked by a controversy between orientalists and anglicists. It started with the issue of the utilization of the grant of 100 000 Rupees for the purpose of education. While the orientalists felt that the grant should be utilized for the spread of oriental learning, the anglicists advocated the use of the grant for the organization of English schools all over the country. The controversy presented an ironical picture in which some British officials strongly pleaded for the preservation of oriental education as well as the use of the oriental languages as the medium of instruction, while some Indian reformists opposed the idea of encouraging oriental learning. For instance, Sir Thomas Munro, who was highly appreciative of Indian culture, said in the House of Commons:

> If civilization were to become an article of trade between the two countries, I am convinced that England would greatly benefit from the import of cargo.[4]

The court of Directors also was in favour of the idea of strengthening links between the British officials and the Indians through oriental learning. The court observed,

> We are informed that there are in Sanskrit language treatises on Astronomy and Mathematics including Geometry and Algebra which, though they may not add new lights to European Science, might be made to form links of communication between the natives and the gentlemen in our service.[5]

The court went a step ahead and recommended that preference should be given in service to those British officials who were willing to learn Sanskrit.

On the other hand, Raja Rammohan Roy, who is described as the father of modern India, strongly protested against the decision of the committee of Public Instruction to start a Sanskrit college in Calcutta. In a letter written in 1923 he argued,

---

[4] Cited after Rawat 1970:137.

[5] Cited after Rawat 1970:138.

> The pupils will there acquire what was known two thousand years ago with the addition of vain and empty subtleties since then produced by speculative men.[6]

Despite the protest the college was started with 35 students and 18 Professors to teach different Indian Śāstras. Gradually two more colleges were added to the list of oriental education institutions, a college in Delhi in 1825 and another college in Agra in 1827. A press was started in Calcutta in 1830 and it started publishing oriental books.

2.4 However, this situation which was conducive to the promotion of Sanskrit education lasted only till June 1834 when Thomas Babington Macaulay was appointed as the law member of the Governor General's Executive Council. Macaulay was consulted for the utilization of the above-mentioned sum of 100 000 Rupees for education. On February 2, 1835 he published his famous minutes in which he despised indigenous education and suggested immediate stoppage of funds for oriental education. His observation, namely, that "a single shelf of a good European literature was worth the whole native literature of India and Arabia," though based on his ignorance, had detrimental effects on Sanskrit education in India. His remarks on the nature of Sanskrit education that was in vogue during his time reflects the ideology of Sanskrit learning current in the first half of the 19th Century. According to him,

> We are to teach false history, false astronomy, false medicine, because we find them in the company of false religion. Can we reasonably or decently bribe men, out of the revenues of the state, to waste their youth in learning how they are to purify themselves after touching an ass or what texts of the Vedas they are to repeat to expatiate the crime of killing a goat?[7]

Macaulay's reaction as recorded above throws light on the nature of Sanskrit learning during that period which was characterised by strict adherence by the Sanskrit teachers to the age-old Śāstras and the predominance of the religious teaching in Sanskrit schools. With Macaulay's recommendations this anachronistic ideology was replaced by an utilitarian ideology and English education was started in the country by William Bentingk. Macaulay's dream to create people "Indian in blood and English in taste" came true. Although the orientalists felt that the

---

[6] Majumdar et al. 1965:34.

[7] Cited after Rawat 1970:157.

baby was thrown with the bathwater, they could not improve the position of Sanskrit education. This situation continued till 1854 when the famous Despatch of Sir Charles Wood brought a revolution in Indian education.

Lord Bentingk implemented Macaulay's recommendation to the extent that English was directly connected with the livelihood of the Indians. Preference in public employment was given to those who were educated in English. According to the Report of the Sanskrit Commission, appointed by the Indian Government in the mid-1950s, there was a rapid decline of Sanskrit education during this period because of

> political and social visicitudes and economic distress, but mainly because of the change of outlook and attitude fostered by a distinctly alien and somewhat haphazard state policy of over a century which was right in insisting on modern learning, but wrong in its apathy towards ancient learning.[8]

2.5 Although traditional Sanskrit learning received a serious blow with the introduction of English as an official medium for higher learning in 1835 all over the country, the famous 1854 Woods Despatch which brought a total revolution in Indian education led to a revival of Sanskrit study. Following the despatch a comprehensive plan of education with a hierarchy from primary school level to the University level was drawn and was gradually brought into force. The despatch expressed its accommodative attitude towards Sanskrit and Arabic. The first three Universities that were established in Bombay, Madras and Calcutta, following in the wake of the Despatch, introduced Sanskrit. Sanskrit was, in fact, from the beginning, one of the compulsory subjects for matriculation or entrance examination in the Bombay University. The three Universities were thus responsible for the popularization of Sanskrit which was, so far, confined to a certain community.

2.6 It must be noted here that at that moment, Indology had already started flourishing in Europe. The gates of the golden treasury of Sanskrit literature were opened to European students through the translation of the Bhagavadgīta, Manusmṛti, Śākuntala etc. Those who studied Sanskrit did not just remain dazed by the glitter of this treasury, but they developed learning aids like dictionaries and translations. When

---

[8] Report Sanskrit Commission, 1956-1957, p. 19.

the Western gates were flung open for the Indians through English education, Sanskrit that had gone abroad, returned through these Western gates in a new garb. This 'return of the native' was heartily welcomed by Indians. Sanskrit re-entered its homeland with a new ideology based on a spirit of inquiry and understanding. This was a turning point in the history of Sanskrit education in India. The widespread movement of Western education which was apparently a curse for the traditional education proved a boon in disguise for Sanskrit. Sanskrit was rid of its obsolete, antiquated character and came to be included in the main stream of Indian education. It was raised to the status of a second language and thus obtained a position among Indian languages.

The contact with the West brought in a new approach to the study of Sanskrit. European orientalists aided by native scholars started collecting and cataloguing manuscripts, undertaking archaeological investigations and doing research in the literature they studied. Thus Sanskrit education started to flourish on all sides.

3.1 Towards the end of the 19th century and the beginning of the 20th century a new dimension was added to the ideology of Sanskrit learning. The encounter between the tradition and modernity led to the rise of what is often described as Neo-Hinduism (cf. Halbfass 1988:239). As remarked by a historian, "the spread of western education and ideals stimulated movements within Hinduism designated to preserve its essential principles and at the same time to remove excrescences."[9] One of the prominent tasks of the Neo-Hindu movement was to reinterpret ancient texts like the Vedas, the Gīta and the Manusmṛti and adjust them to the needs of the modern world and for the wellbeing of the society. The Arya Samaj, founded by Dayananda Sarasvati in 1875, and the Theosophical society, started by Annie Besant in 1899, are among the organizations which were directly or indirectly responsible for the spread of Sanskrit knowledge in this new garb.

3.2 The dawn of the 20th century brought with it new and stronger waves of nationalism, which was quite favourable for Sanskrit study. Different national movements of freedom-fighters evoked patriotic feelings in the minds of the Indians. For instance, the Svadesi move-

[9]Majumdar et al. 1965:93.

ment inspired the social and political leaders to start national educational institutes. Thus Rāṣṭrīya Vidyāpīṭhas were established in places like Pune, Ahmedabad, Patna, Lahore and Banaras to accommodate those teachers and students who quit and boycotted English schools. While the Dakṣiṇā-scheme of Elphinstone's Sanskrit College was discontinued with the fall of the Peshwas, and Pāṭhaśālās were closed down for Sanskrit when their back doors were opened for giving refuge to the freedom fighters in the beginning of this century, traditional religious schools called Gurukulas were also started in places like Haradvar and Vṛndavan in order to revive traditional learning. Sanskrit education started thriving in these schools with Indian ethos. Political leaders like Mahatma Gandhi and Lokamanya Bal Gangadhar Tilak also contributed to the widespread interest in Sanskrit by popularizing works like the Bhagavadgīta and the Upanisads. Yet another factor that led to the advancement of Sanskrit education was the whole-hearted patronage given by Maharajas and philanthropists. The encouragement given by Western Universities and other institutes in the West interested in oriental studies by awarding scholarships to young Indian scholars to go abroad and learn western methods of research in Indology also greatly helped raising the standard of oriental education. Scholars like Dr. Sukthankar, Dr. P.D. Gune, Dr. Suniti Kumar Chatterji, Dr. Taraporewala studied in different Western institutes with great Indologists of that period and returned with new insights and a fresh approach. The healthy collaboration between Western and Indian scholars led to a widening of the horizons of oriental studies. The birth of research institutes like the Bhandarkar Oriental Research Institute (1917) and of national conferences like the All India Oriental Conference (1919) as well as of publication series like the Bibliotheca Indica (Calcutta) and the Government Sanskrit and Prakrit Series (Bombay) accelerated interest in various aspects of Sanskrit study.

3.3 This period is thus marked by a serious and critical inquiry into Sanskrit language and sciences, initiated by western scholars and impelled by the emotional involvement of social, political, and spiritual leaders who were keenly interested in the cultural revival and preservation of the national heritage. This glorious period in the history of Sanskrit education was the result of the working together of several undercurrents of social, economical, political, spiritual and cultural ideologies with the spirit of patriotism and the spirit of inquiry as the foundation. During this period, both nationalism and rationalism, traditionalism and modernism, deism and spiritualism, reason and faith, worked hand in hand.

4. The period of renaissance was, however, followed by a period of stagnation. India's forced participation in the second world war, and the involvement of the Indians in the freedom struggle were among the factors that led to a decline in education in the pre-independence period. Chaos and confusion prevailed over the Country during the decade of provincial autonomy (1937-47). Because of the knowledge explosion on the western horizon the curriculum in the schools became overcrowded. It was imperative for a developing country like India to adopt a utilitarian ideology and make room for modern subjects which were directly connected with the bread and butter. The first to be affected were subjects like Sanskrit which were linked with the past rather than with the present of India.

5.1 The first government of independent India thought of reorganizing the system of education and different commissions were appointed to reexamine the state of education on different levels and make recommendations. Following in the wake of these recommendations, education did make a rapid progress in a multidimensional manner. However, since the aim of the education was to meet the demands of a developing country, there was no remarkable change in the position of Sanskrit and other classical languages. Sanskrit just survived in schools and colleges because of its cultural value.

5.2 The appointment of the so-called 'Sanskrit Commission' by the central government in 1955 in response to the demand by the people as well as by some parliamentarians was an important event in the history of Sanskrit education. The Commission undertook an extensive tour throughout the country, made an exhaustive survey by means of questionnaires and interviews, and prepared a report on the state of Sanskrit education in the country. In the report that was published in 1957 the Commission observed that "Sanskrit has not been allowed to enjoy the status and facilities it had under the British raj."[10] Here is a summary of the state of education of Sanskrit during the post-independency decade as recorded in the report:

On the school level, the study of Sanskrit continued in two types of schools: the Pāṭhaśālās and the Secondary Schools. The number of Pāṭhaśālās throughout the country was about 4000. The largest numbers of Pāṭhaśālās existed in Uttar Pradesh, Bengal and Bihar. While describing the pitiable condition of these Pāṭhaśālās the Commission remarked that, due to poor funding, incompetent teachers and lack of enthusiasm both on the part of teachers as well as students, traditional Sanskrit learning was fast disappearing. The Commission further observed, "most of the students come here because they have nothing else to do".[11] There existed no uniformity with regard to the syllabi, the courses, the mode of education and the grading of examinations amongst the Pāṭhaśālās. A similar lack of uniformity was observed with regard to the teaching of Sanskrit in Secondary Schools. While it was being taught as one of the compulsory subjects in schools in some provinces, its inclusion in the curriculum was optional in some other provinces. Again, in some provinces it alternated with the regional language, whereas elsewhere it was made composite with the mother tongue. Although there was, on the whole, a considerable fall in the number of schools offering facilities for the study of Sanskrit, the situation in the north was better than in the south. With regard to the education of Sanskrit on college and university levels, the Commission observed that it continued to survive in almost all colleges and also in universities as a postgraduate subject.

5.3 The Sanskrit Commission made certain recommendations, such as the accommodation of Sanskrit in the already existing three languages formula, and the establishment of a separate Sanskrit board. The government decided to implement the recommendations of the Commission, and a Central Sanskrit Board came into existence in 1959. After the board worked for more than 10 years and started some new schemes for the promotion of Sanskrit study, it was replaced by Kendriya Sanskṛta Parishad, a body with larger membership and wider activities.

---

[10] Report Sanskrit Commission, p. 7.

[11] Ibid.

In the meanwhile, three Sanskrit universities were established in Puri, Allahabad and Jammu. The Rashtriya Sanskrit Sansthan was established in 1970 to take over the administration of these three universities. In the course of time the Sansthan extended its activities with the objective "to preserve, promote and propagate Sanskrit language and literature in general, and traditional Sanskrit learning in particular." The Sansthan conducts, for instance, teaching of Sanskrit on traditional lines in seven Sanskrit Universities and in about 4000 Pāṭhaśālās. It also conducts teachers training programmes from time to time. Among its other activities are research, publication, collection and preservation of Sanskrit manuscripts, a correspondence course in Sanskrit, the development of a curriculum for traditional Sanskrit teaching, affiliation to Sanskrit institutions awarding scholarships to students and implementing Śāstracūdāmaṇi schemes. The Sansthan has undertaken several programmes such as the modernization of Pāṭhaśālās and the standardization of syllabi in the Pāṭhaśālās.

6.1 At present the department of education which forms part of the ministry of human resources development has a special officer called deputy educational adviser for Sanskrit. According to recent information sent by him, the government of India provides financial assistance to 549 voluntary organizations and Pāṭhaśālās, to 17 Ādarśa Pāṭhaśālās/Śodhasamsthās, and to a project of the preservation of Vedic recitation. In addition to this, the felicitation of Sanskrit Pandits on Independence Day, financial assistance to Sanskrit pandits in indigent circumstances, and to more than hundred Sanskrit magazines, are some of the activities undertaken by the central government to encourage Sanskrit education.

6.2 It will thus be clear that since the establishment of the first Sanskrit Commission, the central government has taken keen interest in the preservation and promotion of Sanskrit. However, its efforts are concentrated more on the preservation of traditional learning. In spite of different measures taken by the government the standard of traditional Sanskrit education has lowered down. The position of Sanskrit in secondary schools got further deteriorated with the rise in different states, at different times, of different political parties with different ideologies. The general degeneration of values in the society and the utilitarian philosophy of life worsened the situation of Sanskrit. Different education commissions appointed during the last four decades reiterated the three language formula. Not only was Sanskrit relegated to the position of an optional subject, but it was possible to completely drop it in the school curriculum. As a result, at least one generation of students has been deprived of the privilege to be acquainted with the language of their culture. This has led further to the scarcity of teachers. Due to this, many schools are unable to provide facilities for teaching Sanskrit, and at least one more generation is feared to be educated without knowing what Sanskrit is.

7.1 For the purpose of this Seminar I had prepared a questionnaire and sent it to about 100 persons in different states. Out of 100, 40 questionnaires were replied and sent back to me. In some cases two questionnaires coming from the same state presented two opposite pictures about the State of Sanskrit. A few persons did oblige by sending back the questionnaire to me; but their answers to most of the questions were of the "I do not know" type. I think, these general observations about the response to my efforts to collect information are enough evidence to show the pitiable condition which Sanskrit education faces today. Here is the summary of the information I received through the questionnaires:

7.2 The reply to the question whether the policy of the state government towards Sanskrit education is encouraging is 'No!' from almost all states except Kerala, Gujarat, Orissa and Andhra Pradesh. In Kerala, Gujarat and Bihar, students belonging to all castes and creeds are coming forward to learn Sanskrit. The number of students desiring admission into postgraduate courses is so large in Puri that admission is denied to quite a few applicants. In one or two places admission is given only to those who pass entrance test. Reason for these occasional encouraging situations are various. For instance, the Arya Samaj which is still dominating in Haryana is responsible for the encouragement of Sanskrit education in that province. In Andhra Pradesh and Kerala, students opt for Sanskrit because of a growing interest in the national culture as well as because of the awareness that the study of Sanskrit is helpful for strengthening the mother tongue. In Bihar, Sanskrit is regarded as a scoring and comparatively easy subject for those who want to pass the public service commission examination. The government policy in the remaining states is not very encouraging for Sanskrit because of the general misconception of Sanskrit as a language of particular caste and religion, because of ignorance about its greatness, as well as because of some political forces. For instance, it has been reported that recently the Uttar Pradesh government has taken the decision to introduce Urdu as a second language in the place of Sanskrit. This move is, according to political observers, motivated by the desires of the ruling party to ensure votes from the minority faction. In West Bengal the lack of modern outlook in preparing syllabi, the outdated method of teaching without creating any interest, and the utilitarian approach of the political leaders, are mentioned as the reason for the downfall in the status of Sanskrit education. Absence of an adequate number of teachers, of adequate library facilities, and of encouragement from the people are among the other reasons given for the general decline in Sanskrit education.

7.3 Although there is in general a fall in the number of schools and colleges offering facilities for the study of sanskrit, the situation is still not entirely discouraging. At the postgraduate level, Sanskrit is still being taught in most of the leading Universities. However, since utility is the only touchstone of education there has been a considerable fall in the number of students opting for Sanskrit which has a low job-potential.

8.1 Although the survey thus draws a gloomy picture about the future of Sanskrit, there is no reason for despair: while Sanskrit has lost its earlier prominence in education in general, it appears from recent events that it is on the way to regain a respectable position in a different way. Moreover, the scope of the study of Sanskrit is no more confined to its character as a literary language. It is being studied more as a *vidyā*, as a 'science', in a number of interdisciplinary projects. A few examples follow:

8.2 Recently, attempts are being made to employ Sanskrit in fields of computer applications such as machine translation and natural language understanding. In 1984, for instance, a NASA scientist advocated Sanskrit, or rather scholarly (so-called Śāstric) Sanskrit, as the best suited interlingua in knowledge representation programmes in the area of artificial intelligence (Briggs 1985). His article triggered a number of projects in this area which involved research into various techniques of sentence interpretation available in different scholarly traditions in Sanskrit such as *Nyāya* (logic) and *Vyākaraṇa* (grammar). Some of the projects in this field are still continuing both in India and in the West. A project of machine translation of the Indian Institute of Technology at Kanpur is concerned with the translation from one Indian language into another and makes use of the Pāṇinian Kāraka-theory in the interlingua.[12] The Centre for Development of Advanced Computing at Pune has developed a number of packages showing how Sanskrit can be exploited as a prototype for launching different projects such as natural language understanding through computer. A new package called Lila is designed in the same institute to teach Sanskrit as a foreign language. Another package known as Desika is meant for generating and analyzing Sanskrit words. Yet another package called Madhava defines the complex relationship between 4200 symptoms and 900 diseases on the basis of the Āyurvedic text Mādhavanidāna.[13]

8.3 Another development emerged in the area of business management with the establishment of the new school of 'dharmic management'. According to the propounder of this school, successful management consists in the application of teachings of philosophy and Vedānta to the field of management.

8.4 Mention should also be made of the 'PP Project' (Pandit Philosopher Project), sponsored by Ford Foundation, which brings together traditional pandits and scholars in Western philosophy in order to establish a dialogue between ancient Indian philosophy and Western philosophy, and especially to revive the Indian tradition of philosophy.[14]

8.5 The projects referred above are responsible for the entry of Sanskrit in interdisciplinary areas. There are also activities taking place which strengthen the position of Sanskrit more directly. Among the re-

---

[12] For further information one may contact Dr. Rajeev Sangal at the Indian Institute of Technology at Kanpur, 208016, India.

[13] Further details could be obtained from Dr. S.N. Bhavsar at the Centre for the Development of Advanced Computing, University of Pune Campus, Pune, 411007, India.

[14] Further details can be had from Prof. M.P. Rege, President, Prajna Pathashala Mandal, Wai, 412 803, Maharashtra, India.

cent activities of the central government to encourage Sanskrit must be mentioned the introduction of Sanskrit on All India Radio as well as on television in news items and cultural items such as dramas. As a result of a recent decision taken by the University Grants Commission to introduce vocational subjects at undergraduate level, a course in functional Sanskrit is introduced in a few universities. This course is primarily a course in the recitation of Vedic mantras, aiming at producing Viadika priests who can perform different rituals of the Hindu religion.

8.6 As on the religious level, so also on the spiritual level the study of Sanskrit is being encouraged by various spiritual movements such as Harekrishna movement, Chinmaya mission and the Maharshi Mahesh Yogi movement. A Sanskrit village called Muttur in South India is a project to establish Sanskrit as a market language.

8.7 Some Sanskrit-lovers with an outstanding interest in Sanskrit have started kindergarten schools in Sanskrit medium. The *Shri Vatsa Balamandiram* of Bombay with a branch in Pune is an example of this type of endeavour in promoting the study of Sanskrit from childhood. A staunch lover of Sanskrit is reported to have trained both his daughters in spoken Sanskrit since their childhood as their mother tongue as an experiment to prove that Sanskrit can survive as a spoken language.

8.8 In fact, on the cultural horizon Sanskrit has found a very respectable position. In addition to numerous audio cassettes or prayers in Sanskrit, classical ragas and semi-classical songs are being presented in Sanskrit by reputed singers like Pdt. Jasraj, Smt. Subbalakshmi and Veena Sahasrabuddhe. Sanskrit is being highly respected as a language of culture not only among the elite but also among the common people. It is being used as a mark of high taste in different communications from marriage invitations to obituary notes. Use of Sanskrit verses as mottos, as headings on different magazines to reflect their ideologies, at the entrance of public institutes and offices such as theatres and even banks, show a growing popularity of Sanskrit.

8.9 The flourishing state of creative literature in Sanskrit is recorded by the fact that there exist at least ten surveys of modern Sanskrit Literature (e.g. Raghavan 1957 and Upadhyaya 1973). Quite a few awards and honours are instituted to encourage creative writing in Sanskrit. In addition to creative literature, news magazines including dailies are also regularly published in Sanskrit. On the cultural scene Sanskrit has achieved a high watermark by entering into the field of cinema and bagging two awards continuously for two years for the two best full length feature films, namely AdiShankaracharya and Bhagavadgita. The third film in Sanskrit on Swami Vivekananda is in the making.

8.10 The traditional Sanskrit theatre is surviving in traditional regional dramatic forms such as Kutiattam in Kerala and partly in forms like Yaksagana. The well known stage performance of the Mahabharata in French and English under the direction of Peter Brook all over the world speaks volumes about the popularity of the ancient Sanskrit epic. Attempts to present ancient Sanskrit literary pieces in a modern garb are a frequent phenomenon. *Aṣṭāvadhāna* or *Śatāvadhāna*, a special cultural feature of Andhra Pradesh, which is based on feats of memory, is presented today in both Sanskrit and Telugu. In addition to these cultural events one may mention festivals like the *Kālidāsamahotsava*, a festival in honour of the Sanskrit poet Kālidāsa organized annually at Ujjain and Pune, recitals of modern Sanskrit poetry, and Symposia in Sanskrit on traditional sciences (*Śāstrārtha*) sponsored by Śaṅkarācāryas or similar religious leaders.

8.11 Because of its prominent religious and spiritual character, Sanskrit is always held with esteem and its use is regarded as adding dignity and solemnity to an occasion by those who respect the cultural heritage of the country. The convocation ceremony in some universities is, for instance, conducted in Sanskrit by reciting the well known convocation address in the Taittirīya Upaniṣad. Often the members of the parliament or different legislative assemblies in different states are found to be taking oaths in Sanskrit. This new ideology, the roots of which can be traced to the emergence of the feeling of self-identity, has proved beneficial for the sustenance of Sanskrit even in the diplomatic world.

8.12 Recently, a new wave of rationalism and modernization has swept over the Hindu religious community. To record a few examples, Pdt. Visvanatha Srouty, an eminent scholar and traditional priest performing sacrifices has categorically opposed the idea of killing animals during sacrifices and accordingly interpreted some Vedic texts.[15] An-

---

[15] He has published a booklet entitled *Paśv-ālambhana-niṣedhaḥ yajñeṣu* (Srouty 1993/4), in which he proclaims that during sacrificial performance *aja* 'goat' should be replaced by *ājya* 'ghee (purified butter)'.

other instance of a modern touch is the emergence of women priests performing Hindu rituals. Women who were denied the right even to listen to the Vedic words are being encouraged in some states like Maharashtra to learn Vedic recitation and work as priests.

8.13 Finally, good prospects for Sanskrit also in school education are indicated by a recent judgement declared by the Supreme Court (Delhi, on 6.10.1994) against the contention of the Secretary of the Central Board of Education in connection with the elimination of Sanskrit from the school curriculum. The supreme court has declared its verdict in favour of Sanskrit, highly emphasizing its importance as the mother of all Indo-Aryan languages.

8.14 There is, however, one faction of Indian society which not only dislikes but despises Sanskrit, because it believes that Sanskrit works like the Manusmṛti teach undemocratic and anti-socialist thought which is contradictory with the modern ideal of social equality and justice. There are reported instances of the Manusmṛti being publicly burnt in protest against its pro-Brahmanic stand. Some social leaders who claim to be reformists are occasionally seen attacking this aspect of Sanskrit.

9.1 In spite of this ambivalence, Sanskrit is gaining popularity and being respectfully studied for the following reasons:

(a) Sanskrit is a language of all-India provenance. Because of its pan-Indian character, serious students of language felt it necessary to study Sanskrit in order to strengthen their knowledge of their mothertongue as well as other Indian languages. In this way it has great cultural value.

(b) It is strongly supported by one of the major political parties of India. The followers of the ideology of this party are seen engaged in many Sanskrit activities such as organizing schools for spoken Sanskrit.

(c) It is the language of one of the prominent religions of India. Since the life of Indians is generally dominated by religious and spiritual forces, the place of Sanskrit is secure in the community of the staunch followers of this religion.

(d) The ideology of Westernization has given a boost to the status of Sanskrit. One comes across the ironical situation that Sanskrit is being respected by those Indians who are the embodiment of Macaulay's ideal of the "Indians in blood and English in thought and behaviour." It is being respected because it is an imported object. The wave of Westernization which has swept all over the country is thus seen to have stabilized the position of Sanskrit in its homeland.

(e) And lastly, Sanskrit has survived because of its intrinsic value. There is something enduring, of a permanent value in Sanskrit which has survived through the ages. Dr. R.N. Dandekar quotes, for instance, from Pandit Jawharlal Nehru's speech in the University of Poona when the degree of Doctor of Letters was conferred upon him in 1961. Referring to the Sanskrit citation that was read out to him Pdt. Nehru said,[16]

> One of my regrets in my life has been that I have had no occasion to learn Sanskrit. Consequently I was unable to follow adequately the citation. But I must confess that I was greatly moved and thrilled by the mellifluous rhythm of the Sanskrit language. Even the mere sound of that language gently touched and stirred the inner cord of my heart. I believe that the history itself has established a kind of innate affinity between Sanskrit and Indian soul.

9.2 I would like to conclude this review of the past and present with a short statement concerning the future of Sanskrit, viz. that it may be expected that in spite of the fluctuations in the position and status of Sanskrit in India in the course of the many centuries of its history, it will survive as long as there is a quest for knowledge, respect for values, faith in culture and interest and love for that which has grandeur and beauty in the world.

---

[16] Dandekar 1993:232. To this citation I may add, that I have also noticed that Sanskrit as an unique linguistic phenomenon with its sonorous character and its richness of inflexions as well as vocabulary, has attracted quite a few persons who want to pursue its study in spite of their non-Sanskrit career. Mention may here also be made of a Pune-based medical surgeon flying his own aeroplane, Dr. S.V. Bhave, who claims that he has succeeded in identifying the path of the cloud in Kālidāsa's poem Meghadūta ('The Cloud-messenger').

CHAPTER EIGHTEEN

CONTEXTUALIZING THE ETERNAL LANGUAGE: FEATURES OF PRIESTLY SANSKRIT

Madhav M. Deshpande

1. *Introduction*

There are some commonly held conceptions about Sanskrit. In terms of theological conceptions held by the Indian tradition, Sanskrit is an eternal language. The notion of an eternal language conceived purely in metaphysical terms may create a picture of a linguistic flatland beyond time and space. The ancient grammarians of this language did observe variation of usage in different domains, and yet struggled hard to reconcile this observed variation within the paradigm of eternal language. Occasionally, even the descriptions of modern linguists unintentionally seem to evoke an image of Sanskrit as a linguistic flatland. Consider the comments of M.B. Emeneau (1966: 123) referring to Classical Sanskrit: "We find in it no dialects, no chronological developments, except loss and at times invasions from the vernaculars of the users, and no geographical divergences." One may, then, be tempted to think of Classical Sanskrit as a linguistic flatland which becomes occasionally uneven due to factors like "invasions from the vernaculars of the users." However, such a perception of Sanskrit overlooks the sociolinguistic dynamics of Indian history within which Sanskrit had to survive along with all other things Indian. More recent sociolinguistic work (Deshpande 1979 and 1993; Hock and Pandharipande 1976) has begun to direct our attention away from such static views of Sanskrit and offer us a realistic understanding of the differing temporal, regional, and societal actualizations of this theologically eternal language.

While the Sanskrit grammarians were loath to admit influences of other languages on Sanskrit, the tradition of poetry was more open to accepting a beneficial relationship between Sanskrit and the vernaculars. Vākpatirāja (*Gaüḍavaho,* verse 65) says that the beauty of Sanskrit blooms with a touch of Prakrit (*payayacchāyā*), and that the effectiveness of Prakrits increases with Sanskritization (*sakkayasakkārukkarisaṇa*). Such Sanskritization or Prakritization of languages may be conscious or unconscious, and it may be due to a number of different factors. At the very basic level, the entire notion of learning a language or acquiring a grammar needs to be reconsidered. If we assume that a grammar exists in the mind of parents, does that grammar get transferred to their child through the process of conceiving that child? Andersen (1973: 767) provides a realistic answer to this question which can be represented by the diagram below:

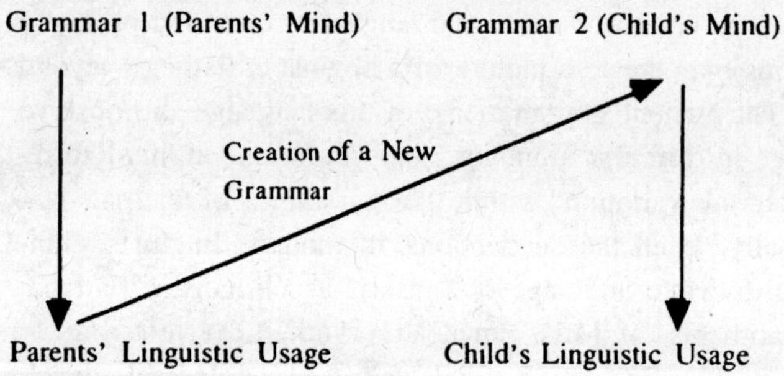

Here the assumption is that a child does not directly inherit its grammar from its parents but builds its own grammar anew by observing the usage of its parents. If we extend this basic process beyond this limited situation, one may say that a child observes the linguistic usage not only of its parents, but of any number of other users it comes into contact with, and hence its newly rebuilt grammar and its own resulting usage of language is bound to be somewhat different from that of its parents. The same analogy can be extended further to the acquisition of a second language like Sanskrit. In spite of the grammarian's best intentions and efforts to inculcate the standardized Sanskrit grammar and language, the language learning process and the process of language use were in actuality complicated by many factors. The totality of such factors may be so complex that it may be indeed very difficult, if not impossible, to pinpoint a specific factor responsible for a specific non-standard usage. However, with a reasonable allowance for complexity and multiple influences, one may still be able to offer what appears to be the most salient reason for a given deviation from some expected norm. This is not necessarily a fully scientific procedure, in that one can never be totally certain whether a given case of deviation from the norm of the classical Sanskrit usage is itself an old inherited pattern, lacking any creativity on the part of the current priestly user, or whether it is an example of the inherited norm of the priestly usage, caused by factors relating specifically to a given priestly performer. However, one must at least initiate the search for a possible cluster of influences. This paper proposes to initiate such an investigation. No suggestions made here are to be treated as exclusive and conclusive solutions, but suggestions for possible influences.

In this paper, I shall specifically focus on the usage of Sanskrit in priestly performances. This presentation is based on a large collection of recordings of priestly performances which I have made, other recordings which are commercially available, printed materials of popular and scholarly varieties, and manuscript materials found mostly at the Bhandarkar Oriental Research Institute and the Vaidika Samshodhana Mandala, Pune. This material is too complex in its diversity, i.e. historical, regional, and social depth. I shall present here a preliminary account of some features which I have detected in this material, and I hope that a more extensive study of this material will be published in the future.

The collected material shows that the priestly performances generally involve three types of language varieties, i.e. Vedic Sanskrit, Classical Sanskrit, and a vernacular language. The ritual performances of the Brahmins generally involve all the three varieties. For groups in the middle range, there is greater variation. Whether a certain group was traditionally considered to belong to Kṣatriya or Vaiśya ranks determined whether their rituals will or will not be performed by using Vedic mantras. Thus, for example, the community of Cāndrasenīya Kāyastha Prabhus (popularly known today as CKP) in Maharashtra wanted to be treated as Kṣatriyas and wanted their rituals to be performed with Vedic mantras. However, the Brahmins of the region often refused to treat them as Kṣatriyas and offered to perform rituals for them only with the Purāṇic mantras. The controversial relations often produced bitter debates to be settled temporarily by referring the dispute to some religious authority. Narendra Wagle (1987) has given a detailed account of these conflicts. The rituals for the decidedly lower castes may or may not involve any Sanskrit, and could be carried out purely in vernaculars by non-Brahmin priests. In the present study, we are concerned with those ritual texts and performances which involve Sanskrit in one form or another.

The individuals who participate in these ritual performances have varying degrees of linguistic abilities. The linguistic performance can be analyzed in terms of whether a person is merely reciting a memorized text, versus whether one is actively using a language variety. An intermediate stage of linguistic performance occurs when one is forced by the contextual factors to modify or manipulate a received memorized text. The factor of linguistic comprehension is almost independent of the ability to recite or 'blurt out' a text. A priest may be able to recite a text flawlessly without comprehending the meaning of that text. If we make a distinction between highly learned priests and low-level priests, we can observe that the high scholar priest may have a flawless recitation of the received Vedic texts, with some low level understanding of the meaning of these texts. However, the same high scholar priest may have a more active control of the classical language. His full control of the local vernacular is simply taken for granted. For a low-level priest, he may have the ability to somehow recite the Vedic texts, with almost zero comprehension of the contents. Such a low-end priest may also have little ability to modify or manipulate the classical language portions. The host, excluding the exceptional scholar-host, generally has some contextual understanding of what is going on and some lexical recognition of Sanskrit expressions. All the participants are primarily working within the outermost frame of the vernacular language. All ultimate comprehension and comunication occurs within this outermost frame of the vernacular language. The use of Sanskrit is situated within the frame of the vernacular language, just as the use of the recited Vedic texts is situated within the frame of the classical language. As it turns out, the Vedic text which is understood the least has the highest sacred value. Next comes the value of the text in classical Sanskrit. Sanskrit is deemed by both the priest and the host to be more sacred than the vernacular. Therefore, a priest not only needs to be able to perform in Sanskrit, or what appears to him and to the host as Sanskrit, but he often needs to get the unlearned host to perform in Sanskrit by prompting him to do so word-by-word or phrase-by-phrase. The kind of Sanskrit one finds in a given text has some direct or indirect relationship to all these contextual factors. The priest needs to make things comprehensible to the host. The priest must produce a sacred atmosphere and must make the host feel that he is participating in something sacred. The use of texts and languages is simply a tool in this process, and a successful priest needs to know how to use this tool to achieve the best results. The contextual factors are presented below in a schematic form:

Comprehension of Different Languages involved in Ritual

	Learned Priest	Non-Learned Priest	Host
Vedic L	Low comprehension	Very Low comprehension	No comprehension
Class. Skt.	High comprehension	Low comprehension	Some Vocabulary
Local L	Full comprehension	Full comprehension	Full comprehension

The observed embedding of language varieties is shown in the diagram below. The outermost frame is that of the local vernacular. Whatever 'comprehension' needs to take place ultimately takes place in relation to this vernacular. Similarly, the Vedic texts exist only as recited segments within a textual frame of classical Sanskrit. In high-end Vedic sacrificial texts, the older Vedic texts are occasionally altered to fit the ritual context, but in most of the latter-day domestic Hindu rituals, the Vedic texts are almost never altered. However, the classical Sanskrit portions are often altered to fit the specific context. Ultimately, the classical Sanskrit portions are a part of the overall performance which is related by the priest to the host/audience through vernacular instructions and explanations. In the diagram below, the inner the circle the more sacred it is, but it also represents the lesser degree of comprehension of meaning. The ultimate goal of the ritual is the creation of the sacred and to this end often the outer linguistic varieties get pulled into the inner circles. The vernaculars get Sanskritized in vocabulary and the classical Sanskrit itself acquires features like pseudo-Vedic accents. Priests often recite vernacular and classical portions with these pseudo-Vedic accents, so much so that an untrained host cannot differentiate these different portions. This is often depicted in the comic situations in Indian films where an unlearned shrewd village priest performs a wedding by reciting Hindi movie songs with a fake Vedic accent.

Spheres of Different Languages

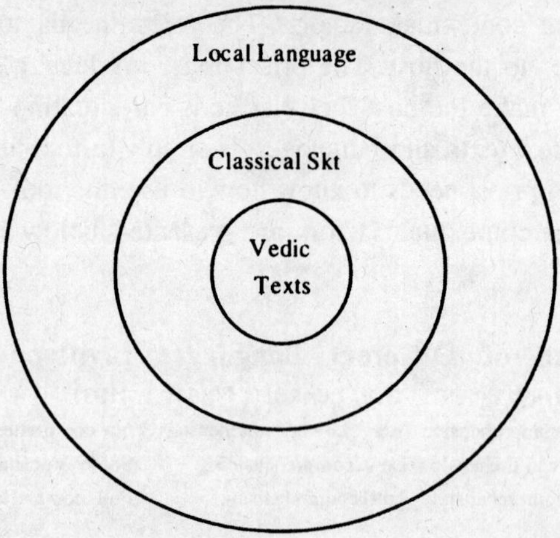

In what follows, we shall examine some salient features of Sanskrit as it is found in priestly performances. As I have already stated, these different features are not historically of the same depth and many vary from region to region and context to context. However, we can learn much about the dynamics of living Sanskrit by examining these features which show us that Sanskrit in its actualization is much more and beyond what is found in the standardized grammars and learned texts edited and published by scholars.

2. Ūha: Linguistic Contextualization of a received ritual formula

We shall begin our exploration with the traditional notion of *ūha.* This term refers to the linguistic contextualization of a received ritual formula. This process already began with the ancient Vedic ritual texts and was continued into the later classical ritual texts. Bronkhorst (1991: 83) explains the original Vedic context of this notion:

> Ūha is the term used to describe the adjustments Vedic mantras undergo to make them fit for other ritual contexts. An original mantra such as *agnaye tvā juṣṭaṁ nirvapāmi*, directed to Agni, can become modified into *sūryāya tvā juṣṭaṁ nirvapāmi*; directed to Sūrya. *Devīr āpaḥ śuddhā yūyam* (*MS* 1.1.11, 1.2.16, 3.10.1; *KS* 3.6), directed to the waters, becomes *deva ājya śuddhaṁ tvam* when directed to clarified butter. Sometimes only the number needs adjustment, as when *āyur āśāste* (*MS* 4.13.9; *TS* 2.6.9.7; *TB* 3.5.10.4) becomes *āyur āśāsāte* or *āyur āśāsate*. Only the gender is modified when *jūr asi dhṛtā manasā juṣṭā viṣṇave tasyās te satyasavasaḥ* (*MS* 1.2.4, 3.7.5; *KS* 2.5, 24.3; *TS* 1.2.4.1, 6.1.7.2; *VS* 4.17; *ŚB* 3.2.4.11; *ŚBK* 4.2.4.9) becomes *jūr asi dhṛto manasā juṣṭo viṣṇave tasya te satyasavasaḥ* because a bull is under discussion.

Bronkhorst also discusses the important question of whether the modified mantras were treated as mantras or as non-mantras, and he shows that while the traditions such as that of Mīmaṁsā reject the mantra status of the modified expressions, there is enough evidence to suggest that "apparently, at one time, modified mantras were mantras."

While we are not directly concerned with this theoretical controversy at this point, it is important to note that at the beginning of his *Mahābhāṣya* (I, p. 1), Patañjali includes the *ūha* among the purposes of studying Sanskrit grammar: *ūhaḥ khalv api / na sarvair liṅgair na ca sarvābhir vibhaktibhir vede mantrā nigaditāḥ / te cāvaśyaṁ yajñagatena yathāyathaṁ vipariṇamayitavyāḥ / tān nāvaiyākaraṇaḥ śaknoti yathāyathaṁ vipariṇamayitum / tasmād adhyeyaṁ vyākaraṇam*, "Ūha as well [is to be included among the purposes]. Mantras are not given in the Vedas with all [possible] genders and case-endings. They need to be appropriately modified by a person involved in ritual. A person not trained in grammar is not capable of properly modifying them. Therefore, one should study grammar." Here, Patañjali brings out the two distinct dimensions: a) the ability to repeat an inherited ritual formula, and b) the ability to modify it to fit a new context. These are clearly distinct abilities. While the first one involves merely the ability of rote memorization and reproduction, the second ability involves comprehension of the received mantra as well as active control over the language of the mantra. With the widening gap between the language of the received mantra and the first language of the priest, the second ability increasingly became problematic. The very expectation that a received formula in an archaic language be appropriately modified, rather than a new formula be produced in the local contemporary vernacular, is indicative of the cultural perception of the different language varieties. The language of the received formula is deemed to be more effective in producing the desired sacred result, but the priest has a relatively lesser control over its grammar, as compared to his own first language.

Formulas in the classical language also had to be appropriately modified to fit the ritual context. Consider the following instruction to the priest/host given in the context of a wedding which involves the giving and receiving of a daughter:

P1: *vācā dattā mayā kanyā putrārthaṁ svīkṛtā tvayā / . . .*
bhrātrādau svīkartari bhrātrartham ityādyūhaḥ kāryaḥ / (C: p. 99)

Here the received formula is stated in the first line: "I have verbally given my daughter and you have accepted her for your son." The second line says: "If the receiver [of the girl] happens to be the brother [of the groom], then the formula should be altered to say, '[you have accepted her] for [your] brother'." Further, the same text suggests that modifications in the formula regarding the age of the girl and other matters may need to be made as well:

P2: *aṣṭavarṣā tv iyaṁ kanyā putravat pālitā mayā / idānīṁ tava putrāya dattā snehena pālyatām // . . .* Footnote: *aṣṭavarṣety atra vadhvā vartamānavatsaroho mātṛpitretarabhrātrādyutsaṅgopaveśane idānīṁ ca tava bhrātra ityādi yathāyatham ūhyam* / (C: p. 114): 'This daughter is only eight years old and has been raised by me like a son. Now she has been given to your son. Please take care of her with love.' [Footnote:] The expression 'eight year old' should be modified to reflect the current age [of the girl]. In case, [the girl, after being given to her in-laws], is going to be seated on the lap of the [older] brother [of the groom] etc., i.e. someone other than the mother and the father [of the groom], then the formula should be appropriately modified to say: '[The girl is given to you] for your brother' etc.

The above instructions are clear indications of the kind of modifications of the received formulas. Insert within this picture the complication that a priest is good enough to repeat the received formulas, but has little active control over Sanskrit. I can refer to two situations which I have observed myself. At the Venkateshwara temple in Pittsburgh, Pennsylvania, (USA), I was waiting in a line of devotees. As each devotee would approach the image of the deity, the priest asked the name of the person and uttered a formulaic blessing: "X+*sya sukham bhavatu.*" The lady ahead of me gave her name as Kamalā, and the priest uttered the blessing: **kamalāsya sukham bhavatu.* The second instance comes from a Hindu wedding I attended in Ann Arbor a few years ago. The priest was a professional engineer with the ability merely to read the printed Sanskrit formulas. During the ritual of giving away the girl to the groom, the priest recited the standard formula: *tava putrāya* "to your son," etc. At that point the person receiving the girl on behalf of the groom said that he was not the father of the groom, but that the groom was his sister's son. The poor engineer priest had to concoct a modified formula on the spot, and after some careful thought, he said: *tava *bhaginīsya putrāya* "to your sister's son."

In both the instances cited above, the priest had little active ability to handle Sanskrit grammar, and produced ungrammatical utterances. However, we must note that neither the priest nor the hosts realized there were any errors, and they were pleased that a proper Sanskrit blessing or ritual promise was carried out. The perception that it all happened in holy Sanskrit was very important to both the performers and the recepients, because it is this perception that leads to the creation of the resulting subjective sacred feeling, and the objective degree of grammaticality or ungrammaticality is of little consequence either to the performer-priest or the host/audience. They are both equally untrained in Sanskrit grammar. Secondly, the linguistic dimension of these modified formulas is worth noting. In both the cases, the ungrammatical forms **kamalāsya* and **bhaginīsya* reflect an extension of the prototypical (masculine) genitive affix *-sya*. This suggests that the priest was either extending this prototypical or most frequent affix to less prototypical contexts, or that the priest, with little understanding of Sanskrit grammar, was merely doing a lexical replacement, maintaining in tact the received *-sya* of the formula. The difference between these theoretical alternatives needs to be tested in ways which are beyond the scope of this paper. Yet the examples reveal the basic linguistic complexity.

3. *Use of honorific* śrī

In middle/late classical Sanskrit, the item *śrī* began its career as an honorific item, along with the elaborate form *śrīmat.* I have extensively dealth with the appearance of the honorific *śrī* in Sanskrit and Prakrit inscriptions in Deshpande 1993c. Here, I shall focus on some dimensions of the behavior of this item in priestly Sanskrit texts. Consider the following instances.

P3. *sarvavighnaharas tasmai śrīgaṇādhipataye namaḥ* / (A)
[Gaṇeśa is the] destroyer of all obstacles. Salutations to him, the honorable [lit. prosperous] lord of the Gaṇa [= tribe, group].

In this passage, the item *śrī* clearly looks like a later add-on to an earlier verse. This is probably the case because the addition of *śrī* creates an extra syllable in the *anuṣṭubh* verse quarter. The eight-syllable segment *gaṇādhipataye namaḥ* perfectly fits the meter. The person who added the item *śrī*, however, may have thought that it was more important to add the honorific *śrī* to the name of the divinity, than to worry about maintaining the metrical pattern. Without going here into a statistical demonstration, I would like to observe that priestly texts which are generally more scholarly have a preference for *OM*, instead of *śrī*.

P4. *OM-kāraḥ sarvatra lakṣmīnārāyaṇābhyāṁ namaḥ* /
umāmaheśvarābhyāṁ namaḥ / (C: Intro., p. 12)

In priestly texts, which are more popular, *śrī* is the most common honorific item, which is added almost to everything, including generic terms like *sarva* 'all' and *amuka* 'so and so'. Besides this, the noteworthy feature of *śrī* is that it is almost never combined in sandhi with the following vowel-initial words. The purpose of this is not hard to see. In sandhi situations, if the audible or visible form of the honorific item is altered, its value as an honorific in the mind of the common listeners may be lost. This feature is found in inscriptions, manuscripts, printed editions and in oral performances. Thus, the pragmatic need to maintain the recognizable identity of this item overrides the grammatical requirement of making the sandhi.

P5. *śrī#iṣṭadevatābhyo namaḥ* /
śrī#etatkarmapradhānadevatābhyo namaḥ /

śrīsarvebhyo devebhyo namaḥ /
śrīsarvebhyo brāhmaṇebhyo namo namaḥ / (D: p. 203)

P6 *śrī#umāmaheśvarābhyāṁ namaḥ* . . . (F: p. 71ff.)

P7. *śrī#umāyai namaḥ* . . . (F: p. 76)

P8. *śrī#arundhatīsahitakaśyapādisapta#ṛṣibhyo namaḥ* (F: p. 102ff.)

P9 śrī *#atraye namaḥ* /, (G: p. 133)

P10. *om ko nāmāsi? śrī#amukaśarmāham bhoḥ* / (K: p. 37)

P11. *aham ācāryas tava śrī#amukaśarman* / (K: p. 12)

P12. *śrī#aṅgirā-ṛṣaye namaḥ* . . . (M: p. 37)

The decision of whether to add *OM* or *śrī*, or both, is a rather subjective decision. Some priests would rather add both the items to gain the maximum effectiveness. In the following passage, the priest not only combines *OM* and *śrī* with the first few salutations, he also replaces the customary *namaḥ* with *svāhā* giving the whole performance a rather archaic Vedic appearance. Such techniques seem to raise the stature of the priest in his own eyes as well as in the eyes of his audiences.

P13. *Oṁ śrīkeśavāya svāhā / Oṁ śrīnārāyaṇāya svāhā / Oṁ śrīmādhavāya svāhā* / [Later *śrī* is dropped] *Oṁ govindāya namaḥ / Oṁ viṣṇave namaḥ / Oṁ madhusūdanāya namaḥ* / . . . (Q)

4. Deliberate splitting of words

In most popular priestly performances, the host has little ability to speak, recite or even repeat Sanskrit. In such cases, at some crucial points, the priest makes the host utter some Sanskrit formulas by prompting him word by word. In such cases of prompting, the long stretches of Sanskrit are broken down into smaller pieces which can be taught one at a time. In the following example, the priest says to the host in Marathi: *mhaṇā* '[Now] say', and then he prompts him phrase by phrase.

P14. *MHAṆĀ - mama # ātmanaḥ # parameśvara # ādnyā[= Skt. jñā] rūpa # sakala # śāstrokta # śrutismṛti # purāṇokta # phalaprāptyartham #*

sakala# durita # upaśama # sarvāpacchāntipūrvaka # sakalamanoratha-siddhyartham... (A)

In the following two instances, first there is a prompted sentence in which the host is made to request the priest to say something, and then the priest says that sentence. In the prompted speech of the host, the long stretches are broken down into smaller pieces. However, when the priest gives the answer, he says it in an unbroken stretch of Sanskrit:

P15. *puṇyāhavācana#phala#samṛddhiḥ astu iti bhavantaḥ bruvantu* / (A), [The priest prompts the host to make the following request]. [O priest], please say: "let there be prosperity as a result of the declaration of an auspicious day."

P16. *puṇyāhavācanaphalasamṛddhirastu* / (A), [The priest responds:] "Let there be prosperity as a result of the declaration of an auspicious day."

Contrast with the above performative sequence the descriptive sequence from a high-end scholarly text, where the scholarly author is addressing the learned priests. Here the text appears with full sandhis and no effort is made to simplify the Sanskrit stretches.

P17 *amukapravarānvitāmukagotrotpannāyāmukaprapautrāyāmuka-pautrāyāmukaputrāyāmukanāmne varāyāmukapravarānvitāma-mukagotrotpannām amukaprapautrīmamukapautrīmamukasya mama putrīmamukanāmnīmimāṁ kanyām*... (C, p. 99). [I give] this daughter of mine, named such and such, [the daughter of me] named so and so, the grand-daughter of so and so, the great-grand-daughter of so and so, born in such and such a Gotra, and possessing such and such Pravaras, to this groom named so and so, born in such and such Gotra and possessing such and such Pravaras, the great-grand-son of so and so, the grandson of so and so, and the son of so and so.

The need to break down the long stretches of Sanskrit to make it easy for the hosts and audiences who repeat those phrases often leads to unexpected breaks in actual performances, as well as in written and printed materials, which show that the prompting priest, or the priestly editor has little comprehension of the contents of the text. The following passage illustrates such unintelligent divisions marked with hyphens in the printed text:

P.18. *agotrākṛti-tvādanaikāntika-tvādalakṣyāgama-tvādaśeṣākara-tvāt prapañcālasa-tvādanārambhaka-vāt tvam ekā parabrahmarūpeṇa siddhā* / . . . *asādhāraṇa-tvādasambandhaka-tvādabhinnāśraya-tvādanākāraka-tvāt avidyātmaka-tvādanādyantaka-tvāt tvam ekā*

parabrahmarūpeṇa siddhā /. . .
(M: p. 69)

4. Simplification to help host-participation

Part of the success of a priest lies in his ability to make the host and the audience feel that they are actively participating in the ritual action as well as in the linguistic exchanges in Sanskrit. Above we have seen certain kinds of simplification in breaking down the sandhis. However, the process of simplification takes many different forms. In the performance recorded in (B), the priest asks the host to recite *OM* 15 times while he himself recites the Vedic mantras. This assumes that the host does not have the ability to recite those Vedic mantras, but that the host can easily repeat the sacred syllable *OM*. In the performance recorded in Q, the priest (= Sant Keshavdas) instructs:

P19. Now offer the flowers one by one as you chant these 108 holy names of God. As I chant the mantra, you devotees chant *namaḥ*.
(Priest:) *oṁ śrī satyadevāya*
(People:) *namaḥ*
(Priest:) *oṁ satyātmane*
(People:) *namaḥ*
(Priest:) *oṁ satyabhūtāya*
(People:) *namaḥ* (Q)

It is clear from the recorded tape, that initially fewer people participate in saying *namaḥ*, and that gradually more and more people participate, and their utterance becomes more and more confident. In the same source (Q), the priest simplifies the request for the declaration of the auspicious day to a single word *puṇyāham*, and asks the audience to say this word three times. Contrast the following with the relatively more elaborate prompting cited above in P15 and P16.

P20. *adya kariṣyamāṇaśrīsatyanārāyaṇavratākhyakarmaṇaḥ puṇyāham bhavanto bruvantu* # say # *puṇyāham* # (audience:) *puṇyāham* # (priest:) *puṇyāham* # (audience:) *puṇyāham* # (priest:) *puṇyāham* # (audience:) *puṇyāham*. (Q)

Another mode of linguistic simplification is to replace the complex verb forms of Sanskrit with verbal nouns followed by a common verb. Thus, instead of using the finite verbs *dhyāyāmi, āvāhayāmi*, etc., it is simpler to have the nouns *dhyānam, āvāhanam* etc. followed by a shared repeated verb *samarpayāmi* 'I offer'. This substitutes the complex verbal syntax of older Sanskrit with a more Middle Indic periphrastic construction type. In the passage below, most finite verbs are replaced by *samarpayāmi.* The only independent verbs in the passage below occur in the phrases *dīpaṁ darśayāmi* and *dhūpam āghrāpayāmi,* and even these are, as I have personally observed, often replaced by the common verb *samarpayāmi.*

P21. *dhyāyāmi / dhyānam samarpayāmi / . . . āvāhanaṁ samarpayāmi / . . . āsanaṁ samarpayāmi / . . . pādyaṁ samarpayāmi / . . . arghyaṁ samarpayāmi / . . . ācamanaṁ samarpayāmi / . . . snānaṁ samarpayāmi / . . . vastraṁ samarpayāmi / . . . yajñopavītaṁ samarpayāmi / . . . gandhaṁ samarpayāmi / . . . puṣpaṁ samarpayami / . . . akṣatān samarpayāmi / . . . dhūpam āghrāpayāmi / . . . dīpaṁ darśayāmi / . . . naivedyaṁ samarpayāmi / . . . maṅgalanīrājanaṁ samarpayāmi / . . . mantrapuṣpaṁ samarpayāmi / . . . pradakṣiṇānamaskārān samarpayāmi / . . . prārthanāṁ samarpayāmi / . . . dhyāna#āvāhanādi#ṣoḍaśopacārapūjā# ārādhanaṁ samarpayāmi / . . .* (Q)

5. Lack of comprehension of the meaning of vedic mantras and their new ritual employment

As one moves from the early period of the Brāhmaṇas and Śrautasūtras to the later period of Purāṇic and Tantrik ritual, one finds that the composers of the later ritual texts had a great need to incorporate the ancient Vedic mantras in the new ritual settings to enhance the perceived sanctity of these latter-day rituals. The late Vedic notion of the ideal employment of mantras (*viniyoga*) in ritual is expressed in the doctrine of *rūpasamṛddhi* 'perfection of ritual form', *etad vai yajñasya samṛddhaṁ yad rūpasamṛddhaṁ yat karma kriyamāṇaṁ ṛg anuvadati, Aitareya-Brāhmaṇa,* 1.13, "This is the perfection of a sacrifice, namely the perfection of ritual form, in that a ritual action being carried out is echoed by the mantra being recited." In an ideal setting, this of course demands that one fully understands the meaning of the mantras and that the ritual employment of the mantras is guided in terms of their understood meaning. However, the situation was different in the period of Purāṇic and Tantrik rituals. Nārāyaṇabhaṭṭa, the author of *Prayogaratna*, refers to many of the difficulties involved:

P22. *idaṁ kāryam aneneti na kvacid dṛśyate vidhiḥ /*
liṅgād evedamarthatvaṁ yeṣāṁ te mantrasaṁjñitāḥ // (C: p. 48)
Sometimes one does not find an exact prescriptive statement that such and such a ritual is to be performed with such and such a mantra. Only from the indications in the mantra does one determine their ritual employment.

P23. *avijñātasvarā mantrāḥ prayoktavyāḥ prayoktṛbhiḥ /*
ekaśrutyaiva homeṣu vijñātāś ca vikalpataḥ // (C: p. 48)
The mantras whose accentuation is not known may be recited by the reciters in monotone while making oblations. Those mantras whose accentuation is known may be recited optionally in monotone.

P24. *yad akṣarapadabhraṣṭam mātrāhīnaṁ tu yad bhavet /*
tat sarvaṁ kṣamyatāṁ devi . . . / (R: p. 16)
This recitation of mine which may lack the proper syllables and words, and which may also lack the proper pronunciation of vowel lengths, O Goddess, please forgive all of that.

Proper pronunciation and comprehension of Sanskrit was already problematic by the time of Patañjali, and I have discussed elsewhere at length how the grammarians tried to improve the situation by proposing to educate the priests in the science of grammar (Deshpande 1993, Chapter II). Here we shall focus on how the lack of comprehension of the original meaning of the mantras combined with the increasing attention to the magical power of sounds, and how this attention to the sounds created new perceptions as to the possible divinities to be propitiated with these mantras. This is indeed similar to what happens in folk-etymologies. The following examples illustrate this new employment of the old Vedic mantras and the likely basis for this new employment. Just to reiterate my caution, these 'new' *viniyoga*s are new only in relative terms. They are several hundred years old, and their actual starting point needs a separate detailed chronological investigation. Here, I am simply pointing out the shifting understanding. For the context of these mantras see Gudrun Bühnemann (1989).

P25. *tatra brahma jajñānaṁ gotamo vāmadevo brahmā triṣṭup / brahmāvāhane viniyogaḥ / Oṁ brahma jajñānam prathamam purastāt . . .* (AV 4.1.1) *anena pālikāmadhye brahmāṇam āvāhayet /* (C: p. 11). For the mantra *brahma jajñānam* (AV 4.1.1), the Ṛṣi is Gotama Vāmadeva, its deity is Brahmā, and its meter is Triṣṭubh. It is used to invoke god Brahmā. With this mantra, one should invite Brahmā to come and reside in the sacrificial plate.

In this mantra, originally there is no reference to the divinity Brahmā, the creator god. The mantra actually contains a reference to the neuter Brahman. However, for the latter-day priesthood, the resemblance between *brahma* and *brahmā* was good enough to use this mantra to invoke Brahmā.

P26. *dadhikrāvṇa ity asya gotamo vāmadevo dadhikrāvānuṣṭup / Oṁ dadhikrāvṇo akāriṣaṁ jiṣṇor aśvasya vājinaḥ / surabhi no mukhā karat pra ṇa āyūṁṣi tāriṣat* / (ṚV 4.39.6) *anena dadhi* . . . (C: p. 22).
For the mantra *dadhikrāvṇa* etc. (ṚV 4.39.6), the Ṛṣi is Gotama Vāmadeva, the deity is Dadhikrāvan, and the meter is the Anuṣṭubh. . . . With this mantra, offer yogurt (*dadhi*)...

The priest even recites the traditional line which says that the deity of this mantra is Dadhikrāvan, which is a name of a horse. There is no reference to *dadhi* 'yogurt'. However, the fact that the priest does not comprehend the original mantra, but that he hears the segment *dadhi* must have led to this latter-day employment of the mantra in offering yogurt to a divinity. The way this passage is framed, it seems that even the explicit statement that the deity of the mantra was Dadhikrāvan was probably not fully understood, and hence had little influence in deciding the employment of the mantra.

P27. *gaurīr mimāyety asya dīrghatamā umāvāhane viniyogaḥ / gaurīr mimāya salilāni takṣaty ekapadī dvipadī sā catuṣpadī / aṣṭāpadī navapadī babhūvuṣī sahasrākṣarā parame vyoman* // (ṚV 1.164.41) (C: p. 24).
For the mantra *gaurīr mimāya* etc. (ṚV 1.164.41), the Ṛṣi is Dīrghatamas, and it is used to invoke [the goddess] Umā.

Here the word *gaurīr* has no connection with Gaurī or Pārvatī. The original word refers to a cow. However, the expression *gaurīr* has sufficient sound-similarity to the word *gaurī* of the classical language, where it can refer to the goddess Umā or Pārvatī. This was apparently sufficient to use the mantra to invoke Umā.

P28. *śukraṁ te anyad ity asya bharadvājaḥ śukras triṣṭup / śukrāvāhane viniyogaḥ / Oṁ śukraṁ te anyad yajataṁ te anyad viṣurūpe ahanī dyaur ivāsi / viśvā hi māyā avasi svadhāvo bhadrā te pūṣann iha rātir astu* / (ṚV 6.58.1), (C: p. 25)
For the mantra *śukraṁ te anyat* etc. (ṚV 6.58.1), the Ṛṣi is Bharadvāja,

the deity is Śukra, and the meter is Triṣṭubh. The mantra is used to invoke the deity Śukra (= Venus).

In mantra ṚV 6.58.1, the word *śukra* has absolutely no reference to the planet/deity Śukra (= Venus). However, the lack of comprehension of the mantra combined with the mere occurrence of the word *śukram* allowed the latter-day priestly tradition to use this mantra to invoke the planet/deity Śukra.

P29. *śam agnir irimbiṭhiḥ śanaiścara uṣṇik / śanaiścarāvāhane viniyogaḥ / Oṁ śam agnir agnibhiḥ karac chaṁ nas tapatu sūryaḥ / śaṁ vāto vātv arapā apasridhaḥ / . . .* (ṚV 8.18.9) (C: p. 26). Of the mantra *śam agniḥ* etc. (ṚV 8.18.9), the Ṛṣi is Irimbiṭhi, the deity is Śanaiścara (= Saturn), and the meter is Uṣṇik. It is used to invoke the deity Saturn.

There is clearly no reference whatsoever to the deity/planet Śanaiścara, or Śani as he is known later, in this mantra from the *Ṛgveda*. At best one can say that the priest who did not fully comprehend the meaning of the mantra heard the sound sequences *śam* and *śaṁ naḥ*, and associated these sound sequences with Śani or Śanaiścara. This sound-similarity was enough to extend the mantra to the new deity.

P30. *sacitram ity asya bharadvājaś citraguptas triṣṭup / citraguptāvāhane viniyogaḥ / Oṁ sa citracitraṁ citayantam asme citrakṣatracitratamaṁ vayodhām / candraṁ rayim puruvīram bṛhantaṁ candra candrābhir gṛṇate yuvasva /* (ṚV 6.6.7) (C: p. 27). For the mantra *sa citram* etc. (ṚV 6.6.7), the Ṛṣi is Bharadvāja, the deity is Citragupta, and the meter is Uṣṇik. It is used to invoke the deity Citragupta.

In the original mantra of the Ṛgveda, there is no reference to the latter-day deity Citragupta, the infamous accountant at the court of Yama, who reads out the Karmic account to the newly arrived souls of the departed. However, the fact that the mantra contains the sound sequence *citram* was sufficient for the priest to extend the application of this mantra to Citragupta.

P31. *jātavedase mārīcaḥ kaśyapo durgā triṣṭup / durgāvāhane viniyogaḥ / Oṁ jātavedase sunavāma somam arātīyato nidahāti vedaḥ / sa naḥ parṣad ati durgāṇi viśvā nāveva sindhuṁ duritātyagniḥ / . . .* (ṚV 1.99.1) (C: p. 27). For the mantra *jātavedase* etc. (ṚV 1.99.1), the Ṛṣi is Mārīca Kaśyapa, the deity is goddess Durgā, and the meter is Triṣṭubh. The mantra is used to invoke goddess Durgā.

In the original Ṛgvedic mantra cited here, there is no reference whatsoever to goddess Durgā or Pārvatī. However, the mantra contains the neuter accusative form *durgāṇi*, which contains the sequence *durgā*. It is this sequence that allows the latter-day priest to extend the mantra to invoke goddess Durgā.

P32. *gaṇānāṁ tvā śaunako gṛtsamado gaṇapatir jagatī / gaṇapatiprītyarthe . . . / Oṁ gaṇānāṁ tvā gaṇapatiṁ havāmahe kaviṁ kavīnām upamaśravastamam / jyeṣṭharājam brahmaṇām brahmaṇaspata ā naḥ śṛṇvann ūtibhiḥ sīda sādanam* / . . . (ṚV 2.23.1) (C: p. 59). For the mantra *gaṇānāṁ tvā* etc. (ṚV 2.23.1), the Ṛṣi is Śaunaka Gṛtsamada, the deity is Gaṇapati (= the elephant-faced Gaṇeśa), and the meter is Jagatī. The mantra is used to propitiate the deity Gaṇapati.

The original Ṛgvedic mantra has most certainly no reference to the latter-day deity, the elephant-faced Gaṇeśa, the son of Śiva. However, the mantra does contain the expression *gaṇapatim*. The priest makes a natural leap from this expression to the identification of the *gaṇapati* in the mantra with the latter-day Gaṇeśa, who is also commonly called Gaṇapati.

In this context, one needs to keep in mind several factors. The first is that these new Viniyogas for the ancient Ṛgvedic mantras go back to a fairly old Purāṇic period, and I do not want to suggest that the modern-day priests are responsible for this transference. Referring to Vedic mantras used to worship the planets, G. Bühnemann says:

> At first sight the selection of the Vedic mantras seems incidental. However, a closer examination of recited mantras reveals that there is a long tradition for their employment in specific contexts, and that their employment is quite meaningful and appropriate in many cases. (G. Bühneman 1989:6)

Bühnemann's last comment is intriguing to me. While I suspect that the ignorance of the meaning of the original mantra may have played an important role in these transferences, there is a sort of traditional authorization for such interpretations found in earlier sources. Elizarenkova (1995: 124ff.) has pointed out that, already in the hymns of the Ṛgveda, one sees a poetic/ritual tendency to incorporate echoes of the name of the deity in the composition of the Ṛgvedic hymns. Thus, in addition to the direct mention of the name of the deity being invoked, one also hears indirect soundings or echoes of that name in the hymns. This is cleverly done through the repeated use of sound-sequences which come very close to the sound-sequence in the actual name of the divinity. Secondly, Yāska does offer as a last-ditch option to explain the meaning of a word through the shared sounds between the word and the possible sources from which this word is built up. As a final last-ditch solution, Yāska says that commonality of even one vowel or consonant may be sufficient to make a connection, and that an etymologist can never say no to a word. He must attempt an etymology (cf. *avidyamāne sāmānye 'py akṣaravarṇasāmānyān nirbrūyāt, na tv eva na nirbrūyāt,* Nirukta 2.1). Medieval Mīmāṁsakas like Someśvara continued to look up to Yāska for guidance in this respect (*niruktād avagato yo dhātv-arthapūrvako nāmārthaḥ / sarvaṁ nāma dhātujam ity arthakalpanā-dvāraṁ nirukte pradarśitam, Nyāyasudhā,* Fasc. III, pp. 225-226). These historical and theoretical antecedents were among the possible factors which allowed the development of new applications for the old mantras. A similar medieval extension of an ancient Ṛgvedic hymn beginning with the words *dve virūpe* (*ṚV* 1.95) to the worship of Viṭṭhala in Maharashtra has been discussed extensively by R.C. Dhere. Dhere (1984: 105-6, 277-79, 283, 338-339) has shown in detail how the worship of Viṭṭhala-Viṣṇu in Pandharpur in Maharashtra is a case of Sanskritization of the folk-tradition centered around the divinity Birobā. The similarity of the name *birobā* and a Prākritized pronunciation and/or understanding of the expression *virūpe* in the Vedic mantra allowed the Brahmins of Pandharpur to claim that the Vedic hymn is in praise of Viṭṭhala/Viṭhobā. There are several medieval commentaries on this hymn composed by priests from Pandharpur to show how the words of the hymn can be applied to Viṭṭhala/Viṭhobā, e.g. see the *Dve Virūpe Sūktabhāṣya* of Kṛṣṇācārya.

6. Vernacularization of sanskrit

Now we shall turn more directly to the signs of linguistic Vernacularization of Sanskrit in the context of its priestly use. Of course, it should be clear that such vernacularization of Sanskrit in the context of its priestly use is only a special case of the more general phenomenon of vernacularization of Sanskrit (cf. R. Salomon 1989 and Deshpande 1993), and hence in many respects this vernacularization is not completely distinguishable from other cases of Sanskritization. The special features of priestly Sanskrit may be noticed in the specific texts, vocabularies, and contexts.

6.1. Vernacular Pronunciation of Sanskrit

In the priestly use of Sanskrit, while one may superficially think in terms of code-switching, the phonetics of the language use seems to be generally seemless, and this seemless phonetics is fully dominated by the vernacular pattern. Often Sanskrit words are uttered as chunks and then vernacularized in divers ways. The Sanskrit sequences *mādhavāya namaḥ* and *keśavāya namaḥ* in the Marathi-speaking areas are heard diversly as *mādhvāyanmaḥ* and *keśvāyanmaḥ*, or as *mādhavāyanmaḥ* and *keśavāyanmaḥ* as in the recorded tape (A).

In the same recorded tape (A), one hears the sequence *akṣatāṁ ca samarpayāmi*, which presents an interesting example. In the original older sources, the expression is *akṣatān*. This word which means 'unbroken' refers to unbroken rice-grains which are offered to the divinity. The word for rice-grains is usually *taṇḍula*, which is a masculine word, and therefore, the accusative plural of the adjective is *akṣatān*. As the priestly reciters of the formulas had little grammatical understanding, the original expression *akṣatān*, with a relatively less frequent word-final *ān*, was generalized to the form *akṣatāṁ*, ending in the more commonplace word-final *anusvāra*. With this *anusvāra*-final pronunciation becoming the most common pronunciation, the expression was reinterpreted as the feminine accusative singular of a reconceptualized new base *akṣatā*. The guess that this is what happened gets strengthened when we notice that the word in Marathi for the unbroken rice-grain used in such ceremonies is the feminine word *akṣatā*. Clearly, the source of this Marathi word must be traced to the standardized mispronunciation *akṣatāṁ* in the Marathi-speaking region. This phenomenon must be fairly old, and can probably be dated by the appearance of the feminine word *akṣatā* in modern Indian languages like Marathi.

Among the verses recited by the priest in the recording (A), one hears the quarter line: *śrīkaraśrīdharaśrīvaraśrīśaṁkara viṣṇo*. This is part of a Sanskrit *ārati* prayer. The metrical pattern actually requires that the repeated syllable *ra* before *śrī* be a light (*laghu*) syllable. This becomes possible through a non-emphatic pronunciation of *śr*. Such a pronuciation of *r*-clusters is attested in languages like Marathi, e.g. *purī / puryā*. In the word *puryā*, the first syllable *pu* is a light syllable. If this were a genuine Sanskrit word, pronounced in the canonical Sanskrit fashion, the first syllable would be a heavy syllable. Such occasional Prakritic pronuciations of Sanskrit consonant clusters are noticed even by the commentators of metrical treatises like *Vṛttaratnākara* (commentary of Nārāyaṇabhaṭṭa, pp. 11ff). Nārāyaṇabhaṭṭa cites examples from works like *Rāmāyaṇa, Kumārasambhava*, and *Śiśupālavadha*. He uses the term *tīvraprayatna* or *atīva tīvraprayatna* to describe this pronunciation of consonant clusters. Perhaps, the word *tīvra* here does not mean 'sharp', but 'quick' or 'rapid'. Though these commentators do not call this phenomenon Prakritic, they notice it in both Sanskrit and Prakrit examples. Similar features have been noticed in the Buddhist Hybrid Sanskrit works by Siddheshwar Varma (1929).

In the pronunciation of Vernacular Sanskrit, we need to recognize that Vernacular Sanskrit is a sort of 'Interlanguage', which stands between the Vernacular and the canonical Sanskrit patterns. The Vernacular Sanskrit is not some stand-alone variety of Sanskrit with entirely consistent grammatical, phonetic, or lexical resources. As an 'in-between' variety, it has a rather 'utilitarian' access to both, the vernacular and the classical language. Thus, depending upon the necessity of the meter etc., one finds that one switches from vernacular to classical pronunciation of sounds. Consider, the two occurrences of the consonant-cluster *pr* in the following example. The Ārati of Gaṇeśa (R: p. 26) contains the line *garuḍaprāñjalisaktaṁ śaṅkarapriyabhaktam*. Here, the syllable *ḍa* in the word *garuḍa* needs to be metrically heavy (*guru*). This is presumably (= my guess based on observation and participation in the recitation of such Āratīs) achieved by pronouncing *pr* after *garuḍa* in the standard Sanskritic fashion. However, the syllable *ra* in *śaṅkara* needs to be metrically light (*laghu*). This is achieved by using the non-emphatic vernacular pronunciation for the following *pr*. Thus, the same line has Sanskritic and vernacular pronunciations for *pr*.

As in the pronunciation of consonant-clusters, the vernacular Sanskrit found in priestly recitations also shows 'need-based' choice in the combination of the word-final *m* with the following vowel. The classical Sanskrit pattern does not allow a hiatus between the word-final *m* and the following vowel, though varius kinds of hiatus-instances are observed in Purāṇic, epic, and other variaties of Sanskrit. If the word-final *m* is not combined with the following vowel, then the word-final syllable ending in *m* becomes invariably a heavy (*guru*) syllable. If the *m* is combined with the following vowel, then the vowel before *m* can be light or heavy, depending upon its own quantity.. In the following Ārati of Śiva, we find instances of both types, used as needed to fulfill the metrical requirements:

P33. Śivan īrājanārtiḥ - (I have marked the hiatus required by the meter with '#'].
Oṁ jaya gaṅgādhara hara jaya girijādhīśā /
tvam mām pālaya nityaṁ kṛpayā jagadīśā //
vāmavibhāge girijārūpam # atilalitam //
avalokayati maheśam # īśam # abhinatvā //
dhyānam # āratisamaye hṛdaye # ati kṛtvā //
rāmas trijaṭānatham # īśam # abhinatvā // (D: 203)

Many modern IA languages show the loss of the final *a* of Sanskrit words. For example, the Sanskrit word *vaṭa* is pronounced as *vaḍ* in Marathi. The NIA loss of final *a* vowels allows the metrically regular pronunciation of the vernacular Sanskrit verse-quarters like *vaṭasāvitryai namas te 'stu /*, (G: p. 10). Here, this quarter-line of a Śloka verse, if pronounced in canonical Sanskrit fashion, would give us an extra syllable. However, a Prakritic pronunciation of *vaṭa* as *vaṭ*, with the loss of the final *a*, allows this line to fit the requirements of the meter.

Prakritic pronunciations create other linguistic variations as well. Both the words *āhvāna* 'invoking, calling' and *āvāhana* 'bringing someone hither' are known to the ancient Sanskrit usage. However, several factors complicate the process of Prakritization or vernacularization of Sanskrit. The Sanskrit cluster *-hv-* gets metathesized to *-vh-* in its Prakritic pronunciation. This reduces the difference between these words and they become phonetically close equivalents. In the Puraṇic verses recited during the Pūjā performances, one finds both the words, e.g. *āvāhanaṁ na jānāmi* 'I do not know *āvāhana*' (B) and *kurve ghaṇṭāravaṁ tatra devatāhvānalakṣaṇam* 'I make the noise of the Ghaṇṭā bell which is a way of invoking the deities' (B). The Marathi glosses (cf. *devatānce āvāhan*) generally render both *āvāhana* and *āhvāna* with the term *āvāhana*, rather than with *āhvāna* (= *āvhān*, in

Marathi pronunciation). At least within the Marathi-speaking region, the choice of *āvāhana* over *āhvāna* (= *āvhān*) for glossing both of these terms is most probably dictated by the peculiar semantics of *āvhān* in Marathi. The word *āvhān* in Marathi has the meaning of 'to extend a challenge', (cf. Marathi: *āvhān deṇe*) and therefore, the priestly usage of *āvāhana* and *āhvāna* makes better sense to the modern audience if rendered with *āvāhana*, rather than with *āhvāna*. One may make a guess that a text such as *kurve ghaṇṭāravaṁ tatra devatāhvānalakṣaṇam* either predates the change in the meaning of the word *āhvāna*, or comes from a community or region where this change was not operative.

6.2. Vernacular Vocabulary in Sanskrit

Inclusion of vernacular vocabulary in changed or unchanged form is indeed very common in the priestly formulas. Thus, referring to the sacred thread which symbolizes the serpent divinity Śeṣa or Ananta, one may find the word *anantasūtra* side by side with the more vernacular expression *doraka*, cf. Marathi *dorā* 'thread'.

P34. *atha DORAKAbandhanamantraḥ* / referring to *anantasūtra* (G: p. 171).

Going a step beyond the mere inclusion of vernacular vocabulary, one finds various patterns of combining vernacular and canonical Sanskrit grammatical patterns. For example, the Sanskrit verb root *khād* 'to eat' is reduced to a mere *khā* in languages like Hindi and Marathi. This vernacular root *khā* is occasionally inducted back into vernacular Sanskrit, and declined like a Sanskrit root ending in *ā*. The verb forms *khāhi khāhi* in the following citation are clearly in imitation of genuine Sanskrit forms like *pāhi*.

P35. *mama śatrūn KHĀHI KHĀHI māraya māraya* . . . (M: p. 37)

The South Indian tradition of Maṇipravāḷam poetry is a well known example of formally combining Sanskrit and Vernacular vocabulary in the same poetic composition. This pattern is, however, not restricted to South Indian languages, but is found in many North Indian languages as well. Many devotional poems composed by Tulasīdās show a fascinating mixture of Sanskrit and medieval dialects of North India. The same sort of mixture is evident in the Āratī literature, which incorporates features of Bhakti and ritual traditions. Here is a sample Āratī of Śiva. The relevant segment contains a description of Gaurī.

P36. *kokilakūjitaKHELATAhaṁsā vanalalitā //*
racayati kalākalāpam nṛtyati MUDAsahitā //
tanmadhye haranikaṭe gaurī MUDAsahitā //
indrādikasurasevita (no case-ending) *nāmayate ŚĪŚAM //*
vibudhavadhūr bahu nṛtyati hṛdaye MUDAsahitā //
DHINAKATA THAI THAI DHINAKATA
mṛdaṅga (no case-ending) *vādayate //*
MUṆḌAI racayati mālā (no case ending) *pannagam upavītam //*
śaṅkhaninādam kṛtvā JHALLARI (no case-ending) *nādayate //*
(D: p. 203)

Here, *khelata* is a vernacular Hindi expression. The word *śīśam* is interesting in that it takes the vernacular Hindi word *śīś* [= Skt. *śīrṣa*], and makes a Sanskritic accusative out of it. The repeated word *mudasahitā* shows that the Sanskritic *mud* has been replaced with *muda*. A genuine Sanskritic combination of *mud+sahitā* would have resulted with sandhi in *mutsahitā*, which would have been essentially unrecognizable to the popular audience of this Āratī composition. Several Sanskrit words like *mṛdaṅga* and *mālā*, which are syntactically accusative, are given without the Sanskrit accusative affix. In the case of *mṛdaṅga vādayate*, one could perhaps suggest that the addition of the accusative affix after *mṛdaṅga* may have led to a metrical violation. But such is not the case with *racayati mālā*. A possible explanation which may account for both of these cases is that this lack of the accusative affix is a reflection of a lack of overt accusative marking in many Hindi dialects, cf. *rām ām* [no overt accusative marking after *ām*] *khātā hai* 'Rām eats a mango'. Thus, even the grammars of Sanskrit and the vernacular are inextricably mixed in this composition.

Many rituals or portions of rituals developed in specific regions and were probably of non-Sanskritic origin. However, these local rituals were inextricably combined with the more Sanskritic rituals recorded in the Gṛhyasūtras and Dharmasūtras. Even these texts admit the great diversity of such rituals in different regions (*janapada*) and villages (*grāma*), and advise that these specific local traditions be honored especially in the course of the wedding ceremony (cf. *atha khalūccāvacā janapadadharmā grāmadharmāś ca tān vivāhe pratīyāt / yat tu samānaṁ tad vakṣyāmaḥ*, Āśvalāyanagṛhyasūtra 1.7.1.2). Following the advice of the Gṛhyasūtras, the latter-day priest class produced new Sanskrit formulas for these local rituals, and these new formulas incorporated the vernacular names of the local rituals. Notice the incorporation of the vernacular Marathi names for the rituals *sākharapuḍā* and *śālamudī* in the Sanskrit formulas for wedding rituals from the region of Maharashtra.

P37. *vivāhāṅgabhūtam SĀKHARAPUḌĀkhyaṁ karma kariṣye* . . . (F: Pt. II, p. 121) I shall perform the rite called *sākharapuḍā*, which is part of the wedding ceremony.

P38. *vivahāṅgabhūtam ŚĀLAMUDĪkarma kariṣye* . . . (F: Pt. II, p. 130)

Every Pūjā begins with a declaration called *saṁkalpa*, which states, among other matters, the specifics of time and place. In specifying the place, the usual formula contains words like: *bharatakhaṇḍe bharatavarṣe dakṣiṇāpathe godāvaryāḥ dakṣiṇe tīre* etc., "In the continent of Bharata, in the land of Bharata, in the southern region, on the southern bank of Godāvarī . . . " As we approach the modern period, we begin to see occasional changes made in this formula to fit the more modern conceptions. For example, the formula cited below refers to *Hindusthānadeśa* as the region where the ritual is going to take place.

P39. *bharatakhaṇḍe HINDUṢTHĀNAdeśe* . . . (F: Pt. II, p. 147)

This reminds me of two situations of Hindu weddings which I observed in the US during the last few years. On one occasion, the priest recited the formula *bharatakhaṇḍe bharatavarṣe* etc. without any modification. After the ceremony was over, I asked the priest for an explanation. The clever priest, who had not thought of this problem before, responded by saying that all the regions of the world where Indian immigrants have settled are now included in the region referred to by *bharatakhaṇḍe bharatadeśe*. On the other hand, I have observed other Hindu priests in my state of Michigan adjusting the traditional formula of *saṁkalpa* to reflect the changed geography: *amerikākhaṇḍe amerikādeśe miśiganrājye anārbarnagare huron-nadyās tīre*, "in the continent of America, in the country of America, in the state of Michigan, in the city of Ann Arbor, on the bank of the Huron river." This is simply an extension of the process that had already occurred in the different regions of India.

6.3. Grammatical Deviations

Often one notices that Sanskrit compositions produced by the priestly class attempt to Sanskritize the local religious tradition by incorporating the local place-names and the local names of divinities. Such compositions often become so popular that they become an inextricable feature of the local ritual traditions. Consider the following verse which is invariably heard in the wedding ceremonies in Maharashtra.

P40. *svasti śrīgaṇanāyakaṁ gajamukham MOREŚVARAṀ siddhidam /*
BALLĀḶAM MURAḌAṀ vināyakaMAHAṂ cintāmaṇiṁ
ŚRĪVARAM // LEṆYĀDRIṂ girijāṭmakaṁ suvaradaṁ/
vighneśvaraṁ VOJHARAM / grāme RĀṀJAṆAsaṁsthito gaṇapatiḥ
kuryāt sadā maṅgalam // (N: p. 46)

This verse is found with several different varient readings. Here, I shall discuss only the version given above. The verse incorporates the names of the famous eight Gaṇeśas regionally known as the Aṣṭavināyakas. Gaṇeśa in *morgā̃v* [= Skt. *mayūragrāma*] is cited as *moreśvara* [< Skt. *mayūreśvara*]. Gaṇeśa in Muruḍ is cited by the name *ballāḷa*. Notice that the name of Gaṇeśa as well as the place name are both in accusative,. which, on the face of it, is not syntactically motivated. One priest expained to me that the word *svasti* is the verb and that it is equivalent to *namaskaromi*, and the names of Gaṇeśa are in the accusative because they are the objects of this verb. Perhaps, some such conception may explain the accusative of the Gaṇeśa names. How about the accusative of the place name? My best guess is that this is a rendering of the Marathi affix *-lā*, which can be added to a place-name in the locative sense. But the same affix is more commonly used as an accusative/dative affix. The priest replaced this Marathi *-lā* with the Sanskrit accusative affix *-am*. The next sequence *vināyakamaham* is somewhat intriguing. If broken into *vināyakam+aham*, one can understand the accusative *vināyakam*, but the following *aham* makes little sense. In fact, this is a reference to Vināyaka in the town of Mahaḍ, which is simply shortened for the sake of the meter into *maham*, and compounded with the deity-name *vināyaka*. After that, we have a reference to Cintāmaṇi in the town of Śrīvara. The word *śrīvara* is a Sanskritization of the Marathi place-name *theür*. This is followed by the reference to

Girijātmaja at Leṇyādri. The word *leṇyādri* is derived from a combination of Marathi *leṇe* 'cave-temple' and Sanskrit *adri* 'mountain'. Then we have a reference to Vighneśvara in Vojhara. The word *vojhara* is a Sanskritization of Marathi *ozar*, where *z* is an alveolar sound non-existent in Sanskrit. The priests actually pronounce the printed word *vojharam* as *vozaram* with the Marathi sound *z*. Additionally, the change of *o* to *vo* was probably metrically motivated. The priestly author probably thought that if he used the word as *ozaram*, the initial *o* would probably combine with the preceding *m*, and that would lead to a metrical deviation. In the final line of the verse, the priestly author shifts to the nominative case for the final reference to Gaṇapati most probably to syntactically link up with the common verse-ending *kuryāt sadā maṅgalam*. However, the portion *grāme rāṁjaṇasaṁsthito gaṇapatiḥ* has its own interesting displacement of constituents. The word *rāṁjaṇagrāma* is a Sanskritized form of Marathi *rāṁdzaṇ gā̃v*. Phonetically, the sound *dz* is alveolar in Marathi, but Marathi uses the same written character for this sound and for the sound *j* of Sanskrit. Secondly, the Sanskrit phrase, grammatically speaking, should have been *rāṁjaṇagrāme saṁsthito gaṇapatiḥ*. However, to fit the meter, this was altered to *grāme rāṁjaṇasaṁsthito gaṇapatiḥ*. This is incomprehensible to a non-Marathi listener. However, a Marathi listener has hardly any doubt as to what the verse is refering to. Additionally, no Marathi priest recites this phrase with a true Sanskritic sound *j*. If one were to pronounce the word *rāṁjaṇa* with a true Sanskritic *j*, the listener would not recognize this as a reference to Ranjangaon. This verse and the extremely high frequency with which it is recited and listened to by Marathi speakers raise interesting issues about the performance and comprehension of the priestly variety of Sanskrit. It is a fact that after listening to the phrase *grāme rāṁjaṇasaṁsthito gaṇapatiḥ*, the Marathi listener recognizes this as a reference to Gaṇeśa in the village of Ranjangaon, and not as "Gaṇapati, in the village, sitting in a *rāndzaṇ* 'clay water-pot'." What this means is that the comprehension and the production of priestly Sanskrit place little value on the strict rules of Sanskrit grammar, and place a higher value on the contextual and situational understanding of a given phrase. Specific vernacular features of the phrase, as it is performed, such as the Marathi alveolar pronunciation (*dz*) for the Sanskritic *j*, aid in the contextual recognition and comprehension of the Sanskrit phrase. In this pragmatic sense, the local vernacular features override the received canonical Sanskrit features.

On other occasions, deviations from the norm of the classical language may be produced either through a lack of proper discrimination between Sanskrit and the Vernacular, or perhaps for specific metrical reasons. In a prayer to Durgā (*namas te sudurge*, etc) popular in the region of Gujarat, most of the composition is in grammatical Sanskrit. However, we hear a vocative form: *sadādhairyateje*. The best way to make sense of this is to say that the vernacular has *tej* for Sanskrit *tejas*, and that using this vernacular *tej*, the poet produced the feminine form *sadādhairyatejā*, leading to its vocative *sadādhairyateje*. Thus, the vernacular forms of the Sanskrit words are more closely linked to the recognition-ability of the listener, than to the canonical Sanskrit forms. In the recorded tape (A), the priest seems to use the phrase *paya+śarkarā*, rather than the canonical Sanskrit *payas+śarkarā* > *payaśśarkarā*. This may be due to the fact that Sanskritized Marathi has the word *paya*, and not *payas*. In the same recorded tape, the priest recites an Āratī of Viṣṇu, which contains the line: *nija-rūpaikavihāraṇaTAMAhāraṇa viṣṇo*. Here, the canonical Sanskrit form derived from Sanskrit *tamas* would have been ... *tamohāraṇa* ... This would have led to a metrical deviation. What probably aided the output *tamahāraṇa* is also the additional fact that Sanskritized Marathi has the word *tama*, but not *tamas*. In some formulas for blessing, one finds the phrase *sauśriyam astu* /(C: p. 7). In other texts, in parallel passages, one finds *sauśreyam astu* and *sauśreyasam astu*. Neither *sauśriyam* nor *sauśreyam* can be derived as proper Sanskrit expressions. The third form, i.e. *sauśreyasam* is closer to canonical Sanskrit, a secondary derivation from *su+śreyas*. The form *sauśreyam* appears to be a vernacularization, related to the fact that a modern language like Marathi has the word *śreya*, but not *śreyas*. Therefore, it is understandable how a medieval priest may derive the Sanskritized *sauśreyam*, from a base of *su+śreya*. The form *sauśriyam* appears to be a further mutilation, perhaps aided by a possible belief that it is derived from *su+śrī*. It is remarkable that the authoritative medieval text of *Prayogaratna* by Nārāyanabhaṭṭa (C, p. 7) contains the reading *sauśriyam astu*.

One also finds cases, where certain older words were replaced by similar sounding other words, perhaps because, in the course of linguistic change, the meaning of the older words was deemed to be inappropriate in the given context. Consider the case of the word *uttare* in ritual formulas. In the older sacrificial texts, one finds the word *utkara* which refers to a place near the ritual enclosure where one discards the sacrificial waste. The modern Marathi words *ker* 'garbage' and *ukirḍā* 'garbage dump' are etymologically related to this old Sanskrit word. However, these modern words evoke a feeling of revulsion, and in modern Hindu practice, one would never think of dumping items like the withered garlands from the images of deities (*nirmālya*) in the garbage dump. One is supposed to take such items to a holy site like a river bank and immerse them in the water (*visarjan*). In the ritual formula current in the modern Pūjā performances, one hears the expression *uttare nirmālyaṁ visṛjya* . . . / (B). Where does this *uttare* come from? If this were a true reference to the northern direction, one would then expect the Sanskrit pronominal locative pattern: *uttarasmin*, cf. *uttarasyāṁ diśi, Kumārasaṁbhava* 1.1. It is my hunch that the word *uttare* in the phrase *uttare nirmālyaṁ visṛjya* is a medieval modification of an earlier *utkare*. Some person thinking that one could not throw the used garlands in the garbage dump thought that the word *utkare* was an error, and corrected it to *uttare*. This modification itself is fairly old and is found in authoritative medieval texts like the *Prayogaratna* of Nārāyaṇabhaṭṭa, and is not to be attributed to a modern priestly performer.

One finds cases where the grammar of a phrase is modified in view of the perceived distinctions which would be obliterated by the canonical Sanskrit form. For example, everyone knows that the neuter *brahma* is different from the masculine *brahmā*, and that in conjunction with the consort Sāvitrī, one invokes the masculine Brahmā, and not the abstract neuter Brahma. Sāvitrī is the wife of Brahmā. With this widespread popular knowledge, the Dvandva compound of *brahmā + sāvitrī* appears in the ritual formulas as *brahmāsāvitrībhyāṁ namaḥ* . . . (G: p. 5, 6, 7, 8, 9 passim). By the canonical rules of Sanskrit grammar, such a form is not possible. One would have to reduce the form *brahmā* to *brahma*. However, to an untrained listener, this makes it appear as if one is invoking the neuter Brahma along with Sāvitrī. That being inadmissible, the formula always reads: *brahmāsāvitrībhyāṁ namaḥ*. I have verified this usage in printed texts, manuscripts, and in recorded and observed performances. A somewhat similar case is noticed in the passage *śrīsavitāsūryanārāyaṇadevatāprītyartham* ... (P: p. 16). Here, the expression *devatāprītyartham* is a genuine classical Sanskrit expression. The specification of the deity is, by contrast, done in the latter-day forms of vernacular Sanskrit. The expression *sūryanārāyaṇa* referring to the sun-divinity is a somewhat late phenomenon. The addition of the honorific *śrī* is also a relatively late phenomenon. The form *savitā* is a hanging nominative form, which cannot be grammatically justified in this context. One would expect the form *savitṛ* to appear in the compound. However, the vernacular-speaking audience, and the priest himself, have a greater recognition of the nominative form *savitā*, than the abstract base-form *savitṛ*. The nominative Sanskrit form *savitā* has been inherited by Marathi, but not the abstract base-form *savitṛ*.

One of the primary purposes of the priestly performance is to generate an atmosphere of auspiciousness or holiness for the host/audience. Among the various tools at the disposal of the priest, language is an important tool. However, language becomes a tool toward this end not exactly by being correct in terms of the elite grammar of classical Sanskrit, but by fitting a pre-existing pattern of cultural expectations on the part of the listener/performers. These expectations have little to do with the rules of Sanskrit grammar. They are more closely linked with the presence of certain well known items of vocabulary or phrases. Among such phrases in the context of a Marathi wedding is the refrain : *kuryāt sadā maṅgalam* (and its minor variations). Many recited verses end with this phrase and it serves as a punctuation during the ritual. Similarly, the recitation of holy names of deities, rivers, etc. also leads to the overall generation of a euphoric feeling of religious well-being. Observe the concatenation of holy river names in the following verse recited during many Marathi weddings:

P41. *gaṅgā sindhu sarasvatī ca yamunā godāvarī narmadā*
kāverī sarayū mahendratanayā carmaṇvatī vedikā /
kṣiprā vetravatī mahāsuranadī khyātā ca yā gaṇḍakī
pūrṇā pūrṇajalaiḥ samudrasahitāḥ kurvantu vo maṅgalam //
(H: pp. 23-4)

Here most of the grammar consists simply of the concatenation of the holy river names. The beginning of the verse creates several problems for a grammarian. How is the sequence *gaṅgā sindhu sarasvatī ca* to be grammatically understood? If it is a compound, then one does not need a *ca*. If it is not a compound, what is the word *sindhu* doing there? One cannot grammatically account for it. Outside of a compound, one might have expected the form *sindhuḥ*. However, the short *u* is metrically required. Anyway, the audience of this verse has never been beset with such questions. The audience is happy to be blessed by all these rivers brought together in this single verse. The next example is even more revealing of this process. Here, a listing of all kinds of diverse holy items is followed by the singular phrase: *kuryāt sadā maṅgalam.*

P41. *gaṅgāgomatigopatir gaṇapatir govindagovardhano*
gītāgomayagorajogirisutā gaṅgādharo gautamaḥ /
gāyatrī garuḍo gadādharagayāgambhīragodāvarī
gandharvagrahagopagokulagaṇāḥ kuryāt sadā maṅgalam // (H: pp. 24)

The only guiding principle in the composition of this verse is that the names of all these different holy entities begin with (the holy sound?) *g*. The guess that the sound *g* is deemed to be particularly holy in the context of weddings and thread ceremonies is justified by the observation that the most important deity on these occasions, and especially connected with verses ending with *kuryāt sadā maṅgalam*, is Gaṇeśa, cf. *oṁ gaṁ gaṇapataye namaḥ, Gaṇapatyartharvaśīrṣa.* Once such a holy listing of *g*-initial names is achieved, one does not worry too much about the rules of grammar. Violations of the rules of classical Sanskrit in this listing are so obvious and numerous, I need not list them individually. A similar concatenation of diverse things occurs at the end of the recitation of the verses ending in *kuryāt sadā maṅgalam.* These are Sanskrit or Sanskritized expressions, but one cannot say with any confidence whether one would regard these passages as Sanskrit passages. However, I have asked both the priests and the audiences what they thought it was, and for them it is all holy Sanskrit. Generation of holiness depends upon such perceptions on the part of the priests, hosts, and audiences. The word that the Marathi audiences immediately recognize is *sāvadhān*, derived from Sanskrit *sa+avadhāna* 'with attention'. However, for the Marathi audience, the word functions almost as a warning, an imperative: "be attentive!" This warning is uttered by the priests several times before the wedding ritual is finally concluded. This is meant to make the participants in the ceremony become aware of the fact that they are entering into this relation of holy matrimony being fully conscious and attentive. The word *sāvadhāna* is not attested in this fuction in the classical language.

P42. *iṣṭadevatākuladevatāgrāmadevatācintanasumuhūrtasāvadhān / lakṣmīnārāyaṇabrahmāsāvitrīumāmaheśvaracintanasulagnasāvadhān / sāvadhān / sāvadhān* / (H: p. 24)

A common pattern of concatenation of Sanskrit words, with a minimal degree of Sanskrit grammar, is found in many texts where one finds a string of vocatives addressed to a certain deity or person, with some concluding phrase like "protect me." This pattern is seen in the following verse. Additionally, in the meter *Śārdūlavikrīḍita*, most of these vocatives, naturally or otherwise, end in long vowels (marked here in upper case), and are metrically important. Vocatives like *śrīrāmĀ*, *puruṣottamĀ* etc. generally do not appear with such long final vowels in classical poems, though Sanskrit grammarians do indeed allow the presence of protracted vowels in vocatives. The lengthening here actually follows the Marathi vocative pattern, rather than the genuine Sanskrit pattern. This is clear from the vocative form *narahar Ī* in this verse. The genuine classical form would have been *narahare*. Metrically, either *narahar Ī* or *narahare* would be acceptable. However, the fact that the verse contains the form *narahar Ī* is an indication of the Marathi element in this composition. However, this is not uniformly present, as is indicated by the form *guṇanidhe*, which does follow the classical Sanskrit pattern. The best explanation is that there is no clear-cut dividing line between Sanskrit, Sanskritized Marathi, and Marathi in the mind of the author. The boundaries of all these categories are permeable and not fixed.

P43. *śrīrāmĀ puruṣottamĀ narahar Ī nārāyaṇĀ keśavĀ*
govindĀ garuḍadhvajĀ guṇanidhe dāmodarĀ mādhavĀ /
śrīkṛṣṇĀ kamalāpate yadupate sītāpate śrīpate
vaikuṇṭhādhipate carācarapate lakṣmīpate pāhi mām // (I: p. 21)

The next passage shows a similar pattern of vocatives combined with the repeated phrase *tava śaraṇam*.

P44. *dattātreyĀ tava śaraṇam / dattanāthĀ tava śaraṇam //*
triguṇātmakĀ triguṇātītĀ tribhuvanapālaka tava śaraṇam //1//
śāśvatamūrte tava śaraṇam / śyāmasundarĀ tava śaraṇam //
śeṣābharaṇĀ śeṣabhūṣaṇĀ śeṣaśāyi guru tava śaraṇam //2//
ṣaḍbhujamūrte tava śaraṇam / ṣaḍbhujayativara tava śaraṇam //
daṇḍakamaṇḍalugadāpadmakara śaṁkhacakradhara tava śaraṇam //3//

śrīgurunāthĀ tava śaraṇam / sadgurunāthĀ tava śaraṇam //
kṛṣṇāsaṅgamataruvaravāsĪ bhaktavatsalĀ tava śaraṇam //5//
kṛpāmūrte tava śaraṇam / kṛpāsāgarĀ tava śaraṇam //
kṛpākatakṣĀ kṛpāvalokanĀ kṛpānidhe prabhU tava śaraṇam //6//
kālāntakĀ tava śaraṇam / kālanāśakĀ tava śaraṇam //
pūrṇānandĀ pūrnapareśĀ purāṇapuruṣĀ tava śaraṇam //7//
jagadīśĀ tava śaraṇam / jagannāthĀ tava śaraṇam //
jagatpālakĀ jagadādhīśĀ jagaduddhārĀ tava śaraṇam //8//
akhilāntarĀ tava śaraṇam / akhilaiśvaryĀ tava śaraṇam //
bhaktapriyĀ vajrapañjarĀ prasannavaktrĀ tava śaraṇam //9//
digambarĀ tava śaraṇam / dīnadayāghana tava śaraṇam //
dīnanāthĀ dīnadayāḷĀ dīnoddhārĀ tava śaraṇam //10//
tapomūrte tava śaraṇam / tejorāśĪ tava śaraṇam //
brahmānandĀ brahmasanātana brahmamohanĀ tava śaraṇam //11//
viśvātmakĀ tava śaraṇam / viśvarakṣakĀ tava śaraṇam //
viśvaṁbharĀ viśvajīvanĀ viśvaparātpara tava śaraṇam //12//
vighnāntakĀ tava śaraṇam / vighnanāśakĀ tava śaraṇam //
praṇavātīta premavardhanĀ prakāśamūrte tava śaraṇam //13//
nijānandĀ tava śaraṇam / nijapadadāyakĀ tava śaraṇam /
nityaniranjana nirākārĀ nirādhārĀ tava śaraṇam //14//
cidghanamūrte tava śaraṇam / cidākārĀ tava śaraṇam //
cidātmarūpĀ cidānandĀ citsukhakandĀ tava śaraṇam //15//
anādimūrte tava śaraṇam / akhilāvatārĀ tava śaraṇam //
anantakoṭībrahmāṇḍanāyakĀ aghaṭitaghaṭanĀ tava śaraṇam //16//
bhaktoddhārĀ tava śaraṇam / bhaktarakṣakĀ tava śaraṇam //
bhaktānugrahagurubhaktipriyĀ patitoddhārĀ tava śaraṇam //17//
Śrīdattaguruśaraṇāṣṭakam (I: p. 167-8)

Note that some of the vocatives end in long vowels, while others do not, even in those cases where the classical grammar would require them to do so. The choice is mostly determined by the metrical necessity. For instance, in this non-Sanskrit meter, each of the first two feet of the verse has the same metrical structure. The pāda breaks down into two units, with the first one with eight mātrās and the second one with six mātrās. The constant portion *tava śaraṇam* consists of six mātrās. The preceding portion must consist of eight mātrās. Thus, in the very first pāda of the passage, we have *dattātreyā tava śaraṇam.* The vocative *dattātreyĀ* ends in a long vowel, because without the long vowel, it will not make eight mātrās. On the other hand, in the second pāda of the third verse, i.e. *ṣaḍbhujayativara tava śaraṇam,* the vocative *ṣaḍbhujayativara* does not end in a long vowel, because a long vowel would create an additional mātrā. The vocative *guru* in the second verse should have been *guro* according to the rules of Sanskrit grammar.

However, that would have created an extra mātrā. Also note that the verses are sung in Marathi phonetics, which allows additional flexibilities. Consider the lines *dattanāthā tava śaraṇam, jagannāthā tava śaraṇam,* and *cidākārā tavaśaraṇam.* Here, the words *dattanāthā, jagannāthā,* and *cidākārā* each would scan only seven mātrās, if counted by the rules of the classical language. However, in the Marathi recitation of these verses, many light syllables get metrically lengthened. I have indicated this lengthening by placing '2 after the vowel: *datta2nāthā, ja2gannāthā,* and *ci2dākārā.* Other acceptable recitational strategies include making long vowels even longer to scan for three mātrās, i.e. *dattanā3thā, jagannā3thā,* and *cidākā3rā.* While singing the same line again and again, the reciters use different alternative patterns of lengthening. [This is comparable to alternative prolation of different heavy syllables in a vocative prescribed by Pāṇini 8.2.86: *guror anṛto 'nantyasyāpy ekaikasya prācām*]. Thus, the vernacular recitational practice makes up for the lack of mātrās. There are reverse cases as well. There are expressions which in their canonical Sanskrit pronunciation would produce extra mātrās, but in their vernacular pronunciation they scan properly. As an example, consider the expression *anantakoṭībrahmāṇḍanāyakā* in verse 16 above. Pronounced in the canonical Sanskrit way, this expression would have an extra mātrā. In the recitational pattern common in the Marathi region, one gets rid of this extra mātrā by reciting the expression as *anantakoṭībrahmāṇḍa-NĀYKĀ.* Such a loss of short *a* is a common feature of the modern IA languages like Marathi and Hindi, cf. Skt. *apavāda* > Marathi/Hindi *apvād.* Anther feature of the vernacular pronunciation of Sanskrit, which is manifest in this passage, is the occasional non-emphatic pronunciation of consonant clusters. In the expression *bhaktānugrahagurubhaktipriyĀ* in verse 17, the canonical Sanskrit pronunciation leads to an extra mātrā. One can get rid of this extra mātrā by using a non-emphatic pronunciation of the cluster *kt.* This allows the vowel *a* in the word *bhakti* in the above expression to be recited as a light vowel with one mātrā.

7. Conclusion

The above demonstration of some features of priestly Sanskrit shows that this variety of Sanskrit is in some respects similar to other varieties of Vernacular Sanskrit, in that this variety stands at the intersection of classical Sanskrit and the given vernacular. However, its specific features result from the specific context of its use and the specific motivations involved in its production. Its many features result from the fact that the priest who is generally quite ignorant of the grammar of the classical language needs to project a Sanskritic holy image to his host and the audience, who are, most of the time, even more ignorant of Sanskrit. The host refers to the priest by names like *paṇḍita* and *guru-jī*, and looks up to him for ritual, if not spiritual, guidance. The priest is caught between his own ignorance of Sanskrit grammar, and the need to simultaneously appear knowledgeable, authentic, and also at the same time be comprehensible to the vernacular-speaking host/audience. The features of priestly Sanskrit result from this peculiar hierarchical context and interaction.

List of Special Primary Sources

A. *Satyanārāyaṇapūjā*, recorded cassette. Recited by Madhav Bhalchandra Karambelkar Shastri. 1984. Pune: Alulkar Audio Video Products.

B. *Gaṇeśapūjā*, recorded cassette. Recited by Madhav Bhalchandra Karambelkar Shastri. 1984. Pune: Alulkar Audio Video Products.

C. *Prayogaratnam, Nārāyaṇabhaṭṭī*. By Nārāyaṇabhaṭṭa. Edited by Vāsudev Paṇśikar. Bombay: Nirnayasagara Press.

D. *Nityakarmaprayogamālā*. Compiled by Caturthīlāl Śarmā. Saṁvat: 2021. Bombay: Kṣemarāja Śrīkṛṇadāsa, Venkateshwar Press.

F. *Svayampurohit*. K.M. Bapat Shastri. 1983. Bombay: Shri Gajanan Book Depot.

G. *Sārthapūjākathāsaṁgraha*. By Kashinath Shastri Josh 1964. Pune: Chitralekha Agency, 724 Budhwar Peth.

H. *Brāhmavivāhaprayogaḥ*. By Govind Ramchandra Moghe. 1938. Bombay: Nirnayasagara Press.

I. *Bhaktimārgapradīpa*. Edited by Lakshman Ramchandra Pangarkar. 16th revised edition. 1938. Bombay: Keshav Bhikaji Dhawale.

K. *Vājasaneyinām upanayanapaddhatiḥ*. By Ramadatta Thakkur. Edited by Pt. Ramchandra Jha. Revised 4th edition. Vikram 2023. *Mithilā Granthamālā* No. 16. Banaras: Chaukhambha Sanskrit Series Office.

M. *Śrīkālīstavamañjarī*. Edited by Ṛtaśīla Śarmā. 1983. Prayāga: Śākta Sādhanā Pīṭha.

N. *Mulāñcā bhaktimārga*. Mahadeva Ananta Bhagwat. Bombay: Mauj Office. (no date, approximately 1950).

P. *Sandhyā*. By Siddheshwar Shastri Chitrao. *Nityakarmamālā*, No. 1. 8th edition. Śaka date 1855. Pune: Lokasaṁgraha Chhāpkhānā.

Q. *Satyanārāyaṇapūjā*. Recorded cassette. Recited by Sant Keshavdas. 1985?

R. *Śuklayajurvedībrahmakarma*. 7th edition. 1928. Pune: Mahadev Bhaskar Godbole.

Other Sources: see General Bibliography

GENERAL BIBLIOGRAPHY

For ease of reference most of the bibliographical information belonging to the different chapters has been collected in this General Bibliography, compiled on the basis of the bibliographies provided by the authors of the chapters. The Bibliography consists of Section I (Abbreviations of Journals and Series), Section II (Primary sources and abbreviated titles) and Section III (Secondary literature and remaining sources). It has been attempted to check the bibliographical data of the publications and to give references to different editions of the same work under a single entry, but this was not always possible. Additional lists of special primary sources are found at the end of chapters twelve and eighteen.

Section I: Abbreviations (Journals and Series)

ABORI — Annals of the Bhandarkar Oriental Research Institute, Poona.

ALB — The Adyar Library Bulletin (Brahmavidyā), Adyar (Madras).

ASS — Ānandāśrama Sanskrit Series, Poona.

BhV — Bhāratīya Vidyā: a review of research on Indian culture, Bombay.

AOH — Acta Orientalia Academiquae Scientiarium Hungaricae, Budapest.

AS/ÉA — Asiatische Studien / Études Asiatiques, Bern.

ASI A/R — Archeological Surv·y of India, Annual Report.

BEFEO — Bulletin de l'Ecole Française d'Extrême-Orient, Hanoi, Paris; from vol. 59: Paris.

BTLV — Bijdragen tot de Taal- en Volkenkunde, Den Haag.

CII — Corpus Inscriptionum Indicarum.

EC — Epigraphia Carnatica, Mysore.

EI — Epigraphia Indica, Calcutta.

GOS — Gaekwad's Oriental Series, Baroda.

HOS — Harvard Oriental Series, Cambridge, Massachusetts.

IA — Indian Antiquary, Bombay.

IC — Inscriptions du Cambodge, Hanoi, Paris; Paris.

IHQ — Indian Historical Quarterly, Calcutta.

IIJ — Indo-Iranian Journal, The Hague.

IJDL — International Journal of Dravidian Linguistics, Kariavattom, Trivandrum.

JA — Journal asiatique, Paris.

JAOS — Journal of the American Oriental Society, New Haven.

JAS — Journal of Asian Studies, Ann Arbor.

JBBRAS — Journal of the Bombay Branch of the Royal Asiatic Society, Bombay.

JBORS	Journal of the Bihar and Orissa Research Society, Bankipore.
JIABS	Journal of the International Association of Buddhist Studies, Madison, Wisc.
JIES	Journal of Indo-European Studies, Washington.
JGJRI	Journal of the Gangānātha Jhā Research Institute, Allahabad.
JIPh	Journal of Indian Philosophy, Dordrecht.
JOIB	Journal of the Oriental Institute, Baroda.
JRAS	Journal of the Royal Asiatic Society, London.
PCASS	Publications of the Centre of Advanced Study in Sanskrit, Poona.
SII	South Indian Inscriptions, Madras.
SLS	Studies in the Linguistic Sciences, Urbana, Ill.
StII	Studien zur Indologie und Iranistik, Reinbeck.
TBG	Tijdschrift voor Indische Taal-, Land- en Volkenkunde, uitg. door het Koninklijk Bataviaasch Genootschap van Kunsten en Wetenschappen, Batavia etc.
TCLP	Travaux du Cercle Linguistique de Prague, Prague.
VIJ	Vishveshwaranand Indological Journal, Hoshiarpur.
VKAW	Verhandelingen van de Koninklijke Nederlandse Akademie van Wetenschappen, Afdeling Letterkunde, Nieuwe Reeks, Amsterdam.
WZKM	Wiener Zeitschrift für die Kunde des Morgenlandes, Bombay, Wien.
WZKS	Wiener Zeitschrift für die Kunde Süd- und Ostasiens (und Archiv für indische Philosophie), Wien.

Section II: Primary sources and abbreviated titles

Abhidh-k-bh(P) = Abhidharmakośabhāṣya of Vasubandhu. Ed. by P. Pradhan. Revised second edition with introduction and indices etc. by Aruna Haldar. (Tibetan Sanskrit Works Series Vol. VIII.) Patna: K.P. Jayaswal Research Institute, 1975.

Aitareyabrāhmaṇa. Ed. by Kāśīnātha Śāstrī Āgāśe. ASS 31, parts I-II. Pune: Ānandāśrama, 1896.

AP = Agnipurāṇa. Ed. Apte, Hari Nārāyaṇa. ASS 41,Poona, 1900

Arthaśāstra attributed to Kauṭilīya. Critical Edition and Translation by R.P. Kangle, *The Kauṭilīya Arthaśāstra* Part 1-2, Second edition, 1969-1972; Reprint Delhi: Motilal Banarsidass, 1986.

Aṣṭasāhasrikā = Aṣṭasāhasrikā Prajñāpāramitā. Ed. by P.L. Vaidya. (Buddhist Sanskrit Texts, No. 4.) Darbhanga: Mithila Institute of Post-Graduate Studies and Research in Sanskrit Learning, 1960.

Āśvalāyanagṛhyasūtra. Āśvalāyanagṛhyasūtra with the commentary by Nārāyaṇa. Ed. by Vasudeva Shastri Panshikar. Bombay: Nirnaya Sagara Press, 1894.

Aupapātika Sūtra. *Uvavāiya Suttam*. Ed. Ganesh Lalwani. Jaipur: Prakrit Bharati Academy, 1988.

Aurobindo Centenary: Sri Aurobindo Birth Centenary Library (30 Vols.). Pondicherry: Sri Aurobindo Ashram.

Autobiography Tagore: The Auto-Biography of Maharshi Devendranath Tagore, translated from Bengali by Satyendranath Tagore and Indira Devi, with a new introduction by Prof. Dilip Kumar Biswas. Calcutta: C.S. Sarkar, 1994.

AV = Atharvaveda. Atharvaveda (Śaunaka): With the Pada-pāṭha and Sāyaṇācārya's Commentary, ed. by Vishva Bandhu, Hoshiarpur: Vishveshvaranand Vedic Research Institute, 1960-4.

Bamkim Racanāvali I: Bamkim Racanāvali, prathama khaṇḍa. Calcutta: Sahitya Samsad, 1399 (Beng. era) [CE 1992/3].

Bamkim Racanāvali II: Bamkim Racanāvali, dvitīya khaṇḍa. Calcutta: Sahitya Samsad, 1397 (Beng. era) [CE 1990/1].

Bamkim Racanavali III: Bamkim Racanavali, English Works. Calcutta: Sahitya Samsad, 1969.

BĀUp = Bṛhad-Āraṇyaka-Upaniṣad. Ed. in Limaye & Vadekar 1958:174-282.

Bharaṭakadvātriṃśikā. Ed. Johannes Hertel. Leipzig: Merkert and Petters, 1921.

BY = Brahma-Yāmala. Palm-leaf ms., National Archives of Nepal no. 3-370 / Śaivatantra 129.

CDNI Corpus Diplomaticum neerlando-Indicum. Heeres, J.E. Vol. 2 (1650-1675) and 3 (1676-1691). Den Haag: Martinus Nijhoff, 1931, 1934. (Vol. 2 also appeared as BTLV 87 (1931), vol. 3 also as BTLV 91 (1934).)

Ceiyavaṃdaṇamahābhāsaṃ of Śānti Sūri. [s.n.] Muṃbaī: Śrī Jinaśāsana Ārādhanā Ṭrasṭ, 1986.

Correspondence Roy: The Correspondence of Raja Rammohun Roy, ed. by Biswas, Dilip Kumar. Vol. I: 1809-1831. Calcutta: Saraswat Library, 1992.

CV = Cāndravyākaraṇa of Candragomin. Ed. by Chatterij, Kshitish Chandra. *Sources of Indo-Aryan Lexicography* 13.1-2, Deccan College, Poona, 1953, 1961.

Daśavaikālika Cūrṇi. *Sayyambhava's Dasakāliyasuttaṃ with Bhadrabāhu's Niryukti and Agastyasiṃha's Cūrṇi*, ed. Muni Puṇyavijaya. Varanasi/Ahmedabad: Prakrit Text Society, 1973.

DED Burrow & Emeneau 1961.

DEDR Burrow & Emeneau 1984.

Dharmabinduprakaraṇa of Haribhadra with Municandra Sūri's commentary. Ed. Muni Jambūvijaya. Muṁbaī: Śrī Jinaśāsana Ārādanā Ṭrasṭ, 1994.

Dve Virūpe Sūktabhāṣya. Dve Virūpe Sūktabhāṣya by Kṛṣṇācārya. Ed. by V.V. Bhide. Pune, 1968.

Gāhārayanakosa of Jineśvara Sūri. Ed. A. M. Bhojak and N. J. Shah. Ahmedabad: Lalbhai Dalpatbhai Institute of Indology, 1975.

Garuḍa Purāṇa. Ed. by R.N. Sharma. Introduction, Text and verse-index. Delhi: Nag publishers, 1984.

Gaüḍavaho by Vākpatirāja. Ed. by S.P. Pandit. 2nd edition by Utgikar. Bombay Sanskrit and Prakrit Series, 34. Pune: Bhandarkar Oriental Research Institute, 1927.

GautDhS = Gautama-dharma-sūtra.

GPM = Gīrvāṇa-pada-mañjarī. Ed. in Shah 1960.

GVM = Gīrvāṇa-vāṅ-mañjarī. Ed. in Shah 1960.

Hīrapraśnottarāṇi. [s.n.] Muṃbaī: Śrī Jinaśāsanā Āradhanā Ṭraṣṭ,1988.

History Dharmaśāstra = Kane, Pandurang Vaman, *History of Dharmaśāstra*; Vol. I (1930), Vol. II, 1 and 2 (1941), Vol. III (1946), Vol. IV (1953), Vol. V, 1 (1958, 2nd ed. 1974), Vol. V, 2 (1962). Poona: Bhandarkar Oriental Research Institute.

India Office MSS Catalogue. Catalogue of the Sanskrit (Vol. 2: and Prākrit) Manuscripts in the Library of India Office, 1887-1935. London: Gilbert, Livington (2: Oxford: Clarendon Press).

Jainendra Siddhāntakoṣa. Volume 2, ed. J. Varni. Varanasi: Bharatiya Jnanpith, 1971.

JST = Jñānasaṃkalanī Tantra. Ed. Gopinath Kaviraj, in: Tantrasaṁgraha, vol. II (Varanasi: Sanskrit Univ., 1970):307-317.

JV = Jainendra Vyākaraṇa. *Jainendra Vyākaraṇam by Pūjyapāda Devanandi with Jainendra Mahāvritti of Shri Abhayanandi.*Ed. Tripathi, Shambu Nath. Jñānapītha Mūrtidevī Jaina Granthamālā, Saṃskrit Grantha 17, Bhāratīya Jñānapītha Kāshī, 1956.

Kāmasūtra of Vātsyāyana. *Kāmasūtra with the Commentary Jayamaṅgala of Yashodhar.* Ed. by Sri Gosvami Damodar Shastri. Kashi Sanskrit Series No. 29. Benares: Chowkhamba Sanskrit Series Office, 1929.

KāmT = Kāmadhenu Tantra. Ed. Gopinath Kaviraj, in: Tantrasaṁgraha, vol. II (Varanasi: Sanskrit Univ., 1970):95-160.

Kāvyamīmāṃsā of Rājaśekhara. Ed. C.D. Dalal and Pt. R.A. Sastry. (Gaekwad's Oriental Series, 1.) Third edition. Baroda: Oriental Institute, 1934.

KS = The Kārakasaṁgraha. Ed. Lévi

KS = Kāṭhaka Saṁhitā.

KT = Kātantra. *The Kātantra with the Commentary of Durgasiṃha, ed. with Notes and Indexes* [by] Eggeling, Julius. Bibliotheca Indica N.S. 297, 298, 308, 309, 396, 397. Calcutta. 1874-1878.

KulT = Kulārṇava Tantra. Ed. T. Vidyāratna, 2nd. ed., Madras: Ganesh, 1965.

KulĀ = Kulālikāmnāya version of the Kubjikāmatatantra. Edition Goudriaan & Schoterman 1988.

Kumārasambhava by Kālidāsa. With the commentary by Mallinātha. Ed. by V.L. Panshikar. Bombay: Nirnaya Sagara Press, 1919.

Līlāvatī-Sāra of Jinaratna. *Līlāvatī-Sāra: A Sanskrit Abridgement of Jineśvara Sūri's Prakrit Līlāvatī-Kahā.* Ed. H. C. Bhayani, with assistance from N. M. Kansara. Ahmedabad: Lalbhai Dalpatbhai Institute of Indology, 1983.

Madhyamakāvatāra of Candrakīrti. Traduction tibétaine publiée par Louis de la Vallée Poussin. Neudruck der Ausgabe 1907-1912. Osnabrück: Biblio Verlag, 1970.

Mahābhārata. Critical edition, by various scholars. 19 vols. Poona: Bhandarkar Oriental Research Institute, 1933-1966.

MaiUp = Maitrāyaṇī-Upaniṣad. (1) Limaye & Vadekar 1958:325-357. (2) Edition and translation, van Buitenen 1962.

Manu = Manusmṛti. *Manusmṛti, with the Sanskrit commentary Manvartha-Muktāvalī of Kullūka Bhaṭṭa.* Ed. J.L. Shastri. Delhi: Motilal Banarsidass, 1983.

Mayrhofer I Mayrhofer 1956-1980.

Mayrhofer II Mayrhofer 1986- . . .

MBh = Patañjali's Mahābhāṣya. References to (number of volume):(page).(line) in F. Kielhorn's edition (Poona: Bhandarkar Oriental Research Institute, 3rd rev. ed. by K.V. Abhyankar, 1962-1972).

MBh (S) = Patañjali's Mahābhāṣya with the commentaries Nāgojībhaṭṭa's Uddyota and Kaiyaṭa's Pradīpa. Ed. by Guru Prasad Shastri, second edition revised by Bal Prasad (Sagar,M.P.: Sagar Univ., 1987-1988). References to (number of volume):(page).(line).

MBhD = Bhartṛhari's Mahābhāṣya-dīpikā. (1) The recent Mahābhāṣya-dīpikā edition (with translation and notes) by a team of scholars (Poona, 1985-1991). Poona: Bhandarkar Oriental Research Institute. Āhnika 1 by J. Bronkhorst (1987), Āhnika 2 by G.B. Palsule (1988), Āhnika 3 by G.B. Palsule (1983), Āhnika 4 by G.V. Devasthali and G.B. Palsule (1989), Āhnika 5 by V.P. Limaye, G.B. Palsule and V.B. Bhagavat (1984), Āhnika 6 part 1 by V.B. Bhagavat and Saroja Bhate (1986), Āhnika 6 part 2 by V.B. Bhagavat and Saroja Bhate (1990), Āhnika 7 by G.B. Palsule and V.B. Bhagavat (1991). Numbers following MBhD refer to this edition as follows: MBhD (number of Āhnika):(page).(line). (2) Manuscript reproduced. Poona: Bhandarkar Oriental Research Institute, 1980. (3) Ed. by K.V. Abhyankar and V.P. Limaye. (Post-Graduate and Research Department Series 8.) Poona: Bhandarkar Oriental Research Institute, 1970. (4) Partly ed. by V. Swaminathan under the title *Mahābhāṣya Ṭīkā.* (Hindu Vishvavidyalaya Nepal Rajya Sanskrit Series Vol. 11.) Varanasi: Banaras Hindu Univ., 1965.

Milindapañha. Ed. V. Trenckner. Pali Text Society. London: Luzac & Company, 1962.

MīmS = Jaimini's Mīmāṁsā-Sūtra. (1) Ed. together with Śābara-Bhāṣya, Prabhā-commentary, Kumārila's Tantravārttikam and Ṭupṭīkā by K.V. Abhyankar - G.A. Joshi and M.C. Apte, AAS 97 [First edition 1930-1934; vol. 1, fourth edition 1976; vol. 2, third edition 1981; vol. 3, third edition 1980; vol. 4, second edition 1972; vol. 5, second edition 1973; vol. 6, second edition, 1974; vol. 7, second edition 1974.]; (2) Translation of MīmS and Śābara-Bhāṣya by Gaṅganātha Jhā, 1973-1974, Baroda, Gaekwad's Oriental Series 66, 70, 73.

MS = Maitrāyaṇīya Saṁhitā.

Namaskār Svādhyāy. *Namaskār Svādhyāy(Saṃskṛt Vibhāg).* Ed. Paṃnyās Dhurandharavijaya Gaṇin, Muni Jambūvijaya and Muni Tattvānaṃdavijaya. Bombay: Jain Sāhitya Vikās Maṇḍal, 1962.

Nāṭyaśāstra of Bharata. (1) Ed. with introduction by R.S. Sagar. (Based on four previous editions.) Volume 1-4. Delhi: Parimal publications 1981-1984. (2) Edited with Abhinavagupta's commentary by Ramakrishna Kavi. Vols. 1-4. GOS 36, 68, 74, 145. Baroda: Oriental Institute, 1926-1964. (3) Ed. by M. Ghosh (Ghosh 1967).

Nirukta = Yāska's Nirukta. 1. Ed. Rudolph Roth. Unveränderter reprografischer Nachdruck der 1. Auflage. Darmstadt: Wissenschaftliche Buchgesellschaft, 1976. 2. Ed. and translated by L. Sarup, 1920-1927; reprint Delhi: Motilal Banarsidass, 1967, 1984. 3. Ed. with the commentary of Durga. ASS 88, Vols. 1-2. Pune: Ānandāśrama, 1921, 1926.

Nirvāṇakalikā. Ed. Mohanlāl Bhagvāndās Jhaverī. Bombay: Seth Nathamalji Kanayyalalji Ranka, 1926.

NKC = Nyāyakumudacandra of Prabhācandra (Digambara). Nyāyakumudacandra (dvitīyo bhāgaḥ). Ed. Mahendra Kumar. Bombay: Māṇik Candra Digambara Jain Granthamālā, 1941.

Nyāyasudhā, a commentary by Someśvarabhaṭṭa on Kumārila's *Tantravārttika*. Ed. by Mukunda Sastri. *Chowkhamba Sanskrit Series* 14. Banaras, 1901-9.

P = Pāṇini's Aṣṭādhyāyī.

Pañcasūtraka. Ed. Muni Jambūvijaya. Delhi: Bhogilal Leherchand Institute of Indology, 1986.

Paṇṇavaṇāsuttam. Ed. Muni Puṇyavijaya, Pt. Dalsukh Mālvaṇiā and Pt. Amritlāl Mohanlāl Bhojak. Jaina-Āgama Series 9.2. Bombay: Shri Mahāvīra Jaina Vidyālaya, 1971.

Piṅ = Piṅgalāmata. Palm-leaf ms., National Archives of Nepal no. 3-376/113.

Prabhāvakacarita of Prabhācandra (Śvetāmbara). Ed. Muni Jinavijaya. Ahmedabad/Calcutta: Siṃghī Jain Granthmālā, 1940.

Prajñāpanā Sūtra = Paṇṇavaṇāsuttam.

Prajñāpāramitāhṛdaya Sūtra. In: *Mahāyāna-Sūtra-Saṃgraha* Part I. (Buddhist Sanskrit Texts, No. 17.) Ed. by P.L. Vaidya. Darbhanga: Mithila Institute of Post-Graduate Studies and Research in Sanskrit Learning, 1961.

Prākṛta-Vyākaraṇam of Hemacandra. Ed. Muni Vajrasenavijaya. Bhāvnagar: Jain Ātmānand Sabhā, 1982.

PraNTA = Pramāṇa-Naya-Tattvālokālaṅkāra of Vādi Devasūri. English translation and commentary by Hari Satya Bhattacharya. Bombay: Jain Sāhitya Vikās Maṇḍal, 1967.

Prasannapadā of Candrakīrti. In: *Madhyamakaśāstra of Nāgārjuna with the commentary Prasannapadā by Candrakīrti*. Ed. P.L. Vaidya. (Buddhist Sanskrit Texts, No. 10.) Darbhanga: Mithila Institute of Post-Graduate Studies and Research in Sanskrit Learning, 1987.

Prayogapārijāta by Nṛsiṁha. Manuscript. Pune: Bhandarkar Oriental Research Institute.

Rāmāyaṇa = (1) The Vālmīki Rāmāyaṇa. Critical edition. Baroda: Oriental Research Institute, 1960-1975; (2) Śrīmad Vālmīki Rāmāyaṇa with the commentary of Sri Govindaraja, ed. by T.R. Krishnacharya. Bombay, Nirnaya-sagar Press, 1911-13.

Rāmmohan Racanāvali: Rāmmohan Racanāvali, pradhān sampādak Dr. Ajitkumār Ghosh. Calcutta: Haraph Prakashani, 1973.

Ravīndra-racanāvali: Ravīndra-racanāvali, 125 tama Ravīndrajayantī upalakṣe prakāśita sulabh saṁskaraṇ. 15 Vols. Calcutta: Visva-Bharati, 1393-1398 (Beng. era) [CE 1986/7-1991/2].

Report Sanskrit Commission. *Report of the Sanskrit Commission, 1956-57.* Delhi, 1958.

RSS Resolves: R.S.S. Resolves: Full Text of Resolutions from 1950 to 1983. Bangalore: Prakashan Vibhag, Rashtriya Swayamsevak Sangh, Karnataka, 1983.

ṚV = Ṛgveda. Ed. with the commentary of Sāyaṇācārya by N.N. Sonatake a.o. 5 vols. Poona: Vaidika Saṁśodhana Maṇḍala, 1933-1951. Transl. K.F. Geldner, *Der Rig-Veda aus dem Sanskrit ins Deutsche übersetzt* (Harvard Oriental Series 33-36), Cambridge Massachusetts: Harvard Univ. Press, 1957-1978.

ŚābBh = Śābara Bhāṣya. In: MīmS = Jaimini's Mīmāṁsā-Sūtra.

Sämtliche Werke: *Schopenhauer, Arthur: Sämtliche Werke*, textkritisch bearbeitet und herausgegeben von Wolfgang Frhr. von Löhneysen. Band V. Darmstadt: Wissenschaftliche Buchgesellschaft, 1976.

Sārasiddhāntakaumudī of Varadarāja. Ed. by Devasthali 1968.

ŚB = Śatapatha Brāhmaṇa. Ed. by Albrecht Weber, London 1855. Transl. by Julius Eggeling (Sacred Books of the East 12, 26, 41, 43, 44), London: 1882-1900.

ŚBK = Śatapatha Brāhmaṇa (Kāṇva recension).

Sekaśubhodayā of Halāyudha Miśra. Ed. Sen 1963.

Śikṣāsamuccaya of Śāntideva. Ed. by P.L. Vaidya. (Buddhist Sanskrit Texts, no. 11.) Darbhanga: Mithila Institute, 1961.

ŚivS = Śiva Sūtra. Ed. (with English translation) Jaideva Singh, Delhi: Motilal Banarsidass, 1979.

SK = Sāṃkhya Kārikā. Edition included in Pandeya 1967.

SM = Saṁskṛta-mañjarī.

SN = Saṃyutta-Nikāya, ed. L. Feer, 5 vols., London 1884-1898 (Pali Text Society), vol. 6 (Indexes by C.A.F. Rhys Davids), London 1905 (Pali Text Society).

ṢSS = Ṣaṭsāhasra Saṃhitā. Edition Schoterman 1982.

STB = Saṃskṛta-tattva-bodhinī.

Suvikrāntavikrāmiparipṛcchā. In: *Mahāyāna-Sūtra-Saṃgraha* Part I. (Buddhist Sanskrit Texts, No. 17.) Ed. by P.L. Vaidya. Darbhanga: Mithila Institute of Post-Graduate Studies and Research in Sanskrit Learning, 1961.

SvT = Svacchanda Tantra. Ed. M. Kaul Śāstrī (in 7 vols.) (Kashmir Series of Texts and Studies, vols. 31, 38, 44, 48, 51, 53, 56), Srinagar 1921-35.

TĀl = Tantrāloka of Abhinavagupta. Ed. M. Kaul Śāstrī (in 12 vols.) (Kashmir Series of Texts and Studies, vols. 23, 28, 30, 36, 35, 29, 41, 47, 59, 52, 57, 58), Srinagar 1918-38. Revised ed. by R.C. Dwivedi and Navjivau Rastogi, Delhi: Motilal Banarsidass, 1987.

Tattvārthādhigamasūtra. Kapadia's edition (Tattvārthasūtram, Śrī Umāsvāti-vācaka-mukhya-sandṛbdham. Ed. by Hiralal Rasikdas Kapadia, Bombay, 1926). Cf. also Dixit, 1974.

TB = Taittirīya Brāhmaṇa.

TI = Taishô Shinshū Daizôkyô or Taishô Issaikyô, 100 vols., Tôkyô 1924 ff.

TRT = Tantrarāja Tantra. Part I (chs. 1-18), ed. Lakṣmaṇa Śāstrī, (Tantrik Texts, Vol. VIII), London 1918. Part II (chs. 19-36), ed. Sadāshiva Mishra, (Tantrik Texts, Vol. XII), Calcutta/London, 1926.

Trikāṇḍī see under VP.

TS = Taittirīya Saṁhitā.

TViv = Tattvaviveka of Abhinavagupta, commentary on Parātriṁśikā. Ed. Mukunda Rāma Śāstrī, (Kashmir Series of Texts and Studies, vol. 18), Bombay, 1918.

UVP = Ukti-vyakti-prakaraṇa. Ed. Jinavijaya, Muni 1953.

Vaiyākaraṇasiddhānta-laghumañjūṣā. *Vaiyākaraṇa-siddhānta-laghu-mañjūṣā of Nāgeśa-bhaṭṭa, up to the end of tātparyanirūpaṇa*. With the commentary Ratnaprabhā and notes by Pt. Sabhāpati Śarmā Upādhyāya. Kashi Sanskrit Series, 163. Varanasi: Chowkhamba Sanskrti Series Office, 1963.

Vajracchedikā Prajñāpāramitā. In: *Mahāyāna-Sūtra-Saṃgraha* Part I. (Buddhist Sanskrit Texts, No. 17.) Ed. by P.L. Vaidya. Darbhanga: Mithila Institute of Post-Graduate Studies and Research in Sanskrit Learning, 1961.

Vidhimārgaprapā of Jinaprabha Sūri. *Vidhimārgaprapā*. Ed. Muni Jinavijaya. Bombay: Jaweri Mulchand Hirachand Bhagat, 1941.

Vikramāṅkadevacarita of Bilhaṇa. *Vikramāṅkadevacaritam mahākāvyam*. Vols. 1-3. Ed. by Pt. V. S. Bharadwaj. Varanasi: the Samskrit Sahitya Research Committe of the Banaras Hindu Univ., 1958-1964.

VP = Bhartṛhari's Vākyapadīya; references to the kārikās (with two or three arabic numerals separated by periods) follow W. Rau's critical edition of the kārikās (Rau, 1977).

VP = Bhartṛhari's Vākyapadīya; references to the kārikās (with two or three arabic numerals separated by periods) follow W. Rau's critical edition of the kārikās (Rau, 1977).

VP I = Iyer's edition (Iyer 1966). [References to this edition: VP I:(page).(line).].

Vṛttaratnākara by Bhaṭṭa Kedāra, with the commentary by Nārāyaṇa Bhaṭṭa. Ed. by Vaidyanath Varkal Shastri. Kashi Sanskrit Series - 55. 1927. Banaras: Chowkhambha Sanskrit Series Office.

VS = Vājasaneyi Saṁhitā

Works Sir W. Jones: *The Works of Sir William Jones, with the Life of the Author* by Lord Teignmouth. Vol. 3. Indian reprint. Delhi: Agam Prakashan, 1977.

Works Vivekananda: The Complete Works of Swami Vivekananda. Himalayan Series. Mayavati Memorial Edition. Revised ed. 8 vols. Mayavati, Almora, Kumaon, Himalayas: The Prabuddha Bharata Press. Several editions from 1907. From 1973-1979: Calcutta: Advaita Ashrama.

Section III: Secondary literature and remaining sources

Abbi, Anvita

1992 *Reduplication in South Asian languages: An areal, typological, and historical study.* New Delhi: Allied Publishers.

Abercrombie, Nicholas et al.

1980 *The Dominant Ideology Thesis.* London: Allen and Unwin.

1990 *Dominant Ideologies.* London: Unwin Hyman

Aklujkar, Ashok N.

1971 "The number of kārikās in Trikāṇḍī, Book I." JAOS 91:510-513.

forthc. a "Sociolinguistic History of ancient and medieval India: need for a paradigm change."

forthc. b "The semantic history of 'Vedānta' and the paradigm for the study of Indian philosophy."

Allchin, F.R.

1995 *The Archaeology of Early Historic South Asia: the Emergence of Cities and States.* With contributions from G. Erdosy, R.A.E. Conningham, D.K. Chakrabarti and Bridget Allchin. Cambridge: Cambridge Univ. Press.

Alper, Harvey P. (ed.)

1989 *Understanding Mantras.* Albany: State Univ. of New York Press.

Altekar, A.S.

1965 *Education in Ancient India.* 6th ed. Varanasi: Nand Kishore & Bros. [1st ed.: Varanasi: Indian Book Shop, 1934; 2nd rev. and enl. ed. Varanasi: Raja Printing Press.]

Andersen, Henning

1973 "Abductive and Deductive Change." *Language* 49:765-793.

Anderson, Benedict Richard O'Gorman.

1983 *Imagined Communities. Reflections on the Origin and Spread of Nationalism.* London: Verso.

1991a, 1993 *Imagined Communities: Reflections on the Origin and Spread of Nationalism.* Rev. ed. [first edition 1983] London: Verso.

1991b *Language and Power: Exploring Political Cultures in Indonesia.* Ithaca: Cornell Univ. Press.

Anderson, Walter K., and Shridhar D. Damle.

1987 *The Brotherhood in Saffron: The Rashtriya Swayamsewak Sangh and Hindu Revivalism.* Boulder: Westview Press / New Delhi: Vistaar Publications.

Annamalai, S.P.

1993 "Ārya in Tamil literature." In: Deo & Kamath 1993:73-74.

Apte, Vaman Shivaram

1957 *The Practical Sanskrit-English Dictionary.* Rev. and Enlarged Edition. Poona 1957 [New edition: Kyoto: Rinsen, 1978].

Auerbach, Erich

1988 *Mimesis. Dargestellte Wirklichkeit in der abendländischen Literatur.* 8. Auflage. Bern-Stuttgart: Francke Verlag.

Bagchi, Prabodh Chandra

1934 *Kaulajñānanirṇaya Tantra and some minor texts of the school of Matsyendranātha.* Calcutta Sanskrit Series, no. 3; Texts from Nepal, 1. Calcutta: Metropolitan.

Balbir, Nalini

1990 "*anadhyāya* as a Jaina Topic. The Precepts." WZKS 34: 49-77.

Ball, Steven E., and Simpson, Richard A.

1977 "Shifts from nominal realism in grade school children as a function of participating in a naming task." *Journal of Psychology* 96, 217-21.

Ballantyne, James R.

1866-67 "The Pandits and their Manner of Teaching." *Pandit,* 1:146ff (cf. Pandit Revisited, ed. by Dr. B. N. Miśra, Varanasi 1991: 44-82).

Belvalkar, Shripad Krishna

1976 *An Account of the Different Existing Systems of Sanskrit Grammar (being the Vishwanath Narayan Mandlik gold medal Prize-Essay for 1909).* 2nd rev. ed. Delhi: Bharatiya Vidya Prakashan.

Benfey, Theodor

1869 *Geschichte der Sprachwissenschaft und orientalishen Philologie in Deutschland seit dem Anfänge des 19. Jahrhunderts mit einem Rückblick auf die früheren Zeiten.* Geschichte der Wissenschaften in Deutschland, Neuere Zeit, 8. Bd. München.

Bhandarkar, R.G.

1877 *Wilson Philological Lectures (on Sanskrit and the Derived languages).* Reprinted from the Collected Works of Sir R.G. Bhandarkar, vol. IV. Poona: Bhandarkar Oriental Research Institute, 1974.

Bharati, Agehananda.

1970 "The Hindu Renaissance and its Apologetic Patterns." JAS 29.2: 267-287.

Bhat, D. N. S.

1971 *The Koraga language.* Poona: Deccan College, Postgraduate and Research Institute.

Bhate, Saroja

1993 "Bhartṛhari on language and reality." AS/ÉA 47.1 (Proceedings of the First International Conference on Bhartṛhari): 67-73.

Bhattacharya, B. and Vrajvallabha Dvivedi

1978 *Śaktisaṅgama -Tantra, Vol.IV.* (GOS) Baroda: Oriental Institute.

Bhattacharya, Kamaleswar

1991 *Recherches sur le vocabulaire des inscriptions sanskrites du Cambodge.* Paris: École française d'extrême-orient.

Bhayani, H. C.

1989 *Apabhraṃśa Language and Literature: A Short Introduction.* Delhi: B. L. Institute of Indology.

1992 "The Problem of the So-Called T-Śruti in the Mss. of Certain Early Jain Prakrit Texts." In *Jain Āgam Sāhitya: Seminar on Jaina Āgama*, ed. K. R. Candra: 278-281. Ahmedabad: Prākrit Jain Vidyā Vikās Phaṃḍ.

Biardeau, Madeleine

1964a *Bhartṛhari, Vākyapadīya Brahmakāṇḍa, avec la Vṛtti de Harivṛṣabha.* Texte reproduit de l'édition de Lahore, traduction, introduction et notes. Publications de l'Institut de Civilisation Indienne, fasc. 24. Paris: E. de Boccard.

1964b *Théorie de la connaissance et philosophie de la parole dans le Brahmanisme classique.* Le Monde d'Outre-Mer Passé et Présent, Première Série: Études XXIII. Paris - La Haye: Mouton.

Bloch, Jules

1911 Review of Denys de S. Bray, "The Brahui language, 1." JA, 10e série, 17: 1: 162-167. Repr. in Bloch 1985.

1925 "Sanskrit et dravidien." *Bulletin de la Société de Linguistique de Paris* 25: 1-21. Repr. in Bloch 1985.

1929 "Some problems of Indo-Aryan philology." *Bulletin of the School of Oriental Studies* (London) 5: 719-756. Repr. in Bloch 1985.

1934 *L'indo-aryen du véda aux temps modernes.* Paris: Adrien-Maisonneuve. Engl. transl. by A. Master, with retention of the 1934 pagination in the margin, Ibid., 1965.

1946 *Structure grammaticale des langues dravidiennes.* Engl. transl. by R. G. Harshé, Poona: Deccan College, 1954.

1950 *Les inscriptions d'Asoka.* Paris: Les Belles Lettres.

1985 *Recueil d'articles de Jules Bloch (1906-1955).* Ed. by C. Caillat. Paris: Collège de France, Institut de Civilisation Indienne.

Bloomfield, Maurice and Edgerton, Franklin

1932 *Vedic Variants*, vol. II. Philadelhphia: Linguistic Society of America, Univ. of Pennsylvania.

Bosch, F.D.K.

1928 "De Inscriptie van Keloerak." TBG 68: 1-64.

Bourdieu, Pierre

1977 *Outline of a theory of practice.* Transl. by Richard Nice. Cambridge: Cambridge Univ. Press.

1991 *Language and Symbolic Power.* Cambridge, MA: Harvard Univ. Press.

1993 *Sociology in Question*. Transl. by Richard Nice. London, New Delhi: SAGE Publications.

1994 *The Fields of Cultural Production*. New York: Columbia Univ. Press.

Bourdieu, Pierre and Loïc Wacquant

1992 *An Invitation to Reflexive Sociology*. Chicago: Univ. of Chicago Press.

Briggs, Charles

1992 "Linguistic ideologies and the naturalization of power in Warao discourse." *Pragmatics* 2:387-404.

Briggs, Lawrence Palmer

1951 *The Ancient Khmer Empire*, Transactions of the American Philosophical Society, N.S. Vol 41, Pt1. Philadelphia: The American Philosophical Society.

Briggs, Rick

1985 "Knowledge representation in Sanskrit and artificial intelligence." *AI Magazine* (Menlo Park CA: American Association for Artificial Intelligence) vol. 6: 22-38.

Bronkhorst, Johannes

1981 "Nirukta and Aṣṭādhyāyī: their shared presuppositions." IIJ 23, 1-14.

1983 "On the History of Pāṇinian Grammar in the Early Centuries Following Patañjali." JIPh 11: 357-412.

1985a "Nāgārjuna and the Naiyayikas." JIPh 13: 107-32.

1985b "On the Chronology of the Tattvārtha Sūtra and Some Early Commentaries." WZKS, 29: 155-184.

1987 *Three Problems pertaining to the Mahābhāṣya*. Post-graduate and Research Department Series no. 30; Pandit Shripad Shastri Deodhar Memorial Lectures [Third Series]. Poona: Bhandarkar Oriental Research Institute.

1988 "Études sur Bhartṛhari, 1: L'auteur et la date de la Vṛtti." *Bulletin d'Études Indiennes* 6:105-143.

1990 "Studies on Bhartṛhari, 2: Bhartṛhari and Mīmāṃsā." StII 15 (1989):101-117.

1991a "Pāṇini and the Veda Reconsidered." In: *Pāṇinian Studies, Professor S.D. Joshi Felicitation Volume*, ed. by Madhav M. Deshpande and Saroja Bhate:75-121. Ann Arbor: Center for South and Southeast Asian Studies, The Univ. of Michigan.

1991b "Studies on Bhartṛhari, 3: Bhartṛhari on sphoṭa and universals." AS/ÉA 45:5-18.

1992a "Études sur Bhartṛhari, 4: L'absolu dans le Vākyapadīya et son lien avec le Madhyamaka." AS/ÉA 46.1 (Études bouddhiques offertes à Jacques May):56-80.

1992b "Quelques axiomes du Vaiśeṣika." *Les Cahiers de Philosophie* 14 (L'orient de la pensée: philosophies en Inde): 95-110.

1993a "Buddhist Hybrid Sanskrit: the original language." In: Mishra 1993:396-414.

1993b "Kathāvatthu and Vijñānakāya." In *Premier Colloque Etienne Lamotte* (Publications de L'Institut Orientaliste de Louvain 42):57-61. Louvain-la-Neuve: Institute Orientaliste, Université Catholique de Louvain.

1993c "Studies on Bhartṛhari, 5: Bhartṛhari and Vaiśeṣika." *Proceedings of the First International Conference on Bhartṛhari* (Univ. of Poona, January 6-8, 1992). AS/ÉA 7.1:75-94.

1995 "A note on zero and the numerical place-value system in ancient India." AS/ÉA 48.4 (1994 [1995]):1039-1042.

forthcoming a "Audumbarāyaṇa revisited."

forthcoming b "Nāgārjuna's logic."

Brook, Judith S.

1970 "A test of Piaget's theory of 'nominal realism'." *Journal of Genetic Psychology* 116, 165-75.

Brough, J.

1954 "The Language of the Buddhist Sanskrit Texts." BSOAS 16:351-375.

Brunt, P. A.

1990 *Roman Imperial Themes.* Oxford: Clarendon Press.

Bühler, George

1864 "On the origin of the Sanskrit linguals." *Madras Journal of Literature and Science*, No. I, Third Series, 116-186. [ref. in Wackernagel 1896: 165 and elsewhere.]

1886 *The Laws of Manu.* (Transl.) Repr. Delhi: Motilal Banarsidass. 1984.

Bühnemann, Gudrun

1989 "The Heavenly Bodies (*navagraha*) in Hindu Ritual." *Saṁbhāṣā* 11:1-10. Nagoya: Univ. of Nagoya, Department of Indian Philosophy.

Buitenen, J.A.B. van

1962 *Maitrāyaṇīya Upaniṣad: a critical essay with text, translation and commentary.* (Disputationes Rheno-Traiectinae, vol. 6.) Den Haag: Mouton.

1978 "A brief history of the languages of India." In Edward Dimock, Jr., et al, *The Literatures of India: An Introduction.* Chicago: Univ. of Chicago Press.

Burgess, Jas.

1886 *Tamil and Sanskrit Inscriptions, with some notes on village antiquities collected chiefly in the South of the Madras presidency* (with translations by S.M. Natesa Sastri.) Archeological Survey of Southern India, vol. IV. Madras.

Burghart, Richard, ed.

1987 *Hinduism in Great Britain: The Perpetuation of Religion in an Alien Cultural Milieu.* London, New York: Tavistock Publications.

Burnell, Arthur Coke

1878 *Elements of South-Indian Palaeography from the 4th to the 17th century A.D., being an introduction to the study of South-Indian inscriptions and mss.* London: Truebner.

Burrow, Thomas

1955 *The Sanskrit language.* London: Faber & Faber. [New and revised edition: 1973.]

Burrow, Thomas, and Murray B. Emeneau

1961 *A Dravidian etymological dictionary.* Oxford: Oxford Univ. Press.

1984 *A Dravidian etymological dictionary.* 2nd ed. Oxford: Oxford Univ. Press.

Caillat, Colette (Ed.)

1989 *Dialectes dans les Littératures Indo-Aryennes.* Publications de l'Institut de Civilisation Indienne, Série in - 8°, Fascicule 55. Paris: Institut de Civilisation Indienne.

Caldwell, Robert

1856 *A comparative grammar of the Dravidian or South Indian family of languages* First edition. London. [Third edition 1913, repr. 1974, New Delhi: Oriental Books.]

Cardona, George

1976 *Pāṇini. A survey of research.* The Hague: Mouton & co. [Indian reprint: Delhi: Motilal Banarsidass, 1980.]

1988 *Pāṇini: His work and Its Traditions. Vol. 1: Background and Introduction.* Delhi, etc.: Motilal Banarsidass.

1990 "On attitudes towards language in ancient India." *Sino-Platonic Papers* 15:1-19. Philadelphia: Univ. of Pennsylvania, Department of Oriental Studies.

Casparis, J. G. de

1956 *Prasasti Indonesia II. Selected Inscriptions from the 7th to the 9th century A.D.* Bandung.

1975 *Indonesian Palaeography.* Handbuch der Orientalistik 3.4.1. Leiden, Köln: E. J. Brill.

1991 *Sanskrit Outside India.* Panels of the VIIth World Sanskrit Conference, Vol. VII. Leiden: E.J. Brill.

Çāstrī, Haraprasāda

1900 *Notices of Sanskrit Mss.* Second Series. Under orders of the Government of Bengal. Vol. I. Calcutta.

Chakravarti, Adhir

1978-80 *The Sdok Kak Thom Inscription: A Study in Indo-Khmer Civilization.* Two volumes. Calcutta Sanskrit Research Series No. CXI-II. Calcutta: Sanskrit College.

Chanthit Krasaesin

1962 *Phrakhamphī Chindāmanī khong Phrahorāthibodī,* Cremation Volume for Phra Phatmuni, Wat Thongnopphakhun, 13 January B.E. 2505.

Charnvit Kasetsiri

1976 *The Rise of Ayudhya, A History of Siam in the Fourteenth and Fifteenth Centuries,* Kuala Lumpur: Oxford Univ. Press.

Chatterjee, Partha

1993 *Nationalist Thought and the Colonial World, A Derivative Discourse.* 2nd ed. [first edition 1986]London: Zed Books.

1993a *The Nation and its Fragments: Colonial and Postcolonial Histories.* Princeton, New Jersey: Princeton Univ. Press.

Chatterji, Suniti Kumar

1926 *The origin and development of the Bengali language.* Calcutta: Univ. Press. [Repr. 1970, London: Allen & Unwin.]

1934 "The Pronunciation of Sanskrit." In: *K. B. Pathak Commemoration Volume,* ed. by S.K. Belvalkar:333-49. Pune: Bhandarkar Oriental Research Institute.

1952 "The Pronunciation of Sanskrit." *Le Maître Phonétique* 97 (Jan-June):2-9.

1962 *Indianism and the Indian Synthesis.* Calcutta: Univ. of Calcutta.

Chhabra, Bahadur Chand

1965 *Expansion of Indo-Aryan Culture during Pallava Rule, as Evidenced by Inscriptions.* Delhi: Munshi Ram Manohar Lal.

Christie, Craig

1983 *Uniformitarianism in Linguistics.* Amsterdam: John Benjamins.

Clifford, James

1986 "Introduction: Partial Truths." In James Clifford and George Marcus, eds., *Writing Culture: The Poetics and Politics of Ethnography.* Berkeley: Univ. of California Press.

Coedès, Georges

1915 "Note sur les ouvrages palis composés en pays Thai," BEFEO Vol 15, 1915: 39-46.

1953 *Inscriptions du Cambodge,* Vol. 5. Paris: E. de Boccard.

1964 *Les États Hindouisés d'Indochine et d'Indonésie.* Nouvelle éd. revue et mise à jour. Paris.

1968 *The Indianized States of Southeast Asia.* Honolulu: Univ. Press of Hawaii.

Colas, Gérard

1994 *Les sources scripturaires des vishnouites Vaikhānasa.* Thèse Paris (typewritten).

Collins, Steven

1990 "On The Very Idea of the Pāli Canon." *Journal of the Pāli Text Society.* 15: 89-126.

Compton, Carol J.

1979 *Courting Poetry in Laos: A Textual and Linguistic Analysis,* (Special Report No.18), Northern Illinois Univ.: Centre for Southeast Asian Studies.

Comrie, Bernard

1981 *The languages of the Soviet Union.* New York: Cambridge Univ. Press.

Conze, Edward, and Iida, Shotaro

1968 "'Maitreya's questions' in the Prajñāpāramitā." *Mélanges d'indianisme à la mémoire de Louis Renou* (Publications de l'Institut de Civilisation Indienne, Fasc. 28.): 229-242. Paris: E. de Boccard.

Cort, John E.

1993 "An Overview of the Jaina Purāṇas." In *Purāṇa Perennis: Reciprocity and Transformation in Hindu and Jaina Texts,* ed. W. Doniger: 185-206. Albany: State Univ. of New York Press.

forthcoming Cort, John E. (ed.)*Open Boundaries: Jain Communities and Cultures in Indian History.*

Crawfurd, John

1828 *Journal of an Embassy to the Courts of Siam and Cochin China.* Repr. Singapore: Oxford Univ. Press, 1987.

Cüppers., Christoph

1992 "Some Remarks on a Tibetan-Newari Lexicon cum Phrase Book." *Tibetan Studies. Proceedings of the 5th Seminar of the International Association for Tibetan Studies,* Narita 1989, ed. by Ihara Shōrun and Yamaguchi Zuihō: 413-419. Narita: Naritasan Shinshoji.

Daalen, Leendert J. van

1980 *Vālmīki's Sanskrit.* Orientalia Rheno-Traiectina, vol. 25. Thesis Utrecht. Leiden: E.J. Brill.

Daivarāta, Brahmarṣi/Maharṣi.

1971 *Vāk Sudhā.* Calcutta: Madana-gopāla Poddāra Cairiṭī Ṭrasṭa, saṁvat 2028.

Damsteegt, Th.

1978 *Epigraphical Hybrid Sanskrit: Its Rise, Spread, Characteristics and Relationship to Buddhist Hybrid Sanskrit.* Orientalia Rheno-Traiectina Vo. 23. Leiden: E. J. Brill.

1989 "The Pre-Kuśāna and Kuśāna Inscriptions and the Supercession of Prākrit by Sanskrit in North India." In *Mathurā: The Cultural Heritage,* ed. by Doris Meth Srinivasan. New Delhi: American Institute of Indian Studies.

Danda, A.K.

1993. "The Aryans: an anthropological approach." In Deo & Kamath 1993:103-107.

Dandekar, R.N.

1993 " Relevance of Sanskrit in Modern Times." In:*Chowkhambā: Sanskrit Series Office Centenary Commemoration Volume, 1892-1992,* ed. by Sudhakar Malaviya (Varanasi: Chowkhamba Series Office):231-235.

Dandekar, R.N. (ed.)

1972 *Sanskrit and Maharashtra, A Symposium.* Pune: Univ. of Poona.

Dasgupta, S.N.

1947 *A History of Sanskrit Literature.* Vol. 1. Calcutta.

D'Cruz, Emil

1988 *Indian Secularism: A Fragile Myth.* Indian Social Institute Monograph Series. First ed. New Delhi: Indian Social Institute.

De, Sushil Kumar

1960 *History of Sanskrit Poetics.* Second revised edition. Calcutta: K.L. Mukhopadhyay.

Debrunner, Albert and Jakob Wackernagel

1930 *Altindische Grammatik, 3. Nominalflexion - Zahlwort - Pronomen.* Göttingen: Vandenhoeck & Ruprecht.

Deleu, Jozef

1970 *Viyāhapannatti (Bhagavaī): The Fifth Aṅga of the Jaina Canon: Introduction, Critical Analysis, Commentary and Indexes.* Brugge: "De Tempel."

Demiéville, Paul

1924 "Les versions chinoises du Milindapañha (I)." BEFEO 24:1-258.

Deo, S.B.; Kamath, Suryanath (eds).

1993. *The Aryan Problem.* Pune: Bharatiya Itihasa Sankalana Samiti.

Deshpande, Madhav

1979a *Sociolinguistic attitudes in India: A historical reconstruction.* Linguistica Extranea, Studia 5. Ann Arbor: Karoma.

1979b "Genesis of Ṛgvedic retroflexion: A historical and sociolinguistic investigation." In: *Aryan and non-Aryan in India,* ed. by M. Deshpande and P. E. Hook, 235-315. Ann Arbor: Center for South and Southeast Asian Studies, Univ. of Michigan.

1979c "History, change and permanence: a Classical Indian Perspective." *Contributions to South Asian Studies* 1, ed. by Gopal Krishna. Delhi: Oxford Univ. Press.

1986 "Sanskrit Grammarians on Diglossia." In *South Asian Languages: Structure, Convergence and Diglossia,* ed. by Bh. Krishnamurti et al.: 312-321. Delhi: Motilal Banarsidass.

1987 "Strategies of Sanskrit Grammarians in defense of Vedic religion." Aligarh Journal of Oriental Studies 4:75-86.

1990 "Semantics of Kārakas in Pāṇini: An Exploration of Philosophical and Linguistic Issues." In *Sanskrit and Related Studies, Contemporary Researches and Reflections,* Ed. by Bimal Krishna Matilal and Puruṣottama Bilimoria: 33-57. Delhi: Sri Satguru Publications.

1991 "Conceptions of Diglossia in the Writings of the Sanskrit Grammarians." (substantially revised version of Deshpande 1986) *Southwest Journal of Linguistics. The Journal of the Linguistic Association of the Southwest.* 10.1:23-40.

1992a "Sociolinguistic Parameters of Pāṇini's Sanskrit." In: *Vidyāvratin, Professor A.M. Ghatage Felicitation Volume,* ed. by V.N. Jha: 111-130. Delhi: Sri Satguru Publications.

1992b *The Meaning of Nouns. Semantic Theory in Classical and Medieval India. Nāmārtha-nirṇaya of Kauṇḍabhaṭṭa translated and annotated.* Studies of Classical India, 13. Dordrecht: Kluwer Academic Publishers.

1993a *Sanskrit and Prakrit: Sociolonguistic Issues.* Delhi: Motilal Banarsidass.

1993b "Aryans, non-Aryans, and brāhmaṇas: Processes of indigenization." JIES 21: 215-235.

1993c "Inscriptional Evidence for Honorific *Śrī* in Indo-Aryan." In: *Perspectives in Indian Aesthetics and Literature, Essays in honour of the Late Prof. Dr. G.K. Bhat,* ed. by Saroj Deshpande and Maneesha Dikshit: 254-278. Pune: Dastane Ramchandra.

1993d "The changing notion of *śiṣṭa* from Patañjali to Bhartṛhari," AS/ÉA 47.1 (Proceedings of the Bhartṛhari Conference, Poona Univ., January 6-8, 1992): 95-115.

1994 "Brahmanism versus Buddhism: A Perspective of Language Attitudes." In *Jainism and Prakrit in Ancient and Medieval India: Essays for Prof. Jagdish Chandra Jain,* ed. N. N. Bhattacharyya: 89-111. Delhi: Manohar.

Deshpande, Madhav M. and Peter Edwin Hook(eds.).

1979 *Aryan and Non-Aryan in India.* Michigan Papers on South and Southeast Asia, no. 14. Ann Arbor: Centre for South and Southeast Asian Studies, The Univ. of Michigan.

Dessein, Bart

1994 *Allerlei betreffende de Kern der Scholastiek (Saṃyuktābhidharmahṛdayaśāstra - T. Vol. 28, Nr. 1552).* Unpublished doctoral thesis, Univ. of Gent, Belgium.

Devasthali, Govind Vinayak (ed.)

1968 *Sārasiddhāntakaumudī of Varadarāja.* PCASS, Class C, 4. Poona: Univ. of Poona.

Devendraswarup

1993 "Genesis of the Aryan race theory and its application to Indian history." In Deo & Kamath 1993:30-39.

Dhere, R.C.

1984 *Viṭṭhala: Ek Mahāsamanvaya* (in Marathi). Pune: Shrividya Prakashan.

Dijk, Alphons M.G. van

1977 "Europese invloeden op het denken van Sri Aurobindo. European Influences on Sri Aurobindo's Thought (with a summary in English)." Thesis Utrecht.

1981 "Neohinduismus und indologie am Beispiel der Beziehung Sri Aurobindo - Max Müller." *Internationales Asienforum* 12, 2/3: 171-187. [Cf. Dijk 1977.]

Dobson Collet, Sophia

1988 *The Life and Letters of Raja Rammohun Roy,* ed. by Dilip Kumar Biswas and Prabhat Chandra Ganguli. 4th annotated edition. [first edition without notes, 1900.] Calcutta: Sadharan Brahmo Samaj.

d'Souza, Jean

1988 "Diglossia in the South Asian Sociolinguistic Area." *ITL: Review of applied Linguistics,* vol. 79-80:25-59.

Dumont, Louis.

1960 "World Renunciation in Indian Religions." *Contributions to Indian Sociology* 4.1:33-62.

Dundas, Paul

1991 "The Digambara Jain Warrior." In: *The Assembly of Listeners: Jains in Society.* In M. Carrithers and C. Humphrey (ed.): 169-186. Cambridge: Cambridge Univ. Press.

1992 *The Jains.* London/New York: Routledge.

forthcoming a "Becoming Gautama: Mantra and History in Śvetāmbara Jainism." In Cort (ed.), forthcoming.

forthcoming b "Somnolent Sūtras: Scriptural Commentary in Śvetāmbara Jainism." JIPh 24 (1996):73-101.

During, Simon (ed.)

1993 *The Cultural Studies Reader.* London, New York: Routledge.

Dutta, Abhijit

1992 *Nineteenth Century Bengal Society And Christian Missionaries.* Calcutta: Minerva.

Edgerton, Franklin

1926/27 *Vikrama's adventures or the thirty-two tales of the throne.* Harvard Oriental Series Nos. 26 and 27. Cambridge, Massachusetts: Harvard Univ. Press.

1953 *Buddhist Hybrid Sanskrit Grammar and Dictionary.* New Haven: Yale Univ. Press.

Eggeling, Julius

1889 *Catalogue of the Sanskrit Manuscripts in the Library of the India Office. Part II Saṁskrit Literature: A. Scientific and Technical Literature. I. Grammar, Lexicography, Prosody, Music.* London.

1885 *The Śatapatha-Brāhmaṇa.* Translation. Part IV (Books VIII, IX and X). Reprint: Motilal Banarsidass, Delhi, 1978.

Elizarenkova, Tatyana J.

1989 "About traces of a Prakrit dialectal basis in the language of the Ṛgveda." In Caillat 1989:1-17.

1995 *Language and Style of the Vedic Ṛṣis.* Albany: State Univ. of New York Press.

Emeneau, Murray B.

1954 "Linguistic prehistory of India." *Proceedings of the American Philosophical Society* 98: 282-292. Repr. in Emeneau 1980.

1956 "India as a linguistic area." *Language* 32: 3-16. Repr. in Emeneau 1980.

1962 *Brahui and Dravidian comparative grammar.* Berkeley and Los Angeles: Univ. of California Press.

1966 "The Dialects of Old Indo-Aryan." In *Ancient Indo-European Dialects,* ed. by H. Birnbaum and Jaan Puhvel: 123-138. Berkeley: Univ. of California Press.

1971a "Dravidian and Indo-Aryan: The Indian linguistic area." in: *Symposium on Dravidian civilization,* ed. by Andrée F. Sjoberg: 33-68. Austin & New York: Jenkins Publishing & Pemberton Press. Repr. in Emeneau 1980.

1971b "Kodagu and Brahui developments of Proto-Dravidian **r.*" IIJ 13: 176-198. Repr. in Emeneau 1994.

1974 "The Indian linguistic area revisited." IJDL 3: 92-134. Repr. in Emeneau 1980.

1980 *Language and linguistic area: Essays selected by A. S. Dil.* Stanford, CA: Univ. Press.

1989 "The language of the Nilgiris." In *Blue Mountains: The ethnography and biogeography of a South Indian region,* 133-143. Repr. in Emeneau 1994.

1994 *Dravidian studies: Selected papers.* Ed. by Bh. Krishnamurti. Delhi: Motilal Banarsidass.

Emeneau, M.B. and Burrow, T.

1962 *Dravidian Borrowings from Indo-Aryan.* (Univ. of California Publications in Linguistics, vol. 26.) Berkeley etc.: Univ. of California Press.

Erdosy, George

1995 "Language, material culture and ethnicity: Theoretical perspectives." In *The Indo-Aryans of Ancient South Asia: Language, Material Culture and Ethnicity,* ed. by George Erdosy: 1-31. Berlin, New York: Walter de Gruyter.

Falk, Harry

1990 "Goodies for India – literacy, orality, and Vedic culture." In: *Erscheinungsformen kultureller Prozesse*, ed. Wolfgang Raible. Tübingen: Gunter Narr. (ScriptOralia, 13.) Pp. 103-120.

1993 *Schrift im alten Indien. Ein Forschungsbericht mit Anmerkungen.* ScriptOralia, 56. Tübingen: Gunter Narr.

Ferguson, C.A.

1959 "Diglossia." *Word* 15:325-340.

Fernández, Mauro

1993 *Diglossia, A comprehensive bibliography 1960-1990, and supplements.* Amsterdam: John Benjamins.

Filliozat, Jean

1972 "Sanskrit as a link language." *Sanskṛit Studies Abroad*: 10-18. New Delhi: Ministry of Education and Social Welfare, Government of India.

1977 "Le Sanskrit et le Pāli en Asie du sud-est." *Comptes Rendus, Académie des Inscriptions et Belles-lettres*: 398-406.

Fishman, Joshua A.

1985 "Bilingualism and Biculturalism as Individual and as Societal phenomena." *The Rise and Fall of the Ethnic Revival: Perspectives on Language and Ethnicity*, ed. by J.A. Fishman: 39-56. Berlin: Mouton.

Fitzgerald, Timothy.

1990 "Hinduism and the 'world religion' fallacy." *Religion* 20:101-118.

Fortson, Ben.

1994 "Prolegomena to a synchronic analysis of the Hittite quotative particle." *Harvard Working Papers in Linguistics* 4: 37-51.

Franco, Eli

1994 "Yet another look at the framework of the Pramāṇasiddhi chapter of Pramāṇavārttika." IIJ 37:233-252.

Frauwallner, Erich

1956 *Die Philosophie des Buddhismus.* Berlin: Akademie Verlag. [4. Auflage 1994.]

Friedrich, Paul

1975 *Proto-Indo-European syntax*. Butte, Montana: JIES.

1976 "Ad Hock." JIES 4: 207-220.

1977 "The devil's case: PIE as type II." In *Linguistic studies offered to Joseph Greenberg on the occasion of his 60th birthday*, ed. by A. Juilland, 3: 463-480. Saratoga, CA: Anma Libri.

Fussman, Gérard

1980a "Nouvelles Inscriptions śaka." BEFEO 67:1-43.

1980b Review of Damsteegt 1978. JA 268:420-426.

Gandhi, L.B. (ed.)

1927 *Apabhraṁśa-kāvya-trayī* [by Jina-datta-sūri]. Baroda: Gaekwad's Oriental Series no. 37. [Reprinted 1967.]

Gerini, G.E.

1976 *Chūlākantamaṅgala or the Tonsure Ceremony as Performed in Siam*, Bangkok: The Siam Society. (Reprint of the 1893 edition).

Gerow, Edwin

1978 "Origins of Poetics." In *The Literatures of India: An Introduction*, ed. by Edward Dimock, Jr., et al. Chicago: Univ. of Chicago Press.

Ghatage, A.M., et al. (ed.)

1976 - *Encyclopaedic Dictionary of Sanskrit on Historical Principles*. Poona: Univ. of Poona and Deccan College.

Ghosh, Manomohan (ed.)

1967 *The Nāṭyaśāstra ascribed to Bharata-Muni*. Vol I (chapters I-XXVII). Calcutta: Manisha Granthalaya.

Gibbons, John

1992 "Sociology of Language," in: *International Encyclopedia of Linguistics* (Oxford, etc.: Oxford University Press, 1992; ed. W. Bright), 22-25.

Giddens, Anthony

1981 *A Contemporary Critique of Historical Materialism*. Berkeley: Univ. of California Press.

Giddens, Anthony, David Held, Don Hubert, et al.

1994 *The Polity Reader in Cultural Theory*. Oxford: Polity Press.

Gil, David

1994 "Conjunctive operators in South-Asian languages." In *SALA XV: Papers from the Fifteenth South Asian Language Analysis Roundtable Conference 1993*, ed. by A. Davison and F. M. Smith. Iowa City: South Asian Studies Program, Univ. of Iowa.

Gode, Parashuram Krishna

1941 "Varadarāja, a Pupil of Bhaṭṭoji Dīkṣita and his works – Between A.D. 1600 and 1650." *A Volume of Studies in Indology presented to P. V. Kane on his 61st Birthday*, ed. by S. M. Katre and P. K. Gode: 188-199. Poona: Oriental Book Agency. [Reprinted in Gode 1954: 316-329.]

1954 *Studies in Indian LiteraryHistory*, Vol. II. Bombay: Bharatiya Vidya Bhavan.

1956 "An Echo of the Siege of Jinji in a Sanskrit Grammatical Work." *Studies in Indian Literary History*, Vol. III: 161-171. Poona: Prof. P.K. Gode Collected Works Committee. [Originally published in the *Journal of the Sarasvati Mahal Library Tanjore*, Vol. V, No. 3, 1-13; year of publ. not available.]

Golwarkar, Madhav Sadashiv.

1966 *Bunch of Thoughts*. Bangalore: Vikrama Prakashan.

Gonda, Jan

1973 *Sanskrit in Indonesia*. Sec. ed. Śata-Piṭaka Series, Indonesian Literatures, Vol. 99. New Delhi: International Academy of Indian Culture.

1975 *Vedic literature*. A history of Indian literature, 1.1. Wiesbaden: Harrassowitz.

1980 *Vedic Ritual. The Non-Solemn Rites*. Leiden-Köln: E.J. Brill.

Goudriaan, Teun and Sanyukta Gupta

1981 *Hindu Tantric and Śākta Literature.* A history of Indian literature, 2.2. Wiesbaden: Otto Harrassowitz.

Goudriaan, T. and C. Hooykaas

1971 *Stuti and Stava (Bauddha, Śaiva and Vaiṣṇava) of Balinese Brahman Priests.* VKAW, deel 76. Amsterdam, London: North Holland Publishing Company.

Goudriaan, Teun and J.A. Schoterman

1988 *Kubjikāmatatantra: Kulālikāmnāya version. Critical Edition.* Orientalia Rheno-Traiectina, vol. 30. Leiden: E.J. Brill.

Gramsci, Antonio

1991 *Selections from cultural writings.* Ed. by David Forges and Geoffrey Nowell-Smith. Cambridge: Harvard Univ. Press.

Granoff, Phyllis

1989 "The Biographies of Siddhasena: A Study in the Texture of Allusion and the Weaving of a Group-Image, Part 1." JIPh 17: 329-384.

1990 "The Biographies of Siddhasena: A Study in the Texture of Allusion and the Weaving of a Group-Image, Part 2." JIPh 18: 261-304.

1991 "Buddhaghoṣa's Penance and Siddhasena's Crime: Remarks on Some Buddhist and Jain Attitudes towards the Language of Religious Texts." In *From Benares to Beijing: Essays on Buddhism and Chinese Religion,* ed. K. Shinohara and G. Schopen: 17-33. Oakville/New York/London: Mosaic Press.

1995 "Sarasvatī's sons: biographies of poets in medieval India." AS/ÉA 49.2:351-376.

Grierson, George A.

1903-28 *Linguistic survey of India,* 11 vols. Comp. and ed. by G.A. Grierson. Calcutta. Repr. 1968, Delhi: Motilal Banarsidass.

1904 Contribution to discussion on the question: "In what degree was Sanskrit a Spoken Language?" JRAS: 471-481.

Griswold, A.B. and Prasert na Nagara

1973 "The Epigraphy of Mahādharmarājā I of Sukhodaya." *Journal of the Siam Society,* January 1973, Vol 61, Pt 1:71-178.

Grossberg, Lawrence, Cary Nelson, Paula Treichler (eds.)

1992 *Cultural Studies.* New York, London: Routledge.

Gumperz, John J., and Robert Wilson

1971 "Convergence and creolization: a case from the Indo-Aryan/Dravidian border." In *Pidginization and creolization of language,* ed. by D. Hymes: 151-168. Cambridge: Univ. Press.

Gupta, S.P.

1993 "Palaeo-Anthropology and Archaelogy of the Vedic Aryans." In Deo & Kamath 1993:153-165.

Gyani, S.D.

1964 *Agni-Purāṇa. A Study.* The Chowkhamba Sanskrit Studies 42. Varanasi.

Hacker, Paul.

1978 "Aspects of Neo-Hinduism as Contrasted with Surviving Traditional Hinduism." (Vortragsmanuskript, diskutiert am 5.5.1970 an der Universität London.) In *Kleine Schriften*, ed. Lambert Schmithausen:580-608. Wiesbaden: Franz Steiner Verlag. Also in Hacker 1995:229-255.

1995 *Philology and Confrontation. Paul Hacker on Traditional and Modern Vedanta.* Ed. by Wilhelm Halbfass. Albany: State Univ. of New York Press.

Hahn, Ferd

1911 *Kurukh grammar.* Calcutta: Bengal Secretariat. Repr. (no date), Delhi: Mittal.

Halbfass, Wilhelm

1988 *India and Europe: An Essay in Understanding.* Albany: State Univ. of New York Press.

1991a "Tradition und Reflexion: Zur Gegenwart des Veda in der indischen Philosophie." In *Beiträge zur Hermeneutik indischer und abendländischer Religionstraditionen*, ed. by Gerhard Oberhammer: 123-146. Wien: Österreichische Akademie der Wissenschaften.

1991b *Tradition and Reflection: Explorations in Indian Thought.* Albany: State Univ. of New York Press.

Hale, Wash Edward

1986 *Ásura in early Vedic religion.* Delhi: Motilal Banarsidass.

Hall, Bruce Cameron

1986 "The meaning of vijñapti in Vasubandhu's concept of mind." JIABS 9.1:7-23.

Hall, Kenneth R.

1976 "An Introductory Essay on Southeast Asian Statecraft in the Classical Period." In *Explorations in Early Southeast Asian History: The Origins of Southeast Asian Statecraft*, ed. by Kenneth R. Hall and John K.Whitmore:1-18. Ann Arbor: Center for South and Southeast Asian Studies, The Univ. of Michigan.

Hannerz, Ulf

1989 "Culture Between Center and Periphery: Toward a Macroanthropology." *Ethnos* 3-4:200-216.

Harris, Ian Charles

1991 *The Continuity of Madhyamaka and Yogācāra in Indian Mahāyāna Buddhism.* Brill' s Indological Library, 6. Leiden: E.J. Brill.

Harrison, Paul

1990 *The Samādhi of Direct Encounter with the Buddhas of the Present. An annotated English translation of the Tibetan version of the Pratyutpanna-Buddha-Sammukhāvasthita-Samādhi-Sūtra with several appendices relating to the history of the text.* Studia Philologica Buddhica, Monograph Series, 5. Tokyo: The International Institute for Buddhist Studies.

1992 "Is the dharma-kāya the real 'phantom body' of the Buddha?" JIABS 15.1:44-94.

Hartmann, J.F.

1984 *Linguistic and Memory Structures in Tai-Lue Oral Narratives.* Pacific Linguistics Series B˘ No.90. Canberra: Department of Linguistics, Research School of Pacific Studies, The Australian National Univ.Hayes, Richard P.

1988 *Dignaga on the Interpretation of Signs.* Studies of Classical India, 9. Dordrecht: Kluwer Academic Publishers.

Hazra, R.C.

1963 *Studies in the Upapurāṇas, Vol. II.* Calcutta Sanskrit College Research Series: no. 2, 20; studies no. 1, 10. Calcutta: Sanskrit College.

Heidegger, Martin

1960 *Der Ursprung des Kunstwerkes.* Stuttgart: Reclam.

Hertel, Johannes

1921 *Bharaṭakadvātriṁśikā* [ed.]. Sächsisches Forschungsinstitut für Indogermanistik, Indische Abteilung, Nr. 2. Leipzig.

1922 *On the Literature of the Śvetāmbaras of Gujarat.* Sächsisches Forschungsinstitut für Indogermanistik, Indische Abteilung, Nr. 1. Leipzig: Markert & Petter.

Hinüber, Oskar von

1986 *Das ältere Mittelindisch im Überblick.* Veröffentlichungen der Kommission für Sprachen und Kulturen Südasiens, Heft 20. Wien: Verlag der Österreichischen Akademie der Wissenschaften.

1988 *Die Sprachgeschichte des Pāli im Spiegel der südostasiatischen Handschriftenüberlieferung.* Untersuchungen zur Sprachgeschichte und Handschriftenkunde des Pāḷi I. Mainz: Akademie der Wissenschaften und der Literatur; Stuttgart: Franz Steiner Verlag Wiesbaden.

1989 "Origin and varieties of Buddhist Sanskrit." In Caillat 1989:341-367.

1993 "From colloquial to standard language: the oral phase in the development of Pāli." In: *Premier Colloque Étienne Lamotte,* Publications de l'institut orientaliste de Louvain, no. 42:101-113. Louvain-la-Neuve: Institut Orientaliste.

1994 "On the History of the Name of the Pāli Language." In O. von Hinüber, *Selected Papers*: 76-90. Oxford: The Pali Text Society.

Hobsbawm, E.J.

1992 *Nations and Nationalism since 1780: Programme, Myth, Reality.* 2nd edition. Cambridge: Cambridge Univ. Press.

Hock, Hans Henrich

1974 "Historical change and synchronic structure: The case of the Sanskrit root nouns." In *Toward tomorrow's linguistics,* ed. by R. W. Shuy & C.-J. N. Bailey: 329-42. Georgetown Univ. Press. Repr. in IJDL 4(1975): 215-28.

1975 "Substratum influence on (Rig-Vedic) Sanskrit?" SLS 5: 2: 76-125.

1979 "Retroflexion rules in Sanskrit." *South Asian Languages Analysis* 1: 47-62.

1982a "AUX-cliticization as a motivation for word order change." SLS 12: 1: 91-101

1982b "The Sanskrit quotative: A historical and comparative study." SLS 12: 2: 39-85.

1984 "(Pre-)Rig-Vedic convergence of Indo-Aryan with Dravidian? Another look at the evidence." SLS 14: 1: 89-107.

1987 "Regular contact dissimilation." In *A Festschrift for Henry Hoenigswald*, ed. by G. Cardona & N. Zide: 143-53. Tübingen: Narr.

1988a "Historical implications of a dialectological approach to convergence." In *Historical dialectology*, ed. by J. Fisiak: 283-328. Berlin: Mouton de Gruyter.

1988b Review article: Finiteness in Dravidian. (Sanford B. Steever (1988): *The serial verb formation in the Dravidian languages*.) SLS 18: 2: 211-31

1989 "Conjoined we stand: Theoretical implications of Sanskrit relative clauses." SLS 19: 1:93-126.

1991a "Dialects, diglossia, and diachronic phonology in early Indo-Aryan." In *Studies in the historical phonology of Asian languages*, ed. by W. G. Boltz and M. C. Shapiro:119-159. Amsterdam & Philadelphia: John Benjamins.

1991b *Principles of historical linguistics*. 2nd revised ed. Berlin: Mouton de Gruyter. [First ed. idem, 1986.]

1992a "Reconstruction and syntactic typology: A plea for a different approach." In *Explanation in historical linguistics*, ed. by G. W. Davis and G. K. Iverson: 105-121. Amsterdam: John Benjamins.

1992b Review of Tikkanen 1987. *Kratylos* 37: 62-68.

1993a "Swallow tales: Chance and the 'world etymology' MALIQ'A 'swallow, throat'." *Papers from the 29th Regional Meeting of the Chicago Linguistic Society*, 1: 215-238.

1993b Review of Abbi 1992. SLS 23: 1: 169-192.

1994a "Discourse linkage in Sanskrit narratives with special emphasis on the story of Nala." In *Papers from the Fifteenth South Asian Language Analysis Roundtable 1993*, ed. by A. Davison and F. M. Smith:117-139. Iowa City: South Asian Studies Program.

1994b "Narrative linkage in the Mahābhārata." In *Modern evaluation of the Mahābhārata: Professor R. K. Sharma felicitation volume*, ed. by S. P. Narang: 295-313. Delhi: Nag Publishers.

Hock, Hans Henrich, and Rajeshwari Pandharipande

1976 "The Sociolinguistic Position of Sanskrit in Pre-Muslim South Asia." *Studies in Language Learning*, Vol. 1.2 (Special issue on Dimensions of Bilingualism: Theory and Case Studies, ed. by Braj B. Kachru):105-138. Urbana: Univ. of Illinois.

1978 "Sanskrit in the Pre-Islamic Sociolinguistic Context of South Asia." *International Journal of the Sociology of Language* 16 (*Aspects of Sociolinguistics in South Asia*, ed. by Kachru, Braj B. and S.N. Sridhar): 11-25. [Condensed version of Hock & Pandharipande 1976.]

Hoffmann, Karl

1941 "Die alt-indoarischen Wörter mit -*ṇḍ*-, besonders im Ṛgveda." Unpublished doctoral dissertation, München.

1956 "'Wiederholende' Onomatopoetika im Altindischen." *Indogermanische Forschungen* 60: 254-264. Repr. in Hoffmann 1975.

1975 *Aufsätze zur Indoiranistik*, ed. by J. Narten, 1. Wiesbaden: Reichert.

Holmström, Mark

1956 "'Wiederholende' Onomatopoetika im Altindischen." *Indogermanische Forschungen* 60: 254-264. Repr. in Hoffmann 1975.

1975 *Aufsätze zur Indoiranistik*, ed. by J. Narten, 1. Wiesbaden: Reichert.

1971 "Religious Change in an Industrial City of South India." JRAS: 28-40.

Hooykaas, C.

1955 *The Old-Javanese Rāmāyaṇa Kakawin, with special reference to the problem of interpolation in kakawins.* Verhand. KITLV, Deel 16. 's-Gravenhage.

1964 *Āgama Tīrtha. Five Studies in Hindu-Balinese Religion.* VKAW, Deel 70.4, Amsterdam: North-Holland Publishing Company.

Hopkins, Edward W.

1902 *The Great Epic of India. Its Character and Origin.* New York: Charles Scribner's Sons; London: Edward Arnold.

Horner, I.B. trans.

1952 *Vinayapiṭaka: The Book of the Discipline*, vol 5: Cullavagga. London: Luzac & Co.

Houben, Jan E.M.

1992 *The Saṃbandha-samuddeśa (Chapter on Relation) and Bhartṛhari's Philosophy of Language.* Doctoral thesis, Univ. of Utrecht. [Cf. Houben 1995a.]

1993 "Bhartṛhari en de structuur van het Sanskrit: 'God's truth' of 'hocus-pocus'?" *Nieuwe wegen in taal- en literatuurwetenschap: Handelingen van het Eenenveertigste Filologencongres.* Ed. J. Goedegebure. Tilburg: Tilburg Univ. Press. Pp. 143-158.

1994a "Bhartṛhari's familiarity with Jainism." ABORI 75:1-24.

1994b "Early Indian authors and linguistic change. Postscript to Bhartṛhari's familiarity with Jainism." ABORI 75:255-256.

1995a *The Saṁbandha-samuddeśa (chapter on relation) and Bhartṛhari's Philosophy of Language.* Gonda Indological Studies, 2. Groningen: Egbert Forsten.

1995b "Liberation and natural philosophy in early Vaiśeṣika: some methodological problems." *Asiatische Studien / Études Asiatiques* 48.2 (1994 [1995]):711-748.

1995c "Bhartṛhari's Perspectivism (2): Bhartṛhari on the Primary Unit of Language". *History and Rationality: The Skövde Papers in the Historiography of Linguistics*, ed. by Klaus D. Dutz and Kjell-Åke Forsgren: 29-62. Münster: Nodus.

forthc. "Bhartṛhari's perspectivism (1) The Vṛtti and Bhartṛhari's perspectivism in the first kāṇḍa of the Vākyapadīya." To appear in *Beyond Orientalism: the impact of the work of W. Halbfass on Indian and cross-cultural studies*, ed. K. Preisendanz and E. Franco. Amsterdam: Rodopi.

Householder, F.W.

1989 Review of *History of Linguistics in the Classical Period*, ed. by D.J. Taylor; Amsterdam & Philadelphia: Benjamins, 1987. *Historiographia Linguistica* 16.1/2:131-148.

Hudak, Thomas John,

1985 "Poetic Conventions in Thai *chǎn* Meters." JAOS 105.1:107-117.

1986 "Toward an Understanding of a Thai Poem." In *Papers from a Conference on Thai Studies in Honor of William J. Gedney*, ed. by Robert J. Bickner, Thomas J. Hudak and Patcharin Peyasantiwong:185-198. Univ. of Michigan: Center for South and Southeast Asian Studies.

1990 *The Indigenization of Pali Meters in Thai Poetry*. Ohio Univ. Monographs in International Studies, Southeast Asia Series, No 87. Athens, Ohio.

Hultzsch, E.

1917 *South Indian Inscriptions*, vol. II, pt. 1, New Imperial Series, vol. X. Archeological Survey of India. Madras: Government Press.

Irvine, Martin

1994 *The Making of Textual Culture: 'Grammatica' and Literary Theory, 350-1100*. Cambridge, Eng.: Cambridge Univ. Press.

Isaacson, Harunaga

1993 "Yogic perception (*yogipratyakṣa*) in early Vaiśeṣika." StII 18:139-160.

Ishikawa, M.

1990 *A critical edition of the Sgra sbyor bam po gnyis pa. An old and basic commentary on the Mahāvyutpatti*. Studia Tibetica 18, Materials for Tibetan-Mongolian Dictionaries 2. Tokyo: The Tokyo Bunko.

Iyer, K.A. Subramania

1964 "Bhartṛhari on Apabhraṁśa." *Vishveshwaranand Indological Journal* (Hoshiarpur) 2.2:242-246.

1977 *The Vākyapadīya of Bhartṛhari, Kāṇḍa II: English translation with exegetical notes*. Delhi: Motilal Banarsidass.

Jacobi, Hermann

1893 *Das Rāmāyaṇa. Geschichte und Inhalt nebst Concordanz der gedruckten Recensionen*. Bonn: F. Cohen. [Repr. Darmstadt: Wissenschaftliche Buchgesellschaft, 1970.]

Jacques, Claude

1986 "Economic Activities in Khmer and Cham Lands." In *Southeast Asia in the 9th to 14th Centuries*, ed. by D. G. Hall and A. C. Milner. Singapore.

Jain, G. C.

1993 "Hybridism in Jaina Sanskrit Literature." In Mishra 1993: 105-115.

Jain, Sagar Mal

1986 *Jain Bhāṣā-Darśan*. Delhi: Bhogilal Leherchand Institute of Indology.

Jakobson, Roman.

1931 "Über die phonologischen Sprachbünde." TCLP 4: 234-240.

Jambuvijaya, Muni (ed.)

1961 *Vaiśeṣika Sūtra of Kaṇāda.* With the commentary of Candrānanda. Baroda: Oriental Institute. [2nd ed. 1982.]

Jamspal, L. (ed.)

1992 *Abhidhānaviśvalocana of Śrīdharasena.* Narita: Naritasan Shinshoji.

Jinavijaya, Muni (ed.)

1953 *Ukti-Vyakti-Prakaraṇa of Pandit Dāmodara.* With an Introduction by Dr. S. V. Chatterji and Dr. Moti Chandra. Singhi Jaina Granthamala 39. Bombay: Bharatiya Vidya Bhavan.

Johnson, B.C.

1986 "Diglossia in Africa." In *South Asian Languages: Structure, Convergence and Diglossia,* ed. by Bh. Krishnamurti et alii: 337-349. Delhi: Motilal Banarsidass.

Jones, Kenneth W.

1976 *Arya Dharm: Hindu consciousness in 19th-century Punjab.* Berkeley and Los Angeles, California: Univ. of California Press.

Jordens, J.T.F.

1978 *Dayananda Sarasvati: His Life and Ideas.* Delhi: Oxford Univ. Press.

Joshi, M. (ed.)

1979 *Bharatīya Sanskṛti Kośa.* 9 volumes. Pune: Bharatīya Sanskṛti Kośa Maṇḍala.

Joshi, S.D.

1989 "Patañjali's views on Apaśabdas." In: Caillat 1989::267-274.

Joshi, S.D., and J.A.F. Roodbergen.

1975 *Patañjali's Vyākaraṇa-mahābhāṣya, Kārakāhnika (p. 1. 4. 23-1. 4. 55).* PCASS. Class C, 10. Poona: Univ. of Poona. 11. 12. 14.

1976 *Patañjali's Vyākaraṇa-Mahābhāṣya, Anabhihitāhnika (p. 2. 3. 1-2. 3. 17).* PCASS. Class C, 11. Poona: Univ. of Poona.

1980 *Patañjali's Vyākaraṇa-Mahābhāṣya, Vibhaktyāhnika (p. 2. 3. 18-2. 3. 45).* PCASS. Class C, 12. Poona: Univ. of Poona.

1981 *Patañjali's Vyākaraṇa-Mahābhāṣya, Prātipadikārthaśeṣāhnika (P. 2. 3. 46-2. 3. 71).* PCASS. Class C, 14. Poona: Univ. of Poona.

1986 *Patañjali's Vyākaraṇa-Mahābhāṣya, Paspaśāhnika.* Introduction, Text, Translation and Notes. PCASS. Class C, 15. Poona: Univ. of Poona.

[1991] *The Aṣṭādhyāyī of Pāṇini with Translation and Explanatory Notes.* Volume I (1.1.1 - 1.1.75). New Delhi: Sahitya Akademi.

Jourdan, Christine

1991 "Pidgins and Creoles: The Blurring of Categories." *Annual Review of Anthropology* 20: 187-209.

Juynboll, H.H.

1907, 1911 *Supplement op den catalogus van de Javaansche en Madoereesche handschriften der Leidsche Universiteits-Bibliotheek.* I, II, Leiden.

Kahrs, Eivind G.

1992 "What is a *tad-bhava* word?" IIJ 35:225-49.

Kak, Subhash.

1994 "On the classification of Indic languages." ABORI 75:185-95.

Kalupahana, David

1986 *Nāgārjuna: The Philosophy of the Middle Way*. Albany: State Univ. of New York Press.

Kale, M. R.

1967 *Kālidāsa's Kumārasaṃbhava. Cantos I-VIII (Complete) ed. with the commentary of Mallīnātha, a literal English translation, Notes and Introduction*. Delhi-Varanasi-Patna: Motilal Banarsidass.

Kane, Pandurang Vaman

1971 *History of Sanskrit Poetics*. 4th rev. edition. Delhi: Motilal Banarsidass.

Kapadia, H. R.

1941 *A History of the Canonical Literature of the Jainas*. Surat.

Kaviraj, Sudipta

1993 "The Imaginary Institution of India." *Subaltern Studies*, vol. 7:1-39. Delhi: Oxford Univ. Press.

Kawasaki, Shinjō

1977 "The Mīmāṃsā chapter of Bhavya's Madhyamaka-hṛdaya-kārikā – text and translation – (1) Pūrva-pakṣa." *Studies 1976, Institute of Philosophy, The Univ. of Tsukuba*: 1-16.

Keith, A. Berridale

1928 *A History of Sanskrit Literature*. Oxford Univ. Press. London: Geoffrey Cumberlege. [Reprints ibidem 1941 and 1948.]

Khing, Hoc Dy

1990 *Contribution à l'histoire de la littérature khmère*, vol. 1: Littérature de l'époque 'classique' (xv-xixième siècles). Paris. Editions l'Harmattan.

Kielhorn, F. (ed.)

1880-85 *The Vyākaraṇa-Mahābhāṣya of Patañjali*. 3 vols. Third edition by K.V. Abhyankar. Poona: Bhandarkar Oriental Research Institute. 1962-72. [Cf. Gen. Bibliography Sect. II under MBh.]

Klaiman, M. H.

1976 "Correlative clauses and IE syntactic reconstruction." In *Papers from the Parasession on Diachronic Syntax*: 159-68. Chicago: Linguistic Society.

Konow, Sten

1906 Discussion in vol. 4: 279 of Grierson 1903-1928.

Kripalani, Krishna

1980 *Rabindranath Tagore, A Biography*. 2nd edition. [first edition 1962] Calcutta: Visva-Bharati.

Krishnamurti, Bh.

1969 "Comparative Dravidian Studies." *Current trends in linguistics*, ed. by T. Sebeok, 5: 309-333. The Hague: Mouton.

1986 *South Asian Languages: Structure, Convergence and Diglossia.* Ed. by Bh. Krishnamurti; assoc. ed.: C. P. Masica, A. K. Sinha. Delhi: Motilal Banarsidass.

1991 "The emergence of the syllable types of stems (C)VCC(V) and (C)$\bar{V}$C(V) in Indo-Aryan and Dravidian: Conspiracy or convergence?" In *Studies in the historical phonology of Asian languages*, ed. by W. G. Boltz and M. C. Shapiro: 160-175. Amsterdam & Philadelphia: John Benjamins.

forthc. "The origin and evolution of primary derivative suffixes in Dravidian." *Historical, Indo-European, and lexicographical studies for Ladislav Zgusta in honor of his 70th birthday*, ed. by H. H. Hock. Berlin: Mouton de Gruyter.

Krom, N.J.

1931 *Hindoe-Javaansche Geschiedenis.* 2nd rev. ed. 's-Gravenhage.

Kuijp, L.W.J. van der

forthc. "Skyogs ston Lo tsa ba Rin chen bkra shis as a Sanskritist and Textual Critic." WZKS.

Kuiper, F. B. J.

1955 "Rigvedic loanwords." In *Studia Indologica: Festschrift für Willibald Kirfel*, ed. by O. Spies: 137-185. Bonn: Orientalistisches Seminar der Universität.

1962 *Nahali: A comparative study.* (Meded. der Kon. Nederl. Ak. v. Wetensch., Afd. Letterk., N.R., 25: 5.) Amsterdam: Noord-Hollandsche Uitgevers Maatschappij.

1966 "The sources of Nahali vocabulary." In *Studies in comparative Austroasiatic linguistics*, ed. by N. H. Zide. The Hague: Mouton.

1967a "The Genesis of a Linguistic Area." IIJ 10: 81-102. Repr. IJDL 3: 135-153 (1974).

1967b "The Sanskrit nom. sing. *viṭ*." IIJ 10: 103-125.

1991 *Aryans in the Rigveda.* Amsterdam and Atlanta, GA: Rodopi.

1992 "Rigvedic loanwords." IJDL 21: 1-49.

Kulkarni, V. M.

1991 *Sarvasena's Harivijaya.* Ahmedabad: L. D. Institute.

Kulke, Hermann

1986 "The Early and the Imperial Kingdom in Southeast Asian History." In *Southeast Asia in the 9th to 14th Centuries*,ed. by David G. Marr and A.C. Milner: 1-22. Singapore: Institute of Southeast Asian Studies.

1990 "Indian Colonies, Indianization or Cultural Convergence: Reflections on the Changing Image of India's Role in South-East Asia." *Semaian* 3: 8-32.

Kulke, Hermann, and Dietmar Rothermund

1990 *A history of India.* Rev. ed. London, New York: Routledge. [1st ed. London: Croom Helm, 1986.]

Kumamoto, H.

1988 *Sanskrit-Khotanese Conversational Manual for Central Asian Travelers.* Colloque Franco-Japonais de Documents et Archives provenant de l'Asie Central. Kyoto.

Kumar, Avanindra

1989 "Apabhraṁśa: Communication of Meaning." *Studies in Indology: Professor Rasik Vihari Joshi Felicitation Volume.* Ed. A. Kumar et alii: 283-291. New Delhi: Shree Publishing House.

Labov, William

1965 "The social motivation of a sound change." *Word* 19:273-309.

1972 *Sociolinguistic patterns.* Philadelphia: University of Pennsylvania Press.

1994 *Principles of Linguistic Change. Volume 1: Internal Factors.* Language in Society 20. Oxford UK: Blackwell.

LaCapra, Dominick

1983 *Rethinking Intellectual History: Texts, Contexts, Language.* Ithaca: Cornell Univ. Press.

Lakshmi Bai, B.

1985 "Some notes on correlative constructions in Dravidian." *For Gordon H. Fairbanks,* ed. by V. Z. Acson & R. L. Leed: 181-190. Honolulu: Univ. of Hawaii Press.

Lamotte, Étienne

1935 *Saṃdhinirmocana Sūtra: L'explication des mystères. Texte tibétain édité et traduit.* Université de Louvain, Recueil de travaux publiés par les membres des Conférences d'Histoire et de Philologie, 2e Série, 34e Fascicule. Louvain - Paris.

1949 *Le Traité de la Grande Vertu de Sagesse de Nāgārjuna (Mahāprajñāpāramitā-śāstra).* Tome II. Bibliothèque du Muséon, 18. Louvain: Bureaux du Muséon.

1970 *Le Traité de la Grande Vertu de Sagesse de Nāgārjuna (Mahāprajñāpāramitāśāstra).* Tome III. Publications de l'Institut Orientaliste de Louvain, 2. Louvain: Institut Orientaliste, Université de Louvain.

1973 *La Somme du Grand Véhicule d'Asaṅga (Mahāyānasaṃgraha).* Tome II: traduction et commentaire. Publications de l'Institut Orientaliste de Louvain, 8. Louvain-la-Neuve: Institut Orientaliste.

Lancaster, L. (ed.)

1977 *Prajñāpāramitā and Related Systems: Studies in honor of Edward Conze.* Berkeley Buddhist Studies Series 1. Berkeley: University of California.

Lang, K.C.

1993 "On the Middle Indic forms found in Candrakīrti's quotations from chapter nine of the *Samādhirājasūtra.*" In Mishra 1993: 426-449.

La Vallée Poussin, Louis de

1910 "Madhyamakāvatāra, Introduction au Traité du Milieu de l'Ācārya Candrakīrti, avec le commentaire de l'auteur, traduit d'après la version tibétaine (ch. VI)." *Le Muséon* N.S. 11, 271-358.

1928-29 *La Siddhi de Hiuan-tsang.* Tomes I-II. Buddhica - Documents et Travaux pour l'Étude du Bouddhisme, Première Série: Mémoires - Tomes I, V. Paris: Paul Geuthner.

1933 "Le Joyau dans la main." *Mélanges chinois et bouddhiques* 2 (1932-33): 68-138.

1937 "Documents d'Abhidharma: les deux, les quatre, les trois vérités." *Mélanges chinois et bouddhiques* 5 (1936-37): 159-187.

1980 *L'Abhidharmakośa de Vasubandhu*, traduction et annotations. Nouvelle édition anastatique présentée par Étienne Lamotte. 6 tomes. Mélanges Chinois et Bouddhiques vol. XVI. Bruxelles: Institut Belge des Hautes Études Chinoises.

Lee, Gina M.

1986 "Diglossia in Ancient India." *Working Papers in Linguistics (Ohio State Univ.)*, 34:151-164.

Leumann, E.

1885 "Die alten Berichte von den Schismen der Jaina." *Indische Studien* 17:91-135.

Lévi, Sylvain

1904 "On Some Terms Employed in the Inscriptions of the Kshatrapas." IA 163-174. [originally JA 1902: 95-125.]

1933 *Bālidvīpagranthāḥ. Sanskrit Texts from Bāli. Critically edited with an introduction.* GOS 67. Baroda: Oriental Research Institute.

Liebich, Bruno

1919 "Zur Einführung in die indische einheimische Sprachwissenschaft. I. Das Kātantra." *Sitzungsberichte der Heidelberger Akad. der Wissenschaften, philos-hist. Klasse*. Heidelberg: Winter.

Likhit Likhitanonta

1980 "The Golden Age of Buddhist Literature in Lanna Thai." In *Buddhism in Northern Thailand, Commemoration Volume of the 13th General Conference of the World Fellowship of Buddhists at Chiangmai, Thailand*: 64-80.

Limaye, V.P., and R.D. Vadekar (ed.)

1958 *Eighteen Principal Upaniṣads*. Vol. I. Poona: Vaidika Saṃśodhana Maṇḍala.

Lindtner, Chr.

1982 *Nagarjuniana: Studies in the Writings and Philosophy of Nāgārjuna*. Delhi: Motilal Banarsidass.

1992 "The Laṅkāvatārasūtra in early Indian Madhyamaka literature." AS/ÉA 46.1 (Études bouddhiques offertes à Jacques May): 244-279.

Lombard, Denys

1990 *Le Carrefour javanais, essai d'histoire globale. III: L'héritage des royaumes concentriques*. Paris: Éditions de l'École en sciences sociales.

Lüders, Heinrich

1940 "Kātantra und Kaumāralāta." *Philologica Indica. Ausgewählte kleine Schriften von Heinrich Lüders*: 659-721. Göttingen.

Macdonnell, Arthur Anthony, and Arthur Berriedale Keith

1912 *Vedic index of names and subjects*, 2 vols. Repr. Delhi: Motilal Banarsidass, 1958.

MacMullen, Ramsay

1990 *Changes in the Roman Empire: Essays in the Ordinary*. Princeton, N.J.: Princeton Univ. Press.

Madhava Krishna Sarma, K.

1943 "Vāk before Bhartṛhari." *The Poona Orientalist* 8:21-36.

Mahalingam. T. V.

1967 *Early South Indian Palaeography*. Madras Univ. Archaeological series, no. 1. Madras: Univ. of Madras.

1988 *Inscriptions of the Pallavas*. New Delhi: Indian Council of Historical Research; Delhi: Agam Prakashan.

1988 *Inscriptions of the Pallavas*. Indian Council of Historical Research. New Delhi: Agam Prakashan.

Mair, Victor H. and Tsu-lin Mei

1991 "The Sanskrit Origins of Recent Style Prosody." *Harvard Journal of Asian Studies*, Vol. 51:375-470.

Majumdar, R. C.

1944 *Hindu Colonies in the Far East*. Calcutta: General Printers.

1953 *Inscriptions of Kambuja*. Calcutta: Asiatic Society.

Mālavaṇiyā, Dalasukha [= Malvania, Dalsukh]

1983 *Jaināgama aura pāli-piṭaka-gata kucha samāna viṣayoṁ kī carcā*. Post-graduate and Research Department Series No. 19. Poona: Bhandarkar Oriental Research Institute.

Mallory, J.P.

1989 *In Search of the Indo-Europeans: Language, Archeology and Myth*. London: Thames and Hudson.

Mansion, Joseph

1931 *Esquisse d'une histoire de la langue sanscrite*. Paris: Geuthner.

Masica, Colin P.

1976 *Defining a linguistic area: South Asia*. Chicago: Chicago Univ. Press.

May, Jacques

1959 *Candrakīrti, Prasannapadā Madhyamakavṛtti*. Douze chapitres traduits du sanscrit et du tibétain, accompagnés d'une introduction, de notes et d'une édition critique de la version tibétaine. Collection Jean Przyluski, Tome II. Paris: Adrien-Maisonneuve.

Mayrhofer, Manfred

1956-1980 *Kurzgefaßtes etymologisches Wörterbuch des Altindischen*. Heidelberg: Winter.

1986- *Etymologisches Wörterbuch des Altindoarischen*. Heidelberg: Winter.

Mehendale

1993 "The Indo-Aryans, Indo-Iranians and the Indo-Europeans." In Deo & Kamath 1993:43-50.

Mehta, Mohanlal, and Chandra, K. Rishabh

1972 *Prakrit Proper Names*, Part II. Lalbhai Dalpatbhai Series, 37. Ahmedabad: L.D. Institute of Indology.

Menon, A.G. and G.H. Schokker

1992 "The Conception of Rāma-Rājya in South and North Indian literature." In: *Ritual, State and History in South Asia; Essays in honour of J.C. Heesterman*, ed. by A.W. van den Hoek, D.H.A. Kolff and M.S. Oort: 610-636. Leiden: E.J. Brill.

Migron, Saul

1993 "Catena and climax in Vedic prose." *Die Sprache* 35: 71-80.

Miller, D. Gary

1975 "Indo-European: VSO, SOV, SVO, or all three?" *Lingua* 37: 31-52.

Miller, R.A.

1966 "Buddhist Hybrid Sanskrit *āli, kāli* as Grammatical Terms in Tibet." *Harvard Journal of Asiatic Studies*, 26:125-147.

Minard, Armand

1932 *Trois Énigmes sur les Cent Chemins*. Annales de l'Université de Lyon. Paris: Société "Les Belles Lettres."

Mirashi, V. V.

1981 *The History and Inscriptions of the Sātavāhanas and the Western Kshatrapas*. Bombay: Maharasthra State Board for Literature and Culture.

Mishra, K.N. (ed.)

1993 *Aspects of Buddhist Sanskrit. Proceedings of the International Symposium on the Language of Sanskrit Buddhist Texts, Oct. 1-5, 1991*. Samyag-Vāk Series VI. Sarnath: Central Institute of Higher Tibetan Studies.

Mitchiner, John

1986 *The Yuga Purāṇa*. Calcutta: Asiatic Society of Bengal.

Mitra, Rājendralāla

1877 *A Descriptive Catalogue of Sanskrit Mss. in the Library of the Asiatic Society of Bengal. Part I: Grammar*. Calcutta.

Moag, Rodney F.

1986 "Diglossia versus Bidialectalism: Hindi in Fiji and in eastern Uttar Pradesh." *South Asian Languages: Structure, Convergence and Diglossia*, ed. by Bh. Krishnamurti et alii: 350-370. Delhi: Motilal Banarsidass.

Mookerji, Radha Kumud

1969 *Ancient Indian Education*. 4th ed. Delhi, etc.: Motilal Banarsidass. [1st, 2nd ed. London: Macmillan and co., 1947, 1951.]

Müller, Max

1883 *India, What Can It Teach Us? A course of lectures delivered before the Univ. of Cambridge*. London: Longmans.

Nadkarni, M. V.

1975 "Bilingualism and syntactic change in Konkani." *Language* 51.672-83.

Naerssen, F. H. van, and R. C. de Jongh

1977 *The Economic and Administrative History of Early Indonesia*. Handbuch der Orientalistik 3.7. Leiden/Köln: E. J. Brill.

Nagaraju, S.

1984 "The Palaeography of the Earliest Inscriptions of Burma, Thailand, Cambodia, and Vietnam." In *Svasti Sri: Dr. B.Ch. Chhabra Felicitation Volume*, ed by K. V. Ramesh et al. Delhi : Agam.

forthc. "Emergence of Regional Identity and Beginnings of Vernacular Literature: A case study of Telugu." In *Literary History, Region, and Nation in South Asia*, a special number of *Social Scientist*.

Nagaswamy, R.

1978 *Studies in Ancient Tamil Law and Society*. Madras: Institute of Epigraphy, Tamilnadu.

Nakamura, Hajime

1989 *Indian Buddhism: A Survey with Bibliographical Notes*. Delhi: Motilal Banarsidass.

Nandy, Ashis

1994 *The Illegitimacy of Nationalism: Rabindranath Tagore and the Politics of Self*. Delhi: Oxford Univ. Press.

Newman, John

1988 "Buddhist Sanskrit in the Kālacakra Tantra." JIABS 11:123-141.

Norman, K. R.

1988 "The Origin of Pali and its Position among the Indo-European Languages." *Journal of Pali and Buddhist Studies* 1:1-27 (= *Collected Papers* 3:225-43).

1991 "The language in which the Buddha taught." In K.R. Norman, *Collected Papers*: Volume II, 84-98. Oxford: The Pali Text Society.

Oetke, Claus

1988 *'Ich' und das Ich. Analytische Untersuchungen zur buddhistisch-brahmanischen Atmankontroverse*. Stuttgart: Franz Steiner.

Oberlies, Thomas

1994 Review of Kuiper 1991. IIJ 37: 333-349.

Ohira, Suzuko

1982 *A Study of the Tattvārthasūtra with Bhāṣya*. Ahmedabad: L. D. Institute of Indology.

Oldenberg, Hermann

1919 *Die Weltanschauung der Brāhmaṇa-Texte*. Göttingen: Vandenhoeck & Ruprecht.

Om Prakash

1987 *Economy and Food in Ancient India*. 2 Pts. Delhi-Varanasi: Bharatiya Vidya Prakashan.

Padoux, André

1990 *Vāc. The Concept of the Word in selected Hindu Tantras*. Translated by Jacques Gontier. [Revision of author's doctoral thesis, Univ. of Paris, 1964.] Albany NY: State Univ. of New York Press.

Pal, Prasanta Kumar

[1982/3-90/1] *Rabijīvanī*. 5 Vols. Calcutta: Ananda Publishers, 1389-1397 (Beng. era).

Palmer, Nigel F.

1993 *German Literary Culture in the Twelfth and Thirteenth Centuries.* Oxford: Clarendon Press.

Pandey, Gyanendra

1990 *The Construction of Communalism in Colonial North India.* Delhi: Oxford Univ. Press.

Pandeya, Ram Chandra (ed.)

1967 *Yuktidīpikā. An ancient commentary on the Sāṃkhya-Kārikā of Īśvarakṛṣṇa.* Delhi: Motilal Banarsidass.

Pandharipande, Rajeshwari

1982 "Counteracting forces in language change: convergence vs. maintenance." SLS 12: 2:97-116.

Panglung, J.L.

1994 "New Fragments of the *sGra-sbyor bam-po gñis-pa.*" *East and West,* 44.1:161-172.

Panneerselvam, R.

1968 "A Dimodel system of Inscriptional and Literary Dialect." In: *Subramoniam* 1968:29-40.

Parpola, Asko

1988 "The coming of the Aryans to Iran and India and the cultural and ethnic identity of the dāsas." IJDL 17: 2: 85-229.

Pathak, V.S.

1993 "Semantics of Ārya: its historical implications." In Deo & Kamath 1993:86-99.

Piaget, J.

1925 "Le réalisme nominal chez l'enfant." *Revue Philosophique de la France et de l'Étranger* 99:189-234.

Pingree, David

1978 *The Yavanajātaka,* Vol. 1. Cambridge: Harvard Univ. Press.

Pischel, Richard

1981 *Comparative Grammar of the Prākrit Languages.* Transl. from German by Subhadra Jha. 2nd rev. ed. Delhi: Motilal Banarsidass.

Pollock, Sheldon

1985 "The Theory of Practice and the Practice of Theory in Indian Intellectual History." JAOS105: 499-519.

1993 "Deep Orientalism? Notes on Sanskrit and Power beyond the Raj." In *The Postcolonial Predicament,* ed. by C.A. Breckenridge and P. van der Veer: 76-133. Philadelphia: University of Pennsylvania Press.

1995 "In Praise of Poets: On the History and Function of the *kavipraśaṁsā.*" *Ānandabhāratī: Dr. K. Krishnamoorthy Felicitation Volume:* 443-457. Mysore: DVK Murthy.

1996 "Making History: Kalyāni, A.D. 1008." In: *M.S. Nagaraja Rao Felicitation Volume* (Bangalore).

forthc. "Literary History, Indian History, World History." In *Literary History, Region, and Nation in South Asia*, a special number of *Social Scientist.*

Popper, Karl R.

1972 *Objective Knowledge. An Evolutionary Approach.* London: Oxford Univ. Press.

Pott, August Friedrich

1833, 1836 *Etymologische Forschungen auf dem Gebiete der indogermanischen Sprachen*, 1 and 2. Lemgo: Meyer.

Pou, Saveros (transl. and ed.)

1989 *Nouvelles inscriptions du Cambodge I.* Collection de textes et documents sur l'Indochine No. 17. Paris: École Française d'Extrême-Orient.

Purani, A.B. (ed.)

1964 *The Life of Sri Aurobindo: A Source Book.* Pondicherry: Sri Aurobindo Ashram.

Quaritch Wales, H.G.

1931 *Siamese State Ceremonies; Their History and Function.* London: Bernard Quaritch.

Radicchi, Anna

1992 "la Greater India, fra ideale e storia." *Annali del la faccoltà di magistero dell'Università di Cagliari.* Nuova Serie Vol. 15. Parte 4· 23-25. Cagliari: Università di Cagliari.

Raghavan, V.

1957 *Modern Sanskrit Literature.* Delhi: Sahitya Akademi.

Ramakrishnarao, K.V.

1993 "Ariyar in ancient Tamil literature." In Deo & Kamath 1993:75-80.

Ramanan, K. Venkata

1966 *Nāgārjuna's Philosophy as presented in the Mahā-Prajñāpāramitā-Śāstra.* Repr. Delhi: Motilal Banarsidass, 1978.

Ramanujan, A. K., & Colin Masica

1969 "Toward a phonological typology of the Indian linguistic area." *Current trends in linguistics*, ed. by T. Sebeok, 5: 543-577. The Hague: Mouton.

Ramasamy, K.

1981 "Correlative relative clauses in Tamil." In *Dravidian syntax* (Annamalai Univ. Publications in Linguistics, 73), ed. by S. Agesthialingom & N. Rajasekharan Nair: 363-80. Annamalainagar.

Ramesan, N.

1972 *Copper Plate Inscriptions of the State Museum*, vol. III. Hyderabad: Government of Andhra Pradesh.

Ramesh, K. V.

1984 *Inscriptions of the Western Gaṅgas.* Indian Council of Historical Research. New Delhi: Agam Prakashan.

Rapson, E.J.

1904 "In what degree was Sanskrit a spoken language?" JRAS: 435-456. (Followed by discussion at the General Meeting by Rhys Davids, F.W. Thomas, G.A. Grierson, Fleet, JRAS: 457-487, 747-749.)

Rau, Wilhelm

1957 *Staat und Gesellschaft im alten Indien nach den Brāhmaṇa-Texten dargestellt.* Wiesbaden: Harrassowitz.

1977 *Bhartṛharis Vākyapadīya.* Wiesbaden: Franz Steiner. (Abhandlungen für die Kunde des Morgenlandes XLII , 4.)

Rawat, P.L.

1970 *History of Indian Education.* 6th edition. (1st edition 1956.) Agra: Ram Prasad.

Raychaudhuri, Tapan

1988 *Europe Reconsidered, Perceptions of the West in Nineteenth Century Bengal.* Delhi: Oxford Univ. Press.

Reid, Anthony

1990 "An 'Age of Commerce' in Southeast Asian History." *Modern Asian Studies* 24.1:1-30.

Renfrew, Colin

1987 *Archeology and Language: The Puzzle of Indo-European Origins.* London: Jonathan Cape.

Renou, Louis

1947a *L'Inde classique,* Vol. 1. (together with Jean Filliozat.) Paris: Payot.

1947b "Les connexions entre le rituel et la grammaire en Sanskrit." JA 233 (1941-42):105-165. Repr. in Staal 1972: 434-469.

1955 "Les pouvoirs de la parole dans le Ṛgveda." *Études védiques et pāṇinéennes* I:1-27. Paris: E. de Boccard.

1956a *Hymnes spéculatifs du Véda.* Gallimard / UNESCO.

1956b *Histoire de la Langue Sanskrite.* Collection Les Langues du Monde. Lyon: IAC.

1960 *Études Védiques et Pāṇinéennes. Tome VI. Le Destin du Veda dans L'Inde.* Paris: E. de Boccard.

1965 *The Destiny of the Veda in India.* Delhi: Motilal Banarsidass [Dev Raj Chanana's transl. of Renou 1960, with some new references by the author.]

1966 *La Grammaire de Pāṇini. Texte sanskrit, traduction française avec extraits des commentaires.* I-II. Bibliothèque de l'École Française d'Extrême-Orient. Paris.

Rhys Davids, T.W.

1890 *The Questions of King Milinda.* Repr. Delhi: Motilal Banarsidass, 1965.

Romaine, Suzanne

1982 *Socio-historical Linguistics. Its Status and Methodology.* Cambridge: Cambridge University Press.

Rosenberg, Klaus

1976 *Die epischen Chan-Dichtungen in der Literatur Thailands; mit einer vollständigen Übersetzung des Anirut Kham Chan.* Hamburg: Gesellschaft für Natur- und Völkerkunde Ostasiens.

Roy, N. Ch.

1960 *The Civil Service of India.* 2nd ed. Calcutta: K.L. Mukhopadhyay.

Rubinstein, R.

1988 "Beyond the Realm of the Senses; the Balinese Ritual of Kekawin Compositions." Unpublished PhD thesis, Sydney Univ.

Ruegg, David Seyfort

1977 "The *gotra, ekayāna* and *tathāgatagarbha* theories of the Prajñāpāramitā according to Dharmamitra and Abhayākaragupta." In: Lancaster 1977: 283-312.

1994a "*Pramāṇabhūta, *pramāṇa(bhūta)-puruṣa, pratyakṣadharman* and *sākṣāt-kṛtadharman* as epithets of the *ṛṣi, ācārya* and *tathāgata* in grammatical, epistemological and Madhyamaka texts." BSOAS 57:303-320.

1994b "La notion du voyant et du 'connaisseur suprême' et la question de l'autorité épistémique." WZKS 38 (Festschrift G. Oberhammer): 403-419.

Saeng Chandrangaam

1980 "Lanna Thai Kingdom and its Religion." In *Buddhism in Northern Thailand, Commemoration Volume of the 13th General Conference of the World Fellowship of Buddhists at Chiangmai, Thailand*: 87-99.

Salomon, Richard

1982 "The Ukti-Vyakti-Prakaraṇa as a Manual of Spoken Sanskrit." IIJ 24:13-25.

1989 "Linguistic variability in Post-Vedic Sanskrit." In Caillat 1989:275-294.

Sankaranarayanan, S.

1993 "Sanskrit education in ancient Tamil country." ALB 57:7-33.

1994 "Sanskrit education in ancient Karṅāṭaka (epigraphical survey)." ALB 58:100-124.

Sāṅkṛtyāyana, R.

1935 "Sanskrit palm-leaf mss. in Tibet." JBORS 21.1:21-43.

1937 "Second search of Sanskrit palm-leaf mss. in Tibet [with plates]." JBORS 23.1:1-57.

1938 "Search for Sanskrit mss. in Tibet." JBORS 24.4:137-163.

Sarangi, Alekha Chandra

1979 "Development of Sanskrit from Pāṇini to Patañjali." *Tokkai Bukyo (= Journal of Tokkai Association of Indian and Buddhist Studies, Univ. of Nagoya)* 24:110-102.

Sarkar, Himansu Bhusan

1934 *Indian Influences on the Literature of Java and Bali.* Greater Indian Studies 1. Calcutta.

1937 "The Cultural Contact between Java and Bengal." IHQ 13: 589-599.

1971, 1972 *Corpus of the Inscriptions of Java (Corpus Inscriptionum Javanicum) (up to 928 A.D.).* Vol. I, II. Calcutta: Mukhopadhyay.

1985 *Cultural Relations between India and Southeast Asian Countries.* New Delhi: Indian Council for Cultural Relations and Motilal Banarsidass.

Sastri, Hirananda

1942 *Nālandā and its Epigraphic Material.* Memoirs of the Archaelogical survey of India, 66. Delhi: Manager of Publications.

Sastri, K.A.Nilakanta

1935-37 *The Colas* Vol. I and II. Madras Univ. Historical Series No. 9-10. Madras: Madras Univ.

1964 *The Culture and History of the Tamils.* Calcutta: Firma K.L.Mukhopadhyay.

1974 *Aspects of India's History and Culture.* Collected articles of Professor K.A.Nilakanta Sastri, ed. by S.P. Gupta. Delhi: Oriental Publishers on behalf of the Indian Archaeological Society.

Saussure, F. de

1916 *Cours de Linguistique Générale.* Geneva. Critical edition (with notes and introduction) by T. de Mauro. Paris: Payot, 1984.

Scarlett, Helaine, and Press, Allan

1975 "An experimental investigation of the phenomenon of word-realism." *Merrill-Palmer Quarterly* 21:127-37.

Scharfe, Hartmut

1977 *Grammatical Literature.* A History of Indian Literature, 5.2. Wiesbaden: Otto Harrassowitz.

Schmithausen, Lambert

1973 "Spirituelle Praxis und philosophische Theorie im Buddhismus." *Zeitschrift für Missionswissenschaft und Religionswissenschaft* 57: 161-186.

Schopen, G.

1975 "The phrase '*sa pṛthivīpradeśaś caityabhūto bhavet*' in the *Vajracchedikā*: Notes on the Cult of the Book in Mahāyāna." IIJ 17:147-181.

Schoterman, J.A.

1981 "An Introduction to Old Javanese Sanskrit Dictionaries and Grammars." BTLV 137:419-442.

1982 *The Ṣaṭsāhasra Saṃhitā: Chapters 1-5, ed., translated and annotated.* Orientalia Rheno-Trajectina, vol. 27. Thesis Utrecht. Leiden: E.J. Brill.

Schrader, Friedrich Otto

1928 "Ein syntaktisches Problem der indischen Sprachfamilie." *Zeitschrift für Indologie und Iranistik* 6, 72-81. [= *Kleine Schriften*, ed. by J. F. Sprockhoff, Wiesbaden 1983, 433-443.]

Schubring, Walther

1935 *Die Lehre der Jainas nach den alten Quellen dargestellt.* Berlin und Leipzig: Walter de Gruyter.

Schwab, Raymond

1984 *The Oriental Renaissance: Europe's Rediscovery of India and the East, 1680-1880.* New York: Columbia Univ. Press.

Schweisguth, P.

1951 *Étude sur la littérature siamoise.* Paris: Imprimerie Nationale.Scott, James

1990 *Domination and the Arts of Resistance: Hidden Transcripts.* New Haven: Yale Univ. Press.

Sen, Amulyachandra

1941 "The Aṇgacūliyā, a sacred text of the Jainas." IHQ 17.4: 472-491.

Sen, Sukumar

1928 "Sekaśubhodayā: A Mediaeval Romance and Collection of Tales from Bengal, written in corrupt Sanskrit." Proceedings of the 4th AIOC, Vol. II, 515-524.

1958 *History and Pre-History of Sanskrit.* Univ. of Mysore. Extension Lectures. Mysore: Mysore Univ.

1963 *Sekaśubhodayā of Halayudha Miśra ed. with Notes, Introduction and translated into English.* Bibliotheca Indica No. 286. Calcutta: The Asiatic Society.

Settar, S., and Gunther D. Sontheimer, eds.

1982 *Memorial Stones: A Study of Their Origin, Significance, and Variety.* Dharwad: Institute of Indian Art History, Karnataka Univ.; New Delhi: South Asia Institute, Univ. of Heidelberg.

Sewell, Robert,

1932 *The Historical Inscriptions of Southern India (collected till 1923) and outlines of political history.* Ed. by S.Krishnaswami Aiyangar. Madras: Univ. of Madras.

Shah, Umakant Premanand

1960 *Gīrvāṇa-pada-mañjarī and Gīrvāṇa-vāṅ-mañjarī.* The Maharaja Sayajirao Univ. Oriental Series, 4. Baroda: Oriental Institute.

Shapiro, Michael C., and Harold F. Schiffman

1983 *Language and Society in South Asia.* New Delhi: Motilal Banarasidass.

Sharan, Mahesh Kumar

1974 *Studies in Sanskrit Inscriptions of Ancient Cambodia.* New Delhi: Abhinav Publications.

Sharma, Rama Nath

1987 *The Aṣṭādhyāyī of Pāṇini,* vol. I. Delhi: Munshiram Manoharlal.

Sharma, Vīrendra.

1977 *Vākyapadīya --- Saṁbandhasamuddeśa. A critical study with special reference to the commentary of Helārāja.* Panjab Univ. Indological Series 9. [In Hindi.] Hoshiarpur: Vishveshvaranand Vishva Bandhu Institute of Sanskrit and Indological Studies.

Shastree, K.K.

1993 "Aryan race: a mis-nomer." In Deo & Kamath 1993:116-119.

Shastri, A.M.

1993 "Āryāvarta and Jambūdvīpa." In Deo & Kamath 1993:135-142.

Shastri, Hara Prasad

1905 *Catalogue of the Palm-leaf and Selected Paper MSS. belonging to the Durbar Library, Nepal. Vol. I.* Calcutta: Baptist Mission Press.

Sikdar, J. C.

1987 *Concept of Matter in Jaina Philosophy.* Varanasi: P. V. Research Institute.

Silverstein, Michael

1992 "The Uses and Utility of Ideology: Some Reflections." *Pragmatics* 2:311-323.

Simonsson, N.

1957 *Indo-tibetische Studien I. Die Methoden der tibetischen Übersetzer, untersucht im Hinblick auf die Bedeutung ihrer Übersetzungen für die Sanskritphilologie.* Uppsala: Almqvist & Wiksells.

1982 "Reflections on the grammatical tradition in Tibet." In *Indological and Buddhist Studies: Volume in honour of Professor J.W. de Jong on his sixtieth birthday*, ed. by L.A. Hercus et al.: 531-544. Canberra: Faculty of Asian Studies.

1986 "A Note on the Knowledge of Indian Grammar Among the Tibetan Translators." *Orientalia Suecana*, 33-35 (1984-86):385-389.

Sircar, D.C.

1939 "Inscriptional Evidences Relating to the Development of Classical Sanskrit." IHQ 15:38-46.

1965 *Indian Epigraphy*. Delhi: Motilal Banarsidass.

1965-83 *Select Inscriptions Bearing on Indian History and Civilization*. Two Volumes. Calcutta: Calcutta Univ. (vol. 1); Delhi: Motilal Banarsidass (vol. 2).

Śiva-nārāyaṇa Śāstrī

1972 *Vaidika vāṅmaya meṁ bhāṣā-cintana. Vārāṇasī - Dillī:* Indological Book House.

Snellgrove, D.L.

1987 *Indo-Tibetan Buddhism. Indian Buddhists and their Tibetan Successors*. London: Serindia.

Southworth, Franklin C.

1974 "Linguistic stratigraphy of North India." In *Contact and Convergence in South Asian Languages*, ed. by F.C. Southworth & M.L. Apte:201-223. IJDL. [Also IJDL 3.2:201-223.]

1979 "Lexical evidence for early contacts between Indo-Aryan and Dravidian." In *Aryan and non-Aryan in India*, ed. by M. Deshpande and P. E. Hook: 191-233. Ann Arbor: Center for South and Southeast Asian Studies, Univ. of Michigan.

1982 "Dravidian and Indo-European: The neglected hypothesis." IJDL 11: 1-21.

Sridhar, S. N.

1981 "Linguistic convergence: Indo-Aryanization of Dravidian." *Lingua* 53.199-220.

Srimannarayana Murti, M.

1993 "On the nomenclature 'Saṁskṛta'." ALB 57:58-71.

Srinivas, M.N.

1952 *Religion and Society among the Coorgs of South India*. London: Oxford Univ. Press.

1989 *The Cohesive role of Sanskritization*. Madras: Oxford Univ. Press, Madras.

Srinivasan, P. R., and S. Sankaranarayanan

1979 *Inscriptions of the Ikshvāku Period*. Epigraphical Series No.14. Hyderabad: Government of Andhra Pradesh.

Srouty, Visvanatha

[1993/4] *Paśv-ālambhana-niṣedhaḥ yajñeṣu*, Pune: Vaidika Saṁśodhana Maṇḍala, Śāka era 1915.

Staal, J.F.

1963 "Sanskrit and Sanskritization." JAS 22 (1962/63):261-275. [Repr. in *South and Southeast Asia: Enduring Scholarship,* ed. by J.A. Harrison. Tucson, 1972.]

1972 *A Reader on the Sanskrit Grammarians.* Studies in Linguistics 1. Cambridge Mass., London: The MIT Press.

Steblin-Kamenskij, M. I.

1965 "Om alveolarer og kakuminaler i norsk og svensk." *Norsk Tidskrift for Sprogvidenskap* 20: 18-27.

Steever, Sanford B.

1988 *The serial verb formation in the Dravidian languages.* Delhi: Motilal Banarsidass.

Steiner, George

1989 *Real Presences. Is there anything* in *what we say?.* London, Boston: Faber and Faber.

Stock, Brian

1990 "Tradition and Modernity: Models from the Past." In *Modernité au Moyen Âge: Le Défi du Passé,* ed. by Brigitte Cazelles and Charles Méla. Geneva: Droz.

Stokes, Eric

1992 *The English Utilitarians and India.* 3rd Indian impression. [First edition 1959.] Delhi: Oxford Univ. Press.

Subrahmanian, N.

1972, 1977 *History of Tamilnad.* Vol. I and II. Madurai: Koodal Publishers.

Subrahmanian, N. et al.

1979 *History of South India.* Vol. I. New Delhi: S. Chand & Company Ltd.

Subrahmanian, T.N.

1966 *Thirty Pallava Copper plates (prior to 1000 A.D.).* [Tamil title: *Pallavar Ceppetukal Muppatu*] [in Tamil], Publications of the Tamil Historical Academy -1. Madras: Tamil Varalatru Kazhagam.

Subrahmanyam, P. S.

1983 *Dravidian comparative phonology.* Annamalainagar: Annamalai Univ.

Subramoniam, V.I. et al,

1968 *Four Papers on Literature and Linguistics.* Madurai: Meenakshi Puthaka Nilayam.

Suppiramaniam, P.

1983 *Meykkīrttikaḷ.* Madras: International Institute of Tamil Studies.

Suzuki, Daisetz Teitaro

1930 *Studies in the Lankavatara Sutra.* London: Routledge & Kegan Paul. 1968.

Syed, Renate

1994 "Das altindische Spiel mit den śāras—Ein Vorläufer des Backgammon und des Trick-Track?" *Beiträge des Südasien-Institutes* (Humboldt-Universität Berlin), Heft 7:85-131.

Takakusu, J.

1896 *The Buddhist Religion as practiced in India and in the Malay archipelago, by I-Tsing* (A.D. 671-695). Translated by J. Takakusu. Oxford. [Reprint Delhi 1966, 1982.]

Tarling, Nicholas, ed.

1992 *The Cambridge History of Southeast Asia, Vol. One: From Early Times to c. 1800.* Cambridge: Cambridge Univ. Press.

Teeuw, A.

1990 Review of Hudak (1990). BTLV, Vol 149 (1993): 188.

Thapar, Romila

1979 *Ancient Indian Social History: Some Interpretations.* Delhi: Orient Longman.

1984 *From Lineage to State: Social Formations in the Mid-First Millenium B.C. in the Gangā Valley.* Bombay: Oxford Univ. Press.

Theraphan L. Thongkum

1979 "Iconicity of Vowel Qualities in Northeastern Thai: Reduplicated Words." In *Studies in Tai and Khmer Phonetics and Phonology in Honour of Eugénie J.A. Henderson*, ed. by Theraphan L. Thongkum et al. Bangkok: Chulalongkorn Univ. Press.

Thieme, Paul

1961 "Chess and Backgammon (Tric-Trac) in Sanskrit Literature." *Indological Studies in honour of W. Norman Brown*: 204-216. New Haven: American Oriental Society. (=*Kleine Schriften*, hrsg. v. G. Buddruss: 413-425. Wiesbaden 1971: Steiner.)

1977 "Bhartṛhari's Allegorie vom Schicksalswürfel." *Beiträge zur Indienforschung, Ernst Waldschmidt zum 80. Geburtstag gewidmet*: 511-522. Berlin: Museum für Indische Kunst.

1985 "Nennformen aus Anrede und Anruf im Sanskrit." *Münchener Studien zur Sprachwissenschaft* 44 (Festschrift Karl Hoffmann I): 239-258.

1994a "Zur Frühgeschichte des Schachs." *Tübinger Beiträge zum Thema Schach*, hrsg. v Dr. Hans Eldinger: 15ff. Tübingen: Promos Verlag.

1994b "On M. Mayrhofer's Etymologisches Wörterbuch des Altindoarischen." BSOAS 57, 321-328.

Thomason, Sarah Grey, and Terrence Kaufman

1988 *Language contact, creolization, and genetic linguistics.* Berkeley and Los Angeles: Univ. of California Press.

Tikkanen, Bertil

1987 *The Sanskrit gerund: A synchronic, diachronic, and typological analysis.* Studia Orientalia, 62. Helsinki: Finnish Oriental Society.

1988 "On Burushaski and other ancient substrata in northwestern South Asia." *Studia Orientalia* 64: 303-325.

Tillemans, T.J.F.

1990 *Materials for the study of _Āryadeva, Dharmapāla and Candrakīrti. The Catuḥśataka of Āryadeva, chapters XII and XIII, with the commentaries of*

Dharmapāla and Candrakīrti: Introduction, translation, Sanskrit, Tibetan and Chinese texts, notes. Wien: Arbeitskreis für tibetische und buddhistische Studien Universität Wien.

Trautmann, Thomas R.

1971 *Kauṭilya and the Arthaśāstra: a statistical investigation of the authorship and evolution of the text.* Leiden: E.J. Brill.

Tripathi, Dipti S.

1986 "Apabhraṁśa in Sanskrit Grammar. An Appraisal of Bhartṛhari's View." *Aligarh Journal of Oriental Studies* 3:81-92.

Tripāṭhī, Rāma-deva

1976 "Vaidika vāṅmaya meṁ bhāṣā-darśana." In *Bhāratīya bhāṣā-śāstrīya cintana*, ed. by Miśra, Vidyānivāsa et al.: 167-75. Jayapura: Rājasthāna Hindī Grantha Akādamī.

Trubetzkoy, N. S.

1931 "Phonologie und Sprachgeographie." TCLP 4: 228-234. (French version in N. S. Trubetzkoy: *Principes de phonologie.* Paris: Klincksieck, 1957.)

Turner, Sir Ralph L.

1921 "Gujarati phonology." JRAS. Repr. in Turner 1973: 88-145.

1924 "Cerebralization in Sindhi." JRAS. Repr. in Turner 1973: 206-227.

1926 "Middle Indian *-d-* and *-dd-*." In: *Festgabe Hermann Jacobi.* Repr. in Turner 1973: 239-250.

1966 *A Comparative Dictionary of the Indo-Aryan Languages.* London: Oxford Univ. Press.

1973 *Indo-Aryan linguistics: Collected papers*, ed. by J. Brough. Repr., Delhi: Disha Publications, 1985.

Upadhyaya, Deendayal

1968 *Integral Humanism.* Delhi: Navchetan Press.

Upadhyaya, Ramji

1973 *Ādhunikasaṁskṛtasāhityānuśīlanam.* Delhi: Meherchand Lacchamandas.

Uray, G.

1990 "Contributions to the date of the *Vyutpatti*-treatises." AOH 43.1:3-21.

Vaidyanathan, S.

1971 *Indo-Aryan Loanwords in Old Tamil.* Madras: Rajan Publishers.

Vajreshwari, R.

1958 "Temples as centres of higher and popular education." *Proc. of the All-India Oriental C.* 18 (Annamalainagar 1955):286-293.

Varma, Siddheshwar

1929 *The Phonetic Observations of Indian Grammarians.* London, 1929. Repr. Delhi: Munshi Ram Manoharlal, 1961.

Verhagen, P.C.

1990 "The *Mantra "Oṁ maṇi-padme hūṃ"* in an Early Tibetan Grammatical Treatise." JIABS 13.2:133-138.

1992 "'Royal' Patronage of Sanskrit Grammatical Studies in Tibet." In *Ritual, State and History in South Asia: Essays in honour of J.C. Heesterman*, ed. by A.W. Van den Hoek, D.H.A. Kolff & M.S. Oort: 375-392. Leiden etc.: E.J. Brill.

1993 "*Mantras* and Grammar. Observations on the study of the linguistical aspects of Buddhist 'esoteric formulas' in Tibet." In Mishra 1993: 320-342.

1994 *A History of Sanskrit Grammatical Literature in Tibet. Volume 1: Transmission of the Canonical Literature.* Handbuch der Orientalistik Abt. 2 Bd. 8. Leiden etc.: E.J. Brill.

1995 "Influence of Indic *vyākaraṇa* on Tibetan indigenous grammar." In *Tibetan Literature. Studies in Genre: Essays in Honor of Geshe Lhundup Sopa*, ed. by Cabezon, J.I. & R. Jackson: 422-437. Ithaca, New York: Snow Lion Press.

forthc. a "Tibetan Expertise in Sanskrit Grammar: A Case-Study: Grammatical Analysis of the Term *pratītya-samutpāda*." *Journal of the Tibet Society*, 21-47.

forthc. b "The influence of the Sanskrit tradition on Tibetan indigenous grammar." In *Geschichte der Sprachwissenschaften. Ein Internationales Handbuch zur Geschichte der Sprachforschung von den Anfängen bis zur Gegenwart*, 3 vols., ed. by S. Auroux, K. Koerner, H.-J. Niederehe & K. Versteegh. Handbücher zur Sprach- und Kommunikationswissenschaft. Berlin-New York: Walter de Gruyter.

Versteegh, Kees

1986 "Latinitas, Hellenismos, 'Arabiyya", *Historiographia Linguistica* 13.2/3:425-448. Also in: *History of Linguistics in the Classical Period* (ed. D.J. Taylor; Amsterdam & Philadelphia: Benjamins, 1987): 251-274.

Vesper, Don

1971 *Kurukh syntax with special reference to the verbal system.* Ph.D. dissertation Univ. of Chicago.

Vickery, Michael

1985 "The Reign of Sūryavarman I and Royal Factionalism at Angkor." *Journal of Southeast Asian Studies* 16.2: 226-44.

Vine, Brent

1987 "Vedic *kūláyati* and 'spontaneous cerebralization' in Sanskrit." *14th International Congress of Linguistics*, Berlin, 1987. (Published in the Proceedings, ed. by W. Bahner, J. Schildt, and D. Viehweger, Berlin: Akademie-Verlag.)

Vološinov, V. N.

1983 "The Latest Trends in Linguistic Thought in the West." In *Bakhtin School Papers* ed. by Ann Shukman.

Vrat, Satya

1994 *Studies in Jaina Sanskrit Literature.* Delhi: Eastern Book Linkers.

Wackernagel, Jakob

1896 *Altindische Grammatik, I.* Göttingen: Vandenhoeck & Ruprecht. [Second edition, 1957, with a new introduction by L. Renou and Nachträge by A. Debrunner, ibid.]

Wagle, Narendra

1987 "Ritual and Change in Early Nineteenth Century Society in Maharashtra: Vedokta Disputes in Baroda, Pune and Satara, 1824-1838." In *Religion and Society in Maharashtra*, ed. by Milton Israel and N.K. Wagle: 145-181. Toronto: Univ. of Toronto, Centre for South Asian Studies.

Wakankar, L.S.

1993 "Random Notes on the 'Aryans' and Indian antiquity." In *Deo & Kamath* 1993:20-29.

Walimbe. S.R.

1993 "The Aryans: the physical anthropological approach." In Deo & Kamath 1993:108-115.

Walle, Lieve van de

1993 *Pragmatics and Classical Sanskrit. A Pilot Study in Linguistic Politeness.* Amsterdam: John Benjamins.

Warder, A.K.

1974 *Indian Kāvya Literature*, Vol. 2: *Origins and Formation of Classical Kāvya.* Delhi-Varanasi-Patna: Motilal Banarsidass.

1980 *Indian Buddhism.* 2nd ed. Delhi: Motilal Banarsidass.

Weber, Eugen

1976 *Peasants Into Frenchmen.* Stanford, CA: Stanford Univ. Press.

Wezler, Albrecht

1985a "Bemerkungen zu Vaiśeṣika-Sūtra 6.1.1-3 (Resümee)." ZDMG, Supplement VI:282.

1985b "Dharma und Deśadharma." *Regionale Tradition in Südasien*, ed. by H. Kulke und D. Rothermund: 3-22. Stuttgart: Steiner.

1993 "A slap on the face of the Brahmins. Introducing a little-known Jain text of polemical objectives." In *Jain Studies in Honour of Josef Deleu*, ed. by Rudy Smet and Kenji Watanabe: 485-501. Tokyo: Hon-No-Tomosha.

1994 "Credo, quia occidentale: A Note on Sanskrit *varṇa* and its Misinterpretation in Literature on Mīmāṃsā and Vyākaraṇa." *Studies in Mīmāṃsā. Dr. Mandan Mishra Felicitation Volume*, ed. R. C. Dwivedi: 221-241. Delhi: Motilal Banarsidass.

Wheatly, Paul

1961 *The Golden Khersonese: Studies in the Historical Geography of the Malay Peninsula Before A.D. 1500.* Kuala Lumpur: Univ. of Malaya Press.

Whitney, William Dwight

1884 "The Study of Hindu Grammar and the Study of Sanskrit." *American Journal of Philology* 5: 279-297.

1893 "On Recent Studies of Hindu Grammar." *American Journal of Philology* 14:171-197.

Williams, Paul M.

1980 "Some aspects of language and construction in the Madhyamaka." JIPh 8:1-45.

1981 "On the Abhidharma ontology." JIPh 9:227-257.

1989 *Mahāyāna Buddhism*. The doctrinal foundations. London / New York: Routledge.

Williams, R.

1963 *Jaina Yoga: A Survey of the Medieval Śrāvakācāras*. London: Oxford Univ. Press.

Williams, Robert

1977 "Nominal realism in the child of the seventies? A replication." *Journal of Genetic Psychology* 130, 161-62.

Winternitz, Moritz

1907-22 *Geschichte der indischen Literatur*. Vol. I-III. Prag. Reprint: Stuttgart, K.F. Koehler Verlag, 1968.

1981 *A History of Indian Literature*, vol. I. Transl. of Winternitz 1907-22, vol. I by Srinivasa Sarma. Delhi: Motilal Banarsidass.

1985 *A History of Indian Literature*, vol. III. Transl. of Winternitz 1907-22, vol. III by Subhadra Jha. Delhi: Motilal Banarsidass.

1988 *A History of Indian Literature*, vol. II. Transl. of Winternitz 1907-22, vol. II by Srinivasa Sarma. Delhi: Motilal Banarsidass.

Witzel, Michael

1987 "On the Origin of the Literary Device of the 'Frame Story' in Old Indian Literature." *Hinduismus and Buddhismus. Festschrift für Ulrich Schneider*, hrsg. von Harry Falk. Freiburg: Hedwig Falk.

1989 "Tracing the Vedic Dialects." In Caillat 1989:97-266.

1995 "The linguistic situation in 1000 B.C." *Symposium on Language and Prehistory in South Asia*, Univ. of Hawaii, March 1995.

Wolters, O. W.

1979 "Khmer 'Hinduism' in the Seventh Century." In R. B. Smith and W. Watson, eds. *Early South East Asia: Essays in Archaeology, History and Historical Geography*. New York, Kuala Lumpur: Oxford Univ. Press.lke

1982 *History, Culture, and Region in Southeast Asian Perspectives*. Singapore: Institute of Southeast Asian Studies.

Woolard, Kathryn A.

1992 "Language Ideology: Issues and Approaches." *Pragmatics* 2:235-249.

Wyatt, David K.

1969 *The Politics of Reform in Thailand: Education in the Reign of King Chulalongkorn*, New Haven: Yale Univ. Press.

Zoetmulder, P. J.

1974 *Kalangwan: A Survey of Old Javanese Literature*. The Hague: Martinus Nijhoff.

Zimmer, Heinrich

1879 *Altindisches Leben*. Berlin: Weidmann.

Zvelebil, K.

1970 *Comparative Dravidian phonology*. The Hague: Mouton.

Zydenbos, Robert J.

1983 *Mokṣa in Jainism, According to Umāsvāti*. Wiesbaden: Franz Steiner.

AUTHOR INDEX

It has been attempted to make this Author Index fairly complete, especially for the body of the text. If an author appears only in the footnotes of a page, the number of the latter is given in *italics*; if in both the body of the text and in the footnotes, the reference is given in regular font. In the case of dual (or plural) authors for a publication, only the first has been indexed (sometimes an exception is made when the other(s) appear(s) as independent author(s) in the list). References to hypothetical or legendary authors, and to translators and editors are often also included. Authors of inscriptions, institutions as authors, and authors of personal communications have generally speaking not been included.

General Index

This General Index is intended to provide a first entrance to some major and secondary themes in the papers of this volume. Completeness (in terms indexed or in references under an entry) has not been aimed at. Texts which can be easily found through the author's name should be searched through the Author Index. References are mainly to the body of text, occasionally also to footnotes (in *italics*).